T0213354

Maintaining and Troubleshooting Your 3D Printer

Charles Bell

Apress®

Maintaining and Troubleshooting Your 3D Printer

Copyright © 2014 by Charles Bell

This work is subject to copyright. All rights are reserved by the Publisher, whether the whole or part of the material is concerned, specifically the rights of translation, reprinting, reuse of illustrations, recitation, broadcasting, reproduction on microfilms or in any other physical way, and transmission or information storage and retrieval, electronic adaptation, computer software, or by similar or dissimilar methodology now known or hereafter developed. Exempted from this legal reservation are brief excerpts in connection with reviews or scholarly analysis or material supplied specifically for the purpose of being entered and executed on a computer system, for exclusive use by the purchaser of the work. Duplication of this publication or parts thereof is permitted only under the provisions of the Copyright Law of the Publisher's location, in its current version, and permission for use must always be obtained from Springer. Permissions for use may be obtained through RightsLink at the Copyright Clearance Center. Violations are liable to prosecution under the respective Copyright Law.

ISBN-13 (pbk): 978-1-4302-6809-3

ISBN-13 (electronic): 978-1-4302-6808-6

Trademarked names, logos, and images may appear in this book. Rather than use a trademark symbol with every occurrence of a trademarked name, logo, or image we use the names, logos, and images only in an editorial fashion and to the benefit of the trademark owner, with no intention of infringement of the trademark.

The use in this publication of trade names, trademarks, service marks, and similar terms, even if they are not identified as such, is not to be taken as an expression of opinion as to whether or not they are subject to proprietary rights.

While the advice and information in this book are believed to be true and accurate at the date of publication, neither the authors nor the editors nor the publisher can accept any legal responsibility for any errors or omissions that may be made. The publisher makes no warranty, express or implied, with respect to the material contained herein.

Publisher: Heinz Weinheimer
Lead Editor: Michelle Lowman
Development Editor: Douglas Pundick
Technical Reviewer: Richard Cameron
Editorial Board: Steve Anglin, Mark Beckner, Ewan Buckingham, Gary Cornell, Louise Corrigan, Jim DeWolf, Jonathan Gennick, Jonathan Hassell, Robert Hutchinson, Michelle Lowman, James Markham, Matthew Moodie, Jeff Olson, Jeffrey Pepper, Douglas Pundick, Ben Renow-Clarke, Dominic Shakeshaft, Gwenan Spearing, Matt Wade, Steve Weiss
Coordinating Editor: Kevin Walter
Copy Editor: Kimberly Burton-Weisman
Compositor: SPi Global
Indexer: SPi Global
Artist: SPi Global
Cover Designer: Anna Ishchenko

Distributed to the book trade worldwide by Springer Science+Business Media New York, 233 Spring Street, 6th Floor, New York, NY 10013. Phone 1-800-SPRINGER, fax (201) 348-4505, e-mail orders-ny@springer-sbm.com, or visit www.springeronline.com. Apress Media, LLC is a California LLC and the sole member (owner) is Springer Science + Business Media Finance Inc (SSBM Finance Inc). SSBM Finance Inc is a Delaware corporation.

For information on translations, please e-mail rights@apress.com, or visit www.apress.com.

Apress and friends of ED books may be purchased in bulk for academic, corporate, or promotional use. eBook versions and licenses are also available for most titles. For more information, reference our Special Bulk Sales–eBook Licensing web page at www.apress.com/bulk-sales.

Any source code or other supplementary materials referenced by the author in this text is available to readers at www.apress.com. For detailed information about how to locate your book's source code, go to www.apress.com/source-code/.

*I dedicate this book to my late father, Richard, who taught
me mechanical, electrical, and automotive skills that I continue to use to this day.
He instilled in me a curiosity to discover how things work and
a desire to repair things that stop working.
I hope my career as an engineer satisfies his aspirations for me.*

— Dr. Charles Bell

Contents at a Glance

Contents

About the Author

Dr. Charles Bell conducts research in emerging technologies. He is a member of the Oracle MySQL Development team as team lead for the MySQL Utilities team. He lives in a small town in rural Virginia with his loving wife. He received his Doctor of Philosophy in Engineering from Virginia Commonwealth University in 2005. His research interests include database systems, software engineering, sensor networks, and 3D printing. He spends his limited free time as a practicing Maker focusing on microcontroller and 3D printing projects.

Dr. Bell's research and engineering projects makes him uniquely qualified to author this book. He is an engineer by trade, hobby, and life choice and has extensive knowledge and experience in building, maintaining, and using 3D printers.

About the Technical Reviewer

Rich Cameron (known online as "Whosawhatsis") is the Vice President of Research and Development at Deezmaker 3D Printers, and the designer of the Bukito portable 3D printer (seen on the back cover of this book). Rich is an experienced open-source developer who has been a key member of the RepRap printer development community for many years. Rich personally built several of the early classic 3D printers, and wrested amazing performance out of even those ancestral machines. When he's not busy making every aspect of his own 3d printers better, from slicing software to firmware and hardware, he likes to share that knowledge and experience so that he can help make everyone else's printers better too.

Acknowledgments

I would like to thank all of the many talented and energetic professionals at Apress. I appreciate the understanding and patience of my editor, Michelle Lowman, and coordinating editor, Kevin Walter. They were instrumental in the success of this project. I would also like to thank the army of publishing professionals at Apress for making me look so good in print. Thank you all very much!

I'd like to especially thank the technical reviewer, Richard Cameron, for his often-profound insights, constructive criticism, and mentoring when I needed it most. I'd also like to thank my friends for encouraging me to write this book. Most importantly, I want to thank my wife, Annette, for her unending patience and understanding during the long hours spent alone writing.

Introduction

It is time to face the facts and one of those facts is 3D printers are here. While they have been around for some time, they are rapidly becoming plentiful and popular enough that anyone with a modest budget can afford and enjoy them. They are no longer relegated to the dark subbasements, garages, and poorly lit workshops of the nerdy—almost maniacal—tinkerers.

Intended Audience

I wrote this book to share my passion for 3D printers with everyone who wants to join the 3D printing world but isn't prepared or has the time to devote to digging through thousands of web posts and poorly written wikis, and slogging through fact and fiction in order to learn the skills needed to use and maintain a 3D printer. It is my hope that this book fills the gap from the thin and in some cases nonexistent user's manual to the accumulation of knowledge and experience of the expert.

This book therefore is for novice and intermediate 3D enthusiasts who want to master their 3D printers. Even enthusiasts who have been using their printers for several years will find information in this book that will help further enhance their skills.

More importantly, I wrote this book to help those who have become frustrated trying to learn how to use their printers. I have talked with and read the remorseful laments of those who have thrown the towel in after failing to get their printers to print more than a useless pile of tangled filament. If I never again see for sale a partially assembled or new printer with less than 10 hours on it, I will have achieved this goal immeasurably. Perhaps that is too much to wish for, but if I get one person to turn his or her lament to enjoyment, I'll be happy.

How This Book Is Structured

The book is divided into four parts. The first part covers general topics, including a short introduction to 3D printing, build tips, configuration, and calibration. The second part covers troubleshooting hardware, software, and print problems. The third part covers printer maintenance and improvements. The fourth part includes topics on designing parts, working with parts after they are printed, and contributing to the growing 3D printing community.

Part I: Getting Started

Part I of the book is designed to get you started in 3D printing and includes a short introduction to 3D printing technology, software, and hardware. Topics include choosing the right filament, getting and building a 3D printer, calibrating and setting up your printer, as well as configuring your software and helpful tips on printing your first objects and fine-tuning your printer.

- *Introduction to 3D Printing*. Chapter 1 presents an introduction to 3D printing, including the anatomy of a 3D printer and the software used in printing and filaments types.

- *Getting a 3D Printer*. Chapter 2 covers the classes of 3D printers, a description of the features found on 3D printers, as well as a discussion on whether to buy or build your own 3D printer.

- *3D Printer Building: Tips for a Successful Build.* Chapter 3 includes a comprehensive discussion on the types of tools needed to build and maintain 3D printers. It also includes a section on building your own 3D printer, in the form of helpful tips for a successful build.

- *Configuring the Software.* Chapter 4 presents how to install the software on your computer and printer. It also presents a detailed look at how to configure the Marlin firmware for your printer.

- *Calibrating the Printer.* Chapter 5 presents the most vital tasks for preparing your printer, including calibrating the hardware to function properly. From axes, endstops, and electronics, this chapter will help you get your printer calibrated correctly.

- *Printing for the First Time.* Chapter 6 will help you prepare your print surface for printing by closely examining the types of print surface treatments, including which to use for each filament type. It also covers setting the Z-axis initial height, configuring the slicer to generate print files, and ideas for some things to test your printer.

Part II: Troubleshooting

Part II provides a look into the sometimes baffling world of troubleshooting 3D printers and print quality. It includes chapters on diagnosing hardware and software problems. You will learn how to diagnose print quality issues like first-layer adhesion (lifting) and other anomalous print artifacts. Also included are many tips on getting the most out of your hardware.

- *Solving Hardware Issues.* Chapter 7 provides an introduction on how to conduct troubleshooting, including tips on how to observe and diagnose problems. Specific problems related to hardware issues are examined in-depth, including those related to the filament, extruder, and axes mechanisms.

- *Solving Software Issues.* Chapter 8 presents those problems that have a software-related cause and include such things as problems generating the .stl file, as well as problems related to incorrect calibration settings in the firmware introduced either by accident, hardware changes, or upgrades.

Part III: Maintenance and Enhancements

Part III will get you familiar with the concepts of maintaining a 3D printer. This includes alignment, adjustment, cleaning, and repairing the components of your printer. You will also learn how to extend the life of your 3D printer by upgrading and enhancing features.

- *3D Printer Maintenance: Inspection and Adjustment Tasks.* Chapter 9 includes an introduction to performing maintenance, as well as a list of things you can do to spot problems before they occur. It also presents a number of routine things you should do before each print to ensure your printer is working correctly.

- *3D Printer Maintenance: Preventive and Corrective Tasks.* Chapter 10 presents a detailed look at those maintenance tasks you need to perform periodically to correct wear and alignment issues, such as cleaning and lubricating the moving parts. It also presents topics on how to fix things that go wrong, including several examples of common failures in 3D printers.

- *3D Printer Enhancements.* Chapter 11 presents a look at how you can improve your printer through the enhancement of existing features, as well as upgrading the printer by adding new features. It also presents a look at several key upgrades for some of the most popular printers.

Part IV: Mastering Your Craft

Part IV concludes the journey through the 3D printing world by presenting how you can become a productive member of the 3D printing community. It also includes topics on how to finish your 3D prints with a surface treatment, as well as how to get started designing your own objects. Finally, examples of solutions to real-world problems are presented to give you fuel for sparking your own creativity.

- *Working with Objects*. Chapter 12 will get you started on working with objects, beginning with a tutorial on how to use OpenSCAD to design your own objects. Included is a section on how to modify existing objects by combining it with your own OpenSCAD code to further enhance the object. You will also discover how to refine your printed objects with paint and other surface treatments.

- *Taking it to the Next Level*. This final chapter presents suggestions and etiquette on how to join the 3D printing community. It also presents some advanced projects for your 3D printing, including how to spawn your own 3D printer and some examples you can use with your 3D printer to solve real-world problems in your home.

Appendix

The appendix contains diagnostic charts to help you zero-in on the cause of a print quality issue, a failure, or other problems with hardware and software.

How to Use This Book

There are several ways you can use this book, depending on your experience level and, of course, the time you have to devote to study. After all, you want to enjoy your new acquisition, yes? The following sections describe some likely levels of experience. You may find that you fit into several categories—that's OK. The sections are not intended as the only ways to read and apply the material presented. Indeed, you can read this book cover-to-cover or a single chapter at a time in any order. Only you know your needs. However, if you want some guidance, I provide such next.

New to 3D Printing

This section is for those who are new to 3D printing and have either just bought a printer or plan to in the near future. It also covers those who want to learn to build their own 3D printer. You will learn all about 3D printers, including the hardware used to build them and the software to run them.

If this fits your needs, I recommend you read through the first two parts of this book before trying to spend a lot of time with your printer. This applies even to those who have purchased a commercial printer. The time you spend reading about and later executing calibration and proper setup may make the difference between buyer's remorse and enthusiasm.

Once you have your printer going and have had success printing several things, you can move on to the third part of this book, which will help you understand the maintenance needs of your printer. There is also a chapter on adding features your printer is missing. When you are ready to learn what more you can do with your printer, including post-print finishing your things, you can dive into the fourth part of the book.

You Own a 3D Printer, but Need Help Getting it Working Well

This section covers topics for those of you who have had some experience with a 3D printer but want to learn about how it works, and more importantly, how to tweak your printer to improve its print quality.

If this is you, I recommend skimming through the first part of the book to ensure that you have learned all of the key concepts of 3D printing. Even if you already have your printer set up and have software installed, it is a good idea to read about those topics in a more general aspect. If nothing else, you will see some of the choices you could make concerning filament, hardware, and software solutions.

From there, I recommend reading through the second and third parts of this book, one chapter at a time, to apply the techniques you've learned. This includes proper calibration, setup, maintenance, and troubleshooting your prints. The troubleshooting chapters alone are the one area where intermediate enthusiasts have a lot of frustration. As I mention in one chapter, there are a lot of opinions and solutions out there for common maladies; some are no more than voodoo or wishful thinking, some work for a few, and most are too specific to a particular model or situation to be a general cure. If you are having print issues, you will learn many solutions that can make almost all of your problems vanish.

Once you have your printer dialed in and your printing woes cured, take a look at the fourth part of the book to learn how you can take your hobby to the next level by finishing your prints with surface treatments, learning to become a member of the 3D printing community by sharing your ideas and designs.

You Own a 3D Printer, but Want More

This section is for those who have been using a 3D printer but feel there is something more out there.[1] In other words, those of you that want to further immerse yourselves into your 3D printing hobby and become more than a user—you want to become a true 3D printing enthusiast.

If you find that you are in this group—and since you are likely to have some experience in most areas, I recommend starting with the table of contents and reading each chapter in which you would like to learn more or perhaps recap your existing knowledge. This applies mainly to the first part of the book.

However, I recommend that you read the second and third parts carefully because good troubleshooting and maintenance are key skills that you must master to achieve the level of enthusiast. Furthermore, the fourth part should become your call to reach out with your newly refined skills to help others.

Downloading the Code

The code for the examples shown in this book is available on the Apress web site (www.apress.com). A link can be found on the book's information page under the Source Code/Downloads tab. This tab is located underneath the Related Titles section of the page.

Contacting the Author

Should you have any questions or comments—or even spot a mistake you think I should know about—you can contact me—the author—at drcharlesbell@gmail.com.

---

[1] I was there once a few years ago so I know exactly what you're thinking!

■ ■ ■

PART 1

Getting Started with 3D Printing

This section provides the basic information that you need to get started in 3D printing, including a short introduction to 3D printing technology, software, and hardware. The section also includes a chapter for those who are planning to build their own printers, with discussions on the tools and supplies required, as well as valuable tips on building 3D printers. The section concludes with chapters devoted to configuring your software and setting up and calibrating your printer, and one that offers helpful tips on printing your first objects and fine-tuning your printer.

CHAPTER 1

■ ■ ■

Introduction to 3D Printing

Three-dimensional (3D) printing has evolved dramatically in the last few years. 3D printers have become plentiful and affordable enough that anyone can own one.[1] Indeed, the cost of 3D printers (as little as $200 USD) makes them an attractive choice for small businesses, researchers, educators, and hobbyists alike. You can use a 3D printer in your business to create prototypes for manufacturing, develop architectural or engineering models, print miniature terrain and figures for gaming, or fix things around the house.

You can experience a lot of pleasure designing things and holding the results in your hand. Even after several years of printing three-dimensional parts, I often find myself watching the printer build the object layer by layer. It's still fascinating to me. I enjoy creating solutions for use in my home or office—especially if it saves me money. I also enjoy designing and printing upgrades and improvements for my printers.[2] But this enjoyment comes at a price. Some of my printers require attention every time I print, whereas others can operate with little effort.

What this means is, while 3D printers and software have become much easier to use, they are neither toys nor maintenance-free. 3D printers must be properly assembled (if you purchased a kit), adjusted, maintained, and repaired when they break. Many of the problems you will encounter when printing are directly related to some mechanical adjustment or software setting. Unless you have been working with 3D printers for some time or have spent countless hours trolling for solutions while trying to discern hokum from fact, it is easy to become frustrated with your printer when things don't work out. When you get to this point, you're well beyond the operators' manual.

This book provides a depth of information that far exceeds the meager documentation provided with some printers. You will discover many secrets, arcane facts, and techniques for getting the most out of your printer. In fact, I take you through the entire 3D printing experience—from choosing or building a printer, to maintaining and troubleshooting your prints, to designing your own objects.

In this chapter, I present a brief primer on 3D printing. I will cover 3D printing techniques, how 3D printers work, the software required, and the types of plastic supplies, including a brief overview of their properties and uses. I will conclude the chapter with some ideas on what you can expect from your 3D printer and where to get ideas for creating objects.

Getting Started

Before we jump into the various forms of 3D printers and their technologies, let's talk a little bit about what defines 3D printing. Whether you have recently acquired or built a 3D printer, or are completely new to 3D printing and about to buy your first 3D printer, I think this section will be helpful to set the stage for the chapters ahead. After all, it is always good to know (or review) the fundamentals and terms before jumping into lingo-infested waters, eh?

---

[1]Most range in price equivalent to laptop computers; the more features it has, the more expensive it is.
[2]At least one of my printers is in a perpetual state of pending upgrade. There seems to be no end to the ways you can improve some printer architectures.

■ **Note**   Henceforth I will use 3D printer and printer interchangeably since I will be talking only about 3D printers.

What Is 3D Printing?

The most fundamental concept to understand 3D printing is the process by which objects are built. The process is called *additive manufacturing*.[3] Conversely, the process that computer numeric control (CNC) machines use to form objects (starting with a block of material and cutaway parts to form the object) is called *subtractive manufacturing*. Both forms of manufacture use a Cartesian plot (X, Y, and Z axes) to position the hardware to execute the build. Thus, the mechanical movements for 3D printing are very similar to the mechanisms used in CNC machines. In both cases, there are three axes of movement controlled by a computer, and capable of very high precision movement.

Additive manufacturing has several forms or types that refer to the material used and the process used to take the material and form the object. However, they all use the same basic steps (called a *workflow*) to create the object. Let's start from a raw idea and see how the idea is transformed into a physical object using additive manufacturing. The following lists the steps in the process at a high level.

An object is formed using computer-aided design (CAD) software. The object is exported in a file format that contains the standard tessellation language for defining a 3D object with triangulated surfaces and vertices (called an .stl file).

■ **Note**   There is a new file format—named *additive manufacturing file* (AMF) format—that is becoming more popular. It was designed to extend the capabilities of STL and may emerge as the choice in the near future.

The resulting .stl file is split or sliced into layers, and a machine-level instruction file is created (called a .gcode file) using computer-aided manufacturing (CAM) software. The file contains instructions for controlling the axes, direction of travel, temperature of the hot end, and more. In addition, each layer is constructed as a map of traces (paths for the extruded filament) for filling in the object outline and interior.

■ **Note**   MakerBot printers use a slightly different file format, .x3g or the older .s3g, instead of .gcode. The use of the file is the same. It contains commands to tell the printer how to print the object.

The printer uses its own software (firmware) to read the machine-level file and print the object one layer at a time. This software also supports operations for setting up and tuning the printer.

This last step is where most 3D printing forms differ. That is, they vary slightly in the mechanism used and the materials used to form the object. However, all additive types use the same concept of taking an object and building it in layers. Table 1-1 lists some of the forms available, describes how the material is used to build the object, and tells what materials can be used.

---

[3]For more information, visit http://en.wikipedia.org/wiki/3D_printing.

Table 1-1. *Types of Additive Manufacturing*

Type	Build Process	Materials
Filament	Objects built layer by layer, where material in filament form is extruded from a heated nozzle.	Various plastics, wood, nylon, and so forth.
Wire	An electron beam is used to melt the wire as it is unspooled to form an object layer by layer.	Most metal alloys.
Granular	Various processes are used to take material in a raw, granular form using a laser, light, or electricity to fuse the granules and build the object.	Some metal alloys and thermoplastics.
Powder	A reactive liquid is sprayed on a power base to form solid layers. Some variations use a multistep process to fuse and then bind materials.	Plaster and similar cranular materials. Emerging solutions can use metal.
Laminate	Material is laid over the object and fused with a heated roller. A laser is then used to cut out the shape.	Paper, metal foil, plastic film.

The most common form of 3D printing is called *fused filament fabrication* (FFF). Since the majority of 3D printers available today for consumer purchase[4] are FFF, I will only discuss FFF in depth in this book. To simplify our discussion, henceforth I consider 3D printing to be synonymous with the FFF process. In fact, all printers discussed in this book are FFF-based.

WHERE DID FUSED FILAMENT FABRICATION ORIGINATE?

FFF is also known as fused deposition modeling (FDM). FDM was developed by S. Scott Crump in the late 1980s, and further developed and commercialized by Stratasys Ltd. in the 1990s. Indeed, FDM is a trademark of Stratasys Ltd. (the owners of MakerBot Industries). Since the majority of 3D printers use this process (the process is not trademarked, only the term *FDM*), we use FFF to avoid confusion with the Stratasys trademark.

How Does FFF Work?

When a 3D printer creates an object, the material used to print an object comes in filament form[5] on a large spool to make it easier for the printer to draw material. The filament is then loaded into an extruder that has two parts: one to pull the filament off the spool and push it into a heating element, and another to heat the filament to its melting point.

The part that pulls the filament and feeds it to the heating element is called the *cold end*, whereas the heating element is called the *hot end*. In most cases, the extruder contains both parts in a single unit, but it is not uncommon to see these as two separate parts. Sometimes manufacturers refer to both parts as the *extruder*, but others distinguish the extruder from the hot end (but they sometimes don't call it a cold end). Just one of the many nuances to 3D printing I hope to explain!

[4] I limit our discussion to printers that cost no more than about $3,000.00 USD. Any more than that amount, and you're in the commercial and manufacturing realm.
[5] Like fishing line, or as my wife says, "fishing twine."

5

■ **Tip** Never buy filament that isn't on a spool or a similar orderly delivery mechanism. Improperly wound filament can introduce a maddening number of extrusion failures. We will see why in a later chapter.

If this sounds like nothing more than a fancy hot glue gun, you're right! The process is very similar, but unlike the hot glue gun that relies on human power to pump glue sticks (however inaccurately) into the heating element, 3D printers use a computer-controlled electric motor called a *stepper motor* to precisely control how much and how fast the filament is fed to the hot end. Most extruders use a geared arrangement to allow the stepper motor to apply more torque to the filament to overcome forces such as the tension of the spool or the weight (and thickness) of the filament.

Figure 1-1 shows a drawing of how the extrusion process works, including a pictorial representation of the components discussed in this section.

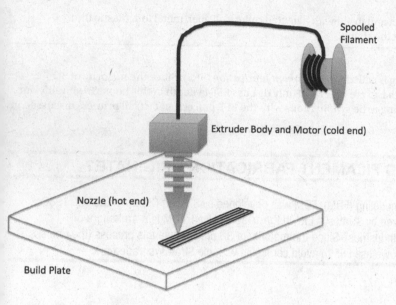

Figure 1-1. *FFF extrusion with nomenclature*

The drawing shows a mock-up of the extruder and a spool of filament. As you can see, the filament is pulled into the extruder (cold end) and then pushed into the nozzle (hot end). Once heated, the filament is extruded onto a *build plate* (a very flat surface used as the base for the object). Typically, the outer edges of an object are printed first, then the interior edges are printed, and finally, the interior of the layer is printed as either a solid layer (for outer-most layers) or as a fill-in matrix for inner layers.

Notice that the filament from the spool is much larger than the heated extrusion. This is because most nozzles (the small part where the filament exits the heater block) have a very small opening ranging from 0.3 millimeters (mm) to 0.5mm. Notice in the drawing I've exaggerated how the layer is built from multiple lines of heated filament. While grossly simplified, this is effectively how a 3D printer takes filament and builds a layer of the object.

Figure 1-2 shows an example of a printed part that was stopped after only a few layers. On the left is the bottom of the part. The part on the right shows what the default fill pattern and density look like. Notice that the edges are made from several passes of the extruder, but the interior is only partially filled. This not only saves filament but also ensures the part will have sufficient strength.

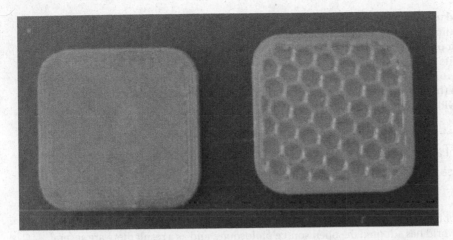

Figure 1-2. Example print

Now that we understand how a 3D printer puts the filament together to form an object, let's take a look at the software required for 3D printing. I will introduce the types of software needed and briefly discuss how they are used, and also provide a short demonstration of how to use the software to print an object. If you want to install the software, refer to the URLs listed for installation instructions.

3D Printing Software

There are three pieces of software involved in 3D printing: software required to create the object and export it as an .stl file (CAD), another to convert it into a G-code file that a printer can read (CAM), and finally, the firmware loaded in the "brain" of the printer itself that reads and executes the .gcode file. We call the printer software *firmware* because it is typically loaded once into a special memory device built into the electronics for the printer and started when the printer is turned on. You rarely ever need to change or modify the firmware (other than an initial load and calibration).

But wait, there's one more piece. Often overlooked, there is a fourth category of software often used in 3D printing and it may be the most important of all to your satisfaction! It's the *printer control application*. This software allows you to connect your computer to your printer (via a USB connection) and perform many operations, such as moving the axes, turning the hot end on/off, and aligning the axes (called *homing*).

I routinely use a 3D printer controller as part of my normal setup routine. Some printers come with an onboard LCD control panel that has controls for moving an axis and setting the temperature. Most support an SD card for reading G-code files. If your printer is already adjusted and ready to go, you can use this feature to print objects without tying up your computer for the duration of the print.

■ **Caution** If you print from your computer, don't disconnect your computer until the job is done! Can you guess what happens if you do? You'll end up with a partially complete part to add to your growing pile of printing horror stories.[6]

---

[6]The box I use to store my failed prints has once again proven that the gas law reigns supreme (also known as the *container maxim*: all containers will eventually fill to capacity regardless of their size).

Many 3D printing experts and manufacturers refer to the software as a "tool chain" because of the way you must use one piece of the software at a time to realize an object. Some manufacturers, like MakerBot Industries (www.makerbot.com), provide their own software that combines an object visualizer and slicer (CAM), as well as a printer controller. MakerBot calls its software suite *MakerWare* (www.makerbot.com/makerware/). Ultimaker calls its software suite *Cura* (http://wiki.ultimaker.com/Cura). Other examples of combined tools are the Repetier suite (www.repetier.com) and Printrun (http://reprap.org/wiki/Printrun). Each of these is an interface to the CAM software (the slicer) and each provides a printer controller feature.

■ **Note**   When I discuss aspects of a type of software in general, I use the term *software*. When I speak of an implementation of the software, I use the terms *program* and *application*.

If you are about to purchase or have already purchased a printer that does not come with software, do not despair! Much of the 3D printing world has adopted the open source philosophy, and as a result there are several options to choose for each software category. I will discuss each of these and show some examples of MakerWare and other solutions in the following sections. I will also explain the types of files you will generate from each step.

WHAT IS OPEN SOURCE?

Open source means the software or hardware is free for anyone to use. Think *free* as in "free speech," not free as in free beer. Most open source products have a license associated with it, designed to define ownership and outline the permissions that users have. For example, if something is marked as open source, it may be that the license allows you to freely use and even distribute. The license may also permit you to modify the product, but require you to surrender all modifications to the original owner. So while you can use it for free, it isn't yours to own. Always check the license carefully before using, distributing, or modifying the product.

Computer-Aided Design

Simply put, *computer-aided design* (CAD) is software that permits you to use a computer to create an object. CAD software typically includes features to realize an object in various 3D views, manipulate the object surface and interior details, as well as change the view of the object (scaling, rotating, etc.).

■ **Note**   CAD is also referred to as *computer-aided drafting*, but in this case it refers to the drawing aspect alone. I spent several years learning the art of mechanical drawing.[7] Computer-aided drafting revolutionized that aspect of the engineering discipline. In fact, learning computer-aided drafting software is what got me interested in the engineering disciplines.

---

[7]I still have my mechanical drawing tools. I can even letter properly when forced to do so. I remember distinctly practicing my letters for hours in preparation for a final exam—much like a second grader learning to write for the first time.

Advanced CAD software has features that allow you to create a number of objects and fit them together to form a complex mechanical solution (called a *model*). Advanced CAD software includes additional features that test fit, endurance, and even stress under load. An ultimate example would be the software that automotive manufacturers use to construct engines. I have seen examples of such software that can animate all of the moving parts and even suggest ways to improve the individual components.

There are many CAD applications available with a wide range of features. To be used with 3D printing, they must, at a minimum, permit you to design shapes in three dimensions, define interior features like holes for mounting the object, and basic tools to add a surface or facing to the object.

The various CAD applications save the models in a specific, sometimes proprietary, format. This limits the possibility of using several different CAD applications to manipulate an object. Fortunately, most permit you to import models and objects from various file formats.

More importantly, the software must permit you to create an object that is *manifold* (has an inside and outside surface with no gaps). This is important because the slicer needs to be able to create paths for the filament to follow, and gaps or holes means there is a break in the path. Attempting to force the slicing and printing of a nonmanifold object will result in an undesirable end result. I tried it once with a whistle and ended up with a solid block in the shape of a whistle—it filled the interior with solid plastic. Tragic.

■ **Tip** If your slicer program displays an error that your object is not manifold, you can use an online tool from NetFabb to fix the holes. Visit http://cloud.netfabb.com, select your object, enter your e-mail address, agree to the terms and conditions, and click "Upload to cloud". After a few moments, you will get an e-mail with a link to the fixed object. I have fixed a number of objects like this. While you are there, check out the cool online 3D printing tools they offer.

Remember, CAD applications for 3D printing must be capable of creating a standard tessellation language (.stl) file so that the CAM software can read the file, slice it, and create a printer instructions (.gcode) file for forming the object in three dimensions.

CAD Software Choices

There are a lot of applications that provide CAD features that you can use to create 3D objects. You can find some that are open source, some free to use (but limited in some way), and those that you must purchase. Most have a graphical user interface that allows you to see the object as you build it. As you will see, there is one that uses a C-like programming language to build a script to create the object. Some applications are available for online use. Furthermore, some are easy to use, whereas others take a lot of time to learn. In general, the more features the software application has, the more difficult it is to use.

If you are just starting out, you may want to try an application with fewer features until you get the hang of it or outgrow its features. Table 1-2 contains a list of some of the more popular CAD solutions, including cost basis, degree of difficulty to learn (how long it takes to create your initial object), and type of interface. This is not an exhaustive list, but it is a list of the choices known to export or save files in .stl format. In the next sections, I highlight the first (most difficult/full-featured) and last (easiest) options available.

Table 1-2. *CAD Software for 3D Printing*

Name	URL	Cost/License	Interface	Difficulty
Blender	www.blender.org	Open source	GUI	High
123D (Autodesk)	www.123dapp.com	Free (limited) Paid (unlimited)	Web	High
SketchUp	www.sketchup.com	Free (limited), Paid (pro version)	GUI	Medium
FreeCAD	www.freecadweb.org	Open source	GUI	Medium
TinkerCAD	https://tinkercad.com	Free (limited), Paid levels	Web	Low
NetFabb	www.netfabb.com	Paid	Web	Low
OpenSCAD	www.openscad.org	Open source	Text	Low*

Requires learning the language and library of functions.

Blender

The Blender CAD application (blender.org) is a veritable Swiss army knife of CAD software. Not only can you create highly detailed 3D models, you can also create 3D animation and more! For 3D printing, it's really overkill for most of the types of objects you will create. On the other hand, if you plan to develop complex models for commercial use or for creating parts for a complex solution, you will want to take a hard look at this application. Figure 1-3 shows a screenshot of the Blender application.

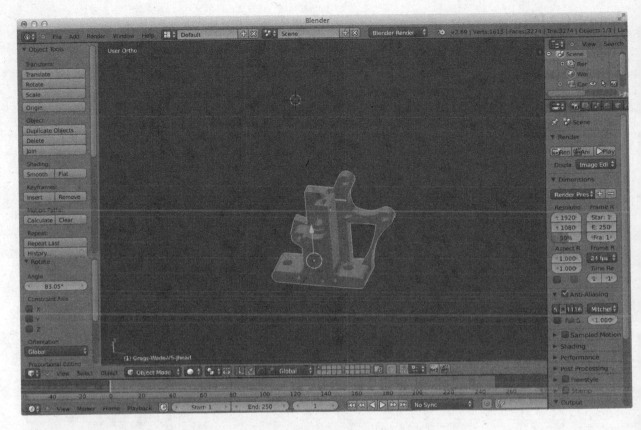

Figure 1-3. *Blender CAD software*

The example shows the editor window in which an object has been loaded. In this case, it is the extruder body for the Greg's Wade hinged extruder. I was able to import the .stl file, and Blender converts it so that I can modify the object however I like. For example, I may want to move the mounting holes or cover the existing legacy mounting holes (the ones for mounting on a Prusa Iteration 2 X-carriage).

If I had modified the object, I could save the object (model) and export it to a different .stl file, slice it, and print it. Clearly, this could be a useful feature if you need to modify an object but do not have the CAD software with which it was created. Perhaps best of all, it is open source!

I rated this application with a high level of difficulty for several reasons. First, there are a dizzying number of features to learn and hundreds of menu choices. It is definitely not something you can sit down and learn in an afternoon. However, it is a first-rate CAD solution—one that you would do well to master if you plan to design highly complex objects.

The good news is that there are a number of books available to learn Blender. If you want to master Blender, I recommend spending some time with the included documentation and seek out one or more of the following books:

- Lance Flavell, *Beginning Blender: Open Source 3D Modeling, Animation, and Game Design* (Apress, 2010)

- Roland Hess, *Blender Foundations: The Essential Guide to Learning Blender 2.6* (Focal Press, 2010)

- Gordon Fisher, *Blender 3D Printing Essentials* (Packt Publishing, 2013)

OpenSCAD

This solution is on the opposite side of the difficulty scale. Indeed, if you know a little programming (or at least the concepts of writing executable scripts), you can create simple objects very quickly without reading tome after tome of instruction manuals.

To build an object, you begin by defining a base object (say a square) and add or subtract other shapes. For example, to build a standoff for mounting a printed circuit board (like an Arduino or a Raspberry Pi), you start with a cylinder (the outer perimeter) and "subtract" a smaller cylinder (the inner perimeter). While this sounds simple, you can use this very simple technique to create very complex objects.

In fact, this is the process that was used to create the plastic parts for a popular variant of an open source printer created by Josef Prusa. Figure 1-4 shows an example of one of the models that Josef Prusa created.

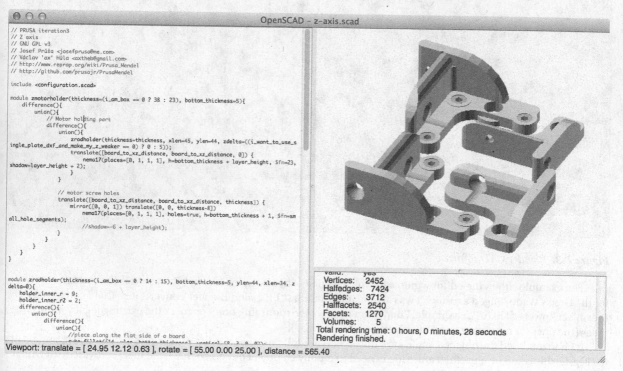

Figure 1-4. OpenSCAD example (GPL v3)

Take a moment to observe the figure. Notice that there are three parts to the interface. On the left is the code editor window where you enter all of the statements for defining your objects. On the right, at the top, is a view of the model (generated when the script is compiled) and below that is a list of feedback and messages from the OpenSCAD subprocesses and compiler.

As you can see, you can create very complex objects and even several in the same file. When you save the file, you are actually only saving the statements and not a rendered model. This enables you to save a lot of disk space (CAD-based files can be quite large), but you must compile the script to visualize the object(s).

OpenSCAD allows you to export the compiled model in a variety of formats that can be opened by other CAD applications for further manipulation. More importantly, you can generate the required .stl file for use in a CAM (slicer) application, permitting you to use OpenSCAD as the first stop in your 3D printing tool chain.

Even if you do not know the language, it is not difficult to learn and there are many examples on the web site (www.openscad.org) to help you get going. If you are looking for something to get started quickly, you will want to consider using OpenSCAD until you need the more advanced features of the larger CAD applications.

Thingiverse: An Object Repository

If you are thinking that learning a CAD program is a lot of work, you're right, it can be. Learning Blender can be a steep curve but if you favor a GUI with advanced features, the learning curve comes with the territory. The other GUI-based CAD programs have varying demands for learning to use, but most require you to learn a specific set of menus and tools. On the other hand, OpenSCAD is easier to use if you think in code, and therefore you may not need to use a complex GUI and all of its trappings to design your own objects.

But what if you don't have the time or the inclination to design your own object? Wouldn't it be great if there were a place where you could download .stl files of interesting and useful objects for printing? That's exactly what the nice people at MakerBot were thinking when they created a site called Thingiverse (thingiverse.com).

Thingiverse is a place where anyone can upload and post information about their objects (ones they have created or modified by permission) for anyone to view and use. Most of the objects on Thingiverse are open source, so you need not worry about intellectual property violations—but always read the license! Figure 1-5 shows a snapshot of the Thingiverse web site.

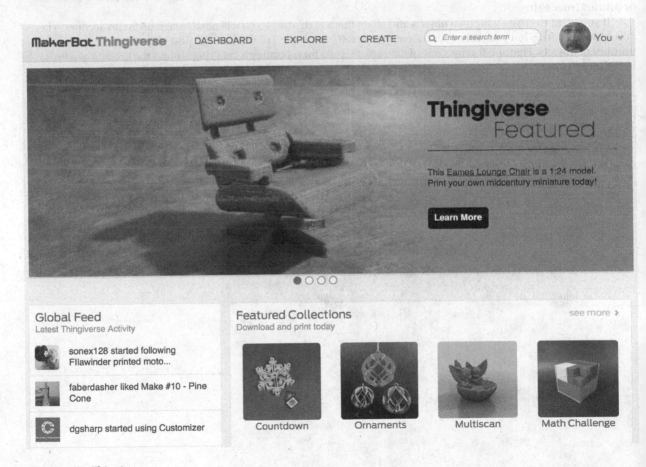

Figure 1-5. *Thingiverse*

The site is free for anyone to browse, search, and download objects. You don't even need to create an account! Once you find an object you want to use (print), simply click the Download button and save the files to your hard drive. Most files are in the .stl format, so you need only slice it and print it.

Registered users can create objects, mark objects for printing later, tag things that they like, organize things into collections to keep a virtual file of these things, and keep tabs on any objects uploaded. You can also share with others the objects you have printed (made). It is always nice to find a thing you like and see examples of it printed by others.

■ **Tip**   The best objects are those that a lot of people like. Watch for things that have been made often. This is indicative of a well-designed (and useful) thing.

When you find a part you want to see in more detail, simply click on it. You will then see a detailed page with a list of photos of the thing (a 3D view and one or more photos that the creator has uploaded). The page also includes a menu or tabs (varies among platforms) that include entries for a description of the object (thing info), instructions for assembly (optional), a list of the files available, and a comments section where anyone can comment or ask the creator questions. There are also statistics on the number of people that have liked the object, added it to a collection, or printed (made) it.

If you want to create your own objects and share them with others, you will need to sign up for an account. The account is also free, but you will need to identify yourself (name, etc.) so that you can post objects. I have posted a number of objects. Figure 1-6 shows one of my early designs for mounting a light ring around the hot end of a Prusa Iteration 2 printer.

Figure 1-6. *An object on Thingiverse*

This is a nifty upgrade that makes watching the print much easier. I use the LED to help me determine early on whether I am getting good adhesion to the build surface. It has helped me stop a number of prints that would have failed (corner lift or loss of adhesion altogether) had I not had more light to catch the problem before too much of the part was printed.

The Thingiverse web site works for most browsers and platforms. There is even a Thingiverse app for your iPhone or Android device so you can see what has been added since your last visit. Simply go to the site, click the Explore menu item, and choose Newest. I find myself checking for new objects at least once a day. I've found many useful objects and inspiration for other objects. Thingiverse is a great asset. I recommend searching Thingiverse before you create any object yourself. Chances are you will find something similar that you can download, slice, and print right away!

You can find all manner of objects on the site. Even though the predominant objects are suitable for 3D printing, you can also find files for laser and water-cutting 2D shapes. Thingiverse is also a major site for hundreds of modifications to many open source 3D printer designs. I have found dozens of interesting upgrades, many of which I have adopted with little or no modification. I will show you some of these upgrades in a later chapter. For now, let's return to the next step in the tool chain—slicing (CAM).

Computer-Aided Manufacturing

There are many aspects to CAM, but the one process we need is the ability to take a 3D object definition (an .stl file) and convert it into a file that contains instructions for the printer to build the object layer by layer (a .gcode file). More specifically, the slicer uses numerical control code in the standard tessellation language to create canonical machining function calls in the form of G-codes.

What is G-code?

G-code is a shorthand notation for a set of machine functions that govern the movement of the various parts of the machine. While 3D printers read G-code files, the codes themselves are not limited to 3D printers. In fact, the codes cover a wider range of machines, including CNC machines. Moreover, the G-code definition has been modified to include new codes specifically for 3D printing.

The codes are formed by a letter that signifies the class of command, a number (index), and one or more parameters separated by spaces (optional). There are codes for positioning the hot end, setting the temperature, moving the axis, checking sensors, and many more. Let's look at a few examples in Table 1-3, and then see what a .gcode file looks like, as shown in Listing 1-1.

Table 1-3. Common G-Codes

Code	Description	Parameters	Example
G28	Travel to X, Y, and Z zero endstops. This is the homing command.	None	G28
M104	Set temperature of hot end.	Snnn: temp in Celsius	M104 S205
M105	Get temperature of hot end.	None	M105
M106	Turn on fan.	Snnn: fan speed (0–255)	M106 S127
M114	Get position of all axes.	None	M114
M119	Get status of all endstops.	None	M119

Listing 1-1. Example G-code File

```
; generated by Slic3r 0.9.9 on 2014-01-05 at 15:53:58

; layer_height = 0.2
; perimeters = 3
; top_solid_layers = 3
; bottom_solid_layers = 3
; fill_density = 0.4
; perimeter_speed = 30
; infill_speed = 60
; travel_speed = 130
; nozzle_diameter = 0.35
; filament_diameter = 3
; extrusion_multiplier = 1
; perimeters extrusion width = 0.52mm
; infill extrusion width = 0.52mm
; solid infill extrusion width = 0.52mm
; top infill extrusion width = 0.52mm
; support material extrusion width = 0.52mm
; first layer extrusion width = 0.70mm

G21 ; set units to millimeters
M107
M104 S200 ; set temperature
G28 ; home all axes
G1 Z5 F5000 ; lift nozzle

M109 S200 ; wait for temperature to be reached
G90 ; use absolute coordinates
G92 E0
M82 ; use absolute distances for extrusion
G1 F1800.000 E-1.00000
G92 E0
G1 Z0.350 F7800.000
G1 X78.730 Y91.880
G1 F1800.000 E1.00000
G1 X79.360 Y91.360 F540.000 E1.02528
G1 X79.820 Y91.060 E1.04227
G1 X80.290 Y90.800 E1.05889
...
G1 X92.051 Y96.742 E6.11230
G1 X92.051 Y96.051 E6.12185
G1 F1800.000 E5.12185
G92 E0
M107
M104 S0 ; turn off temperature
G28 X0 ; home X axis
M84 ; disable motors

; filament used = 164.4mm (1.2cm3)
```

The G-code file is a text file that contains all of the machine instructions to build the file, including the setup and teardown mechanisms as defined by the slicer. Listing 1-1 shows an excerpt of a .gcode file. Notice that the first lines are preceded with a semicolon. This indicates a comment line and is commonly used to define the parameters for the print operation in plain English. Notice that the comments indicate layer height, solidity of the top and bottom, density, and much more. This makes it easy for you to determine the characteristics of the file without having to translate the G-codes.

■ **Tip** If you plan to print with more than one type of filament, you might want to name the sliced file (the .gcode file) with a code or phrase to indicate what filament is used. This is because each filament type requires different temperature settings. It is also likely that filament of the same type will vary in size or have slightly different melting characteristics.[8] All of this data is stored in the G-code file. You may also want to consider making folders, like PLA_3.06 or ABS_BLACK, and store all of the .gcode files by filament type, size, or color.

If you would like to know more about G-code and the various commands available, see http://reprap.org/wiki/G-code for a complete list of codes supported by most 3D printer firmware. We will see several of the more commonly used G-codes in later chapters.

WHAT IS REPRAP?

RepRap stands for *replicating rapid prototyping*.[9] The RepRap movement began as a vision of Dr. Adrian Bowyer at the University of Bath in 2005, with the goal to build a 3D printing platform that can print a clone of itself.

The term is used to categorize a number of open source 3D printer designs. Most popular and ubiquitous with RepRap are the Prusa iterations created by Josef Prusa. The RepRap world is very large, and supported by a number of communities with some very passionate contributors.

To learn more about RepRap, keep reading this book and visit the wiki at http://reprap.org/wiki/RepRap.

CAM Software Choices

Unlike CAD software, there are few choices for CAM software designed specifically for 3D printing. Recall that the primary function is slicing an object and producing the G-code file that 3D printers require. However, the choices available vary in how much you can control the generation of G-code.

Table 1-4 lists some of the most popular choices for CAM software for use in 3D printing. I will discuss the two most popular choices in the following sections.

---

[8]I have two reels of the same color from different suppliers, but one melts at about 8 degrees cooler than the other.
[9]No, it isn't a new style of music.

Table 1-4. *CAM Software for 3D Printing (Slicing)*

Name	URL	Cost/License	Notes
MakerWare	www.makerbot.com/makerware/	Free	Premier choice for MakerBot printers. Can generate G-code files for use with other printers, but it is optimized for MakerBot printers.
Slic3r	http://slic3r.org/	Open source	Wildly popular among RepRap enthusiasts. Very customizable.
Skeinforge	http://fabmetheus.crsndoo.com/ wiki/index.php/Skeinforge	Open source	Simple interface, but can be tedious to use.
KISSLicer	http://kisslicer.com/	Free (limited) Paid (Pro features)	Free edition has minimal features for 3D printing. Pro adds multiextrusion and advanced model control.

MakerWare

MakerBot has developed an application called MakerWare (makerbot.com/makerware/) that uses a 3D view that depicts the build platform and its maximum build volume. It allows you to position objects anywhere on the build platform (other CAM applications automatically center the object), generate sliced files (X3D or S3D) for use on their printers, and even gives you an option to see a layer-by-layer preview of the object before printing.

The MakerWare application is optimized for use with MakerBot printers. Indeed, MakerBot has done all of the really hard work for you. Simply stated, it just works—no fuss, no fiddling. Unlike other solutions, there are very few settings you can change—they aren't needed. However, if you need to fine-tune your prints (the G-codes) beyond the available settings or if you want to print on a non-MakerBot printer, you may want to explore other solutions that offer more customizability and control over the G-code generation.

MakerWare allows you to add objects (.stl files) to your build plate, move and rotate them, and even scale them to fit in the build area. You can also rotate the view in any direction, and zoom in or out. Figure 1-7 shows a snapshot of the MakerWare main interface.

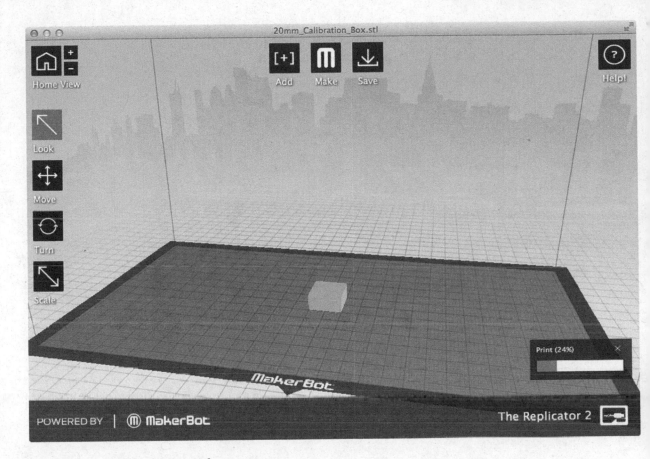

Figure 1-7. MakerWare main window

By permitting you to place the objects anywhere on the build platform, you can overcome the problem when the Kapton or blue tape gets damaged—just put the object somewhere else! Once you have your objects arranged on the build platform, you can click the Make button to enter the slicing function. The slicing feature of the software is highly optimized and streamlined. Unlike other software (as we will see), you can change only a few settings. Figure 1-8 shows the slicing dialog.

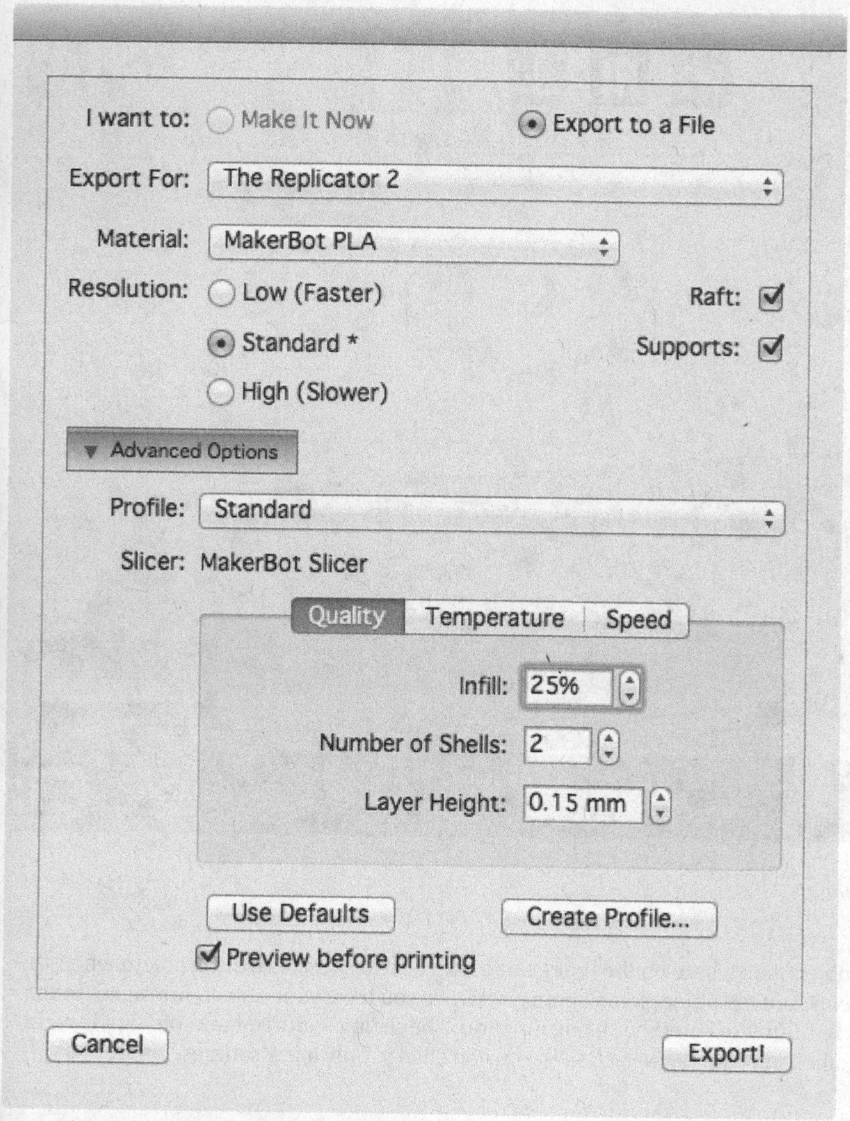

I want to: ○ Make It Now   ● Export to a File

Export For: The Replicator 2

Material: MakerBot PLA

Resolution: ○ Low (Faster)   **Raft:** ☑

● Standard *   **Supports:** ☑

○ High (Slower)

▼ Advanced Options

Profile: Standard

Slicer: MakerBot Slicer

| Quality | Temperature | Speed |

Infill: 25%

Number of Shells: 2

Layer Height: 0.15 mm

Use Defaults   Create Profile...

☑ Preview before printing

Cancel   Export!

Figure 1-8. MakerWare slicing control

The dialog permits you to select which printer you have (Replicator, Replicator 1 Dual, Replicator 2, or Replicator 2X), the material (ABS or PLA), and quality. You can also turn on support material and rafting. You can also print to a file or print directly to the printer (requires a USB connection between the computer and the printer).

Support materials are bits of plastic used to bridge large gaps or add support for extreme overhangs. Think of it as scaffolding used to shore up a portion of the object that would otherwise fail. For example, suppose you wanted to print an object that had a large empty interior. Rather than having the printer attempt to bridge (apply filament across a gap, which can lead to drooping or even failure to bridge the gap) the area, you can turn on support to prevent the filament from drooping in the middle. Adding support means you will have to remove the extra bits to get the part cleaned for use (or admiration of your brilliant design). Dual extruder machines can print using a second filament for support material. In this case, the filament can be dissolved rather than having to be removed or cut away.

Rafting, on the other hand, is a special technique used to improve cooling to prevent portions of the object from cooling faster than others. When this happens, the part can lift off of the print bed itself (called *lifting* or *curling*). Rafting is several layers of filament laid down on the print bed prior to printing the object. In the case of MakerWare, the rafting peels away from the part very cleanly.

If you want a bit more control over the print, you can click the Advanced button, which reveals finer control settings for quality, temperature of the hot end, and even the speed of extrusion. Figure 1-8 shows what this looks like. You can also save your customized settings and retrieve them later. This permits you to set up profiles for certain filaments (heat properties for colored filament can vary). Lastly, you can choose to see a preview of the print prior to generating the file. Select the "Preview before printing" check box to see the preview.

The build preview dialog allows you to see a graphical representation of the paths the printer will use to extrude filament. Use the slider on the left side of the dialog to show a range of layers starting from the first layer. Figure 1-9 shows an example of the build preview dialog.

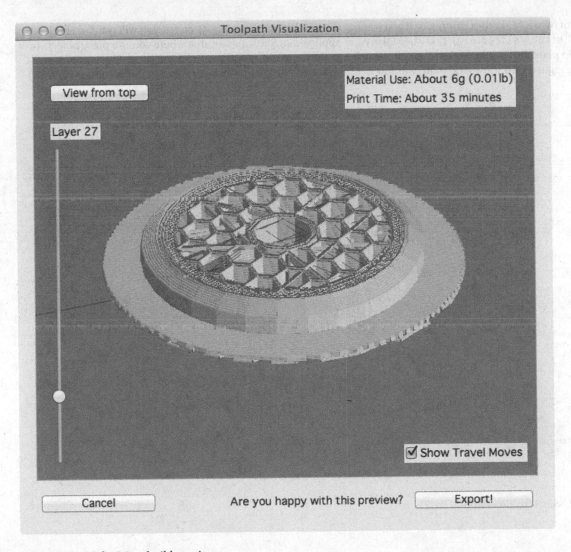

Figure 1-9. MakerWare build preview

Notice in the figure that you can also choose to show the tool paths (Show Travel Moves). This highlights the paths that the extruder will take when moving the hot end into position for printing. For complex or multiple objects, this may generate many lines. For simple objects as shown in the example, it reveals little.

Take another look at the example. Notice I've set the layer bar to 27. It shows how the printer will manage the infill and layers. Interestingly, it also shows the raft that is built under the object. To finish your export (slicing action), click Export!.

Finally, not only does MakerWare generate the sliced files, you can also use it to control a MakerBot printer. Thus, it combines the CAM and printer control functions. All of these features mean MakerBot printers are supported from the CAM step onward by a very robust, easy to use application. In many ways, MakerBot has made all of the hard decisions for you ensuring you have a successful print any time you want to print an object.

Slic3r

If you do not own a MakerBot printer, or if you want to control the creation of the G-codes, you will want to check out the Slic3r[10] (http://slic3r.org). Like the MakerWare application, Slic3r has an area where you can place objects on a virtual build plate, but unlike MakerWare, the view is top-down, two-dimensional, and automatically centered on the build plate. Figure 1-10 shows the main window in expert mode (simple mode hides many of the advanced controls).

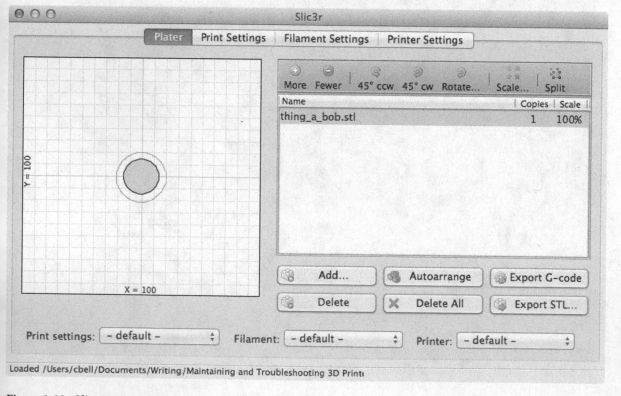

Figure 1-10. *Slic3r main window*

---

[10]No, it isn't spelled wrong. The name includes the number 3.

■ **Note**   The latest releases of Slic3r will include a three-dimensional view option.

Slic3r allows you to have complete control over the generation of the G-codes. There are dialogs for controlling the print, such as specifying infill (quality), perimeters, skirt, brim, and also rafting. There are so many settings, in fact, that you could spend a lot of time fine-tuning your slicing. Don't worry about those for now. We will explore all of these terms in a later chapter that discusses how to fine-tune your print. There is also excellent documentation online for you to explore every nuance of the software (`http://manual.slic3r.org`).

Like MakerWare, you can also store profiles, but in this case, you store a separate profile for each of the three major categories: print settings, filament settings, and printer settings. The print settings section permits you to set parameters for how the object will print (e.g., infill). The filament settings section permits you to set the temperature of the hot end (and build platform), as well as the size of the filament. The printer settings dialog allows you to control the printer, including adding custom G-codes—like moving the print bed, turning off fans, and so forth—at the beginning or end of the print job.

You can save your settings for each of these three areas individually. Thus, you can set up special filament settings for each roll of filament you own, as well as set up different printer profiles if you have different printers. More likely, you will set up different print settings to correspond with different levels of print quality, speed, and so forth.

Filament Properties

Not only is it likely that filament will have different heating properties, it also can vary in size from one manufacturer to another. It is not unusual to find filament that measures 1.8mm (it should be 1.75mm) or even 3.1mm (it should be 3.0mm). You should always measure your filament and set the dialog accordingly.

■ **Caution**   Check the size of your filament as you consume it. If it varies in size by more than 0.01mm–0.03mm, you may want to reconsider buying filament from the same vendor. Wildly varying size can indicate inferior filament and can lead to extrusion failures, poorly filled (filament too small) prints, or over-filled (filament too big) prints.

The main settings you will use to control the print are located on the print dialog. This includes the fill density (infill), print speed, and support material. Figure 1-11 shows and example of the print settings dialog. Notice on the left is a long list of topics. When you click each of these, you can see all of the advanced settings for that category.

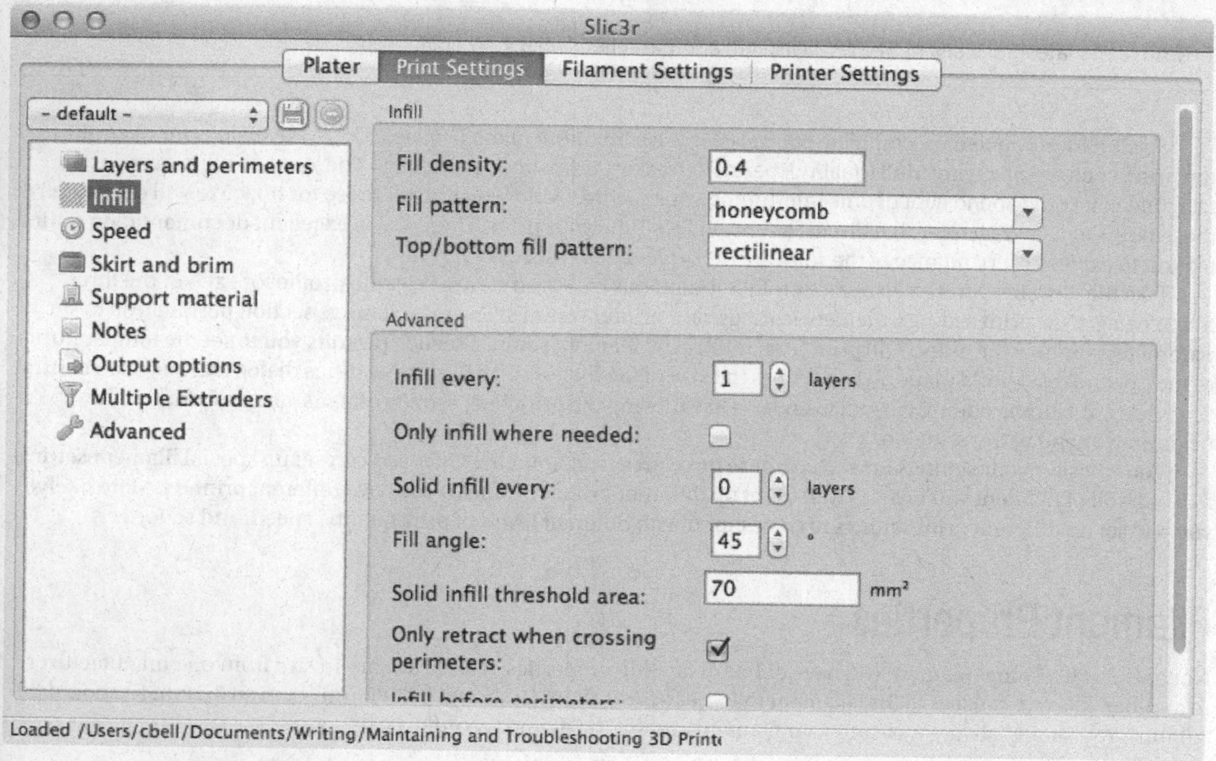

Figure 1-11. *Slic3r print settings window*

Figure 1-12 shows an example of the printer settings dialog depicting the entry page for setting custom G-codes at the start and end of the print job. In this example, I tell the printer to home all axes and lift the nozzle (hot end) 5mm at the start. Then at the end, I tell the printer to turn off the heater(s), move the X axis to home, and disable the motors. You can add your own custom commands here too.

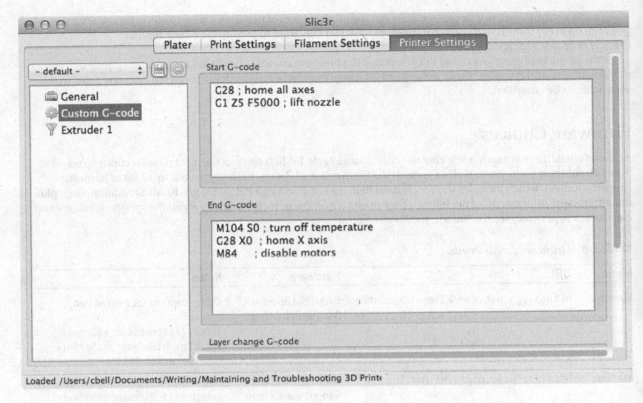

Figure 1-12. *Slic3r printer settings window*

In many ways, Slic3r is more of a professional tool than MakerWare. This is because Slic3r gives you far more control over the generation of the G-code file, and thus the printer itself. All of this power comes with a price, however. You should tread carefully when modifying the many settings, making sure you change only certain areas at a time.

In fact, I recommend testing your ideas using a simple test cube of about 10mm–20mm square. This will save you a lot of frustration (and filament) by letting you see the effects of the change more quickly than, say, printing something for several hours—only to discover you don't have the right settings for your needs.

Now that we have seen examples of the CAM software, I will discuss the firmware and then look at printer control options.

Firmware

All the object generation (CAD) and machine controller/slicing (CAM) can get you only so far. It is at this stage where the printer takes control. The software (called firmware because it is loaded into non-volatile RAM) on the printer is therefore responsible for reading the G-code file and providing controls for managing prints, controlling temperature, resetting the printer, and so forth.

If you purchased a complete printer like the MakerBot Replicator 2, you do not have to worry about the firmware—it is already loaded and configured for you at the factory. Similarly, if you built your printer from a kit, the choice of what firmware to use has been made for you. You may still need to load the firmware, but typically all of the hard work has been done for you. Consult your printer documentation for more information about the specifics of loading the firmware. On the other hand, if you are building your own printer from scratch or are considering changing the firmware on you printer, you need to know what options are available.

In this section, I will briefly present the more common choices of firmware. There seems to be a new variant popping up every month so if you want the very latest, you may want to consult the online forums (`http://forums.reprap.org`).

One of the first things you need to know is that the firmware comes to you in the form of source code that you must configure and compile. There are some cases where this has been done for you, but the firmware listed in this section must be compiled.

Firmware Choices

As mentioned, there are only a few choices for firmware. Table 1-5 lists some of the most popular choices and notes about their features, as well as some of the hardware it supports. Each supports a small set of hardware (the electronics), which includes the widely used RepRap Arduino Mega Pololu Shield (RAMPS) Arduino Mega plus daughterboard solution. All of the following are open source. For more information about the specific hardware and electronics supported, see the links in the Notes column.

Table 1-5. *Firmware for 3D Printers*

Name	URL	Hardware	Notes
Sprinter	`https://github.com/kliment/Sprinter`	RAMPS, Ultimaker, Sanguiololu, Gen6.	Offers support for heated bed, SD card. `https://github.com/kliment/ Sprinter/blob/master/Sprinter/ Configuration.h#L6`
Marlin	`http://reprap.org/wiki/Marlin`	RAMPS, Ultimaker, Sanguiololu, Gen6, and similar.	Offers support for multiple extruders, as well as LCD panels, auto bed-leveling, and more. A variant/fork of Sprinter. `https://github.com/ErikZalm/ Marlin/blob/Marlin_v1/Marlin/ Configuration.h#L35`
Repetier	`https://github.com/repetier/ Repetier-Firmware`	RAMPS, Azteeg X3, Gen6, Sanguinololu, Gen7, Printrboard, RAMBo, and many more.	Combines the best of many firmware options, with enhancements for speed, greater control, and a wider range of hardware support. Features an automatic configuration utility to allow you to build a firmware for your specific printer without digging through the source code. `https://github.com/repetier/ Repetier-Firmware/tree/master/ boards`
Teacup	`http://reprap.org/wiki/Teacup_ Firmware`	RAMPS, Ultimaker, Sanguiololu, Gen6, and similar.	An early version of 3D printing firmware. `https://github.com/Traumflug/ Teacup_Firmware`

Except for Repetier-Firmware, all of these options require you to edit the source code directly before compiling it for loading on the Arduino (or similar) electronics board. Listing 1-2 shows a small portion of the Marlin source code. In this case, it is an excerpt from the Configuration.h file. This is the only file you need to modify. I show only a few parts of the file—it is quite a bit larger than this!

Listing 1-2. Configuration.h: Settings for 3D Printing Hardware

```
...

//================================================================================
//============================Mechanical Settings============================
//================================================================================

// Uncomment the following line to enable CoreXY kinematics
// #define COREXY

// coarse Endstop Settings
#define ENDSTOPPULLUPS // Comment this out (using // at the start of the line) to disable the
endstop pullup resistors

#ifndef ENDSTOPPULLUPS
  // fine Enstop settings: Individual Pullups. will be ignored if ENDSTOPPULLUPS is defined
  // #define ENDSTOPPULLUP_XMAX
  // #define ENDSTOPPULLUP_YMAX
  // #define ENDSTOPPULLUP_ZMAX
  // #define ENDSTOPPULLUP_XMIN
  // #define ENDSTOPPULLUP_YMIN
  // #define ENDSTOPPULLUP_ZMIN
#endif

#ifdef ENDSTOPPULLUPS
  #define ENDSTOPPULLUP_XMAX
  #define ENDSTOPPULLUP_YMAX
  #define ENDSTOPPULLUP_ZMAX
  #define ENDSTOPPULLUP_XMIN
  #define ENDSTOPPULLUP_YMIN
  #define ENDSTOPPULLUP_ZMIN
#endif

// The pullups are needed if you directly connect a mechanical endswitch between the signal and
ground pins.
const bool X_MIN_ENDSTOP_INVERTING = true; // set to true to invert the logic of the endstop.
const bool Y_MIN_ENDSTOP_INVERTING = true; // set to true to invert the logic of the endstop.
const bool Z_MIN_ENDSTOP_INVERTING = true; // set to true to invert the logic of the endstop.
const bool X_MAX_ENDSTOP_INVERTING = true; // set to true to invert the logic of the endstop.
const bool Y_MAX_ENDSTOP_INVERTING = true; // set to true to invert the logic of the endstop.
const bool Z_MAX_ENDSTOP_INVERTING = true; // set to true to invert the logic of the endstop.
//#define DISABLE_MAX_ENDSTOPS
//#define DISABLE_MIN_ENDSTOPS
```

```
// Disable max endstops for compatibility with endstop checking routine
#if defined(COREXY) && !defined(DISABLE_MAX_ENDSTOPS)
  #define DISABLE_MAX_ENDSTOPS
#endif

// For Inverting Stepper Enable Pins (Active Low) use 0, Non Inverting (Active High) use 1
#define X_ENABLE_ON 0
#define Y_ENABLE_ON 0
#define Z_ENABLE_ON 0
#define E_ENABLE_ON 0 // For all extruders

// Disables axis when it's not being used.
#define DISABLE_X false
#define DISABLE_Y false
#define DISABLE_Z false
#define DISABLE_E false // For all extruders

#define INVERT_X_DIR true    // for Mendel set to false, for Orca set to true
#define INVERT_Y_DIR false   // for Mendel set to true, for Orca set to false
#define INVERT_Z_DIR true    // for Mendel set to false, for Orca set to true
#define INVERT_E0_DIR false  // for direct drive extruder v9 set to true, for geared extruder
set to false
#define INVERT_E1_DIR false  // for direct drive extruder v9 set to true, for geared extruder
set to false
#define INVERT_E2_DIR false  // for direct drive extruder v9 set to true, for geared extruder
set to false

// ENDSTOP SETTINGS:
// Sets direction of endstops when homing; 1=MAX, -1=MIN
#define X_HOME_DIR -1
#define Y_HOME_DIR -1
#define Z_HOME_DIR -1

#define min_software_endstops true // If true, axis won't move to coordinates less than HOME_POS.
#define max_software_endstops true // If true, axis won't move to coordinates greater than the
defined lengths below.

// Travel limits after homing
#define X_MAX_POS 205
#define X_MIN_POS 0
#define Y_MAX_POS 205
#define Y_MIN_POS 0
#define Z_MAX_POS 200
#define Z_MIN_POS 0

#define X_MAX_LENGTH (X_MAX_POS - X_MIN_POS)
#define Y_MAX_LENGTH (Y_MAX_POS - Y_MIN_POS)
#define Z_MAX_LENGTH (Z_MAX_POS - Z_MIN_POS)

...
```

```
// The position of the homing switches
//#define MANUAL_HOME_POSITIONS  // If defined, MANUAL_*_HOME_POS below will be used
//#define BED_CENTER_AT_0_0      // If defined, the center of the bed is at (X=0, Y=0)

//Manual homing switch locations:
// For deltabots this means top and center of the cartesian print volume.
#define MANUAL_X_HOME_POS 0
#define MANUAL_Y_HOME_POS 0
#define MANUAL_Z_HOME_POS 0
//#define MANUAL_Z_HOME_POS 402 // For delta: Distance between nozzle and print surface after homing.

//// MOVEMENT SETTINGS
#define NUM_AXIS 4 // The axis order in all axis related arrays is X, Y, Z, E
#define HOMING_FEEDRATE {50*60, 50*60, 4*60, 0}  // set the homing speeds (mm/min)

// default settings

#define DEFAULT_AXIS_STEPS_PER_UNIT   {78.7402,78.7402,200.0*8/3,760*1.1}  // default steps per unit
for Ultimaker
#define DEFAULT_MAX_FEEDRATE          {500, 500, 5, 25}          // (mm/sec)
#define DEFAULT_MAX_ACCELERATION      {9000,9000,100,10000}   // X, Y, Z, E maximum start speed
for accelerated moves. E default values are good for skeinforge 40+, for older versions raise
them a lot.

#define DEFAULT_ACCELERATION          3000    // X, Y, Z and E max acceleration in mm/s^2 for
printing moves
#define DEFAULT_RETRACT_ACCELERATION  3000    // X, Y, Z and E max acceleration in mm/s^2 for
retracts

...

// Preheat Constants
#define PLA_PREHEAT_HOTEND_TEMP 180
#define PLA_PREHEAT_HPB_TEMP 70
#define PLA_PREHEAT_FAN_SPEED 255   // Insert Value between 0 and 255

#define ABS_PREHEAT_HOTEND_TEMP 240
#define ABS_PREHEAT_HPB_TEMP 100
#define ABS_PREHEAT_FAN_SPEED 255   // Insert Value between 0 and 255

...

#endif //__CONFIGURATION_H
RUNAWAy!!!
```

If this file is scary or if you think you're in way too deep, do not despair! While it requires you to know all of the specifics of your hardware, like the mechanics (and mathematics) of each axis, there are a great number of people who have done this before. If you get stuck, consult the forums and similar online sites. With a little digging, you can find the correct values to use for just about any hardware configuration.

Setting all of the correct variables and constants can be a challenge. If you purchased your printer as a kit or without the firmware loaded, you should have received instructions on what values to set in this file. Consult your printer documentation or your vendor's web site for help.

On the other hand, if you are building your own printer, there are a couple of tools that can make configuring the firmware for your printer much easier. The first is the excellent online RepRap Calculator 3 page that Josef Prusa created to help you supply the correct values for many of the critical attributes (http://calculator.josefprusa.cz/).

Another tool you should consider using is the Repetier-Firmware configuration tool (www.repetier.com/firmware/v091/). This allows you to step through the setting of the hardware variables in a guided form. You can use the results from the hardware calculator to complete the process.

Whether you need to load firmware for the first time or want to modify your firmware (if you changed the hardware), this book will help you do that. Rather than diving into that realm here, I will talk more about configuring the firmware in a later chapter.

Now that we've had a brief glance at the firmware, let us now talk about the last piece in the software tool chain: printer control software.

Printer Control

Printer control applications are designed to allow you to move the axis and turn on/off the heaters (extruder, bed), fans, and more. Most printer control software allows you to send ad hoc G-code commands to the printer. For example, you can check the status of the endstops or check the temperature of the extruder.

The software for controlling a printer is becoming more of an option than in years past. It used to be that you had to have a printer control application to send the G-code files to the printer. However, most 3D printers (and kits) have LCD panels that have a number of features, like setting the temperature for the extruder and print bed, moving the axis, and even reading from an SD card. As mentioned previously, printing from an SD card means you don't need the printer control piece of the tool chain.

However, there is still a need for this software. For example, if you want to set your Z axis endstop or check movement of an axis, I find it easier to use a printer control application. Perhaps it's more likely you will want to issue a special command to interrogate some aspect of the printer—through custom G-codes. Another example is that some printer firmware allows you to preheat the printer, but doesn't allow you to turn on only the extruder or bed—it turns on both at the same time. Printer control applications, on the other hand, give you finer control of the hardware.

There are only a few choices for printer control software. Table 1-6 shows the most popular choices. I present two of the more popular choices for non-MakerBot printers in the following sections. I omit the MakerWare option since it is very streamlined, with little feedback other than percent complete, and tailored exclusively for MakerBot printers.

Table 1-6. *3D Printer Control Software*

Name	URL	Cost/License	Notes
MakerWare	www.makerbot.com/makerware/	Free	Premier choice for MakerBot printers.
Pronterface	http://reprap.org/wiki/Printrun	Open source	Wildly popular among early RepRap enthusiasts but is losing popularity.
Repetier-Host	www.repetier.com	Open source	Simple interface but can be tedious to use. Has been gaining popularity since its release.
OctoPrint	http://octoprint.org	Free	Web-based printing. Designed for use on small computing like Raspberry Pi.

Pronterface

Pronterface is a Python-based application for controlling your printer. It is actually a suite of tools that includes Printrun, which includes a G-code protocol (Printcore), a command-line G-code protocol interface (Pronsole), a GUI printer controller (Pronterface), and a number of helpful scripts. Basically, when you use Pronterface, you are actually using many of the other pieces of the suite, but most people use only the Printrun application.

Printrun provides a unique graphical interface for controlling the axes of your printer. You can set the temperature of the extruder and print bed independently to whatever value you want. You can also turn off the motors (great for cancelling a print in a hurry) and even set up your own custom buttons to execute G-code commands or other actions. You can also see a layer-by-layer view of the print job before it is printed.

What I like most about Printrun is how easy it is to move each axis at a time and set up the printer for a print job. Figure 1-13 shows the Printrun interface.

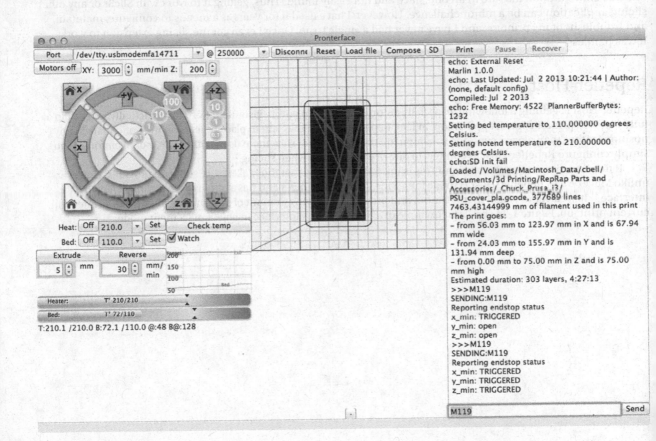

Figure 1-13. *Printrun*

Notice the segment of the window to the right. This is a running list of feedback from the printer. Look at the last few lines. This is the result of me issuing the M119 G-code command to get the status of the endstops. As you can see, they are all triggered. This tells me the printer has homed (all axes are at position 0), so I don't have to turn my chair or even look at the printer to verify.

Also, the panel in the center (the print bed) will show you a 2D display of the object as the G-codes are being sent to the printer. It effectively lets you check on the print job without having to visit the printer. Cool, eh?

Notice that the listing also tells me some statistics about the print job. In this case, the print job is going to take a while—almost four and a half hours! This tells me that I may have chosen too fine of a quality or have failed to set my print speed properly. In this example, I am printing on a Prusa Iteration 2 with a fairly slow extruder. The print quality is really good, but it isn't very fast. I use this feedback to help me decide whether to print the object or perhaps reconfigure the G-codes for faster printing.

Sadly, while the application works well, it can be a bit tedious to install and get configured. For example, on a Mac the configuration files are in an odd place and not easily found. Thus, getting it to work with Slic3r or any other slicing application can be a minor challenge. However, I have used it for years as a means to configure, maintain, and troubleshoot my printers, and I have never had a single issue. Once I even got the slicing extension to work. It was painless.

Repetier-Host

Repetier-Host is gaining a following, especially among the RepRap enthusiasts. Repetier-Host is actually more than a fully featured printer control application. In fact, Repetier-Host allows you to place objects on the build plate in any position (rather than always centered), manipulate them, and even slice them using either Slic3r or Skeinforge. You simply configure Repetier-Host to connect to one of these for use when slicing.

If this sounds familiar, you're right! This is the same workflow that the MakerWare software provides. However, unlike MakerWare, Repetier-Host is made for a wide variety of printers and has a much more technical feel to its interface.[11] It is easier to install than Printrun and provides a dizzying amount of information about your printer and current print job. Figure 1-14 shows an example of a Repetier-Host interface in object placement mode.

---

[11]In other words, it's a bit nerdy or tinker-inspired. 3D printing veterans will appreciate the level of detail in feedback and printer control.

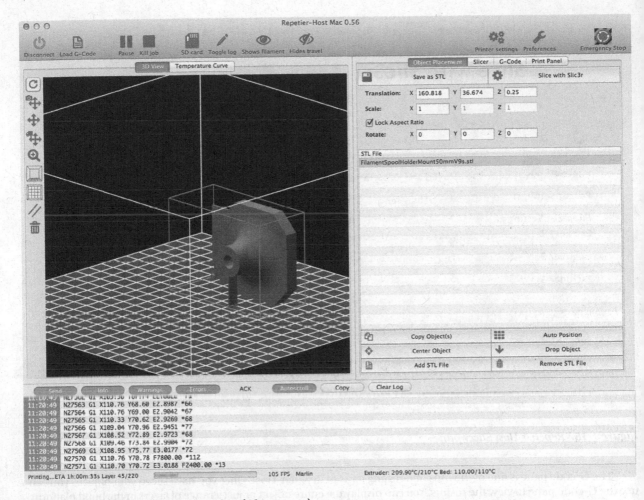

Figure 1-14. *Repetier-Host main interface (Object pane)*

The interface is divided into several parts. Toolbars are located at the top and left for common operations such as connecting to the printer, manipulating the build plate views, and so forth. In the center is the build plate view. Unlike Printrun (but like MakerWare), this is a 3D view that is very easy to zoom and rotate to orient the view.

To the right is a multitab panel that provides controls for loading and manipulating objects, slicing the objects (using Slic3r or Skeinforge), another for working with the G-code, and finally a printer control panel. I will present an example of each of these. As you can see, Repetier-Host is much more than a simple printer controller, but is categorized as such.

The slicing pane allows you to configure the slicer used to generate the G-code. Unlike Printrun, you have a very easy way to choose which profiles to use. For example, you can choose the specific profiles for each category with Slic3r. Figure 1-15 shows the Slicer pane.

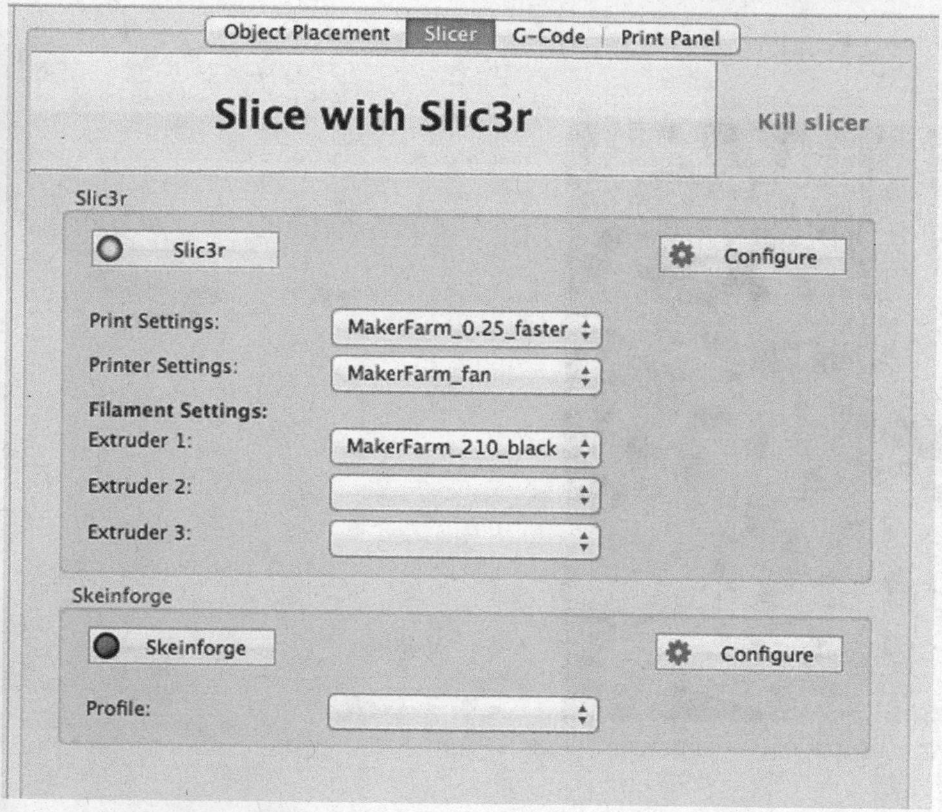

Figure 1-15. *Repetier-Host Slicer pane*

The G-code pane is one of the most interesting parts of Repetier-Host. Once you have sliced your objects, you can use the G-code pane to view the results. You can display the entire object or just a range of layers in the build platform panel. This allows you to check the print job before it prints—just like you can in MakerWare.

But the really interesting for-experts-only feature is the ability to edit the G-code directly. I have not found another application that permits you to do this. Thus, if you know what you are doing, you can change the G-code without reslicing. For example, I often print the same object in PLA and ABS (for various reasons). However, since the temperature settings are different, as well as a few other parameters—like filament thickness, I can simply change those settings and not run the slicer again. Very nice! Figure 1-16 shows the G-code pane.

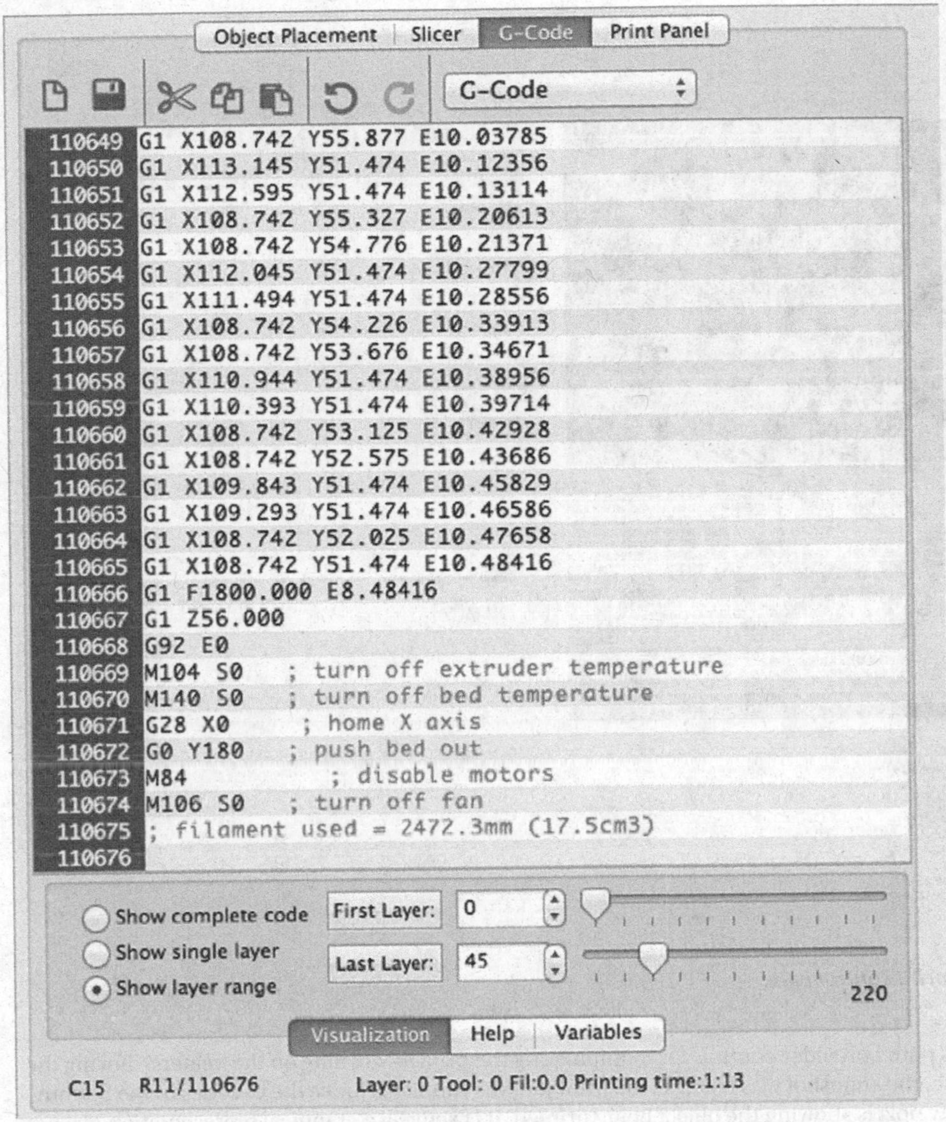

Object Placement	Slicer	G-Code	Print Panel

```
                                    G-Code

110649  G1 X108.742 Y55.877 E10.03785
110650  G1 X113.145 Y51.474 E10.12356
110651  G1 X112.595 Y51.474 E10.13114
110652  G1 X108.742 Y55.327 E10.20613
110653  G1 X108.742 Y54.776 E10.21371
110654  G1 X112.045 Y51.474 E10.27799
110655  G1 X111.494 Y51.474 E10.28556
110656  G1 X108.742 Y54.226 E10.33913
110657  G1 X108.742 Y53.676 E10.34671
110658  G1 X110.944 Y51.474 E10.38956
110659  G1 X110.393 Y51.474 E10.39714
110660  G1 X108.742 Y53.125 E10.42928
110661  G1 X108.742 Y52.575 E10.43686
110662  G1 X109.843 Y51.474 E10.45829
110663  G1 X109.293 Y51.474 E10.46586
110664  G1 X108.742 Y52.025 E10.47658
110665  G1 X108.742 Y51.474 E10.48416
110666  G1 F1800.000 E8.48416
110667  G1 Z56.000
110668  G92 E0
110669  M104 S0    ; turn off extruder temperature
110670  M140 S0    ; turn off bed temperature
110671  G28 X0     ; home X axis
110672  G0 Y180    ; push bed out
110673  M84        ; disable motors
110674  M106 S0    ; turn off fan
110675  ; filament used = 2472.3mm (17.5cm3)
110676
```

Show complete code   First Layer: 0

Show single layer   Last Layer: 45

Show layer range   220

Visualization   Help   Variables

C15   R11/110676   Layer: 0 Tool: 0 Fil:0.0 Printing time:1:13

Figure 1-16. *Repetier-Host G-code pane*

■ **Caution**   Tread lightly when editing the G-code file! One wrong command and you could end up with a strange object or a ruined print.

One of the interesting features of Repetier-Host is that it allows you to see all of the messages to and from the printer. You can see the actual G-codes scroll by as they are sent to the printer. While this is fascinating at first, it can become a bit of a novelty. Fortunately, you can turn off classes of feedback messages to clean up the display. Figure 1-17 shows the Repetier-Host print control panel.

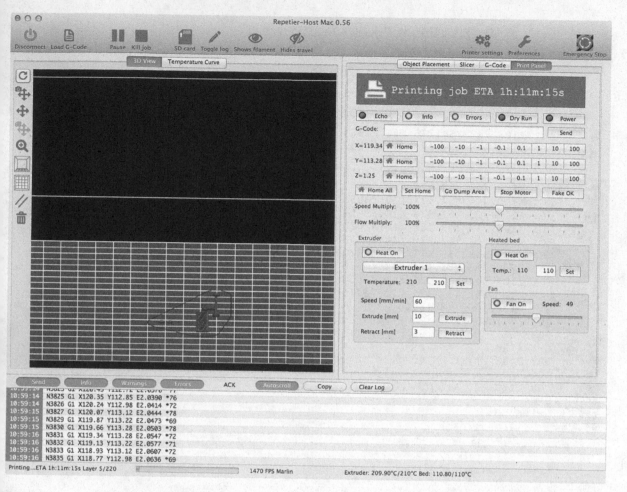

Figure 1-17. *Repetier-Host print control pane*

Similar to Printrun, this panel provides controls for manipulating the printer—turning on the heaters, moving the axis, and so forth. In this case, the snapshot was taken as the print job was running. Notice the G-codes in the bottom pane. Notice also the 3D view port is showing the object being printed. It is actually a graphical representation of what the printer is doing. This could be very handy if your printer is located away from your computer.

Well, that's it for the software. Most references on 3D printers either spend too little or too much time talking about the software, and rarely offer you options to consider. I hope that the previous sections have given you a lot to consider if you want to try other options or are shopping for what software to use.

Now let's turn our attention to the really cool parts of our printers—the hardware!

3D Printer Hardware

The hardware used to construct 3D printers varies greatly, despite some fundamental concepts. You can find printers that are made from clear and colored Plexiglas or acrylic, some made almost entirely from wood, others constructed with major components made from plastic (e.g., RepRap varieties), and some that are constructed from a sturdy metal frame. Not only do the materials used in constructing the frame vary, so do the mechanisms used to move the print head and extrude the plastic.

Some may scoff at this claim, but a 3D printer is essentially a special type of machine called a *robot*. You may think of robots as anthropomorphic devices that hobble around bleeping and blinking various lights (or bashing each other to scrap in an extremely geeky contest), but not all robots have legs, wheels, or other forms of mobility. Indeed, according to Wikipedia, a robot is "a mechanical or virtual agent, usually an electromechanical machine that is guided by a computer program or electronic circuitry." As you will see, 3D printers fit that description quite well.

Recall from the previous section that it is vital to know all of the specifics of your hardware in order to configure the firmware correctly. But to do that, you must understand how the printer as a whole is constructed. In this section, we explore the basic hardware components in a generic sense (no particular vendor or configuration).

The following sections introduce the hardware in six basic groups: the axes (parts that move horizontally and vertically), the types of electric motors used, the hardware used in extruding plastic, the build platform, electronics, and finally, the frame. Each section will describe some of the variants you can expect to find and some of the tradeoffs for certain options.

Axis Movement

A 3D printer gets its name from the number of planes it uses to construct objects. Technically, the axes movement is called a *three-dimensional Cartesian coordinate system*. The three axes are labeled X, Y, and Z. They are typically oriented where X moves left and right, Y forward and backward, and Z up and down. Figure 1-18 depicts a cube that illustrates the planes of movement. As you can see, a cube is an excellent shape to use to think about how the printer moves.

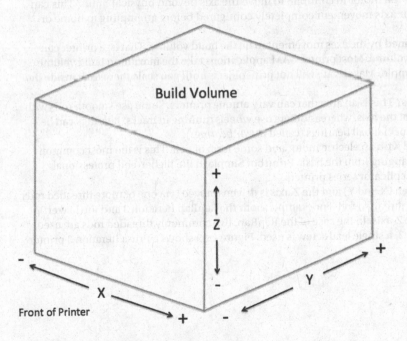

Figure 1-18. Axes movement and orientation

Notice that in the drawing, the end points of the axes are labeled with a plus or minus sign. This is representative of how the printer moves. For example, as the printer moves the X axis to the left, its position is reduced, and as it moves to the right, the position is increased.

The starting point or "home" for all axes is position [0,0,0], which orients in the lower-left corner of the drawing. Printers vary in how they locate this position. Some use mechanical or optical switches at the "minus" side or starting point of each axis. When the printer moves the axis to this point (called an *endstop*), the printer sets its counter or position indicator to 0. Conversely, other printers place the endstop at the "plus" side of the axis, and count back movement of the axis from there to reach 0. When a printer moves all three axes to their starting points, it is called *homing*.

■ **Note**   3D printers have a fourth axis. Some printer firmware and software refer to the movement of the extruder as the *E axis*. It is not uncommon to see this in reference works.

Minimum and Maximum Endstops and Crashes

When you examine the firmware or documentation for some printers, you will see that some use endstops at both ends of the axis, referred to as the *minimum endstop* and the *maximum endstop*. Other printers (most RepRap variants) use only minimum endstops and a setting in the firmware for maximum travel.

Care should be taken when adjusting endstops or changing the firmware. If the endstop switch does not work or the software defines an invalid end position (too large), the printer may cause the axis to crash into its mechanical components; or worse, cause the motor to continue to move the axis beyond physical limits. This can cause serious damage. It is best to get your axis movement completely configured before attempting to home or print for the first time.

We consider the cube (or cuboid) defined by the axes movement to be the build volume. That is, a printer can create any object that fits inside the build volume. Most printer CAM applications take the maximum build volume into account when slicing objects. For example, MakerWare will not print objects until you scale them to fit inside the build volume.

So how does the printer move the axes? This is an area that can vary among printers. Some use smooth rods with bearings to support the mechanical parts of the axis, whereas others use wheels running in tracks. Bearings can be made from plastic, oil-infused bronze, or special ball bearings (called *linear bearings*).

Movement of the axis is accomplished with an electric motor and some form of belt. This is the most common mechanism and can be found in printers ranging from the basic Printrbot Simple to the higher-end professional consumer (dubbed *prosumer*) MakerBot Replicator series printers.

Typically, two of the axes are belt driven (X and Y) and the Z axis is driven (moved) via one or more threaded rods or lead screws—a special type of precision threaded rod. For example, both the RepRap iteration 3 and the MakerBot Replicator 2 use threaded rods to move the Z axis. In the case of the RepRap, two commonly threaded rods are used, and in the case of the MakerBot Replicator 2, a single lead screw is used. Figure 1-19 shows a Prusa Iteration 3 printer with the axes labeled.

Figure 1-19. *Prusa Iteration 3 printer*

Each axis on the Prusa Iteration 3 rides on two smooth rods with bearings (typically linear bearings). It uses a belt-driven X and Y axes and a threaded rod mechanism for the Z axis. Notice in the drawing that the X axis is the part that moves the extruder (located in the center of the photo) left and right. The Y axis moves the build plate (the part with the binder clips attached) forward and backward. Both axes use a belt driven by an electric motor. If you look between the two rods, you will see the belt and idler pulleys. The Z axis uses two electric motors and two threaded rods to move the Z axis up and down. You can see the motors mounted at the bottom of the frame. The small vertical rods are the threaded rods.

Whichever mechanism is used to move the axis, the geometry of that mechanism must be known and entered into the firmware. For example, the size of the drive pulley (the one mounted on the electric motor) and the number of teeth per millimeter of the belt are critical to determining how far the firmware must turn the motor to move the axis a fraction of a millimeter. Similarly, the movement of the threaded rods or lead screw must be programmed in the firmware.

Lastly, the most vital part of the mechanism is the electric motor, called a *stepper motor*.

Stepper Motors

A stepper motor is a special type of electric motor. Unlike a typical electric motor that spins a shaft, the stepper is designed to turn in either direction a partial rotation (or step) at a time. Think of them as having electronic gears where each time the motor is told to turn, it steps to the next tooth in the gear.[12] Most stepper motors used in 3D printers can "step" 1.8 degrees at a time. Figure 1-20 depicts a typical stepper motor.

Figure 1-20. Stepper motor (image courtesy of MakerFarm.com)

Another aspect of stepper motors that makes them vital to 3D printers (and CNC machines) is the ability to hold or fix the rotation. This means that it is possible to have a stepper motor turn for so many steps, and then stop and keep the shaft from turning. Most stepper motors have a rating called *holding torque* that measures how much torque they can withstand and not turn.

Up to five stepper motors are used on a typical 3D printer. One each is used to move the X and Y axes, another is used to drive the extruder (E axis), and one or two are used to move the Z axis.

---

[12]Metaphorically speaking. Even if you open one up, you won't see any actual gears.

Extrusion Mechanism (Extruder)

The extruder is where the plastic hits the, er, plastic. As we discovered in an earlier section, the extruder is the component that controls the amount of plastic used to build the object. The extruder is moved and the plastic is extruded based on the G-codes in the file. The paths that the extruded plastic takes are called *runs* or simply *paths*. Other terms you may encounter include *road*, *threads*, or *beads*.

Figure 1-21 shows a photo of a 3D printer extruder assembly. The filament is fed into the top of the extruder. In the background, you can see the stepper motor. On the bottom of the extruder, you can see the hot end, and the extruder itself is mounted on the X carriage. Notice that the motor turns a shaft via a small gear and a large gear. The shaft is a special bolt with area that is machined to grip the filament. This bolt is called a *hobbed bolt*. Figure 1-22 shows an example of a hobbed bolt.

Figure 1-21. *Extruder assembly (Prusa Iteration 3 with Greg's Wade hinged extruder by misan:* thingiverse.com/thing:65939*)*

Figure 1-22. *Extruder assembly (image courtesy of MakerFarm.com)*

This is just one form of extruder. There are many variants, including some that do not use a gear-drive hobbed bolt. Instead, they use a special pulley that has been machined to grip the filament. Figure 1-23 shows the special drive pulley, called an *Mk7 direct drive pulley* (sometimes called a *direct drive gear*). In fact, these extruders are also called *direct drive extruders* or even *compact extruders*, because they require very few extra parts and a small body to mount the motor. I have enlarged the photo so you can see the machined grooves for gripping filament.

Figure 1-23. *Direct drive Mk7 gear (image courtesy of MakerFarm.com)*

In almost all cases, extruders use a tension mechanism to help the extruder grip the filament. For example, the Greg's Wade hinged extruder uses a door with an idler pulley (a bearing) with two springs held under tension by bolts. Similarly, a direct drive extruder for the MakerBot Replicator 2 uses a spring-loaded arm to apply pressure against the direct drive gear. Figure 1-24 shows an example of a custom extruder body made from machined aluminum by Karas Kustoms (karaskustoms.com). We will see more upgrades for 3D printers in a later chapter.

Figure 1-24. *MakerBot Replicator 2 extruder body upgrade (image courtesy of Karas Kustoms)*

The hot end, if you recall, is responsible for accepting the filament fed from the extruder body and heating it to its melting point. You can see one of the latest hot end upgrades for 3D printers in Figure 1-21. The bit at the bottom with the fins is a Prusa Nozzle made especially by Josef Prusa's company (http://prusanozzle.org). I will discuss different types of hot ends and why you would choose one over another in Chapter 2.

Now that we have an idea of how the extruder heats and extrudes plastic to form objects, let us talk briefly about where all that plastic goes.

Build Platform

All 3D printers (FFF or FDM types in particular) use either a stationary or moving platform to build the object. Hence it is called a *build platform*. Those printers that use a moving platform isolate movement to one axis. For example, a Printrbot Simple moves the build platform on the X axis (left and right), a Prusa variant moves the build platform on the Y axis (forward and backward), and the MakerBot Replicator 2 moves on the Z axis (up and down).

The build platform (sometimes called *print bed* or simply *print platform*) can be made from wood, Lexan, aluminum, and composite materials as the base. Placed on top of this is an aluminum, glass, or composite plate called the *build plate*. Glass is the most common choice. It is to this surface that the first layers of the object are extruded. Some build platforms include a heater element, called a *heated build plate*, placed under the glass. The heated plate is used to help some filament stick to the build plate. A built platform with the heated element is called a *heated build platform*. Figure 1-25 shows a heated build plate.

Figure 1-25. Heated build plate (image courtesy of MakerFarm.com)

It is common practice—and indeed sometimes essential—to use another medium on top of the build platform to help objects adhere to the build plate. Like the decision to use a heated build plate, the medium used varies with the filament used. For example, some plastics adhere better to blue painter's tape, whereas others adhere better to Kapton tape (a special heat-resistant film).

Electronics

The component responsible for reading the G-codes and translating them into signals to control the stepper motors is a small microcontroller platform utilizing several components. Most notably are the microprocessor for performing calculations, reading sensors (endstops, temperature), and controlling the stepper motors. Stepper motors require the use of a special board called a *stepper driver*. Some electronics packages have the stepper drivers integrate, and others use pluggable daughterboards.

While most commercial printers use a proprietary electronics package, there are several types available for RepRap and similar DIY printers (RAMPS, RAMBo, Printrboard, etc.). The most common is RAMPS, which uses an Arduino Mega, a special daughterboard (called a *shield*), and separate stepper driver boards. Figure 1-26 shows the components for a typical RAMPS package. The photo shows the optional LCD display with an integrated SD drive that enables computerless operation.

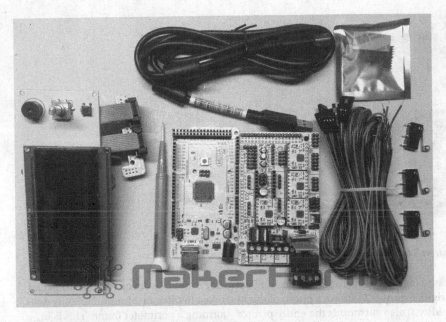

Figure 1-26. *RAMPS kit (image courtesy of MakerFarm.com)*

Now that we have discussed the axes, how they are moved, the electric motors that move the component, the extruder, the build platform used to form the object, and the electronics, it is time to discuss how a frame holds all of these parts together.

Frame

The choice of frame material is another area that varies from one printer to another. The best frames are those that are rigid and do not flex when the extruder is moving or when the printer moves an axis in small increments. As you can imagine, this is very important to a high-quality print.

Early open source 3D printers (like the Prusa variants) used a series of threaded rods and printed parts to form the frame. They used two triangular frame members joined by another series of threaded rods. You can see the evolution of the RepRap variants at http://reprap.org/wiki/Build_A_RepRap.

The most recent RepRap Prusa iteration can be built with either laser-cut wood or a single sheet of aluminum. Figure 1-21 showed a single sheet aluminum version. Figure 1-27 shows an example of a wooden version of the same printer. It is actually made from melamine, which is a wood composite that offers better rigidity than plywood without the effects of humidity (swelling).

Figure 1-27. *Malamine Prusa Iteration 3 frame (image courtesy of See MeCNC.com)*

Another common choice for frame material is steel. The MakerBot Replicator 2 and newer versions use a special rectangular steel frame that is very rigid. Figure 1-28 shows a photo of the MakerBot Replicator 2 frame. Not only does the steel frame provide excellent rigidity, it also surrounds the entire printer—forming a perimeter frame. This is in stark contrast to the Prusa Iteration 3 that has a very minimal, mostly internal frame.

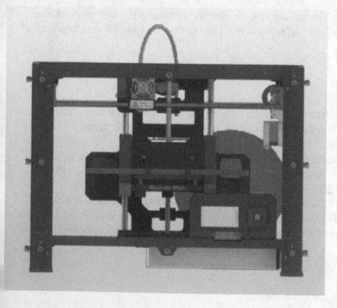

Figure 1-28. *MakerBot Replicator 2 steel frame (image courtesy of MakerBot.com)*

Other printers use thick acrylic for the frame components: laser-cut wood panels that are bolted together, or a combination of various materials. Aesthetics are sometimes employed so that the printer itself resembles more of a household appliance and less of a mash-up of a blender and a lawnmower.[13]

---

[13]Which is precisely what my first 3D printer looked like.

If you are buying a prebuilt printer or a commercial offering, you won't have a choice of the frame materials. However, if you are building your own printer or deciding which kit to buy, you can choose the frame material. As I mentioned, the Prusa Iteration 3 variant can be found as a kit with a wooden, composite, or even aluminum frame. Whichever material you choose, the frame is the only part of the printer that isn't directly moved. It should be as rigid as possible and provide strong anchorage for each axis.

Now that we have discussed how 3D printers are constructed, let us now look at the types of filaments that are available to use in building objects.

Filament Types

There are many forms of filament and more being created every year. Filament comes in a variety of sizes (usually 1.75mm or 3.0mm) and dozens of different colors. You can get filament that has a slight sheen or even a flat (think matte) filament that glows in the dark, and even filament that has small bits of metal flake to make it appear to sparkle in the light. Indeed, you can build up quite a pallet of colors to express your creativity. Filament is normally wound on a plastic or wooden spool.

■ **Note**   The diameter of the filament required is governed by the size of the extruder. Printers come with either a 1.75mm or 3.0mm hot end. Check your documentation before ordering new filament.

The most common types of filament are plastics called *polylactic acid* (PLA) and *acrylonitrile butadiene styrene* (ABS). Each type of filament has certain heating properties and requirements for build platforms. Table 1-7 lists the more common filaments available, along with their abbreviations and brief descriptions. The melting point (in this case, the temperature that the filament becomes soft enough to extrude) is listed in degrees Celsius.

Table 1-7. *Filament Types*

Type	Abbrev.	Melting Point (Celsius)	Description
Polycarbonate	PC	155	Impact resistant. Can print clear.
Aliphatic polyamide	Nylon	220	Low friction. Somewhat pliable.
High-impact Polystyrene	HIPS	180	Similar to ABS but can be dissolved with limonene. Sometimes used for support material.
Acrylonitrile butadiene styrene	ABS	215	Flexible, easy to modify (carve, sand, etc.).
Polyethylene terephthalate	PET	210	Made from food-grade substrate. Completely recyclable.
Polyvinyl alcohol	PVA	180	Dissolves in cold water. Used for support material.
Laywoo-D3		180	Wood blend. Similar to PLA. Looks like light pine when printed.
Polylactic acid	PLA	160	Derived from plants and biodegradable.

■ **Note**   Actual melting points for your printer may vary slightly.

No matter what type of printer you buy or build, the choice of filament will be dictated by the printer hardware. Specifically, the following components determine which filament the printer will support.

- Size of extruder and hot end

- Hot end heating characteristics, such as the maximum heat range

- Heated print bed support

The size of the extruder feed mechanism and the size of the hot end will determine whether you can use 1.75mm or 3.0mm filament. The material used to make the extruder body and the heating characteristics of the hot end will also factor into which filament you can use. Lastly, whether the printer has a heated print bed will also determine which filament you can use.

Recall a heated print bed helps the filament adhere to the print bed. Filaments that require a heated print bed (those that perform best with a heated print bed) are ABS, HIPS, nylon, and PC. PLA and other filaments with a lower melting point typically don't require a heated print bed. However, it can be shown to help with PLA.

If you are planning to build a printer or want to be able to print with a number of filament types, you should look for a printer that has a hot end that can heat efficiently to 265 degrees Celsius (or higher), and has a heated print bed option.

Another, less frequently cited, criteria is the sort of gases that the filament exudes when heated. Some filament produces a noticeable odor when heated. Some have an odor that is neither harmful nor noxious (to some), whereas others have an odor that can cause irritation for those with sensitivity or are allergic to certain chemicals.

Some filament, like ABS, can be extruded in an open environment and are not susceptible to air movement that can cause the object to cool too quickly (none can withstand the effects of the air currents from a house fan, for example). Cooling ABS too quickly can cause print failures. Other filament, like PLA, retains heat and requires a small fan to cool. Figure 1-29 shows one example of how a fan is used when printing PLA.

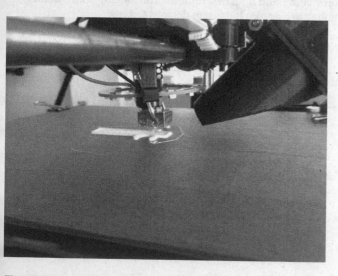

Figure 1-29. Using a fan when printing with PLA

Most printers and kits on the market today are designed to print in PLA or ABS. Since ABS has a higher melting point than PLA, a printer that has a small fan to cool the filament can print ABS and PLA.

ABS vs. PLA: Which Is Best?

The choice of whether to print with ABS or PLA can sometimes be emotionally charged. Those enthusiasts who have perfected their printing of either choice can be quite insistent that theirs is the best choice. Rather than supply yet more rhetoric, I will present arguments for and against each. With this information, you can make your own choice. That is, provided you haven't locked in on a printer that prints only one type of filament (not that there is anything wrong with that).

ABS is a very good choice if you plan to create objects that are going to be in close proximity to heat sources like a hot end. ABS is also somewhat flexible and can withstand forces that would break PLA objects. It is also easily modified—you can cut it with a hobby knife and glue it together with either ABS glue or acetone. In fact, ABS dissolves in acetone. You can make your own ABS glue by dissolving a small amount of ABS in acetone. As the acetone evaporates, it leaves hardened ABS that forms a strong bond. Lastly, ABS flexes well—forming strong bond layers.

However, ABS exudes a very noticeable odor that can cause some people irritation. It is always a good idea to use a fume extractor when printing with ABS. In fact, some people build special enclosures or fume hoods to vent the gases to the outside. ABS is also not as rigid or as strong as PLA and can wear more quickly than PLA. For example, gears are best made from PLA, since gears made from ABS can wear out quickly. If your printer came with ABS gears, check them often for wear, and replace them when tolerance becomes too great (the gears have excessive play).

Lastly, ABS requires a heated print bed and Kapton tape or similar for the best bond. This fact alone makes ABS harder to print objects with no warping. Furthermore, Kapton tape can be a bit of a challenge to get to stick to a glass plate without air bubbles or wrinkles. There are many techniques that can help, and that alone should be enough to conclude ABS is more difficult to use.

PLA is a very good choice for those who plan to use their printers in their home or office. The odor it exudes smells a lot like pancakes, so unless you abhor that type of breakfast food, it is not an unpleasant experience. PLA is harder and more rigid, making it a good choice for components that must be strong and do not permit too much flexing. It is recommended to use a fan when printing PLA. A fan forces air over the filament as it is extruded. This helps the filament cool more quickly, forming a stronger bond and reducing lift. PLA is also more forgiving when it comes to adhering to the print bed. PLA adheres well to common blue painter's tape, which is much easier to apply than Kapton tape. The ease of printing makes PLA a good choice for beginners.

However, since PLA does not flex well, it isn't a good choice for clamps and similar objects that must flex. Also, since PLA has a lower melting point than ABS, PLA is not a good choice for extruder bodies and similar parts for printers that print ABS.

So, which is best? That depends. If you are starting out, you might want to stick with PLA until you've mastered some of the calibration techniques for achieving high-quality prints. On the other hand, if you want to build things that you can customize or use *adaptive prototyping*,[14] you may want to choose ABS. Again, it is your choice, and now that you know the major ins and outs of each, you can make an educated choice.

Switching Filament

You may be wondering if it is possible to switch from one type of filament to another. The answer is simply, "Yes, you can." The only issue is making sure the old filament is completely removed from the nozzle before loading and using the new filament. The same is true for changing colors of filament, as we will see in a later chapter.

Now that we've explored the software, hardware, and filament types used in 3D printers, I want to set some expectations for you if you are just entering the world of 3D printing.

---

[14]Which goes something like this: cut, drill, sand, glue, repeat.

What You Can Expect from a 3D Printer

If you have never owned a 3D printer or are experiencing 3D printing for the first time, there are some expectations you should consider adopting. The following are areas where most novice 3D printing enthusiasts experience disappointment, or shall I say less than ideal enthusiasm. I discuss each in the following paragraphs.

- Ease of use

- Print quality

- Reliability

- Maintenance

These areas may seem intuitive, but there are surprises awaiting you if you do not consider each as you plan your purchase or learn to live with what you have. Don't be tempted to give up and sell your printer or force the vendor to accept it in a return (most will not anyway). I've seen a number of incomplete printers, and printers with very low use, for sale. I often wonder if they are for sale because the owners' expectations of the 3D printing experience are misguided. Perhaps the following will help you avoid a similar fate.

Ease of Use

This is the one area where things can go wrong quickly. If you've read or otherwise been convinced 3D printers are easy to use, you should reevaluate that assessment. The CAD software alone can be a challenge to learn and master. Vendors like MakerBot have achieved a high level of user friendliness, but that can be deceiving. You still must know where to find objects to print (Thingiverse) or learn how to use CAD software.

Aside from the software, some 3D printer vendors claim "click and print" capability, which is a bit misnamed. Even the best, most reliable 3D printers require a certain amount of calibration and maintenance to achieve good prints every time (which is unrealistic because there are so many things that can go wrong).

Ease of use, therefore, is a qualitative term. If you are already an experienced 3D printing enthusiast or if you enjoy tinkering, adjusting, upgrading, and general fiddling with hardware, the vast world of RepRap variants will seem like a treasure trove. On the other hand, if you are just starting out or do not have the patience (or skills) to tinker with your printer to get it to print well, you will want to steer clear of DIY kits and RepRap-like variants, and instead choose a well-established commercial option, like a MakerBot Replicator 2.

Once again, even the best printers require a certain amount of work to get the most out of them. Keep this in mind and avoid the temptation to blame the vendor when things don't work so well. Most likely the problem is something you have forgotten to do, or do not know must be done. For example, leveling (tramming) the print bed is often overlooked; this is the source of a host of print failures that can be corrected by the very simple process of adjusting the print bed.

■ **Note** The term "leveling" isn't a correct term. We don't level the bed, as in making it even with the horizon (or floor); rather we make the print bed the same distance from the X axis across the bed. That is, the hot end is the same distance away from the print bed at all locations. While *tramming* is the correct term, many vendors, including MakerBot, use "leveling" and "tramming" interchangeably.

Print Quality

This category is one that can cause even the most hardened 3D printing fan consternation. Many things can contribute to poor print quality, so sometimes it is hard to know where to start to diagnose and correct the problem. Indeed, there are 3D printer reviews I've read that rated the quality of printers based on skewed results. In one case, I noticed a clear indication that had the author or tester followed a few simple precautions, the print quality would have been better than what was reported.

What this means is you cannot expect to unbox (or assemble) your printer, click Print, and see a finished, perfect object appear before your eyes. You must start out with relatively low quality settings, modify them to perfection while calibrating your printer, and then increase those settings in increments until you achieve a good print.

One major factor to consider is the hardware itself. For example, a commercial printer is unlikely to arrive with incorrectly installed or damaged components. For example, building a RepRap Prusa Iteration 2 requires the use of 8-millimeter or 5/16-inch threaded rods for the Z axis. If the rods are not perfectly straight, and the threading is wound incorrectly (I once found a rod where the threads were deeper on one side than the other), you can experience Z wobble, which produces a washboard affect (the sides are not perfectly flat).

Similarly, the build platform must be level with the X axis. Adjusting it so that it is level (again, called *tramming*) requires moving the extruder to each corner of the build platform, and raising or lowering the print bed in that corner until the nozzle is the same distance from the print bed in all four corners (assuming the build plate is flat). Some printers are easier to tram than others. For example, the MakerBot Replicator 2 has an automated process that moves the extruder for you, whereas most printers require you to move the print head with either a printer controller application or through an LCD interface. However, you can move the axes by hand if the printer is powered off and you do not move them too quickly. Moving the axes quickly can cause the stepper motor to generate electricity and feedback through the electronics.

There is much more to consider with respect to hardware, and we will see more of this in other chapters. For now, keep in mind that print quality is something you must earn through careful calibration and attention to detail. The ease of which depends largely on the capabilities of your hardware and your willingness to tinker to perfection.

Reliability

Another area that can sometimes be an issue is reliability. Even if you devote the proper attention to detail to get the printer calibrated and ready to print, you can sometimes experience hardware and software failures—especially over a relatively short period of use.

One such example is the X axis ends on one of my Prusa Iteration 2 printers. The part cracked, causing a host of random print quality issues. I replaced it, only to have it crack again. I finally fixed the problem by grafting a brace for the affected area. Fortunately, the part was made of ABS, making it very easy to add the brace. If it were PLA, it would have been harder to do (but not impossible).

As part of my diagnosis of the part failure, I made sure that the smooth rods that the part rides on were straight and that everything on the axis was aligned properly. The part is simply too fragile for long-term use. You may find that this is the case for a number of different printers.

Another example is the routing of the X axis wiring on some MakerBot Replicator 2 machines can break over time due to a stress point. Should the wire break, your printer will become inoperable. Careful research and preventive maintenance can avoid this problem.

There are more examples of reliability issues that I could discuss, but what you should keep in mind is that 3D printers are not quite to the level of the average toaster—or even the famous battery spokesrabbit. Some are more reliable than others, but all require periodic preventive and regular corrective maintenance for proper function.

Generally speaking, the more expensive commercial varieties offer better reliability than the DIY kits, but there are always exceptions. I've had almost no reliability problems with one of my older Prusa printers, but one of the latest ones has driven me to have a conversation or two with it. It never listens and stubbornly refuses to obey my commands.

Maintainability

Closely related to reliability is maintainability, or simply how easy it is to maintain and repair the printer. I've found my RepRap printers to be easier to work on, but they require work more often than my MakerBot Replicator 2. Indeed, regular maintenance on the RepRap printers takes about 10 minutes each time I start a series of print jobs (that day) and as much as an hour per month to clean, lubricate, and adjust. However, my MakerBot Replicator 2 requires only periodic adjustment and only 20 minutes or so to fully clean, and I lubricate it every couple of months. Similarly, the RepRap printers require regular leveling of the print bed, whereas the MakerBot rarely needs any adjustment.

The takeaway here is if you want to be able to use a printer for hundreds of hours of relatively good printing experiences, you will want to consider how easy it is to work with the printer. If the vendor doesn't provide examples, how-tos, and the like for maintaining their printers, be sure to ask so that you know what you are getting into. Regardless, you should consider it your job to do certain preventive procedures (e.g., cleaning, lubricating) as part of your ownership experience.

Summary

If you are thinking there is a lot more to 3D printing than you originally thought, you're right on track. Most articles and blogs about 3D printing barely cover some of the fundamentals discussed in this chapter. Indeed, most focus on the tool chain, and heighten the reader's expectations by convincing her about all of the wonderful things she can print. While not expressly a fairy tale, this is only part of the knowledge you need to become successful in 3D printing. However, in this chapter I provided a lot more information about the hardware and how it works. As you will see in later chapters, this information forms the basis for understanding how to get the most out of your printer.

In this chapter, we discovered how 3D printers work and what software is required, and learned about the hardware components and the different types of filament available. I also presented some sound advice for setting expectations for your printing experience and how to get started with exploring the exciting world of shared objects (things).

In the next chapter, I discuss your options for getting a 3D printer. If you already have a completed 3D printer, you might want to skim the next chapter. I think it is still valuable to learn what options you have, in case you decide to make 3D printing a hobby.[15]

---

[15]Like all good enthusiasts, most of us end up with several 3D printers of various designs—despite the good (and common sense) question, "Why do you need five printers?" While your spouse may never understand your answer, other 3D printing enthusiasts will.

CHAPTER 2

■ ■ ■

Getting a 3D Printer

The 3D printing world is rapidly expanding with new printer vendors, models, and features being added almost daily. This is especially true given how fast printer designs change. Part of this is because there is a very large (also growing) community of developers, engineers, artists, and laymen who are building, contributing, or providing ideas for new features. Knowing when to jump in or even how to jump in can be a challenge.

That is, how do you know which printer to buy, or even whether one printer design is a better choice than another? Even if you already have a 3D printer, chances are you will either discover features you would like to have or eventually decide you need a different model with certain features. For example, if you have been printing with PLA and discover you need to print with ABS; your existing PLA-optimized printer may not have either a heated print bed or a sealed heated build chamber (required for high-quality ABS printing).

Sometimes when you reach a stage of wanting or needing a certain feature, you can upgrade your existing printer, but this depends entirely on the platform (hardware design). For example, adding a heated build platform to a RepRap variant is very easy, but adding a heated build platform to a commercial, prebuilt printer may require specialized parts or even additional external electronics. It may also void your warranty!

Whether you are looking to buy your first 3D printer or looking to move on to a newer model with more features, this chapter will guide you in the right direction. I will discuss the options for getting a 3D printer (including some specific hardware designs) and present advice on whether to buy or build a printer. I will also present some advice for those considering building their own printer. Let's get started with a discussion of the options for getting a 3D printer.

Classes of 3D Printers

Unlike conventional ink-on-paper printers, there are few 3D printers that have become available in retail stores. While there are some available from major retail chains such as Microsoft (MakerBot) and Staples (Cube), you won't find a 3D printer at your local big-box home electronics store (but you may soon).

So where do you go to find a 3D printer if not in a store[1]? Why, the Internet of course! A quick Google search for "3D printer" will result in many different printers—from ones that resemble a mash-up of random parts, to the loveable animated sanitation robot Wall-E, to early versions of the replicators on *Star Trek*. But how do you know which one is right for you?

---

[1]MakerBot has opened its own stores in the New York City area, and Deezmaker has opened a store in Pasadena, California. Yes, you can walk in, get a full demo by a professional staff member, and go home with a 3D printer.

53

I will answer these questions by first discussing the options available. I have classified the various 3D printers and vendors into three categories. While there are certainly other options available (like inventing your own 3D printer, as well as other types of 3D printers, like a UV-cured resin printer), the vast majority of the FFF printers fall into one of these categories. I describe each of these in more detail in the following sections.

- *Professional grade*: Closed source options with advanced features and paid support
- *Consumer grade*: Commercial offerings available as a kit or preassembled
- *Hobbyist grade*: Pure open source designs for DIY enthusiasts

PROSUMER, PROFESSIONAL, OR INDUSTRIAL?

I use the label *professional grade* to describe a range of printers that are purpose-built, require little setup, and are backed by warranties and accessible technical support. However, some may disagree with this label because there are other printers of even greater sophistication that are designed for use in industrial design and manufacturing. That is, what I call professional grade is too broad and blurs the line between what is available to the consumer and what must be purchased through industry channels.[2]

Thus, some people would say the top consumer 3D printers are "prosumer"—meaning they are meant for consumers who need higher-grade printers than, say, a hobbyist or home user. However, since this book is written for 3D printer enthusiasts who may range from novices to professionals, I feel the professional-grade label is fitting.

To complete the discussion on the range of printers available, I refer to the level above professional grade as *industrial grade* because the price, features, and sophistication of these printers are targeted at industries.

A case in point is the new Z18 printer from MakerBot. The features, size, and price of this printer exceed the budget of all but the most fortunate. Few 3D printing enthusiasts would need all of the capabilities of this new printer. With the Z18, MakerBot is entering the world of its parent company by offering an industrial-grade option in its portfolio of excellent 3D printers.

Professional Grade

The first category contains those vendors who offer 3D printers that have been manufactured for commercial sale to consumers. That is, they offer printers of their own design with mass-produced parts (from minor parts to the entire unit) that arrive with a warranty and support options. Such vendors have elaborate, professional web sites where you can not only buy their products, but also purchase parts and even get help using the products.

While these qualities may (and often do) apply to other 3D printer options, these printers are typically built with a higher level of quality and precision. Vendors typically do not offer a full parts catalog; rather, they typically offer only those parts that are considered wear-and-maintenance items. As you can expect, they are typically more expensive. What you get for the extra cost is directly reflected in the quality and ease of use of the product.

For example, a professional-grade 3D printer normally does not need much in the way of setup and configuration. You won't eagerly unbox your new purchase and find "some assembly required" stamped on the inner packaging. In fact, some printers arrive so well packed that it takes longer to get it out of the box than it does to get it to print!

That doesn't mean commercial printers are ready-to-print out of the box. You can assume any printer you buy will require some amount of setup to use it the first time. You can also expect to have to adjust the printer periodically.

---

[2]Or better, that are affordable. Have you seen the price of industrial-grade 3D printers? Ouch!

WHAT IS READY-TO-PRINT?

Some vendors market their printers as "just click print"—meaning the printer requires little or no setup once it is unboxed. There has been mixed success with these claims. This is because a 3D printer is a very specialized machine that requires a great deal of precision to print properly. However, the setup is typically much less than one you've assembled yourself. Even the MakerBot Replicator 2, arguably one of the best professional-grade offerings, requires no more than about 10 to 15 minutes to set up. I think we are a year or so away from having offerings that can truly print right out of the box without any calibration or setup procedure.

The "higher quality" that I mentioned refers to how well the printer is constructed rather than how well it prints, but in general the two go hand in hand. Despite being well made, some professional-grade printers are more finicky to get good quality prints than others. That doesn't mean you won't get a good quality print. Rather, it means you may need to spend some time to properly adjust or calibrate the printer in order to get a good quality print. Unfortunately, you may not always find this information without experiencing it yourself.

Before buying a printer, I recommend searching for reviews first. You do this with everything you buy online, right? When you read a review, pay attention to the relative experience of the reviewer. If the reviewer is a professional and has experience with 3D printers, her outlook on what is easy to set up will be quite different than someone who knows little about 3D printing. I have read and dismissed a few negative reviews by inexperienced reviewers because I recognized the skipped step (or more) in setting up their printers.

It is also a good idea to visit the vendor's web site and carefully examine the manuals, paying attention to the procedure for unboxing and setting up the printer. If the manual discusses a lengthy setup procedure, you may want to spend extra time going over it carefully.

In general,[3] you will find a commercial 3D printer to be a rewarding buying and owning experience. They do cost more, but the higher cost may be worth considering if you need to get started printing objects quickly. Whether for your organization or for personal enjoyment, a professional-grade 3D printer is by far your best investment.

Vendors

There are several vendors who offer professional-grade 3D printers. Table 2-1 lists some of the more popular choices, along with some specifics about their services and products. Before buying a professional-grade 3D printer, I recommend visiting each of these vendors and reading the product descriptions thoroughly. You should also check out the support portal for the type of information the vendor makes available to customers. I think you will find that there is a lot more information than you expect.

Table 2-1. *Commercial 3D Printer Vendors*

Name	URL	Products	Services
MakerBot Industries	makerbot.com	Offers a full line of 3D printers from beginner to professional. They also offer a 3D scanner.	Online technical support articles, paid support, free CAM software (MakerWare).
Ultimaker	ultimaker.com	Offers a professional version of their successful Ultimaker line.	Online technical support, free CAD/CAM software.

(continued)

---

[3]There are always exceptions and the occasional quality-control issue, but these are rare with professional-grade 3D printers.

Table 2-1. (*continued*)

Name	URL	Products	Services
Delta Micro Factory Corporation	pp3dp.com	Offers several midpriced printers, including one with automatic calibration.	Online technical support articles, paid support, proprietary printer controller.
3D Systems	cubify.com	Offers a wide range of printers, including cartridge-based filament printers, as well as esthetically enhanced designs.	Online technical support articles, proprietary software. Quirky product offerings.
Lulzbot	lulzbot.com	Offers one printer with very high speeds and a large build volume.	Online technical support articles, wide selection of parts for their printers and RepRap printers.

■ **Tip** You can find complete reviews and more about each of these vendors in *Make: Ultimate Guide to 3D Printing* (Maker Media, 2012). Despite the name, it is a condensed overview of 3D printing technologies and vendors, and reviews of popular 3D printers. But you won't find much about DIY kits or RepRap. For that, read on!

Vendor Spotlight

Rather than describing each of the printers in Table 2-1, I will spotlight one of the printers from MakerBot. Arguably the top dog in professional-grade 3D printers, the MakerBot Replicator Desktop 3D Printer and its predecessors have consistently won "best of" categories when compared to other 3D printers. Figure 2-1 shows the latest MakerBot Replicator Desktop 3D Printer.

Figure 2-1. *The MakerBot Replicator Desktop 3D Printer (Fifth Generation)*

This new model is a step-wise improvement over the previous model. It offers more features, including an onboard camera, network-capable printing, a graphical LCD panel, easier to access mechanicals, and more. It also features a build platform that extends for easier removal of prints. In typical MakerBot fashion, they've taken a superb printer and kicked it up a notch with more features, while retaining print-quality superiority.

MakerBot launched a lower-priced entry-level printer, the MakerBot Replicator Mini. It has a smaller build volume but incorporates many of the newer features. MakerBot also has a larger form-factor model, the MakerBot Replicator Z18. It has a huge build volume (and a price tag to match). Clearly, the larger model is aimed at the growing application of 3D printing in manufacturing and engineering.

While the new models are sure to become as popular as the previous models, fortunately, much of the knowledge in this book is applicable to the new versions, with minor differences in mechanical procedures only. For example, the extruder is mounted differently but the need to clean the drive gear and how to do that is the same. The current models—the Replicator 2 and Replicator 2X—are the MakerBot 3D printers that I will use to demonstrate when I discuss troubleshooting and maintenance. Figure 2-2 shows the MakerBot Replicator 2.

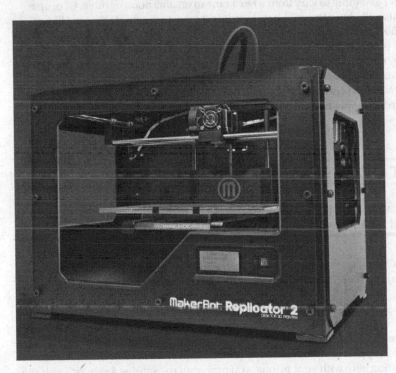

Figure 2-2. *MakerBot Replicator 2*

In summary, professional-grade 3D printers are a wise choice for those seeking a product that they can use without any assembly or lengthy configuration. Professional-grade 3D printers also provide ample documentation and software for using the printer, are covered by a warranty, and vendors offer access (paid or free) to experienced technical support personnel.

Consumer Grade

The next category contains those 3D printers that are available as partial kits (some parts preassembled), full kits (requires you to do all of the assembly work), or fully assembled. They aren't full, professional offerings since vendors typically don't offer the same level of services and support (although some come close).

This category is also larger than the professional-grade 3D printer category. One reason for this is that many of these vendors either gather their components from suppliers and assemble the kits for you (while offering an assembly option) or are smaller organizations that do not yet have the capital to implement and produce their own designs. That doesn't mean these aren't excellent choices! In fact, many of the printers that fall into this category are considered on par with professional-grade 3D printers, having the same print quality and attention to detail in their components.

So don't be tempted to think an assembled option of one of these 3D printers is something you must settle for if your budget doesn't permit a more expensive professional-grade 3D printer. Furthermore, some of the printers in this category are priced competitively with some of the printers in the professional-grade category. However, it is the kit format that permits vendors in this category to offer some of their 3D printers at lower prices.

If you purchase a 3D printer that comes as a kit, you can expect it to be fairly easy to assemble, requiring a small number of tools and a moderate level of skill. These printers aren't quite as simple as assembling a tricycle, but can sometimes require the same level of patience required for assembling furniture from Scandinavia.[4] The time it takes to assemble varies, but in general you can expect assembly to vary from a few hours to an afternoon or three. Of course, your own skills, patience, and time constraints will play a factor in how long it takes you to assemble the kit. I like to double the vendor's estimate, and then add 50% more for those "oh, drat" moments.

One of the motivations for requiring the buyer to assemble part of the components is to reduce shipping cost. A portion of the shipping cost is calculated by weight, but it is also based on the size of the box. The smaller the box, the cheaper it is to ship (well, sort of). One extreme case of this is the Printrbot Simple. In kit form, it packs down to a box that is surprisingly small. While the assembled printer itself is small, the shipping box is quite a bit smaller yet. Shipping a product partially assembled also reduces the need for sophisticated packaging, and therefore reduces the risk of being damaged during shipment.

THE EFFECT OF SIZE ON SHIPPING COSTS

I once shipped a guitar to someone, and despite it weighing no more than about 20 pounds, the size of the box made it many times more expensive than if I had shipped a 20-pound lead weight in a shoe box!

Another reason the kit form is cheaper is because it saves the cost of labor required for an assembly line. This is likely to be the case for small (and growing) companies. The kit form therefore offers you a price break in exchange for a few hours of your time.

So what do 3D printers in this category have in common besides the fact that they require some assembly? As you may surmise, it has to do with how the product is offered and the level of support available. Some vendors offer the same level of services as professional-grade vendors, but more often, vendors in this category have limited support on their web sites and either do not offer any paid support or do not offer any phone support. While this may not be an issue for some, if you are concerned about getting help with your printer, you may want to examine a vendor's web site carefully, and before buying one of their 3D printers, ask them if they provide any level of support.

Another aspect of 3D printers in this category is the material used in construction. While most use commodity components (e.g., stepper motors, bolts, etc.), the material used for the major frame components can range from laser-cut wooden platforms, like the Printrbot line of printers, to the professionally manufactured components found in the SeeMeCNC Delta printers.

None of this should affect or prevent you from buying a consumer-grade 3D printer. If you have some mechanical and electronics skills, as well as the desire to tinker, and you don't mind having to spend a little time putting the printer together yourself, you can save some money and have some fun at the same time!

---

[4]The kind where every joint requires fiddly turn-bolts (dreadfully fragile), dowels, or nails, and things only go together one way, despite the fact all of the pieces look identical.

Vendors

There are simply too many 3D printer vendors in this category to form any reasonable coverage. Rather than attempt to describe all of the available options (and fail), in Table 2-2 I include a list of some of the more widely known vendors, along with a summary of their products and services. All of these vendors offer assembly of their 3D printer kits for a fee.

Table 2-2. *Assembly-Required 3D Printer Vendors*

Name	URL	Products	Services
Printrbot	printrbot.com	Entry-level to mid-level	Online technical support, but no phone support.
Airwolf	airwolf3d.com	RepRap-derived, mid- to high-end printers	Online technical support, extensive knowledge base, phone support available.
SeeMeCNC	seemecnc.com	Delta printer kits, extensive parts catalog, filament	Online technical support forums, product manuals, and assembly guides.
Maxbots	makerstoolworks.com	RepRap-derived mid-level printers with customizable configurations, extensive parts catalog	Extensive assembly and getting-started forums, online technical support, no phone support.
Deezmaker	deezmaker.com	RepRap-derived small, portable printer, mid- to high-end printers, including dual extrusion	Retail store in Pasadena, CA, online blogs and articles. Technical support forum and wiki available at Bukobot.com.
MakerGear	makergear.com	Mid- to high-end printers, parts	E-mail technical support, online manuals.

Vendor Spotlight

Since the assembly requirements and type of components used in this category can be quite diverse, I will spotlight two extremes. The first is a simple kit made from laser-cut plywood that can be assembled with a small set of tools—those found in a typical kitchen junk/fix-it drawer. The other is an example of a high-quality printer that requires more skill and time to assemble.

Let's start by examining a printer from Printrbot. Printrbot offers a complete range of 3D printers that are sure to meet the needs of enthusiasts and professionals alike (see printrbot.com for more details). Figure 2-2 shows the Printrbot Simple.

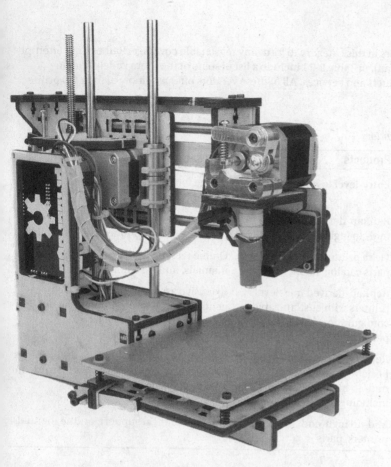

Figure 2-3. *Printrbot Simple (courtesy of* printrbot.com*)*

The Printrbot Simple is a very special DIY kit. It was conceived as an inexpensive, entry-level 3D printer. It is a minimalist's machine—with as few moving parts as possible, while still retaining many of the features of larger, more complex, and more expensive 3D printers. One of the side effects of being a minimalist's design is the build volume is rather small at approximately 4"×4"×4".

The Printrbot Simple uses a unique Y-axis arm that doubles as a gantry for the Z axis. Thus, the entire Y axis is raised up and down. The print bed moves left-to-right for the X axis. It also uses a peculiar string-and-drum mechanism to move the X and Y axes. A traditional threaded rod is used for the Z axis.

Another interesting feature of the Printrbot Simple is that it is open source. That means you can find the designs on the vendor's web site and make any part of the frame and related parts yourself. As such, it uses only commodity hardware that is readily available (you don't have to buy specially made parts from the vendor). About the only thing on the printer that you would have to buy from Printrbot is the electronics board, the hot end, and the extruder. Interestingly, the electronics board is open source, so other electronics boards can be used—you aren't tied to using the Printrboard.

The next examples from SeeMeCNC are delta printers (http://reprap.org/wiki/Rostock). Their Rostock Max line of 3D printers is sold in kit form and their higher-end fast-printing Orion Delta 3D printer is sold preassembled. The major components of all of their 3D printers are a combination of laser-cut melamine and extruded aluminum. The build volume is about average but can typically print objects taller than other printers can due to the vertical configuration of the delta mechanism. Figure 2-4 shows the Orion 3D printer from SeeMeCNC.

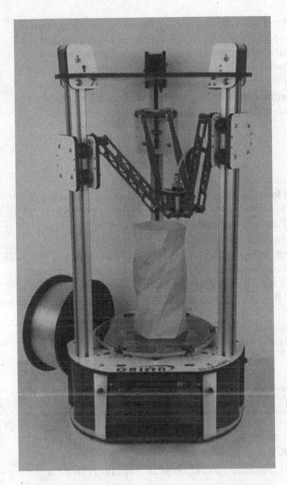

Figure 2-4. *SeeMeCNC's Orion Delta printer (courtesy of* seemecnc.com*)*

Aside from the fact that they look odd, they are fully featured 3D printers. They have LCD panels and a heated print bed, and the quick-release extruder makes maintenance a breeze. The delta mechanism allows the Orion printer to achieve higher speeds than most 3D printers, while also achieving a very high resolution.

If you are looking for a fast, accurate 3D printer that can print tall objects, you should consider the SeeMeCNC delta printers. I should note that SeeMeCNC offers more than printer kits for sale. Indeed, SeeMeCNC offers many high-quality parts for RepRap and similar 3D printers, as well as filament. SeeMeCNC is one of the best examples of this category because they offer a full portfolio of products, making them a one-stop shopping experience. I have used a number of their RepRap components myself with great satisfaction.

WHAT IS A DELTA PRINTER?

A delta printer is a special design that uses three vertical tracks or rods to control each of the axes. Each axis is moved up and down in its tracks (or on the rods) using a special link that ties the axis to a print head. The print head is moved by a combination of the movement of all three axes. Needless to say, delta printers look quite different from most 3D printers.

In summary, consumer-grade 3D printers are a good option for those who want or can handle a 3D printer that requires some assembly, for those who don't mind working on the printer, and for those who don't need technical support (free or otherwise). These 3D printers are a mix of customized designs with some open source derivations. The quality of the printers ranges from a bit below (but still considered good) to comparable with professional-grade 3D printers. They are sometimes cheaper than professional-grade 3D printers and parts are more readily available. Some vendors offer warranties, but those that do, have shorter warranty periods than professional-grade vendors. Lastly, consumer-grade 3D printers require more time and skill to operate and maintain.

Hobbyist Grade (RepRap)

The vendors in this category offer 3D printers that are implementations of one or more RepRap designs. They are open source and almost entirely DIY. That is, the printers are in kit form, requiring assembly from scratch. As a result, they are not designed for those who want to open the box and start printing. This is one of the tenets or perhaps rules of the RepRap world—you are expected to have the technical skills to put it together. Those with less skill can assemble some kits, but most kits require some mechanical skills, soldering, and a zeal for tinkering.

If you do not have these skills and you don't want to learn them, or if you don't have the time to devote to assembling your own 3D printer, you may want to consider a consumer-grade printer kit or an assembled 3D printer. You should also consider the fact that RepRap 3D printers require a fair bit of maintenance and tinkering to get working well. Thus, you may still need to repair and maintain it.[5] If this isn't for you, you may want to consider a professional-grade 3D printer.

Most of the vendors in this category do not offer much in the way of services, but most at least make their manuals and assembly guides available for download. While a few offer phone support, most will answer your questions via e-mail within a day or so.

REPRAP FAMILY TREE

There have been a number of variants of the RepRap 3D printer movement since its inception in 2005. If you would like to know more about the RepRap project, and especially the timeline for when certain variants came to be or were updated (like the Prusa Mendel), you can visit `http://reprap.org/wiki/RepRap_Family_Tree` for a chronological map of designs.

The main reason for this is that the vendors are striving to make RepRap printers more widely available. They've done all of the hard work for you by sourcing the various parts and ensuring that the parts will work together. Consequently, most vendors will allow you to pick and choose options when ordering their kits.

For example, if you decide to use a different electronics board, you can usually specify that when you order the kit. Similarly, you can often find kits that have part of the components omitted, permitting you to buy only what you need. I find this very convenient because it allows me to upgrade a RepRap printer from one iteration to another, reusing the motors, electronics, and extruder. If you are thinking about getting another printer because your old one is a bit dated or it doesn't have some of the latest features, look for vendors that offer partial kits so that you can save some money and get a new printer in the bargain.

■ **Tip** If you go with the partial kit to upgrade you printer, you can often recover a portion of the cost by selling your old parts.

---

[5]While your mileage may vary, all 3D printers need maintenance and repair to ensure proper operation.

You can find RepRap vendors—such as MakerFarm (makerfarm.com) or NextDayRepRap (nextdayreprap.co.uk)—that offer printers in kit form, as well as a vast array of parts and options to keep even the most enthusiastic tinkerers among us happy. You can also find vendors that offer assembled or partially assembled RepRap printers, such as IC3D Printers (www.ic3dprinters.com).[6]

Why RepRap?

The RepRap designs are considered to be the largest segment of the 3D printer market. Whether this is true or not (I cannot substantiate or refute), it is easy to see why some would consider this to be true. That is, the Internet is chock full of blogs, articles, forums, and wikis dedicated to discussing and promoting RepRap printers.

You can see this trend on a popular online auction site. Searching for RepRap generates thousands of hits, whereas searching for Ultimaker, MakerBot, Printrbot, and other commercial printers generates only a few hundred hits each. That doesn't necessarily mean RepRaps are everywhere, but it is a good indication that the RepRap world is alive and prospering.

In fact, one survey[7] of 3D printer owners—both commercial and consumer—suggests that the RepRap community is the largest segment of the 3D printing universe. Figure 2-5 shows a pie chart from this survey. Clearly, RepRap holds a large percentage of the market share.

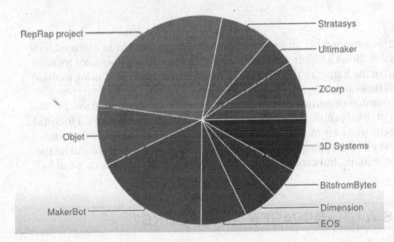

Figure 2-5. Survey of 3D printer owners (courtesy of Stephen Murphey, http://stephenmurphey.com)

This rising popularity has a downside. RepRap designs are rapidly evolving. New features, designs, redesigns, and even revolutionary designs appear almost daily.[8] Part of this is due to how much data there is available for anyone wanting to build a RepRap printer. However, they are popular for a more profound reason: RepRap printers are open source.

The hardware and software is freely shared under various open source licenses. For example, you can freely download, print, and build any variant of a RepRap printer you wish. You can also modify the various printer components, provided you share them with others.

---

[6]Despite the whimsical name, IC3D are quality printers. They also stock very high-quality filament and are embarking on a mission to manufacture their own filament.

[7]Conducted by Jarkko Moilanen and Tere Vadén and appearing in "Manufacturing in Motion: First Survey On the 3D Printing Community," *Statistical Studies of Peer Production*, May 31, 2012.

[8]Which is why there are so few books written about building 3D printers—they are almost out of date by the time they are published.

■ **Note** Never modify and attempt to sell a component unless you have verified with the owner that the license governing the component permits you to do so. To do otherwise isn't playing nice in open source land and could get you flamed (at the very least) or result in legal action.

If you are wondering why I keep saying "RepRap variant," it is because RepRap designs have changed rapidly over a relatively short time. In fact, there are over a dozen evolutionary (and some not so evolutionary) designs to choose from—and that's limiting your choices to popular designs. If you include all of the minor variants and abandoned designs, it probably totals several dozen.

For the purposes of this book, and to try to keep as current as possible and avoid killing every tree in the Northern hemisphere,[9] let us consider only the RepRap variants based on Josef Prusa's designs (http://josefprusa.cz/). They represent the largest and most popular RepRap designs.

Consequently, the designs are a family of RepRap printers called simply *Prusa* or *Prusa Mendel*. The latest iteration of the Prusa design is named *iteration 3*, meaning it is the third version of Prusa's original Mendel design. However, since the iteration 2 is still very much in demand (I have several myself) and parts are readily available—more so than the Prusa iteration 3, I will include both iteration 2 and iteration 3 design details in the following sections.

Prusa Mendel i2

The Prusa Mendel iteration 2, hence Prusa i2, is most notable for its triangular frame assembled from threaded rods bolted to printed plastic components. Figure 2-2 shows a highly modified Prusa i2 printer. It has one motor for each X and Y axis, and two motors mounted on top of the frame for the Z axis. The X and Y axes are moved using toothed belts, and the Z axis by two 8mm or 5/16-inch threaded rods.

As you can see in Figure 2-2, there are a number of printed parts. In the base version (without all of the modifications), there are over 36 parts. If you plan on printing a set of plastic parts using your existing (or a friend's) printer, it is likely it will take a while. Some of the parts are quite large and each could take several hours to print.

The frame itself is very sturdy, and despite all of the plastic, it does not wiggle, shake, or bounce around on the table. Some people have cited breakage or loose joints, but careful inspection and preventive maintenance can help you avoid those rare cases.

MY PRUSA I2 IS A GRANDPARENT— IS YOURS?

There is a certain satisfaction one gets when the last part of a new Prusa 3D printer has finished printing. This is amplified when you pass on the plastic kit to a friend or start your own build. In this way, you are demonstrating the original intent of the RepRap—to self-replicate. Thus, the printer you build using a set of printed parts is called the *child* and the original printer is the *parent*. Using this terminology means one of my Prusa i2 printers is a grandparent. I used its child to print a Prusa i3.

---

[9]I suppose in the digital age I should say, "to avoid running out of digital paper."

Most Prusa i2 kits are complete printers, but lack some of the nice-to-have or advanced features. What that means is that it has all of the basic components for you to assemble and start printing. Most even come with heated print beds and high-temperature hot ends. What most kits lack most are adjustable build platforms, belt tensioners, and a fine-adjustment Z endstop. I would consider all of these features essential for sustaining good-quality prints (nearly) every print.

Figure 2-6. *A Prusa i2*

MY PRUSA I2 MODIFICATIONS

The Prusa i2 in Figure 2-6 includes the following modifications. I describe many of these in later chapters.

- Adjustable feet for keeping the printer stable on uneven surfaces

- Adjustable print bed

- Fine-adjustment Z-height (endstop)

- LED light
- Filament filter/cleaner
- Nozzle fan
- Y-belt tensioner
- Relocated RAMPS (electronics)
- Onboard power supply (most are external like a ball and chain)
- LCD panel with SD card reader
- Spool holder

Many of these modifications improve print quality, but some (like the onboard power supply and filament holder) are designed to make the printer self-contained. This allows you to move the printer more easily and makes it easier to maintain since you don't have to disconnect a bunch of things to move it.

The Prusa i2 improved greatly on previous designs by providing a more stable Y and Z axis, as well as far more freely moving axes due to the use of linear bearings. The bearings alone improved the quality over the previous version. But the Prusa i2 is not without its drawbacks.

One of the drawbacks of this design is the use of threaded rods for the Z axis. If your threaded rods are not perfectly straight and wound correctly, and both ends of the Z axis are bolted or fixed to the frame, you may experience Z wobble, which manifests as slightly offset layers. If you are fortunate, the offsets are very minor, and noticeable only upon close inspection. However, perusing the various things on Thingiverse will reveal the norm to be more noticeable. There are a number of treatments for Z wobble, but the best way to eliminate it is to use flexible shaft couplers that permit either the motor or the rods to move slightly, such as a flexible shaft coupler or stepper motor mounts that permit the motor to move freely horizontally. For an excellent in-depth analysis of Z wobble, see the article by Richard Cameron titled "Taxonomy of Z Axis Artifacts in Extrusion-Based 3d Printing" in *RepRap Magazine* (`http://reprapmagazine.com/issues/1/index.html`).

While it may seem like the Prusa i2 isn't a good choice, that isn't exactly true. Given how long this variant has been around (longer than most), there are a great number of upgrades and options you can install. Aside from those mentioned in the preceding sidebar, other examples include tool holders, accessory drawers, and dual extruders. If you want to build your own printer, and you enjoy tinkering and refining, the Prusa i2 may be a good choice.

Prusa i3

The Prusa iteration 3, hence Prusa i3, is most notable for its fewer and smaller plastic parts and a distinctive frame. There are three different frame designs for the Prusa i3. You can opt for a single-sheet aluminum frame ("single sheet" as in cut from a single sheet), wood or composite braced frame, and a boxed frame. The boxed frame is become less used and it is rare to see it as a kit.

■ **Note** Some vendors refer to the braced wood or composite frame as the "boxed" version, but that is not correct. The distinction is important because the plastic parts for the Z axis are slightly different. Be sure to check if you are buying your plastic parts separately.

The new frame design accomplishes another important function. It improves access to the print bed. I find working with parts on the Prusa i3 to be much easier than the Prusa i2. For example, when I have a part that is stuck really well to the print bed (perhaps stuck too well), on the Prusa i3 I am free to attack the part from multiple angles, whereas on the Prusa i2 the frame can sometimes get in the way.

No matter which frame material/version you choose, the design includes a compact horizontal sub frame made from several threaded rods. These rods are shorter, and the ones that run parallel with the Y-axis smooth rods are larger in diameter. Once bolted together, it makes for a very strong platform. Figure 2-7 shows a modified Prusa i3 3D printer.

Figure 2-7. *A Prusa i3, single-sheet aluminum frame*

Like the Prusa i2 example, this Prusa i3 has many of the same features—onboard power supply, adjustable Z-height, adjustable print bed, filament filter/cleaner, and more.

Perhaps the most significant improvement over the Prusa i2 is the use of smaller-diameter threaded rods for the Z axis. Unlike the Prusa i2, where the stepper motors are mounted on top, the Prusa i3 Z-axis stepper motors are mounted on the bottom with the threaded rods mounted to the stepper motor side only.

Since the Prusa i3 is a fairly new design, there hasn't been as much stabilization on revisions to the printed parts. Many people use Prusa's original designs (as shown in Figure 2-7), but others use a slightly different design. The main difference is how the X axis mounts to the Z-axis rods. The original Prusa design mounts the rods behind the

X-axis mounts, whereas recent revisions mount them in front of the X-axis mounts. Another difference concerns the addition or omission of belt tensioners (and how they work). Lastly, the designs differ on how the extruder mounts to the X axis. Most use a Greg's Wade extruder (also shown in Figure 2-7), whereas newer revisions use either a modified Greg's Wade extruder or a version of a compact extruder. Again, be sure you know which plastic kit you are buying if you are not buying a full kit.

Vendors

The vendors in this category offer more than just kits. They often include a full range of parts, and even filament choices. After all, many of the vendors are people who have turned their passion and hobby into a business designed to support others with the same passions. Table 2-3 lists some of the more popular RepRap 3D printer vendors.

Table 2-3. RepRap 3D Printer Vendors

Name	URL	Products	Services
MakerFarm	makerfarm.com	Wood-framed Prusa i3, parts, filament	Online assembly manuals, prompt e-mail responses for help
DIY Tech Shop	https://shop.diytechshop.com	Aluminum-framed Prusa i3 and Prusa i2, parts, filament	Online assembly manuals
NorCal-RepRap	http://norcalreprap.com	Aluminum-framed Prusa i3, parts, filament	Online assembly manuals
Ultibots	ultibots.com	RepRap-inspired MendelMax 3D printers	Online assembly manuals, online technical support, phone support
NextDayRepRap	nextdayreprap.co.uk	Prusa i2 3D printers, parts, filament	Extensive online support, build manuals, and detailed step-by-step assembly guides, and e-mail technical support

■ **Tip** The NextDayRepRap site contains one of the richest repositories for help on RepRap printers. If you own or plan to build a RepRap, you should consider this site a valuable resource.

Vendor Spotlight

RepRap 3D printer vendors are more plentiful than the other categories. Some offer kits and a few of the parts needed. Others offer only parts and no kits. In fact, it can be a challenge to find a single vendor that has all of the components you need to put together your own kit. One notable exception (among the several listed) is MakerFarm, which is a one-stop shopping site for those who want either a kit or to buy all of the components for their own kit.

They offer two Prusa i3 kits—a normal-size 6" build plate and a larger 8" build plate. Their kits are unique wood laser-cut frames. In fact, the printer doesn't use the normal Prusa i3 printed parts. Indeed, only the extruder and extruder gears are printed plastic. Figure 2-8 shows an 8" MakerFarm Prusa i3 3D printer.

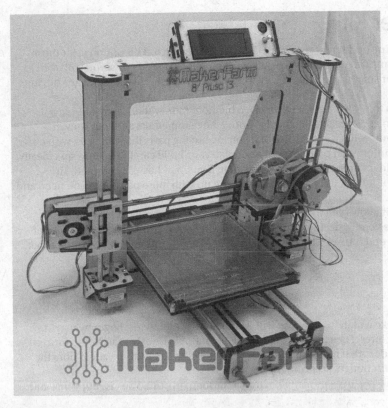

Figure 2-8. *A Prusa i3, wooden frame (courtesy of makerfarm.com)*

MakerFarm has taken the same tactic as Printrbot with using wood for all of the major components. All of the mounting points for the stepper motors, the Y axis, and even the X-axis mounts are wood. This makes assembly of the kit much quicker than a kit like the one used to build the printer in Figure 2-7.

The kits still retain the Prusa i3 design, but are priced a bit lower than an aluminum single-sheet frame version. The absence of the plastic parts, fewer threaded rods, and the wood frame components contribute to this price break. This makes choosing a MakerFarm kit a good choice for those who want to build their own 3D printer but may not have the skills or time needed for a more complex kit.

In summary, RepRap printers are pure and simply DIY. The vendors that support RepRap 3D printers typically offer kits or parts only, and little or no online technical support. Most provide excellent documentation for their kits, but seldom include any help for assembly. Did I mention that they're DIY?

A RepRap kit is a good choice for someone who wants to learn how a 3D printer works and those who want to tinker. Due to the lower cost of the kits, a RepRap kit can be a good way for someone to enter the 3D printing world, but success or failure lies in the hands of the buyer. You can find a lot of help on the Internet, including the RepRap wiki (reprap.org), but you should not expect to be able to pick up the phone and ask your vendor for help. Did I mention it's DIY only?

Now that we've had a merry jaunt down DIY lane, let's go a bit further and discuss how you can go about putting together your own RepRap 3D printer from scratch.

Sourcing Your Own Printer Kit

If you are reading this, then you are considering building your own 3D printer from scratch. This option is for those of us who enjoy a challenge.[10] Instead of buying a kit of matched or at least compatible components, you will need to spend the necessary research time to discover sources for each of the components needed. This often means buying pieces and parts from multiple vendors.

The biggest benefit of doing it this way is that you can end up saving a bit more money than if you bought a complete DIY kit. Of course, you will also gain considerable knowledge about the components and how they fit together. This is because, unlike the DIY kit, you will have to ensure that you are buying parts that can work with other parts. However, there is the risk of incurring unforeseen costs if you do not plan your build carefully. More specifically, if you make multiple orders of parts, you could incur more shipping costs than if you purchased a complete kit. Furthermore, if you purchase incompatible (or the wrong) parts, you could end up with more parts than you need and thus have paid more in the long run.[11]

Another advantage of this option is that it allows you to pick and choose the best components for your new printer. Most DIY kits come with whatever the vendor decides to include, and you do not normally have a choice of manufacturers or even which extruder or hot end is used. The sky is the limit as to what you can achieve with proper planning and a well-thought-out source list.

Make a Plan

Like all successful endeavors, you need to make a plan for how you will gather your components. Begin by making a list of the major components of a RepRap printer. Then use my vendor list or your own Google searches to find vendors. Beside each component, list the vendors that have the component in stock. You may also want to note the cost of the component so that you can plan your budget accordingly.

We call this a *bill of materials*. Table 2-4 shows an example bill of materials for a Prusa i3. You can copy this and make a new column for vendors.

Table 2-4. Prusa i3 Bill of Materials

Component	Quantity	Price Ranges	Notes
Frame	1	$45–$135	Wood sets are cheaper and easier to modify.
Hardware (bolts, nuts, etc.)	1 set	$35+	Look for vendors who sell a complete kit for a Prusa i3. Beware of SAE (Society of Automotive Engineers – a machining standard) kits—they don't apply and can only make life difficult for you (and waste your money).
Plastic parts	1 set	$35+	PLA is fine for some frame components and gears, but insist on ABS for the extruder and any parts exposed to heat, such as the hot end and stepper motor mounts.
RAMPS or equivalent controller	1	$125+	An assembled RAMPS kit normally includes the Arduino Mega.

(continued)

[10]In other words, the never-say-can't crowd. Guilty as charged.
[11]This is especially true for the first-time builder. Do your homework and plan carefully.

Table 2-4. (*continued*)

Component	Quantity	Price Ranges	Notes
threaded rods	1 set	$45	Be sure to check that all threaded rods are included. Check lengths to ensure that they meet the Prusa i3.
Smooth rods	1 set	$45+	Check lengths to ensure that they meet the Prusa i3.
Nema 17 stepper motors	5	$15+	Size varies but generally a 54 oz-in[12] or better is safe. Make sure that they are prewired for RepRap printers. Also, make note of the voltage requirements. Look for motors in the 1–1.5A range. You will need this data to calibrate your printer.
Hot end kit	1	$55+	Ensure that the thermistor and wiring is included.
Heated print bed	1	$25+	Needed if you want to print in ABS; helps with PLA too!
wiring and thermistor kit for print bed	1	$4+	Some vendors of heated build plates will supply these with the heated build plate.
endstops	3	$5–$12	Use simple switches. Some of the endstops with LED indicators can be more difficult to wire.
Zip ties (small, medium)	varies	$4+	Required component that is frequently overlooked. You will need these for taming your wiring and securing the smooth rods and bearings.
Power supply 20-30A 12V	1	$35+	Most opt for an LED power supply, as shown in Figures 2-6 and 2-7. A PC power supply with a switch works well too.
Power socket, switch, and cord for power supply	1	$12+	Required to the LED power supply. You can wire the AC cord directly to the power supply, but it is not recommended (there's no way to turn it off).
Belts and pulleys	2	$35+	You need (2) GT2 or similar pulleys and approximately 3 meters of belt. Look for vendors who sell them as a set.
Filament	1	$40+	Yes, you need this too! Get a roll of your favorite color, but be sure it is the right size and type of filament to match your extruder and use.
LCD panel	1	$115+	Optional but highly recommended. Get one with a built-in SD card reader.
40mm fan	1	$6+	Optional. Strongly recommended for printing with PLA.

■ **Tip** RAMPS kits can come assembled or unassembled. If you do not know how to solder or have little experience in soldering small components, you may want to get a preassembled RAMPS kit. On the other hand, if you do solder, you can save as much as 50% on the cost if you assemble it yourself.

---

[12]Or ounce-inch; a measure of holding torque (http://www.numberfactory.com/nf_torque.html).

Once you have your list completed, you can begin acquiring your components. I like to start with the most expensive ones first, making it easier to complete the list if you cannot buy the components all at once.

Another strategy is to first buy the components for the frame and then assemble it. This can help you focus on achieving your goal. I've tried this myself and it does indeed help to see your project come to life early rather than waiting for your parts bin to fill up.

Whichever method you choose, this is also part of the plan that you should decide early on. Knowing where you are going to get the parts and the order you plan to acquire them can help a lot when sourcing your own printer kit. It also helps avoid getting almost entirely through the build only to discover that you don't have any endstops or that you're missing a thermistor. Hey, it happens!

Rules of Acquisition[13]

Yes, there are some unofficial rules out there in the RepRap world. While some may be of my own imagination, it has been my experience there are limits to what you can expect from a vendor and the RepRap community in general.

Vendors who supply RepRap components vary—ranging from those who have an online presence to sell components in large quantities to those with a higher purpose of fulfilling the needs of RepRap owners. The best way to tell the difference is by what the vendor offers on its web site in the form of documentation. If you see detailed descriptions, manuals, specification sheets, or technical forums, chances are you have a winner. Beware of those that don't specify the features of their components or offer vague descriptions. You simply must do your homework and buy from vendors that have good reviews in the community and that will answer your questions.

Assuming you are buying from a respectful vendor, you can and should ask them questions about their products. Most are very patient with buyers who may be new to building a RepRap 3D printer. But there are limits. Don't expect the vendor to tutor you on how to assemble your printer with their components. You can ask them about how best to assemble, or even what other parts they recommend, but it is not OK to ask them how to adjust your axes when leveling the print bed.

If you use the RepRap forums (and you will), you should expect those who monitor the forums and participate (answer questions) to be no different than other forums. That is, you must keep your topics on track and not meander in thought or try to ask a host of questions in the same or the wrong forum. All of these are likely to get you a stern, negative response.

You can also expect to encounter responses that may not apply to your postings. With so many people commenting on the forums, it is easy for someone to offer advice for fixing various problems, but confuse the situation or circumstances. For example, if you are having trouble getting your endstops mounted, be sure you are looking at forum posts that match your choice of design; the mounting of the endstops for a Prusa i3, while in the same general location, use different mounting tabs than other Prusa variants.

Similarly, when asking for advice, make sure to provide as much information as you can so people can help you zero in on the problem. Don't write a book about it, but do make a list of your pertinent hardware. Sometimes knowing which stepper motor you are using will help immensely in solving a calibration problem (discussed shortly). Again, ask questions about your problems, but one at a time, and provide all of the symptoms.

As far as etiquette goes, be courteous, and similar courtesies will be returned. You will likely see some instances of where this doesn't happen, but do not let this hamper you in any way. Like most hobbies, the RepRap world has its share of opinions, including some that come close to an obsession. For example, there are those who would stake their reputation on one hot end over another, and there are others who would argue the opposite. Another example is the question of which filament to use, as I discussed in Chapter 1. Until you have experience with a component yourself, you should not take commentary too seriously beyond the advice and reviews presented.

Finally, there are two more pieces of advice when it comes to sourcing your own kit. First, visit and read every forum and technical blog or discussion about RepRap that you can find the time to read. While you may not understand all of what you read at first, the more you read, the more it will become clear. Second, if you happen to be

---

[13]No, not the Ferengi Rules of Acquisition (see http://en.wikipedia.org/wiki/Rules_of_Acquisition).

in a city that has a Maker group—or better, a 3D printer user group—join it! Go meet other RepRap enthusiasts and talk with them! You will gain considerable knowledge very quickly if you are fortunate enough to make a friend or two who shares your passion. You will find all types—from beginners to experienced RepRap-ers—who will take the time to help you (but you have to take the initiative).

Danger Ahead

The RepRap world can be very rewarding and educational. You will encounter people who are very helpful and will gladly offer advice. You will also find vendors who are very responsive and supply customers with quality RepRap components. All you need to succeed is a desire to learn and a little patience. Your reward at the end of your journey is a printer, but it is often the journey itself that is most enjoyable.

Sadly, this isn't always the case. There are downsides to sourcing your own kit. I've already mentioned the lack of guidance by vendors (generally—there are exceptions) and I've warned you about making sure the components are designed for RepRap use. What I haven't discussed yet are some of the bad things that you may encounter.

What I mean are the things that can go wrong unexpectedly, which can lead to a host of problems. In other words, the downsides and pitfalls to building a RepRap 3D printer from scratch. While I cannot cover them all (I'm sure I'll encounter more myself), I can give you some examples to help illustrate what you can expect.

The biggest drawback is that it simply takes a while to gather the parts for a RepRap before you can start assembling it. This could be because you need time to research vendors or because some of the parts are not currently available (there was a drought of stepper motors for a while in 2012). More likely, it will take time to *pay* for the parts—especially if you are doing so on a limited budget or with discretionary funds set aside for hobbies.[14]

There can also be long build times if you encounter incompatibilities. For example, I bought a RAMPS board from what I was led to believe was a respectable vendor, but the result was a maddening calibration session concerning the motors I chose. It turned out that the stepper driver boards I purchased would not output the current needed for the motors, despite the documentation and the vendor's claim to the contrary. The result was that my axis movement was jerky and the motors would fail (seemingly) at random. Once I discovered the problem, I purchased better stepper driver boards and all was well.

Another example concerns buying bargain components. Early in my immersion into the RepRap world, I ordered a set of stepper motors in "like new" condition (I was OK with that) in order to save some money. The vendor specifications listed respectable performance characteristics and 5mm shafts (the standard). Furthermore, the supplied specification sheet (a PDF document that describes all of the details) met the minimum specifications for a RepRap (see `http://reprap.org/wiki/Stepper_motor`).

When the motors were delivered, they had been clearly used in a very dirty environment (probably a CNC machine), had 4mm shafts with pressed on pulleys, and were not wired correctly for use with a RepRap. Despite my arguments, the vendor told me "no returns," so I was stuck with the motors. I had to either try to make them work or toss them away as an expensive lesson learned. Whereas the motors were easily cleaned and the wiring easily resolved, the 4mm shafts and pulleys proved to be quite a challenge. Even once I had the pulleys removed (I had to destroy the pulleys to remove them),[15] it took me a long time to find a source for 4mm pulleys. Once I had acquired the pulleys, I later discovered the stepper motors would not hold torque.[16]

The end result was that one of my early built-from-scratch RepRap 3D printers took about three months to complete—far from typical. I managed to build two other printers while waiting to get the problem child sorted out. I am wiser now and won't make those mistakes again!

---

[14]For example, diverted from other hobbies, mad money, turtle breeding sales, eBay profits, etc.
[15]Magnesium is brittle. Go figure.
[16]Which really torqued me off!

■ **Caution**   You really must do your homework on each and every component you buy. Don't take the vendor's word that the product is compatible. Ask other customers or do a search on the Web to see if others have had problems with the components. You will be glad you did!

Please don't think I am suggesting that building a RepRap 3D printer is a bad idea—it isn't. But as I demonstrated in examples from my own experience, it isn't always going to be smooth sailing. That being said, sourcing your own kit and building it from scratch can be extremely rewarding. This is especially so if your results yield a higher print quality. The first time I did this, I went a bit overboard and included about a dozen minor upgrades in the process. While some ultimately didn't work, the end result was a printer that exceeded the print quality of my last DIY kit and it cost about $200.00 USD less! Of course, it took about eight months to complete.

3D Printer Features

Let us now discover the features and some common options of 3D printers. While not all vendors or printers have all of these features, it is important to be familiar with them when considering your first (or next) 3D printer. The more common options and their benefits are included in the following list and subsections. Some of these will be discussed in greater detail in the maintenance and troubleshooting part of the book.

- Build volume
- Filament
- Hot end
- LCD panel
- SD card reader
- Filament cartridge system
- Network connection
- Wireless support
- Adjustable print bed
- Filament cleaner
- Filament spool holder
- Heated print bed
- Cooling fans for print bed
- Electronics cooling fan
- Auto bed leveling

Build Volume

The size of the object you can create with a 3D printer may be something you want to consider carefully when evaluating which printer to buy. If you want to print large objects, you will want to look at 3D printers that are designed with a large print area (build volume). For example, if you want to print tall objects, you may want to consider a delta 3D printer—their design is best for tall objects. Most RepRap printers have a rather limited build volume compared to professional- or consumer-grade printers. Some of the lower-cost 3D printers have a smaller build volume.

REALISTIC BUILD VOLUME OF REPRAP 3D PRINTERS

While some RepRap designs are billed as having a certain build volume, the actual build volume is often smaller. For example, a combination of the Prusa i2 frame components, the size of the extruder, and the clips used to hold the glass build plate to the heated bed can reduce the size of the build volume considerably.

Filament

If you have chosen a filament type you want to use (e.g., ABS or PLA), make sure that the printer you are evaluating for purchase or to build from a kit is optimized for your choice. Keep in mind that most 3D printers that can print with ABS can also print with PLA provided they have a print bed cooling fan (or you can add one). Similarly, if you want to print with ABS, the printer must have a heated print bed.

Hot End Types

There are dozens of hot end designs available for 3D printers. This may seem like an exaggeration, but it isn't. My research revealed several sites listing 10 or even 20 designs. The site that seems most complete, but incomplete, is at https://sites.google.com/site/3dprinterlist/home/hot-ends. You will find links to details about each of the more than 50 hot ends listed.

With so many hot end designs, how do you know which one to choose or even which one is best for your printer, filament, and object design choices? Fortunately, most hot end designs can be loosely categorized by their construction into two types: all-metal and PEEK body with PTFE (polytetrafluoroethylene) liner. There are some exceptions, like an all-metal design with a PTFE liner, but in general they either are all one material or use a liner of some sort. I will discuss some of the characteristics of each in the following sections.

All-Metal

All-metal hot ends are made from one or more metal types. Typically, this includes a stainless steel core, aluminum, or brass heater block, and a brass or stainless steel nozzle. They are relatively maintenance-free since they do not contain any parts that wear out from normal use. A stainless steel core permits filament to glide with little friction. In some cases, the hot end can be certified for use with food, which could come in handy if you want to print with chocolate.

Some all-metal hot ends have a body with fins so that the body can be cooled with a fan. This is necessary because all-metal designs need a sharp heat transition to keep the filament from jamming. However, it is possible the entire hot end could reach the temperature of the heater block (or nearly so). If you use the hot end without a fan and the body isn't long enough to dissipate enough heat, it is possible these hot ends can transfer heat to your extruder body or mount. This could make the plastic parts soft and they could deform. Thus, most all-metal hot ends are used with a fan.

These hot ends have one distinct advantage: they can handle much higher temperatures and thus can be used to print higher-temperature filament. As I mentioned, all-metal hotends are lower maintenance because there are no internal parts that must be replaced when they wear out.

Examples of all-metal hot ends include the proprietary MakerBot Mk8 (makerbot.com), the Prusa Nozzle (http://prusanozzle.org/), and the E3D (http://e3d-online.com/E3D-v5). Figures 2-9 and 2-10 show the MakerBot Mk8 extruder and hot end.

Figure 2-9. *MakerBot Mk8 extruder (upgraded with aluminum body)*

Figure 2-10. *MakerBot Mk8 hot end*

PEEK Body with PTFE Liner

This construction type uses a metal heater block with a brass, aluminum, or stainless steel nozzle connected to a special plastic body made from polyether ether ketone,[17] a.k.a. PEEK (http://en.wikipedia.org/wiki/PEEK), which has a PTFE liner. There are a lot of hot ends in this category, so consequently, they are more widely available.

The peek, or body, of the hot end has low thermal conductivity and normally does not need a fan to cool it. Some versions of this type of hot end may add fins or slots in the peek to further aid in dissipating heat.

One advantage that some manufacturers provide is the ability to change the PTFE liner for use with 1.75mm or 3mm filament. However, the PTFE liner has a couple of limitations. It can deform over time and will need to be replaced periodically. The liner also limits the heat range to a maximum of about 240 degrees Celsius. Any more than that and the PTFE liner will fail and the material may degrade. Regardless of these limitations, this type of hot end is very popular and can be found on a lot of printer designs.

Examples of this type of hot end include the J-head (http://hot-ends.com), Budaschnozzle (www.lulzbot.com/products/budaschnozzle-20c-w-035mm-nozzle), and Merlin (www.reprapdiscount.com/hotends/59-merlin-hotend-set.html). Figure 2-11 shows the J-head hot end from MakerFarm.

Figure 2-11. *J-head hot end*

Mounting Orientation

Hot ends can also be designed expressly for direct drive, Bowden drive, or both. Hot ends designed for direct drive extruders mount close to or in the same body as the extruder. Examples of these are the J-head and MakerBot MK8 hot ends. There are a few hot ends that can be used only with Bowden extruders, but these require a special mount or come with their own mount.

---

[17]You may also see it spelled *polyetheretherketone*.

■ **Note**   The J-head is commonly used for Bowden extruders, particularly on deltabots. In some cases, the hollow-set screw used to lock the PTFE tube in place can be replaced with a push-to-connect fitting, which allows you to attach the Bowden tube in a secure manner.

Most hot ends can be used with either a direct or Bowden drive extruder. Only the mount (extruder body) and installation differs, where the direct drive is mounted together with the hot end and the Bowden drive mounts the hot end and extruder separately.

Choosing a Hot End

If you are building your own printer or upgrading, you can change the hot end easily. Those printers build with vendor-specific extruders and hot ends may not be so easily upgraded.

So which one should you use? That depends on what you want to do with it. If you want to print higher-temperature filament, you should choose an all-metal hot end. If you want a hot end made for PLA or ABS that is reliable and doesn't need a fan to operate, choose a peek body hot end.

This may seem noncommittal since I don't list specific hot ends that you should use. The reason is also simple: I think there are so many hot ends (well, variants on a theme) because each one is designed to perform to the needs driving that particular design. In fact, you will encounter some people who feel one particular hot end is superior to all others. It seems there are as many different opinions as there are hot ends!

If you decide on the construction type and make a list of the features or capabilities, such as range of filament, mounting type, and so forth, you should be able to narrow down your selection.

Your criteria should also consider whether a vendor is the original designer or manufacturer—that is, make sure to buy a hot end from someone who manufactures it. For example, the J-head hot end is very widely used in RepRap printers; so much so that there are many vendors who make copies or clones of the design. Some are very well made, others not so much. Before buying a new hot end, do some research and read reviews from previous buyers.

Thus, you should buy the hot end that best meets your needs, is designed to fit your printer (or the one you are building), is well made, and has a reputation for reliability.

LCD Panel

Most commonly a text-based multiline display, an LCD panel allows for computerless operation of the printer. Since most LCD panels include either a rotary selector or buttons, the firmware provides menus that you can use to select options, such as moving the axes, turning on the heaters, and more. Having features like this on the printer itself helps with routine adjustments and maintenance, without the need for connecting to a computer. Now that I've converted all of my older 3D printers (except one) to have an LCD panel (and software to use it), I cannot imagine having a printer without it. In fact, I have plans to add one to my Printrbot Simple so that even my entry-level example can be used without a computer.

SD Card Reader

If you don't want to tie up your computer or dedicate a computer to printing, you should consider buying a printer that has an SD card reader. Not only will this permit you to disconnect your printer from your computer, if the printer has an LCD interface, it allows you to print without ever having to turn on your computer. Which means you can take your printer anywhere and amaze your friends.

Filament Cartridge System

A few 3D printers incorporate a filament loading system that uses a cartridge or similar enclosure to confine the filament. This promotes easy filament loading and unloading, and can also eliminate the need for a filter or cleaner to ensure that the filament is clean.

Network Connection

A network connection would permit you to print over the network and share your printer with others on your network. The newest 3D printers from MakerBot include this feature.

Wireless Support

Wireless support is the same as having a network connection, but without the wires!

Adjustable Print Bed

I consider this feature another must-have for any 3D printer. It permits you to tram the print bed quickly, thereby making routine maintenance a bit easier. Some mechanisms (like the MakerBot 3D printers and the one I designed for my Prusa i2) can be adjusted without tools.

Filament Cleaner

If your 3D printer doesn't have a hood or some covering for the spool of filament, you should consider opting for a 3D printer with a filament cleaner. Even if the printer you want doesn't have this option, it can be added to just about any 3D printer. A quick search on Thingiverse reveals a number of options. For example, I use thingiverse.com/thing:16483 for my RepRap printers and thingiverse.com/thing:52203 for my MakerBot printers. The major benefit of filament cleaner is that it prevents small pieces of lint, dust, and other contaminates from entering the extruder, and eventually the nozzle. If you are having frequent filament extrusion failures, try adding a filament cleaner.

Filament Spool Holder

A lot of printers have this feature. Not only does it keep the area around the printer tidy, it also helps reduce extrusion failures by relieving tension on the extruder motor. That is, the filament spool holder allows the spool to unwind filament by rolling on some form of roller or other low-friction device. This is another item I feel is essential to a good printing experience. If you are having extrusion failures and don't have a spool holder, it is likely there is too much tension on the filament, causing the extruder to strip the filament.

Heated Print Bed

If the printer you are considering doesn't have a heated print bed, it is not optimized for printing ABS and other high-temperature material. If you want to (perhaps in the future) print with ABS, insist on having a heated print bed. Not only does it ensure that the printed object retains heat, it also helps the object stick to the build plate. It can also help with PLA adhesion, so you really cannot go wrong here.

Cooling Fans for the Print Bed

If you want to print with PLA, you simply must have a print bed fan. Blowing air over the printed object helps keep the PLA stable by making it cool faster.

Electronics Cooling Fan

This option isn't normally something you find on professional-grade and most consumer-grade options. Indeed, the need for cooling the electronics should have been solved by the manufacturer. Thus, this applies mainly to RepRap 3D printers. In this case, it can help keep things working properly, such as avoiding skipped steps when the stepper drivers get too hot. I had this happen once on a really big print. Sadly, it happened at about 90% complete, ruining the part entirely. If you build your own RepRap, consider carefully how you will house and cool the electronics.

Auto Bed Leveling

One of the hottest new features is called *auto bed leveling*. This feature permits the printer to discover its Z-height (how far the nozzle is from the print bed) and detect and correct for bed misalignment. In fact, vendors are starting to equip their printers with this feature. It is becoming a popular option for RepRap printers too (see thingiverse.com/thing:182889). It is likely that this technology or something similar will become more prevalent in the coming year. I will talk more about this particular feature in Chapter 11 as I demonstrate some of the ways you can upgrade your RepRap printer.

LEVELING VS. TRAMMING: IS THERE A DIFFERENCE?

Like any industry, the 3D printing world has its share of misused, mangled, and otherwise misspelled words, terms, and acronyms.[18] One case that has a lot of experts baffled is the misuse of the terms *level* or *leveling* when referring to adjusting the print bed. For better or worse, the industry as a whole seems to be accepting of the term *leveling* to describe the process of making the print bed parallel to the X axis. Indeed, several well-known vendors use *level* in this manner.

The goal is to make sure the nozzle is the same distance from the print bed throughout the range of movement of both the X and Y axes, while the Z axis remains fixed. This process is called *tramming*. It has nothing to do with leveling as in the process of making an object parallel to the horizon (perpendicular to gravity)[19] nor does it involve a bubble, line, or plane level or any such device.[20]

In fact, you should avoid and ignore any description of a similar process that uses these devices to adjust the print bed. Similarly, don't bother buying or printing any device that is designed to make the print bed level with the horizon. However well intended, these processes and devices are likely to make your print bed issues worse. Unless, of course, you are lucky enough to have a printer whose X axis is actually level with the horizon.

Personally, I am OK with the use of the word *leveling* when referring to adjusting the print bed, but some experts are not so accepting. So long as you understand the goal of the process, it should not matter that it is technically misnamed. Furthermore, if you encounter a process that is described as "tramming the print bed," you know it has the same goal as the process presented here and should be interchangeable.

---

[18]For example, "framily" = friends and family, which is a particularly bothersome word mash up.
[19]In case you live in areas with strange gravitational illusions (mysteryspot.com).
[20]This does not mean you should never level your printer. Making sure your printer's frame is level or is sitting on a level surface is a good practice, but it isn't critical. A degree or two out of level will not affect your printer.

Build or Buy?

The answer to the question of whether to build your own printer or buy a ready-to-go printer lies in your assessment of your skills and your desire to learn. If you are confident you can handle any electrical or mechanical task needed to build a 3D printer, and you have the time necessary to devote to the task and learn new skills, then a 3D printer kit is an option you will want to consider. On the other hand, if you don't have the skills or you don't have the time to learn those skills, much less the time to build the printer, you may want to consider buying a printer that is ready-to-print.

In this section, I provide advice for choosing whether to build or buy a 3D printer. I also present a condensed summary of the list of the characteristics for each category of 3D printer option. While you are ultimately the one who needs to make the choice, the information in this section should help you make your choice a bit easier.

Reasons for Building Your Own 3D Printer

Let us set some expectations about a 3D printer build. Building your own 3D printer encompasses all of the RepRap class of printers, as well as any of the consumer-grade class 3D printers that require some form of assembly.

There are two main reasons why you would want to opt to build your own printer. First, you enjoy working on a project that requires you to spend a lot of time during construction and configuration. Second, you want to save some money. Other reasons include wanting to build a 3D printer with specific unique features or you want to be able to upgrade the printer in the future.

If you want to embark on a build option, you should plan to spend anywhere from a single afternoon (for some assembly-required kits) to about 40 to 60 hours for a built-from-scratch RepRap 3D printer. While this estimate may seem very high (and some would say it is), realistically you should anticipate it taking more than a long weekend to complete—and that's if you have all of the parts and they all work! In addition, you should plan to spend some time configuring and calibrating your new printer. The next chapters will help you to prepare so that you spend less time than if you had to do it without help.

However, you should not try to rush through the build, but take your time to get things right. You will be glad you did. Once you have your printer whirring away, laying down plastic to make a whistle or another small gewgaw, you will be glad you took the time to get it right. So if you want a challenge and time isn't an issue, building your own printer is a good option.

Reasons for Buying a Ready-to-Print 3D Printer

Ready-to-print 3D printers encompass all of the professional-grade class of 3D printers and any 3D printer in the consumer-grade class that comes assembled or can be ordered assembled.

There are several reasons for choosing a professional-grade 3D printer. One reason is time. If you need to get started printing objects quickly and do not have time to learn how to build (and then build) your own 3D printer, either from a kit or from scratch, you will want to choose a professional-grade option.

Another reason you may want to buy a printer that is ready-to-go concerns quality. The print quality is generally better than what you may achieve if you built your own 3D printer. This isn't always the case, however, and it is more often applicable to professional-grade options. Regardless, if quality is a concern, you may want to buy a printer with a good reputation for high-quality prints.

Additionally, a ready-to-print option is easier to use and more reliable. That is, a ready-to-print option means all of the hard work of configuration and calibration has been done for you. Although you may need to spend some time to get the printer set up properly once you've unboxed it, this is typically a small fraction of the time required to *build* your own 3D printer. That is, you don't have to invest the time required to get everything fit together and working. This goes far beyond the mundane mechanics of the assembly.

Perhaps the most important factor in buying a ready-to-go printer is technical support. If you do not have or do not want to learn the skills required to diagnose or fix problems with your 3D printer, you should buy your printer from a vendor who offers a support option.

How Do I Decide?

So how do you decide which to choose if none of these reasons apply to you or perhaps aren't that big of a deal to you? To help you decide, Table 2-5 is a list of the more important characteristics of each class of 3D printer offerings. It includes a rating in each class of printer for each characteristic.

Table 2-5. Considerations for 3D Printer Categories

Characteristic	Professional Grade	Consumer Grade	RepRap
Setup difficulty	Low	Medium	High
Cost	High	Medium	Low
Support options	Yes	Maybe	No
Specialized components	Yes	Some	No
Available as a kit	No	Yes	Yes
Phone support	Yes	Few	Almost never
Technical skills	Low	Some	High
Ease of upgrading	Low	Medium	High
Documentation included	Yes	Sometimes	None
Warranty	Yes	Some	No

You can use this table to circle the ratings that best apply to you, and then sum up which class aligns with your own assessment. For example, if you consider a difficult setup as something that you want to avoid, you would circle the cell marked "Low" for that characteristic. Try it now.

I think you will find that one class stands out for you. If it happens to be the professional-grade class, you can conclude that you should buy a 3D printer. Similarly, if the RepRap class stands out, you can conclude that building your own 3D printer is a good option.

However, if your assessment isn't definitive, focus on those characteristics that matter most to you, and base your decision on that. For those of us who are truly ambivalent, a 3D printer kit from the consumer-grade class can be a good choice. You will have a bit of fun putting it together and can expect very little additional work to ensure a good quality print.

Buying a Used 3D Printer

If your budget limits your buying power or you are looking for a bargain, a used printer may be a good choice. You can often get a slightly used 3D printer for about 75% of the price of a new one. However, like all used purchases, you need to do your homework to ensure that you are getting a well-maintained and reliable printer. The following lists several considerations and some advice on how to buy a used 3D printer. If you follow this advice, you should be able to find a good printer to fit your budget.

- Online auction sites are an excellent place to look for a 3D printer. If you apply a little patience and avoid the temptation to join a bidding frenzy, you will find the printer you want at the price you are willing to pay.

- Set your expectations based on your budget. Remember, real bargains are hard to come by. If the price is too good to be true, chances are there is something wrong with it.

- Find the printer with the lowest usage. I've seen cases where used printers have no more than a few hours of use. Avoid printers with hundreds of hours of use.

- Beware of highly modified printers. Buying a well-tuned printer is a good idea, but don't pay extra for all of the add-ons and upgrades. It is possible those upgrades could be useless or even detrimental to your print quality.

- If you are seeking a professional-grade printer, check to see if there is an extended warranty and that it can be transferred to you (most cannot).

- Ask if the seller is the original owner. If the printer has passed among several owners, you may want to pass on it as well.

- Check for the original accessories. Look for printers that come with the original manuals and accessories. Consumables may not be included, but the original tools and whatnot should.

- Be very careful if buying from a seller who doesn't have the original shipping box. This shouldn't be a deal breaker, but you should insist on shipping insurance and ask the seller to explain how they plan to prepare the printer for shipping. You should also ensure that they secure the axes for shipping.

- Ask to see hi-res photos of printed objects. Check the quality carefully. If you see any anomalies or quality issues (described in Chapters 7 and 8), don't buy the printer.

- Good communication is the key to a good sale. If the seller is willing to exchange e-mails and answer questions promptly, it is a good sign. Don't buy from a seller who won't return your e-mails, dodges questions, or takes a long time to respond.

- Lastly, ask the seller whether he will take the printer back for a full refund if there is something wrong with it. You may have to pay return shipping.

I'd like to present two examples from my own experience of buying a used 3D printer. In fact, both printers are MakerBot printers. The first one is a Replicator 2 and the second a Replicator 1 Dual.

The Replicator 2 was listed with less than 20 hours of use. The seller described it as being in excellent condition. The price was also very good. Aside from missing the original box, the printer met all of my criteria (as listed earlier). The printer was packed well and the axes secured. In fact, it took me almost 10 minutes to free it from its cocoon of packing material.

However, when I unpacked the printer, I found that it was very dirty and in need of a full maintenance overhaul. Fortunately, a few hours of cleaning and partial disassembly proved that the printer was still a good buy. Had I known the printer needed so much work, however, I would have negotiated a lower price.

The lesson here is that another person's idea of "excellent" may not meet your own. The only way to avoid this mistake is to ask for hi-res photos taken from every angle. Specifically, ask for photos of the axes and look for dust, dirt, and other signs of neglect. While my purchase turned out OK in the end, I was a bit disappointed.

The Replicator 1 Dual was a different story. It had only four hours of use. The seller was very understanding and answered all of my questions, including requests for additional photos. I could tell from the photos that the printer was in excellent like-new condition. The seller had the original box, all accessories, and even the consumables were included. It arrived packed exactly as MakerBot originally shipped it. Best of all, the sale price was less than half of the original sale price. I saved so much money that I was able to upgrade this printer with some top-of-the-line options. In fact, it is now one of my most reliable and best-quality printers.

Summary

Getting a 3D printer isn't at all like buying a toaster. There are so many 3D printers to choose from that a random choice may be out of the question (it's far too risky that you'll end up hating your purchase). Furthermore, deciding whether to buy a 3D printer or to build your own can be a difficult decision process.

In this chapter, I presented three classifications of 3D printer options for you to consider, ranging from sourcing your own printer kit piece by piece, to acquiring a commercial printer with very high quality, paid support, and a warranty. I also presented some advice for those considering a RepRap printer.

The chapter also provided some insight into some of the most common features available for 3D printers. This information isn't always available and can sometimes read more like a marketing pitch. Knowing what the features are can help you decide which 3D printer to choose.

In the next chapter, I discuss tips for building 3D printers. If you are in the middle of or about to start a 3D printer build, you might want to wait until you've read the next chapter. It will help you succeed in getting your 3D printer built with a minimum of fuss, and help you head off bad choices.

CHAPTER 3

■■■

3D Printer Building: Tips for a Successful Build

Building your own 3D printer can be a really cool project. Building a 3D printer requires basic mechanical skills and the ability to work with wiring (crimping, soldering). It also requires a certain set of tools to build the printer. Finally, there are a number of things you can do to help make the build more productive and successful. I cover all of these topics and more in this chapter starting with the tools and skills required.

While this chapter is intended for those who want to build their own 3D printer, the chapter also covers the types of tools and supplies needed for using and maintaining your printer. If you have little desire to build your own printer or are just getting started, you should still read the tool section to familiarize yourself with the tools and supplies you will need to get the most out of your 3D printer.

Tools and Skills Required

If you are concerned you will have to sink a huge wad of cash into a full set of gleaming chrome tools and their assorted bits and bobs of handheld contrivances, your fears will not be realized. While it is true you will need more than the average kitchen junk drawer assortment,[1] the only specialized tool you must have is a caliper for precise measurement.

There are some tools that you will need for building, and others that you will need for maintenance and repair. There are also some tools you must have for using the 3D printer. Finally, there are tools and supplies needed as part of the printing process. I cover all of these in this section. I will also discuss briefly the skills you need to complete a build. As you will see, the requirements are not so great.

■ **Note**   Although the lists may seem complete, some printers may require tools not listed in this chapter. It is also possible you may find a substitute for one or more of the tools—like a really good multitool[2] instead of a set of pliers, wrenches, screwdrivers, and so forth.

Before we get into that, I want to discuss tool quality and how some of the brands stack up with respect to quality. As you will see, you need not spend a lot of money on tools but you should be aware of the better brands.

---

[1]In other words, you will need more than a hammer, wobbly pliers, and a screwdriver that has seen its share of opening cans and prying open boxes.
[2]I sometimes get multitools for gifts. They're really handy but I'm running out of places to put them.

Tool Quality: Does it Matter?

There are many tool brands. Some are sold through various retail centers ranging from department stores to hardware stores. Others are sold only through specific retailers, and a few are sold only through door-to-door salesmen. The better quality brands have a lifetime replacement warranty. The prices of these tools range greatly, and so does the quality and durability. Some would suggest that the more expensive tools are no better than the cheaper tools. But that is not the case.

At the high end of the range are tools made and sold by Snap-on (http://store.snapon.com/) and other high-end, precision tool manufacturers. The quality of these tools is superior to most other brands. In fact, professionals who rely on tools for their craft often choose Snap-on knowing they are more precise and durable than other brands. They also come with a lifetime replacement warranty.

Middle-range tools are those made for home mechanics. An example brand is Craftsman sold by Sears. These tools are very good and built very well. The tolerances are tight (a 13mm tool is 13mm exactly), and they have reasonable durability. Sears backs their Craftsman tools with a free replacement warranty. Although they are very good, they do not have the durability of Snap-on tools. What this implies is if you do not rely on your tools for your trade, Craftsman tools will serve you well.

At the next level are the tools manufactured for sale at retail stores such as those sold at home improvement stores like Lowe's and Home Depot. The quality of tools varies from fair to good, with most falling in the middle. While some would disagree and there are exceptions, I've found these tools to be a bit lower in quality and less precise than Craftsman. These store brands are good enough for tasks that do not require precision and are only used occasionally. Some of the tools sold have a limited warranty. You should ask about the warranty if you plan to purchase one of these brands.

There are also innumerable off-brands that can sometimes be decent quality but in general are not the best choice when precision or durability is a concern. For example, I typically buy off-brand tools for use in emergency kits or for situations where I know the tools will be exposed to the elements (like in the toolbox of my tractor). That isn't to say they aren't worth buying—just don't expect them to last very long.

So which tools should you buy for building and maintaining a 3D printer? That depends on your budget, really. It can also depend on whether you use your tools for other things. For example, I perform my own maintenance on everything I own—from blenders to my sports car. But that is because of my training as an engineer and a lifetime of being a motorhead.

I have several grades of tools—I reserve some tools (namely my Snap-on tools) for work on my motorcycles and sports car, which require a very high level of precision, other tools for general automotive and small engine maintenance (namely Craftsman), and other tools household work (a mixture of Craftsman and Kobolt).

Thus, I have several toolboxes and locations for storing my tools. All of the tools I use to work on my 3D printers are store brands like Kobolt with a few Craftsman pieces (namely screwdrivers). These tools are stored in my office so that I do not have to fetch them every time I want to work on one of my printers.

■ **Tip** Watch for occasional in-store sales. Stores often run sales on overstock items—especially after a holiday like Christmas or Father's Day. Indeed, most of my Kobolt tools were bought at 40%–50% off the regular price.

In conclusion, the choice of tool brand is yours. If you consider the fact that you will not be using the tools every hour of the day, and that you will only use them occasionally, the major store brands are of sufficient quality and are a good choice for those who want decent quality without the higher price tag.

TOOL SNOBBERY OR JUST PARTICULAR?

It may seem like I'm being too picky about my tools. Once you have experienced the brands like I have, you will understand. For example, I have worn out Craftsman tools when I was active in motorcycle racing because they did not stand up to the wear of frequent use. Similarly, I've found I need a very precise socket for some of the bolts on my BMW motorcycle. In this case, only the Snap-on tools fit properly, preventing accidental slippage, or worse—stripping. Once again, experience suggests the old adage is true: use the best tool for the job. Sometimes that means the $300 tool instead of the $10 one. Of course, sometimes a hammer is just a hammer.

Tools

The vast majority of tools you will need to build and maintain your 3D printer are common hand tools (screwdrivers, wrenches, pliers, etc.). There are a few tools you may want to have that would make the job easier. There are also a few tools that I recommend having, but depending on the type of plastic you need, the tool may not be applicable. I describe the tools associated with 3D printing in three categories in the following sections: required (general and building), recommended, and optional.

You cannot go wrong if you prefer to buy a complete toolset. You can often find basic toolsets at larger retailers such as Lowe's, Home Depot, and Sears. However, you may need to buy an electronics toolkit as well as a basic mechanic's toolkit to get all of the tools described here. It may be cheaper to buy them individually.

Required Tools: General

This section describes those tools I feel are essential for every 3D printer owner. While some printers require fewer tools than others, the following list is what your basic 3D printer toolkit should contain. I list the tools first, and then discuss some of the less common tools later.

- Needle-nose pliers
- Small flat-blade (slotted) screwdriver
- Small and medium-sized Phillips screwdrivers
- Side cutters
- Hex wrenches: 1mm, 1.5mm, 2.5mm, 3.0mm
- Digital caliper with metric scale
- ESD tweezers
- Hobby knife set
- Rulers (metric), (1) 300mm or more, (1) 100mm–150mm
- Wrenches: a combination of 8mm, 10mm, 13mm, and 17mm (Prusa i3)
- Square

■ **Note**   Some vendors include the tools you need for regular maintenance. For example, the MakerBot Replicator comes with the hex wrenches needed to adjust the print bed and extruder.

The digital caliper is used in a variety of ways. It makes setting up your printer easier and more precise. That is, the caliper can reliably measure small distances. It can also measure outside and inside dimensions as well as depth. It is also very handy to use when modeling or creating objects that will be mounted to other objects. For example, you can use a digital caliper to measure thickness or depth of mating surfaces. Figure 3-1 shows a typical digital caliper from Kobalt.

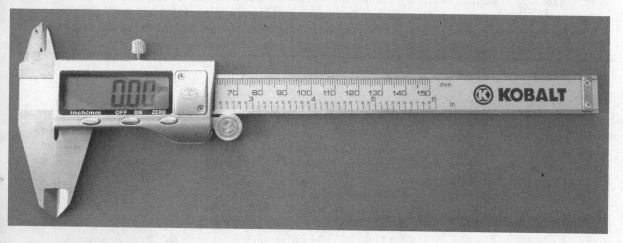

Figure 3-1. *Digital caliper*

■ **Tip** When you use a digital caliper, always make sure to close the jaws and press the zero or reset button to calibrate the scale to zero, as shown in the photo.

Electric static discharge (ESD)–safe tweezers are another handy addition. I prefer tweezers with an angled head. You can use these to safely remove excess hot filament from the nozzle and build plate without fear of a static discharge (or getting burned).

With some printers, such as some Prusa designs, contacting the nozzle or extruder with non-ESD tweezers can result in a small static discharge that can cause the LCD interface to become corrupt. This is normally not fatal, but why risk it? Get an ESD-safe set instead.

A hobby knife (known by its more common name X-Acto[3]) set is another very handy tool every 3D printer owner must have. You will need a hobby knife to remove plastic filament from your objects, cut and reshape objects, and more. Figure 3-2 shows a comprehensive Kobalt hobby knife set that includes a variety of blades. I recommend looking for a set like this. The molded case is a nice touch and helps keep the sharp things neat and safe to handle.

---

[3]Just like *Xerox* is a synonym for copier, *X-Acto knife* is a synonym for a small, sharp, and guaranteed-to-make-you-bleed if you're careless hobby knife.

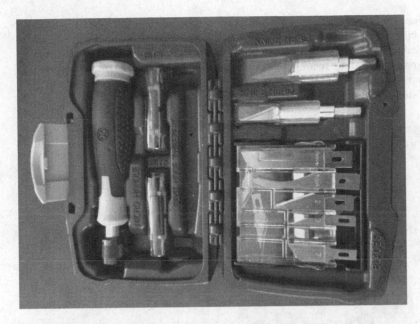

Figure 3-2. *Hobby knife set*

I have listed a number of wrench sizes, but the ones that you will need depends entirely on the printer you have. For example, if you own a MakerBot Replicator or Printrbot Simple, you won't need any of the wrenches. Before buying a set, check the vendor's bill of materials and build instructions, or observe your printer first. You can save some money by buying only those wrenches you need. On the other hand, if you plan to build a 3D printer now or in the future, the sizes listed should cover most printer designs.

An adjustable wrench can be a good compromise if you want to keep your toolkit small. A medium, six-inch adjustable wrench will do for most printers. However, keep in mind that cheap adjustable wrenches may be more trouble than they are worth since they tend to not hold their settings very well and can slip under moderate force. So if you want to get one, get one of the better brands (like Craftsman or Kobalt).

A small carpenter's square can be very helpful when assembling frame components by keeping the frame parts at the proper angle. For example, if there are frame components that are mounted 90 degrees to other components, the square can be used to keep the parts at the proper angle when tightening the hardware.

Required Tools: Building a 3D Printer

There are also a number of tools you will need if you plan to build your own 3D printer or if you plan to upgrade your existing printer. While you could use some of the following tools in the course of repairing your printer, you should consider adding these items to your toolkit eventually. For example, if you are not planning to build your own 3D printer, you can wait until you see these tools on sale, so that you can save some money and have the tools when you need them in the future.

- Wire stripper
- Soldering iron and solder
- Multimeter
- Ceramic screwdriver

There are several types of *wire strippers*. In fact, there are probably a dozen or more designs out there. But there really are two kinds: ones that only grip and cut the insulation as you pull it off the wire manually, and those that grip, cut, and remove the insulation automatically. The first type is more common and, with some practice, will do just fine for most small jobs (like repairing a broken wire); but the second type makes a larger job—such as wiring 3D printer electronics from bare wire (no prefab connectors)—much faster. As you can imagine, the first type is considerably cheaper. Figure 3-3 shows both types of wire strippers. Either is a good choice.

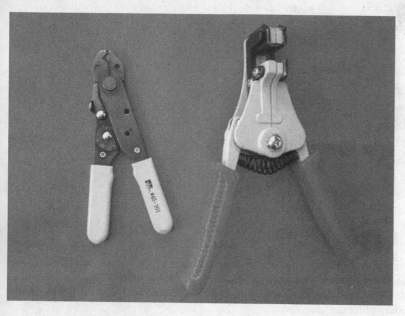

Figure 3-3. *Wire strippers*

A *soldering iron* is required for most 3D printer kits—especially those that do not have prefabricated electronics and cables. If you are going to build a printer that requires you to solder wires together, or maybe a few connectors, a basic soldering iron from an electronics store such as Radio Shack is all you will need. On the other hand, if you plan to assemble your own electronics, you may want to consider getting a good, professional soldering iron such as a Hakko. The professional models include features that allow you to set the temperature of the wand, have a wider array of tips available, and tend to last a lot longer. Figure 3-4 shows a well-used entry-level Radio Shack. Figure 3-5 shows a professional model Hakko soldering iron.

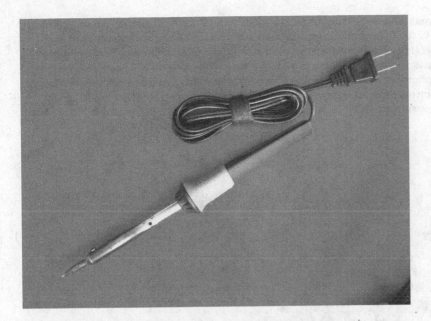

Figure 3-4. *Entry-level soldering iron*

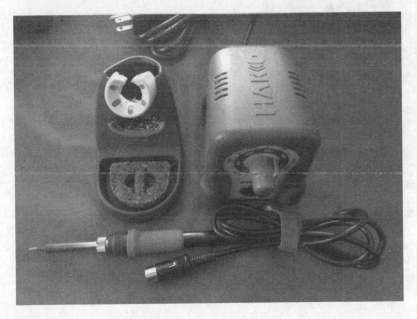

Figure 3-5. *Professional soldering iron*

■ **Tip**   For best results, choose a solder with a low lead content in the 37%–40% range. If you use a professional soldering iron, adjust the temperature to match the melting point of the solder (listed on the label).

A *multimeter* is another tool that you will need when building your own printer. You will also need it to do almost any electrical repair on your printer. Like soldering irons, there are many different multimeters available. And like soldering irons, the prices of multimeters range from inexpensive basic units to complex, feature-rich, incredibly expensive units. For most 3D printer tasks, including building most kits, a basic unit is all you will need. However, if you plan to build more than one 3D printer or want to assemble your own electronics, you may want to invest a bit more in a more sophisticated multimeter. Figure 3-6 shows a basic digital multimeter (costing about $10) and Figure 3-7 shows a professional multimeter from BK Precision.

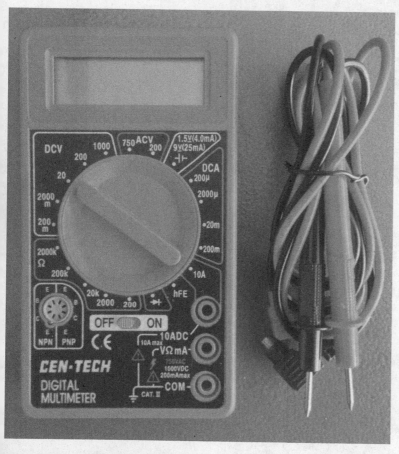

Figure 3-6. Basic digital multimeter

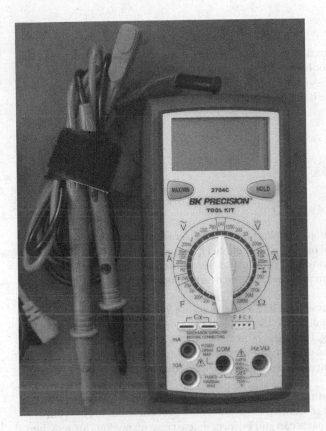

Figure 3-7. Advanced digital multimeter

Notice the better meter has more granular settings and more features. Again, you probably won't need more than the basic unit. You will need to measure voltage and resistance at a minimum. Whichever meter you buy, make sure it has modes for measuring AC and DC voltage, continuity testing (with an audible alert), and checking resistance.

■ **Tip** Most multimeters including the inexpensive ones come with a small instruction booklet that shows you how to measure voltage, resistance, and other functions of the unit.

A *ceramic screwdriver* is used to adjust small potentiometers found on some electronics components. Since it is ceramic, it does not conduct electricity and therefore makes adjusting potentiometers while the electronics are powered-on safer. The primary reason for having one of these screwdrivers is to adjust the stepper motor driver current. You would need to do this during a build if you purchased a RAMPS (or similar) electronics set that is not prematched to your stepper motors. If you have to change a stepper motor with a different model, you may need to adjust your stepper motor driver.

■ **Note** Some vendors include a ceramic screwdriver with their RAMPS set.

Recommended Tools

The tools mentioned in the previous sections are the minimal sets you should have for working with and building 3D printers. This section lists and describes some additional tools you should consider adding to your kit if you plan to make 3D printing a hobby. While not explicitly required, they can improve your experience over the long term. Some may seem obvious, but others not so much. I'll describe the benefits of using each.

- Fire extinguisher

- Fume extractor

- Electric screwdriver and bits

- Drill bits

- Heat gun (also called a *hot air gun*)

At the top of my list of recommended tools is a *fire extinguisher*. You may think it a really strange thing to have in your 3D printer kit, but let me assure you it is the proverbial ounce of protection. I have not had the need to use one myself with any of my printers (thankfully), but I have encountered people who have. Indeed, I've read a couple forum posts about cases where the heaters on the printers have run away and caused overheating, and in at least one case, a small fire.

The closest I've come to needing a fire extinguisher was when I had a small fracture in one of the power supply cables supplying power to my electronics board (RAMPS). I detected the problem the old-fashion way—something smelled funny. While I could not visibly see anything wrong, I definitely smelled something burning. Closer inspection (by touch) revealed the culprit—one of my mains power cables was overheating. Once I powered everything off, I was able to confirm I had a short in the cable itself. Had I not detected something amiss, I may have needed that fire extinguisher!

Considering the fact that the nozzles on 3D printers routinely heat to temperatures in excess of 180 degrees Celsius, and even the heated print beds run at over 60 degrees Celsius, there is a lot of heat generated. Even if your printer is made mostly of metal, the electronics and plastic parts can still burn, or at least give off noxious fumes when smoldering. It is best to not take chances.

■ **Caution**   This is a good time to warn you to never leave a newly built or substantially upgraded printer running unattended. You need not watch it every second, but you should at least be in the same room so you can detect problems either by smell or sound. Once the printer is well broken-in, you may not need to check on it so often—but I would still not leave it unattended for long periods.

If you are going to print with filament that potentially emits irritant fumes when heated (like ABS), or if you plan to do a lot of soldering, you should consider getting a *fume extractor*. A fume extractor is a small but powerful fan that draws air through a charcoal filter to eliminate much of the smell and irritant fumes. If you are like me and have more allergies than any one person should ever have, you will appreciate having a fume extractor.

In fact, I have two—one for soldering and one mounted on an articulated arm near the printers I use for printing ABS. The articulated arm allows me to move the extractor from one printer to the other (they are side by side on one of my worktables). Figure 3-8 shows a Hakko benchtop fume extractor that you can use for soldering or for collecting fumes from your printer. Figure 3-9 shows the arm-mounted fume extractor I use with some of my printers. Notice that I locate the extractor above the extruder but near the rear of the printer. This keeps it far enough away from the printer as not to affect it with air currents, while still eliminating much of the odor and irritants associated with printing with ABS.

Figure 3-8. *Benchtop fume extractor*

Figure 3-9. *Fume extractor on articulated arm*

One tool that you will find very handy if you plan to build more than one printer or you plan to build a printer with a lot of bolts is an *electric screwdriver*. While not expressly required, it will save you a lot of work. One task where this is evident is opening the door on a Greg's Wade extruder. There are two bolts that take more than a few turns to remove. An electric screwdriver can make this a lot faster and relieves you from the stress of turning the screwdriver manually.

■ **Tip**   For those of us suffering from carpal tunnel syndrome[4] or similar injuries, an electric screwdriver is a must.

If you plan to get an electric screwdriver (only a cordless rechargeable will do), get one with a variety of bits, such as a Phillips, slotted, hex, Torx, and the like. You can often find these at reasonable prices in most hardware and home improvement centers. On the other hand, if you do not want an electric screwdriver, you should consider a bit driver instead. Bit drivers have a built-in ratchet that makes it easier and faster to use than a fixed handle. You can get them with various bit assortments.

You may also want to consider getting a *drill bit set*. There are many uses for drill bits. When building a printer, you may need to drill out some plastic or wood pieces if the holes are not quite large enough (or you need to enlarge holes because you only have SAE bolts—because your hardware store thinks metric bolts are just a fad). You may also want to have some drill bits on hand to work with your own objects. Sometimes printed objects can be distorted (for a variety of reasons) where holes may need reaming a bit. A drill bit of the correct size makes short work of that task.

METRIC DRILL BITS?

Sadly, it is almost impossible to find metric-sized drill bits in most hardware and home improvement stores in the United States. Fortunately, the SAE sizes included in most drill bit sets will do. The following lists the frequently used sizes and their metric equivalent (not exact in some cases).

- 1/8 inch = 3 millimeters

- 11/64 inch = 4 millimeters

- 13/64 inch = 5 millimeters

- 1/4 inch = 6 millimeters

- 5/16 inch = 8 millimeters

This is another example of where a digital caliper can help. Use it to measure your drill bits to make sure you have the correct size before drilling through something that took hours to print.

Of course, having a drill bit set means you will need a drill, right? Not really. There are drill bit sets available with a hex shank that makes using them in electric screwdrivers and bit drivers very handy. Figure 3-10 shows a drill bit set along with a reasonably priced electric screwdriver.

---

[4]The scourge of the modern geek, nerd, and active computer user! See http://www.ninds.nih.gov/disorders/carpal_tunnel/detail_carpal_tunnel.htm for more details.

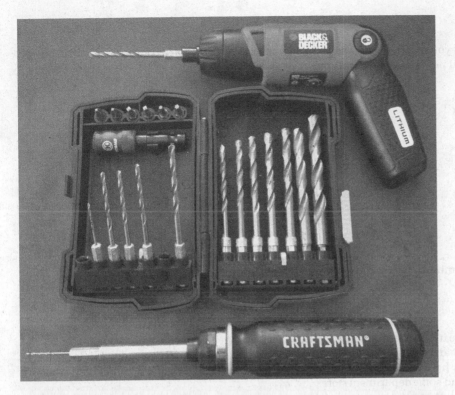

Figure 3-10. *Electric screwdriver and drill bit set*

Notice how well the drill bits fit the bit driver. Speaking of which, I've found the Craftsman bit driver a really good addition to my toolkit. This version has on-tool storage for a host of bits, making it a one-stop choice for screwdrivers. Figure 3-11 shows the bit driver storage compartment. Cool, eh?

Figure 3-11. *Bit driver from Sears*

The last recommended tool is a *heat gun* (sometimes called a *hot air gun*). If you plan to do any wiring more than crimping pins to build connectors, you will want to use shrink-wrap to cover the connections (You did solder them, right?). A heat gun is the best tool for applying heat to shrink wrap to make it constrict. You can use a butane torch, a lighter, or a match to do the same, but you need to be very careful that you do not apply too much heat or get the wire too close to the flame.

The next section lists some other tools you may want to consider having, but these tools are not strictly necessary to build, use, and maintain 3D printers.

Optional Tools

The following is a list of tools that you may need at some point. In some cases, it is a tool of convenience, and in other cases, it is a tool of necessity if you perform a certain task often.

- Canned air
- Small brush/sweeper
- Vacuum
- Hobby saw
- File set
- Sandpaper
- Small level
- Dial gauge
- Small wrenches: a combination box and open 3mm, 4mm, 5mm, etc.
- Butane torch
- Scissors

A can of compressed air, while it may sound strange, can help clear away debris and dust from your printer. In fact, it is the only method I consider safe for cleaning dust from electronics. You can also use canned air to cool objects more quickly (tread lightly here—cooling parts too fast can cause cracking). You can find canned air in most hardware, home improvement, and some department stores.

Similarly, for cleaning your print bed and surrounding areas, I recommend *a small brush*—like those used by artists, mechanical engineers, and architects.

■ **Caution** Never attempt to clean your build plate while the printer is powered on—especially if hot.

Perhaps the best optional tool is *a small vacuum*. This can be somewhat of a personality thing. For example, I am of the type that doesn't like dirt and debris on my work surfaces. Thus, I clean my printers and work surfaces after my printer(s) has cooled.

■ **Caution** You should never use a vacuum around a printer that is actively printing. The suction will affect cooling of the part and can hasten or increase warping and lift. Wait until the printer has stopped and cooled before getting that annoying extra bit of plastic off the build plate.

Once you have printed for some time, you will notice that small bits of filament seem to litter the area around and under your printer. Whether this is from your working with shaping plastic parts or from just the usual excess print, a vacuum will make short work of the cleanup.

If you buy a hobby knife set, you may also be able to purchase *a small saw blade* to fit the handle. Conversely, you can buy *hobby saws* with handles. What would you cut with a small saw? If you are building a printer with a wood frame, it is likely the vendor will ship you laser-cut parts. Sometimes these parts are still joined together in small areas. A saw will make cutting them apart easier than using a hobby or utility knife. I've also used a small saw to cut parts or to remove large sections in order to modify them to fit or to join two parts. For example, I wanted to move an endstop adjuster out a little farther from the X-end axis. Rather than render and print a new part (which would have taken a couple of hours), I simply created a small rectangle part sized to move the adjuster out. I then cut the adjuster off the X-end with the saw, and then glued the pieces back together using ABS glue. Easy!

Two other tools that you may want to work with plastic or wood parts are *a file set* and *sandpaper*. I use a small metal file set that includes a number of files with different profiles—flat, round, triangular, and so forth. You may need to file parts for fit. Often the areas needing to be modified are interior areas. A file can make reaching these areas much easier than sandpaper. If you plan to get some sandpaper, look for medium and fine grades. You generally do not need the coarser grades, and unless you plan to paint your parts, you won't need the finishing grades.

You may read about leveling your printer in various forums and in blogs, instructions, and commentaries. What most of these are discussing is leveling the print bed—that is, making the print bed parallel to the X axis. While it is not strictly necessary, you could consider keeping the printer itself level. If your printer comes with leveling feet, you can easily make it level on almost any work surface. You don't need to use a level—a sighting is all you need. If your printer doesn't have leveling feet, check out Chapter 11 for ideas on how to make your own. To whet your appetite, Figure 3-12 shows leveling feet that I created for my MakerBot Replicator 2.

Figure 3-12. *MakerBot Replicator 2 leveling feet*

One tool that is often overlooked is *a dial gauge*. This is a precision tool designed to measure depth. Mechanics and engineers use it to measure the tolerances of parts. A dial gauge is used with 3D printers in several ways. The two most common uses are to help level the print bed and to measure fine axis movement for calibration. The gauge comes without a mount but often includes a common mount loop on the back. Savvy 3D designers have designed several clips and mounts that allow you to mount a dial gauge on the X axis for leveling the print bed. Figure 3-13 shows a dial gauge mount I created for leveling the print bed on a Prusa i3.

Figure 3-13. *Dial gauge and mount for leveling the print bed*

You may think that smaller (7mm and smaller) open-end or combination wrenches should be on the required tool list. However, since most small bolts can be easily over tightened or stripped, you can often hold the nut with your fingers or a small pair of pliers when tightening. Further, some wood and plastic parts incorporate nut traps, eliminating the need for small wrenches.

Thus, *small wrenches* for tightening nuts and bolts are not really needed, but in some cases they can be beneficial. For example, I use a RAMPS fan mount that mounts to the RAMPS board itself. This is great if I don't need to remove it, but if I do, I need to reach the nuts underneath the RAMPS but above the Arduino board. A small wrench makes this operation a bit easier.

A butane torch can be very handy when making your own parts. If you plan to make parts that bolt together and you plan to make nut traps (small pockets to hold a nut in place), you can use a butane torch to heat up the nut before placing it in the part. Thus, you can make the nut traps a bit smaller, and once the heated nut is in place, it will not come loose or fall out (a common hassle for wood or acrylic parts with nut traps).

A butane torch can also be used to heat a part for flexing. For example, some Prusa i2 parts need to be heated before bearings are inserted so that you don't break the part. A heat gun can do the same thing, and honestly is a bit easier to use.

Scissors are needed if you plan to print on Kapton tape. Unless you have found a source that I am unaware of, Kapton tape comes in rolls that you must cut to length. I'll talk more about the specifics of how to apply the tape in a later chapter. If you do plan to use Kapton tape, look for scissors that are nonstick. The nonstick coating helps prevent the tape from sticking to the scissors when you cut it.

WHAT, NO HAMMERS?

It is very rare that you would need a hammer to build a 3D printer. Conversely, you may need *a small mallet* either made of wood, plastic, or rubber to press together some components (those intended to be pressed together, that is), but in general, no metal hammers are needed.[5]

---

[5]Do you know how to tell if an auto mechanic is well trained? Ask him how many hammers he has. If he says, "I think my wife has one in the kitchen," hire him!

Now that we've talked about the required, recommended, and optional tools, let us now discuss the common supplies you will need for 3D printing.

Recommended Supplies

This section describes those supplies that you will likely need while using your 3D printer. The following list includes the more common consumables.

- Acetone (for working with ABS)

- Plastic adhesive (for PLA)

- Light sewing machine oil or PTFE grease

- Lint-free cloth

- Brass brush

- Blue painter's tape

- Kapton tape

First on the list is *acetone* for working with ABS. Since ABS dissolves in acetone, you can directly apply acetone on two parts and press them together. When the acetone evaporates (dries), the parts are bound together. You can also soak the parts' ends in acetone for a few seconds to achieve a stronger bond. Another use for acetone is to finish parts. A light swipe of *a lint-free cloth* soaked in acetone can smooth a sanded ABS part, giving is a satin sheen. The best use of acetone is in making ABS slurry—dissolved ABS that is painted on Kapton tape as a means to reduce lifting and warping.

If you don't print with ABS and use PLA instead, know that there isn't a solvent that is quite as versatile as acetone. However, *dichloromethane* has been used by some as a solvent for PLA. If you want to shape and glue PLA parts, you will need to find an adhesive that is made specifically for light plastics. Check your local hardware or home improvement store and ask the clerk for *plastic cement* (not model airplane glue).

■ **Note** I've had limited success using some brands of epoxy to glue PLA parts. More specifically, some epoxies can weaken the plastic near the bond, making it pliable (spelled *ruined* in most situations).

As part of a regular maintenance routine, you should have some *light sewing machine oil* or *PTFE grease* on hand. Check with your printer vendor for the type they recommend. The light oil is used on the smooth rods to keep them moist, and the seals on the bearings pliable. The grease is often used on threaded rods or lead screws. I talk more about cleaning and lubricating your printer in Chapter 10. You should use lint-free cloths or rags to clean the smooth rods and apply the oil.

DISPOSE OF OILY RAGS PROPERLY

Always store oily rags in an approved container. Oil-soaked cloth can generate enough heat to combust. Although it is unlikely you will use enough oil for this to be a danger, it is still a risk. This isn't a fairy tale either. A friend of a friend once lost his prized antique BMW motorcycle because he left out a can of oily rags while he went away on vacation. Yes, his garage burned down!

If you do not have a used oil container or a similar container for oiled cloth, you can use a glass jar filled with water. Simply place the oily rag in the water and close the lid. Regardless, it is best to dispose of the oily rags as soon as you can and in a manner that complies with your local ordinances on waste disposal. Call your local landfill or sanitation department if you are unsure.

I would recommend getting *a brass brush* for cleaning plastic off the nozzle. It makes the job very easy—especially when the nozzle has been heated to temperature (and powered off). However, brass brushes have small bristles that can bend and get clogged with bits of filament over several uses. Hence, eventually you will need to get a new one. Look for one with a wooden handle so that you can use it with a hot nozzle and not risk contaminating the nozzle with yet more melted plastic.

Lastly, you will need to get *blue painter's tape* for printing PLA on glass or metal and *Kapton tape* for printing ABS and other higher-temperature filament. When buying blue painter's tape, get the widest size you can find and avoid brands with the logo on the tape surface. The logo printing can transfer to light-colored parts, which can ruin the perfectly printed object you planned to give as a gift. Guess how I know this? Get the logo- and writing-free tape. You won't be sorry. Make sure you choose a brand name such as ScotchBlue (by 3M) or similar.

Similarly, when buying Kapton tape, look for the widest you can find. The prices vary greatly and can be much more expensive for wider widths. Look for vendors that sell quality tape or have favorable reviews from other customers. A cheap roll of Kapton tape can make life difficult. Cheap, imitation Kapton tape can come loose from the print bed when heated, it can be difficult to install or remove, or simply be too thin to work well.

■ **Note**   Wider Kapton tape can be harder to apply. If your print bed can withstand water, a soap solution can make applying wider Kapton tape easier. If you cannot use a soap solution, you may want to use 2-inch wide Kapton, which is easier to apply without the soap solution.

Kapton tape is also required for some installations of nozzles and heated print beds. Check your build instructions to see if you need Kapton tape to complete the build.

Now that we've discussed the tools used in building, maintaining, and using 3D printers, let's discuss the skills you will need should you decide to build and maintain your own printer.

Skills

The skills needed to build a 3D printer are somewhat dependent on the type of kit you buy. I will highlight the skills needed to build a typical RepRap kit next, but let's consider the skills needed for kits that come with all of the necessary components. In this case, I am focusing on the Printrbot Simple (actually, any Printrbot kit) or the MakerFarm Prusa i3, which are two of the easiest kits to assemble.

The area where most kits differ is in mechanical skills. Fortunately, if you can successfully negotiate tightening a bolt with a wrench, pliers, or a screwdriver, then you have the basics covered. More specifically, most kits come with instructions that guide you through the mechanical assembly and rarely require more than bolting together parts and using zip ties to attach pieces.

Similarly, if you are building a printer based on a kit that has the electronics preassembled and the wires cut to length, you may not even need to solder anything. Indeed, it is likely you won't have to do anything more difficult than plugging in the wires to their respective points on the electronics board.

Now let's see the other end of the spectrum: the skills needed for building a RepRap printer.

Mechanical

RepRap kits are unlikely to be optimized or refined to the point of the Printrbot kits. Indeed, most require you to solve fit issues with the frame components in particular. For example, kits with wooden frames may require you to sand or cut pieces for a better fit. Kits with plastic components sometimes need to have the pieces trimmed and holes reamed out to allow clearance for bolts. Some kits with metal frames, like the single sheet aluminum Prusa i3, may require drilling or even tapping holes for bolts (sometimes called *threading holes*).

Thus, the mechanical skills needed for a typical RepRap printer include simple mechanical assembly, cleaning plastic and wood parts of excess material, resizing holes for bolts, sanding, filing, drilling holes, and, in rare cases, tapping holes for bolts. Thus, you should be competent with using a drill and similar handheld power tools.

Electrical

The electrical skills needed for RepRap kits can vary from nothing more than plugging in wires—as we saw with the Printrbot kits—to needing to solder components to printed circuit boards (PCBs).

Beyond plugging in wires, most kits require you to assemble cables either using crimped connectors, or by soldering together connectors or soldering wires. For example, some RepRap kits require you to use crimped connections for *thermistors* (temperature sensors), and possibly the resistor for the *hot end* (the heater) and heated print bed. Thus, you should have had practice with connecting wires together with solder, assembling connectors with crimped pins, and securing the connections with shrink wrap.

If you chose a kit that does not include an assembled RAMPS board, you will need to be able to solder components to the PCB. Most RAMPS kits have the harder components (surface mount) presoldered. Thus, you will need to be proficient with using a soldering iron for small work.

DO YOU NEED TO LEARN TO SOLDER?

If you do not know how to solder or it has been a while since you've used a soldering iron, you may want to check out the book by *Learn to Solder* by Brian Jepson, Tyler Moskowite, and Gregory Hayes (O'Reilly Media, 2012) or Google how-to videos on soldering. Or you could buy the Learn To Solder Kit from Maker Shed (makershed.com/product_p/mkel4.htm), which comes with a soldering iron, wire cutters, and supplies—better still, the exercises include building a sample emergency siren. Cool. Not only will you get feedback that you're doing it right, but you will also you get to annoy your friends and family.

Regardless of whether you need to assemble the electronics, you will also need to be able to use a basic multimeter to measure resistance and check voltage and current. The most frequent case is adjusting the stepper drivers to match the current requirements (via the reference voltage) of your stepper motors.

■ **Caution**   This is one area where most RepRap beginners fail to heed the instructions. Be sure to take the time to check and adjust your stepper drivers so that they are set correctly. If they are set too low, the steppers may fail to move or miss steps. If they are set too high, they become noisy and can overheat.

As you can see, the more DIY a kit is (how much of it comes preassembled), the more skills it is likely to require to build. I present some categories of kits in the next section and talk more about what you can expect from each.

3D Printer Kits Revisited

Before I discuss a number of tips for building 3D printers, I'd like to discuss the types of kits available. In the last chapter, I presented how to source your own kit and I briefly discussed the range of kits available. However, there is a bit more to understanding 3D printer kits. More specifically, what you can expect when building certain kits. I have categorized printer kits into three types: complete, parts only, and component. I describe each in more detail next.

Complete

A complete kit contains all of the parts you need to assemble a printer. Some kits also include some of the tools needed, but that is not the norm. However, most complete kits include a full or partial set of instructions (or are made available on the vendor's web site).

You can also expect a complete kit to be packaged so that the parts are cataloged in the form of a bill of materials and labeled or packaged in such a way to make identification of the parts easy—either with numbered parts or a parts layout with reference numbers. Kits in this category often include a full instruction manual with detailed photos and step-by-step explanations. Figure 3-14 shows an excellent example of a complete kit—the Printrbot Simple.

Figure 3-14. *Complete Printrbot Simple kit (image courtesy of* Printrbot.com*)*

The Printrbot Simple kit represents one of the best complete printer kits. All of the wood parts are laser cut and go together well without need to trim or fiddle with drilling out holes. It comes complete with a preassembled electronics board—the Printrboard made by Printrbot, and includes all of the cables needed. You don't need to solder or otherwise modify any of the wiring to complete the assembly. The kit also includes a bill of materials that is clearly hand-checked prior to shipment (as is evident by the handwritten remarks), and includes a link to a complete set of documentation.

Not only is the kit easy to assemble, the little printer is fun to use, portable, and produces prints of surprising quality. The Printrbot Simple is priced at only $299 USD for the basic kit and $349 USD for the upgraded aluminum extruder (a must if you can go the extra $50). If you are looking for a no-fuss, complete 3D printer kit, you will be hard-pressed to find a better alternative.[6]

---

[6]Except maybe another Printrbot model.

PRINTRBOT SIMPLE: THE BEST KIT FOR BEGINNERS

I decided to try a Printrbot Simple to evaluate an entry-level printer kit. I found the kit very easy to assemble, requiring a single afternoon to complete.[7] The instructions are clear albeit a bit terse, but offer ample photos and many tips to help you succeed. You don't need soldering skills—just basic mechanical skills. If you can tie a knot, use a knife, and turn a screwdriver, you've got all the skills needed to build a Printrbot Simple.

The only task where a beginner might stumble is tying the fishing line for the X and Y axes. To do it properly, you need to follow the instructions carefully, measuring the line before you tie it off on both ends. Once you tackle this task, you're home free!

Whether you have your own printer already and want to experience building a 3D printer, or you want to get started with 3D printing but have a limited budget, the Printrbot Simple is the best choice bar none.

Parts Only

The next category is a kit where all of the components are supplied, but may or may not include the hardware, such as bolts, nuts, washers, threaded rods, and so forth. Some vendors offer hardware kits to go along with the printer kit for an additional cost. It is also possible the kits in this category will not include all of the miscellaneous supplies, like zip ties, tape, and shrink-wrap. This permits vendors to sell the kits at a bit of a discount. Unlike the complete kits, these kits often need more work in the form of cleaning and fitting pieces together. You are likely to need to spend more time to test-fit components and correct any anomalies. Lastly, I would not expect kits in this category to come with instructions (but some do). Figure 3-15 shows a typical parts-only kit.

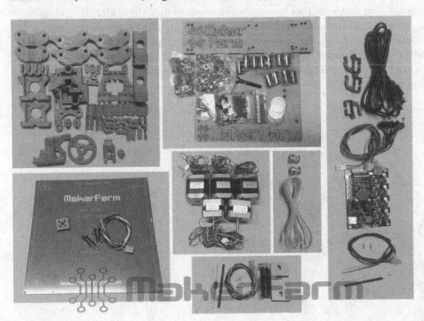

Figure 3-15. *Parts-only Prusa i2 Deluxe RepRap kit (image courtesy of MakerFarm)*

---

[7] This included 20 minutes to find the superglue that I was sure I put in a specific drawer. It is funny how things like that can move around. It must be the work of gnomes or house elves.

Notice that the kit includes everything you need to build a Prusa i2 3D printer except for the smooth and threaded rods. In fact, at the time of this writing, MakerFarm does not stock the rods, so you have to source those from another vendor. While the kit does include all of the nuts and bolts, washers, and bearings, it doesn't have any zip ties or other miscellaneous bits.

Despite that, MakerFarm provides extra components, such as extra hardware, extra-long wiring, and even extra-small electrical parts. Kits from other vendors sometimes have the precise number of 3mm nuts needed. Lose one and you're in a work-stoppage situation.

Unlike a complete kit, the Prusa i2 Deluxe kit requires a bit more electronics skills and the mechanical build is also more difficult (but not overly so). You will need to know how to build connectors, solder wires, bolt together parts, align parts during assembly, and adjust the build on the fly. Also, the plastic parts may need trimming to fit properly.

Perhaps the most attractive aspect is that MakerFarm allows you to choose some of the components when you order the kit. You have your choice of color for the printed parts, with or without stepper motors, with or without electronics and choice of electronics, and choice of size of the nozzle. Due to the choices available and the fact that all of the small hardware is included, the MakerFarm Prusa i2 kit is a step above most RepRap printer kits. Better still, MakerFarm has a set of clear instructions with all parts identified available on their web site.

Overall, the MakerFarm kit is a better choice than most RepRap kits. If you are looking for the RepRap experience, get a MakerFarm Prusa i2 kit.

■ **Note** MakerFarm also has complete kits for their Prusa i3 printer. Similar to the i2, you can customize your order by choosing which nozzle you want to include. Nozzle options are listed together with the types of filament they support.

Component

Component kits aren't really kits in the sense that they contain everything you need. Rather, these kits are actually a collection of smaller kits. For example, a vendor may sell a hot-end kit or an extruder kit, a frame kit, an electronics kit, and so forth, but no single kit that contains everything. Furthermore, the component kit may come preassembled. Vendors who do this are making it possible for you to tailor the kit to your needs. Thus, you are completely on your own for any parts that are not included, like hardware and consumables that can make sourcing your own kit easier. Figure 3-16 shows an example of a component kit.

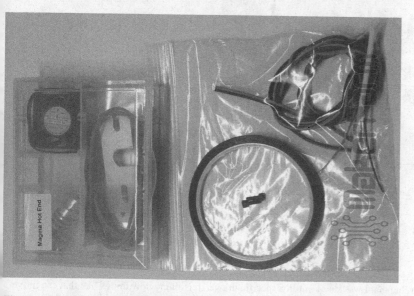

Figure 3-16. *Component kit: hot end (image courtesy of MakerFarm)*

The kit shown is only one part of a printer, but it shows how some vendors package the component to include everything you need. Another example is the RAMPS 1.4 Ultra Set from Gadgets3D (gadgets3d.com). Figure 3-17 shows the kit as sold by Gadgets3D (`http://gadgets3d.com/index.php?route=product/product&path=61&product_id=70`).

Figure 3-17. Component kit: RAMPS kit (image courtesy of Gadgets3D)

Notice how all of the electronic components (not just the RAMPS bits) are assembled and packaged with all of the wiring needed. I have used a number of their kits and they are superior to most.

■ **Tip** Look to kits like these if you want to source your own RepRap printer. They can save you a lot of time, and in most cases, a bit of money too.

They also have an outstanding web site with complete documentation on all of their products. All of their products are shipped quickly and come in well-packaged plastic boxes that have wonderful recycle opportunities for use as storage of spare parts.

Gadgets 3D also sells other kits for RepRap printers. They have smaller kits that include fewer electronics components, kits with stepper motors, and even complete printer kits. Their LCD units are the absolute best I've found anywhere, so even if you don't need to buy a RAMPS setup, get their LCD add-on. You won't be sorry.

Now let's turn our attention to some very helpful tips for building your printer.

3D Printer Build Tips

So you have decided to build your own 3D printer. Great choice! It will be a fun adventure. You need only have the desire to see it through and the drive to succeed. A little help from someone who has made a lot of mistakes and learned a trick or two cannot hurt either.

In fact, that is exactly what I will present in this section. I will present a set of tips and tricks you can use to help avoid some of the pitfalls associated with building a 3D printer. I will limit the discussion to the build tasks and save the maintenance tips and tricks for a later chapter. I have arranged the tips into the following categories to make it easier to use as a reference.

- General notes
- Frame components
- Moving parts
- Electronics
- Preflight checks

I recommend reading through all of the tips prior to starting your build. Even if you have already started building a printer, reading through the tips may help get you past a troublesome point.

The following is not intended to replace any set of instructions that your kit may contain or that your vendor provides. I think writing any set of general printer building instructions is not helpful, given how often printer designs change—not to mention the many variants out there. However, there are a few things that are common to all builds. I include these in the following lists as well.

General Notes

This section includes tips for things you should do prior to starting your build.

Organize Your Small Parts

One of the most time-consuming things I've experienced is finding the right small part—be that a bolt, nut, washer, or that one small grub screw among 50 small screws of the same diameter. The best thing you can do when building your printer is to organize your small parts using a plastic storage bin. If you purchased a kit that has the hardware included, or perhaps you bought a hardware kit, it is worth the extra time to organize the small parts in this manner. Figure 3-14 shows the small parts from a Printrbot Simple kit.

Not shown in the photo is the fact that the tray has a hinged lid. This means that I can stop my work at any time, close the lid, and put the project away. If you plan to buy trays for small parts, get one that has a lid. This tip alone may help you avoid a most dreadful case of missing or scattered small parts if you drop or knock the box over.

If you plan to build more than one 3D printer (that is, make it an obsession), you may want to invest in a set of storage trays for storing an assortment of bolts. For example, I have storage trays with a wide assortment of 2mm, 3mm, 4mm, 5mm, and 8mm nuts, bolts, washers, and more. Figure 3-18 shows my 2mm and 3mm tray.

Figure 3-18. *Using a storage tray for your small parts*

Not only does this make it easier to find the size bolt you need, it can also be cheaper in the long run to buy your small hardware in bulk. For example, to fill out the kit in Figure 3-19, I purchased sets of 50 or 100 pieces for each size bolt. This could be considered overkill if you are building a single printer, but a necessity if you plan to build many.

Figure 3-19. *Large assortment of hardware for multiple builds*

WHICH IS BEST: HEX, SLOT, OR PHILLIPS?

If you are sourcing your own printer kit, you may wonder which type of screws to use—socket cap (hex), slotted, or Phillips? I and many other builders use hex or hex-cap head bolts. Indeed, most kits come with them. They are easier to use because the hex wrench fits snugly in the cap head. But this is a matter of preference. It turns out it really doesn't matter so long as you have the correct size, thread, and lengths needed.

Read the Instructions

If your vendor has provided you with a set of build instructions, be sure to read through them front-to-back at least once. If this is your first 3D printer build, read through the instructions several times so that you are familiar with each step.

This is important because it will decrease the possibility that you will miss a step or perhaps assemble parts in the wrong order, or worse—in the wrong orientation. For example, if you fail to orient some of the parts of the frame on a RepRap printer, especially the Prusa i2, you could find yourself disassembling the entire frame to get that one lousy washer in place. Yes, it does happen. Reading the instructions can help avoid this and similar calamities.

Lastly, reading the instructions will help confirm you have the correct tools for the job. Most build instructions include a required tools list. Check this against your own toolkit to make sure you have everything you need. This too will help avoid frustration late in the build when you discover your own hex key is just a wee bit too small, forcing you to abandon your build in order to acquire another tool.[8]

Use a Clean, Clear Workspace

This is one tip that can save you some consternation if planned in advance. Make sure your choice of workspace for your build has no other small parts, tools, or projects that can interfere with your build. It also helps to choose a workspace where you can leave your project in place should you not be able to finish it in one sitting.

It also helps to clean the workspace before you lay out your parts. You need not be able to eat off the surface, but it should be clear of any dirt, debris, grease, and other contaminants. Keep in mind that the smooth rods, and certainly the bearings, will come oiled. Placing these on a dirty worktop will result in transfer of the dirt to your printer. You do not want that.

As to how large a workspace you will need depends on the size of the printer you are building and how organized you are. For example, all of the parts for a Printrbot Simple can be laid out on a typical computer worktable—with plenty of room for tools and the printer itself. Conversely, due to the number of parts, a RepRap printer needs a larger table—perhaps more like the size of a normal desk.

Your work habits may also be a factor. If you like to keep your workspace clear, you may want to store parts in boxes (or the shipping box) stacked in order of the build instructions. That way, you can remove only the parts needed. Keep in mind that every kit has stages where you will need to set aside a partial assembly. Leave some room for those.

Also, keep in mind the type of frame your printer uses. This is an important point if your workspace happens to be the family dinner table. Your spouse will not appreciate the character your metal frame printer inflicts on the wood surface. Thus, you should consider covering the workspace to avoid scratches, or choose a difference workspace to build your printer.

Lastly, make sure all liquids, beverages, and other messy things are well clear of your work area and parts. Accidental spills can be quite a bother to clean up, especially if you need to dry off a hundred little bolts and nuts.

---

[8]This reminds me of a theory of mine concerning home repair. It seems the difficulty of the repair is directly proportionate to the number of trips to the home improvement store. A corollary suggests this rate is also directly proportional to the time you would have saved hiring a professional to do the job right the first time.

Check the Bill of Materials

If you purchased a kit with a bill of materials, lay that aside and refer to it as you unpack your kit. This helps to ensure you aren't missing any parts, but it also helps you take inventory of the parts. Lay each part or package of parts on your workspace. Try to arrange them in order of the build instructions.

If your kit came with small hardware such as nuts and bolts, be sure to count them to ensure you have enough to complete the build. Most vendors will send you extra in case you lose one or thirteen small nuts and washers.

Lay Out Your Tools

Once you have read the instructions and checked the bill of materials, you should lay out those tools you will need for the build. I like to keep mine in small trays to make them easier to get to and easier to put away, should I need to stop before I am finished. It can be frustrating to spend a lot of time contorting your hands into position to place a nut on the back of a component, only to realize the bit driver is out of arms' reach or has the wrong bit installed. Keep your tools close by.

Don't Mix SAE and Metric

All jocularity about hardware stores and metric sizes aside, don't be tempted to force a SAE bolt in place of the proper metric bolt (or vice versa). While it is fine to use SAE bolts for some components and metric for others, mixing them can be a problem. I recommend sticking with all metric hardware. It may be harder to find, but at least you only need one set of wrenches.

Keep Your Hands Clean

If your frame has laser-cut wood parts, be advised some of these parts may have ash on the cut edges that can transfer to the face of the wood. If this doesn't bother you, then you can safely ignore this tip. However, if it does, you should also consider the fact that small hardware, bearings, and rods often have a thin coat of oil applied by the manufacturer. Unless you want to transfer that oil to your plastic and wood parts, you might want to keep a damp washcloth (preferably one your spouse won't mind getting oil on) and some paper towels to clean up after handling the parts.

I once built a Prusa printer using white PLA parts. When I placed the parts out on my workspace and viewed them with the aluminum frame components, the all-white parts looked pretty cool. Sadly, once I handled a few bolts and a smooth rod or two, I realized too late how easy it is to soil PLA plastic. No, it does not wash off. Even soap and water won't remove all of the smudges from dirty hands. This is because plastic parts have many small cavities that trap dirt. Darker plastic parts tend to hide light smudges better.

No Duct Tape Allowed

That's right. Duct tape ("high-speed Bondo" to NASCAR fans[9]) is strictly prohibited. OK, maybe just one small piece—but that's all you get! Joking aside, there really is no reason to use questionable bonding practices such as duct tape to join parts of your printer together.

However, there is one possible use of duct tape that you might consider safe. When you encounter situations where you need to hold a bolt or a nut in place, and you don't have enough hands or reach to do so while using a tool to assemble a component, a small piece of duct tape attached to a screwdriver can work wonders; for example, holding a small nut in place long enough for you to get the bolt started.

---

[9]Yes, I am one of those too. So I have eclectic tastes. If only we can get them to broadcast a race in Klingon, it would be the perfect sport!

Give Me a Break!

If you find yourself getting frustrated or trying to rush through a build step, stop and give yourself a break. Sometimes stepping away from the problem—even overnight or over a weekend—can work wonders in solving your particular frustration. I recommend taking a break every two hours or so. Do something different during that time, like talking to your family and friends so they don't think you're a complete nerd. But they still might.

Don't Force Components Together

Test-fit all parts before bolting or snapping them together. Some only go one way easily, but can be forced together the wrong way. Just ask any parent the day after Christmas what this means.

Don't Vary From the Plan

If you are like me and always thinking about ways to improve your printers, don't be tempted to alter the design or build midstream to add some gizmo or upgrade you found on Thingiverse. While these upgrades and convenience accessories may improve your printer, adding them before the printer is finished can be more trouble than you expect. For example, if you add a new endstop adjuster in place of the one that came with the kit, and you encounter problems when calibrating the printer later on, how do you know there is something wrong with the kit and not your new addition? Also, if you need help from the vendor and you've deviated from their instructions, you may not find they are as sympathetic as you'd expect. And you should expect them to request you remove the upgrade as a first step in solving the problem. It is best to wait to add embellishments.

FARKLING YOUR PRINTER

In the luxury touring motorcycle world, we call accessories that perform a function, but are not essential to the operation of the motorcycle, a *farkle*—a combination of function and sparkle. This is because while they have a function, they are mostly for show. I must admit some of my printers have been farkled a bit with cool-looking filament guides, extra lighting, and so forth. Basically, if it doesn't come in the kit and isn't required for good print quality, it's likely to be a farkle. There's nothing wrong with that, but you should wait to farkle your printer once you have it built and it is working correctly.

Keep an Engineering Logbook

Many developers, engineers, and scientists keep notes about their projects in paper notebooks or digital notebooks using apps like Evernote (http://evernote.com/). A voice recorder can also be handy in catching those impromptu ideas when you don't have time or it is too dangerous to use pen and paper. Some people are more detailed than others, but most take notes during meetings and phone conversations, thereby providing a written record of verbal communication.

If you aren't in the habit of keeping an engineering logbook, you should consider doing so. You will find a logbook especially handy for building a 3D printer if your build will take more than one sitting. Not only can you record what you've done—settings, measurements, and so forth, but you can also record your thoughts on what worked and what did not. Perhaps more important for a project that requires more than a few hours and a single session is having a place to write down where you are and what you need to do next.

Naturally, you can use any type of notebook you desire; but if you want to class up your notes a bit, you can purchase a notebook made especially for keeping engineering notes. These typically have subdued gridlines and sometimes text areas for recording key information like the project name and page number. Two of my favorite notebooks include the small project-sized notebooks from SparkFun and the larger Maker's Notebook from Maker Shed.

The SparkFun notebooks come in red or gray and feature 52 pages of white-grid on light-gray pages. They are semiflexible, lightweight, and just the right size (10" × 7.5") for recording your notes for all but the largest, world-domination-level projects. The links for these notebooks are as follows:

- Red: www.sparkfun.com/products/11064

- Black: www.sparkfun.com/products/11063

If you are looking for a notebook with more pages and more features—one specially designed for multiple small projects—you may be interested in looking at the Maker's Notebook (makershed.com/Maker_s_Notebook_p/9780596519414.htm).

This notebook features 150 numbered pages of graph paper, each with a special header for noting the project name, date, and page reference pointers. It also includes such nice additions as a space for a table of contents, and a pocket for those small notes you write to yourself but later cannot read due to your own handwriting. This notebook is a bit more expensive than a run-of-the-mill lined or grid-filled notebook, but it is worth a look if you desire a good tool to help manage notes for multiple projects.

It's Not a Toy!

As tempting as it may be to buy your gifted son or daughter a 3D printer kit and say, "Have at it, kid," you should resist this temptation. 3D printers are not toys. They have parts that can get hot enough to burn and scar human tissue. That does not mean your gifted offspring should be denied the pleasures of 3D printing. On the contrary, just make sure you provide adult supervision during the build and use of the 3D printer.

Frame Components

This section contains tips that are related to assembling the frame of a 3D printer. Some of these apply only to wooden frames while others apply to any frame material.

Cleaning Bolt and Rod Holes

If the hole or shaft that a bolt or rod must pass is too small, you can make the hole larger (also called *reaming*) by using a drill bit of the correct size. For plastic parts in particular, be sure to use a bit that is only marginally larger than the existing opening.

It is also important to use the drill bit manually instead of popping it into a high-speed drill and letting the bit eat away at the plastic. As tempting as this may be, it can be hazardous to the structural integrity of the part. There are two reasons for this. First, plastic parts are built with several layers on external surfaces. If you drill beyond these layers, you will expose the internal fill volume and weaken the part. Second, a drill bit can easily bite into the plastic, putting excessive pressure on it. This can result in broken parts.

■ **Tip** You can also use drill bits in an electric drill but here you should place the drill in reverse to prevent the bit from biting into the plastic. If a bit bites too deeply, it can cause cracks and similar damage.

If the opening is significantly smaller, you may need to either use a smaller bolt, or correct the part and reprint it. It is always better to use a smaller bolt if possible.

Test-Fit Parts Before Assembly

While there are many examples to the contrary, some printer kits are not laser or water-jet cut, milled, or printed with enough accuracy that all of the pieces bolt together without any problems. That doesn't mean you will always need to cut, trim, or sand pieces to fit. However, it does mean you should test the parts first so that you don't discover too late that one of the seven tabs, grooves, or screw holes needs a bit of trimming to fit properly after tightening the first six.

I would test-fit two, or no more than three, pieces together at a time. This gives you an opportunity to modify those parts individually rather than trying to trim some area on a larger assembly that may be harder to hold or to reach the area needing attention, or worse—force you to disassemble.

Once you have them mating well, you can assemble them and move on. A side effect of this practice is that the build is usually tighter, making for stronger joints and ultimately a bit better printer. I once saw a wooden frame printer assembled so poorly that the frame itself could be flexed slightly from side to side.[10] That's horrible for print quality given how 3D printers shake under the small, rapid movements of the extruder.

Measure Twice

The RepRap Prusa i2 (and similar designs that use a frame made from metal rods or extruded aluminum that are bolted to plastic connecting parts) is assembled according to a specific measurement. If your printer falls into this category, be sure to measure the frame subassembly twice—once as you are assembling it and again after you've tightened the fasteners. This can help you avoid ill-fitting subassemblies.

You should also check the frame for alignment—that is, the parts are assembled with the correct orientation to one another (e.g., right angles are 90 degrees) and the parallel subcomponents are indeed parallel.

Clean Threaded Rods

Don't force a nut onto a cut threaded rod. Use a file or a grinder to clean up the threads at the end of the rod. It is OK if the threads are a little tight; just don't use a nut as a substitute for a *die* (a special tool to cut threads on round stock). It also helps to clean out the thread grooves. Sometimes the cutting tools used will fold back a small section of the thread over the next rotation. Use a small triangular metal file to clear the starting groove(s).

Nut Traps

If your printer is made from laser-cut wood, acrylic, or a composite, it is likely the design uses nut traps cut into one piece of the material. The idea is you use a bolt through one piece threaded into the nut held in place. This works really well and is an excellent alternative to nails and other error-prone fasteners.

However, it can be maddeningly difficult to keep the nut in place if the nut trap is larger than the nut itself. In other words, the nut trap won't hold the nut in place. This makes it frustrating to work with nut traps in pieces oriented so that the nut falls out.

To combat this, you can place a small piece of blue tape (You did buy a roll, didn't you?) on the side facing the direction of the earth's gravitational pull (er, down). This way, you can put the nut in the nut trap and it won't go kerpkunk! into the inner workings of your printer.

Another method is to use a pair of needle-nose pliers to place the nut in the nut trap and hold it there while you thread the bolt through. In this case, you grip the outer edge of the nut and hold it firmly. Figure 3-20 demonstrates this technique.

---

[10]Just like cheap pressboard furniture. College students know this all too well.

Figure 3-20. Working with nut traps

How Tight?

I sometimes get this question from inexperienced and experienced alike. How tight do I make the bolts? While there are tested limits for torque of each fastener (see the manufacturer's data sheet if you are curious), building 3D printers is not like building a spaceship. You don't need a torque wrench.

However, you should be aware that too much torque can be bad. For example, don't tighten bolts and nuts on wood and plastic parts so much that you crush the material. In other words, your wooden frame should not appear to be using countersunk bolts.

To give you an idea of how much is enough, the parts you are bolting together should make for a strong connection without any play. Parts should not be loose or be capable of shaking loose. An example is the Prusa i2 frame where threaded rods meet plastic parts. You should not tighten these nuts any more than it takes to keep the plastic parts from turning around the threaded rod. One gauge I stumbled on when trying to solve a loose frame problem on a Prusa i2 is to use lock washers. The torque required to compress the lock washer is just about right for keeping the frame components tight.

Fixing Stripped Bolts

If you make a mistake and overtighten a bolt, you could strip it. That is, the threads can cross, making it difficult to remove the bolt. If this happens when the nut is in a nut trap made from plastic, it can also damage the plastic. This most often happens with smaller 3mm and 2mm bolts. When it does happen, and you cannot get the bolt to unthread without damaging the plastic or wood, you can use a small metal file to cut the bolt off. You can also use a small bolt cutter to cut the head off. However, you should not use an electric hobby tool with a cutting wheel for bolts in plastic. The bolt could get hot enough to melt the plastic.

Locate Lost Nuts and Other Small Bits

Given the small size of 2mm and 3mm nuts and bolts, and their proclivity for falling onto the floor and disappearing under furniture, you may be tempted after the first dozen or so cases to just ignore it and let the vacuum cleaner find it later. Avoid this temptation and keep close tabs on the small hardware!

I did this once myself. I looked and looked for a missing 3mm nut and never found it. I even used a magnetic pickup to reach behind my workspace, but it simply wasn't there. That is, until I powered my printer on. Yes, you guessed it. That small nut had fallen into my electronics and shorted out my Arduino Mega board. Well, at least two good things came from this. I saw some very interesting smoke complete with a small light show and I learned the importance of always locating that lost little bit of metallic hardware.

Paint or Stain with Caution

If you are thinking about staining or painting the wood parts of your printer before you've assembled it, you are on the right track. That is a definite must if you want to customize your printer with a cool coat of paint or wood stain. Just be careful about what kind of paint or stain you use. If you are not sure which to use, take one of the frame parts to your hardware or home improvement store and ask the professionals what they recommend. Ask them if there will be any chance of warping or changes in the dimensions. Even a slight warp or swelling can be a problem.

For example, I once painted the Y carriage base, and despite using the right paint for the material (MDF), I have a slight warp on one corner. This wasn't a problem because I used print bed adjusters, but it did mean one corner had a slightly lower adjustment than the others. Keep this in mind if you plan to paint your frame.

The Moving Parts

This section concerns the mounting and alignment of the stepper motors, belts, and assorted bits for the moving parts of your printer.

Working with Oiled Parts

We will talk more about keeping the moving parts oiled as part of a regular maintenance regimen, but it is also important for assembly. The smooth rods, bearings, and even some of the bolts and other hardware will come from the factory with light oil covering them. Resist the temptation to clean this away. Your smooth rods need to be damp with a thin layer of oil for most bearings. Naturally, this oil will transfer to your hands. I have already discussed the need to keep your hands clean, but handling the rods themselves makes that complicated.

However, you can wear tight-fitting rubber, Nitrile, or similar latex gloves when handling these parts. This allows you to work with the oily bits and still have clean hands for handling the other bits. I keep a box of Nitrile gloves on my worktop for just those occasions.

Keep Smooth and Threaded Rods Clean

A related tip concerns keeping the threaded rods, bearings, and smooth rods free of dirt and other debris. Using gloves can help in this endeavor, but the best way to keep them clean is to store them in a plastic bag or under a sheet of plastic during assembly. This way, they won't accumulate dust and debris from your build, like particles of wood, bits of plastic, and so forth. If they do get dirt or dust on them, use a lint-free rag to wipe them clean. Reapply a thin coat of oil once the part is installed.

Use of Belt Tensioners

If your printer design incorporates belt tensioners, leave them a little slack until your printer build is complete. Chances are you will have to adjust them again anyway, so leaving them a little slack saves you from having to do it twice. Plus, if you have to adjust the axis in any way during the build, you won't have to loosen it first. I once fussed and fumed for several minutes over an X axis that just would not line up with the Z-axis rods, until I realized I had tightened the belt tensioner. Had I left it slack, I would have been able to make the small adjustment without resorting to threatening my printer.[11]

Align Pulleys with the Belt

This is one area where most instructions fail to illustrate or even mention. When building a printer that uses belts for axes movement, you need to align the pulley, idler, and fixed belt mounts so that the belt does not wander on the idler, or worse—the pulley. There is a very easy way to do this. Once you have the axis assembled, sight down the belt and check the alignment as it moves. The belt should not move to one side or the other. If it does, you must adjust the location of the idler or pulley.

The method I use is to loosen the idler and the pulley, and then move the axis back and forth, adjusting the idler and pulley as needed. Once I get both aligned, I tighten them in place. This makes for a smoother moving axis and can also improve sidewall alignment (a problem with filament is that it may be displaced a tiny fraction on some rows, causing a wavy or grooved look to the part).

Don't Stress the Plastic

During assembly it may be tempting to flex the axis to align the rods and the axis ends. This is normally the case for an axis that uses press-fit connections for smooth rods, like the X axis in the Prusa printer designs. If you need to do this, take care. Too much flex will likely result in broken plastic. If you hear a creak or crack, you've gone too far and have just broken the bond between filament layers or the filament itself. If you must flex the axis to get things to line up, take it apart and use a flat work surface to assemble the axis as close to alignment as possible.

What Is Backward?

If you examine photographs and sample instructions for building RepRap printers, you may notice one small detail that seems to spark debates of a most passionate nature: the location of the X- and Y-axes motors. It doesn't really matter which side they are mounted.

For example, many Prusa i2 printers are assembled with the Y-axis motor in the front, but others have the motor mounted in the back. The bottom line is that it really doesn't matter. The stepper motor can turn both directions, so there is no "right" direction and therefore no "right" end to place the motor. The only issue comes with the firmware. You must set the firmware to orient the motor of the stepper motor to correspond with its orientation. Similarly, the location of the X-axis motor isn't that important.

If you'd rather follow convention, it appears that the X-axis motor is traditionally mounted on the left side of the axis (facing the printer), and the Y axis is mounted in the front of the printer. But again, it really doesn't matter. For my Prusa builds, I've placed the X-axis motor on the left and the Y-axis motor in the rear.

Don't Mix Part Repositories

If you are building a RepRap or other open source printer, and planning to print your own plastic parts, make sure you are using the moving parts from the same repository. For example, consider the Prusa i3. It can sometimes be tempting to use a seemingly better set of X-axis ends from a different repository. However, I have found some

---

[11]Trust me, you'll do this at least once. It won't help, but it might make you feel better.

incompatibilities between some of the repositories. Some of these have been resolved with later versions of the parts, but you should still use caution when mixing and matching parts from different repositories. One version of a part isn't really better if it forces you to reorient or change the hardware in your kit. Stick with the parts from the same repository.

GOT BOX OR SHEET?

A special note is warranted for the Prusa i3 designs. Recall that there are at least two main versions—one with a wood box frame and another for a single-sheet aluminum design. Some of the plastic parts are specific to the frame type. For example, the Z-axis ends are different. Be sure to check the `.stl` files to make sure you are using the right version of the parts. If you are buying a set of plastic parts from a vendor, ask them to verify which version they are selling.

Electronics

This section contains tips for assembling the electronics for your printer. If you have little experience with electronics, you might want to reread some of these before working with the printer's electronics.

ESD Is the Enemy

You should take care to make sure your body, your workspace, and your printer are grounded to avoid electrostatic shock (ESD). ESD can damage your electronics. The best way to avoid this is to use a grounding strap that loops around your wrist and attaches to the frame of the equipment you are working on.

Test Your Components Separately

Whenever possible, it is a good idea to test your electronics components prior to assembly. This can add significant time to your build but it is worth it. This is especially true if you either bought your kit from several component kits or sourced them yourself. I used to trust that certain components—like power supplies and Arduino clone boards—were rarely dead on arrival (DOA); that is, despite being new they don't work or work incorrectly.

Thus, it is a good idea to plug in the power supply and check its voltage when the item arrives. But be sure to test the components individually. If that power supply is putting out too much voltage, you could damage other components.

You can test your Arduino and RAMPS simply by installing the shield on the Arduino and connecting it to your computer (and loading the firmware). I sometimes do this when I use components from vendors that I haven't used in the past.

You can take this tip to an extreme and wire up all of your electronics, and then run tests like moving the axis (to see the motors spin), checking the hot end for proper heating, and even checking the LCD panel for proper operation. This process is called *bench testing*, and savvy electronics enthusiasts do this as a matter of practice.

If you do nothing else, I recommend testing the power supply. It is the one component that can quickly ruin a build—either by not working or working too well. A quick test can avoid that unpleasant (and depressing) moment of stolen eureka when you flip the switch on your newly built printer, only to have nothing happen.

Don't Rush Assembly

Rushing the assembly of your electronics can be very bad for the life of your equipment. For example, if you mistakenly plug a component in the wrong way, you could risk burning out the component, or worse—shorting out your RAMPS or similar board altogether. Especially if this is your first build, take your time and study the instructions carefully to make sure you've got everything wired and connected properly.

You Cannot Use Too Many Zip Ties

Well, I suppose you can but that would be a lot of zip ties! That aside, don't hesitate to use zip ties to tame your wiring to keep it clear of moving parts or parts that get hot—or that may otherwise interfere with the normal operation of your printer.

You should also avoid the temptation to cinch everything up before you've done the preflight checks. Imagine the frustration level incurred if you have to take your RAMPS apart to change the orientation of one wire connection.

Similarly, I would not let your wires lay about wherever they fall. Aside from keeping them away from moving parts, it makes for a more professional build to have all of the extra wire bundled up and tucked away.

Cutting Wires to Length

You may also want to avoid the temptation to cut wires to length if your kit requires you to make your own cables or to attach the connectors. There are two reasons for this. First, if you discover you need to reroute a cable to add an accessory later, you may find the cable is too short to accommodate the accessory, forcing you to redo the cable. Second, if you ever have to replace your electronics board with another, where the connectors are in a different location, you may not be able to if the cables are too short. It is best to leave them a little long and bundle them with zip ties.

Cut Zip Ties Close to the Nub

This is something you may not think about. When you use as many zip ties as most printer kits tend to, the point where you cut off the excess can vary based on how fast you go through the build. For example, if you are in a hurry to trim the zip ties, you may not position the side cutters close enough to the nub, leaving a small, often angled bit of tie sticking out. For really small zip ties this isn't a problem (but it might not look as nice), but for larger zip ties, especially those made from hard plastic, it can be a problem. I have scratched my hands and arms on zip tie nubs several times. I could have avoided those minor injuries if I had taken the time to cut the tie off closer to and flush with the nub. It also looks a lot neater.

Use High-Temp Wire for Heaters

The heaters on your printer (the extruder hot end and the heated build plate, if provided) can generate a lot of heat. You must use special wire designed for use in heater circuits. The wire is often labeled as being high temperature (or it gives a temperature rating). If you bought a kit, make sure the vendor has included high-temperature wiring for the hot end and build plate.

Use ESD Shielding for LCD Cables

I have found that some LCD panel components are sensitive to radiation from other wires. I had this problem on one of my early Prusa printers. It seemed that if I got anywhere near the printer when it was printing, the LCD panel became corrupt. This didn't seem to affect the printer, and I traced it to a small electrostatic discharge. Despite grounding everything properly, this particular LCD panel was very sensitive to ESD or EMI. You can combat this by making sure your LCD cables are routed away from wires carrying mains (5v or 12v) power.

The best method is to wrap the LCD cables in ESD shielding. I use peel-and-stick wire wrap that has a braided core and an aluminum inner sheet. McMaster sells a variety of shielding. The type I used is for EMI/RF (www.mcmaster.com/#standard-cable-sleeving/=rxbz4z).

Be sure to mark your cables! Once you wrap them in the shielding, it may not be obvious which end corresponds to one on the other end. I use a small permanent marker to mark both ends of one of the cables (most LCD panels use two cables). Figures 3-21 and 3-22 show the cable before and after the wrap is applied. You will want to keep the dark (black) side facing out.

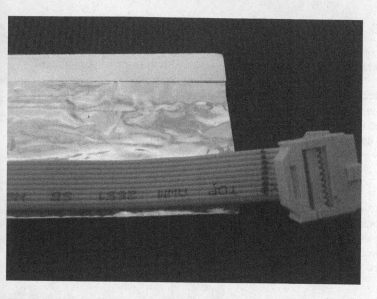

Figure 3-21. *Before wrapping the LCD cables*

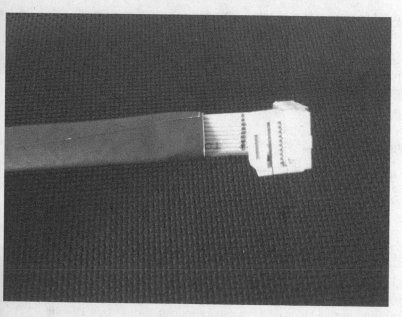

Figure 3-22. *After wrapping the LCD cables*

Insulate Mains

If your printer kit does not include a self-contained power supply or if you plan to use a typical LED 12v 30a power supply, you will need to take care in how you wire it for plugging into your household power—that is, the AC power connector should be deliberately protected.

A popular method is to use an AC plug with a switch, such as IEC320 C14 (or similar), and mount that to the printer in some manner—either as part of a cover for the power supply or as a separate mount. I've used both and I can say I feel a lot safer with those AC wires tucked away.

Even if you don't have an enclosure-like mounting point, keeping the higher voltage wires covered is always a good idea to avoid accidental experiments in hair follicle growth.

Another reason may be to avoid accidental shorts. For example, I have a cover I made for one of my Prusa printers that covers the end of my LED power supply. Incorporated into that design is the power plug and switch. When I mount the plug, the wires on the back that connect the switch and lead to the power supply get compressed. Clearly, if one of those connectors came loose, it could cause a short.

The best way to insulate these wires is to use heat-shrink tubing to cover the ends of the connectors. This ensures all higher voltage wires are covered as much as possible. Figure 3-23 shows a "before" photo of the plug and Figure 3-24 shows an "after" photo of the improved plug. The first photo screams "Look out!" while the second photo looks much safer.

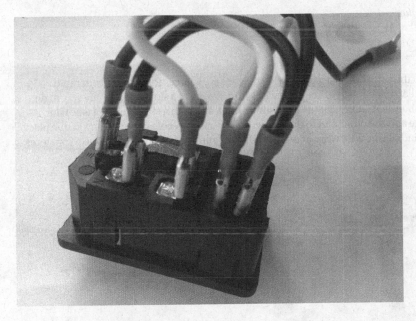

Figure 3-23. Before wrapping the mains plug

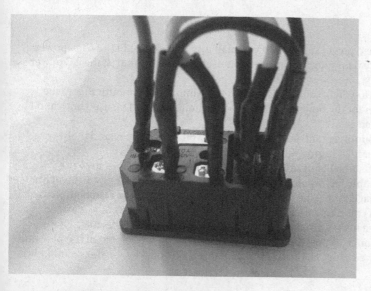

Figure 3-24. After wrapping the mains plug

Use Stress Relief

Cables that attach to moving parts such as the print bed, extruder, and some axes are sources for failures from rapid movement. For these areas, use a stress relief mechanism to keep the wires from flexing at a single point. One way to do this is to use plastic wire wrap around the bundled cables. Figure 3-25 shows the X axis with a stress relief plastic wire wrap. One end is attached to the X carriage and the other end to the frame. This keeps the cables from flexing in one place, which can cause them to break. You can find plastic wire wrap at most hardware stores, as well as automotive parts stores.

Figure 3-25. Strain relief of extruder cables

■ **Caution** When using plastic wire wraps, be sure to tie down the ends of the wrap so that the stiffness added doesn't create a flex point beyond the ends of the warp, thereby making the problem worse.

Did you notice something interesting in this photo, or maybe the lack of something? If you're wondering where the extruder (cold end) is, it's because this is a Bowden setup, where the cold end is separated from the hot end and connected with a PTFE tube. This permits the X carriage to have a higher travel speed, making for faster prints.

Spread the Load

If you are wiring your own power supply, be sure to use a different lead from the power supply for each major component. Use two leads for your RAMPS (most have two sets of mains power) and one for your accessories. If one of those accessories is a heater, use a separate lead for it. Some people wire the RAMPS to the same output lead from the power supply. Depending on how powerful your power supply is, it may not matter, but it is always better to distribute the load.

Preflight Checks

This section includes tips for things you should do once your build is complete and before you begin calibrating it. Note that these tips assume the firmware is already loaded on the printer controller electronics. If it has not been loaded, come back to these tips once it is loaded.

Smoke Test

The first thing I like to do is called a *smoke test*.[12] What this means is plugging in the power supply and powering on the printer. Stand by the switch just in case, but you should be rewarded with an LED or two glowing, and if you have a LCD panel, it should illuminate too. In fact, if the firmware is loaded on the printer, you should see the menus appear on the LCD panel.

If you smell or see any smoke, or otherwise hear any strange noises, you should immediately cut the power and investigate. Assuming you don't smell, see, or hear anything strange, you can proceed to the next check.

Set Endstops Conservatively

Next, I like to make sure the endstops are set further than the absolute minimum. This allows you to make fine adjustments once the printer is properly calibrated. For the X and Y axes, loosen the endstop mounts and move them toward the center of the axis about 5mm to 10mm. For the Z axis, you can set the endstop adjuster to its maximum. If your kit has a fixed Z-axis endstop, you can loosen the mount and raise it about 5mm.

Connect Your Controller Software

Now comes the fun part. Go ahead and launch your printer controller software (e.g., Repetier-Host), insert the USB cable into your computer, and connect the other end to your printer. You can then press the connect button to permit the printer software to talk to the printer.

---

[12] No tobacco or electronic equivalent required.

If you cannot get the software to connect, check the port settings of the printer software and try again. If you still have problems, check the communication speed. Some versions of firmware (like Marlin) allow you to set the communication speed. Check your documentation for the correct speed or check your firmware configuration if you loaded the firmware yourself.

Check the Endstop Status

Endstops are one of the most simple components on your printer, and yet vital to its operation. Recall the endstops are switches that, when closed, prevent the axis from moving. Failure to check the endstops for correct operation can result in the axis crashing into the frame or other bits that it should never come into contact with (like fragile wires, electronics, your fingers, small animals, and so forth—all very bad).

BASIC ENDSTOP WIRING

If you are using standard endstops with three pins, take a look at the side of the endstop (or the documentation). You should see three sets of letters; NO, NC, and C. These represent *normally open*, *normally closed*, and *common*. You want to use the NO and C connectors for your wiring so that when the switch it triggered, it makes a connection between the C (common) and NO (normally open) pins. For all other endstops, check with your vendor for proper wiring.

The best way to check your endstops is with a special G-code. The code you need is M119. Issue this command via your printer controller software. Figure 3-26 shows the command issued on Repetier-Host.

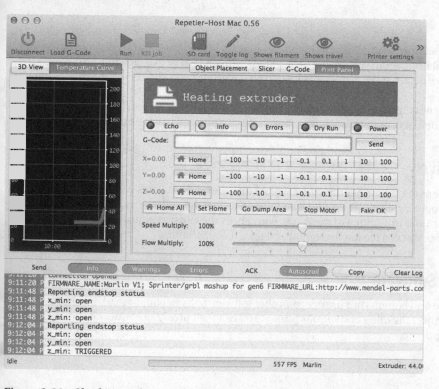

Figure 3-26. Checking endstops with M119

Notice the firmware returned the status of each endstop. Notice at the bottom of the screen—the messages window—that I ran the command twice. The first time, all endstops were marked open, but the second time the Z endstop is marked as TRIGGERED. This is because I manually pressed the endstop. You have to use two hands—one with the mouse ready to click the Send button, and another holding the endstop closed.

If the endstop you have closed does not register as triggered, check your connections to make sure the endstop is connected properly. In rare cases, especially when using Marlin or similar firmware, you may need to change the configuration to match your endstop behavior. If you use normal endstops that make a contact when closed (and you've wired it correctly), you should not have to adjust the firmware.

Check Axis Movement

Next, try moving the axes, one at a time, about 10mm toward the positive side. Recall that for the X axis this means to the right, the Y axis is to the rear, and the Z axis is up. However, before attempting to move the axes and while the printer is turned off and the stepper motors unplugged, slowly set the axes in their center position or near to the center.

Reconnect all of the axes and power the printer on. Use your LCD panel or your printer controller software to move each axis 10mm in the positive direction. If one of the axes does not move in the correct direction, you can fix the problem in one of two ways. If the connectors are not polarized (can be plugged in only one direction), you can simply reverse the stepper motor connector on the electronics board. This will effectively reverse the direction. If the connectors are polarized, you will have to either change the direction in firmware or changing the wires at the motor (some motors have connectors at the motor, others have only wire leads).

■ **Caution**   Never unplug any components, especially stepper motors, when the printer is powered on. Power the printer off before working with connections.

You can also change the direction in the firmware. For example, the Marlin software has settings for reversing the axes direction in the Configuration.h file.

■ **Caution**   Do not attempt to move your axes to their maximum yet. You will set this value as part of the configuration process once you have set the endstop correctly. If your calibration is off and the axis is moving faster than it is supposed to (say 110mm instead of 100mm), you can damage your printer by overextending the travel of your endstop.

Once all of the axes move correctly, go ahead and home each axis. Since you set the endstops conservatively, the axis should stop well short of the minimum range. Just for fun, you can check the endstops again. You should see all of them triggered, as shown in Figure 3-27.

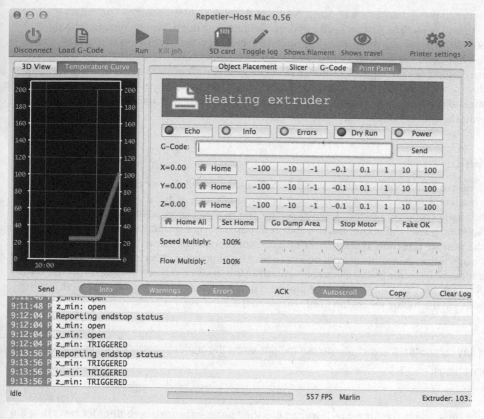

Figure 3-27. Checking endstops after homing all axes

■ **Tip**   Always home the axis before attempting to move it. If you are building a RepRap printer, the firmware (unless you've changed it) assumes the axis is at position 0. Thus, by default, the printer thinks its axes are at the home position when you power on the printer. Watch for this when you are working with the printer—either through the printer controller software or via the LCD menus.

Check Heaters

The next step is to test the heaters. You can turn on the hot end and heated bed from the printer controller software. Set the hot end to 200 degrees Celsius and the heated bed (if installed) to 100 degrees Celsius. Check them one at a time. You can use an infrared temperature meter to ensure they are heating. Remember, the temperature settings are in Celsius, so the hot end gets plenty hot enough to burn you.

■ **Caution**   Some hot ends can smoke a bit when heated the first time. This is normal. Do not hose it down with your fire extinguisher. On the other hand, if the smoke becomes a small plume and you hear crackling or popping sounds, unplug your printer immediately and check your electronics for wiring faults.

Test Extrusion

The last preflight check you should perform is testing your extruder. Begin by inserting filament in your extruder following the vendor's instructions. For example, spring-loaded extruders require you to press down on a plunger and insert the filament past a drive gear and into the hot end.

Since you already have the heaters warmed up to temperature, go ahead and use your printer controller software to extrude a small amount of filament. Depending on how far you were able to insert the filament, you may need to extrude about 30mm to 50mm. But don't do that all at once. If your hot end isn't heating properly, you will only result in stripping the filament—filling the teeth of the drive gear or hobbed bolt with filament.

Once you've extruded a small pile of filament, you can do your victory dance. You are not officially a 3D printer builder. Don't celebrate too long. You've still got the calibration process to go through before you can print your first object. But you are nearly there!

Well, that's about it. I've prepared you as much as one can to take on the challenge of building your own 3D printer. Now, go order that kit or open the box and dive in![13]

Summary

If you thought that owning a 3D printer was much like owning a modern 2D printer, you may be a bit surprised to see this chapter list a bunch of tools—some of which you may have never seen. Fortunately, I've listed all of the tools you are most likely going to need to build, use, and maintain a 3D printer.

I revisited the types of kits available to help you choose the kit that is right for you. This should prepare you for selecting a kit that will give you the best opportunity to experience the build yourself. I also presented a set of tips and tricks for getting the most out of your build should you decide to build your own printer. If you were considering building a 3D printer but were concerned about the skills needed and the general lack of instruction, I hope that this chapter has alleviated those concerns.[14]

In the next chapter, I will show you how to take your newly built 3D printer and set up the software to use it on your computer, as well as the printer itself.

---

[13]To all you Klingon fans out there, Qapla'! http://en.wiktionary.org/wiki/Qapla%27.
[14]And I hope to see the number of partially complete printers for sale drop dramatically.

CHAPTER 4

■ ■ ■

Configuring the Software

Building a 3D printer and seeing the mechanical bits together for the first time is quite an accomplishment. However, you aren't done yet. To make the most of your new printer, you need to configure and load the firmware on your printer as well as install software on your computer to control the printer.

This chapter will show you how to configure the firmware for your printer and show you an example of printer controller software for your computer. I will use the Marlin firmware and the Repetier-Host printer controller software to demonstrate how to complete the software setup for a typical RepRap printer. I will also demonstrate some simple modifications to the firmware to add new functions for the LCD panel menu.

If your printer is not a RepRap design or your printer was delivered fully configured, you may want to skim the section on firmware. The section contains a number of insights into how the firmware directs the motors to move the axis. You may find this interesting if you plan to build your own RepRap printer in the future.

I will first discuss printer firmware. If you are building your own printer, you will have to install the firmware before you can use the printer controller software to test the printer for correct orientation of the axis.

Setting up and Configuring the Firmware on Your Printer

Recall the firmware on your printer is responsible for accepting connections from your computer and receiving and executing the G-code commands via the connection. The firmware therefore is the software installed on your printer that makes it work. But it is a bit more complicated than that. The firmware must be configured to execute the commands that control the printer's axes based on the geometry of those axes. For example, the firmware must know how many steps to turn the motor in order to move a fraction of a millimeter in each direction. Fortunately, there are some excellent tools for figuring out the specifics of the geometry.

In this section, I will demonstrate how to set up and configure the Marlin firmware on your printer. I will show you how to get the firmware, how to configure it for your printer's geometry, and how to load it on your printer.

Choosing Your Firmware

If your printer arrived without any firmware installed, or you built your own printer, you will need to decide which firmware to use. There are a few firmware choices you can use and Chapter 1 listed the more popular choices. I have found the Marlin firmware to be the best choice for my RepRap printers. Marlin is derived from the Sprinter firmware that was popular among early RepRap adopters. Marlin combines a number of features from Sprinter and other firmware, providing a more comprehensive set of printer functions. It is also one of the few that seem to have regular contributions and are continuing to evolve.

WHICH MARLIN?

It may surprise you to know there are many variants of the Marlin firmware. Most variants are designed for a specific printer vendor or to support a specific hardware feature (like a particular LCD or electronics board). I use the Marlin variant originally developed by Erik van der Zalm (`https://github.com/ErikZalm/Marlin`). Other variants include the following (listed by printer model/design):

- Rostock Max: `https://github.com/johnoly99/Marlin-for-rostockmax-rambo`

- Tantillus: `https://github.com/Intrinsically-Sublime/Marlin`

- Printrbot (PxT): `https://github.com/PxT/Marlin`

- Deltamaker, Kossel (uses a fork of): `https://github.com/jcrocholl/Marlin`

- LulzBot: `http://download.lulzbot.com`

- RepRapPro: `https://github.com/reprappro/Marlin`

- MakerGear M2: `http://makergear.wikidot.com/m2-firmware`

The bottom line here is if your printer vendor (kit or assembled) has its own variant of the Marlin firmware, you should refer to that repository to download and use when configuring your printer.

You may not think this important if all you want to do is operate your printer, but if you are thinking about adding new features to your printer over time, you may find some of those features are supported in Marlin before others. For example, the auto bed leveling feature was added to Marlin as it was being developed.

Getting Started with Marlin

Marlin is written for a number of microcontrollers, including the Arduino Mega. The newer Arduino Mega 2560 microcontroller is a popular choice for hosting Marlin. As such, Marlin is a large, multiple-file sketch that you must download, modify, and compile before uploading it to your printer. In order to compile Marlin, you will need to first download and install the Arduino Integrated Development Environment (IDE). The following sections present a short tutorial on how to download, install, and use the Arduino environment.

WHAT IS AN ARDUINO?

The Arduino is an open source hardware prototyping platform supported by an open source software environment. It was first introduced in 2005 and was designed with the goal of making the hardware and software easy to use and available to the widest audience possible. Thus, you don't have to be an electronics expert to use the Arduino. This means you can use the Arduino for all manner of projects—from reacting to environmental conditions to controlling complex robotic functions to controlling a 3D printer. The Arduino has also made learning electronics easier through practical applications. For more information about Arduino, visit `http://arduino.cc`.

Arduino Tutorial

This section is a short tutorial on getting started using an Arduino. It covers obtaining and installing the IDE and writing a sample sketch. Rather than duplicate the excellent works that precede this book, I cover the highlights and refer readers who are less familiar with the Arduino to online resources and other books that offer a much deeper introduction. Also, the Arduino IDE has many sample sketches that you can use to explore the Arduino on your own. Most have corresponding tutorials on the Arduino.cc site.

The Arduino IDE is available for download for the Mac, Linux (32- and 64-bit versions), and Windows platforms. There is also a download for the source code itself so that you can compile it for other platforms or even customize it for you own needs. The current version is 1.0.5. You can download the Arduino IDE from http://arduino.cc/en/Main/Software. There are links for each platform, as well as a link to the source code.

Installing the IDE is straightforward. I omit the actual steps of installing the IDE for brevity, but if you require a walkthrough of installing the IDE, you can see the Getting Started link on the download page, or read more in *Beginning Arduino* by Michael McRoberts (Apress, 2010). Figure 4-1 shows the Arduino IDE with one of the sample sketches loaded.

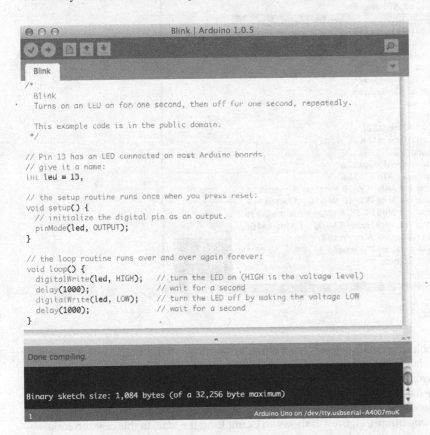

Figure 4-1. *The Arduino IDE*

Once the IDE launches, you see a simple interface with a text editor area (a white background by default), a message area beneath the editor (a black background by default), and a simple button bar at the top. The buttons are (from left to right) Verify, Upload, New, Open, and Save. There is also a button on the far right that opens the serial monitor. You use the serial monitor to view messages from the Arduino sent (or printed) via the Serial library. You see this in action in your first project.

Notice that in Figure 4-1 you see a sample sketch (called *blink*) and the result of a successful compile operation. Notice also at the bottom that it tells you that you're programming an Arduino Uno board on a specific serial port.

Due to the differences in processors and supporting architecture, there are some differences in how the compiler builds the program (and how the IDE uploads it). Thus, one of the first things you should do when you start the IDE is choose your board from the Tools ➤ Board menu. For most 3D printers, you will want to choose the Arduino Mega 2560 entry. Figure 4-2 shows a sample of selecting the board on the Mac.

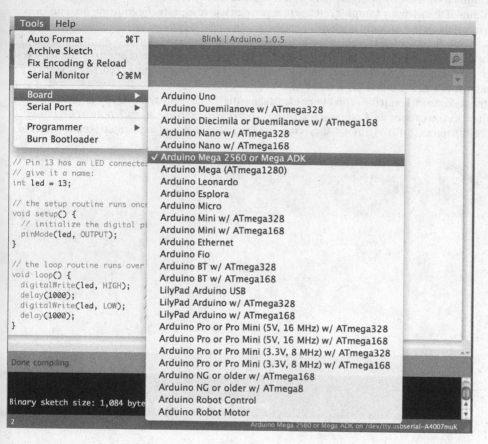

Figure 4-2. Choosing the Arduino board

Notice the number of boards available. If your 3D printer uses a different board, check the manufacturer's site for the recommended setting to use. If you choose the wrong board, you typically get an error during upload, but it may not be obvious that you've chosen the wrong board. Because I have so many different boards, I've made it a habit to choose the board each time I launch the IDE.

The next thing you need to do is choose the serial port to which the Arduino board is connected. To connect to the board, use the Tools ➤ Serial Port menu option. Figure 4-3 shows an example on the Mac. In this case, no serial ports are listed. This can happen if you haven't plugged your Arduino in to the computer's USB ports (or hub), or you had it plugged in but disconnected it at some point, or you haven't loaded the FTDI drivers for the Arduino (Mac and Windows). Typically, this can be remedied by simply unplugging the Arduino and plugging it back in and waiting until the computer recognizes the port.

Figure 4-3. *Choosing the serial port*

■ **Note** If you use a Mac, it doesn't matter which port you choose: either the one that starts with tty or the one that starts with cu will work.

■ **Tip** See http://arduino.cc/en/Guide/Howto if you need help installing the drivers for Mac and Windows.

OK, now that you have your Arduino IDE installed, you can connect your printer electronics to your computer using the appropriate USB cable. When you plug in the board, you should see some of the LEDs illuminate, and if your printer has an LCD panel, it may also power on. This is because the electronics board (the Arduino Mega) is getting power from your computer's USB port. This is normal.

■ **Note** While your USB connection can power the Arduino and, in most cases, the LCD panel, it is not enough power to enable the motors, heaters, or any of the 12v systems. This is because the USB port produces only 5v, which is not enough to power all of the components. Thus, all printers require an additional power supply wired through the electronics board.

Go ahead and open the Arduino IDE and choose the correct board and serial port if you have not done so already. Try out the blink sketch by opening it, compiling, and uploading it to your Arduino. Once the sketch starts, you will see the hard-wired LED on pin 13 blink periodically. Once your IDE is installed and you are able to compile the simple blink sketch, you are now ready to open the Marlin firmware and start configuring it for your hardware.

Downloading Marlin

To download the latest version of the Marlin firmware, visit https://github.com/ErikZalm/Marlin and click the Download Zip button located on the right side of the page. Once the file is downloaded, unzip the file and copy or move it to your Documents/Arduino folder.

By default, the Arduino install creates the Arduino folder for you. However, if it does not exist, you can find the default location for project files by checking the preferences and looking for the sketchbook location entry, as shown in Figure 4-4. For example, on Mac OS X, the default location is in your Documents folder.

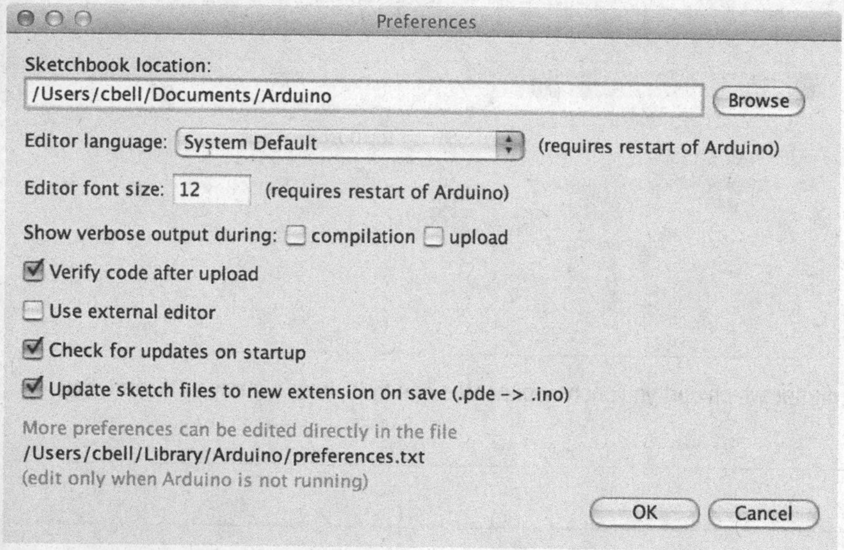

Figure 4-4. Arduino IDE Preferences

In the next section, I discuss the prerequisite values you will need in order to successfully configure Marlin. More specifically, you must calculate the values used in the axis movement. This is one area most 3D printer builders struggle with. If you take the time to gather the correct data and perform the calculations in advance, you will be in a much better state to calibrate your printer.

Indeed, if your calculations are accurate, you may not need to alter the values during calibration. In other words, your axis movement will move precisely 100mm when instructed to do so. I present techniques for calibrating and fine-tuning your printer in the next chapter.

Prerequisite: Do the Math

There are a number of areas that you will need to modify in the Marlin firmware (but you will only be modifying one file). One of those areas involves calculating the value for steps per millimeter that controls axis movement. Another involves calculating how far your extruder motor must turn to move the filament a given distance (also expressed as steps per millimeter).

There are two ways to go about this. First, you can perform the calculations using a formula for each type of axis movement: belt, threaded rod, and geared. Second, you can use the excellent online RepRap calculator from Josef Prusa.

So why would you do the math by hand if you could use a calculator? Is that cheating[1]? Perhaps, but being one of those type-A personalities, I like to know what is going into the calculations even if I do use a calculator to get the right answer. At least afterward I know it is the right answer (again, type-A). So let's see how the calculations are done first, and then look at the same calculations using the calculator.

---

[1]Check out the features of the average high school and college-level graphing calculator. Those things can solve complex calculus problems with a few simple entries. Now, that's cheating!

But before we do that, you must gather a certain amount of data about your hardware. You will need to know the number of teeth on each of your drive pulleys (the ones mounted on the motors for belt-driven mechanisms), the spacing or pitch of the belts, the thread pitch for threaded rod–driven mechanisms, and the number of teeth on the gears of your extruder. You will also need to know the number of steps-per-revolution for your stepper motors and the microstep for your stepper motor driver. Typically, 3D printers use Nema 17 stepper motors with 200 steps per revolution and 1/16th microstep. To summarize, you need the following data.

- Stepper motors
  - Steps-per-revolution
  - Microstep
- Belt-driven axes
  - Number of teeth on drive pulley
  - Belt pitch (distance between belt notches)
- Threaded rod-driven axes
  - Thread lead (for single-start screws, thread pitch for multistart screws)
- Geared extruders
  - Number of teeth on small gear
  - Number of teeth on large gear
  - Effective diameter of the hobbed bolt

■ **Note**   If you are using a direct-drive or other extruder mechanism, consult your documentation for specifics on calculating the steps per millimeter for the extruder.

Method 1: Manual Calculations

Belt driven mechanisms for Marlin and similar firmware are calculated using the following equation. Here we derive the steps per millimeter using the number of steps the motor has per a single revolution multiplied by the microstep setting for the driver. This value is then divided by the pitch of the belt (the spacing between the teeth) and the number of teeth in the drive pulley. Wow!

```
steps_per_mm = (motor_steps_per_rev * driver_microstep) /
               (belt_pitch * pulley_number_of_teeth)
```

For example, let's say we have a typical Nema 17 stepper motor common to almost all 3D printers. It has 200 steps per revolution and the driver microstep is 1/16th. We use the denominator for the value of the microstep. Now, let's say our drive pulley has 16 teeth and the belt pitch is 2.0mm (GT2). The steps per millimeter is therefore calculated as follows.

```
100 = (200 * 16) / (2.0 * 16)
```

Let's see another example, but this time we will use a T2.5 belt with 20 teeth on the drive gear. Our steps per millimeter is calculated as follows.

```
64 = (200 * 16) / (2.5 * 20)
```

Threaded rod-driven mechanisms are calculated a little differently using the following formula. Here we still need the stepper motor steps per millimeter and the stepper motor driver microstep, but we also need to know the thread pitch—that is, the number of threads to turn one increment (number of millimeters, inches, etc.). We divide the same calculation for the stepper motor by the thread pitch.

```
steps_per_mm = (motor_steps_per_rev * driver_microstep) / (thread_pitch * thread_starts)
```

■ **Note** The formula is in millimeters. If you use SAE rods, you will have to convert the units. For example, a 5/16-inch threaded rod has 18 threads per inch or 25.4/18 = 1.4111[2] threads per millimeter.

For example, using the same Nema 17 stepper motors and a 5mm threaded rod (common among Prusa i3 variants) with a 0.8 mm thread pitch, we calculate the steps per millimeter as follows.

```
4000 = (200 * 16) / 0.8
```

Let's see another example but this time we will use a SAE 5/16" threaded rod. Notice I have rounded the value up (the actual value is 2267.735)

```
2268 = (200 * 16) / 1.4111
```

Gear-driven axes (the extruder) require a few more calculations. In this case, we need the same values for the stepper motor but also the gear ratio (the number of teeth in large gear divided by the number of teeth in the small gear), which we divide by the diameter of the filament drive (the hobbed bolt) times pi. The formula is as follows.

```
e_steps_per_mm = (motor_steps_per_rev * driver_microstep) *
                 (big_gear_teeth / small_gear_teeth) /
                 (hob_effective_diameter * pi)
```

This is the one calculation that trips almost everyone up when building a 3D printer. If you miscount the number of teeth in the gears or measure your hobbed bolt incorrectly, your calculation will be off a bit. This can result in either too much or not enough filament extruded during a print.

For example, your extruder may extrude only 95mm of filament when instructed to extrude 100mm. Since this is such an issue, I will go over the calibration of the extruder in much greater detail in the next chapter. For now, let's get the calculation as close as possible.

■ **Tip** To measure the hobbed bolt diameter, use a digital caliper set to millimeters and measure the inside-most diameter of the bolt at the center of the hobbed area. This will provide a good starting point for finer calibration of the extruder.

---

[2] Note the repeating decimals. This indicates a slight rounding error in the calculations. This is usually not a big deal, but may be the source of very minute differences.

For example, using the same Nema 17 motor and a Greg's Wade hinged extruder with a large gear of 51 teeth and a small gear with 11 teeth, and a hobbed bolt diameter of 7mm, we calculate the steps per millimeters as follows.

```
674.65 = (200 * 16) * (51 / 11) / (7 * 3.1416)
```

Let's see another example. This time, we will use gears with 49 and 13 teeth. Clearly, the difference in gear ratio has a profound effect on the steps per millimeter that the extruder will turn. This is why this calculation is the most error-prone of the three. But never fear, we will get this right in the next chapter.

```
548.47 = (200 * 16) * (49 / 13) / (7 * 3.1416)
```

If you feel a little overwhelmed at this point, don't worry. This is really the hardest part of configuring the firmware. Everything else will be much easier to deal with. If you take your time and get the data right for the calculations, the resulting values should be sufficient to get you close to the correct values and a great deal closer to having the printer calibrated. If, on the other hand, you do not know some of the values for the calculation, you may need to dig a little deeper in your documentation or ask your vendor for the specifics.

Method 2: Using the RepRap Calculator

You may also be thinking that there simply must be a better way. Well, there is! In fact, the online RepRap calculator has many of the common values for axes movement in a drop-down list, making it very easy to calculate the steps per millimeter for the most common drive mechanisms. The only one curiously absent is the gear-driven calculations. I suppose that is because there are so many different extruders out there.

To use the RepRap calculator, navigate to http://calculator.josefprusa.cz/ and observe the formula areas. Figure 4-5 shows the RepRap calculator. Go to the site now and scroll through the calculations available. Notice there are four: belt-driven, gear-driven, layer-height, and acceleration (but no geared calculator). I will go through each of these in turn.

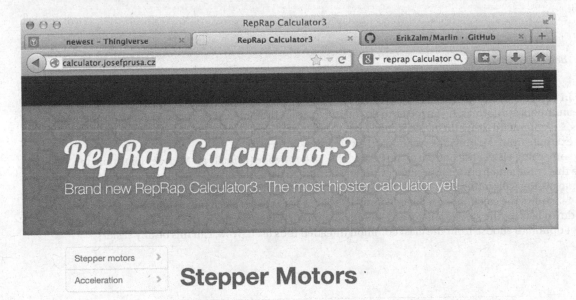

Figure 4-5. RepRap calculator

Figure 4-6 shows the calculator for belt-driven mechanisms. Notice there are text boxes for belt pitch and the number of teeth for the drive pulley. There are also drop-down boxes for the stepper motor, stepper motor driver, and belt presets. This last drop-down box will automatically fill in the belt pitch for you, so if you are not sure what the belt pitch is but know the type of belt, the calculator has saved you a possible headache later if you accidentally thought the belt pitch was 2.0, but it was really 2.5. Mistakes like this are a bane for those trying to calibrate their printer. Which is all the more reason to get it right the first time!

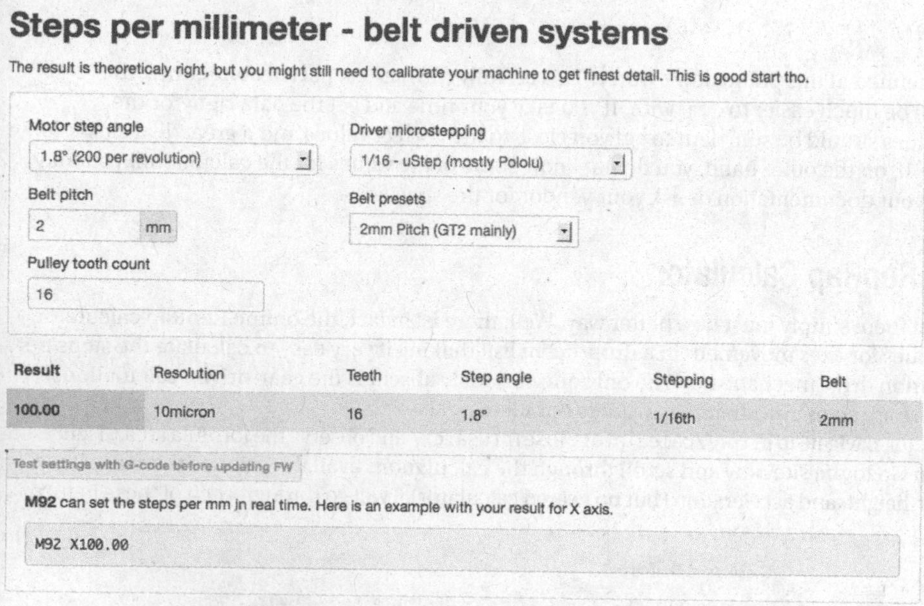

Steps per millimeter - belt driven systems

The result is theoreticaly right, but you might still need to calibrate your machine to get finest detail. This is good start tho.

Motor step angle

| 1.8° (200 per revolution) | ▼ |

Driver microstepping

| 1/16 - uStep (mostly Pololu) | ▼ |

Belt pitch

| 2 | mm |

Belt presets

| 2mm Pitch (GT2 mainly) | ▼ |

Pulley tooth count

| 16 |

Result	Resolution	Teeth	Step angle	Stepping	Belt
100.00	10micron	16	1.8°	1/16th	2mm

Test settings with G-code before updating FW

M92 can set the steps per mm in real time. Here is an example with your result for X axis.

```
M92 X100.00
```

Figure 4-6. *Belt-driven axis calculations*

Notice in Figure 4-6 I have entered the same values from the sample calculation in the previous section. As you can see, the numbers are correct. If you prefer to do the calculations by hand or if you want to check any previous calculations, I recommend using the RepRap calculator to check those values. Go ahead and try out the second belt-driven example from the previous section. Is the value shown correct?

Notice something else in the bottom of the figure. This is the G-code (actually an M-code) for setting this value. You can use this command from your printer controller software to make the change on the fly and test it. We will use this technique during calibration.

Figure 4-7 shows the calculator for threaded rod–driven (or lead screw) mechanisms. Once again, we have the same drop-down lists for the stepper motor and the stepper motor driver. Similar to the belt-driven calculator, we have a preset option to choose from the most common threaded rods used. Wow, can this be any easier?

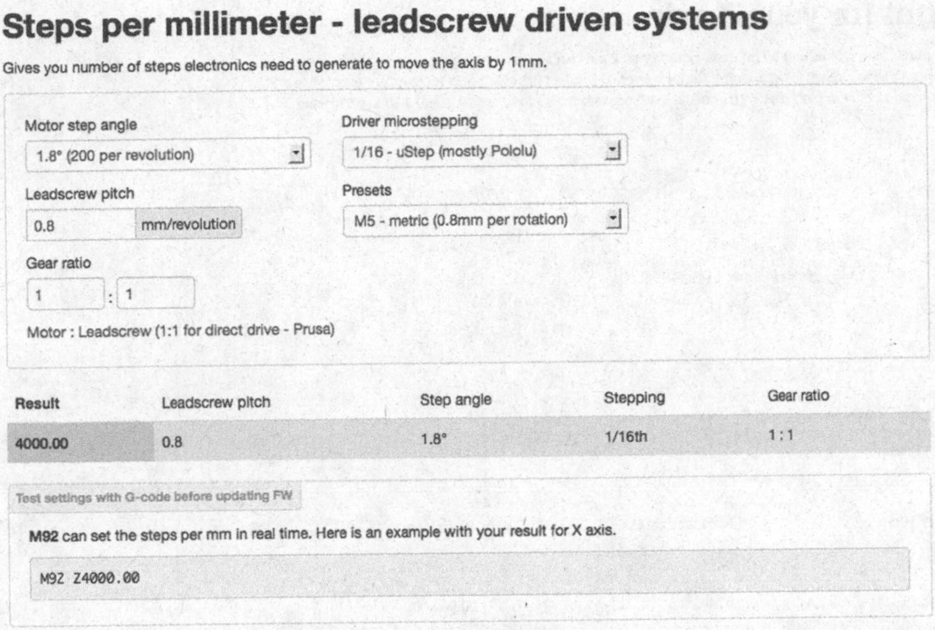

Steps per millimeter - leadscrew driven systems

Gives you number of steps electronics need to generate to move the axis by 1mm.

Motor step angle

| 1.8° (200 per revolution) | ▾ |

Driver microstepping

| 1/16 - uStep (mostly Pololu) | ▾ |

Leadscrew pitch

| 0.8 | mm/revolution |

Presets

| M5 - metric (0.8mm per rotation) | ▾ |

Gear ratio

| 1 | : | 1 |

Motor : Leadscrew (1:1 for direct drive - Prusa)

Result	Leadscrew pitch	Step angle	Stepping	Gear ratio
4000.00	0.8	1.8°	1/16th	1 : 1

Test settings with G-code before updating FW

M92 can set the steps per mm in real time. Here is an example with your result for X axis.

```
M92 Z4000.00
```

Figure 4-7. Lead screw–driven axis calculations

Notice the gear ratio text boxes. This calculator also allows you to calculate the steps per millimeter for threaded rods driven by gears. That is, some 3D printers use a stepper motor connected via a gear-driven rod. For those, use the large gear divided by the small gear to get the gear ratio. Use 1:1 as shown in the figure for threaded rods mounted directly to stepper motors. Once again, the M-code for setting the value on the fly is provided for us.

Go ahead and plug in the data from the previous section to check the calculations. Are they correct? You bet! ·

The next calculator shown in Figure 4-8 is used to calculate the optimal layer height for your Z axis. This allows you to calculate what the best layer height is for your Z-axis mechanism. Since most Z-axis systems are threaded rod-driven, the values for the calculations use many of the same variables: stepper motor steps per revolution, thread pitch, and gear ratio. You can also specify your desired layer height to check its accuracy estimate.

139

Optimal layer height for your Z axis

Helps you to select layer height in a way, that Z axis moves only by full step increments. Z axis isn't usually enabled during inactivity. If the axis is disabled during micro-step, axis jumps to the closest full step and intorduce error. This effect is occuring to some extent even while leaving the Z axis motors enabled. This is most usefull to machines with imperial leadscrews but also for unusual layer heights with metric leadscrews.

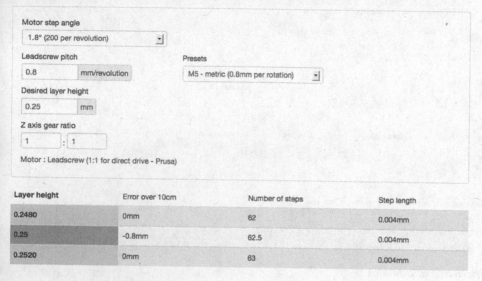

Layer height	Error over 10cm	Number of steps	Step length
0.2480	0mm	62	0.004mm
0.25	-0.8mm	62.5	0.004mm
0.2520	0mm	63	0.004mm

Figure 4-8. *Optimal layer height calculations*

■ **Note**   As of this printing, the calculator is not accurate. I explain choosing an optimal layer height next.

I have read some 3D printer build documents that suggest using a layer height of 0.25 because it is easier to calculate the number of layers there are in a calibration object. For example, there are exactly 40 layers in a 10mm tall object. Other build documents suggest using a layer height of 0.3mm to do calibration. Neither of these may be optimal in the sense you will get a perfectly sized object. It will depend on the actual height of the object.

For example, if you use 0.2mm or even 0.25mm to print a 10mm tall object, we expect it to print exactly 10mm tall because 0.2 and 0.25 divide evenly into 10. However, if you use 0.3, it cannot be divided evenly into 10 and thus if you print a 10mm tall object with a 0.3mm layer height, it will be only 9.9mm tall. This is considered a nonaccumulating error because it affects the final height of the object due to the rounding error on division. Figure 4-9 shows the measurement of a 10mm tall test cube printed with a 0.3mm layer height next to the same cube printed with a 0.25mm layer height.

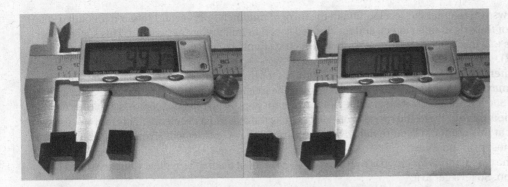

Figure 4-9. 10mm cube printed with 0.3mm and 0.25 layer heights

Notice that the cube on the left is slightly shorter than the one on the right.[3] The one on the left measures 9.97mm while the one on the right measures 10.08mm. To avoid printing objects that are too short, I use a layer height that is closest to producing an accurate height. That is, a layer height with the lowest rounding error.

The last calculator is another calculation that is used to set expectations. Figure 4-10 shows the maximum acceleration calculator.

Max speed

Input your acceleration settings, distance/length of axis and you can see you your printer will hit your desired speed and for how long.

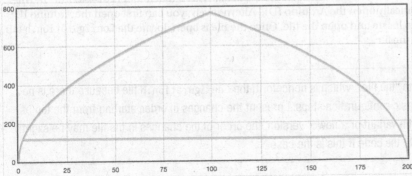

Figure 4-10. Acceleration calculations

---

[3]Granted, this is a very small difference. Interestingly, since it is not an accumulated error, a 100mm object with a 0.3mm layer height would be 99.9mm tall.

This calculator allows you to enter the acceleration in the form of millimeter per second squared (default if 3000), the maximum distance of the axis in millimeters, and the desired speed in millimeters per second. This speed is the speed at which your axis will move across its range. For belt-driven systems, 120mm/s is considered a fast but stable speed (consider it a goal).

Notice I chose to enter 200mm for the axis length and 120mm/s for the desired speed. The chart shows a vertical axis that represents the maximum speed the axis can achieve over the maximum length. As you can see, even with an acceleration value of 3000, the axis can at most achieve a movement peak of just under 800mm/s, but only when the axis reaches its midpoint. From there, the speed drops off because the axis must decelerate. This may not see very interesting or important at this point (and you're right), but it is something to consider when you start fine-tuning your prints to get the fastest print possible.

Now that we have the calculations for our axis movement, we have all of the mathematical values we need to perform the configuration. So let's get to it!

Configuring Marlin

Configuring Marlin for use with your printer involves modifying the Configuration.h file in a number of places. Depending on the hardware used in your printer, you may need to modify only a few locations. The areas most often modified include the following (listed in the order they appear in the file). I explain how to modify each of these in the following sections.

- Author and Version

- Baudrate

- Electronics Board

- Temperature

- Endstops

- Axes Movement

- EEPROM

- LCD Panel

Begin by opening the Marlin firmware by navigating to the folder you unzipped and placed in your Arduino folder in your Documents folder. Under that folder is another folder named Marlin. Within that folder is the Marlin.ino file. Double-click the file. This will automatically open the Arduino IDE. Alternatively, you can first open the Arduino IDE and then use the File ➤ Open menu to locate and open the file. Once the file is open, locate the Configuration.h tab and click it. You are now ready to edit the file.

■ **Note** The following sections refer to "the file," which is henceforth the Configuration.h file because there is no other file you should be changing for basic configuration steps. I present the changes in order, starting from the top of the file. If you are using a different Marlin variant or a newer version, the order of the changes in the file may be slightly different. Use the search option to locate the code if this is the case.

I recommend making one change at a time and saving the file after each change. Use the File ➤ Save menu item to save the files.

Author and Version

Changing the author and version is optional, but can be very helpful if you have several printers or if you plan to modify the printer at a later date. I don't change the date and time values. Rather, I allow the firmware to compile with the __DATE__ and __TIME__ directives, which are the defaults. This means the date and time will be filled in when the firmware is compiled.

However, I do change the author. This helps me identify printers that I have made custom firmware changes (or I just set up myself). The following code shows the lines changed in the file. Find those lines and change the author to yourself.

```
#define STRING_VERSION_CONFIG_H __DATE__ " " __TIME__ // build date and time
#define STRING_CONFIG_H_AUTHOR "Dr. Charles Bell" // Who made the changes.
```

So how do you read these values on your printer? When you connect to your printer using a printer controller software like Repetier-Host and have the log turned on, you can use the M115 code to see these values in the lower panel, as shown in Figure 4-11.

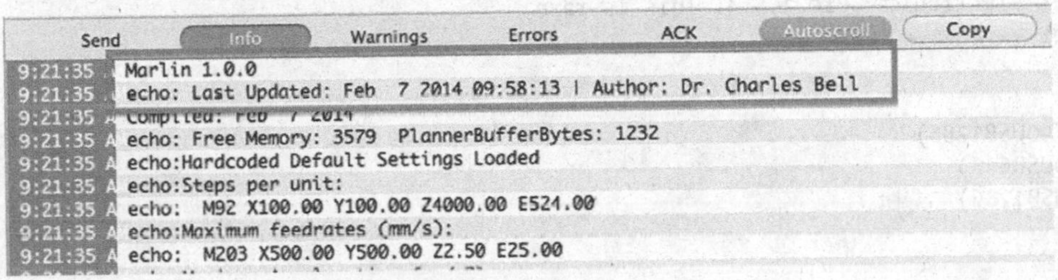

Figure 4-11. *Showing author, version from firmware in Repetier-Host*

Baud Rate

The next area to change sets the baud rate of the serial (USB) connection. Most will choose 250000 but in some cases you may want to set it slower. Locate the code to change it as follows.

```
#define BAUDRATE 250000
```

Electronics Board

The firmware must know what electronics board you are using. You can find a long list of the types of boards supported (called *motherboards*) in the file near the top. Listing 4-1 shows the code comments that define the list and an example of how to set the motherboard value to a RAMPs setup with a single extruder, a fan (pointed at the extruder nozzle), and a heated bed. Choose the value that matches your own board.

Listing 4-1. Selecting the Electronics Board

```
//// The following define selects which electronics board you have. Please choose the one that
matches your setup
// 10 = Gen7 custom (Alfons3 Version) "https://github.com/Alfons3/Generation_7_Electronics"
// 11 = Gen7 v1.1, v1.2 = 11
// 12 = Gen7 v1.3
// 13 = Gen7 v1.4
```

```
// 2  = Cheaptronic v1.0
// 20 = Sethi 3D_1
// 3  = MEGA/RAMPS up to 1.2 = 3
// 33 = RAMPS 1.3 / 1.4 (Power outputs: Extruder, Fan, Bed)
// 34 = RAMPS 1.3 / 1.4 (Power outputs: Extruder0, Extruder1, Bed)
// 35 = RAMPS 1.3 / 1.4 (Power outputs: Extruder, Fan, Fan)
// 4  = Duemilanove w/ ATMega328P pin assignment
// 5  = Gen6
// 51 = Gen6 deluxe
// 6  = Sanguinololu < 1.2
// 62 = Sanguinololu 1.2 and above
// 63 = Melzi
// 64 = STB V1.1
// 65 = Azteeg X1
// 66 = Melzi with ATmega1284 (MaKr3d version)
// 67 = Azteeg X3
// 7  = Ultimaker
// 71 = Ultimaker (Older electronics. Pre 1.5.4. This is rare)
// 77 = 3Drag Controller
// 8  = Teensylu
// 80 = Rumba
// 81 = Printrboard (AT90USB1286)
// 82 = Brainwave (AT90USB646)
// 83 = SAV Mk-I (AT90USB1286)
// 9  = Gen3+
// 70 = Megatronics
// 701= Megatronics v2.0
// 702= Minitronics v1.0
// 90 = Alpha OMCA board
// 91 = Final OMCA board
// 301 = Rambo
// 21 = Elefu Ra Board (v3)

#ifndef MOTHERBOARD
#define MOTHERBOARD 33
#endif
```

Temperature

The next area to change concerns the temperature sensors. More specifically, the type of temperature sensor you have to measure the temperature of the extruder or print bed. Listing 4-2 shows the documentation with the possible values and the code changes to choose a 100k thermistor, which is the most common type for RepRap kits. Check with your vendor to choose the correct sensor.

■ **Caution**   This is another area where novice 3D printer builders sometimes get confused. If you choose the wrong sensor type, your printer may heat the extruder to the wrong temperature, possibly even overheating it. Take some time to make sure you get this part right. Don't hesitate to contact the vendor to verify the setting.

Listing 4-2. Setting the Temperature Sensors

```
//=============================================================================
//========================Thermal Settings  ============================
//=============================================================================
//
//--NORMAL IS 4.7kohm PULLUP!-- 1kohm pullup can be used on hotend sensor, using correct
resistor and table
//
//// Temperature sensor settings:
// -2 is thermocouple with MAX6675 (only for sensor 0)
// -1 is thermocouple with AD595
// 0 is not used
// 1 is 100k thermistor - best choice for EPCOS 100k (4.7k pullup)
// 2 is 200k thermistor - ATC Semitec 204GT-2 (4.7k pullup)
// 3 is mendel-parts thermistor (4.7k pullup)
// 4 is 10k thermistor !! do not use it for a hotend. It gives bad resolution at high temp. !!
// 5 is 100K thermistor - ATC Semitec 104GT-2 (Used in ParCan & J-Head) (4.7k pullup)
// 6 is 100k EPCOS - Not as accurate as table 1 (created using a fluke thermocouple) (4.7k pullup)
// 7 is 100k Honeywell thermistor 135-104LAG-J01 (4.7k pullup)
// 71 is 100k Honeywell thermistor 135-104LAF-J01 (4.7k pullup)
// 8 is 100k 0603 SMD Vishay NTCS0603E3104FXT (4.7k pullup)
// 9 is 100k GE Sensing AL03006-58.2K-97-G1 (4.7k pullup)
// 10 is 100k RS thermistor 198-961 (4.7k pullup)
// 60 is 100k Maker's Tool Works Kapton Bed Thermister
//
//     1k ohm pullup tables - This is not normal, you would have to have changed out your 4.7k for 1k
//                        (but gives greater accuracy and more stable PID)
// 51 is 100k thermistor - EPCOS (1k pullup)
// 52 is 200k thermistor - ATC Semitec 204GT-2 (1k pullup)
// 55 is 100k thermistor - ATC Semitec 104GT-2 (Used in ParCan & J-Head) (1k pullup)

#define TEMP_SENSOR_0 1
#define TEMP_SENSOR_1 0
#define TEMP_SENSOR_2 0
#define TEMP_SENSOR_BED 1
```

Notice there are four settings. The values support up to three extruders and one for the bed. If your printer does not have a second (or third) extruder, set those to 0. Likewise, if your printer does not have a heated bed, set that to 0 to turn off monitoring of the sensor. In this example, there is a single extruder and a heated bed, both with 100k thermistors.

■ **Note** If your printer has multiple extruders, you should also change the #define EXTRUDERS 1 statement to indicate the number of extruders that are included.

Endstops

The next area is another area that can cause some hiccups. This is partly because the variable names are a bit confusing.[4] In this case, we may need to do several things, but it depends on your choice of electronics and the type of endstops. For example, if you are using a typical RAMPS setup with mechanical endstops that are opened until triggered, you may need to enable the endstop pull-up resistors and set the endstop behavior to the opposite of the default. That is, the default is normally closed, which means closed until triggered. If you use a mechanical endstop that is normally open, which means open until triggered, you need to invert the logic. Listing 4-3 shows the lines involved, with the ones I changed in bold.

Listing 4-3. Endstop Settings

```
// coarse Endstop Settings
#define ENDSTOPPULLUPS // Comment this out (using // at the start of the line) to disable the
endstop pullup resistors

#ifndef ENDSTOPPULLUPS
  // fine Endstop settings: Individual Pullups. will be ignored if ENDSTOPPULLUPS is defined
  // #define ENDSTOPPULLUP_XMAX
  // #define ENDSTOPPULLUP_YMAX
  // #define ENDSTOPPULLUP_ZMAX
  // #define ENDSTOPPULLUP_XMIN
  // #define ENDSTOPPULLUP_YMIN
  // #define ENDSTOPPULLUP_ZMIN
#endif

#ifdef ENDSTOPPULLUPS
  #define ENDSTOPPULLUP_XMAX
  #define ENDSTOPPULLUP_YMAX
  #define ENDSTOPPULLUP_ZMAX
  #define ENDSTOPPULLUP_XMIN
  #define ENDSTOPPULLUP_YMIN
  #define ENDSTOPPULLUP_ZMIN
#endif

// The pullups are needed if you directly connect a mechanical endswitch between the signal and
ground pins.
const bool X_MIN_ENDSTOP_INVERTING = true; // set to true to invert the logic of the endstop.
const bool Y_MIN_ENDSTOP_INVERTING = true; // set to true to invert the logic of the endstop.
const bool Z_MIN_ENDSTOP_INVERTING = true; // set to true to invert the logic of the endstop.
const bool X_MAX_ENDSTOP_INVERTING = true; // set to true to invert the logic of the endstop.
const bool Y_MAX_ENDSTOP_INVERTING = true; // set to true to invert the logic of the endstop.
const bool Z_MAX_ENDSTOP_INVERTING = true; // set to true to invert the logic of the endstop.
#define DISABLE_MAX_ENDSTOPS
//#define DISABLE_MIN_ENDSTOPS
```

---

[4]To me, they are named strangely.

OK, so if you read the code changes, you may see something odd. Notice that the only thing I did was uncomment out the #define to disable the maximum endstops. This is because my printer does not have any maximum endstops. You don't see other changes because it just so happens the default settings will work for me—only minimum, mechanical normally open endstops.

As I said, this is one area that can be an issue. If you get the settings wrong, your endstops will not be triggered correctly. Recall from Chapter 3 we used the M119 code to get the values of the endstops. If you perform this preflight test and the endstops do not behave correctly (they aren't reporting "triggered" or "open" in response to your tests), try changing the ?_MIN_ENDSTOP_INVERTING value to false.

■ **Tip** Always double-check your wiring connections before changing these values! It can be wildly irritating to switch the settings and retest, only to discover nothing has changed. If your wiring is wrong, no amount of fiddling with the source code will fix it.

Another thing to check if the endstops are not triggering correctly is whether you need the pull-up resistors. This may be dependent on the type of endstops. For example, I used the MakerBot mechanical endstops on one of my printers (they are normally open). They needed the pull-up resistors enabled to work correctly. Sometimes fiddling is the quickest way to get the endstops working. If in doubt, leave the pull-up resistors on.

There is one other portion of the code that you may need to change with respect to endstops, shown as follows. This defines how the endstops are used in the homing process. If your endstops are at the minimum position of the axes, make sure you check these settings and set them accordingly. If you fail to do so, or they get changed incorrectly, the axis will ram into the frame/mechanical portions during homing. You do not want that to happen.

```
// ENDSTOP SETTINGS:
// Sets direction of endstops when homing; 1=MAX, -1=MIN
#define X_HOME_DIR -1
#define Y_HOME_DIR -1
#define Z_HOME_DIR -1
```

Axes Movement

The next segment of code to change is the place where you will need those values from the calculations in the last section. But first, we need to set the min and max values for each axis. Locate the following code. This is where you set the build volume for your printer. For example, if you are building a Prusa i3 printer, your values may be similar to these.

```
// Travel limits after homing
#define X_MAX_POS 180
#define X_MIN_POS 0
#define Y_MAX_POS 180
#define Y_MIN_POS 0
#define Z_MAX_POS 80
#define Z_MIN_POS 0
```

So how do you know which values to use? For the X and Y axes, it is a simple matter of measuring the size of your build plate where the left-to-right length is the X axis and the forward-to-back length is the Y axis. You should check the movement of all of your axes to double-check that they move through their entire available length.

■ **Tip**   It is especially important to check the Z axis because the movement can generate enough mechanical force to cause damage if it runs into the hard parts (frame).

However, you should also consider how your build plate is configured. That is, if you are using a glass build plate on top of the heated build platform (the most common setup), consider where you are going to use binder clips or some other clip to hold the glass to the heated build platform. More specifically, make sure you subtract the length that these clips use. We need to do this so that the extruder nozzle will not run into the clips during movement.

For example, I use metal binder clips on my Prusa i3 printers on the front and back of the build platform. I set the Y-axis minimal endstop to stop the axis prior to when the extruder nozzle reaches the binder clip. I then measure from that point to the binder clip on the back of the build platform. This distance measures 180mm on my printer. You should check your setup equally as careful.

My X axis also has a travel limitation, but this is because I am using a belt tensioner set to the absolute minimum (so I can adjust it throughout its entire length). This also restricts movement of the X axis by about 20mm.

The Z axis is a little harder to determine and may take some careful measuring. I like to set the Z-axis travel really low (for example, 80), and then when I experiment with the axis during preflight checks I can adjust it. For example, I raise the extruder to its maximum after homing, and then measure the remaining clearance to hard obstructions and increase the max for the Z axis incrementally until I establish the maximum safe Z-axis travel distance. This is the safest way to do this.

■ **Caution**   Setting any axis to travel beyond its maximum length after homing is asking for trouble! If your axis runs into a hard obstruction, it can damage the movement mechanisms. For belt-driven systems, this can be a damaged belt or a damaged belt retention clip. For threaded rod–driven mechanisms, it can result in one of the Z-axis motor connectors slipping and therefore canting the axis, which can lead to breakage of plastic parts. It is always best to set these values conservatively and adjust them during preflight checks.

OK, so now I've scared you. Never fear, it isn't all that bad and your printer won't explode if you get the settings wrong. Just follow the advice as I've given by using conservative values until you can confirm the actual values.

■ **Tip**   If you use conservative values for your axis movement, but have the axis positioned more than 1.5 times the maximum movement, the home action for your axis and the mechanism may not run all the way to the endstop. You can simply home the axis again if this occurs. Once you have the correct maximum range, homing should work no matter where the axis is positioned on its travel.

Next, we need to enter those values from the calculations. It's just a single line of code as shown next. Here we see an array of values that represent the X, Y, and Z axes, and extruder steps per millimeter settings in that order (X, Y, Z, extruder). Plug those in place of the defaults. For example, my Prusa i3 belt-driven X and Y axes have 100 steps per millimeter, my Z axis is 4000, and my extruder value is 524. Notice I use two decimals. Had any of my values needed to be expressed with more, I would likely use only four decimal places.

```
#define DEFAULT_AXIS_STEPS_PER_UNIT    {100.00,100.00,4000.00,524.00}
```

Wow, is that it? Yep. Once you do the calculations and get that right, you only need to enter the values in the array. However, there is one other line you may need to change. For printers that use smaller, finer threaded rods, you may need to change the feed rate (sometimes called *acceleration multiplier*) to match.

For example, a Prusa i3 with 5mm threaded rods cannot handle the default acceleration settings. You can tell if this is a problem when you hear your Z motors chatter, skip steps, or simply refuse to turn more than a few microns at a time. That is, the axis moves OK slowly, but fast movement (say over about 4–5mm at a time) doesn't work. The first line is the default settings and the second is the maximum values that I determined for my Prusa i3.

```
#define DEFAULT_MAX_FEEDRATE          {500, 500, 5, 25}     // (mm/sec)
#define DEFAULT_MAX_FEEDRATE          {500, 500, 2.5, 25}   // (mm/sec)
```

Note the change in bold. This is for the Z axis. Set this to 1 if you experience movement problems and you have double-checked that the voltages on your stepper driver match your stepper motors. Increase it slowly by 0.5 until you reach an acceptable, reliable feed rate.

EEPROM

The next area concerns the behavior of the EEPROM. The EEPROM is a special nonvolatile memory area on the Arduino where the firmware can store the values for much of the variables. For instance, we can set the maximum travel for an axis on the fly as we saw in the RepRap calculator examples. Without using EEPROM, using the commands only updates the value in runtime memory. When the printer is turned off, the value reverts to what was specified in the code. Thus, using EEPROM can be very helpful in fine-tuning your printer calibration. Listing 4-4 shows the code for turning on the EEPROM feature (it is off by default).

Listing 4-4. EEPROM Settings

```
// EEPROM
// the microcontroller can store settings in the EEPROM, e.g. max velocity...
// M500 - stores paramters in EEPROM
// M501 - reads parameters from EEPROM (if you need reset them after you changed them temporarily).
// M502 - reverts to the default "factory settings".  You still need to store them in EEPROM
afterwards if you want to.
//define this to enable eeprom support
#define EEPROM_SETTINGS
//to disable EEPROM Serial responses and decrease program space by ~1700 byte: comment this out:
// please keep turned on if you can.
#define EEPROM_CHITCHAT
```

Notice we have comments that tell us there are a number of codes we can use to control the EEPROM (if enabled). There is a code to store values, read them, and revert them. Thus, with these values enabled, we can do a preflight check of the Z-axis travel and adjust it accordingly, and then save it to EEPROM. You can at any time see the values stored in EEPROM or revert to the defaults if something goes wonky.

■ **Tip** If you make changes during calibration and write them to EEPROM, always change your file to match any adjustments you make using the EEPROM feature. This will avoid nasty surprises if you later compile some unrelated feature and reupload the firmware. Imagine finding your Z axis won't travel more than 80mm after a minor change to your firmware.[5]

---

[5]Can you guess how I know how this feels? It only took me a day to discover my blunder. Do as I say, not as a I do (have done).

149

LCD Panel

Finally, if your printer has an LCD panel, you must change the firmware to enable it, else your LCD will either power on but display lines of solid blocks, or perhaps display garbage, or partial or no data. Locate the code shown in Listing 4-5. It should be down the file a ways.

Listing 4-5. LCD Settings

```
//LCD and SD support
//#define ULTRA_LCD  //general lcd support, also 16x2
//#define DOGLCD  // Support for SPI LCD 128x64 (Controller ST7565R graphic Display Family)
//#define SDSUPPORT // Enable SD Card Support in Hardware Console
//#define SDSLOW // Use slower SD transfer mode (not normally needed - uncomment if you're getting
volume init error)
//#define ENCODER_PULSES_PER_STEP 1 // Increase if you have a high resolution encoder
//#define ENCODER_STEPS_PER_MENU_ITEM 5 // Set according to ENCODER_PULSES_PER_STEP or your liking
//#define ULTIMAKERCONTROLLER //as available from the ultimaker online store.
//#define ULTIPANEL  //the ultipanel as on thingiverse

// The MaKr3d Makr-Panel with graphic controller and SD support
// http://reprap.org/wiki/MaKr3d_MaKrPanel
//#define MAKRPANEL

// The RepRapDiscount Smart Controller (white PCB)
// http://reprap.org/wiki/RepRapDiscount_Smart_Controller
#define REPRAP_DISCOUNT_SMART_CONTROLLER

// The GADGETS3D G3D LCD/SD Controller (blue PCB)
// http://reprap.org/wiki/RAMPS_1.3/1.4_GADGETS3D_Shield_with_Panel
//#define G3D_PANEL

// The RepRapDiscount FULL GRAPHIC Smart Controller (quadratic white PCB)
// http://reprap.org/wiki/RepRapDiscount_Full_Graphic_Smart_Controller
//
// ==> REMEMBER TO INSTALL U8glib to your ARDUINO library folder:
http://code.google.com/p/u8glib/wiki/u8glib
//#define REPRAP_DISCOUNT_FULL_GRAPHIC_SMART_CONTROLLER

// The RepRapWorld REPRAPWORLD_KEYPAD v1.1
// http://reprapworld.com/?products_details&products_id=202&cPath=1591_1626
//#define REPRAPWORLD_KEYPAD
//#define REPRAPWORLD_KEYPAD_MOVE_STEP 10.0 // how much should be moved when a key is pressed,
eg 10.0 means 10mm per click

// The Elefu RA Board Control Panel
// http://www.elefu.com/index.php?route=product/product&product_id=53
// REMEMBER TO INSTALL LiquidCrystal_I2C.h in your ARUDINO library folder:
https://github.com/kiyoshigawa/LiquidCrystal_I2C
//#define RA_CONTROL_PANEL
```

As you can see, there are a lot of LCD panel options. Fortunately, this is one of the best-documented areas of the code. Notice there are links to most of the LCD panels supported. Choose the one that matches your LCD and uncomment the #define as I have done. For example, RepRap Discount Smart Controller made the LCD panel I used for this example.

■ **Tip** If you sourced your parts yourself but don't recall the vendor of your LCD panel, look at the PCB that it is mounted on. The manufacturer typically imprints their name on the PCB. If there it is not there, check with the vendor to make sure you get the right settings.

I have used some of the other panels listed here and even some clever clones. For example, I once had a RepRap Discount Smart Controller that was reproduced by another vendor. It had all the right parts in all the right places but the PCB was red, not white. It did not work with the RepRap Discount Smart Controller setting, so I did some further research and discovered it was not up to specification. Thus, it pays to make sure the parts you are buying are indeed the genuine article.

Notice also that some LCD panels require additional Arduino libraries. You can find these libraries in the ArduinoAdditions folder in the folder you unzipped and copied to your Documents/Arduino folder. If you need any of these, close the IDE and copy the subfolders to the Libraries folder for your platform, and then restart the IDE. The new libraries will be detected and used on the next compile.

If you scroll down a bit more, you will see a number of lines of code about the LCD panels. Ignore those. You need only set the correct #define from the preceding listing to enable your LCD. However, if you choose the wrong value, you most likely will encounter strange behavior on the display (wrong data, corrupted values, not refreshing, etc.), or the rotary button won't work. If this happens, check your setting, correct it, compile, and upload the firmware.

WHAT ABOUT THE OTHER STUFF?

As you can see, there are a lot of other variables and definitions that you can change. What I've shown here are the typical ones you will need to change. Fortunately, the file contains a lot of comments that can help you determine if you should change the settings. Some, like the endstops, can be a little confusing but most are straightforward. If you are building a typical RepRap Prusa-style printer, what is shown here will suffice. Consult your vendor's instructions or ask them if there are other settings you should change.

Now that we have our Marlin code configured, we must now compile and upload it to our printer.

Compiling and Uploading

I like to compile the firmware before I attempt to upload it. You can use the Compile button on the toolbar (the leftmost button) in the Arduino IDE to do this. You may see a few warnings in the other Marlin files. These are OK and are not normally an issue. What you want to make sure is that there are no errors and you see a successful compile message like the one shown here.

```
Binary sketch size: 133,188 bytes (of a 258,048 byte maximum)
```

If you encounter errors, scroll up in the messages window and read the error messages. Try to find the first error listed. Since the only file you changed was Configuration.h, you should only see errors related to your editing of the file. If you get errors, consult the examples and correct them, and then recompile. Sometimes a single error can produce a number of false errors, such that when the first one is fixed the false hits vanish. For example, unbalanced curly braces or a missing semicolon can cause false errors in several lines.

Now that the firmware compiles, it's time to connect to your printer and upload the sketch. To do so, click the Upload button (second from the left). Even though you just compiled the code, the upload process will compile it again and begin transferring it to your printer's electronics. When it is done, you should see a message stating that the compile is complete, and the progress bar will disappear.

Once the upload is complete (the progress bar in the lower right of the edit screen is gone), check the LCD panel. After a brief reboot, you should see the initial information screen on the display. For example, if you have a character-based LCD, you should see a menu similar to the one shown in Figure 4-12.

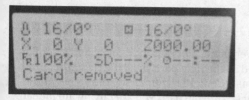

Figure 4-12. *Information screen (Marlin LCD support)*

Once your upload is complete, your printer is now ready to use! You can now perform your preflight checks as described in Chapter 3.

For the really adventurous types (you know how you are), I've included some minor modifications that you may find interesting. The following sections briefly describe some simple modifications to extend the Marlin LCD menus.

Project: Customizing Marlin

One of the cool things about open source software and indeed firmware based on the Arduino platform is that it is easy to modify. But why would you?

If you have built your printer and included an LCD panel, you may encounter cases where there isn't a menu item or you'd like to change one or more menu items. Take some time to explore the various menus on the LCD panel. Don't select any for execution, rather, just scroll through them.

LCD? WHAT LCD?

LCD panels are a relatively new feature for some printers. If your printer doesn't have an LCD panel, you have been using the printer via your printer controller software. What an LCD panel can do for you is allow you to manage the printer without the computer. You can do things like print from an SD card, home the axes, preheat the heaters, and more.

One of the things that I noticed when I first began working with the Marlin firmware (and most RepRap printer firmware) is the lack of some operations that I performed regularly using the printer controller software. For example, in Marlin, there isn't a separate home operation for each axis—only one for auto homing all three axes. Similarly, there is no menu item to move the build plate "out" of the printer by moving the Y axis to its maximum.[6]

---

[6]Interestingly, this feature can be found on the fifth-generation MakerBot Replicator Desktop 3D printer.

■ Note The extend function assumes your Y axis moves your print bed. This is the most common RepRap design, but it may not apply to other printers. For example, the Printrbot Simple moves the build plate on the X axis and the extruder arm as the Y axis. However, moving the extruder arm back out of the way on Printrbot has the same effect as moving the print bed out on RepRap designs. That's because all movements are considered as movements of the extruder relative to the platform, and regardless of which piece is actually moving, a move to Y-maximum will "move" the extruder at the back of the platform.

Wouldn't it be nice if you could add these functions? Well, you can! I will show you how to add these features to the LCD menus in the following sections.

Adding Custom Menu Items

To add custom menu items, we will first need to define a text string to use for each menu item, and then add code to insert the menu item in the Prepare menu. I used the Prepare menu because that is where the auto home function is located. Adding the per-axis homing seems to fit with it, and indeed I will show you how to add the items after the auto home function.

First, we need to add the #define statements.[7] Locate the language.h file (by clicking the tab) and search for the MSG_AUTO_HOME label. Listing 4-6 shows the new menu items in bold in context within the file. Here we add the new lines to define the menu item text along with a label to match. Remember these labels because you will need them in the next step.

■ Tip Use the small down arrow located on the right side of the tab bar to pull down a menu of all of the files associated with the project. Locate the file you want and click it. This will make it the focus of the edit window in the Arduino IDE.

Listing 4-6. Adding Message Strings

```
#define MSG_AUTO_HOME "Auto Home"
#define MSG_X_HOME "Home X Axis"
#define MSG_Y_HOME "Home Y Axis"
#define MSG_Z_HOME "Home Z Axis"
#define MSG_EJECT "Extend Bed"
```

Next, we need to add the menu items. Locate the ultralcd.cpp file, open it (by clicking the tab), and locate the MSG_AUTO_HOME label. Listing 4-7 shows how to add the new menu items. Notice I included the appropriate G-code and variable for each.

---

[7]You don't strictly have to do this because you can hard-code the text string, as you will see in the next project, but it is convention to use #define statements to locate all of the text strings in a single file. It makes for easier maintenance, especially if the strings are reused in several places.

Listing 4-7. Adding New Menu Items

```
MENU_ITEM(gcode, MSG_AUTO_HOME, PSTR("G28"));
MENU_ITEM(gcode, MSG_X_HOME, PSTR("G28 X0"));
MENU_ITEM(gcode, MSG_Y_HOME, PSTR("G28 Y0"));
MENU_ITEM(gcode, MSG_Z_HOME, PSTR("G28 Z0"));
MENU_ITEM(gcode, MSG_EJECT, PSTR("G0 Y180"));
```

The way the `MENU_ITEM()` function works with the gcode option is the menu item is added with the text described in the next parameter (e.g., MSG_X_HOME), and when the menu item is selected, the G-codes in the next parameter are sent to the printer via the serial interface. For example, when you choose the auto home X function, it executes the G28 X0 to move the X axis to its 0 position (home.)

Go ahead and compile the firmware. You should not see any compilation errors. If you do, check your code modifications to make sure they match the ones in Listing 4-7. Once it compiles, upload it to your printer. When the printer is rebooted, use the rotary wheel to select the Prepare menu and scroll down to the new menu items. You should see them appear as shown in Figure 4-13.

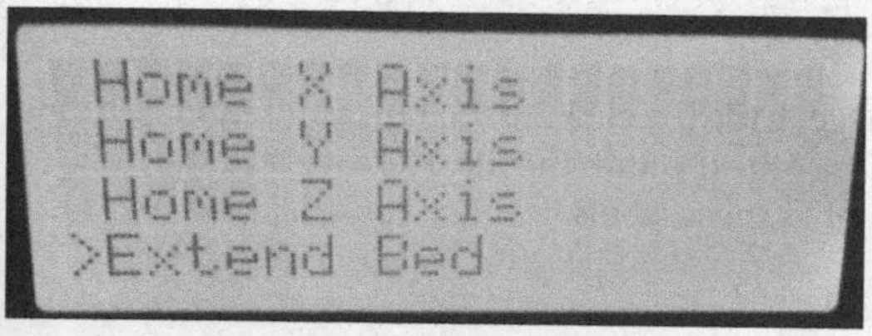

Figure 4-13. *Custom menu items*

Go ahead and try each one out. But make sure your printer axes are clear before you do! Also, make sure you have homed the Y axis before executing the Extend Bed menu item.

■ **Caution**   Never move an axis without first homing it. Failure to home the axis first either by a home function, like the ones demonstrated here, or with G-code commands, can result in the axis trying to run past its maximum travel limit. Failing to home the axes before moving them can damage your printer.

There you have it—four new menu items to make using the printer without a computer a bit easier. Now you can home each axis individually, as well as extend the bed to make removing objects easier.

But wait, let's get really nerdy and add a welcome message. The next section shows you how to do it.

Displaying a Welcome Message

Another thing you can do is to add a greeting message to the LCD panel so that when the printer is started, it will print a short message before showing the main menu. In this case, we simply want to display the message, "Welcome, <yournamehere>!". Once again, we need to add the message text to the language.h file and edit the ultralcd.cpp file. First, open the language.h file and add the following code. If you completed the last project, just add it after those lines.

```
#define MSG_WELCOME_SCREEN "Welcome, Chuck!"
```

Next, open the file with your Arduino IDE and scroll down to about line number 176. We will edit the lcd_status_screen() method. Listing 4-8 shows the method with the new lines of code shown in bold.

Listing 4-8. Adding a Welcome Message

```
boolean welcomed = false;

/* Main status screen. It's up to the implementation ... */
static void lcd_status_screen()
{
    // do a simple welcome screen.
    if (!welcomed) {
        START_MENU();
        MENU_ITEM(gcode, MSG_WELCOME_SCREEN, PSTR("M119"));
        delay(1000);
        welcomed = true;
        END_MENU();
    }
    if (lcd_status_update_delay)
        lcd_status_update_delay--;
    else
```

Here we add a Boolean variable and set it to false. We then add a condition to the status screen method so that if the Boolean is false, we show the message and set the Boolean to true. This way, we only show the screen once. This is important because this method is called whenever you return to the main menu on the LCD. You really don't want to see the welcome message each time, do you?

Notice the code block after the conditional. We use a new menu as a means to display the menu.[8] Thus, we initiate a new menu, display a menu item with the welcome message, and if the message is selected, simply execute the endstop status command. This is harmless because it doesn't move any axes or affect the hot end—or anything else for that matter. Notice right after this is a delay method call. This is a timer that will do nothing for one second. Thus, the menu will disappear after one second. Cool, eh? The code block ends with the closing of the menu.

Once you type this code in, compile, and upload the firmware, your printer will reset and you should see the new welcome message appear like shown in Figure 4-14.

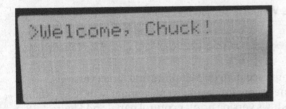

Figure 4-14. Welcome message on printer

Now that we've compiled the firmware and uploaded it, and then modified it to include some new features, let us return to the computer software, install it, and then run the preflight tests discussed in Chapter 3. But before you do that, you need to make sure you have a printer controller program installed on your printer. The following sections describe how to prepare your computer for working with your printer.

---

[8]OK, so it is a hack. It works!

Installing Software on Your Computer

Recall that the software needed for using a 3D printer involves a CAD program to create objects (.stl); a CAM program to convert the objects into a file that the printer can use to create the object (.gcode); and a printer control program to send the G-codes to your printer, control the axes, set the temperature of the hot end, and perform other maintenance operations. If the printer has an LCD panel, the printer controller program may not be used much, but I find the printer controller program very helpful to use when preparing the printer for printing, as well as for some maintenance procedures. This is especially true for calibration tasks.

In this section, I will demonstrate how to set up the Repetier-Host software on your computer. I will delay a discussion about CAD software and return to that topic in a later chapter. For now, we will explore using existing objects from Thingiverse.

Choosing Your Printer Controller

Chapter 1 discussed the various alternatives for printer controller software. Among the more popular choices are Printrun and Repetier-Host. Both of these permit you to integrate with CAM software. In the case of Printrun, the access to the CAM functions and printer controller features into the interface. Repetier-Host uses a series of dialog panels to arrange the features.

Despite the popularity of Printrun, I think Repetier-Host is a better choice. I base this on the fact that Repetier-Host has features that Printrun lacks, including direct editing of the .gcode file, the ability to arrange objects on the build platform, configuration files for different printers, and logging of the codes sent to the printer and its responses. Esthetically, Repetier-Host seems more complete than other alternatives.

Thus, I have chosen to use Repetier-Host to demonstrate how to use printer controller software to get the most out of your printer. For example, if you want to execute the preflight checks from Chapter 3, Repetier-Host will make those tasks easy.

Repetier-Host is available for download from www.repetier.com/download. You will find downloads for Linux, Mac OS X, and Windows. All of these are open source products and free for you to use. The documentation for installation is available at www.repetier.com/documentation/repetier-host/rh-installation-and-configuration/.

■ **Note** The Linux version actually runs a special installation of the Windows version and Mono to execute the .NET Framework.

Currently, the Mac OS X version has a slightly different user interface than the Windows and Linux versions. However, despite a different layout, the features are largely the same except for the object placement features available on Windows but not Mac. For example, Figure 4-15 shows the Windows version printer control panel and Figure 4-16 shows the Mac OS X printer control panel. While the Windows version has graphical controls, the Mac OS X version has simple buttons. Neither is necessarily easier to use.

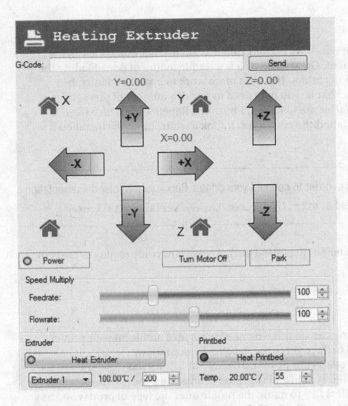

Figure 4-15. *Printer control panel (Windows)*

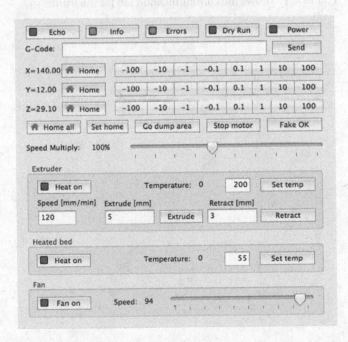

Figure 4-16. *Printer control panel (Mac OS X)*

Installing Repetier-Host

Fortunately, installing Repetier-Host is very easy. The Windows version contains an installer that is easy to use, requiring the usual install dialogs and license agreement. On Mac OS X, it is a simple matter of downloading the ZIP file, opening it, and dragging it to your Applications folder. It is a bit more work to install on Linux, but nothing a savvy Linux user would be surprised to see. That is, you may need to install a number of prerequisites depending on whether Mono and a host of other libraries are installed. I installed Repetier-Host on a fresh Ubuntu machine and the installer automatically installed the resources. It took a while, but once installed it worked correctly.

■ **Tip** You may need to install a USB driver on Windows in order to connect your printer. Check your printer documentation for any required drivers. You can also try the driver located at `http://pjrc.com/teensy/serial_install.exe`.

Once you have your printer controller software installed (Repetier-Host), you are now ready to plug in the USB cable from your computer to your printer.

Connecting Your Printer

The next step is to connect to your printer. But before you can do this, you need to set up a profile for your printer. Click the Printer Settings button on the toolbar located to the right of the Repetier-Host window.

There are four tabs on the dialog you can use to set up your printer. The first tab allows you to set the communication parameters, as well as create the profile. To add a new printer profile, click the Add button and give the new printer configuration a name. For example, I like to name the profile after the type of printer and any information about the printer configuration. Thus, I have profiles for PrintrBot, Prusa i2 PLA, Prusa i2 ABS, and Prusa i3. If you haven't opened the dialog, do so now. Figure 4-17 shows the communication tab for the Printer Settings dialog.

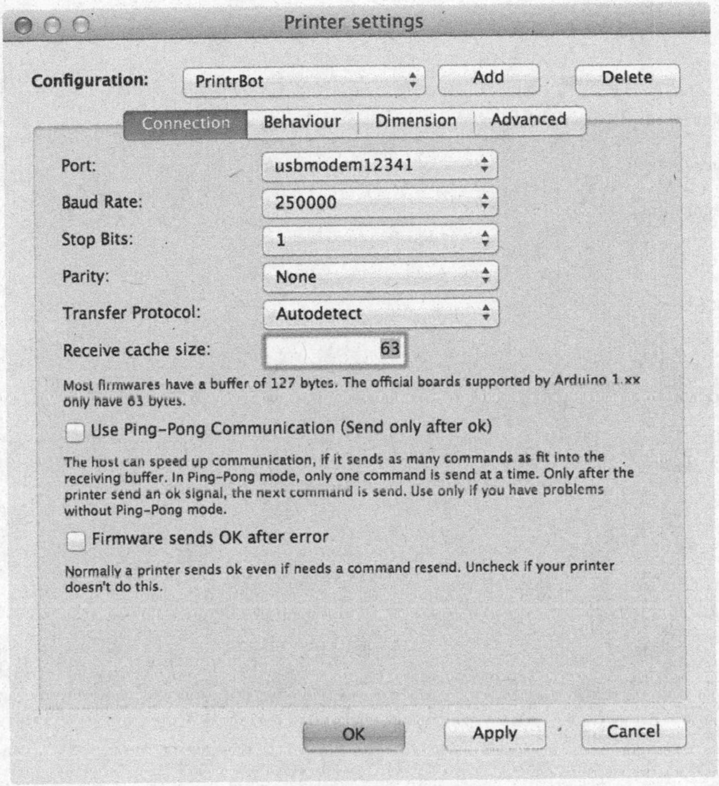

Figure 4-17. Communications tab for printer settings dialog

As I mentioned, click the Add button and name the profile, and then click Create. Next, modify the parameters to match the configuration of your printer and USB port. For example, choose the port, speed, stop bits, and so on. Check your printer documentation to ensure you have the right settings. Once you have those settings correct, click the Behavior tab. Figure 4-18 shows the Behavior page.

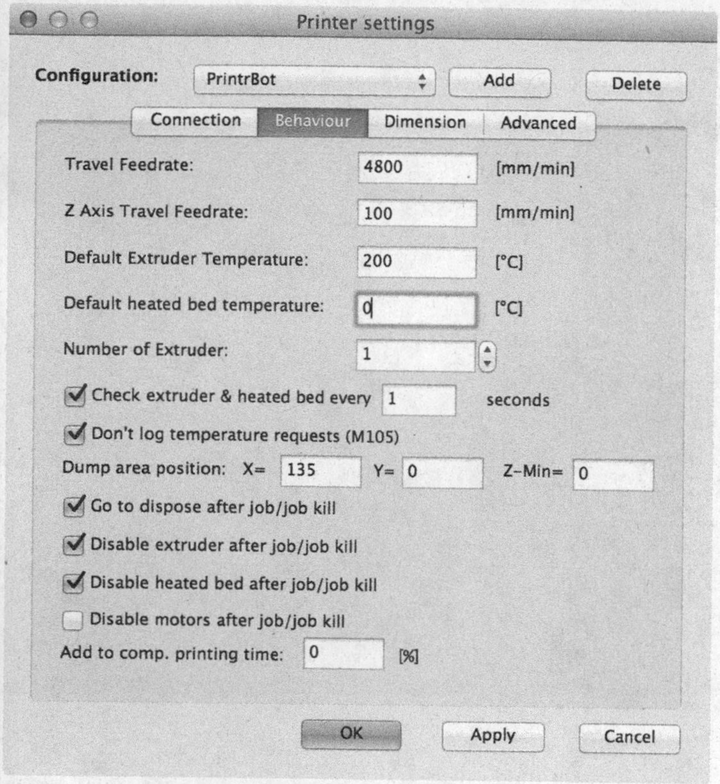

Figure 4-18. *Behavior page for printer settings dialog*

On this page, you can set the defaults for a variety of printer settings. Most of the defaults are fine, just change the heat settings to match your printer. Note that you can change these values manually and set them in the G-code file when the object is sliced. Click the next tab. Figure 4-19 shows the Dimension tab.

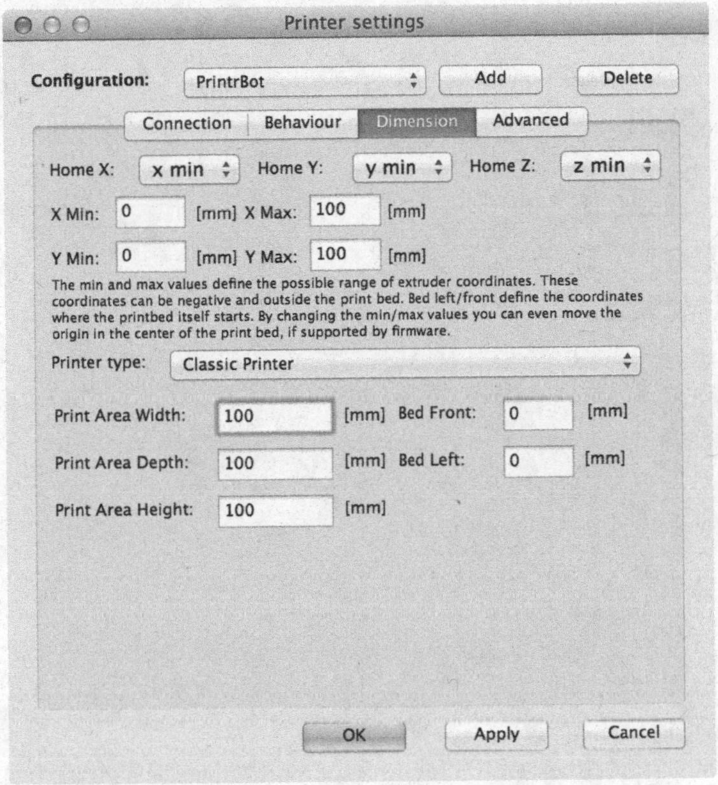

Figure 4-19. *Dimension page for printer settings dialog*

This is where you set the maximum dimensions of your build area. Be sure to verify that the values match your settings in the firmware. The example shows the settings for my PrintrBot Simple. When you have those values, click the next tab. Figure 4-20 shows the Advanced page.

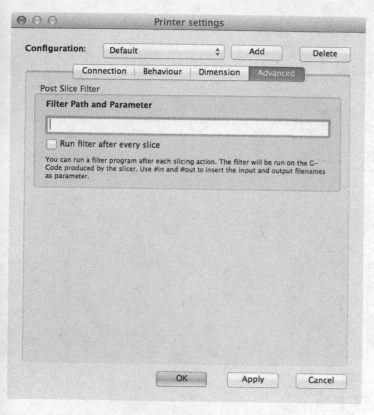

Figure 4-20. Advanced page for printer settings dialog

You can use this page to call a filter script to call after slicing. You might want to do this if you want to modify the G-codes in any way. This is really an advanced technique that you can safely ignore for all but the most unique prints.

Once you have all of the settings checked, click the Apply button and then close the dialog. You can now connect the USB cable to your printer if you haven't already, and then use the Connect button on the toolbar to connect to your printer.

When the printer connects, you will see the connection response in the lower portion of the screen. If you do not get a connection, go back and check your settings. The most common issue is with which port you need to use. Check the following Repetier-Host documentation for platform-specific walkthroughs.

- Windows, Linux: www.repetier.com/documentation/repetier-host/rh-installation-and-configuration/

- Mac OS/X: www.repetier.com/documentation/repetier-host-mac/installation-and-connection/

Once you get a successful connection, you can start running your preflight tests, as described in the next section.

Running the Preflight Tests

The preflight tests in Chapter 3 are ideal for checking out your printer for the first time. I summarize these as steps you can follow to execute the checks. Except for the first two steps, you can do these in any order.

1. Move all of the axes to their center locations. For the Z axis, make sure it is at least 30mm above the print bed.

2. Turn on the main power for your printer.

3. Use the printer control panel in Repetier-Host to set the extruder temperature to 100 and turn it on, and then click the `temperature curve` tab to the left. This opens a special chart that displays the temperature of all the hot bits in your printer. You should see the heat for the extruder rising and you should feel heat radiating from the extruder nozzle after a few moments. If you do not see any temperature values increasing, turn off the printer and wait for the extruder to cool. This indicates the temperature sensor is either not set properly in the firmware or is not connected properly. Correct the problem and repeat the process.

■ **Caution** Never touch the extruder or heated print bed while it is heating. They can and do get hot enough to burn flesh. If you have a temperature probe for your multimeter, use that instead. Somewhat less reliable are infrared heat detectors. They will work for this task—to tell if the item is getting hot, but due to the reflective properties of the components, they may not give an accurate reading. A temperature probe is a better tool for measuring precise temperatures.

---

4. Check the heated print bed (if installed). Set the temperature to 60 and turn it on the printer control panel, and then click the `temperature curve` tab. You should see the temperature increase and should be able to feel heat radiating from the print bed. If you do not see any temperature values increasing, turn off the printer and wait for the extruder to cool. This indicates the temperature sensor is either not set properly in the firmware or is not connected properly. Correct the problem and repeat the process.

5. Move each axis 10mm in the positive direction. Verify that they all move in the correct direction; the X axis should move to the right, the Y axis toward the front, and the Z axis upward.

6. Manually trigger each endstop and use the M119 code to check their status. All should read `TRIGGERED` when closed.

7. Last, but not least, load filament into your extruder and heat your extruder to 180 for PLA or 210 for ABS. Wait for the extruder to reach the desired temperature (as shown in the temperature curve display) and use the printer control panel to extrude a small amount of filament.

Congratulations! Your printer is moving its axis in the right directions and the hot end is heating. Let us take a brief detour and talk about one feature that is becoming standard on newer printers: printing over the network.

Project: Building a 3D Printer Print Server

If you have looked at the latest printers from MakerBot and some other professional-class printer vendors, you may have noticed they are starting to outfit the printers with networking and wireless connectivity. This is really cool, but does it mean you need to upgrade to the new printers to get these features?

Fortunately, for RepRap printers the answer is no, you do not have to buy a new printer! The OctoPrint software (http://octoprint.org) is a 3D printer network print server that allows you to control your printer remotely. OctoPrint is also available for the Raspberry Pi (https://github.com/guysoft/OctoPi), which allows you to use a lightweight computer as a network print server to control your printer. In fact, you can set it up to be wireless!

■ **Note**   OctoPrint works only with printers that use G-codes. MakerBot printers can accept G-codes, but as of this writing, OctoPrint did not officially support MakerBot printers. Look for this to be added in future versions (or send the developer lots of fan e-mails asking for it).

This section will explain how to use a Raspberry Pi computer to run a special version of the OctoPrint software that will enable you to print and control your printer over the network. As an added bonus, if you also add the Raspberry Pi camera (or equivalent), you can monitor your printer by watching a streaming video of the print process. You can also set up time-lapse photos so that you can make a short time-lapse video of your build. How cool is that?

WHAT IS A RASPBERRY PI?

The Raspberry Pi is a small, inexpensive personal computer. Although it lacks the capacity for memory expansion and can't accommodate onboard devices such as CD, DVD, and hard drives, it has everything a simple personal computer requires. That is, it has two USB ports, an Ethernet port, HDMI (and composite) video, and even an audio connector for sound.

The Raspberry Pi has an SD drive[9] that you can use to boot the computer into any of several Linux operating systems. All you need is an HDMI monitor (or DVI with an HDMI-to-DVI adapter), a USB keyboard and mouse, and a 5V power supply—and you're off and running.

■ **Tip**   You can also power your Raspberry Pi using a USB port on your computer, provided it can provide at least 700mA (raspberrypi.org/wp-content/uploads/2012/04/quick-start-guide-v2_1.pdf). In this case, you need a USB type A male to micro-USB type B male cable. Plug the type A side into a USB port on your computer and the micro-USB type B side into the Raspberry Pi power port.

The board is available in several versions and comes as a bare board costing as little as $35.00 (for the version with Ethernet). It can be purchased online from electronics vendors such as SparkFun and Adafruit. Most vendors have a host of accessories that have been tested and verified to work with the Raspberry Pi. These include small monitors, miniature keyboards, and even cases for mounting the board.

---

[9]Secure Digital (SD): A small removable memory drive the size of a postage stamp (see http://en.wikipedia.org/wiki/Secure_Digital).

Raspberry Pi Tutorial

The Raspberry Pi is a personal computer with a surprising amount of power and versatility. You may be tempted to consider it a toy or a severely limited platform, but that is far from the truth. With the addition of onboard peripherals like USB, Ethernet, and HDMI video, the Raspberry Pi has everything you need for a lightweight desktop computer. If you consider the addition of the GPIO header, the Raspberry Pi becomes more than a simple desktop computer, and fulfills its role as a computing system designed to promote hardware experimentation.

The following sections present a short tutorial on getting started with your new Raspberry Pi, from a bare board to a fully operational platform. A number of excellent works cover this topic in much greater detail. If you find yourself stuck or wanting to know more about beginning to use the Raspberry Pi and more about the Raspbian operating system, see *Learn Raspberry Pi with Linux* by Peter Membrey and David Hows (Apress, 2012). If you want to know more about using the Raspberry Pi in hardware projects, an excellent resource is *Practical Raspberry Pi* by Brendan Horan (Apress, 2013).

Getting Started

As mentioned in the "Required Accessories" section, you need an SD card (or a microSD with the microSD adapter), a USB power supply rated at 700mA or better with a male micro-USB connector, a keyboard, a mouse (optional), and an HDMI monitor or a DVI monitor with an HDMI adapter. However, before you can plug these things into your Raspberry Pi and bask in its brilliance, you need to create a boot image for your SD card.

Installing a Boot Image

The process of installing a boot image involves choosing an image, downloading it, and then copying it to your SD card. The following sections detail the steps involved.

Once you select an image and download it, you first unzip the file and then copy it to your SD card. There are a variety of ways to do this. The following sections describe some simplified methods for a variety of platforms. You must have an SD card reader/writer connected to your computer. Some systems have SD card drives built in (Lenovo laptops, Apple laptops and desktops, and so on).

Windows

To create the SD card image on Windows, you can use the Win32 Disk Imager software from Launchpad (https://launchpad.net/win32-image-writer). Download this file, and install it on your system. Unzip the image if you haven't already, and then insert your SD card into your SD card reader/writer. Launch the Win32 Disk Imager application, select the image in the top box, and then click WRITE to copy the image to the SD.

■ **Caution**   The copy process overwrites anything already on the SD card, so be sure to copy those photos to your hard drive first!

Mac OS X

To create the SD card image on the Mac, download the image and unzip it. Insert your SD card into your SD card reader/writer. Be sure the card is formatted with FAT32. Next, open the System report (hint: use the Apple menu ➤ About this Mac).

Click the card reader if you have a built-in card reader, or navigate through the USB menu and find the SD card. Take note of the disk number; for example, it could be disk4.

Next, open the Disk Utility and unmount the SD card. You need to do this to allow the Disk Utility to mount and connect to the card. Now things get a bit messy. Open a terminal and run the following command, substituting the disk number for *n* and the path and name of the image file for <image_file>:

```
sudo dd if=<image_file> of=/dev/diskn bs=1m
```

At this point, you should see the disk-drive indicator flash (if there is one), and you need to be patient. This step can run for some time with no user feedback. You will know it is complete when the command prompt is displayed again.

Linux

To create the SD card image using Linux, you need to know the device name for the SD card reader. Execute the following command to see the devices currently mounted:

```
df -h
```

Next, insert the SD card or connect a card reader, and wait for the system to recognize it. Run the command again:

```
df -h
```

Take a moment to examine the list and compare it to the first execution. The "extra" device is your SD card reader. Take note of the device name; for example, /dev/sdc1. The number is the partition number. So, /dev/sdc1 is partition 1, and the device is /dev/sdc. Next, unmount the device (I will use the previous example):

```
umount /dev/sdc1
```

Use the following command to write the image, substituting the device name for <device> and path and name of the image file for <image_file> (for example, /dev/sdc and my_image.img). Set the size of the image to match the size of your SD card; for example, I use 4M for my 4MB card.

```
sudo dd bs=4M if=<image_file> of=<device>.
```

At this point, you should see the disk-drive indicator flash (if there is one), and you may need to be patient. This step can run for some time with no user feedback. You will know it is complete when the command prompt is displayed again.

Setting up the Raspberry Pi Hardware

The hardware you need includes a Raspberry Pi (type B with 512Mb RAM), a Raspberry Pi camera, and a case for each. You can find the Raspberry Pi and case, as well as a Raspberry Pi camera from SparkFun (sparkfun.com/categories/233), Adafruit (adafruit.com/category/105), or Maker Shed (makershed.com/Raspberry_Pi_Boards_and_Accessories_s/227.htm). You may also be able to purchase these on online auction sites. Figure 4-21 shows a Raspberry Pi assembled in a case.

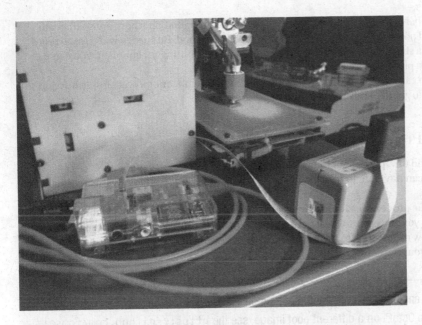

Figure 4-21. Raspberry Pi hardware setup

Notice that I placed the Raspberry Pi near the printer and mounted the camera on an impromptu mount. If you were mounting this permanently, you may want to consider making a fixed mount for the Raspberry Pi and camera. Notice also that I have a light illuminating the build area. I recommend using the brightest light you can find, like an LED light on a flexible shaft.

■ **Note** I normally use my Raspberry Pi on my Prusa i3. I moved it to my Printrbot Simple to give you an idea of the versatility of the Octopi server.

The case for the camera is also available on one of these sites, but you may want to consider getting an inexpensive one to start with and make a better one sourced from Thingiverse once your printer is fully operational. I will show you one such example next.

The figure shows a Raspberry Pi mounted in a clear case and the camera mounted in a special case I printed on another printer. The camera case is a customized version (called a *Remix*) of a case by alexspeller (thingiverse.com/thing:192364); I added a bolt to the clamp for a more secure mount. The clear Raspberry Pi case was purchased from Adafruit (adafruit.com/products/1140).

Notice how the camera is oriented. Since the printer used in the example is a Printrbot Simple, the print build is small enough that I can mount the camera fairly close to the print area. If you are adding the OctoPi to a printer with a larger print volume, you may need to position the camera in a location out of the way of the print bed so that printed objects don't run into it.[10]

---

[10]Talk about your extreme close-ups! Sadly, this will likely reposition your camera so that it is taking pictures of the wall or your own mug staring at the print (we all do it) or depending on how firm your camera mount is, it can knock parts off the print bed.

Go ahead and assemble your Raspberry Pi and camera in whatever case you decided on (there are so many to choose). Mount it near your printer and point the camera at the middle of the print bed. Be sure to leave some room for the axis movement. If you are using a simple camera case that doesn't have a mounting mechanism, you can use good old gray camera tape to secure it in place (or the ever-ready zip tie).

Once the unit is positioned and the camera pointed correctly, plug in your network and power supply but don't plug it into your home power. We need to get the software ready to go first.

Setting up the Raspberry Pi Software

To set up the software, first download and unzip the boot image from `https://github.com/guysoft/OctoPi/archive/devel.zip`. Alternatively, you can navigate to `http://octoprint.org/download` and follow the instructions and links there.

OK, now the file is unzipped. Use the procedures for loading a boot image onto the SD card to expand the image to your SD card. Once you've done that, you're ready to boot up the Raspberry Pi. Go ahead and insert the SD card and power everything on. We've got a few more steps to do, but these require connecting to the OctoPi server. Make sure your Raspberry Pi is connected to your network.

■ **Note** If you are using a Raspberry Pi and camera, the OctoPi boot image is already set up and ready to go. If you are using a different camera or want to set up OctoPi on a different boot image, see the `https://github.com/foosel/OctoPrint/wiki/Setup-on-a-Raspberry-Pi-running-Raspbian` page for detailed instructions on setting up OctoPi manually. You can connect to the server via a terminal with the `ssh pi@octopi.local` command using the default password of `raspberry` (unless you changed it).

Connecting and Using OctoPi

To connect to the OctoPi server, you should first ensure that the network cable is plugged in, and then wait for the Raspberry Pi to boot. This can take about 3–5 minutes. If you have access to the Raspberry Pi LEDs, wait until all of the LEDs for networking illuminate or begin blinking. Once fully booted, open your browser on your laptop and use the URL `octopi.local` to connect.

■ **Note** The octopi.local address will work on Mac and Windows, however, not all Linux distributions come with the tools needed to make this work. If you use Linux, check to ensure the Avahi software is loaded.

The first thing you need to do is click the Connection link and connect to the printer. Figure 4-22 shows the OctoPi connection area. You should be able to leave the defaults and click Connect. Once you connect, the connection area will close. Now, take a look at the main window, as shown in Figure 4-23.

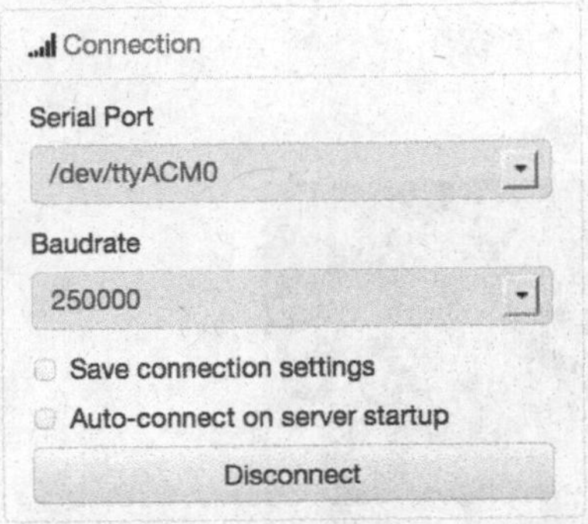

Figure 4-22. *Connection area*

Figure 4-23. *OctoPi main window*

Before you can print, you need to upload one or more G-code files to the server. I have uploaded a test cube to the server. Notice in Figure 4-23 that I've hovered over the file and the server has given me a few statistics on the file.

I have also activated the printer's extruder heater, which is depicted in the Temperature tab, also shown in the figure. To do this, you click the Control tab to reveal the printer control functions. Figure 4-24 shows the Control tab view. As you can see, there are controls for moving the axes, homing, and setting the temperature of the extruder and print bed. Notice the coolest part of this—the camera view! When you use this tab, you will see a streaming, live video feed from the Raspberry Pi. You can use this page to watch your printer over the network.

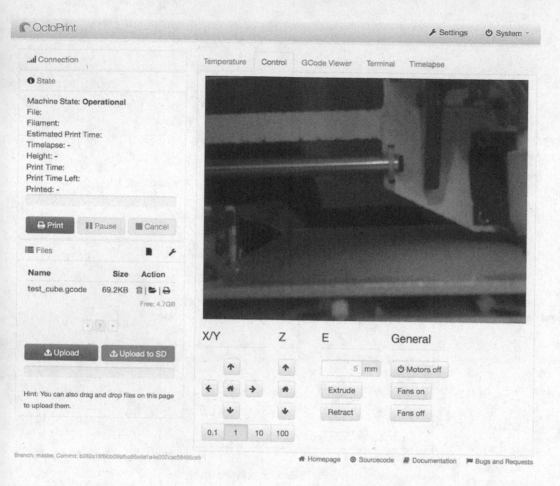

Figure 4-24. *Control tab*

The GCode Viewer tab lets you view the layers of the file you are printing. You can also get a bunch of statistics about the print from the links on that page. Figure 4-25 shows the GCode Viewer tab.

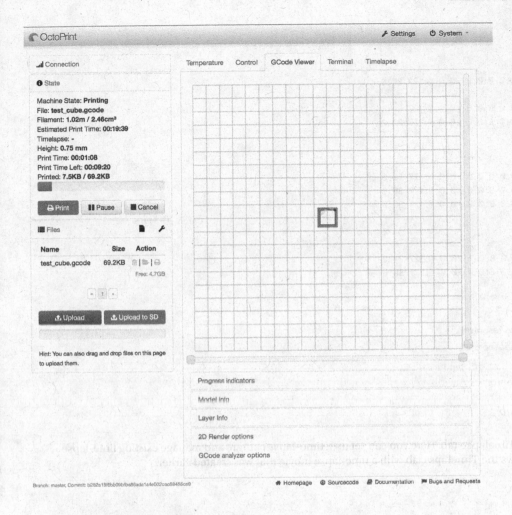

Figure 4-25. *GCode Viewer tab*

The next tab is a terminal viewer that you can use to watch the G-Codes being sent to the printer, as well as any messages being received from the printer. This is the same sort of information you see at the bottom of the Repetier-Host application. Figure 4-26 shows the Terminal tab.

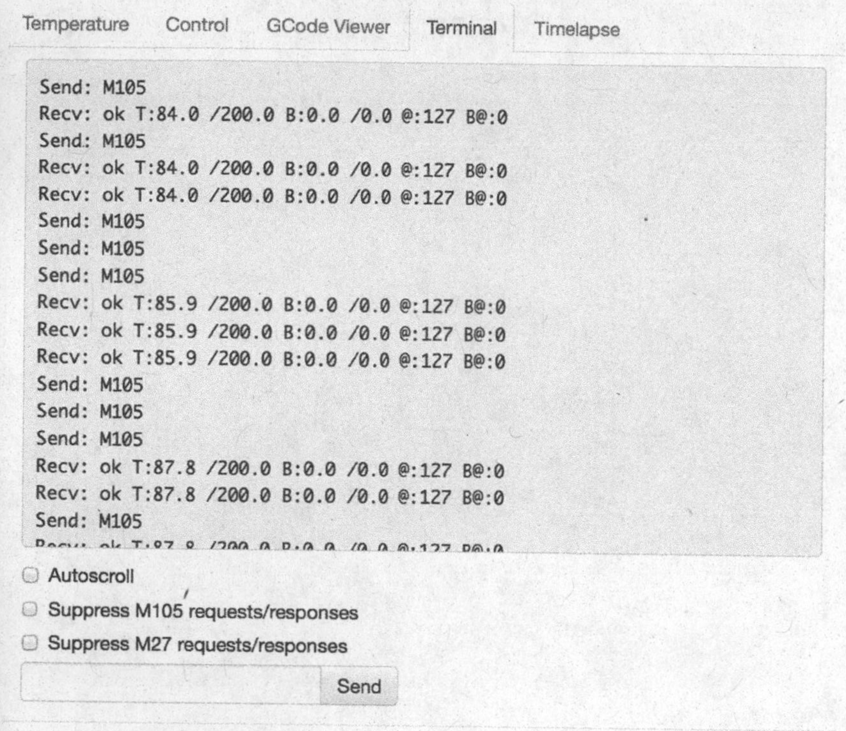

Temperature　　Control　　GCode Viewer　　**Terminal**　　Timelapse

```
Send: M105
Recv: ok T:84.0 /200.0 B:0.0 /0.0 @:127 B@:0
Send: M105
Recv: ok T:84.0 /200.0 B:0.0 /0.0 @:127 B@:0
Recv: ok T:84.0 /200.0 B:0.0 /0.0 @:127 B@:0
Send: M105
Send: M105
Send: M105
Recv: ok T:85.9 /200.0 B:0.0 /0.0 @:127 B@:0
Recv: ok T:85.9 /200.0 B:0.0 /0.0 @:127 B@:0
Recv: ok T:85.9 /200.0 B:0.0 /0.0 @:127 B@:0
Send: M105
Send: M105
Send: M105
Recv: ok T:87.8 /200.0 B:0.0 /0.0 @:127 B@:0
Recv: ok T:87.8 /200.0 B:0.0 /0.0 @:127 B@:0
Send: M105
Recv: ok T:87.8 /200.0 B:0.0 /0.0 @:127 B@:0
```

☐ Autoscroll

☐ Suppress M105 requests/responses

☐ Suppress M27 requests/responses

[_____]　Send

Figure 4-26. *Terminal tab*

The next tab is the Timelapse tab. Here you can set up a time-lapse capture and manage existing time-lapse movies. Figure 4-27 shows the Timelapse tab with a time-lapse movie that was created earlier.

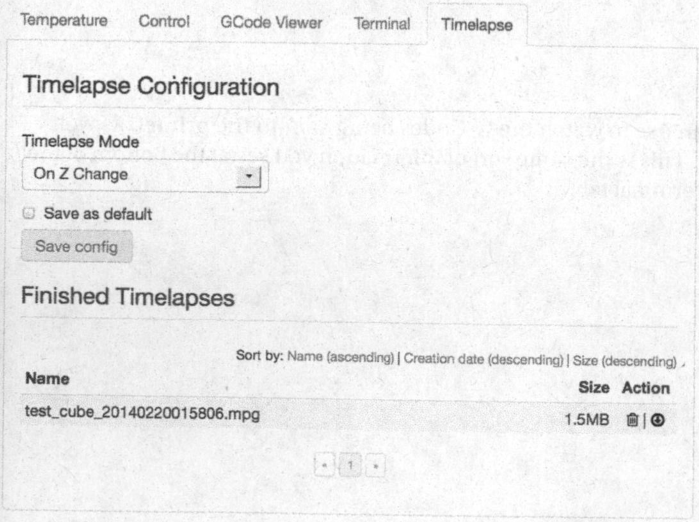

Temperature　　Control　　GCode Viewer　　Terminal　　Timelapse

Timelapse Configuration

Timelapse Mode

[On Z Change ▾]

☐ Save as default

[Save config]

Finished Timelapses

Sort by: Name (ascending) | Creation date (descending) | Size (descending)

Name	Size	Action
test_cube_20140220015806.mpg	1.5MB	🗑 | ⊕

‹ 1 ›

Figure 4-27. *Timelapse tab*

The use of this tab and its controls are not very clear in the documentation. You cannot change the time-lapse settings if there is a print in progress or if a printer is not connected. You must therefore wait until after you have connected to a printer and before you start to print to turn on the time-lapse feature. Notice in the figure that I have it set to record a snapshot in a frame of the movie on each Z-axis change. This creates a small, fast movie of your print.

To see a time-lapse movie, wait until the print is done and visit this tab. If the movie isn't ready yet, you may have to refresh the page after a couple of minutes. OctoPi names the movie using the name of the object you printed. To view the movie, click the tiny icon to the right of the file name. The first one deletes the movie. Figure 4-28 shows the movie in progress.

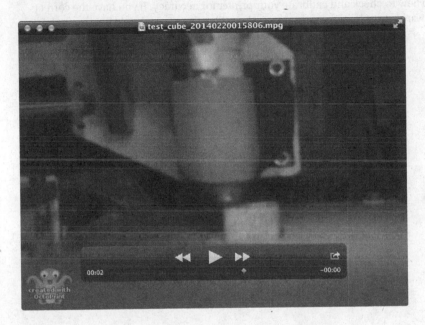

Figure 4-28. *Time-lapse movie*

Notice how the movie has the OctoPrint icon branded. If you'd like, you can turn this off in the Settings dialog (see the link in the upper-right corner of the dialog).

Well, that's it! When you complete this project, you will have a fully functional network-enabled printer. What we've done is move the printer controller software from our computer to the small Raspberry Pi (which is clearly up to the task), letting us control our printer without tying up a USB connection on our laptop. Oh, and we get some really cool video capabilities in the bargain!

If you have not tried this project, I encourage you to do so at your first opportunity. You may want to wait until your printer is fully calibrated, but as you can see, the OctoPi has all of the controls you need to run the preflight tests—even over the network! How cool is that?

Summary

This chapter has covered a lot of ground. Not only did I present the Marlin firmware and how to configure it for a new printer (or to replace the firmware on an existing printer), I also showed you some cool ways to modify Marlin to add new menus. This is the most important part of building a 3D printer. Getting the values in Marlin set correctly, or at least close, will make calibration a lot easier.

I also showed you how to install a printer controller program on your computer. I took a minor detour (still related to printer control software) and showed you how to make almost any Marlin- (or similar variant) enabled printer into a network printer (or wireless if you prefer). The best part was the camera action. Way cool trick there![11]

In the next chapter, I will show you how to check and calibrate your printer for accuracy. If you have the correct geometry and calculations in your firmware—or at least are very close—the calibration steps should be a matter of fine-tuning your settings.

---

[11] It is a rare and precious gem of a gadget indeed that doesn't require us to spend thousands of dollars replacing a perfectly good and functional printer for the swanky new model (not that there is anything wrong with that).

CHAPTER 5

■ ■ ■

Calibrating the Printer

The most important aspect of setting up your printer for the first time is calibrating the mechanisms to produce the correct movement in all three axes and the accurate extrusion of filament. Failing to do this or rushing through this process can result in a number of issues with your printer. Some of these may not be obvious until you print a very large object or even an object with sufficient detail, such as overhang or gap coverage.

Calibration-related inaccuracies can be subtle and thus almost undetectable. They can also become serious and affect the quality of your prints. Significant inaccuracies can result in a wide range of problems, including inaccurate object size (too large, too small), excess filament (resulting in globs of filament), insufficient filament (weak layer bonds), and adhesion problems. I've read a number of articles and requests for help, and heard general misery from people who have struggled with one or more of these maladies. More often than not, the owner is treating the symptoms rather than the source of the problem. Proper calibration won't solve all of your printing woes, but it will go a long way toward improving your experience and the quality of your prints.

This chapter is therefore an effort to help you avoid the worst of these calibration-related problems by introducing a step-wise procedure for setting the endstops, calibrating each of the axes and the extruder, and leveling (tramming) the print bed. Once all of these elements are working like they are supposed to, you can then turn your attention to fine-tuning your print files for even better, faster printing. But let's get that printer dialed-in mechanically first!

Setting the Endstops

Recall that endstops are used to set either the minimum or maximum travel of the axis. They are mounted so that a physical part of the axis movement forces the endstop to close, thereby triggering the firmware that the axis has reached a specific point in its movement.

The mount for the endstop should be either a clamp that can be tightened or a press-fit arrangement that permits the endstop to be mounted in a stationary position. Endstops that can be moved easily (say, by sliding along one of the smooth rods) can cause a host of issues, not the least of which is inconsistent homing. Check each of your endstops to ensure that they cannot be moved easily. As mentioned, press-fit is fine provided it is a very firm fit that cannot be moved when triggered.

In previous chapters, I discussed setting the endstops in a general location far enough from the hard bits to avoid a crash. In this section, we examine setting the endstops to the proper location by fine-tuning their position on the axis.

■ **Note** I am referring to mechanical endstops in this section. There are also optical and hall-effect endstops. Optical endstops use a special sensor to detect when an obstruction passes through two points. Hall-effect endstops detect the proximity of a magnet. These other endstop types achieve the same goal but have different signaling mechanisms.

X-Axis Endstop

The X-axis endstop should be set so that the X carriage (that holds the extruder and hot end) arrests its movement prior to the nozzle leaving the print bed surface or prior to the nozzle striking any clips or fasteners on the print bed.

The most common location for this endstop (for single extruder machines) is on one of the smooth rods for the X axis. Figure 5-1 shows the X-axis endstop for a Prusa i2 printer. Notice how the endstop is oriented so that the X carriage itself is used to close the switch. Notice also that it is held in place with a clamp that doubles as the endstop holder.

Figure 5-1. *X-axis endstop location Prusa i2*

■ **Note** Printers with multiple extruders offset on the X axis will be set up so that the rightmost nozzle can travel to the edge of the print surface.

The X-axis endstop for a Prusa i3 is similar, as shown in Figure 5-2.

Figure 5-2. *X-axis endstop location Prusa i3*

The endstop holder in this example is mounted using a press-fit mount. In this case, the endstop can be moved by hand, but the force of the extruder closing the switch does affect the location of the mount.

You may also notice that the Prusa i3 is using an endstop with four wires instead of two. This is because these are endstops modeled after the MakerBot version 1.2 endstop. The endstop includes an LED that illuminates when the switch is closed. This requires two additional wires to power the LED. Actually, it uses a common ground between the center pins, which means you can connect only three wires to use this endstop: ground, positive 5v, and signal for the endstop.

To adjust the endstop, power off your printer first.[1] Then, slowly move the X carriage until you hear the switch close. You should be able to hear an audible click.

■ **Caution** When manually moving axes, always move them very slowly so as not to generate current that will feed back to your electronics. Alternatively, you can disconnect the stepper motor during the move, but remember to plug it back in while the printer is turned off.

Next, observe where the nozzle is in relation to the print bed. Does it appear that the nozzle tip is clear of any obstructions, such as binder clips or similar on the print bed surface? Similarly, is the nozzle located within the dimensions of the heated print bed (if equipped)? If you need to change the position of the endstop, move the axis away from the endstop and reposition it. Repeat the process until the nozzle stops inside all obstructions, as well as inside the heat zone for the print bed. Figure 5-3 shows an example of the correct location for a Prusa i3 X-axis endstop.

---

[1]As well as any loud music, neighbors, cats playing the trombone, and so forth, so you can hear the "click."

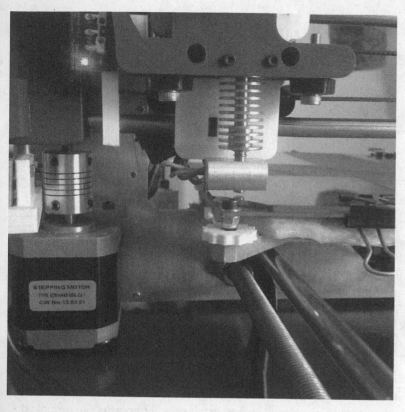

Figure 5-3. *Correct X-axis endstop location for a Prusa i3*

Y-Axis Endstop

The Y-axis endstop should be set so that the print bed arrests its movement prior to the nozzle leaving the print bed surface or prior to the nozzle striking any clips or fasteners on the print bed.

The most common location for the Y-axis endstop is under the print bed at the rear of the Y-axis mechanism. Sometimes you will see endstops mounted on the smooth rods; other times they are mounted on the threaded rods or similar frame components. Figure 5-4 shows the Y-axis endstop for a Prusa i2 and Figure 5-5 shows the Y-axis endstop for Prusa i3.

If you can have even just two options, it is useful. I explain these options here. This means the endstop must be mounted so that leaving the bed all the way toward where the gantry is, or away from the gantry (this is typically referred to as bed or motor retract has a preventing up for the Y-axis. Adjusting this entails to enter where you before used for the X-axis. For the Y-axis, back it out so that, as you slowly turn move the gantry back and forth, adjust the endstop so that the switch engages the carriage with precision so that the bed is fully toward the motor retract. Remember to look for the position of the X-axis switch as you do so for the X-axis.

Figure 5-4. *Y-axis endstop location Prusa i2*

Figure 5-5. *Y-axis endstop location Prusa i3*

■ **Note**   The view for Figure 5-5 is taken from above. The arrows show the location of the endstop.

In each of these examples, the endstop is oriented so that the bearing or bearing holder is used to close the switch. This means the endstop must be mounted so that the print bed can pass over the endstop. You may see other orientations that place the Y-axis endstop such that the print bed itself is used to close the switch. For example, a variant of the Prusa i3 Y motor mount has a mounting point for the Y-axis endstop.

Adjusting this endstop is the same procedure used for the X axis—only in this case, we are concerned about how far the print bed itself can move. Again, move the print bed slowly until it closes the endstop (listen for the click). Adjust the endstop so that the nozzle remains in the heat zone but does not come into contact with any obstructions like binder clips. Figure 5-6 shows the proper orientation of the Y-axis endstop with respect to the location of the nozzle over the print bed.

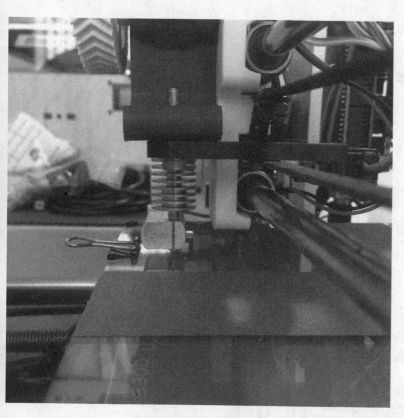

Figure 5-6. *Correct Y-axis endstop location Prusa i3*

HEAT ZONE

Most heated print beds have a colored line drawn around the border. This is more than simple border dressing. It demarcates the outer perimeter of the heated surface. That's right, most heated build plates do not heat all the way to the edge. Keep this in mind when setting your X- and Y-axes endstops.

Z-Axis Endstop

The Z-axis endstop should be set so that the Z carriage (that also moves the X-axis mechanism) arrests its movement prior to the nozzle touching the print bed surface.

The most common location for this endstop is on the smooth rod on either the left or right side of the Z axis. Typically, you will find the endstop mounted loosely so that it can be more easily adjusted. More recent incarnations of RepRap printers use an endstop with a fine adjustment that allows you to alter the location in small increments. This allows you to set the Z-height quickly.

While it is true that the Z-axis endstop is just another switch and works the same way as the endstops on the other axes, there is a bit more to it than that. Unlike the X and Y axes, whose location does not affect print quality (only starting location), the Z-axis endstop is used to set the initial height of the first layer. If the endstop is set too high, the filament may not stick to the build surface, causing low adhesion for the first layer (and a maddening array of adhesion maladies). If the endstop is set too low, it can cause the first layers to appear "squished," and if set low enough, can cause filament extrusion failures from obstruction (filament extrusion is blocked by build surface).

Let us take a moment to examine the types of Z-axis adjusters available and to discuss the correct Z-height for the first layer.

Z-Height Adjusters

Unlike the X and Y axes, you are likely to need to adjust the Z axis periodically. Most people do this before they use the printer for the first time each day. Having to adjust one axis may seem odd, but there are several reasons for this.

Chief among these are the effects of humidity on build platforms that use a wood base. The wood can expand and contract, depending on the humidity. While typically this is only a very small amount, if you consider the proper Z-height is about 0.1mm, it doesn't take much to throw that gap off.

Another possibility concerns changes induced by the application of different adhesion techniques. For example, blue painter's tape is not the same thickness as Kapton tape. If you use another technique such as ABS slurry, the Z-height can be uneven across the build surface.

No matter the reason, you will have to make fine adjustments to the Z-height. Early RepRap printers, and indeed many early commercial printers, used a fixed endstop for the Z axis. Adjusting the Z-height means loosening the endstop mount and moving it slightly up or down, and then testing the height and repeating the process until you get the Z-height set. This is very error-prone and can take some practice to master. But there is a better way.

One of the first modifications most people make to their RepRap printers is to change the fixed endstop mount for the Z axis to an adjustable mount. There are many versions of Z-axis adjusters on Thingiverse. Some are better than others, and it really doesn't matter how they work—provided they are not prone to loosening from vibration, and provide an even, linear movement, and can allow for fine adjustment (I've seen some that have preset detents that seem to never be quiet right). I will show you an example of a Z-axis adjuster in Figure 5-7.

Figure 5-7. *Z-axis endstop location Prusa i2 with fine adjuster*

Proper Z-Height

One of the challenges for a beginning 3D printer enthusiast is setting the proper Z-height. No matter what class of printer you are working with, there will be a mechanism you can use to set the Z-height. On older printers or printers that have not been upgraded, you may need to loosen and move the entire endstop mount. This is very error-prone. If you have this setup, you should consider getting a Z-axis adjuster to replace the endstop mount.

So what is the correct Z-height? The easiest and simplest method of setting the Z-height is using a sheet of paper. Most common weight paper is about 0.01mm thick. Thus, you use a piece of paper as a gauge to set your Z-height by positioning the Z axis to its lowest point and sliding the paper under the nozzle. If the paper slides under easily, lower the Z-axis endstop a very tiny amount and try homing the Z axis again. Repeat the process until the paper is very slightly gripped by the nozzle (between the nozzle and the print bed).

■ **Tip** Make sure there is no filament protruding from the nozzle. Use a hobby knife to cut away the filament so that you are measuring the distance from the nozzle to the print bed.

You may also find that heating the print bed and the nozzle to their proper temperature may permit you to make more accurate measurements. Again, this has to do with what materials are used in the print bed and hot end. Some materials expand more than others when heated.

Z-Axis Endstop Location

Typically, the Z-axis endstop is located on the left side of the printer and mounted to the smooth rod underneath the X-axis mechanism (called the *X-ends*). The X-axis motor is normally mounted on the same side. Figure 5-7 shows the Z-axis endstop for a Prusa i2. Notice that the endstop is mounted on a fine adjuster assembly.

The adjuster used in the photo is a customized version of thingiverse.com/thing:16380. More specifically, it is mounted so that the arm is to the left, allowing the X-axis stepper motor to act as a mount point for the tall foot that activates the endstop. In this case, the adjuster moves the endstop itself. The use of a fine threaded bolt and nylon lock nut permits very fine adjustment, as well as not being affected by vibrations (it won't come loose).

There are also a number of options for mounting the Z-axis endstop on a Prusa i3. One of the more popular methods is modifying the left X-end to include a long M3 bolt, which is used to trigger a fixed endstop. If you already have your X-ends printed, you can print a small bracket to hold the 3mm bolt. A spring and a nylon lock nut are used to both keep tension and reduce risk of changes due to vibration.

Like the Prusa i2, the endstop on the Prusa i3 is mounted on the left smooth rod. Depending on what type of Z-axis threaded rod clamp you use, you may need to use a narrow endstop mount. Notice that the LED is on in the figure. This indicates that the endstop is triggered, which can be really handy when adjusting the Z-height.

Figure 5-8. *Z-axis endstop location Prusa i3*

I have mentioned some RepRap enthusiasts are adopting *auto Z-probing* (sometimes inaccurately described as auto bed leveling). Auto Z-probing is a solution for automatically setting the Z-height, as well as compensating for uneven print beds. The most common mechanism uses a servo with the endstop mounted on a short arm. When the firmware's auto Z-probing code is triggered, it deploys the servo arm to lower the endstop and performs probing (lowers the Z axis until the switch engages) at several points across the print bed. The arm is retracted once the Z-height is determined. Figure 5-9 shows one example of how the Z-axis endstop can be mounted on a servo with a short arm. In this photo, the endstop is deployed for probing. The endstop is normally rotated away from the heat bed.

Figure 5-9. *Z-axis endstop location Prusa i3 with auto bed leveling*

While this sounds like a dream solution (especially if you've been setting your Z-height manually for a long time), you should know this is not a simple modification. It requires firmware changes, as well as additional hardware and a fairly tedious set-up procedure. I will discuss this feature and how to add it to your RepRap printer in more detail in a later chapter.

Calibrating the Stepper Drivers

There is one thing that you should do before you attempt to calibrate your axes. You should check the stepper drivers to make sure they are sending the right voltage to your stepper motors. It is OK if you haven't done this step yet, but I highly recommended that you do it again as a double check.

The following presents procedures for setting A4988 stepper drivers. There are other stepper driver boards available. While the basic logical process is the same, the actual steps may differ for other boards. You should check your vendor's web site for the correct procedure if you are using non-A4988-based stepper drivers.

First, check your stepper motor specifications to see what operating amperage the vendor recommends. You should be able to find this on the data sheet for the stepper motor. Next, check your stepper drivers to see what value resistors are used. For example, Pololu stepper drivers normally have 0.05 ohm resistors (but you need to check your vendor's data sheet to know for certain). Finally, you can plug this data into the following formula to calculate the reference voltage (VREF).

```
VREF = Max_Amps * 8 * Resistors
```

For Pololu stepper drivers, the formula is:

```
VREF = Max_Amps * 8 * 0.05
```

Let's suppose your stepper motors are rated at 1.0 amps. The reference voltage should be:

```
0.4V = 1.0 * 8 * 0.05
```

To measure the VREF, power on your printer and locate the small potentiometer on the stepper driver. Figure 5-10 shows a Pololu stepper driver. I have highlighted the potentiometer with an oval and the ground pin with a square.

Figure 5-10. Stepstick stepper driver module

To measure the voltage, use a multimeter set to measure DC voltage. If your multimeter has several settings, choose the one that measures up to 10 or 20 volts. Power on your printer and carefully place the positive probe on the center of the potentiometer and the ground probe on the ground pin. Read the voltage and compare it to your calculations.

If you need to increase the voltage, use a ceramic screwdriver to rotate the potentiometer clockwise a small fraction at a time. It only takes a small movement to increase or decrease the voltage. Measure the voltage again and repeat the process until you get the correct voltage. If you turn the potentiometer too far, you may cycle back around to 0 volts. Just keep turning the potentiometer, but do so using smaller increments. Repeat the process for each of your axes and the extruder printer driver.

■ **Caution** Be careful where you put that probe! If you are using a RAMPS setup, the X-, Y-, and Z- stepper drivers are placed side by side. It is easy to accidentally touch the wrong pin. If you do, you may see a small spark, and if you are really lucky you won't damage your stepper driver.[2]

Now that the stepper drivers are calibrated, we can work on getting the axes calibrated properly. I discuss procedures for adjusting all three axes in the next section.

Calibrating the Axes

The next step in the calibration process is adjusting each axis so that movement is accurate. The basic process involves choosing a starting point (typically the home location if the endstops are set correctly), marking the location of the nozzle, measuring a predetermined distance out and marking that location, and then moving the axis a distance and measuring the actual distance traveled. The process is repeated using several starting locations and lengths.

If differences are found, you should check your calculations. If they are correct, and the axis movement is assembled correctly, you should not have to make adjustments. However, those axes that use toothless belts and similar mechanisms may require manual calibration. This is true for the extruder mechanism, but is not true for a threaded rod mechanism.

---

[2]Can you guess how I know this? Yep, the stepper driver in the photo is a dead stepper driver module.

To calibrate non-mathematically predictable axes mechanisms, you would calculate the difference so that you can modify the firmware settings accordingly. For example, if the axis moves only 90% of the distance, you can adjust the firmware setting using a ratio to increase the steps per millimeter.

■ **Caution**   Axes calibration requires a stable chassis that has been assembled correctly. If your frame is loose or has parts that can come loose or oscillate, you can expect accuracy to suffer. Similarly, if the frame is out of square, it can cause odd behavior. Thus, before calibrating your axes, ensure that your frame is correctly assembled and true. See the "Frame and Chassis" section for tips on checking your frame.

However, before I get into the specifics of each axis, I will discuss the tools you will need so that you can have them ready when you perform the calibration.

Tools Required

The tools you need include any wrenches that fit the bolts securing your axis mechanism. Depending on the hardware used in your printer, you may need a screwdriver, hex key, and so forth, to loosen and tighten the components. If the axis is belt-driven, you may also need wrenches to tighten the belt tensioner. Check each axis prior to attempting the calibration steps to make sure you have the right tools at hand.

You will also need masking or blue painter's tape and a pen or pencil. If you use blue painter's tape, choose a fine point pen of contrasting color (e.g., black) so that it shows up well on the tape. You will be making marks on the tape to measure movement of the axis. Thus, a fine point will make measuring easier and a bit more accurate than a typical wide-tip permanent marker. Of course, a metric ruler is also required. Choose a shorter one (say, 100mm–150mm) for measuring lengths in confined spaces and a longer one (say, 300mm) for measuring the range of the axis. You may also find a digital caliper helpful when measuring the Z-axis travel.

In summary, you will need one or more of the following tools. Check your printer for the proper sizes of screwdrivers, wrenches, and hex keys.

- Wrenches
- Hex keys
- Screwdriver
- Ruler
- Digital caliper

Remember to update your firmware files (e.g., the Configure.h file in Marlin) with the new values. I like to annotate the code so that I capture the original values. The following shows an example.

```
// Refined settings. E steps was 524, now 552.5
#define DEFAULT_AXIS_STEPS_PER_UNIT    {100.00,100.00,4000.00,552.5}
```

X Axis

Let's start with the X axis. Place a strip of blue painter's tape or masking tape on the print bed. The tape should extend from one edge of the print bed to the other. Power the printer on (if not already) and home the X axis with either your printer controller software or the LCD menu on the printer. Once homed, move the axis out about 20mm. This should place the hot end well within the edge of the print bed.

■ **Tip**   I find it easier to use the printer controller software when calibrating. Sometimes the sensitivity of the rotary switch can cause you to move the axis too far or too little, which is annoying. It is better to use presets in the printer controller software or even use the Go code to move the axis. For example, Go X50 moves the X axis to position 50.

Next, you should lower the Z axis so that the nozzle is within about 5mm–10mm of the print bed. Use either the nozzle tip or the edge of the heater block to make a mark on the tape. This will be your starting point. Next, measure exactly 100mm to the right along the X axis and make another mark. Figure 5-11 shows how to mark the print bed.

Figure 5-11. *Measuring the X-axis movement*

Now move the X axis exactly 100mm using your printer controller software or the LCD menu. Observe the mark you made at 100mm. Did the edge you used to measure the starting point stop at the 100mm mark? If so, try moving the axis back about 50mm or 75mm, and make a second mark, and then measure another 100mm and try the movement again. Figure 5-12 shows an example of the X axis moving correctly to the 100mm mark on the print bed.

Figure 5-12. *Accurate X-axis movement*

It is best to test the movement in several locations along the axis to make sure you don't have a mechanical problem that restricts movement.[3] If the value is not exactly 100mm, make a mark where the axis stopped and measure the distance. Write that number down. Repeat at least three times total. Figure 5-13 shows an example of several measurements taken on a Prusa i3.

---

[3]A bent smooth rod can cause inaccurate movement across the "bend."

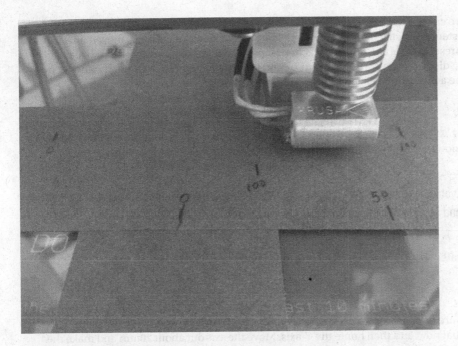

Figure 5-13. *Multiple tests on the X-axis movement*

If your axis moved consistently on all three measurements and it moved exactly 100mm, you are done! On the other hand, if you find that the axis moved somewhat less or more than 100mm, you must correct the issue. Before you fire up your Arduino IDE and start changing things,[4] take some more measurements using a different scale. Try 50mm or even 150mm. Record those values. Now, make a ratio for each test. Take the value of the actual movement and divide it by the desired movement. For example, 95/100 = 95%. All of your measurements should be within two decimal places. That is, they should all be the same ratio.

WHY IS MY AXIS MOVEMENT WRONG?

If you used the RepRap calculator and you are absolutely positive that the variables you used are correct (the number of teeth in the drive gear, belt pitch, etc.), but the axis is not 100%, you may be wondering why this can happen. There are a number of reasons that the axis may be a bit off. The diameter of the drive pulley may not be exactly to specification or your axis uses idler pulleys that change the geometry slightly. The cause is usually a very small factor and the distance off should also be very small. If it is more than 5%, you should go back and check your hardware and calculations, but even then it is rare to be as much as 5% off. I normally find variances of 1% to 2% when I build a printer using different hardware.

---

[4]You must resist, Grasshopper!

Recall from Chapter 4 that we can use the M92 command to set the steps per millimeter for a given axis, and that the measurements are consistent for each length tested.[5] For example, let's suppose your axis moved only 95mm instead of 100mm. This value represents 95% (95/100) of the actual steps per millimeter. If you confirm that all of your other tests moved 95% of the distance, you can adjust your original calculation for the steps per millimeter by calculating 95% of 79.75. Thus, the actual value needed is:

```
Steps_per_millimeter = 79.75 / 0.95 = 83.95
```

You can use the command M92 X83.95 to set the X-axis steps per millimeter. Once that is done, try your measurements again. The axis movement should now be exactly 100mm. Repeat at least twice more in different locations to verify.

■ **Tip** Once you have fine-tuned your steps per millimeter, open your Marlin firmware and change the value in there. If you don't save the values in EEPROM, and you ever reload the firmware, you will have to recalibrate. No one wants to do that!

OK, now your X axis is calibrated. Let's turn to the Y axis.

Y Axis

We use the same method to measure the Y axis as we do the X axis, only we place the tape so that it runs from front-to-back. Go ahead and do that now, and then home the Y-axis. Move the axis out about 20mm and make the starting mark, and then measure out 100mm. Figure 5-14 shows an example of measuring movement on the Y axis.

Figure 5-14. Measuring the Y axis

---

[5]If the tests are not consistent, you may have problems with your axis drive mechanism, or you are using a non-mathematically predictive mechanism.

Like the X axis, you want to take several measurements and note the distance actually traveled. If it is off, do the measurement again for 50mm or 75mm and write those values down.

If you have a difference ratio, use the ratio to calculate a new value for the Y-axis steps per millimeter and change it with the M92 command. For example, if you experience a 98% ratio for the Y axis and originally had a value of 80 for the Y steps per millimeter, your value and command would be the following.

```
81.63 = 80/.98
M92 Y81.63
```

■ **Tip** Remember, update those values in Marlin!

Well, that wasn't so bad, eh? Now let's look at the Z axis. This is usually easier, but sometimes it can be a problem, as you will see.

Z Axis

A threaded rod normally drives the Z axis. As such, the threaded rod should be very precise and have almost no deviation. That is, the thread pitch is constant throughout its length. Thus, no matter where the Z axis is at the moment, it should move the same distance.

Measuring Z-axis movement, however, is a bit harder to do. I've seen some examples where people have used a small square or drafting triangle covered with tape to measure how far the Z axis moves. This will work fine if you want to do it that way, but I've found a digital caliper to be the best tool for the job. The trick is to find a location that allows you to consistently measure the distance traveled.

To do this, I use a dial gauge holder that I designed for leveling (tramming) the print bed. Figure 5-15 shows the dial gauge mount that I designed; it is available on Thingiverse (thingiverse.com/thing:232979). Use the link to download the gauge for your use. There is a version for lower-profile hot ends and another for taller hot ends.

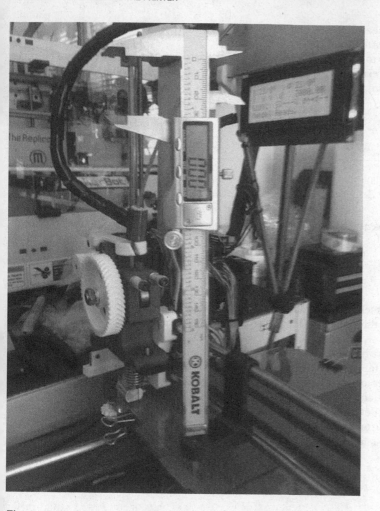

Figure 5-15. *Measuring Z axis with a dial gauge mount at zero*

Notice that I set my digital caliper to zero after placing the depth gauge on the print bed. It is important to not move your mount or print bed. Doing so can change the measurement slightly.

What I've done is clip the dial gauge mount to the X-axis smooth rods. I use the depth probe on my digital caliper to measure the distance to the print bed.

To measure the travel, I jot down that figure, and then I move the axis 50mm. Why 50mm and not 100mm? Recall that in Chapter 3 I recommended setting the maximum travel of the Z axis (for example, 80mm) until you have a chance to calibrate. Thus, depending on where the axis is to start, you may not have 100mm to work with.

■ **Tip** If you can find a fixed point on your X axis, you can also use a simple ruler to measure the distance traveled.

Your measurements should be very close to 50mm of movement. It may not be exactly 50mm due to the measuring technique, but it should be very close. If it is not, you either have the wrong thread pitch or you calculated the steps per millimeter incorrectly. Very rarely, and I've only seen it once, will you find a threaded rod that has a thread pitch that varies. Figure 5-16 shows the results of measuring the Z height after moving the axis.

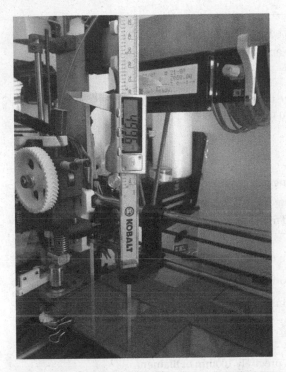

Figure 5-16. Measuring Z axis with a dial gauge mount at 50mm

However, if your movement is off, you can use the same ratio calculation we used for the X and Y axes to adjust the steps per millimeter. In this case, the command would be `M92 Znn.nn`.

OK, now all three axes move precisely as far as they should. You're almost there. Now it is time to calibrate the extruder.

Calibrating the Extruder

The extruder is the most challenging component to calibrate. Recall the number of variables in the formula from Chapter 03. One of the variables is the diameter of the drive pulley or hobbed bolt. If this measurement is off, the extruder will extrude less or more filament than desired.

An improperly calibrated extruder can cause a range of problems that may tempt you to think there is something wrong with the objects you are attempting to print. For example, extruding too little filament can cause poor layer adhesion. Similarly, extruding too much filament can cause stringing and globs of filament being deposited during slower movement. There are other similar problems related to extruder calibration. However, if your extruder is calibrated properly, it becomes easier to diagnose problems related to filament size, heat settings, or slicer options.

Calibrating the extruder is not like the other axes. There is some trial and error involved since the measurement of the hobbed bolt is not precise. Part of the reason for this is how much the filament fills the hobbed area. For example, if the hobbed area (the indentation with the striation marks) is narrow, the filament will be located nearer the outside of the bolt making the actual diameter larger. Conversely if the hobbed area is wide, the filament will be located nearer the center making the actual diameter smaller. The size of the filament itself will also affect the measurement. I suppose this is why there is no extruder calculator on the RepRap calculator.

■ **Tip** Check with the vendor from whom you purchased the hobbed bolt or drive pulley. They may have a more accurate value to use for the diameter given the size filament you plan to use (3mm or 1.75mm).

To measure the amount of filament extruded, we will measure the distance the filament travels as it enters the extruder. The basic process is as follows. I will describe the steps in more detail next.

1. Remove the hot end.

2. Load filament in the extruder.

3. Make a mark on the filament aligned with a nonmoving part of the extruder (e.g., the body or door).

4. Use a ruler to measure 100mm along the filament and make a second mark on the filament.

5. Use your printer controller software to extrude 100mm of filament.

6. You're done if the filament stops at the second mark; otherwise, measure the distance.

7. Calculate a ratio based on your existing steps per millimeter for the extruder and modify it with the `M92 ENN.NN` command.

8. Advance the filament past the marks.

9. Repeat starting with step 3 until the extruder extrudes precisely 100mm of filament.

The first step is to unload your filament and remove the hot end. This will save you from wasting a lot of filament and avoid having to wait for the hot end to heat up. If you have already loaded filament and tested the extruder, that's great and you do not strictly have to unload the filament and remove the hot end, but it is a bit easier.

If you removed the hot end, you must use the M302 code to disable the cold extrusion prevention. This is because most firmware has a setting that prevents attempts to extrude filament if the hot end is cold. If you get the message "cold extrusion prevented", use the code. Otherwise, you will have to heat the hot end before you can extrude.

■ **Caution** Place the loose hot end on the print bed in a location where you won't accidentally touch it. If you turn on the heater, it will get hot enough to burn!

With the filament loaded and the extruder idler closed and tightened, make a mark on the filament that aligns with a fixed portion of the extruder. A good choice is the extruder body or extruder idler edge. Figure 5-17 shows how to do this with a Greg's Wade hinged extruder.

Figure 5-17. Marking filament at 0mm

Next, measure a distance 100mm away from the first mark and mark the filament at this point. Figure 5-18 shows measuring and setting the mark. Make a second mark at 120mm. Make the 120mm mark distinct with a wider mark or a different color. We will use the second mark if the extruder extrudes too much filament. This is because you won't be able to see the 100mm mark if there is an overrun.

Figure 5-18. Marking filament at 100mm and 120mm

■ **Tip** I use different color markers for each mark so that I can tell which mark is the starting, 100mm, and 120mm mark, and so that if I do the test a second or third time, I won't confuse the marks.

Using your printer controller software, set the extruder to extrude 100mm of filament. Figure 5-19 shows the screen and controls for the Repetier-Host software.

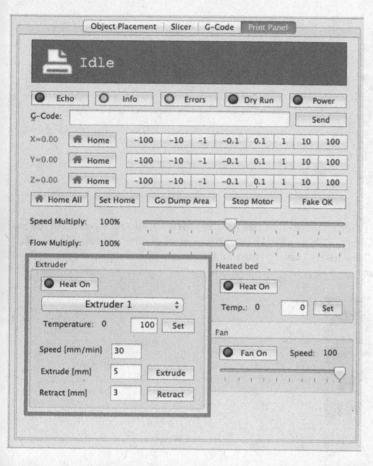

Figure 5-19. *Repetier-Host filament extrusion on printer control panel*

Once the extruder stops, take a look at where the mark on the filament at the 100mm mark is in relation to your reference point. If it is aligned with your reference point, congratulations, you're done! If not, you must determine if you have an underrun condition where not enough filament was extruded or an overrun where the extruder extruded too much filament.

If underrun, the 100mm mark is above the reference point. Use a digital caliper or a small ruler to measure the distance from your reference point to the 100mm mark. Formulate a difference calculation using your existing extruder steps per millimeter. You can find this value by looking in your Marlin firmware files or by searching the log window in the Repetier-Host software. As part of the connection handshake, Repetier-Host requests the steps per millimeter settings using the M503 command. The following is an example of the data returned from the printer.

```
2:28:23 PM: echo:  M92 X100.00 Y100.00 Z4000.00 E524.00
```

Let's say your extruder extruded 96mm of filament. That is, there was a 4mm gap from the reference point to the 100mm mark (100–4=96), or you extruded 96% of 100mm. Using the steps per millimeter shown in Figure 5-19, we can calculate the new steps per millimeter as follows. Figure 5-20 shows an example of underrun.

```
545.83 = 524 / .96
```

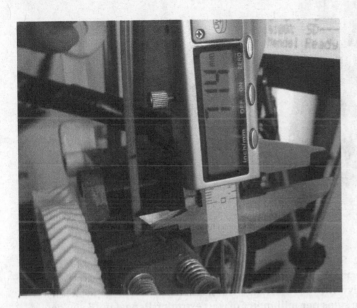

Figure 5-20. *Extruder underrun*

On the other hand, if the 100mm mark is below your reference point, you have overrun. In this case, measure the distance to the 120mm mark, and subtract it from 120 and add it to 100. For example, if the distance to the 120mm mark is 10mm, the actual run of filament was 110mm or 110% of 100mm. Using the steps per millimeter shown in Figure 5-20, we can calculate the new steps per millimeter as follows. Figure 5-21 shows an example of overrun.

```
476.36 = 524 / 1.10
```

Figure 5-21. *Extruder overrun*

Once you calculate the correct value, use the M92 EN.NN command to set the new steps per millimeter for the extruder (E axis), and run the test again. Make a new mark for 0mm and a new mark for 100mm and extrude 100mm. The 100mm mark should now align perfectly with your reference point. If it doesn't and it is just a few millimeters off, try the process again to fine-tune the steps per millimeter of your extruder. Repeat until you get consistent results.

Let's look at a real example. Figure 5-22 shows the result of my calibration test for one of my Prusa printers. Notice here that I measured 5.24mm of underrun. More specifically, the extruder extruded only 94.76mm of filament. Given my original calculation of 524mm for the steps per millimeter, I must calculate a new value, as follows.

```
552.98 = 524 / .9476
```

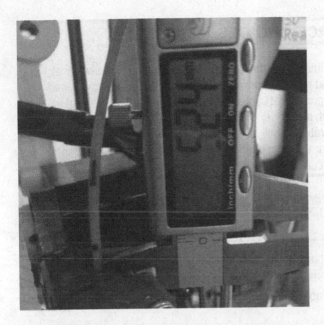

Figure 5-22. *Measuring the underrun*

I then used the command M92 E552.98 to set the steps per millimeter for my extruder and reran the test. I discovered this time the measurement was off by a very small fraction. Not wanting to leave that as "good enough,"[6] I ran the original test several more times and averaged the runs to 5.16mm of underrun. I then recalculated the steps per millimeter as follows.

```
552.51 = 524 / .9484
```

Once again, I used the M92 E552.50 command to set the steps per millimeter and ran the test again. This time, the extruder extruded exactly 100mm of filament. You may find you will have to run several tests to ensure that you have accurate measurements.

Now that the extruder is calibrated, we're almost ready to try printing an object. The next step is to level (tram) the print bed.

Leveling the Heated Print Bed

This is one area where it pays to take your time to get it right. Unless you have auto bed leveling turned on, you will need to make sure your print bed is on a parallel plane to your X axis. We use the term *leveling*, but that isn't entirely correct. We are not making the print bed level with the horizon. Rather, we are making sure the nozzle is the same height above the print bed at all points. You must install your choice of print surface prior to executing the procedure.

■ **Note**   This procedure would be done prior to using the normal paper feeler gauge process to set your Z-height.

---

[6]Did I mention the type-A element?

PRINT SURFACE CHOICES

The common choice for a printing surface is glass. Most kits use common household glass (think window pane) of about 3/8" thick. While glass of this type is plentiful and relatively inexpensive, it often has flaws. I have found several pieces of glass from different glass and home improvement shops that were not nearly flat. They had a noticeable convex shape (or concave, depending on which side is up). This can cause problems when setting Z-height. In fact, you may not even know you have this problem until you use a center point in your bed leveling (tramming) technique. I discovered it because objects near the edge of my print area had lower adhesion than those in the center. A convex glass print surface was the culprit.

A good way to level (tram) the print bed is to use a dial gauge mounted to the X axis. Set each print bed adjuster to its middle position (about half way down/up the threads). The process to level the print bed is as follows.

■ **Tip** If you are working with a new printer, you may not have a dial gauge mount available (or you cannot print it because your printer isn't ready). In this case, you can still perform the procedure, but instead of using a dial gauge, you can use your calipers to measure the height of the axis above the print bed. Just be sure to use the same location for all measurements.

---

1. Place the dial gauge on the left side of the X axis near the edge of the print bed.

2. Move the Y axis to the home position.

3. Read the value and note it (or rotate the dial or one of the pins to this point).

4. Move the Y axis to the maximum position. Adjust the print bed until the dial reads the same value as step 2. Take the measurement as close to the four corners as possible.

5. Gently move the dial gauge to the right side of the X axis. Adjust the print bed until the dial reads the same value as step 2.

6. Move the Y axis to the home position. Adjust the print bed until the dial reads the same value as step 2.

7. Repeat steps 2–6 until all four positions read the same.

Use the same dial gauge mount that we used to measure the Z axis. Mount the gauge and clip it onto the X axis. Be careful as you adjust the print bed. Depending on the materials used, you may be able to flex the bed slightly by pressing down on the print bed. Similarly, be careful not to press on or bump the dial gauge or X axis during the procedure. Figures 5-23 through 5-26 illustrate the leveling process with relative X- and Y-axes positions. Notice that some positions are a little off. I adjusted these points so that the dial reads zero.

Figure 5-23 shows the dial gauge at the minimum position for the X and Y axes.

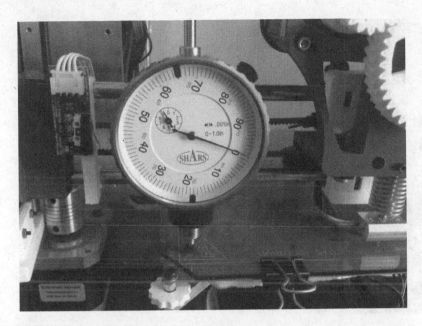

Figure 5-23. *Measuring point one (X:MIN, Y:MIN)*

Figure 5-24 shows the dial gauge at the minimum position for the X axis and the maximum position for the Y axis.

Figure 5-24. *Measuring point two (X:MIN, Y:MAX)*

Figure 5-25 shows the dial gauge at the maximum position for the X and Y axes.

Figure 5-25. *Measuring point three (X:MAX, Y:MAX)*

Figure 5-26 shows the dial gauge at the maximum position for the X axis and the minimum position for the Y axis.

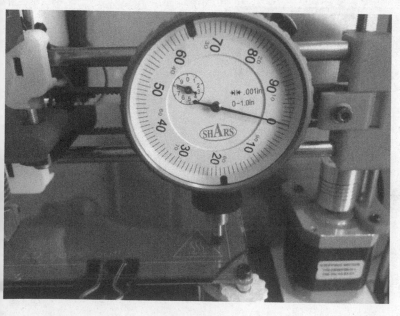

Figure 5-26. *Measuring point four (X:MAX, Y:MIN)*

You should go through the procedure at least twice to ensure your print bed is the same height at all four corners. It is OK if the measurement is off by a very small amount, but this should not exceed 50 microns. Any more than that and it could affect adhesion at the corners of the print bed. However, you may find your printer can tolerate slightly higher deviations.

OK, you are almost done! One final check needs to be made: you should double-check your frame to ensure that it is rigid and not easily flexed. I describe some things to look for in the next section.

Frame and Chassis

You may not think the chassis as something you should consider calibrating. However, if you have built a RepRap printer, especially one with many frame components, you would do well to ensure that the chassis is stable. More specifically, the frame is not loose, does not shake or oscillate, and all axes mechanisms are securely fastened and properly adjusted (e.g., belt tension).

Take a few moments to check the tightness of all bolts and the tension of your belts. Tighten and adjust as needed. Next, check the frame to see if it flexes. Some flex is normal, especially if the metal bits are joined by plastic parts, but you should not be able to see any movement of the frame.

PRUSA I3 SINGLE-SHEET FRAME RIGIDITY

One of the things that attracted me to the new (at the time) Prusa i3 design was the openness of the new frame. I liked the idea of having a print bed unencumbered by frame components. Many times I would find myself shifting my arms to get access to the print bed and other components in the older Prusa designs. So I was eager to build my first Prusa i3.

However, after having built an aluminum single-sheet frame, I discovered what I consider a minor flaw regarding a popular accessory. If you mount a spool holder on top of the frame, the added weight can induce a very small amount of flex during rapid movement, no matter how tight you manage to tighten the threaded rods for the Y axis. What this means is as your Z axis raises, rapid movements of the X axis can induce a very small amount of flex or wobble in the aluminum frame. This manifests as a slight back and forward movement that induces a slight, inconsistent wave in the objects.

To combat this problem, you can add additional braces on the backside of the frame. There are several examples, but the one I've found that cures the problem is the Prusa i3 Aluminum Frame Brace by iPrintIn3D on Thingiverse (thingiverse.com/thing:251890).

If you are considering building a Prusa i3, you may want to rethink the aluminum single-sheet version and consider a hybrid frame like the one from SeeMeCNC (http://seemecnc.com/collections/parts-accesories/products/prusa-i3-lasercut-melamine-frame).

This frame does not suffer from the same flex problem of the single sheet aluminum frame and allows you to use the single-sheet plastic components. In fact, I have considered swapping out my frame for one from SeeMeCNC. It will allow me to solve the Z-axis wobble and reduce the number of frame components at the same time.

Summary

As you can see, calibrating your printer involves not only making sure the axes move the correct distance, but also that the stepper motor drivers are set properly, the endstops are configured correctly, and even that the frame and extruder do their jobs correctly. I covered all of these topics and provided instructions on calibrating each.

If you've reached this point and have done all of the calibration steps outlined in this chapter, congratulations! Now that your printer is calibrated, it is time to print your first object!

Aha, gotcha there, eh? You thought all of your wrenching and monkeying around with Marlin was over. Well, it sort of is. But we really need to check how the printer performs when printing objects. That is, if asked to print a 15mm cube, is the resulting object exactly 15mm in size on each axis?

In the next chapter, I will discuss printing test objects to verify your calibration, as well as ideas on what to print and where to find print files.

PART 2

■ ■ ■

Troubleshooting

This section provides a look into the sometimes baffling world of troubleshooting 3D printers and print quality. You will discover techniques for the successful analysis and diagnosis of problems in both hardware and software that lead to print quality issues. Many problems and solutions are presented and discussed to help you recognize common ailments and correct them quickly. Also included are many tips on getting the most out of your hardware.

CHAPTER 6

■ ■ ■

Printing for the First Time

At this point, you either have a new 3D printer[1] or you have just finished calibrating the hardware of the printer you've built yourself. Either way, you are now looking at the exciting possibilities of printing your first object. To get the most out of your printer and indeed your first printing experience, you need to take some time to prepare your printer. Yes, there are still more things you need to work on—even for a printer right out of the box. While this sounds like more tedious procedures and fiddling, that isn't the case.

This chapter begins with the steps you need to take to ensure that your printing surface is prepared properly. This is an essential step to ensure that you eliminate yet another source of problems that can masquerade as other problems. A properly prepared print surface can help you avoid contributing to one of the worst and most frequent printing problems—lifting.

The chapter also presents tips on preparing your slicer and printing your first object. In this case, I discuss starting out with simple calibration objects that can help you fine-tune your printer. You will see how to use simple geometric shapes (e.g., cubes) to ensure that your printer is calibrated correctly. Let's get started!

Preparing the Printer for Printing

There are certain things you need to do before you print. Whether it is the first time you've printed with a new printer or the hundredth object on a well-maintained printer, there are certain steps you need to do before you power on the printer.

This is one area that most 3D printing books skim over or mention in a few sentences. However, taking time to get your printer prepared will save you from a host of printing problems. There are three preparation tasks you should perform prior to printing: you should ensure that your print surface is prepared and the preparation matches the filament type you want to use, you must set your Z-height, and you must ensure that your slicer settings match your filament requirements for temperature and diameter.

I present each of these in more detail in the following sections. Once you have taken the time to execute these steps, you will be ready to print.

Preparing Your Print Surface

There are several types of print surfaces. The filament type dictates which of these you can use. For example, recall from Chapter 1 that the best surface for PLA is blue painter's tape, and the best surface for ABS is Kapton tape. These are surface treatments that work best for PLA and ABS filament. I will discuss one alternative for ABS that is used to combat lifting.[2]

---

[1]Or new to you.
[2]It is as close to a magic cure as you're likely to get for ABS lifting.

207

There are some additional considerations if you have a printer that permits you to choose the print surface itself. For example, aluminum is better for using blue painter's tape, and glass is a good choice for Kapton tape. However, glass works well for both.

The following sections present various surface treatments. I include notes about the surface so that you can consider which is best for your needs.

■ **Tip** I like to have a different print surface for each surface treatment. For example, I have one for blue painter's tape, another for Kapton tape, and a third for Kapton tape plus ABS juice (see the following sections).

Prerequisites

To get the most out of your surface treatment, you should ensure that the surface is clean and free from any dirt, smudges, and oils from your hands, and that it is dry. If your print surface is glass or aluminum, clean the surface with acetone followed by 90% or better isopropanol, which cleans the surface well— without leaving any residue like soap and other cleaners. You may also use window cleaner, but make sure that it is safe to use on your print surface first. If you use a water-based solution, make sure that it is completely dry before printing.

If you are replacing the surface treatment, make sure that you remove all of the old treatment first. Using several layers of surface treatment—more specifically blue painter's or Kapton tape—is not recommended. Figure 6-1 shows what can happen if you use blue painter's tape on top of Kapton tape. While it saved me from having to remove the Kapton tape first, it created a lifting problem because blue painter's tape does not adhere well to Kapton tape. The same is true for multiple layers of the same type of tape.

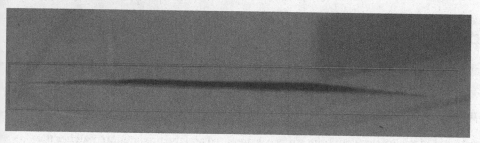

Figure 6-1. *Multiple layers of surface treatment*

Blue Painter's Tape

If you visit your local hardware or home improvement store, or even a specialty paint store, you will find a number of tape products that are specifically designed to be used to mask out areas for painting (also called *masking tape*). The best tapes for painting are those that prevent paint from bleeding along the edge, which helps painters create precise lines when painting with multiple colors or around trim, electrical components, and just about anything they don't want painted.

There are several types of painting masking tape. Some are nothing more than common masking tape (tan or brown in color), others are blue, while others are a combination of tape and plastic sheeting.[3] While some are certainly

---

[3]Never, ever attempt to use painter's tape that is made of plastic of any variety. It will not survive application on a heated print bed and may make a mess of your prints because it may stick to your objects.

better than others, they all have one attribute that is a must for painters: they can be removed easily without peeling away the paint or wallpaper to which they were adhered. The type of tape we will use is called *blue painter's tape*. We call it that because, well, it's blue and it is used for painting.

GOT THE BLUES?

There are some new vendors making painter's tape, and some of these are not—gasp!—blue! Indeed, I have found green and yellow painter's tape—called FrogTape. The green is equivalent to typical blue painter's tape. The yellow is a low adhesion version for sensitive surfaces. Some people have reported mixed results with the green tape. I have found it works OK with a heated print bed, but it is not as good as blue painter's tape without a heated print bed because parts do not stick to it as well. However, the yellow is not as good for 3D printing because it can become loose and pull off with the part.

Blue painter's tape is a very good surface material for print beds. It works well for PLA and can work fine for ABS if a heated printed bed is used (but not as good as Kapton tape for ABS). The tape comes in a variety of widths and can be applied to glass or aluminum easily, and can be removed and replaced quickly without special applicators or tools.

■ **Note**   Objects printed on blue painter's tape will have a matte finish for the bottom and will show the stippling of the tape.

Parts can be removed easily once they have cooled, and the tape can be reused a number of times. Due to its lower cost, removing parts is not a stressful affair, even if you tear the tape. You can just cut away one strip or a part of a strip and replace that portion.

■ **Tip**   Objects can be removed from blue painter's tape more easily once they have cooled.

But not all blue painter's tapes are created equal. I recommend avoiding the really inexpensive, little-known manufacturers. Some of these may be just fine, but if they do not adhere well to the print surface, it can make a lifting problem worse. Similarly, if they adhere too well, they may not be easily removed from the print surface, making it harder to replace the tape.

HOW WIDE IS WIDE ENOUGH?

In general, it is best to get the widest tape you can find. However, be sure to do some comparative shopping. For example, I once found some four-inch-wide blue painter's tape, but it was priced nearly four times the cost of the two-inch tape and was only 75% as long as the two-inch rolls. In this case, wider is not cheaper. Also, really wide tape can be harder to apply if your print bed surface is not removable, especially if there are frames or electronics that prevent you from accessing the print surface easily. Thus, I use 2-inch-wide tape and make several passes to cover the entire surface. This, for me, is the most economical choice.

Another consideration is whether the tape has the manufacturer's logo imprinted on the tape surface. You should avoid using these tapes if you plan to print with light-colored filament. This is because the logo can transfer to the filament. For example, I used a major manufacturer's "best" blue painter's tape for printing white PLA. When I removed my objects from the printer, I discovered the logo was prominently displayed on each of my objects. If you use dark colored filament, you may not notice, but I would still avoid tape that has logos imprinted on the surface.

You will have to do your own cost analysis based on the cost of the tape in your area, but generally, you should look for a balance of cost, width, and adhesive qualities. For example, I use two-inch-wide tape that features a nonbleed edge and does not have any logos. It costs a bit more, but makes for a good bond to glass and has a much better durability than cheaper brands.

Applying blue painter's tape to your print surface is really easy. You simply cut a length of tape a bit longer than your print surface and apply the tape to the surface one row at a time until the surface is completely covered. Don't worry about overhang—you can cut that away with scissors or a hobby knife after the surface is covered. I like to leave a bit of an overhang so that I can more easily remove the tape. But don't leave so much as to affect movement of the printer axes. That is, blue painter's tape overhang can curl on heated print beds. If you leave so much that it curls and strikes the hot end, it could stick and peel away the tape—or even obstruct the nozzle, causing extrusion failures.

The hardest part of applying the tape is getting the seams even and as close as possible. Fortunately, the tape can be removed easily, so if you need to adjust it, you can. I like to start by holding the length of tape just beyond the print surface or at least near the edge. Position one side of the tape so that there is no gap, and then slowly lower the other side, keeping the tape straight and tight against the edge of the previous strip. Again, this is easier to describe than do, but once you've practiced it a couple of times, you'll get the hang of it.

Once I have the tape applied, I trim the edges and use a flat edge to press down across the seams. This allows you to firmly adhere the tape to the print surface, even if there is a small bit of overlap.

Figures 6-2 through 6-6 present the process for applying blue painter's tape. I used a special milled aluminum print surface for a MakerBot Replicator 2. The procedure is the same for glass, nylon, and similar materials. The only possible deviation would be if your print surface is soft (like Plexiglas). In that case, you may not want to use a hobby knife to trim the edges. That is, if you slip and cut the blue tape, you may also mar the print surface.

Figure 6-2. *Applying the tape in rows*

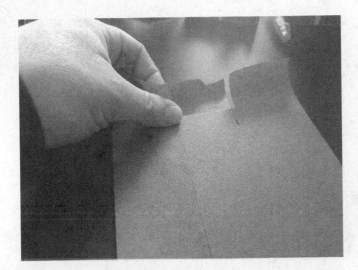

Figure 6-3. *Align one side first*

Figure 6-4. *Align the other side*

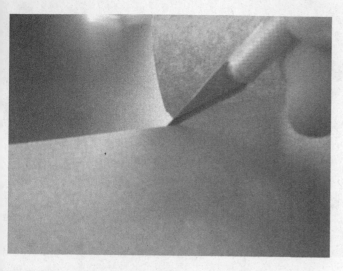

Figure 6-5. *Cut away the excess tape*

Figure 6-6. *Smooth over the gaps*

Notice in Figure 6-3 that I pulled the tape taught and aligned the outer edges. This helps avoid creating wrinkles and ensures that the seam is even across the surface. Notice that I also left a little overhang.

In Figure 6-5, I apply the finishing touches of trimming the excess and smoothing the seams. If your tape overlaps, you may see the effect on the bottom of your prints.

■ **Caution**   Try to avoid overlapping the tape. The thickness of the tape may be enough to cause the nozzle to strike the tape on the first layer, which can lead to problems such as lifting, or at the very least a crease on the underside of your object. Similarly, avoid gaps between the strips of tape. Gaps will cause creases on the bottom of your prints, but can also lead to lifting if the filament does not stick to the build surface.

Printing with blue painter's tape requires no special settings on your printer. So long as the Z-height is set correctly (the width of a standard weight sheet of paper), filament should stick to the tape easily. Blue painter's tape is great for printing with PLA and can also be used for printing ABS if there is a heated bed (but this may be harder to control lifting). Using blue painter's tape with PLA and a heated bed works equally well, however, it has known to reduce the effectiveness of the adhesive, so you may have to change the tape more often when using with a heated print bed.

■ **Tip** Using blue painter's tape with ABS requires a very precise Z-height setting. I have found I need to set the Z-height lower when using ABS on blue painter's tape than Kapton tape. ABS doesn't stick as well to blue painter's tape as it does to Kapton tape.[4]

You should change the tape when you see distortions on the surface. After several prints (perhaps as few as five), you may also start to notice a change in the color of the tape. Some discoloration is fine, so long as the tape is still attached to the print bed. We are most concerned about any damage from removing parts or distortion of the tape surface, which can happen over many prints.

This is especially so if your slicing software positions the objects in the center by default. In this case, the center of the tape will wear out sooner. On the other hand, even if there is no distortion, if your prints start losing first-layer adhesion—or worse, you start experiencing lifting at the edges and corners, you should replace the tape.

If you used two-inch-wide tape like I do, you may be able to replace only a strip or two of the tape. That is, if you've only printed in the center and the size of the objects printed do not extend past the center two strips, just replace those. You do not need to completely strip the surface every time. This is also another good reason to choose tape that isn't as wide as your print surface—you can replace only those areas that are worn.

Kapton Tape

Have you ever seen the inside of a modern laptop, tablet, or smartphone?[5] Did you notice some transparent yellow tape in there? Most likely you were seeing Kapton tape. Kapton is a brand-name tape made by DuPont. Kapton tape is a polyimide film with an adhesive on one side. It is highly heat resistant across a range of temperatures from –269ºC to +400ºC (degrees Celsius). In the 3D printing world (and likely others), the name Kapton has become synonymous with the product (like Xerox). Indeed, you may find several vendors who sell polyimide film, but do not call it Kapton tape (for obvious trademark/product restrictions).

Kapton tape is best used for printing ABS. It may also work for other higher-temperature filaments. Kapton tape is more difficult to apply because the adhesive is designed to stick really well. In fact, the adhesive is stronger than the film itself. Thus, if you apply Kapton tape to a dry aluminum or glass print surface, you may not be able to remove it without tearing the film. Figure 6-7 shows a typical roll of Kapton tape.

---

[4] This is one of those YMMV situations. It is harder to control lifting and adhesion problems, and for that reason alone I'd recommend waiting to use blue painter's tape with ABS until you've had some experience controlling lifting and similar adhesion problems.

[5] Every Apple device I've seen has several pieces inside.

Figure 6-7. Kapton tape roll

■ **Note**   Objects printed on Kapton tape will have a smooth finish on the bottom. Some don't like this because it is different from the other sides of the object.

Removing parts from Kapton tape can be a bit of a challenge. For the best results, you should wait until the parts cool completely before attempting to remove them. They remove more easily when cool. There are a number of techniques for removing parts from Kapton tape. Some are to use a sharp knife, or a craft blade, or a putty knife to pry the parts off. Any of these will work, but you risk damaging the Kapton tape. Given that Kapton tape is relatively expensive and harder to apply, you may want to use these tools as a last resort.

The technique I use for small objects is an adjustable wrench tightened around the object perpendicular to the print bed. I apply a slight force to the wrench to twist the object—just enough to flex it—and the object usually pops off, or that side pops loose enough for me to use a dull plastic blade to pop the object off the print surface.

■ **Caution**   Do not attempt the following without wearing thick gloves and eye protection. If you get this wrong, you can break your glass print bed!

Another technique that works for objects that are really stuck to Kapton tape on normal glass is to remove the glass print surface and place it on a towel on a workbench or a desk. Move the print surface so that half is on the desk and half is not. Press down very softly, gradually increasing pressure until you hear a pop. Do not use quick, energetic pressure—this can break your glass print bed! Repeat this for each edge or until enough of the part is free for you to pry it off.

Like blue painter's tape, you will find Kapton tape in a variety of widths. However, unlike blue painter's tape, I prefer the wider widths because it is harder to get pieces to align well enough to avoid gaps or overlap. Once again, you have to do some comparative shopping, as the wider widths can be a bit more expensive than the narrower widths. I use 200mm width rolls and make two passes (two strips) when applying the tape. This leaves only a single seam down the center of the print surface.

Applying Kapton tape requires some practice and a fair amount of patience. I have found a technique that works well for most print surfaces. It works best for glass and aluminum. I would not recommend using it on porous print surfaces or in situations where you cannot remove the print surface (like the MakerBot Replicator 1). See the sidebar for special instructions on the Replicator 1. The technique I use is as follows. Figure 6-8 through Figure 6-13 show the process in action.

Figure 6-8. *Getting ready*

Figure 6-9. *Applying the water mixture*

Figure 6-10. *Apply one strip at a time*

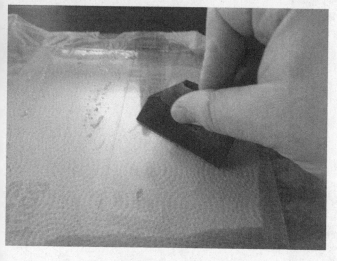

Figure 6-11. *Apply remaining strips until surface is covered*

Figure 6-12. *Go over the seam(s)*

Figure 6-13. *All done!*

1. Remove the print surface and place it on a flat, water-resistant surface. I like to put a couple of paper towels down first to absorb extra liquid.

2. Use a mixture of 1 drop of baby shampoo to 4 ounces of distilled water.

3. Spray a liberal amount of the water on the print surface. Use a spritzing sprayer to distribute the water as evenly as you can.

4. Cut a long strip of Kapton tape that is at least 2 inches longer than needed.

5. Spray a small amount of the water on your fingers and carefully grip the tape on each end.

6. Hold the tape over the print surface and allow it to droop, forming a "U" shape.

7. Slowly and evenly (without pulling), lower your hands so that the tape spreads out evenly.

8. If the tape isn't applying evenly, remove it and try again. The water solution will make the tape much easier to remove. Spray more water if the tape is sticking to the glass.

9. Using a rubber or similar soft-edge squeegee, start in the center of the tape and press lightly and outward to one edge to squeeze out the water. Repeat for the other direction. If there are large bubbles or wrinkles, carefully lift the tape back to the point where the anomaly begins and reapply by pulling (but not stretching) to remove the crease.

10. Continue to squeeze out all of the water you can. It is OK if you cannot get all of the bubbles out. Small bubbles (say, about 4mm–5mm in diameter) are fine and will disappear as the water dries.

11. Repeat the process for the next strip, carefully aligning the tape next to the applied strip. You will find the water makes it easier to remove and even move the tape so that it joins the first strip.

12. Use the squeegee to remove as much water as possible. Go over the seams again with the squeegee to remove water trapped near the edge.

13. Use a hobby knife to cut off all the excess Kapton tape.

14. Dry the print surface with paper towels, place the print surface in sunlight, and allow it to dry. Any small bubbles will disappear in a few hours or, at most, overnight.

■ **Tip** It is fine to spray a lot of water on the surface. The water keeps the tape from sticking to the glass.

Starting in the center, use smooth even strokes to press the water out to the edges.

Try to get the strips as close together as possible. Overlap should be avoided. If you do leave a small gap, make sure that it is no more than a few tenths of a millimeter at most. Any more than that and you will get a ridge on any objects that cross the gap.

USING THE APPLICATION TECHNIQUE ON THE REPLICATOR 1

You can use the preceding technique on the MakerBot Replicator 1, but it requires more work and a fair amount of caution. You must first remove the print bed from the printer. This requires disconnecting the heated print bed (the connector is located in the center of the back of the print bed) and removing the four bed leveling thumbscrews. Once removed, you can lift the print bed off of the arms and out of the printer.

Carefully cover the heated bed connector with electrical tape or similar water-repellent tape. With the electrical connector covered, you can use the preceding technique to apply the tape. Try to use as little water mixture as you can to avoid filling the screw heads with water. Allow the print bed to dry overnight and inspect it for any traces of water. Never use the print bed if there is any moisture anywhere.

Clearly, this is a deviant procedure that solves the problematic dry application of Kapton tape for Replicator 1 machines, but it takes much more time since you must allow the bed to dry before using it and you must relevel the print bed when you reinstall it.

This is one reason why some owners have replaced their heated print bed with a removable version. If you own a Replicator 1, you may want to watch the online auction sites for an old heated print bed. Having two will allow you to keep a dry, prepared surface in reserve.

Printing with Kapton tape requires a very precise Z-height—more so than blue painter's tape. You should check your Z-height for the first few prints on newly applied Kapton tape (if not at least once per day of use).

While ABS sticks very well to Kapton tape, it is not a cure for lifting. Some people have switched from blue painter's tape to Kapton tape in order to solve lifting problems, only to discover it made it worse. This is most likely because the print surface wasn't the problem. For example, if ABS is subjected to cooling air currents, the higher layers can shrink faster than the lower layers (which are heated by the print bed), forcing the lower layers to bend and curl—hence, lifting.[6]

■ **Note** Delamination of layers can occur not only from cooling too fast but also when printing on a layer that has cooled. In this case, the temperature of the two layers is too low for a sufficient bond.

To get the most out of printing ABS on Kapton tape, you should use a heated print bed set to a range of 90ºC to 110ºC. The proper temperature may take some experimentation to get right and can vary based on the filament used. I have some lighter-color filament that requires lower heat on the print bed. The best thing to do is start at 100ºC and watch how well the first layer adheres. If there is some lifting on smaller-diameter parts or the edges, increase the heated print bed by 5 degrees and run another print. This isn't a terribly scientific process. I tend to use 100ºC to 110ºC when I print with ABS on Kapton tape, using the lower range for large objects and the higher for smaller objects or objects with thin protrusions. You can set these values in your slicer program.

Replacing Kapton tape is required less frequently than blue painter's tape. It is more likely you will damage the tape when removing objects before the adhesion properties degrade. Even then, you can revive Kapton tape by using a small amount of acetone and a lint-free cloth to remove any ABS from the surface. I have had Kapton print surfaces last for more than 40 hours of printing. In fact, I have yet to wear the tape out without first damaging it.

ABS Juice

If you are printing with ABS and want to improve your first-layer adhesion, or you don't want to use Kapton tape (or you ran out), there is a surface treatment called *ABS juice*.[7] You can apply it to glass or on top of Kapton tape.

Simply dissolve about 10mm–20mm of thin ABS scrap from discarded skirts, brims, rafts, and so forth (filament can take a long time to dissolve) per 10ml of acetone in a glass jar with a lid. To apply, spread the solution evenly on a glass surface, allow it to dry (it only takes a few minutes), set your Z-height, and start printing. This technique will significantly reduce lifting problems with ABS on Kapton tape and is a great alternative to building a full enclosure to reduce drafts.

The proper mixture of ABS juice should be watery and free of clumps (the ABS is fully dissolved). Application can be made with a cotton tip, a cloth, or a paintbrush. You should apply the juice in a thin layer. It is OK if there are streaks of juice because this will not affect adhesion, and some users have actually reported that it helps adhesion. I've found it helps with the removal of parts. The proper application should make the glass opaque and it should have a slight tinge of the color of filament used. For example, you should see a very faint blue glaze when using blue filament juice. Figure 6-14 shows a print surface treated with ABS juice.

---

[6]It can also cause larger objects to develop cracks where layers separate during cooling.

[7]Not to be confused with ABS slurry, which is a thicker concoction used to glue parts together.

Figure 6-14. *ABS juice applied*

■ **Tip** For better flow, you can apply the ABS juice to a heated surface of around 50ºC.

When you mix your juice, you should use the same color filament that you use to print. This is because each time you remove an object from the print surface, the layer of juice normally comes off because it is stuck (bonded) to the first layer of your print. Thus, if you want to print a blue object, you should use blue juice. This is one reason some do not like to use juice—you have to remix it whenever you change filament. This is a drawback, but if you are like me, you tend to keep the same color of filament in the printer for several prints, so it isn't that much of a burden. Figure 6-15 shows what happens when you remove parts from a juice-treated print surface.

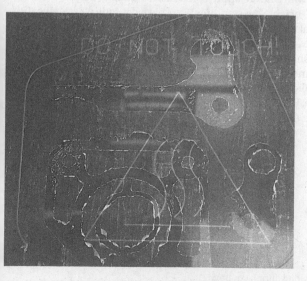

Figure 6-15. *Parts removed from juice-treated surface*

■ **Tip** An alternative to the acetone-based solution is methyl methacrylate-acrylonitrile butadiene styrene (MABS), which is a hybrid of ABS and acrylic. It produces a milky-white ABS juice that dries clear, allowing it to be used for any color of ABS. However, MABS may not be as easily obtained as acetone.

Notice that the juice has pulled completely away with the parts.[8] The really great thing about ABS juice—aside from the fact that it helps to reduce (or in my case, completely eliminate) lifting—is that you can simply reapply more juice over the print surface where you removed the parts, and keep on using the surface. There is no need to completely remove and resurface!

If you ever wanted to remove the juice from a glass print surface, a simple razor tool can be used to scrape off the juice. If you have painted windows in your home, you already know what to do! You can also use a rag and acetone to wipe away the juice. This works best when the juice is thin. If you decide to use a thicker layer, it may require more elbow action to remove the juice with acetone alone (but it can be done).

When mixing and storing the juice, be sure to use a jar that has a seal that can withstand acetone vapor. I use jars with a spring-loaded lid and a rubber gasket. Acetone vapor will damage and in some cases destroy synthetic gaskets. Figure 6-16 shows a glass jar I used for one batch of juice. The jar has a nice screw on the lid, and a sturdy gasket. What you see in the photo is the result of leaving that jar on a shelf for a week. At the start of the week, the jar was about half full. By the end of the week, there was only a small puddle of juice at the bottom, and worse, a dissolved gasket. Sadly, I had to discard the entire jar.

Figure 6-16. *Good juice gone bad*

Another option is to use an empty nail polish bottle. It can withstand the acetone and even has a small brush inside. Clearly, if you want to store juice, make sure your container can withstand the corrosive effects of acetone. On the other hand, if you only plan to use a little juice, you can either allow the acetone to evaporate (leaving a layer of ABS in the bottom that can be reused) or rinse out the jar with more acetone when you are done.

---

[8]Can you tell what I printed? Hint: it is for a MakerBot Replicator 2.

If you use a paintbrush to apply the juice, make sure to use one made from animal hair. If it dissolves or the bristles stick together,[9] it isn't made with hair! I use a paintbrush that is cut straight across the edge (in other words, not round or angled) and is ½-inch wide. When I apply the juice, I make sure to use long, even strokes in the same direction. This helps form a smooth layer with just enough ridges to make removing the parts easy.

■ **Caution**   When using a paintbrush that has lacquer or a similar coating on the handle, be sure to avoid getting any juice on the brush handle. The acetone can make the surface tacky. It can also dissolve paint. The best brushes to use are those made with bare wood handles and animal hair bristles.

The problem with using a paintbrush—beyond the construction of the brush—is cleaning it between uses. I use two jars for acetone. One contains my ABS juice mixture and another is pure acetone. I use the second jar to clean my brush after every use. I simply swish it around a few times, and then dry the bristles with a paper towel and allow it to dry. This method will work well if your juice is thin. If you make it too thick, it may be difficult to clean the brush properly.

Some people prefer to use cotton swabs or cotton tips rather than paintbrushes. Whatever works best for you is fine. The point is to get the juice on the glass as evenly as you can. Again, streaks are OK provided they are not wider than a millimeter or so.

There is one other thing I'd like to mention about ABS juice. Recall that you apply it directly to a glass surface. You can use it on other surfaces, but it isn't nearly as good, and in some cases it can make the surface unusable. For example, I would not apply juice directly to a heated bed (some printers have no glass covering over the heater) because it can damage the circuit board. I would also not use it on an aluminum surface, but some people have reported success with this.

Applying the ABS juice over Kapton tape may sound wasteful or perhaps eccentric, but it is neither. It is a matter of convenience. Not only does it mean I can remove the juice completely by removing the Kapton tape, it also means I can use the juice sparingly using thinner layers. Not only that, but if I accidentally tear the Kapton tape, I can fill in that tear (if it is small) with a bit more juice. So in a way, it means I can repair torn Kapton with ABS juice.

I have also experimented with applying the juice only near the edges of the object. What I do is let the printer lay down the outer border of the object. The outer border is set up in the slicer and is used to clear the nozzle of filament before starting the print. It is a great way to demarcate where the objects are on the print surface. You can see an example of this in Figure 6-15. Once the printer is stopped, I move the axes away and apply juice (about 10mm wide) around the inner perimeter. This saves a little juice while reducing lift.

Whether you use ABS juice directly on Kapton tape as is recommended or apply it on top of glass, you will find it a better alternative than using walls or similar barriers to reduce lifting. I will talk more about how to control lifting in Chapter 7.

■ **Caution**   Remember, acetone is corrosive and can be harmful if ingested or inhaled. Use extreme care when handling acetone because it can cause skin irritation.[10] Perhaps worse, acetone is flammable. Never use it near a flame or devices that can spark. Always have a fire extinguisher nearby when working with flammable liquids.

---

[9]Animal hair does not dissolve in acetone.
[10]It will also dry your skin almost instantly. Guess how I know this? Don't go there!

Other Treatments

There are a number of surface treatments that people have used with varying degrees of success. I won't cover them because many are, well, a bit strange. However, there is one that is worth mentioning. Some people have reported using hairspray on glass as an alternative to ABS juice. Others have used hairspray on aluminum with the same effect. If you are like me and are allergic to some hairsprays (and indeed some solvents), make sure you consider the environmental effects before experimenting.

If you are adventurous and decide to experiment with using alternative surface treatments, I recommend waiting to do so until you have first mastered one or more of the traditional surface treatments. It will also help to have your printer sorted out to the point where all of your prints are high-quality with little or no issues. Don't make the mistake of thinking blue painter's tape, Kapton tape, or ABS juice is inadequate or the source of your problems. Many printing enthusiasts use these surface treatments successfully every day. Fix what is broken first before applying any unorthodox techniques.[11]

Now that we have seen the most common print surface treatments, how they are used, and how to apply them, let's discuss setting the Z-height again.

Setting the Z-Height

I mentioned this in the last chapter and indeed several times throughout the previous chapters. I'll repeat it here in more detail to reinforce the concept and to get you used to the idea of making this a prerequisite step to printing. My main motivation stems from my early experiences. I did not check the Z-height often enough and chased lifting and other problems for many weeks before a very kind soul on one of the forums reminded me of this key step.

■ **Note**   I use the term *Z-height*, but others use *nozzle-height* or sometimes *first-layer height*.

You should always check your Z-height before printing for the first time on a given day, or when you have changed the print surface (especially if you switched print surfaces, since the surface can be a different thickness), or whenever you have performed any manual movement of the axes. We do this because any of these things can cause minor changes to the height of the print bed. Interestingly, you may find that the materials used in the frame of your printer can cause minor changes from one day to the next due to atmospheric or environmental effects. I have a printer with a wood surface for the Y axis. The heated bed is mounted on top, with a glass surface clamped to that. Some days I find the Z-height is off by as much as 0.025mm–0.050mm, which is sufficient to introduce first-layer adhesion problems.

There are several procedures that you can use to check and set your Z-height. Which you use depends on which printer you have. If your printer has a built-in bed leveling (tramming) setting, use that. If your printer documentation includes a procedure, you should use that. On the other hand, if there is no procedure in the manual (or you built it yourself) and the printer has a Z-height adjuster, you can use the following procedure.

1. Turn the Z-height adjuster a few turns to lift the nozzle. We do this to avoid crashing the nozzle into the print bed if the Z-height is too low.

2. Home all axes.

3. Tear off (or cut if you're a type-A like me) a piece of standard weight copy or printer paper (about 20lbs. weight) about 2" × 4". You can also use a Post-it note, but make sure to leave the sticky side up. In fact, you can use the sticky strip to hold it. Slide the paper under the nozzle at the home position.

---

[11]OK, so maybe ABS juice on top of Kapton is unorthodox to some, but it does work well for me.

4. Adjust the Z-height until the paper can be removed without binding or tearing. Binding or tearing means the Z-height is too low. To adjust the Z-height, turn the Z-height adjuster about one-eighth of a turn in the proper direction and rehome the Z axis. Repeat this until the paper can be removed with a small amount of friction.

5. Lift the nozzle about 5mm and move the X and Y axes to the center. Repeat step 4.

This procedure works well for me on all of my RepRap printers. My commercial printers have their own procedures that also work well.

If your printer has a fixed Z-axis endstop and you do not yet have or you do not want to add a Z-height adjuster, you can still set the Z-height, but the procedure depends on your print bed. If your print bed has adjusters for leveling (tramming) the print bed, you can use these to set the Z-height. In this case, you must set the Z-height at each of the four corners for a four-point mounted bed. If your bed is mounted with only three points, you should use the front, back center, and left and right edges for measuring points. I also recommend checking it in the center.

If your printer does not have an adjustable print bed, you will have to set the Z-height the hard way by moving the Z-axis endstop. This may require loosening the bracket or clamp and moving the end stop slightly up or down. This is very error-prone and it can take several attempts to get it right. I am sure once you have done it this way a few times, a Z-height adjuster will be on your must-print list.

With our print surface prepared and our Z-height set, we are now ready to print our first object! Let's begin with a look at how the slicer is calibrated for your printing.

Slicer Calibration

The first step in preparing an object for print is to configure your slicing software. Recall from Chapter 1 that the slicer is designed to take an `.stl` file and convert it to a `.gcode` file. As such, the slicer is where you specify the printer hardware, filament characteristics, heater controls, and print quality. In this section, I use the Slic3r application to demonstrate how to calibrate the application for printing on your printer.

■ **Note** Some documents call this step a setup procedure, but most call it calibration.

Fortunately, the nice people who wrote Slic3r have included a setup wizard called the Calibration Assistant. You will find it on the Help menu. Simply click Help, and then Calibration Assistant… to launch the wizard. Figure 6-17 shows the initial dialog. If you haven't set up Slic3r, now is a good time to open it and follow along as I demonstrate how to use the wizard in the following paragraphs.

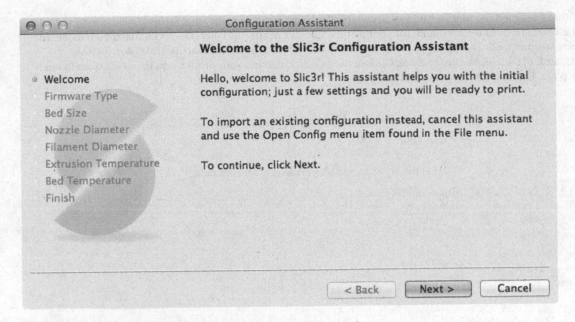

Figure 6-17. *Calibration wizard welcome page*

Notice that there are several steps along the way. You will be asked to enter information about the firmware used in the printer, the size of the print bed, the size of your extruder nozzle, details about the filament used, and temperature settings.

Go ahead and click the Next button to move to the Firmware Type page. Figure 6-18 shows the page with the setting for my Prusa i3 printer.

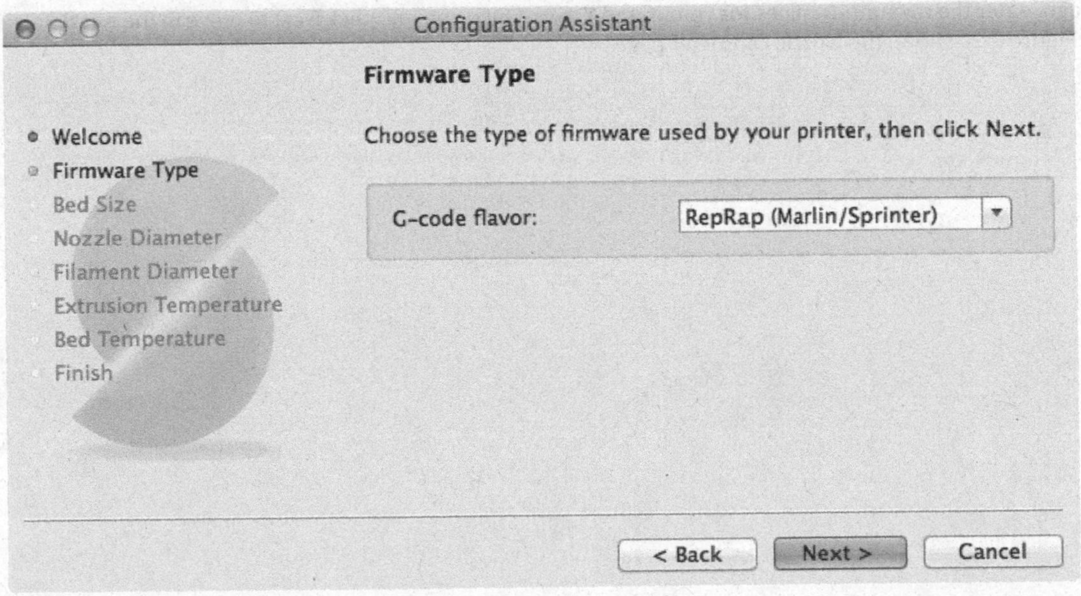

Figure 6-18. *Firmware Type selection page*

Notice that I selected the Marlin/Sprinter firmware. The slicer needs to know what firmware you are using so that it can use the correct machine commands for your printer. In other words, the correct G-codes that match those that your firmware supports. Slic3r has selections for a number of firmware, including Teacup, MakerBot, Sailfish, Mach3/ENC, and, of course, Marlin/Sprinter. Choose the one that matches your printer, and then click Next to open the bed size page. Figure 6-19 shows the bed size page.

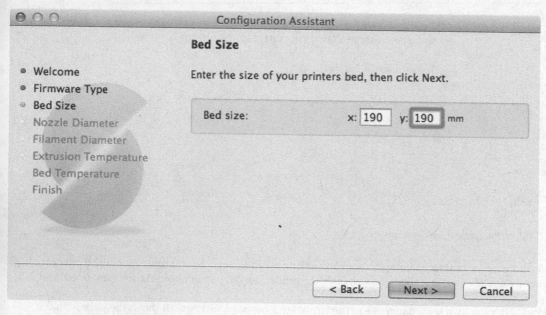

Figure 6-19. Bed Size page

On this page, enter the maximum values for your X and Y axes. Once entered, click Next to move to the nozzle settings page. Figure 6-20 shows the Nozzle Diameter page.

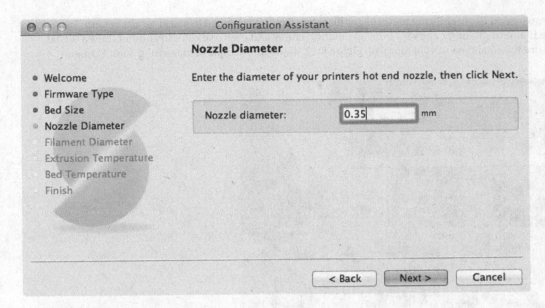

Figure 6-20. Nozzle Diameter page

Refer to the documentation for your printer or your hardware invoices to check the diameter of the nozzle, and then enter it in the dialog. The slicer uses this information for calculating how much filament to extrude to obtain the proper layer thickness, fill values, and so forth. Enter the value and click Next to move to the filament page. Figure 6-21 shows the Filament Diameter page.

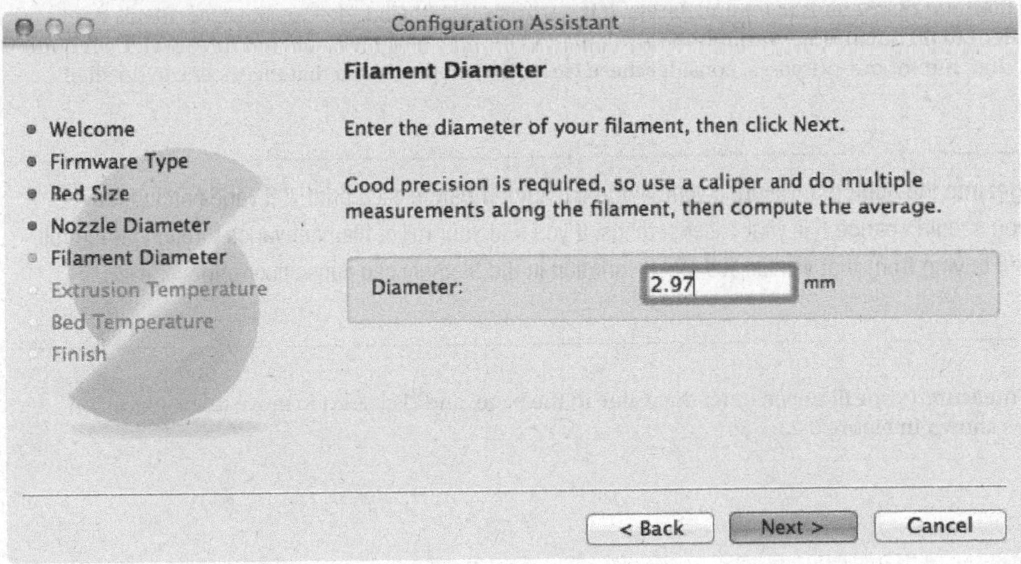

Figure 6-21. Filament Diameter page

On this page, we need to enter the diameter of our filament. Don't be tempted to just enter the generic 3mm or 1.75mm, because filament diameter can vary from one manufacturer and even one color to another. Take a digital caliper and measure the thickness of your filament. Figure 6-22 shows an example of measuring 3mm filament.

Figure 6-22. *Measuring filament diameter*

Notice that the filament diameter is not 3mm. Rather, it is 2.97mm. Like the nozzle size, the slicer needs the diameter of the filament to fill out another variable in its calculation for how much filament to extrude. There is quite a bit more to it than that, but for our purposes, consider these variables you provide so that the slicer can do all of the hard work.

■ **Tip** You should get into the habit of measuring your filament diameter before each print. If it varies more than 0.01mm–0.02mm, you should change it in your slicer settings. If you find your roll of filament varies throughout the roll, you may want to avoid buying from that vendor. Too much variation in the filament can cause poor prints or even extrusion failure.

Once you have measured your filament, enter that value in the page, and click Next to move to the Extrusion Temperature page, as shown in Figure 6-23.

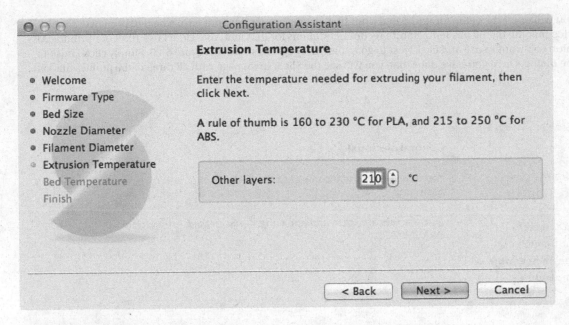

Figure 6-23. *Extrusion Temperature page*

This page is where you enter the temperature value for your hot end that matches the type of filament you are using. In Figure 6-23, I entered 210ºC for ABS filament. You can set it higher if you need to, but you should either follow the recommendations in your printer documentation or those by the manufacturer of your filament. Notice that the dialog has temperature recommendations for PLA and ABS. Enter the value and click Next to move to the Bed Temperature page, as shown in Figure 6-24.

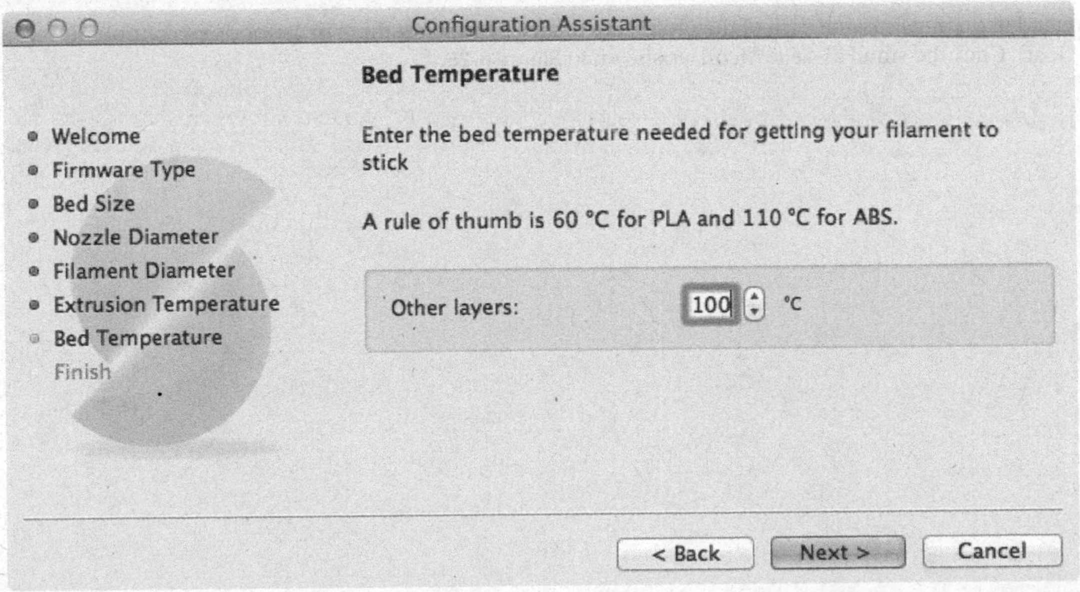

Figure 6-24. *Bed Temperature page*

Here you will enter the value for the heated print bed. If your printer does not have a heated print bed, simply enter 0. Notice that the dialog has temperature recommendations for PLA and ABS. Here I use 100°C for printing ABS. Enter the value you want to use and click Next to go to the final page, as shown in Figure 6-25. Simply click Finish to complete the dialog. Once you have done that, you will see the Slic3r main page with all three of the profiles marked as modified.

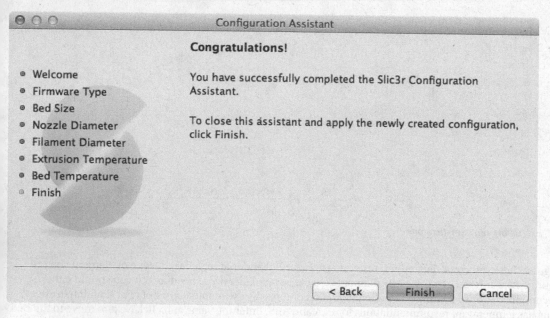

Figure 6-25. *Final page*

What you need to do now is name each of the profiles so that you can select them in your printer control software (like Repetier-Host). Click the small diskette[12] icon, as shown in Figure 6-26.

---

[12]Diskette? What's a diskette? Wonderfully antiquated, isn't it?

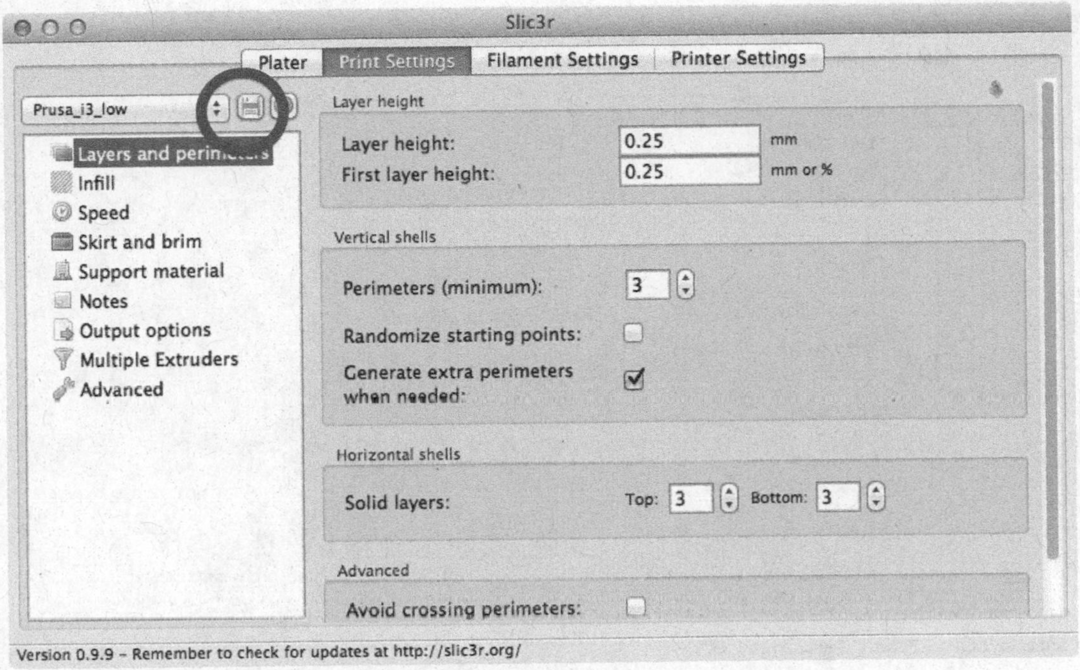

Figure 6-26. *Saving the Print Settings profile*

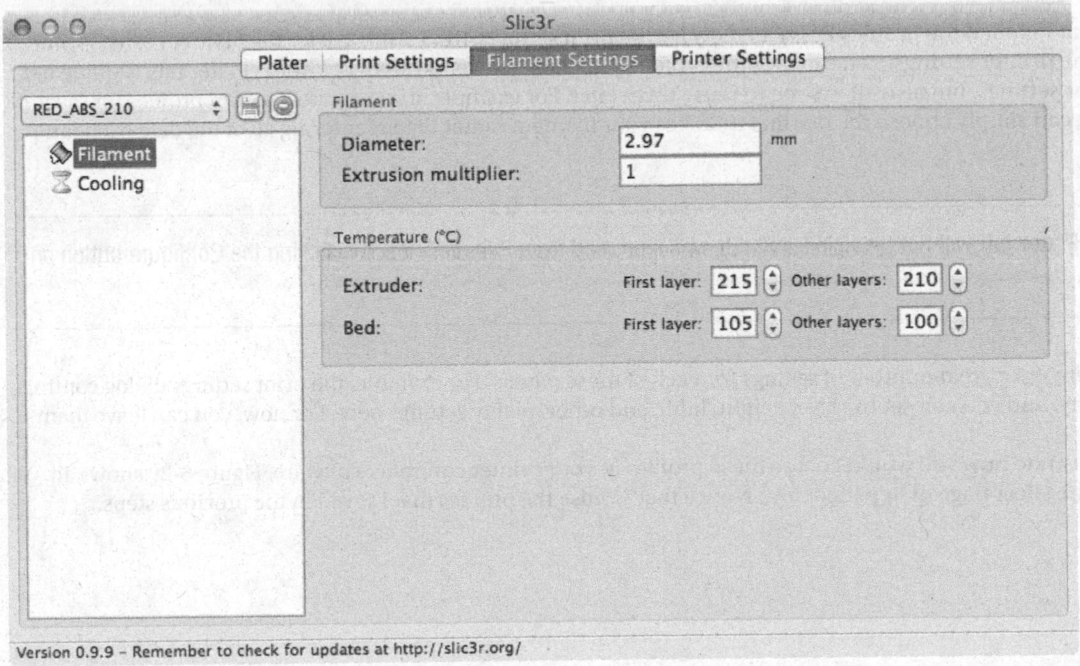

Figure 6-27. *Saving the Filament Settings profile*

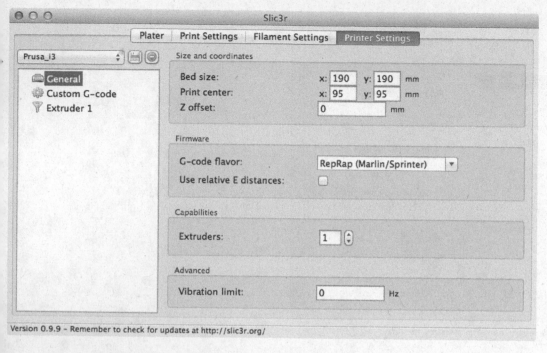

Figure 6-28. *Saving the Printer Settings profile*

Notice that I named the profiles Prusa_i3_Low for the print settings, RED_ABS_210 for the filament settings, and Prusa_i3 for the printer settings. You can save the profile by clicking the disk symbol below the Plater tab. Naming not only saves your settings, but also allows you to reuse them later. For example, if you create filament profiles for several filaments, you can simply choose the one that matches your filament rather than reentering all of the data each time you print.

■ **Note**   The Plater tab will not be visible if Slic3r was launched from Repetier-Host by clicking the Configure button on the slicer page.

Recall there are a great number of settings for each of these panels. For example, the print settings dialog controls the print quality, and you can set the layer height, infill, and other quality settings here. For now, you can leave them as the default.

To demonstrate how you would choose these profiles in your printer controller software, Figure 6-29 shows an excerpt from the slicer page of Repetier-Host. Notice that I chose the profiles that I saved in the previous steps.

Figure 6-29. Choosing Slic3r profiles in Repetier-Host

Now that you have your slicer application configured and the profiles saved, let us discuss some considerations for printing your first object.

Printing Your First Object

Now that you have your print surface prepared, your Z-height set correctly, and your slicing options set, you're ready to print! This section will present an overview of how to print objects with your 3D printer.

While it is possible that you can start printing whatever you want at this stage, you should consider one more calibration step—printing objects to test your calibration settings. I know that seems like a waste of good plastic, but I hope the following sections will reveal how important it is to do this step. Indeed, it will help temper your expectations concerning the print quality capabilities of your printer.

I'll present a brief overview of the printing process, and then discuss printing calibration tests in more detail.

■ **Note** If your printer is of sufficient quality, you may not need to print calibration objects. For example, the MakerBot printers come fully configured and ready to print after a few short setup tasks (including tramming the print bed).

Printing Process

The process to print is as follows. Note that it can vary from one printer to another, because some may not have heated print beds, or may require different software (e.g., MakerBot and MakerWare), or want to print without a computer (via an SD card). However, the following is general enough to represent most printers. I explain the steps in more detail in the next sections.

1. Power on the printer.

2. Check and set the Z-height.

3. Load the filament.

4. Launch your printer controller software.

5. Home all axes.

6. Choose your slicer settings.

7. Turn on the heaters (extruder, print bed).

8. Load and slice the object.

9. When your heat goals are reached, print the object.

■ **Tip** You can complete some of these steps in parallel. As you become more comfortable with the process, you could perform the slicing of your object, including changing profiles while you wait for the heaters to warm up.

First, you need to load filament in the extruder. If your printer does not have a spool holder, make sure you have unwound a length of filament and that it is laying in such a way that it can be pulled by the extruder without snagging. If you want, you can cut off about two to three loops of filament from the spool and drape it across the back of the printer. The important thing is that the filament should have little or no friction and that the extruder can pull it easily.

Follow the instructions in your printer documentation to prepare the extruder for printing. This will require heating the extruder and advancing the filament until it, well, extrudes. I like to extrude about 30mm to ensure that the filament moves freely through the extruder and hot end.

■ **Tip** A must-have accessory is a spool holder. If your printer doesn't have one, check Thingiverse for the many variants of spool holders. Most are ones you print and assemble, but some are clever uses of common materials like small-diameter PVC pipe and fittings. Choose one that introduces as little friction as possible. You can also use a lazy Susan with the spool on its side.

Next, power on the printer (if you haven't already), check the Z-height, and then home all axes.[13] Then, start Repetier-Host on your computer. Once Repetier-Host is running, connect to your printer and turn on the hot end in the print panel. You may need to enter the temperature setting in the extruder section of the Repetier-Host print panel. Be sure to use the value you specified in the slicer.

While the extruder is heating, go back to the object placement page and click the Add STL File button. Locate your cube (the .stl file), and choose it. You should see the cube in the center of the platform.

Next, click the Slicer page and choose the profiles you created previously. Once set, click the Slice with Slic3r button. Once this is complete, you will see the G-code listing.

You are all set to start printing once the extruder heats up. Click the Temperature Curve button to watch a graph of the extruder.

---

[13]I cannot understate how important these steps are to print quality. Always check your Z-height and home all the axes before doing any other operations on your printer.

Once the heat goal is met, click the Run button on the toolbar. Your printer will start printing the object within a few moments. Depending on the speed of your printer (and the speed settings you set in your slicer), it may take 15 to 20 minutes to print the cube. Allow it to cool for about 5 to 10 minutes before removing it from the print surface.

Calibration Prints

A calibration print is a special object designed to test how well your printer performs on certain tasks. For example, you can print a cube to test the accuracy of your axes movement, print an object with several round holes to check precision, print an object with overhangs to test how well your extruder performs, print a hollow object to check bridging, and much more.

I recommend starting with the cube. It is the best way to see how well you've done in setting up your printer. This can be very rewarding for those who have built their own printers. The cube will allow you to measure how well your axes are moving. That is, if you print a 20mm cube, you would expect to measure the resulting object and see that it is 20mm on each side.

Well, that's the goal. In reality, most printers will be slightly off, but only by a tenth of a millimeter or so. Any more than that and you will have to go back and perform axis calibration. The objects may be slightly off for several reasons. Most notably may be because the filament may have slightly different cooling properties or there may be small imperfections in the layers. Whatever the cause, it is generally acceptable for objects to be a few tenths of a millimeter or so off.

You can find calibration cubes on Thingiverse or you can create your own using OpenSCAD. I will discuss OpenSCAD in more detail in a later chapter; however, creating a simple cube requires only the basics of how to use OpenSCAD. Let's do that now. If you have not installed OpenSCAD, do so now.

Begin by opening OpenSCAD. Notice that it launches with a new window. Type the following in the edit box on the left side of the screen.

```
cube([20,20,20]);
```

This will generate a cube 20mm on each side. The order of the sides are X, Y, and Z. For example, if you wanted a cube that was 10mm wide (X), 20mm deep (Y), and 5mm tall (Z), you would use this command.

```
cube([10,20,5]);
```

Now we need to compile it. You can choose the Design ➤ Compile and Render menu item to compile the code and generate a rendering of the object. You should see the cube appear to the right. That's it! You've just written code to generate a 20mm cube. Cool, eh?

Now we need to generate a .stl file for use in the slicer. Choose the File ➤ Export ➤ Export as STL... menu[14] and give the file a name—like cube_20 or similar. If you want to save the OpenSCAD file, you can do so, but given how simple the code is, you may want to skip saving it. You can always type the code again if you want to make a different cube. OK, we're all set! I will show you how to slice the cube in the next section. But first, I want to present some test cases.

In each test case, I discuss the implications of the results of measuring the cubes. I begin with a look at a 20×20×10mm cube printed on a new MakerBot Replicator 2. Figure 6-30 shows the first test case as a collage of the measurements in the order of X, Y, and Z axes.

---

[14]Older versions had the feature under the Design ➤ Export as STL... menu.

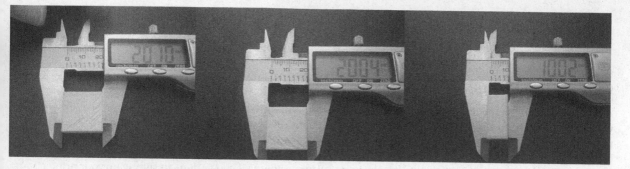

Figure 6-30. *MakerBot Replicator test cube*

Notice here that the size of the cube is very close to what was expected. Specifically, the X axis measured only 0.1mm larger than 20mm. The Y and Z axes measure even closer to the desired size. In my opinion, there is no need to further calibrate this printer because it generates objects that are sized with a low tolerance.

HOW CLOSE IS CLOSE ENOUGH?

Depending on how you will use your printer, the objects you print may not need to be exact. For example, if your objects are used as parts to build another printer, so long as the object prints correctly and tolerances allow for slightly larger outer dimensions, you may not need to adjust your printer calibration settings. So how close is close enough? I think it depends on the printer. For instance, a factor of 0.2mm–0.4mm is acceptable for most entry-level and RepRap printers. For consumer- and professional-grade printers, 0.0mm–0.2mm is acceptable.

The next test case shows a 15×15×15mm cube printed on a Printrbot Simple. Figure 6-31 shows the results. Here we see the measurements are a bit more than expected. For the X and Y axes, the object printed 0.36mm and 0.38mm larger, whereas the Z axis printed only 0.19mm larger.

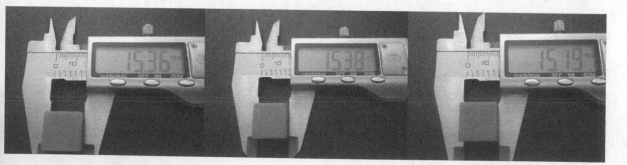

Figure 6-31. *Printrbot Simple test cube*

While this may sound like a very large error factor, if you consider the printer hardware, it really isn't that bad. Overall, the test case result on the Printrbot Simple is reasonable for an entry-level printer. Specifically, the Printrbot Simple uses a friction wheel and fishing line to move the X and Y axes. As a consequence, the mechanism is not as accurate as the MakerBot Replicator. However, if you factor in the cost difference, the slightly large result is still impressive. Conversely, the Z axis uses a threaded rod, which permits a better accuracy. Here we see the accuracy is within 0.20mm (2 tenths of a millimeter, or 200 microns).

The next test case was printed on a poorly calibrated RepRap Prusa i2. It illustrates one of the problems early RepRap builders faced when relying on inaccurate calculations. Figure 6-32 shows a 20×20×20mm test cube.

Figure 6-32. *Uncalibrated RepRap test cube*

At first glance, the X and Y axes appear to be slightly larger, but otherwise are not too bad. However, there is one element to this test case that is unique. If you look closely, you may notice the cube sides are concave. You can see this by looking at the left arm of the X- and Y- inset photos. Notice the slight curve. Figure 6-33 shows the measurement of the cube along the center of the sides.

One thing that tipped me off to something being wrong is the measurement of the Z axis. Here we see that the measurement is significantly less than 20mm. In this case, the error factor is too significant and requires recalibration.

Notice that the figure shows a measurement perpendicular to the axis to be only 0.13mm larger. A closer examination of the cube shows that the edges of the X and Y axes bulge. This is caused by too much filament extrusion. If you look at Figure 6-33 again, you can see the irregular layers.

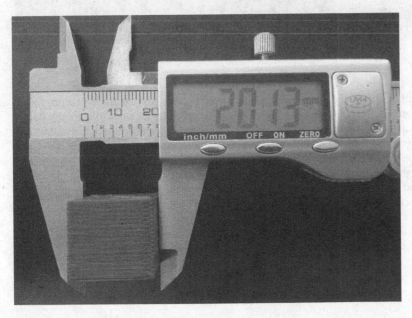

Figure 6-33. *Measuring the axis perpendicular to the axis*

So in this test case we have two problems. First, the Z axis is not calibrated correctly and the filament settings need to be checked. When I acquired this printer and discovered these anomalies, I recalibrated the Z axis by checking the calculations against the firmware. I found a minor difference (error) that, once corrected, produced much more accurate Z-axis measurements.

For the filament issues, I changed the settings in the slicer to match the filament in the printer, and the concave problem improved dramatically. I kept this cube to demonstrate how calibration issues can sometimes be related to other settings—in this case, filament settings. Furthermore, this test cube shows a worst-case scenario that should not happen for you if your calculations and firmware settings are accurate.

■ **Note**   It is possible the error could have been caused by the Z error alone. That is, the layers could be more compressed and therefore bulge more than expected.

Now let's redeem the trusty RepRap variants with an example from a properly calibrated Prusa i2. Figure 6-34 shows a 15×15×15mm cube printed in ABS plastic. Notice that the measurements are much closer to what you would expect for a properly calibrated printer.

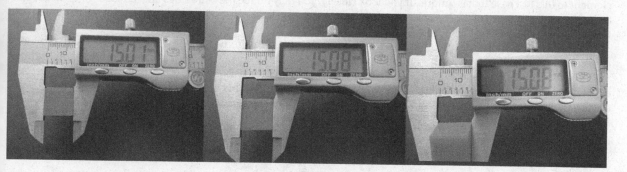

Figure 6-34. *Calibrated RepRap test case*

If you print several calibration test cubes and find your measurements are off by more than 0.2mm–0.4mm, you may want to consider recalibrating your printer. You should also observe the print carefully for sides that are not flat or have similar aspects that can cause your measurements to be inaccurate. If you find these characteristics and your measurements are within about 0.2mm, you should not recalibrate until you explore solutions for those problems. For example, if the first layers appear to be squished, it can cause your Z-axis measurement to be less than what you expect. In this case, it indicates the Z-height is too small, causing the first layer to smash into the print bed.

But before you do that, print a second (or even a third) cube to ensure that you are seeing consistent results. If so, try printing a larger cube. If the error factor remains constant from a small to a larger cube, I would not recalibrate because the inaccuracy may be related to other, less significant factors. However, if the inaccuracy scales with the cube, it is definitely a calibration issue. If you do decide to adjust your printer settings, be sure to adjust one axis at a time, reprint the cube, and check the measurements.

Finding Things to Print

OK, so you've got your printer dialed in and calibrated. Now what? Well, find something to print! In Chapter 1, I briefly discussed Thingiverse, a repository for 3D objects and designs. It is an excellent source for finding objects that someone else has designed and shared with the world. The objects range from rather simple and easy to print, to very complex and challenging to print. You should look at the easier-to-print objects for your first real object. This is especially true if you are new to 3D printing. After all, you want to show off your new hobby to your friends, right? So what should you try to print?

Getting Started

There are some popular objects that you may want to consider printing first. Start with objects that are small, have no overhangs or bridges, and no small diameter protrusions. All of these features can be harder to print and prone to a number of printing problems. In other words, don't expect to be a master 3D printer right out of the gate. You need to spend time learning how your printer responds to different filaments, heat settings, and so forth. Only time and experience will give you these answers.

The following lists a few objects that I recommend you try as your first print. Some of these are quite impressive despite their simplicity. Figure 6-35 shows an example of each object.

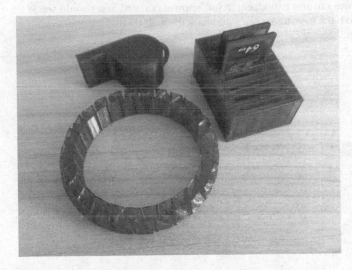

Figure 6-35. *Example first prints*

- *Stretch bracelet* (thingiverse.com/thing:13505): A nice, wearable 3D object. Good for a first, real print job. Prints quickly in about 20 to 30 minutes.

- *SD card holder* (thingiverse.com/thing:9218): A practical tool for organizing SD cards. This will take a little longer to print due to its size. Expect print time to be about 1 to 2 hours, depending on your print settings.

- *Whistle* (thingiverse.com/thing:1046): A bit more of a challenge, but well worth the effort and time to print. Creates a real whistle that you can give away to friends. Make a bunch of them! Print time is under an hour. See the thing information page for details on how to make the pea work (it's printed inside the whistle).

If you print an object and encounter problems, don't worry. I cover how to troubleshoot common printing problems in later chapters. For now, you should check you Z-height, slicer settings, and print surface to make sure all is well there.

That being said, some printers, such as the MakerBot Replicator 2, will likely give you good prints right out of the box. If you built your own printer from a kit or from scratch, and followed the advice in the book, you should get a decent print. Don't feel bad if it takes you more than two attempts to get one of the objects to print correctly—it is part of the learning curve associated with 3D printing.

Searching

Once you've printed these objects successfully, it is time to start looking for something else to print. With so many things available on Thingiverse, you could easily spend hundreds of hours printing your favorite things. Fortunately, MakerBot added a feature to Thingiverse called "like". It is available to anyone who signs up for an account. You use it to mark things you like so that you can quickly revisit them in the future. I like to browse through the things, and when I see something I like, I mark it by clicking "like". You can then navigate to your "Things I Like" page and quickly find those objects you want to print.

You can simply browse through the objects on Thingiverse or you can also search for keywords like *duck*, *bunny*, *shower curtain*, and so forth, to find things. There is a search text box at the top of the web page. Type in what you want to search and press Enter.

For example, if you want to make some new shower curtain rings, search for "shower curtain". You should see several examples. Mark the ones you like, and then go back to your account and look through them. Figure 6-36 shows an excerpt of the results for a search of *shower curtain*.

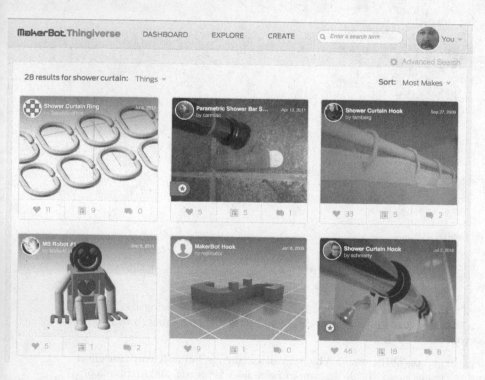

Figure 6-36. Thingiverse search page

Notice the Sort setting in the upper-right corner. The default sort is Relevant, which shows the results that most closely match your search terms. Here I have sorted by Most Makes, which ranks the results (in descending order) by the number of people who have made the object. Use this setting to show the items that are most popular. It is usually the case that these objects are generally the better examples. That is, the more people that have made them, the more likely these objects are the better examples—either for accuracy or applicability. You can also sort by Newest to show those objects that were uploaded to Thingiverse most recently. You can use this setting to see the most up-to-date versions of those objects that have been modified.

Downloading

Once you have found an object you like, just click it in the search results. This will show the details for the object. Figure 6-37 shows one of the shower curtain rings from the example search.

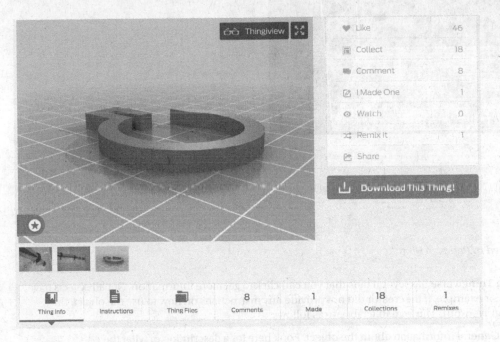

Figure 6-37. *Example object (created by schmarty)*

To download the thing, click the Download This Thing button, which will open the Thing Files panel. Once there, click the Download All Files button and save the `.zip` file some place on your system. From there, you can extract the `.zip` file, and then import the `.stl` file into your slicer or into Repetier-Host for slicing and printing. Figure 6-38 shows the same object loaded in Repetier-Host and ready for printing.

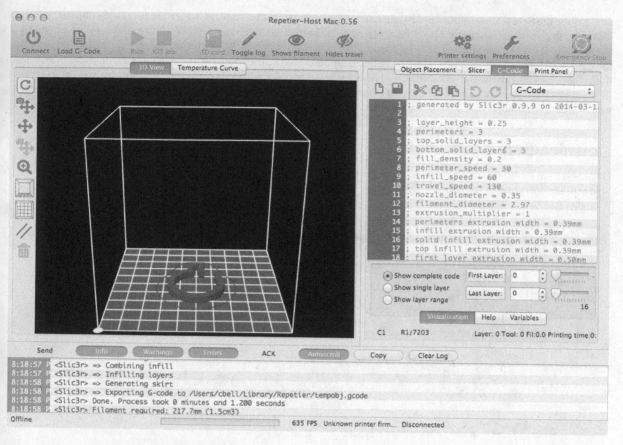

Figure 6-38. *Object sliced in Repetier-Host*

The details page on Thingiverse has several tabs that you can click to get more information. Not all objects have all of the tabs enabled. For example, if the creator did not provide any instructions on how to use the object, the instructions tab will be grayed-out. The available tabs are as follows.

- *Thing Info*: General information about the object. Look here for a description of what the object was designed to do.

- *Instructions*: More details about how to print, assemble, or use the object. Creators of objects typically include recommendations on infill, number of shells, and so forth, related to quality.

- *Thing Files*: The location of all files associated with the object. You will find the .stl files here and sometimes the source files. It can be good to have the source files if you want to modify the object to fit your needs. Note that sometimes the source files are specific to certain graphics software. For example, if the object was created with OpenSCAD, you will see a file with an .scad extension.

- *Comments*: This lists all of the comments other users have made about the object. Registered users can use this as a forum to ask the creator questions or to offer suggestions for improvement, or even better, to encourage the creator with your praise of his work.

- *Made*: This lists the entries created by users who have made the object and uploaded their results to Thingiverse. Use this list to see examples of how others have printed the object. Sometimes it is good to see what the object would look like in other colors. If you make the object yourself, you can log in to Thingiverse and click the I Made One link in the upper-left portion of the details page, and then upload a photo and a brief description of your results.

- *Collections*: This lists the collections other users have created to store your object.

- *Remixes*: This list is updated any time someone creates a new iteration of an existing object. You can use this list to see if there are any variations of the object that you may like better. Remixes usually improve the objects in some unique way. For example, you may find a remix that adds more rigidity or additional features. Remixes are sometimes called *derivatives*.

OK, so now it's your turn. Visit Thingiverse and look for something to print, download it, and then upload an image of your results. Doing this makes you a member of the rapidly expanding world of 3D printing.

Once you have used Thingiverse for a while, and especially once you have an account, you will find it a very useful site. Indeed, I find I check Thingiverse before I design my own objects to make sure there isn't already an object similar that I can use or if there is an object that I can modify in some way to avoid having to design from scratch. In a later chapter, I will show some examples of reusing things.

Summary

If you built your own 3D printer from scratch or from a kit, and have been following along in this chapter to calibrate your printer, you've learned some valuable information for ensuring that your printer is properly prepared for printing. If you have a manufactured printer, you may not have done the calibration prints (but you should to ensure that there are no problems). However, the preparation topics in this chapter also apply.

In this chapter, I covered how to complete the calibration of your printer by explaining the types of surface treatments, setting the Z-height, and testing your printer for accuracy. Performing all of these steps may seem like a lot of extra work, but it is worth the effort, as it will ensure that your printer is configured and working correctly. I also covered the steps for printing an object, as well as how to use Thingiverse to find other objects to print.

The next chapter begins a new part of the book that focuses on troubleshooting your printer. I start with focusing on troubleshooting your printer hardware to find the sources of things that can cause print failures or poor print quality.

CHAPTER 7

■ ■ ■

Solving Hardware Issues

I hope no one would be so bold as to tell you that 3D printing is a carefree experience. While it is true you should expect your printer to perform as designed, a lot of your success will be whether you perform the necessary maintenance and know how to fix the printer when things go wrong. And things will occasionally go wrong. That's part of the charm of owning a leading-edge innovation. In other words, your success should be measured by your ability to maintain, repair, and tune your printer, as well as your learned skills in producing quality prints.

That is not to say all 3D printers will have problems, nor do I insinuate they will self-destruct when you least expect it.[1] Some printers will be better than others. I have read where people have had problems with every grade of printer. Most times the problem can be solved with a simple adjustment, replacing a worn or broken part, or altering your software settings (e.g., slicer). Again, knowing what to focus on when trying to solve a problem is key, but knowing how to properly diagnose the problem will lead you to success quickly.

Keep in mind that we are seeking the best print quality possible. Anything that affects our print quality (or expectations of quality) is a problem that must be fixed. In some cases, the problem causes the print to fail (the part is unusable). In other cases, the part is still usable but may not be of sufficient quality. Also consider that most problems can have more than one cause. For example, layer shifting can be caused by loose axis mechanisms, as well as failing electronics and software.

In this chapter and the next, I present some of the tools that you will need to solve problems as they arise. I focus on the hardware in this chapter and software in the next. I present general ideas and techniques rather than step-by-step directions. I've found knowing why you do something is more important than what you do. Reading these chapters will help give you a broader idea of what to look for when troubleshooting.

It also helps to know which area to focus on. For example, if the hardware isn't working properly, no printing technique or amount of slicing will overcome the problem if it is severe enough.

In this book's appendix, I also present a set of tables that you can use to narrow down the possible remedies for many of the most common problems. After reading this chapter and the next, the appendix will become your guide to applying the knowledge presented.

Before I jump into the types of hardware problems you may encounter, let's discuss some basic techniques for troubleshooting. I present only one form of troubleshooting technique—a technique that has worked well for me. You may find other techniques, or variations of the same, that can work equally as well. However, if you haven't had a lot of experience in troubleshooting, what follows should help you avoid a lot of missteps and headaches.

---

[1]I once had a car in college that would do that. Failures were random, always dramatic, and when you least expected or needed to rely on it for transport.

SOLUTIONS VS. MAGICAL CURES

There is something I learned early on when troubleshooting problems with my 3D printers. It seems there is no end to differing ideas for how to solve some problems. For example, it doesn't take too many web searches to find dozens of solutions for lifting. Some will offer some very good advice—a few may actually work well for most. However, there are others that resemble voodoo or magic. While it is possible some of these will work for you, I present only those techniques that others and I have found to work well. That does not mean there are no other techniques; only that the ones listed here are the most tried and true.

Troubleshooting Techniques

Troubleshooting is not a new method, process, art, or science. Essentially, troubleshooting is determining the source of the problem and solving it. How you go about that can contribute greatly to the success of your solution. You may be able to fix your problem by randomly changing things until the problem gets better. Or you may instinctively know what to do.

■ **Note** The information presented here assumes the problem is repeatable. Random failures can be very difficult to repair due to the inability to re-create the problem. Without the ability to re-create the problem, you won't know whether you have fixed the problem or introduced a new one.

Some have learned good troubleshooting techniques the hard way by suffering many failures and frustrations before adapting strategies that minimize failure and maximize success. That is, they learn the hard way to approaching problems with methodical, proven techniques. Others have learned good troubleshooting techniques from wise tutors. Others still, like myself, have learned from a combination of life experience and academic training. I hope that this section fills in some niche or void in your own experience. If nothing else, you should be able to use these techniques to greater success when facing problems.

THE WHITE X

I once encountered someone with a television that had two pieces of white tape in the form of an X on one side of the chassis. When I asked about it, the owner told me it was the spot that worked the best. When I asked the owner to elaborate,[2] the owner told me it was the spot that worked best to strike the TV with your palm to get it to turn on. While I admired the owner's ability to reason out the best solution, the implementation of the solution was flawed. Don't do this with your 3D printer—or any mechanical or electrical device. Ever.

The following sections describe several tasks you should do prior to trying to solve a problem. If you follow these tasks when approaching a problem, especially a problem with a 3D printer, you will find a solution more quickly and with less frustration and fewer headaches.

---

[2]Fearing the inevitable answer.

Create a Baseline

A baseline will establish many things for you. First and foremost, it will allow you to set a standard or set of observations that define the normal operation of your printer. A baseline is a set of observations made under normal (or initial) operation. Any observation that changes beyond normal parameters can be an indication that something is wrong. As an example, let us consider a garden pond. Depending on weather conditions, some evaporation is common and expected. Similarly, the water level can increase due to precipitation. However, how do you know whether it is a problem when the water level changes? If you kept records of your observations concerning water level—when it decreased or increased, and the weather conditions at the time, you would be able to form patterns from the data. Furthermore, you can form a range of how much the water level can vary under normal conditions. If you encounter a situation where the water level drops inconsistently within this range, you will know there is something wrong. The same is true for your 3D printer. If you ever detect a deviance from the normal operation, you will know not only that there is something wrong, but also where to start looking.

Most people skip this step and it is truly a pity because they often fail to notice when something is starting to wear or requires maintenance. For example, how would you know that the belts on your belt-driven axes need adjustment? You could wait until your printer starts skipping steps and ruining prints, but that seems silly. Wouldn't it be better if you measured the slack in the belts while the printer is operating correctly? If you have data like this, you would be able to tell when the belts needed adjustment. That is, you know you need to tighten the belts when the slack becomes considerably more than your baseline measurement.

A baseline for a 3D printer is a list of observations about a fully configured and properly functioning 3D printer. You should create this baseline as soon as you are comfortable with the print quality of your printer. You can record the observations before that—say when your printer is assembled—but if you make major changes to components during calibration, the values may become invalid.

You can capture all kinds of observations from measuring the length of travel for each axis, belt tension, frame size, and so forth. However, some of these may not be of much use because they measure things that should never change (but there is nothing wrong with recording them).

To give you a starting point, I recommend making the following observations for your printer and recording them in your engineering notebook (or suitable recording device). You may want to include these and any other observations you can think of. Consider all aspects of your particular printer, especially those components that have any form of adjustment. For example, some MakerBot owners are unaware that their X and Y axes can be adjusted.[3]

- *Belt tension*: Establishes minimal tension values

- *Height of each end of the X axis*: Establishes that they are the same values at a known Z position)

- *With bed leveled (trammed), measure height of each corner of the bed adjustors*: Establishes starting point for bed leveling

- *Actual vs. reported temperatures for the hot end and heated print bed*: Lets you check to see if heaters or sensors fail

- *Tightness of axes mechanisms*: Establishes whether they become loose and affect printing

- *Thickness (diameter) of new filament rolls*: Lets you know if there is a quality problem with your filament

Once you have these values and any others you can think of recorded, you can refer to them when something goes wrong. The next sections discuss a process to follow when problems occur. Whether you record a baseline or not, the following process will help you to methodically find the best solution (or at least one that works). I discuss each in more detail later.

---

[3]Indeed, on first glance it appears all belts are nonadjustable, but this isn't the case for the Replicator 1, 2, and 2X.

1. Observe and record relevant data.

2. Consider all possibilities.

3. Choose and implement a strategy.

4. Observe changes and compare data.

    a. If problem solved, stop and record new baseline data.

    b. If problem not solved, return setting to original value and return to step 3.

I present each of these using a concrete example of a layer shift during printing an object.

Observe and Record

The key to successful troubleshooting is making observations and recording them at the time the problem occurs. Recording your observations will help you understand what is wrong. Having a written record of the problems you encounter will also allow you to diagnose and repair the problem more quickly should the problem reoccur.

Let's look at an example. Suppose you notice your object layers are shifted a little. Figure 7-1 shows an example of this problem. There are many observations that you could make about this situation. More generally, I recommend starting with observing the state of the printer at the time of the error. When this problem happened to me, I stopped the printer and noted the obvious things.

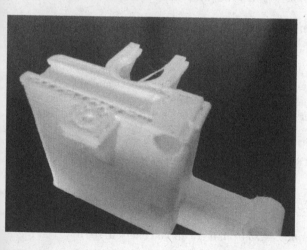

Figure 7-1. Layer shift

Specifically, I noted which axis the shift occurred on and that it occurred more than once. In this case, it was the Y axis. I also noted the state of the axis mechanisms. Initially, all seemed well and nothing seemed out of place. Next, I homed all the axes, one at a time, to their home positions and noted how they moved and whether there were any noises (beyond the usual), and if everything moved smoothly. I then checked the stepper motors for excessive heat. I performed a general check, without touching anything, to ensure I didn't change anything by accident. Listing 7-1 shows the observations made when the layer shift occurred.[4] Notice that I record a problem description, the date the problem occurred, and a list of my observations.

---

[4] I would normally write this in my engineer's notebook, but I list it here electronically. Otherwise, you would need a decoder ring to read my handwriting.

Listing 7-1. Layer Shift Problem: Observations

Problem: Layer shifted several times.
Date: 3 June 2012

Observations:
- Occurred on Y-axis
- Stepper motors are warm but not more than expected
- No heat, odor, noise, or smoke from electronics
- Axis movement is normal, no binding
- Problem occurs only on taller objects

So how do you know what to observe? While you may be able to discern which observations are more likely to point to the problem—and only experience will give you this knowledge—you should record as many as you can. This may sound more like an art form than scientific analysis, and there is some truth to this. The best diagnosticians I've met sometimes use their creativity when problem solving. This includes thinking of all possible things that can go wrong, as well as observations of the state of the machine when the problem occurs.

Consider the Possible Causes

Once you have noted your observations, it is time to consider a list of causes. You should always try to think of as many causes as you can, because while sometimes the cause is obvious (e.g., user error), this isn't always the case. You should consider all of the components involved. In the layer shift example, this includes all of the components of the axis movement—from loose or broken parts—to failed electronics.

While you may not know what to list, you should try to list anything that comes to mind. Experience or a good diagnostic chart like those found in the appendix will help you. I like to make a list of the possible causes and write them underneath the observations. Listing 7-2 shows the updated problem entry in my engineering notebook.

Listing 7-2. Layer Shift Problem: Causes Added

Problem: Layer shifted several times.
Date: 3 June 2012

Observations:
- Occurred on Y-axis
- Stepper motors are warm but not more than expected
- No heat, odor, noise, or smoke from electronics
- Axis movement is normal, no binding
- Problem occurs only on taller objects

Potential Causes:
- Loose belt on Y axis
- Belt clamps broken
- Stepper motor failure
- Stepper driver failure
- Loose drive gear
- Obstruction in axis mechanism

The next step is to consider each cause in turn and decide which to explore first. I like to start with the most likely cause. From experience, it usually has something to do with the mechanics of the axis movement.

Choose a Cause and Implement a Strategy to Correct

When considering potential causes to explore, one strategy is to first focus on those that are the most likely. If the problem is a new one (one you have not experienced before), you may not know which to choose, but you can start with any of them.

Another strategy you could adopt is to check those causes that are least likely to be the problem. In the layer shift example, this includes the broken clamp, loose gear, and obstructions in the axis mechanism. All of these are easy to check. As you test each possible cause, make a tick or check mark next to it on your observations list so that you know you've tested and eliminated it as a cause.

Regardless of which strategy you implement, you should follow the simple technique of adjust, observe, and readjust. More specifically, you make a change, test to see if the change fixed the problem, and if not, return the adjustment back to the previous setting. This is another very handy use of a baseline—how do you know what the initial setting was if you didn't record it? It also applies to anything you do, from adjusting belts and other mechanical items to changes in software (as we will see in the next chapter).

This technique of adjust, observe, and readjust works well to successfully diagnose and repair. It reduces the chances of introducing other problems. If you did not use this technique, you may still fix the problem by changing several things at one time, but you may not learn which repair fixed the problem. In this case, if the problem occurred again, you would not have learned how to fix it—merely how to throw a box of wrenches at a problem.[5]

Choosing what to change is dependent on the cause you've decided to correct, and it is usually intuitive. Some causes may not require any changes; rather, you may just need to check something. For example, if you suspect the cause is a broken clamp, you can simply observe the clamp. If it isn't broken, loose, or so forth, then you can cross off that potential cause and move on to the next.

■ **Caution**   Change one—and only one—setting at a time. Changing more than one thing before observing the effects can lead to making unnecessary changes—or worse, introducing other problems.

Once you choose a cause to try to fix, work on that cause and that cause alone. The best approach is to check and fix the cause, changing only one thing at a time. For example, if you chose to explore the possibility that the belt is loose, you first check the tension on the belt and, if slack, adjust it accordingly. But you don't go any further! You test the condition again before looking at another cause.

When the problem is fixed, you should make a notation in your engineering notebook that describes how you fixed the problem. I like to describe what I did and how it affected the problem. It is sometimes the case that making a change reduces the problem but may not completely fix it. In this case, you would try the repair again until the problem is fixed. For example, if you need to increase the temperature of the hot end, and changing it by 5 degrees helps, increase it another 5 degrees and repeat until the problem is fixed.

Listing 7-3 shows the completed entry for the layer shift example. Notice that I tried several causes before I found the source.

Listing 7-3. Layer Shift Problem: Solution Added

Problem: Layer shifted several times.
Date: 3 June 2012

Observations:
- Occurred on Y-axis
- Stepper motors are warm but not more than expected

---

[5]This is akin to throwing money at a problem. For example, don't throw that clogged nozzle away without first knowing why it clogged and how to unclog it!

- No heat, odor, noise, or smoke from electronics
- Axis movement is normal, no binding
- Problem occurs only on taller objects

Potential Causes:
- Loose belt on Y axis
- Belt clamps broken
- Stepper motor failure
- Stepper driver failure
- Loose drive gear
- Obstruction in axis mechanism

Solution:
This problem was caused by a failed stepper motor.

Notes:
I was able to repeat the problem but it only occurs on tall objects when the printer has run for more than an hour. I checked the belt tension and while it was a little loose, it wasn't loose enough to cause such a large step failure. All clamps, bolts, and other mechanical items are working correctly.

Notice that in this example the problem was a failing stepper motor. That is very unusual; the stepper motors generally don't fail very often. In fact, I had never seen a stepper motor fail in this manner (actually, ever). Normally, a loose belt or other mechanical failure in the axis mechanism causes this problem. But since I listed all of the problems I could think of, including all of the components involved, I was able to include this test. Had I not considered the stepper motor, I may have spent a lot more time finding the source of the problem.

Now that we have a good understanding of good practices for diagnosing and repairing problems, let us look at some specific hardware problems that you could encounter with your 3D printer.

Hardware Problems

There are a number of hardware-related problems that can occur. In this section, I present discussions of the most common hardware failures that can induce a number of problems in 3D printing. These include those related to the filament and its feeding to/through the extruder; adhesion of the heated filament to the print surface, axis and chassis; and electrical failures.

In the following sections, I present discussions of each of these areas. I also include environmental influences in these categories because environmental influences affect how some of the hardware performs. Consider the fact that the hot end must heat to a specific temperature and that the filament extruded must cool in a controlled manner. If there are environmental factors that affect that balance, such as air currents, they can cause the filament to cool too quickly, or in extreme cases, they can cause the hot end temperature to fluctuate.

Filament

You may think filament-related issues are software related. That is, how the slicer builds the objects from settings concerning the filament. However, there are a number of things that can go wrong with filament that is hardware related. Filament is also very sensitive to environmental factors. The following sections describe some of the problems you could encounter, along with recommended remedies.

Quality

The most common issue concerns the quality of the filament. Poor-quality filament can vary in diameter. Some variation is normal, but in this case we are talking about variances of more than a few tenths of a millimeter. This can cause the extruder to extrude too much or too little filament during printing. This manifests in a number of ways, including globs of filament deposited in corners or small curved parts of the object, as well as poor layer adhesion. In extreme cases it can also cause extrusion failures.

Another issue with poor-quality filament is the possibility of weak areas or portions of the filament that are hollow—or worse, portions that have contaminants embedded in the filament. Contaminants, in particular, can block the nozzle, resulting in extrusion failure.

Clearly, the best way to avoid these problems is to use a higher quality of filament. I have found the filament sold by major online retailers such as Maker Shed (`makershed.com`), MakerBot (`makerbot.com`), and IC3D (`ic3dprinters.com`) sell filament of very high quality. I have switched to using their filaments exclusively. I have had only one small issue with a roll of colored filament that was not tinted correctly near the end of the spool. The filament was still usable, only it did not have any tint for the last 20 feet or so.

Filament Spool Tension

When we buy filament, it is usually delivered on a spool. Most printers have accommodations for filament spools to ensure the extruder can pull the filament with as little tension as possible. If your printer does not have a spool holder, you should consider getting (or printing) one. Choose a design that incorporates bearings or rollers that allow the spool to unroll filament easily.

When the spool has too much tension, the extruder can strip the filament. When this happens, you will likely not catch it right away (unless you stare into your printer while it prints). The result is called an "air print," where the printer happily continues to move the axes as if the filament were extruding. There really isn't any way to detect this problem other than observing it.

CHOOSING A SPOOL HOLDER

If your printer did not come with a spool holder and you decide to print one yourself, you will find there are hundreds of different spool holder designs available. In fact, a recent search on Thingiverse revealed over 1400 hits for "spool holder". Most use bearings or rollers that permit the spool to roll freely. Where a design differs most is in the size of the spool it supports, and how it mounts to your printer or if it is free-standing.

You can choose whichever spool holder design you want. Just make sure it is designed to attach to your printer (in a way that you like) and accommodates the spool sizes you own. This is another reason to choose a filament vendor with quality filament—their spool sizes rarely vary. However, some designs permit a variety of spool sizes. The ones I like best have two cones that ride on bearings. They allow me to use a horizontal rod to mount the spool. The outer diameter, thickness, and size of the hole are all easily adaptable using the cones. The following image shows an example of such a spool holder incorporated into a Prusa design.

Filament sold in bundles or coils are susceptible to tangles—where one or more loops are intertwined so that the filament cannot be uncoiled. When this occurs, it will have the same effect as having a spool holder that has too much tension. Extreme cases can result in having to untangle the filament by unraveling the entire coil.

■ **Tip** Don't toss those used spools! If you ever encounter a coil or partial spool of filament, you can always roll it up on an empty spool and use your spool holder.

If you buy coiled filament, I recommend rolling onto a used spool and using a spool holder. This will reduce the possibility of the filament tangling. But be careful and do not allow the filament to come into contact with dirty surfaces, such as your shop floor. This will introduce contaminants that can cause extrusion failures.

Contaminants

You should store your filament in a clean, dry storage bag or plastic container. Make sure your filament is not in a position to have dust or other debris fall onto it. Dust and other debris can stick to the filament and be fed into the hot end. If the particles are large enough, they can cause extrusion failures.

When this occurs, it usually isn't obvious that there is any contamination. That is, you normally clean the extruder and test extrusion. Typically, filament will seem to feed normally, but when you start your print again, you may have another extrusion failure a short time later. If you get several extrusion failures and cannot find any reason for it, you probably have dust and debris on your filament.

The best way to eliminate external contaminants is to use a foam filament filter (sometimes called a *filament cleaner*) that mounts on the filament. The foam or sponge wipes off external contaminants off as the filament slides through the filter. Like spool holders, filament filter/cleaner designs are plentiful. Figure 7-2 shows a filament filter (circled) that I've found works best for me. It mounts on the filament above the extruder. I use a dense sponge in my filters.

Figure 7-2. *Filament filter*

Environmental Factors

Another thing that can cause filament problems is moisture. Filament can absorb a certain amount of moisture if exposed to high humidity. The result can be popping or hissing sounds, steam, and even moments where the filament spurts from the nozzle (rather than flowing evenly).

Should these problems occur, you must stop your printer and remove the filament. Continued use of filament with a high level of moisture is likely to produce poor-quality objects. It also isn't good for your hot end.

If you are thinking you will have to throw the filament away, you can relax because that isn't necessary. You need only place the filament in a plastic bag with a drying agent for a day or so. Once it dries, you can resume printing with it.

■ **Tip**   Always store filament spools that are not in use in a clean, dry plastic bag with a small amount of drying agent (desiccant). I always save those little white packets you get in many products these days and drop a few in the bag with each spool of filament. Since I started storing my filament this way, I haven't encountered a problem with humidity. Also, do not store the desiccant in the open air because this can reduce its effectiveness. You should keep it in a sealed bag when not in use.

I have referred to clogged nozzles and extrusion failures, but I have not explained them or how to fix them. The next sections will do exactly that—describe the types of problems you could encounter with your extruder and hot end.

Extruder and Hot End

The extruder and hot end can be a source of problems and frustration for new enthusiasts. I have already described a number of them in the previous section. In this section, I will list the most common problems and include some suggestions on how to fix or avoid them.

Extruder Mechanism

Recall that the extruder is responsible for feeding filament to the hot end. The extruder is driven by a stepper motor and a drive pulley or hobbed bolt. The drive pulley or hobbed bolt may be driven by a set of gears. These components can sometimes fail, and when they do, there are a number of ways it can affect your print quality.

If you encounter a situation where you observe the extruder gears turning but there is a delay with filament beginning to extrude, you could have a loose or worn gear. Depending on how worn or loose the gears are, this may not affect print quality for some time; and when it does start affecting quality, you may notice small gaps in the start of print layers. Again, this can be very subtle. Where it can matter more is if you use a retraction setting. In this case, the retraction will be cancelled out by the delay induced in the worn or loose gears.

WHAT IS RETRACTION?

Retraction is a setting some slicers provide to allow you to turn the extruder backward for a short period. This "retracts" the heated filament and can be used to treat cases where the filament oozes from the nozzle or there are thin strings between moves. The oozing can be caused by residual pressure in the nozzle after the motor stops. This is more common in nozzles with small openings and large bores. Retraction can relieve the pressure and avoid oozing and stringing.

Fixing this problem for geared extruders begins with observing the gears with the printer powered off. Try turning the extruder manually or checking the gears for wobble. If one or both gears are loose, you should try tightening them. In one case, I found the large gear on a Greg's Wade extruder had its nut trap rounded out. No amount of tightening can fix the problem, but I did find a temporary fix that allowed me to print a new gear.

■ **Note** If your extruder is direct drive where the filament drive pulley is connected directly to the stepper motor, you may not be able to see the gear turning. Similarly, if the extruder uses an enclosed gear box, you may not be able to observe the gears. Thus, you may need to partially disassemble the extruder to check all pulleys and gears to make sure they aren't loose.

When a nut trap rounds out, you can fix the problem temporarily by heating the head of a bolt, rod, or similar blunt metal tool. Heat it with a butane torch or similar heat source. Place the nut in the nut trap and then use the heated tool to press the plastic around the nut trap against the nut. This effectively "squishes" plastic back into the nut trap and should be good for a short-term fix until you can print a new gear.

Worn gears, on the other hand, are easier to spot. You will typically see the teeth of the gear rounded or ground down. You may also see tips or even teeth broken off. For gears that wear evenly, you can check wear by powering off the printer, and holding each gear to try turning them in opposite directions. If there is any play (there shouldn't be any), you should replace both gears as soon as you can. In extreme cases, the gears can become stripped, thereby stopping filament extrusion and leading to air prints.

If you use an extruder with a door, lever, clamp, or arm that you have to tighten to apply tension to the drive pulley, you could encounter problems if the door is tightened too much or too little—either of which can result in extrusion failures. Too much tension can result in the filament pressing into the drive pulley and eventually clogging it. Too little tension can cause the drive pulley to strip the filament, also clogging it. If your drive pulley gets clogged often and there are no spool holder issues (no tension, tangles, etc.) and the hot end is operating correctly, you may want to check the tension on the extruder door, lever, clamp, or arm.

Nozzle Obstructions

There are several problems that can occur with the nozzle. Obstructions are normally the cause for filament extrusion failure in cases where the hot end is heating properly. We've seen this in the section that discussed filament contamination. However, there is a possibility you could encounter other forms of obstruction.

For example, if the nozzle drags on the print surface, it can damage the small opening or the nozzle can pick up some debris. In these cases, you may see the filament curl when exiting the nozzle. When this occurs, you should remove the filament and let the hot end cool. Once cool, remove the nozzle and use a wire brush (brass or aluminum bristles) to clean off the nozzle, and a micro drill bit to reshape the opening. You can also use a piece of emery cloth to lightly sand the nozzle tip, but be careful not to get any shavings in the nozzle itself. Use compressed air to blow out any such contaminants.

■ **Caution**   Some hot ends are easier to disassemble than others. For instance, a J-head hot end is easy to disassemble, but a Buko-style hot end is not. Disassembly of complex hot end designs should be a last resort to clearing nozzle jams. Be sure to check with your vendor for recommendations on how best to service your hot end.

An alternative to removing the nozzle would be to use a cold pull method where you heat the hot end to a temperature slightly below glassing and pull the filament out by hand. This will remove the majority of the filament stuck in the hot end and often the obstruction as well. Temperatures for this technique are 160–180ºC for ABS and 140ºC for PLA (see http://bukobot.com/nozzle-cleaning for a complete analysis of this technique).

Fixing Filament Feed Failures

When your drive gear gets clogged with filament, it can no longer grip the filament and pull it from the spool and feed it to the hot end. The following presents a process you can use to clean out the extruder.

1. Open the extruder door.

2. Bring the hot end to temperature.

3. Remove the filament manually (watch out—it's hot!).

4. Turn off the printer.

5. Use a pointed object to scrape out the filament from the drive pulley, turning the pulley to get to all areas.

6. Use a vacuum to remove all of the filament shards.

7. Reload the filament and resume printing.

Figure 7-3 shows an extruder that has stripped filament clogging the drive pulley (hobbed bolt in this case). Notice how there is excessive buildup of filament on the hobbed bolt. This prevents the grooves from gripping the filament, and thus no filament is extruded.

Figure 7-3. Clogged extruder

Also shown is the use of a hobby knife to clean out the grooves. Depending on how accessible your drive gear is, you may be able to use a brush to clean out the filament.

Now that we have seen what can go wrong with the extruder and hot end, the next section presents hardware related problems that can cause adhesion problems.

Adhesion

Adhesion is the number-one bane of 3D printer enthusiasts. This is especially true for those printing with ABS. Adhesion problems are manifested as portions of the object that have started to curl and pull away from the print surface (hence, it appears to have "lifted" off the print bed). Figure 7-4 shows a large gear that has suffered significant lifting. In this case, the resulting part was unusable.

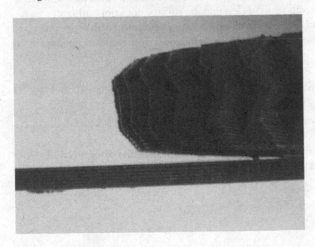

Figure 7-4. Lifting example

■ **Tip**   Lifting may be worse for larger objects or objects with a small surface area that contacts the print surface. Increase the surface area by using a brim (set in the slicer) to print several loops of filament to extend the outer layer of the object. You can peel or cut away the brim once the object is removed from the print surface.

Conquering this problem involves tackling the three most common causes for lifting: leveling the print bed, ensuring that the print surface is prepared correctly, and eliminating environmental factors. I describe each of these in the following sections.

Print Bed Adjustments

If your parts are lifting in such a way that the lifting occurs more toward one edge, it is possible your bed is not trammed (level). You may not notice this if you are printing small parts on a common area (like the center of the print bed). However, the larger parts you print, or the more parts that you have positioned toward the side that is lower, the more lifting can occur. Lifting occurs because the Z-height is too high and the first layer of filament is not being pressed onto the print surface. Conversely, having the nozzle too close to the print surface and compressing the filament can also cause warping.

If you set your Z-height at one spot (say the center), a print bed that is not trammed (level) could be lower at the front, rear, left, or right side. Conversely, it is likely the opposite edge of the print bed could be higher (a lower Z-height), which can cause the first layer to be pressed out, and the object may appear squished. If the Z-height is so low that the nozzle makes contact with the print surface, it can block the nozzle and cause extrusion failures.

The cure for this form of adhesion problem is to level the print bed. Once you have tested your printer and ensured any mechanical issues are resolved, I recommend leveling the print bed on new printers (especially ones that were built from a kit) before you print for the first time each day.

Print Surface

Another common problem that can cause lifting is a print surface that is worn or dirty. If you have touched your print surface with your fingers or other body parts,[6] you could have transferred oils from your skin to the print surface, which will reduce adhesion. Similarly, a printer that has not been used for some time may have a layer of dust built up on the print surface. Finally, the print surface could have been used enough to need replacing.

You can improve adhesion when printing ABS on Kapton film by cleaning the film with acetone. This will remove oils and other contaminants, and renew the surface for better adhesion. If cleaning the surface does not improve adhesion, you should replace the Kapton film. I find Kapton tape has a very long life when compared with other print surface treatments. Indeed, I only replace the Kapton tape when I've accidentally damaged it from removing parts.

■ **Tip**   You can also use ABS slurry to increase adhesion on Kapton tape. In fact, if the bed is level (trammed) and the Z-height is set properly, ABS slurry can nearly completely cure lifting for ABS prints.

Blue painter's tape with PLA can lose its adhesive properties much sooner than Kapton film. Fortunately, blue painter's tape is easier and cheaper to replace. I recommend replacing blue painter's tape after 5 to 10 prints, or when parts show any signs of lifting.

---

[6]Properly cooled, of course.

Another strategy that works very well for PLA is to use a *raft*, which improves first-layer adhesion. A raft is a series of layers printed on the print bed and the object is printed on top. Some CAM software includes settings to generate a raft. For example, MakerWare has a setting to print a raft, which is printed in such a way that it peels off the object once it has cooled. Slic3r also allows you to print a raft, but it is not as sophisticated as the MakerWare option and can be harder to remove. Figure 7-5 shows the raft setting in Slic3r.

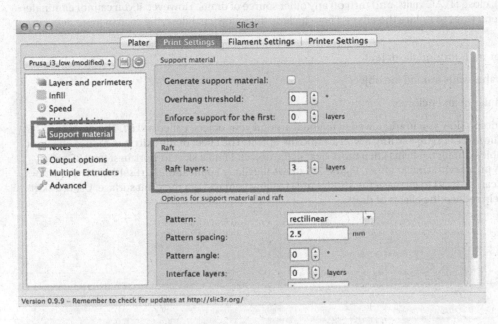

Figure 7-5. *Raft settings in Slic3r*

■ **Tip** The slicer software generates the raft. Some slicers are better at printing rafts. You should experiment with rafts to be sure your slicer will generate rafts that are easy to remove.

Environmental Factors

The effects of environmental factors that can cause lifting include unstable room temperature and air currents or simple drafts. If the room temperature is too low, it can cause parts to cool unevenly and can cause parts to lift off the print surface. Likewise, air moving across the print bed can cause the filament on some layers to cool faster than others. This causes the part to curl and the curling can cause the part to pull away from the print surface. Furthermore, it is possible for upper layers on larger objects to lose layer adhesion, which causes cracks, because some areas cool faster than others.

■ **Note** Lifting, cracking, and layer adhesion problems are more prevalent with ABS than PLA.

You should always ensure your room temperature is stable. The exact temperature isn't that important (as long as it's comfortable for human occupation), but it should remain the same for the duration of your prints. For example, do not use your printer near air conditioners or space heaters. If your room needs to be cooled or heated, allow time for the temperature to stabilize before printing.

You may think "drafts" mean any air driven by a fan or a breeze from an open window, but it doesn't take that much air movement to cause lifting. In fact, you may not even notice the draft. Fans and open windows should be turned off and closed. However, detecting or eliminating all drafts may not be possible. Thus, we need to try and reduce their effects.

The best way to reduce the effects of drafts is to eliminate the sources. You can move the printer away from open windows (or close them), close HVAC vents, and turn off any other source of drafts. However, if you cannot eliminate the source, there are several ways to reduce the effect. These include the following. I describe each in more detail in the following sections.

- Print skirts or walls around the object

- Place removable walls around the object

- Place the printer in an enclosure

Some slicer applications allow you to add a wall of filament around your object, called a *skirt*. The skirt is printed as a single row to a specific layer height, forming a wall around the object. The effect of the skirt is to reduce effects of drafts from cooling the object. In fact, it helps keep more heat in the object. I find a skirt to work best for ABS prints, but I have used it for PLA prints with similar effect. Figure 7-6 shows the Slic3r application skirt settings. It also shows the brim settings, which can be used to increase the surface area making contact with the print surface. Using a skirt and brim together can help reduce the effects of drafts.

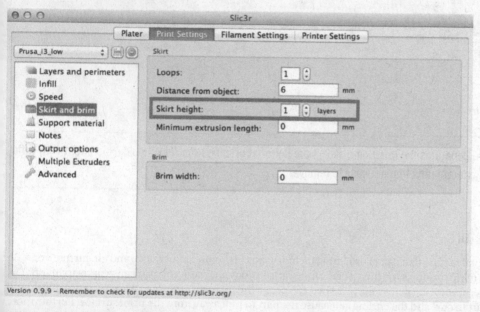

Figure 7-6. *Skirt settings in Slic3r*

If your slicer does not have a skirt feature or you do not want to expend that much filament, you can use removable walls made from blue painter's tape.[7] This may sound low-tech, but you'll be surprised how well it works. In fact, I find it a better treatment than printing a skirt.

---

[7]Use that roll of tape with the logo imprinted, or that less expensive roll you were sure would work just as well as the one twice the price. At least, that's what I do.

To build a removable tape wall, cut a length of blue painter's tape and fold one-third of it over lengthwise and press it down. Next, cut the adhesive side every inch or so. This will allow you to form the tape around the object. Figures 7-7 and 7-8 show the steps for preparing the tape.

Figure 7-7. *Folding the tape*

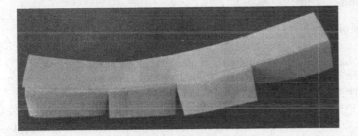

Figure 7-8. *Cut adhesive side every inch*

The best way to apply the tape is to allow the print to print the first couple of layers, and then pause the printer. This ensures you can place the tape so that it will not interfere with the movement of the printer. When the print is done, you can remove the walls and then remove the object. Figures 7-9 and 7-10 show the steps in applying the removable blue painter's tape wall.

Figure 7-9. *Pause and apply the tape around the object*

Figure 7-10. *Continue printing with wall around the object*

The best way to combat lifting caused by drafts that cannot be eliminated is to place the printer in an enclosure. I will show several examples of how to add panels to a MakerBot printer to transform the printer into an enclosed printer in a later chapter. If your printer does not have any external frame or ways to accommodate panels, you will have to improvise. For example, there are a number of designs for printer enclosures on Thingiverse. Here are just a few that I found promising.[8]

- *Big acrylic box* (thingiverse.com/thing:55065): Acrylic panels joined with printed parts.
- *Thermal enclosure* (www.thingiverse.com/thing:269586): Panels made from insulation board that can be used to retain heat in rooms with unstable temperatures.
- *Wooden box* (thingiverse.com/thing:40080): An enclosure made with wood frames and acrylic panels; great for wood working enthusiasts.

I have also seen a very inexpensive enclosure made from a simple, large plastic container where the lid was used as the base with the printer placed on the base in the center and the box placed on top. It won't win any craftsmanship awards, but it will get the job done.

■ **Tip** Another use of a full enclosure is *fume extraction*. You can use a low-power fan connected via a duct to a charcoal filter to remove a lot of the fumes from heating some filament. For example, if you are sensitive to the odor of printing ABS, an enclosure with a fume extractor can greatly reduce the irritants. Search Thingiverse for examples of fume extractors.

Now let's turn to the axes and chassis for the source of print failures or quality issues.

---

[8]I have not created any of these myself, but I recommend trying these if skirts or removable walls do not work for you.

Axes and Chassis

When diagnosing print quality problems, we often don't consider the possibilities that the mechanical components of your printer can fail or come out of adjustment. Sometimes this is because of normal wear or part failure, other times it is from accidental events or changes, and still other times from neglect. I discuss each of these in the following sections.

Obstructions

The most obvious hardware problems are those things that cause the axes to fail to operate properly or move from its minimum to maximum positions.

Sometimes the obstruction is accidental,[9] but other times it can happen that a part of your printer comes loose or an object is knocked off the print bed, only to obstruct one or more axes. When an obstruction falls into the axis mechanism, you are likely to hear chattering, bumps, and other undesirable sounds. Should this occur, you should stop your printer as soon as you can. Use the reset button or simply turn it off. The print will be incomplete and therefore useless, but it is better than your printer breaking a component, belt, or bending some vital part of the printer.

To correct the problem, clear the obstruction and make sure your printer is not damaged. Ensure all axes can be moved freely for their full range. In some cases, the obstruction can bend or dislodge endstops or cause minor changes in the axis adjustments. Be sure to check all components in the area. Power on the printer and home all axes then resume your print.

■ **Caution**   Never attempt to adjust your printer while it is printing. Likewise, never attempt to access your objects on the print bed while the printer is printing.

Adjustments

Every printer differs, but most have several components that can be adjusted to accommodate changes or wear. These often include tension adjustments for belt-driven axes—either at the stepper motor or the idler pulley. There also cases where the printer mechanisms are required to be aligned properly. For example, the print bed must be level in order to ensure that the nozzle moves across the print bed at the same height.

Certain events—such as obstructions, mechanical or electrical failure, or major overhaul or upgrades—can cause changes that foil your adjustments. For instance, if you have a printer that uses two stepper motors for the same axis, such as the Prusa variants, the mechanism is susceptible to misalignment of the threaded rods. If you do something to move one of the threaded rods and not the other, the X axis becomes misaligned.

We have already seen the effects of print bed that isn't level (trammed). This will cause adhesion problems, which can lead to lifting. However, if the print bed gets too far out of adjustment, it can cause the nozzle to come into contact with the print surface. Recall that this can cause extrusion failure as the print surface obstructs the nozzle.

Likewise, loose belts can cause layer shifts if they skip a cog on the drive pulley. If the belt is moderately loose, some backlash may be noticeable. As the belt becomes looser, it begins to introduce a delay—much like a stripped or worn gear. You can tell a belt needs tension by simply testing it by moving the belt up and down. If you can move it up and down so much that the axis moves, it is too loose. On the other hand, once the belt becomes very loose, it can cause the belt to slip over a notch (or more). This will introduce an immediate and extreme layer shift.

---

[9]You should treat your printer the same as any other piece of equipment. Specifically, keep your hands, other robots, drones, and loose clothing away from the printer while it is operating.

Z AXIS WOBBLE

Variations of the Prusa-style RepRap printers (Prusa i2 and prior) that have fixed mounts for the Z-axis threaded rods suffer from Z wobble. The threaded rods for the Z axis may be bent, have inconsistent threading, or simply be out of round. All of these can contribute to minute shifts of the X axis. This is because the X axis is part of the Z-axis lift mechanism. As the threaded rods wobble and shift, so does the X axis. Later versions of the Prusa style have greatly improved this problem by fixing only one size of the threaded rod with a flexible coupling, which allows the rod to wobble around a bit and not transfer to the X axis.

Part Failure

When parts of your printer fail, you often notice the problem immediately and it is usually clear what failed. For example, if a belt or other vital component of the axis movement breaks, that axis will also fail to operate properly and the print will fail.

Sometimes a part will crack from stress or wear. Most times the failure isn't severe enough to cause print quality issues. For example, it is common for the X-axis ends on Prusa i2 printers (and perhaps others) to crack after several to many hours of printing. This normally doesn't affect how the printer operates. Regardless, when you detect a part failure, you should fix or replace the part as soon as possible. Figure 7-11 shows a close-up of an X-end failure. More precisely, it shows how the part was fixed. I used a piece of ABS filament soaked in acetone for 20 seconds. The ABS becomes very soft and can be pressed into the crack. Once the acetone evaporates, the part is mended.

Figure 7-11. *Repaired part*

Whenever I encounter a print quality issue or print failure, I check the parts of the affected axes to ensure there are no broken parts. I also check all of the parts when I perform maintenance on the printer. As you will learn about your printer, there are some parts that fail occasionally. For example, endstop holders for RepRap printers are susceptible to breakage.

Another common part failure, which I have mentioned previously, concerns stripped or broken gears on the extruder. As mentioned, this can cause inconsistent layers in the vertical direction, or even a lack of extrusion altogether.

Far less common are minor part failures that affect only a small portion of the part. For example, the nut trap in the large gear for a Wade-style extruder can sometimes round out, permitting the nut to turn slightly. This can lead to the nut becoming loose. A rounded out nut trap will eventually cause the part to delay action. For example, if the nut trap for a gear rounds out, it may cause the mechanism to appear to pause or hesitate. This can cause delayed extrusion for extruder gears and layer shift for gear-driven axis mechanisms.

Keep in mind that each printer design varies and some may not have any recurring part failures. Likewise, wear can also vary. Some printers are more susceptible to wear than others. While some may have longer periods before wear is an issue, wear is normal for most mechanisms—especially those that must slide or make contact with other parts (e.g., bearings and gears). But how do parts break? Wear can be a cause of breakage, but other factors include maintenance (preventive vs. corrective). I discuss lack of proper maintenance in the next section.

Lack of Maintenance

Keeping your printer running well can be achieved through proper and regular maintenance. I discuss routine and periodic maintenance tasks in upcoming chapters. However, sometimes your printer needs maintenance (or even repair) more often. This need can manifest as noises from your printer axes movement such as squeaks, clunks, or metallic sounds; all of these are early warning alarms.[10]

The most common cause of these issues is lack of lubrication. For example, when bearings become dry or the smooth rods or roller channels become dirty, it is possible for friction to increase. Too much friction may cause stepping errors from too much stress on the stepper motors. If your object seems to have inconsistent layer alignment, you should ensure all axes move freely and that your stepper motors are not overheating. Lubricating the axes, or more specifically, performing maintenance on the axes should return the printer to proper operation.

You can also experience problems if you do not maintain your printer properly. More specifically, if parts wear down or become loose, your printer may start to lose some quality. I have already mentioned loose belts. If you do not adjust your belt-driven mechanisms regularly, they could become loose enough to cause axis shifts. Similarly, if you never adjust your Z-height and print bed, you will eventually experience lifting and similar adhesion problems.

Another example is loose frame components. These can cause the entire frame to shift, causing slight shifts in the layers as viewed vertically. This is the same effect as the Z-wobble problem for Prusa-style printers. If you notice slight variations in how layers are aligned, and the vertical walls are not even, check your frame components for tightness. However, if you add checking the frame for loose components to your maintenance routine, you are not likely to encounter this problem.

In fact, if you follow good maintenance practices, you can normally eliminate maintenance as a cause for the problem. For example, if you adjust your print bed and Z-height, and tighten your belts before printing the first print (that day or session), you do not have to consider lack of maintenance as a cause for print quality problems. Proper maintenance also permits you to detect and correct potential problems. For example, if you discover a part has cracked or is worn, you can replace it, even if it has yet to cause any print quality issues. Clearly, the importance of proper maintenance has significant benefits, which is why I devote two chapters to the subject.

Now that we have explored problems related to filament, extrusion, adhesion, and the mechanics of the printer, let us look at the electrical components for sources of printing problems.

Electrical

Should an electrical component fail, it is the same as when a physical part breaks. That is, the mechanism fails to perform properly. For example, if a stepper motor stops turning, the axis (or extruder) will not move. However, electronic components fail intermittently, which can be much harder to diagnose. An electronics failure, even an intermittent one, does not always manifest as print quality issues. For example, when an LCD fails, your printer may continue to print.

---

[10]Normally early warning. Ignore them long enough and they become "told you so" sounds.

Before testing any electrical component, you must ensure you are properly grounded and follow all safe practices for working with electricity. Most importantly, know where the mains and high power connections are and take care to avoid touching anything when powered on.

IS THIS THING ON?

One thing novices usually forget (and even some of us "mature" enthusiasts) is to check that the power supply is plugged in, the unit is powered on, and the USB cable is attached to both the printer and the computer (if that is how you print). I learned this lesson very early on and always check the cables when diagnosing a problem. If your printer is in a lab or other open area where others can interact with it, someone could have simply turned the thing off and, gasp!, unplugged it.[11] A properly seated plug and a firm click of the switch can fix a host of "dead printer" problems.

I explore a few of the more common problems related to the electronics in the following sections. As you will see, there are several categories of problems: stepper motors, wiring, the main electronics board, and other components, such as switches. I also give suggestions for how to diagnose intermittent problems.

Stepper Motors

Stepper motors do most of the work of the printer. When one fails or begins to operate erratically, it will have an immediate effect on the print. It can manifest as layer shifts, missed steps, and even complete failure.

There are two things to consider when focusing on the stepper motors as a source of print problems: the stepper motor itself and the stepper motor driver. If the stepper motor driver fails, it normally fails completely and the stepper motor will not turn. In some cases, this may fail so that insufficient voltage is sent to the stepper motor. This can be detected by excessive noise when the motor is turning, or even stuttering of the motor. If you correct the problem by adjusting the voltage but it occurs again, you should replace the stepper motor driver.

Another symptom of an incorrectly set current is excessive heat. If the motors are getting really warm and the current is set correctly, you could have a stepper motor problem. If the stepper motor is too small, meaning it doesn't have sufficient power to move the mechanism, installing a larger motor can solve the problem. However, if the printer was working correctly, with no or little heat buildup in the motors, it is possible you will need to replace the motor.

As I mentioned previously, I encountered a layer shift problem with a failed stepper motor. It was such a unique experience (I thought they would run forever, pending no abuse like too much voltage) that I was able to observe something interesting. The failing stepper motor had very little torque. In fact, I could hold the shaft and turn it even when power was applied.[12] From experience, if your stepper motor is very easy to turn and you are seeing skipped steps or layer shift, replace the stepper motor.

In rare cases, you could also notice problems with filament extrusion, where the filament seems to feed at different rates. That is, the filament extrudes sluggishly for short periods, freezes, or even stutters. In this case, you could have a stepper motor failing from overheating or a simple electrical failure. If the stepper motor is overheating, you should check your stepper driver's current settings to make sure it matches the stepper motor.

---

[11]Unpluggers unite! It's one of my OCD quirks. I unplug things. There, I've said it.

[12]This is one of those "do as I say, not as I do" moments. Never handle electronics that are powered on unless you know precisely what you are doing.

Wiring

We do not think of wiring as being a part that can fail. However, consider the way the axes on your printer moves. Any axis that has electronic components that move with the axis has one thing in common—a potential stress point for the wiring powering those components. This could be an endstop, stepper motor, hot end, and so forth.

Wiring can break in two ways. It can simply break away from its solder or clamp, and it can break internally from stress.

A broken wire that has come loose is easy to find and fix. Simply reattach the wiring by removing any bits of broken wiring, and then resolder. If it is a clamped connection, try adding a bit of solder to the end of the wiring to give the clamp something to grip.

When building a printer, you should consider the wiring stress points. Failure to ensure that the wire can move freely and not bind or bend in only one area can result in broken wires. More specifically, as the axis moves, the wire is bent back and forth in a small area (the stress point). Over time, this will cause the copper filaments[13] to break. If the flex continues and enough (as in all) filaments break, the component will stop working.

If you encounter a situation where a stepper motor turns in one direction but not the other, the axis does not stop when the endstop is engaged, or a hot endstops heating, it is possible your wiring is damaged or your driver is malfunctioning.

Unfortunately, the break in the wire isn't so easy to see, and in some cases you won't be able to see it. When looking for broken wiring from stress, look at the stress points. You can locate the break by flexing the wire slightly. The place that flexes more easily than others is the location of the break.

When you find the break, do two things. First, replace the wire, and second, use a stress relief to prevent future breaks. I like to use flexible plastic wire wrap to wrap all wiring that must flex. The wrap gives the wire more strength and is designed to distribute the flex over a larger segment of wire. I also secure both ends of the wrap to ensure that it can flex along the length and not at the attachment points. Figure 7-12 shows an example of a wiring run with flexible plastic wrap.

Figure 7-12. *Using plastic wrap as a wiring stress relief*

---

[13]As in stranded wire. You would not choose solid-core wiring for components that require flexible wire.

Electronics Board

When your electronics board fails, it is normally an all-or-nothing affair. That is, your printer will go dark and you won't be able to communicate with it via USB (or over the network). In some cases, the host board (the Arduino) may still be functioning properly, but the rest of the devices—the hot end, stepper motors, and so forth—do not. In this case, I like to always check the power supply first before considering an electronics board as the source of failure, because sometimes it is a question of power.[14]

For those printers that use a RAMPS or similar setup, you have two boards to test—the Arduino and the RAMPS. If the Arduino board fails, you are likely to encounter a dead printer. However, if the RAMPS fails, you may still be able to communicate with the printer via USB. I had the RAMPS board fail once, and in that case, even the LCD panel, lights, fans, and so forth, all worked; just no motors and no heaters. I originally thought this was a power problem, but as it turns out, my RAMPS board failed (a blown polyfuse).

I have also seen where the electronics board can fail intermittently. This has many possible manifestations—all of them not good. If it is truly random, it may be very inconvenient and fail at the most inopportune times. If you suspect an intermittent problem with your electronics board, try replacing it with a new or known-good component.

Other Components

This category concerns the rest of the electronics components in your printer, including switches (endstops), SD card readers, LCD panels, and so forth. When these components fail, it is usually clear what is wrong (like no display on the LCD), but in other cases it may not be so clear.

Endstop failures are rare, but when one fails, it can be a dramatic event. That is, the axis will slam into the home (or max depending on the configuration) side of the axis mechanism, which can cause damage to your printer. Fortunately, we discover such failures when homing the printer before printing, so it generally won't affect your print. Naturally, the fix is to replace the endstop and rehome your printer.

Endstop holders can break, causing axis problems. If the holder breaks or comes loose, it may allow your axis to travel beyond its limits. Always inspect the endstop holder if you suspect a problem with axis homing.

SD cards are not as robust as other media and can fail. They are also susceptible to corruption from electrostatic discharge (ESD). When an SD card fails, your printer will likely present an error message stating it cannot read the card. Reformatting the card usually fixes the problem, but requires you to reload the card with all of the files you want to print.

In rare cases, the print file itself can become corrupt. This normally manifests as a print that fails in the middle in some bizarre manner, such as suddenly printing out in limbo land (away from the part), dropping the temperature unexpectedly, or just halting. If this occurs, and you've checked all other potential causes, try using a new SD card to see if it is the card or the file on the card.

Sometimes the SD card reader itself can fail with the same result—unable to read the card. In this case, reformatting the SD card or using a second (or third) known-good card will result in failures. The only recourse is to replace the SD card reader. Most printers include the SD card reader with the LCD panel, and thus you may need to replace the whole unit. However, even if the SD reader itself fails, you can still print from a computer until your replacement part arrives.

When an LCD panel fails completely, you will likely not see any text (or graphics) displayed. You may also see a display with all the block characters or several lines illuminated. The printer may even continue to function and print normally. You can even use the printer via a computer. Replacing the LCD is the only option when this occurs. Consult your documentation and contact your vendor to order a new LCD.

However, it is more common—especially on RepRap printers—to see corrupt displays on the panel. This is caused by an electrostatic discharge. If your printer is not properly grounded, your LCD can become corrupted if there is an ESD. If you have ever touched your printer and gotten a mild spark or shock, this is an ESD, which can be deadly to sensitive electronics. Fortunately, the printer will continue to print normally—you just won't be able to read the screen.

---

[14] You checked to see it if is plugged in and the power switch is in the "ON" position, didn't you?

Corrupt LCD displays can also be caused by electromagnetic interference (EMI). This can manifest in a number of ways, but higher power electrical wiring placed too close to the LCD ribbon cable normally causes it. I treat this problem two-fold. First, I wrap the LCD panel cables in shielding, and second, I route the mains power away from the LCD panel. Doing both greatly reduces the possibility of EMI corrupting your LCD panel.

In rare cases it is possible for your heating element to fail. In this case, your printer may never reach its target heat and therefore never start printing. Or in the case of the hot end, the print could fail in the middle. If you suspect your printer is not heating properly, use an infrared temperature sensor or a contact sensor to measure the temperature of your heater. If it is not heating properly, replace the heater. If that does not correct the problem, you may need to consider either a software issue or an electronics board failure.

Another possible reason for not reaching the correct temperature is that you are using a power supply set to 220VAC when plugged into a 110VAC outlet. This can cause the output of the power supply to be too low (around 10V), and therefore not enough to heat the hot end.

■ **Caution**   Never attempt to use your fingers, palms, or any appendage to test heaters. Some heaters can heat up very quickly to temperatures that can cause severe burns. Always use a sensor to measure heaters.

BROTHER, CAN YOU SPARE A PART?

I will talk more about having a set of spares on hand in Chapter 10. However, it is worth mentioning you may want to consider building a spares kit to include printing some of the parts for your printer,[15] which is a great way to start using your printer.

The contents of your kit may depend on how much you want to spend, or more importantly, how long you can wait for a replacement part. For electronics, I like to have at least one stepper motor that matches the other motors in the printer, as well as an electronics board, at least one stepper driver, and plenty of wiring. If the printer is going to be used in a business, I like to also keep on hand a spare hot end and a heated build platform. On the other hand, if you have more than one printer, you can harvest parts from one printer should another fail and require parts.

Summary

Hardware problems can cause a host of print quality issues. As we have seen, finding the cause of the problem requires you to consider several possibilities, because most problems can be caused by several different sources.

In this chapter, I presented some basic best practices for troubleshooting problems, and I presented a host of hardware problems you could encounter. While it is my hope that you never encounter any of these problems, knowing what could fail is a key to being able to detect and repair the problem.

In the next chapter, I present potential problems related to software settings. As you will see, fixing these problems involve changing one or more settings in your slicer, printer settings, or firmware.

---

[15]This was one of the original goals of the RepRap project—to be able to reproduce itself by printing a new set of plastic parts.

CHAPTER 8

∎∎∎

Solving Software Issues

In the last chapter, I presented a host of potential causes and solutions for hardware-related problems. Software issues, as well as hardware issues, can cause many of those problems. I have split the discussion into two chapters because software causes are quite different than hardware causes. Similarly, solving software issues takes very different forms.

Like the last chapter, I will present discussions on the various aspects of software that can cause print quality issues. And like the last chapter, I will present categories of problems and discuss the possible causes and solutions. These include changes you can make in the slicer, printer controller, and firmware.

Hardware problems can sometimes be easy to detect and even correct. Even the less obvious hardware problems, once correctly diagnosed, typically have a visible and logical solution. For example, a broken part or a loose belt are things you can see and replace or adjust. However, software problems are not always that obvious.

In some cases, the software or its settings are not the actual cause of the problem. Thus, I recommend you explore all hardware causes before jumping directly into changing the software settings. For example, if your print bed is not level (trammed), objects could lift when placed in one corner of the print bed but not others. Changing the temperature via the slicer software is not going to fix this or similar problems.

However, there are situations where software settings can be changed to help correct a printing problem. For example, increasing the temperature of the hot end to ensure better layer adhesion. In other cases, the software can be the cause of the problem. For example, incorrectly specifying the diameter of the filament in the slicer can cause very poor prints, including extrusion failures.

Like the hardware problems discussed in the last chapter, knowing the software settings that can be used to treat and cure print quality issues can help you fine-tune your software so that you can get the most out of your printer.

In the following sections, I present discussions of each of these areas, with examples of how the software can be changed, as well as example screenshots of some of the more obscure settings. Let's begin with the settings that you can change in the slicer to correct printing problems.

Slicer

The slicer, or CAM software, can be considered the most important step in the 3D printing tool chain. Recall that the slicer is responsible for taking input in the form of printer configuration settings such as filament size, temperature settings, and so forth, and an object file (.stl) to form a file that contains commands to direct the printer. This file is a .gcode file (or .x3g for MakerBot printers) that is either read from an SD card or sent to the printer directly from the computer.

Clearly, if there are any printer settings in the slicer that do not match your printer hardware, the resulting file will also not match your printer. Printing a file with incorrect printer or slicing settings will result in improperly printed objects. In the most extreme case, this means the printing fails. At the least, it means one of several print quality issues.

Even if the settings are valid and match your printer hardware, you can use the slicer to change certain parameters to help combat some of the more common printing problems. That is, objects that print poorly can sometimes be fixed with slicing changes. In similar fashion, you can use the slicer settings to help combat problems such as adhesion, as you will see in the next section.

First-Layer Adhesion

Adhesion problems most often occur between the first layer and the print surface. When the print pulls away from the print surface, it is called *lifting*. Adhesion problems can also occur between other layers of the object. Poor layer adhesion at higher layers is sometimes called *cracking* or *warping*.

Lifting can be controlled in a number of ways. The last chapter presented several possible causes of lift related to hardware. You also saw how the print surface treatment can affect lifting. However, there is another element to consider: controlling the temperature of the heated print bed.

If your printer has a heated print bed, you should consider using it when printing objects. While a heated print bed is required for ABS, it is often considered optional for PLA and other filaments. The generally accepted heated print temperature for ABS is around 110ºC and PLA is around 60ºC.

■ **Note**   The combination of printer hardware and filament may vary slightly from these estimates. Experimentation and vendor recommendations should be your guide. For example, you may find you can lower the temperature if your printer has an enclosure.

Remember, the temperature settings are stored in the print file. Setting these values on your printer or through a printer controller application is possible, but most printers will override these settings as soon as the codes are read from the file. The following is a sample command (or code) to set the temperature.

```
M190 S60 ; wait for bed temperature to be reached
```

REMEMBER, SLICER FILES ARE PRINTER SPECIFIC

One of the common mistakes for those who print with ABS and PLA is to attempt to print a file that was generated for PLA with ABS. In this case, the heated bed is too cold and lifting is much more likely to occur. The temperature for the hot end is also likely to be wrong, so you can also risk extrusion problems. On the other hand, if you attempt to print a file sliced for ABS with PLA, the print bed will be too high, which can cause the print to sag and print very poorly. Since the hot-end temperature for ABS is normally higher, you could also encounter burning smells from the extruder.

If the print bed is too cold, it can cause the first few layers to cool too quickly, causing the layers to contract and pulling the object away from the print bed, which happens more often with ABS. In this case, it isn't a matter of having a properly prepared print surface, rather it is a case of not enough heat stored in the layers to ensure a slower and more even cooling of the object layers.

If lifting is severe enough, it can even cause the object to come into contact with the hot end. This can cause the entire object to get knocked off the print bed, ruining the print. However, if it has lifted that much already, it is likely to get worse. Sadly, if you are not watching your printer, this can result in a partially printed object and a nesting of filament as the printer happily continues to extrude filament into the air. If the loose filament comes into contact with the hot end, it can melt and stick to places you don't want it to. Not only does this result in a big mess, it also wastes a lot of filament.

If you are experiencing lifting, check the temperature of your heated print bed. If it is lower than the preceding estimates, try raising it 5 degrees, and then check the results on your next print. In rare cases, I've found that lowering the temperature 5 degrees can help print quality in other ways. For example, having the print bed too hot can cause the object to retain too much heat, making it harder to print extreme overhangs. In this case, the overhang layers will curl at the end, giving the overhand a stair-step look rather than a smooth transition. If you are printing with your print bed in excess of 110 degrees, consider lowering it 5 degrees at a time until you have the lowest setting possible that does not cause (or make worse) lifting.

LIVING WITH LIFT

If you have followed the advice here and elsewhere to combat lifting, you should have reduced your lifting problem significantly. However, it is possible you may not completely eliminate the problem. This is especially true for ABS, which requires more effort to perfect. For example, a small amount of lifting—such as a small corner or other part that lifts slightly off the print bed but does not ruin the part—may be acceptable. If you examine Thingiverse carefully, you may find signs of lifting on many things posted to the site. If you have treated your lifting problem using as many techniques as you can, but you still have an occasional small amount of lifting, you may want to declare success.

So how do you set or change the heated print bed temperature? Recall from earlier chapters that the bed temperature can be set in Slic3r on the Filament Settings tab, as shown in Figure 8-1. Similarly, in MakerWare, you set the bed temperature on the Make dialog Temperature tab, as shown in Figure 8-2. Notice in these figures that you can also set the hot-end (extruder) temperature on these screens.

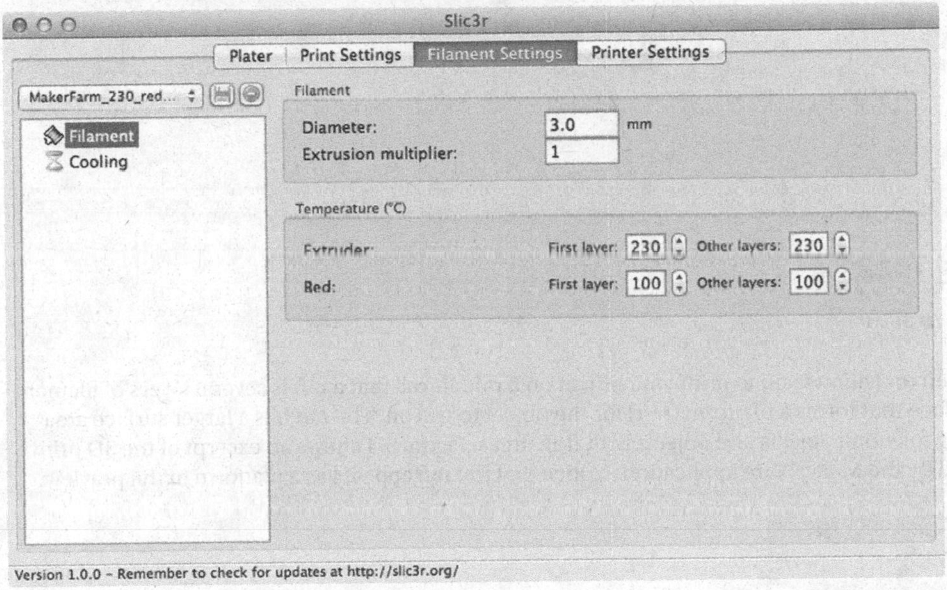

Figure 8-1. Temperature settings in Slic3r

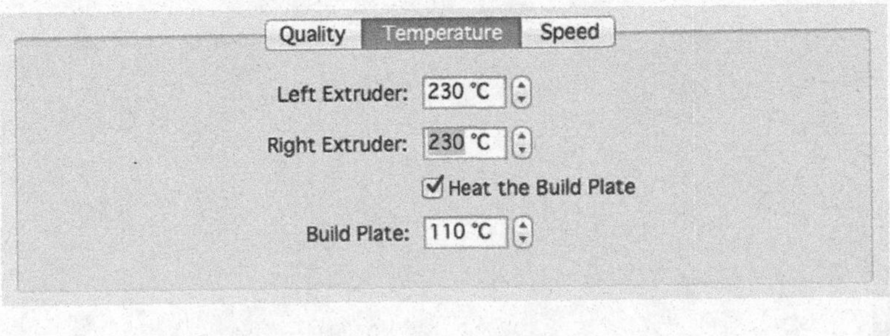

Figure 8-2. Temperature settings in MakerWare

Once again, if you need to change the temperature settings in a print file, you must rerun the slicer. It is possible to edit the `.gcode` file directly, but make sure you do not introduce any errors. However, you cannot easily edit other formats, such as `.x3g`.

Another contributor to lifting is when the object has too small of a surface area that is not enough contact with the print surface. If the object has small protrusions or thin areas, you may not have enough filament that makes up the first layer to make a strong bond with the print surface.

The best way to treat this problem is to enhance the object with a brim. Recall that a brim is additional loops of filament laid down around the perimeter of the object, which increases the surface area. Figure 8-3 shows the brim settings in Slic3r.

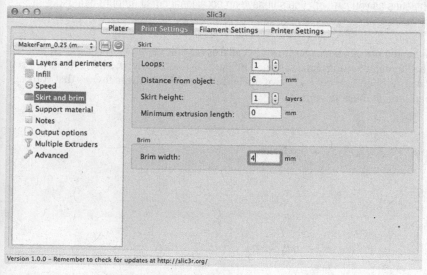

Figure 8-3. *Setting a brim in Slic3r*

Another software-based tool allows you to print your object on a raft. Recall that a raft is several layers of filament laid down on the print surface that forms a platform (raft) for the object to rest on. The raft has a larger surface area and can help prevent lifting for small objects and objects with thin areas. Figure 8-4 shows an excerpt of the 3D print preview for an object sliced by the MakerWare application. Notice that the raft appears as a platform in the preview.

Figure 8-4. *Raft printed with object in MakerWare*

A less frequently used heated print bed technique to combat first-layer adhesion is to set the first layer temperature higher than upper layers. Notice that in Figure 8-1 you can do that with the Slic3r (but not with MakerWare). This setting allows you to set the first-layer temperature high enough to treat your lifting problem, and to set the other layers lower to retain heat in the object and to control cooling (and prevent warping and cracking).

Aside from heated print bed temperature, you can also treat lifting problems by slowing the print speed for the first layer. You can control this easily in Slic3r (MakerWare does this itself) using the Speed dialog on the Print Settings tab, as shown in Figure 8-5.

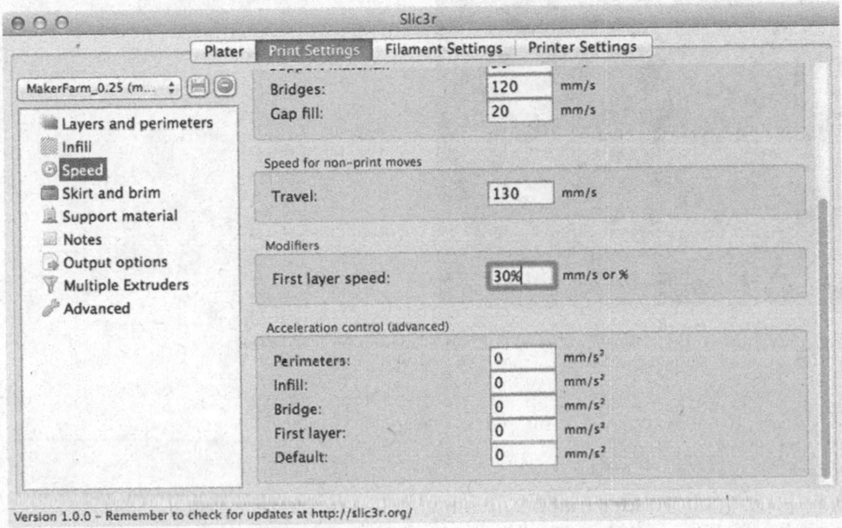

Figure 8-5. *Setting first-layer speed*

Notice that in this case I set the speed of the first layer to 30% of the normal speed. Slowing the print speed can improve first layer adhesion by allowing the filament more time to bond to the print surface. If you notice filament peeling away from the print surface, or small perimeters not sticking well, slowing the print speed of the first layer can help you avoid these problems.

Another way to combat lifting is to use *anchors* (also called *mouse ears* or *lily pads*). These are normally small round discs placed on each corner or protrusion of the object to increase the surface area around the corner without increasing it everywhere like a brim would do. You can create anchors however you like and add them to your slicer platter when slicing. The downside is that these anchors must be cut away from the final part.

Creating anchors is easy. Just use OpenSCAD to create a disc about 0.5mm thick (or two layers, depending on your layer thickness). Some prefer to make their anchors three or four layers thick for really strong bonds. However, the thicker the anchor, the harder it is to cut away. The following is the code for creating a disc-shaped anchor.

```
cylinder(0.5,5,5);
```

To use the anchors, open your slicer and place the object on the platter. Then add as many anchors as you need and place them on the corners, as shown in Figure 8-6. Notice that I placed the anchors on each corner of the object. Some slicers will allow you to combine the anchors and your object into a single part. This is known as a *mashup* and it is something I will demonstrate more fully in a later chapter.

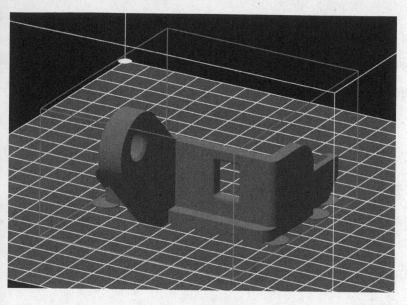

Figure 8-6. *Use anchors to combat lifting*

Print Quality

Closely related to first-layer adhesion are print quality issues that occur at higher layers. These are often layer adhesion problems that are treated in similar fashion as lifting. The layer adhesion problems discussed here include warping, splitting, and sagging.

All of these problems can be treated with changing the temperature of the print bed and hot end. However, they are caused by filament cooling unevenly. Thus, like adhesion, you should fix any hardware problems before experimenting with temperature as a means to fix these print quality issues.

■ **Caution** Never set the temperature higher than the maximum safe settings of your hot end. Check your documentation or contact your vendor to find the limits of your hot end heating range.

Examples of where to set the temperature of the hot end in the slicer are shown in Figures 8-1 and 8-2. Recall also that the hot end temperature is another setting that is maintained in the printer file, and not something you can change on the printer itself.

In most cases, you will raise the temperature of the hot end 5 degrees at a time, and then check the results. In rare cases, you could lower the temperature of the hot end 5 degrees at a time. Before changing your hot end temperature, be sure that you are familiar with the hot end features and capabilities. Never set the hot end higher than its maximum setting.

■ **Tip** Most firmware incorporates a maximum temperature to keep you from accidentally setting the temperature higher than what the hot end can endure. Check to make sure this value is set to your manufacturer's maximum recommended temperature.

FILAMENT TEMPERATURE LIMITATIONS

When the temperature is too low, extrusion failure is likely. However, raising the temperature of the hot end can improve adhesion and extrusion. But you can go too far. If the temperature is too high, you will see the filament oozing from the hot end. Some ooze is possible, but the filament should not ooze more than a slight seeping over a few minutes. If it continues to ooze from the nozzle, you may want to lower the temperature. Another possibility is that the filament could burn.[1] In some cases you may even seem some steam from the hot end.[2] If either of these occurs, stop your printer and reduce the temperature.

Warping

Warping is when the higher layers of an object cool more quickly than the lower layers. When this happens, there may be too high a temperature in the object. Lowering the temperature of the print bed can help combat warping. If you are printing with PLA and using a fan, you may want to slow the fan speed to force less air over the object. Too much air can cause the higher layers to cool more quickly than the lower layers.

As I briefly mentioned earlier, warping can also occur on areas with *overhang*, which is a portion of the object that protrudes from the base at a low angle. Overhangs can be hard to print because they tend to cool much more quickly and can warp at the ends of each layer. When this occurs, you cannot do much about it while the object is printing. Most times the object is still usable because the hot end will tend to push out the thin layers on the next pass. However, the quality of that portion of the object will suffer.

The best way to treat overhangs is to use *supports*. Supports are thin layers of filament extruded to form a scaffold to support the object during printing. You can turn on supports in Slic3r on the Print Settings page, as shown in Figure 8-7. Supports can be enabled in MakerWare on the Make dialog by checking the *Supports* checkbox.

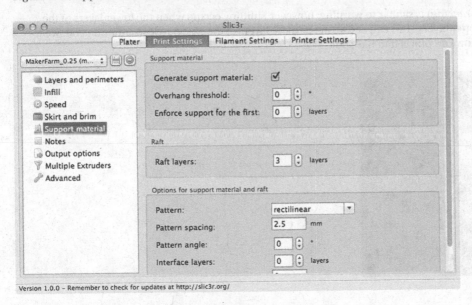

Figure 8-7. Enabling rafting and supports in Slic3r

---

[1]Bad burning smells are always bad. Even ABS should not smell burnt when extruding.
[2]Steam may be normal for some exotic filaments. Steam can also indicate that the filament has absorbed too much moisture, in which case you should attempt to dry the filament with desiccant in a sealed bag.

Using supports effectively creates a false portion of the object that allows thin layers to be printed with greatly reduced warping. These supports are very thin and can be easily removed from the printed object by breaking them away, and then trimming with a hobby knife. Figure 8-8 shows an example preview of an object sliced with support turned on. Notice in this case that there appear to be vertical walls that form bridges for the overhangs.

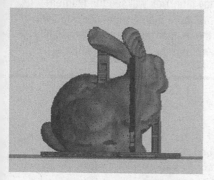

Figure 8-8. Print preview of an object with supports for overhangs

Lastly, you should check that you are not turning off the print bed during printing. Take another look at Figure 8-1. Notice you can set the print bed temperature for lower levels differently than with higher levels. If you neglected to turn on the heated print bed for higher levels, this could cause warping, as described here.

Splitting

Splitting (sometimes called *cracking*) is similar to warping; however, splitting occurs when the lower layers of the object cool faster than the upper layers. This can cause one or more layers of the object to lose adhesion and, well, split the object. Figure 8-9 shows an object that has split.

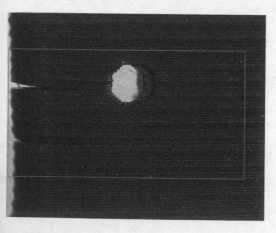

Figure 8-9. Splitting example

Splitting is often caused by drafts. Eliminating drafts can help considerably. However, you can also treat splitting by ensuring that your heated print bed is at the proper temperature and that the hot end temperature is set correctly. In some cases, slowing the print speed can also treat splitting. Slower speeds tend to improve the layer bonds. Again, the problem occurs when the object cools much faster than the newest layers. Raising the heated print bed by 5 degrees may help.

When objects split like the one shown in Figure 8-9, chances are the split or crack isn't isolated to those areas where the split is visible. I have seen objects that have had a small split in one area fail from layer-sheering forces (stress placed on the object parallel to the layers). This revealed that the object had poor layer adhesion throughout. In fact, when I removed the object and applied layer-sheering force, it broke in other places. Thus, when you encounter splitting or cracks in your prints, treat the problem and reprint the object.

Sagging

Sagging occurs in one of two ways: when bridging large gaps and when the object is too hot. Bridging small gaps is not usually a problem. Indeed, the slicer has accommodations for that. For example, a small hole or nut trap can be covered with a layer of filament without too much of a problem. However, large areas or areas without any form of support can be a problem for some printers.

If the gap is really big—more than a few centimeters—the slicer may not be able to compensate, and the only solutions are to use supports in the form of the slicer option or to use artificial supports (parts designed into the object itself).

Figure 8-10 shows an object with a large gap (bridge) that I decided to experiment with. It is a small air dam to be mounted on a power supply to redirect air away from the print bed. Rather than adding supports, I decided to try to print the object without them to see if the sagging filament could be removed or repaired. Fortunately, that was exactly the case; only the one layer sagged. The other layers were able to bridge the gap and printed reasonably well. Figure 8-10 shows the end result.

Figure 8-10. *Bridging a gap*

If the sagging is limited to a single layer under the gap or bridge, you can repair the sag. For PLA, simply use a hot air gun to heat the sagging filament and press them into the object. Be careful not to get it too hot because it can warp the object. You will not be able to get the filament hot enough to reform the layer bonds, but at least you won't have to cut away the filament or toss the object.

For ABS, use a lint-free rag soaked with acetone and rub it on the sagging filaments until they become soft, and then press them into the object. Within a few moments the acetone will evaporate, and the object will be repaired and likely just as strong as if it had not sagged. Figure 8-11 shows the repaired gap for the object in Figure 8-10. In this example, the sag was extreme (and intentional). Some of the filament broke and fell onto the print surface. Hence there are some places where there is no filament. While the surface may not be smooth, it permitted me to use this test object, even though I expected it to fail.[3]

---

[3]Hey, that's part of the joy of 3D printing. Sometimes things you think will never work turn out pretty well, all things considered. Don't be afraid to experiment!

Figure 8-11.   Repaired sagging filaments in gap

Consequently, I reprinted this object with supports turned on in the slicer. The problem was the support option printed supports the entire length of the object making it a pain to clean and wasting a lot of filament.

I then redesigned the object to include supports as part of the object itself. This printed much better, and since the gaps were much smaller, I was able to print without turning supports on in the slicer. Figure 8-12 shows a rendering of the redesign.

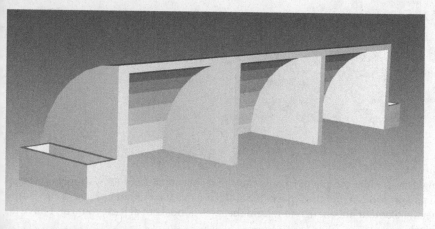

Figure 8-12.   Designing supports into your models

If your heated print bed is too hot, it can cause the object to remain soft and sag. That is, the filament does not cool enough to become firm enough to support the weight of the layers above. When this occurs, lower the heated print bed temperature by 5 degrees and try the print again.[4] If the sagging is severe, you may want to lower the temperature by 10 degrees at a time.

---

[4]Actually, this can be one of the side effects of using an ABS print file with PLA. Check the file to make sure that you are using the right filament.

When printing with PLA, sagging can also be treated by increasing the fan speed on higher layers. This will ensure that the filament that is used to bridge the gap is cooled faster, and thus can keep its shape. You can also increase the number of shells, or in some slicing applications, increase the number of top layers. But these techniques only work if the gap is at the top of the object.

It can help to change the print speed for printing gaps (bridges). If the print speed is increased; it will reduce the chances of the bridge drooping, but may increase the likelihood that it will break.

Lastly, printing supports is the best way to avoid sagging in bridges and gaps.

Scaling

If your object prints well but it isn't the right size (it's too big or too small), you may be able to solve the problem by using a slicing feature called *scaling*. Scaling allows you to shrink or enlarge the object by a certain percentage. Figure 8-13 shows the scaling settings in Slic3r and Figure 8-14 shows the scaling option in MakerWare. In each case, you can scale the object proportionally.

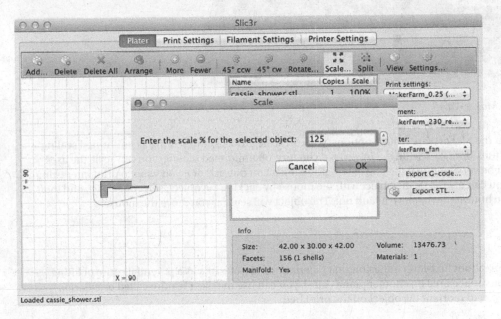

Figure 8-13. *Scaling in Slic3r*

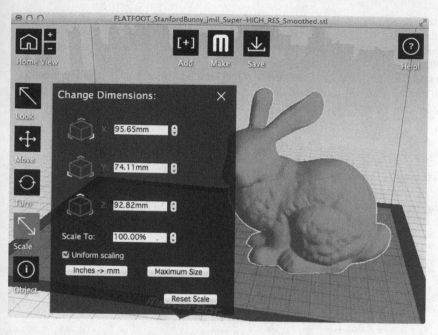

Figure 8-14. *Scaling in MakerWare*

As you can see from the MakerWare scaling options, you can scale any axis, and so long as uniformed scaling is checked, it will adapt the other axes settings. However, if you turn off uniformed scaling, you can scale the axes independently. This can be very helpful if the object is just slightly off on one axis or if you want to print interesting distortions of objects. You can also scale the object with the mouse by clicking the object, selecting Scale, and then while holding the mouse button down, move in and out. The object will scale as you move the mouse.

Orientation

Recall from the discussion about first-layer adhesion that I mentioned surface area as a potential cause of lifting. If your object has a larger surface area on another plane (side), you can use the slicer feature called *orientation* (sometimes called *rotation*) to reorient the object on the print bed.

■ **Tip**   If you design the object yourself, it is best to set the orientation before you export the file.

For example, suppose you have designed the dollhouse table shown in Figure 8-15. It is a simple design and presented in the orientation that you envisioned it—right-side up.

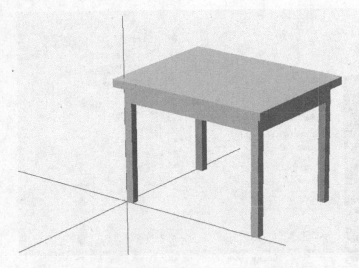

Figure 8-15. *Dollhouse table*

Notice the legs of the table. They're small and only a fraction of the object touches the print surface. Not only that, but there is a large area that will have to be bridged (the table top). You could add supports to ensure that the gap doesn't sag; however, if you flip the object over, you have a much larger surface area and the small bits (legs) are pointing up. Figure 8-16 shows the reoriented object.

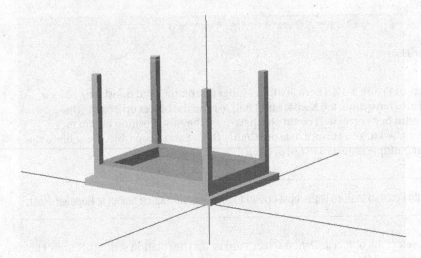

Figure 8-16. *Dollhouse table reoriented*

Sadly, there is no straightforward way to rotate an object like this in Slic3r. However, you can rotate the object in Repetier-Host and MakerWare. Figure 8-17 shows the rotation settings for Repetier-Host and Figure 8-18 shows the rotation dialog in MakerWare.

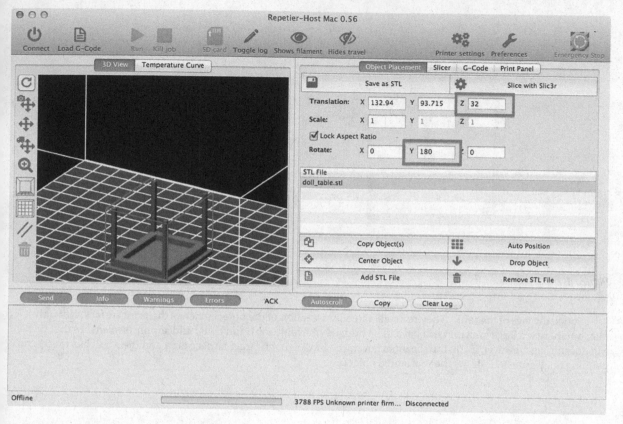

Figure 8-17. *Rotating objects in Repetier-Host*

Notice the two highlighted text boxes in Figure 8-17. These are the settings for rotating and translating objects. Notice I rotated on the Y axis (but could also have done the X axis) and I had to raise the object up 32mm. This is so that the object will position on the print bed correctly. I could also have used the Auto Position button to automatically position the object once I rotated it. You can also use the Center Object and Drop Object to achieve this result. Auto Position will also ensure that multiple objects will not overlap.

■ **Tip**   If you do not know the size, the Auto Position feature is the best option to reposition a rotated object in Repetier-Host.

Notice in Figure 8-18 that you must select the object and then select Turn to see the rotation settings. Simply click the plus or minus sign for whatever axes you want to change, 90 degrees at a time. Or you can enter the value as I have done. Notice in the background the object is oriented correctly. Like Repetier-Host, the Lay Flat button ensures the object will lay flat on the print bed.

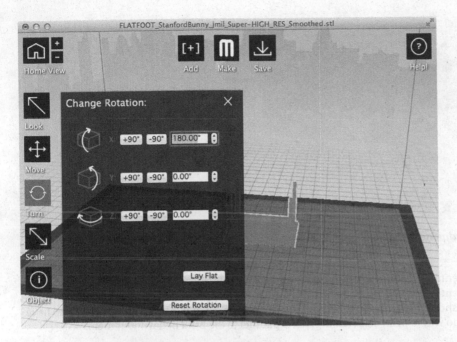

Figure 8-18. *Rotating objects in MakerWare*

As you can see from this simple example, orientation can also be used to eliminate bridging and to help prevent warping. Figure 8-19 shows an object that can be printed easily and, in most cases, well. However, you may experience some sagging and even warping on the overhang (the rounded portion). If you reorient the object as shown in Figure 8-20, you not only increase the surface area but also eliminate the overhang and its possible issues.

Figure 8-19. *Object with overhang*

Figure 8-20. *Reoriented object reducing overhang*

Another example of how orientation can help is with printing supports. Consider the object from Figure 8-19. Sometimes designers want to orient curved sides in the Z axis because they can print slightly better that way.[5] In this case, the object would appear as shown in Figure 8-21. In order to print this object in this orientation, you would have to use supports because there is no way to print an overhang that is parallel to the print bed without them.

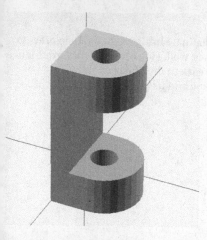

Figure 8-21. *Reoriented object without overhang requiring support*

Figure 8-22 shows what this object looks like with supports added. As you can see, there will be a lot of cleanup necessary to remove the supports.

[5]Actually, this may be compensating for axis issues.

Figure 8-22. Object print preview with supports

However, you should still consider this option if you need to use it. In fact, one reason you might want to reorient an object in this manner is for sheering. The layers in the object in Figure 8-21 will run perpendicular to the layers in the object in Figure 8-20. If you need to consider sheering forces, you may want to reorient your object to ensure that the layers run perpendicular to the sheering force.

For example, if the object in Figure 8-20 is going to be used as an anchor for supporting a pulley or as an idler bearing for a belt-driven mechanism, and thus the forces will be pulling away from the base, this orientation could be slightly stronger than the orientation of the object in Figure 8-20. This is because the layers run perpendicular to the sheering force in Figure 8-21, but parallel in Figure 8-20. Think of it this way: it is easier to break layer bonds than it is to break filament.

When creating your own objects, or printing objects made by others, check the orientation of the object before printing it. Consider not only how much surface area is needed for a strong first layer bond, but also reducing overhangs and gaps (bridges). In some cases, sheering force may determine how you orient the object. Better still, you can avoid using supports—and thereby reduce sagging!

Filament and Extrusion

Problems with filament and extrusion, in general, can sometimes be difficult to diagnose. This is because of the slight variations that exist among filament. Recall our discussion about filament and how it can vary in size and temperature settings. PLA does not have the same properties as ABS. In some cases, even the same type filament, but of different colors, can have different heating properties.

The most common problems are poor extrusion, oozing of the filament from the nozzle,[6] and layer inconsistencies. All of these can be controlled, or at least reduced, with key settings in the slicer. I discuss each in more detail in the following sections.

Poor Extrusion

If your slicer is set up to match the settings of your printer and the filament you are using, extrusion should occur normally without much issue. Hardware-related issues are still a concern (obstructions, blocked nozzle, etc.), but once those issues are solved or eliminated, you should be fine. However, if your slicer settings do not match your filament, you can encounter poor extrusion.

The most common issue is filament that extrudes too much or too little. This is caused by using the incorrect filament diameter in your slicer. Figure 8-23 shows the filament settings for the Slic3r application.

---

[6]Yes, just like an infant's runny nose. Not quite as repulsive, but it still has a certain "ick" element.

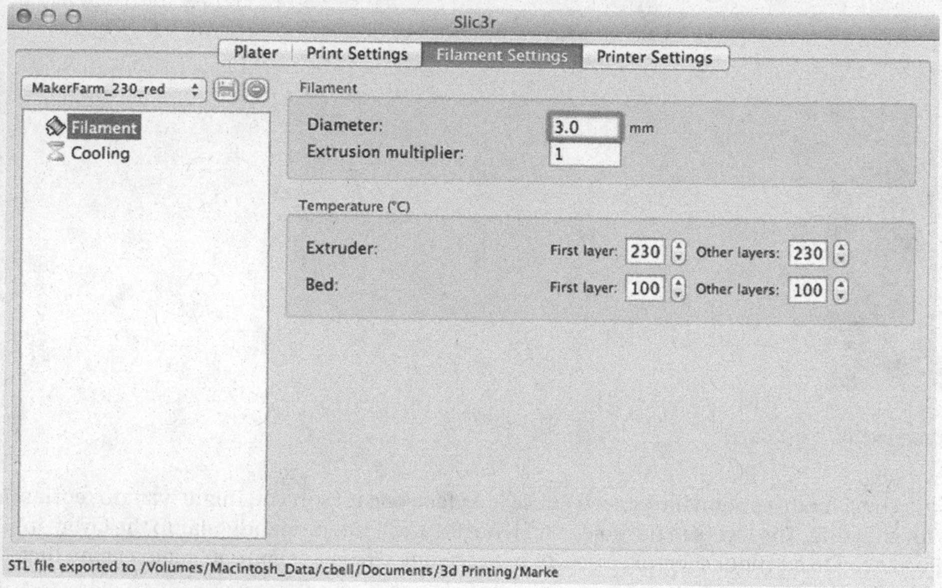

Figure 8-23. Filament settings in Slic3r

■ **Tip** Be sure to measure your filament each time you slice an object.

If you enter a value that is too large, the extruder may not extrude enough filament. In this case, the layer adhesion may suffer and the part may be easier to break with sheering force. In the case where you use a setting that is too low, the filament may clump, or strings (sometimes called *threads*) may appear as the hot end moves from one place to another. If you see a lot of stringing, check your slicer for the proper setting for the filament diameter.

Another cause of poor extrusion is using the wrong settings for your hot end temperature. Too high a setting can cause the filament to extrude more easily, which also causes clumping and stringing. Too low and the filament may not extrude properly. Signs of the wrong temperature can manifest as the extruder drive pulley slipping or chattering. You may also see cases where the filament comes out in spurts or with short sections of thinner filament. In other cases, you may see the filament appearing as dots. If the filament is not extruding in a clean line, you likely are experiencing problems with hot end temperature.

In the extreme, this problem can cause the filament to strip and extrusion to stop. I upgraded one of my printers recently with a really nice set of milled aluminum extruder hardware, only to discover that the spring I used was just a wee bit too stiff. This caused the stepper motor to strip for only one of several spools of filament. The filament was a bit softer than the other spools. I fixed the problem temporarily by increasing the hot end temperature. The correct resolution was to replace the spring.

If your filament seems to clump or string among the part, reduce the hot end temperature by 5 degrees and try the print again. If it gets better, try another 5 degrees until you find the correct setting for that filament.

Similarly, if your filament does not extrude well and there are no obstructions or blockages in the hot end or nozzle, increase the hot end temperature by 5 degrees at a time until the filament extrudes well.

When I encounter situations like this, where I know it is a slicer setting, especially with hot end temperatures, I use a printer controller application to test extrusion by heating the hot end to the new value and extruding between 30mm and 100mm of filament. You can tell everything is going well by observing the extruder and the filament as it exits the nozzle. If it flows well and the extruder turns without stopping, stuttering, or any noise of stripping, I then retry my print. This saves me a lot of filament and doesn't ruin as many parts. Fortunately, you only have to do this if you encounter a new filament or filament from a different vendor.

Oozing

One of the side effects of having the hot end set to the optimal temperature for extrusion is oozing. If the printer sits idle with the hot end heated to temperature, you can observe a small amount of filament oozing from the nozzle. This is normal, so long as it isn't more than a few millimeters. And depending on how long your printer will be idle, this should not be a problem. The filament that oozed out will be expelled when the printer does its purge around the object or along the front of the print bed, as with a MakerBot.[7]

However, if you are experiencing a lot of ooze, you may have your hot end set too high. Too much oozing can transfer to the object in the form of extraneous bits of filament, rounded corners that should be sharper, and odd deposits of filament in places where the hot end has moved from one location to another. This is normally not the thin strands, strings, or threads like you see with a hot end that is a little too hot. In this case, the hot end is much hotter than necessary. If this happens, reduce the hot end temperature by 5 degrees at a time until the oozing slows to only a small amount. If your filament is oozing more than 5mm to 10mm in a few seconds, your hot end is too hot.

It should be noted that some hot ends have a larger heat chamber or are designed in such a way that oozing is more prevalent. For hot ends like this, the slicer application can be helpful in controlling the effects of oozing. The Slic3r application has a feature that can help: retraction. Figure 8-24 shows the Extruder settings on the Printer Settings tab. This is the same location that you enter the nozzle size to match your printer.

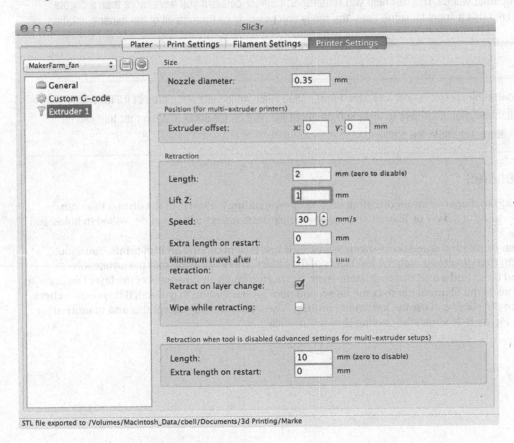

Figure 8-24. Treating oozing with Slic3r

---

[7]This is one of my favorite features of the MakerBot. Even a longer ooze of 25mm can be purged during that long sweep across the front of the print bed.

Notice the Retraction section. Here you can use settings to retract a certain amount of filament, for lifting of the Z axis, to set speed, and more. The two most common options to set are lift and retraction length. As you can see in the example, I have set retraction to 2mm and a lift of 1mm. This will cause the extruder to turn backward for 2mm, sucking in the filament.

The lift is primarily used to prevent the nozzle from striking areas of the print that may be higher than the current Z position. Lifting also gives the filament a chance to break away from the layer, and thereby reduce stringing from the retraction. Use retraction if your hot end oozes a bit more than you'd like or if there is significant stringing (small threads stretching across movements without extrusion) but your hot end temperature settings are correct.

NOT ALL FILAMENT IS CREATED EQUAL

As I mentioned in earlier discussions about filament types and heat characteristics, filament can vary. In fact, different colors and even different vendors of the same type (PLA, ABS, etc.) can have different heating properties and even vary in diameter. Once you zero in on the heated print bed (if equipped) and hot end settings that work best for the filament, make a note of these settings and the diameter on the spool itself. I like to use a sticky label to write down the optimal values. This can help you remember the finer details if you have more than a couple of spools or you do not use a spool for some time. You really don't want to go through all of the experimentation again, do you?

■ **Note**   There is a community project underway called the Unified Filament Identification project (UFID) working on an open standard for filament manufacturers to include data about filament on the spool in a manner that can be machine-read, and therefore automate the process.

Layer Inconsistencies

One of the hardest things to diagnose are inconsistencies that appear among the layers of the print. These can manifest as missing portions of a layer or filament run, gaps in the print layer, extra filament deposited in holes, and poorly formed objects.

The most common cause for some of these inconsistencies is insufficient cooling on PLA prints. You should always use a cooling fan that directs air onto the top layers of the object. This will ensure that the layer cools fast enough to make a good bond and a firm and consistent layer. Having too much air flowing over the layer can cause the layer to deform, portions of the filament run to come loose, and poor layer adhesion in general. If this occurs, check the speed of your fan in the slicer and use the automatic settings. These are generally acceptable and optimized for properly cooling PLA. Figure 8-25 shows the cooling settings in Slic3r.

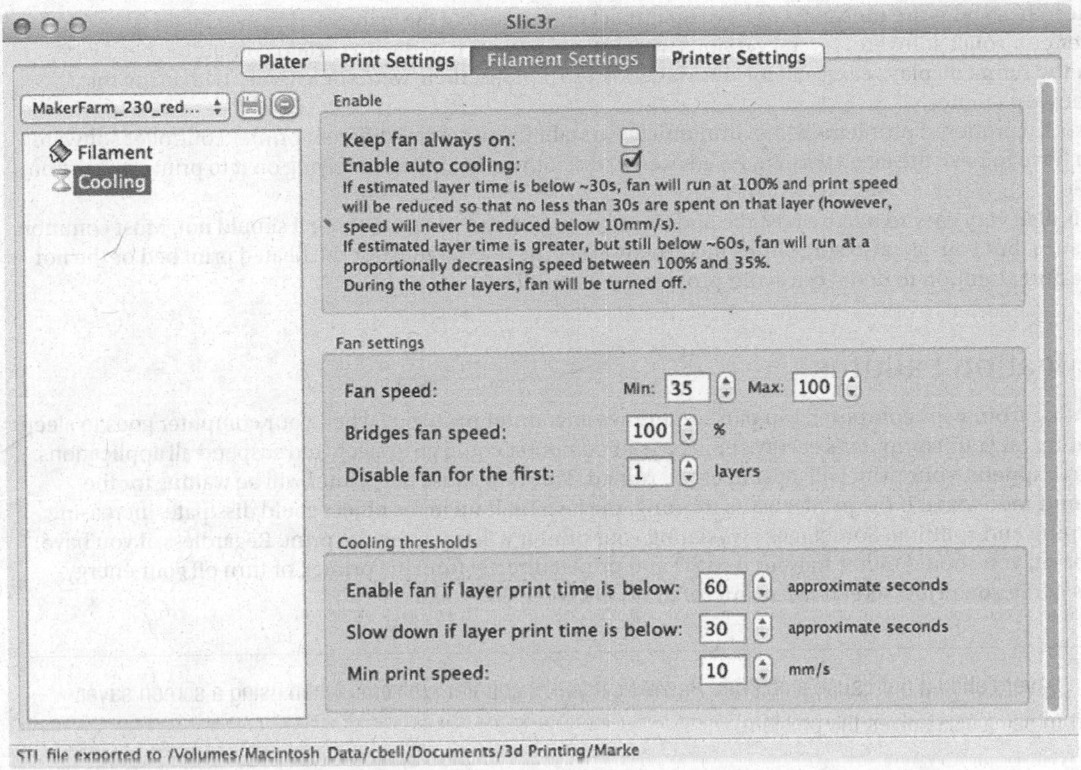

Figure 8-25. *Cooling settings in Slic3r*

Notice that you can choose to keep the fan on at all times. This will keep the fan running at whatever speed you set as the default (see the center of Figure 8-25). So far, I have not found a need to use this setting. The setting you want to use for PLA is the "Enable auto cooling" check box. This will ensure that the fan changes speed as the object is printed (see Figure 8-25 for a description of how this works).

For some objects, the print speed may contribute to inconsistent prints. I have seen this in tall objects with intricate portions at the higher levels (small protrusions, small holes, tall, thin columns, etc.). Slowing the print speed can improve quality for objects with these features.

Another possible cause for inconsistent prints is using a layer height that is too coarse for your hardware. Recall from the calibration chapter that some layer heights can introduce errors in the layer calculations. If you are printing an object with a high layer height, try using a lower value to see if it improves consistency.

Lastly, it is possible that when printing large objects (particularly those printed with PLA) can cool too much before the layer is complete and the next layer is applied. To combat this issue, increase the temperature of the heated print bed, slow the fan, or use an enclosure to ensure that more heat remains in the object at lower levels.

Printer Controller

The printer control software can be very useful, and for the most part (and most vendors' variants), it is very reliable. However, I have found that certain early releases and, in some cases, major releases of printer controller software contain bugs.

Most times, these bugs are nuisances or have no impact on your use of the features. However, in the case of one popular printer controller software, several versions were known to have issues with certain computing hardware. Indeed, when the retina displays came out for the MacBook Pro laptops, there were some issues with using the software on these machines.

I have also encountered problems with communication stability on several different printer controller software. If you feel you have to have the latest version, be advised to test it thoroughly before relying on it to print objects from your computer.

Lastly, it is also very easy to make a mistake and direct your printer to do something it should not. Most common are homing issues, but you can also sometimes incorrectly enter the temperature for the heated print bed or the hot end. Only care and attention to detail can avoid problems such as these.

Communication Failures

If you are printing from your computer, you can sometimes encounter problems when your computer goes to sleep. In fact, depending on your computer's energy settings, your computer could go to sleep and suspend all applications.

When that happens, your print will most likely be ruined. This is because the printer will be waiting for the computer to send more data. If the printer waits too long, the heat built up in the object could dissipate, increasing the risk of warping and splitting. Sometimes awakening your printer will not harm the print. Regardless, if you have a large file to print, you should either transfer it to SD and print it directly from the printer, or turn off your energy-saving settings while you print (screen savers are generally OK).

■ **Tip** Screen savers should not cause problems. However, if you encounter problems when using a screen saver, try turning it off to see if this solves the problem.

In the rare event your printer controller software freezes or goes wonky,[8] you may have little choice but to terminate the application and restart your print. Once again, if you want to print from your computer, be sure you are using the latest and most stable release of your printer controller software.

Axis Crashes

A very common and accidental problem those new to 3D printing sometimes encounter[9] concerns crashing the axis into its mechanical bits. This occurs when you have started your printer for the first time but have not homed the axes, and then use the printer controller software (or the LCD panel) to move the axis.

Failing to home the axes means the printer can consider its current location as (0,0,0). Moving the axes in the positive direction could mean it attempts to travel farther than physically possible, resulting in the mechanical bits coming into contact with the frame or other parts of the printer. This is bad, and you should avoid it by always ensuring that you home all axes before trying to move (jog) any axis.

Also consider that if you reset your printer (for whatever reason) while it is printing, it can also lose its home orientation, and then it must be rehomed before resuming printing or printing another object.

---

[8]A highly technical term used to explain unexplained behavior. Not to be confused with *hinky*, which is altogether more serious and sometimes terminal.

[9]Once is usually enough to train us to avoid this in the future.

Firmware

The firmware isn't normally something that goes wrong. This is most fortunate because you rely on the firmware working correctly. If it were to fail, so too would almost every feature of the printer! However, there are some cases where the firmware can be used to solve problems. First and foremost is upgrades. If you modify your printer with a new LCD panel or change the axis movement, you will need to change the firmware. Sometimes the problem isn't obvious until you notice print quality issues or odd noises.

I once came across someone who changed the belt type on one of his axes. This user experienced major problems on the axis that was changed. The problem was that he failed to make the changes to his firmware. For example, if you change from a T2.5 belt and pulley to a GT2 belt and pulley, but keep the pulley sizes the same, you may think you do not need to change the firmware. But that isn't the case—a 16-tooth T2.5 pulley is not the same size as a 16-tooth GT2 pulley. You should always modify the firmware settings to correspond to the exact hardware.

You may not think that changing the LCD panel is a big deal, but it can be. If the new panel is not compatible with the old one, you could encounter a problem where the LCD is unreadable, has garbage characters displayed, or has no display at all. Be sure to check with your vendor for the correct firmware settings.

Another possibility concerns problems encountered after repairs. If you changed the electronics or repaired them in some way, you may inadvertently erase the firmware settings in nonvolatile memory. If you made any changes by way of a G-code, you could lose those settings when the nonvolatile memory is erased. If you repair your printer and it suddenly acts strangely, especially components you did not modify, try reloading the firmware with the correct settings.

Summary

Software changes can help you solve a number of problems—from controlling the temperature of the hot end or print bed to changing the size of the object (scaling). Make sure your printer controller software is stable, or in the case of upgrades, make sure your firmware settings are changed to match the new hardware; this can solve more specific problems.

In this chapter, I presented some of the more common solutions to printing problems that you can implement in software. As you have seen, the slicer is the most commonly used vehicle for correcting problems, followed by things you can fix with the printer controller, and finally, firmware changes are the least common source of problems and solutions.

While knowing what can cause problems and how to fix them will help you keep your printer going when it breaks or when your print quality suffers, you can prevent some problems from occurring by keeping your printer adjusted, cleaned, and lubricated.

In the next chapters, I cover a topic that is rarely covered in books about emerging technologies: maintenance. In fact, maintenance seems to be missing from some 3D printer manuals. I will discuss maintenance tasks that you should do regularly (every time you print) and in the following chapter, I discuss maintenance tasks you should do periodically to keep your printer in top working order.

PART 3

Maintenance and Enhancements

This section introduces the concept of maintaining 3D printers. Topics include the proper alignment of the print bed, as well as cleaning, adjusting, and repairing your printer. Many examples with photos are provided to help you learn how to perform maintenance on your own printer. Finally, there is a chapter to help you learn how to extend the life of your 3D printer by upgrading and enhancing features. You may find that adding a new feature is a lot easier and cheaper than ditching your old model for a shiny new one.

CHAPTER 9

■ ■ ■

3D Printer Maintenance: Inspection and Adjustment Tasks

Owning a 3D printer can be very rewarding—especially once the printer is calibrated correctly and you are achieving high-quality prints. You should take pride in creating things for your household, family, and friends. Whether you are creating new gadgets, fixing things around the house, or just creating things for gifts,[1] the enjoyment factor is quite high.

However, keeping your printer running well requires vigilance and the judicial application of proper maintenance. You have to learn to pay attention to the printer mechanicals and understand the tasks needed to keep things running properly. Even the best-calibrated printer will eventually have problems if you never adjust or repair it when things go a little wrong (or worse, break).

Indeed, if you let the maintenance of your printer slip far enough, you could encounter a myriad of minor print problems that will be more difficult to diagnose and repair. That is, several minor things that are off by a bit, become dirty, lack proper lubrication, and so forth, can have a cumulative effect. It is our job as responsible 3D printer owners to keep that from happening. This chapter is an introduction to the tasks you need to keep your printer in top shape.

I like to categorize maintenance tasks into two groups: tasks that you should perform before each print (or at least once each day that you use your printer) or as needed (*basic maintenance*), and tasks that should be performed at certain milestones (*periodic maintenance*). The frequency of these depends largely on how much you use your printer, as well as the general reliability of your printer design.

I present basic maintenance tasks in this chapter. I will also discuss some basics about maintenance for those who need a primer or an introduction to performing maintenance.

The next chapter will present more complex, preventive maintenance tasks that you need to do on a periodic basis, as well as some of the more complicated corrective maintenance tasks (or simply how to fix things that go sideways).

Let's begin by looking at some of the basics of performing maintenance and the basic 3D printer maintenance tasks you will need to master.

■ **Note**   Some of the practices and tasks discussed in this chapter may seem familiar. That is no accident. I discussed these either in brief or in some detail in previous chapters. I repeat the information here and build on it so that this chapter can be used as a general reference, keeping all of the information in one place.

---

[1]This Easter, I printed an impressive horde of rabbits and a small flock of bird figurines in all colors and sizes. Some were even given names by their new owners. The figurines brightened a few faces; mine included.

Getting Started with Maintenance

Maintenance of 3D printers involves a lot more than some may think and yet not nearly as much as others fear. That is, there are certain things you should do every time you use your printer or as needed, things you need to do regularly (e.g., every 50 hours), and things you need to do after significant use (e.g., every 250 hours). However, none of the maintenance tasks are very difficult nor do they require any extensive skills or familiarity with complex procedures.

There is no magic behind learning how to perform maintenance on your 3D printer—especially if you built your own printer. While some tasks require a modicum of skill with basic hand tools, nothing is so complicated as to require years of experience. The best tool is your desire to keep your printer working at its best. If you have that in mind, none of the maintenance tasks will be difficult. You may find some tasks tedious perhaps, but not very difficult.

Like most things, there are some maintenance tips that can help you succeed. I've already mentioned the desire to maintain your printer. Beyond that, you should also be aware of certain best practices for maintenance in general. The following sections outline some of the common practices for performing maintenance. These apply to almost any type of maintenance, from automobiles to Zamboni machines.

Keep Your Area Clean and Free of Clutter

Have you ever heard the phrase that suggests the degree of clutter on the desk corresponds with the degree of clutter of the mind? I don't strictly believe in that adage, but there is some merit to it. I've known some academics, researchers, and engineers who have completely spotless work areas cleaned to a near surgical level of sanitation. Amazingly, many of these people maintain their office area using a completely different philosophy. Indeed, I've witnessed a major book and file folder quake and landslide on several occasions. Perhaps more amazing is the fact that these brilliant minds can locate anything on their desk within seconds of the request.

Sadly, I am not in this league. While I have been accused of being slightly obsessive when it comes to organization, I have also been known to have moments of shameless clutter. Let's face it: things tend to pile up after a while. This is especially true for hobbies like 3D printers. As you have learned from a previous chapter, there are all manner of tools needed to use and maintain the printer. And it isn't just the tools that can clutter your work area.

Indeed, it doesn't take long for printed parts (prototypes or otherwise) and little bits of filament to litter the area around your printer. Be it from discarded rafting, shavings from finishing your pieces, or simply trimmings for cases when things need a little adjustment to fit properly. Whatever the source, you should avoid the temptation to let things pile up to the point where you are spending time looking for things, or pushing things around.

Not only does the clutter make it harder to work around your printer, but it can also interfere with the normal operation of your printer. I once discovered that I had inadvertently left a pair of ESD tweezers on my build platform. I don't recall having done so, but I was clearly in a hurry at some point and forgot to secure all of my tools. Suffice it to say, it became very obvious when I homed the axes. Fortunately, no harm was done, but I learned a valuable lesson: even if you don't put your tools away, take inventory to make sure all are accounted for.

Consequently, I've formed the habit to make sure the area around my printers is cleaned once per day. That is, I discard unwanted filament and parts, use a vacuum to remove the little bits of filament, and put my tools away. If you do this once per day, you can avoid unexpected surprises and always know where things are stored.

■ **Caution**   If you have pets, you need to vacuum regularly. I discovered one of our miniature dachshunds has a knack of finding small parts of filament on the floor. He would also seek out discarded wire insulation. I reasoned that these things look like his food (small rods) and were therefore fair game in his doggy brain. Since this discovery, I also make sure I vacuum the floor area around my workspace and keep a watch on my pets.

Organize Your Tools for Quick Access

If you have friends and family that are mechanically inclined, you may have encountered a variety of garage and tool organizational styles or methods. There are the compulsive types that like to keep everything in its place—with a place for everything, those that group things in similar yet somewhat disjointed containers, the free spirits who let things fall where they may,[2] and of course, everyone in between.

No matter which style you subscribe to, you can make maintenance tasks easier by gathering the tools you need ahead of time and placing them nearby. Not only will this save you time, you won't have to drop everything—sometimes literally—to find the tool you need. Experience and familiarity with your printer will teach you which tools you need for certain tasks.

For example, if you are cleaning the extruder drive gear, you will need whatever tools you need to disassemble the mechanism to expose the drive gear, as well as tools for cleaning the gear and removing loose plastic. For the MakerBot Replicator 1 and 2, you need an Allen wrench to take off the extruder fan, a pointed hobby knife or similar object to remove filament from the grooves in the drive gear, and compressed air or a vacuum to remove the debris.

You don't have to lay your tools out like a dental hygienist's tray, but placing them in a shallow basket, or even on the table near the printer, is a good plan. When maintaining or repairing my printers, I like to gather my tools and lay them in front of the printer so that I can reach them easily and quickly.

In fact, as I mentioned in a previous chapter, I keep a complete set of tools to perform all maintenance and repair tasks on my 3D printers in my workshop near my printers. I keep them organized into several groups to make it easier for me to select a subset for whatever I want to do. It takes only a small amount of discipline to return the tools to their proper places when the task is complete.

Unplug Your Printer

Most maintenance tasks should be performed while your printer is turned off and unplugged from mains power. This may seem like a very prudent thing to do (and it is) but you would be surprised at how tempting and easy it is to think your off switch can save you from a nasty electrical surprise. In most cases, this simply isn't true. Even if the switch was designed to interrupt power completely, the fact remains that power is still live on the mains side of the switch.

The best practice is to simply unplug the printer when working on it. For those cases where you need power to manipulate the axes, you should take care to avoid areas of your printer that contain electronics and power connections. If you must come into contact with the electronics, use a grounding strap to avoid ESD damage.

■ **Tip**   Use an electronics enclosure to help protect against accidental damage to your electronics from foreign objects such as small animals and insects, fingers, arms, and other miscellaneous human tissue. While most of the printer uses 5v and 12v systems, even 5v power should be treated with a degree of caution. Don't assume low DC voltage is harmless.

Take Your Time

With the risk of sounding like your elementary school science teacher (or your grandmother), you should not rush yourself when working on your printer. A rushed task will lead to mistakes and, often, rework. Rushing can also result in misplaced tools, added clutter—or worse, mistakes. While very easy to say (write), this is one area many of us struggle to overcome. I can say with few exceptions that every time I've rushed through a procedure, I didn't do quite as good of a job as I preferred.

---

[2]Hey, it's still in the garage, right? Plus, you can always tell what they worked on last—just find the pile of tools.

The best way to avoid rushing is to give yourself plenty of time to complete your work. For example, if you are planning to do some maintenance on your printer before a print job, plan to set aside an hour so that you can be sure to get your printer going in time to complete whatever print you need. If you find yourself rushing because you have other things to do (be it with family, your job, etc.), take a break and take care of the more important tasks first, and then return to your printer when you are done and can take the time you need to do it properly.

Record Your Observations

An earlier chapter demonstrated how to make observations about your printer when things go wrong. The topic was encouraging you to record observations about the printer to help you diagnose and repair something that has broken or become misaligned. The same philosophy applies to performing maintenance on your printer.

More specifically, you should make observations about your printer each time you use the printer. Visually inspect things to make sure that they have not become unfastened, broken, or loose. Like the diagnostic tasks, I recommend keeping a journal and recording anything you observe about your printer. For example, you may notice some wear on one of the gears, a belt starting to get a little loose, or even some buildup of filament on the nozzle. None of these things are necessarily things that need to be fixed immediately, but entering the observation in your journal will help you stay aware of what your printer is doing. Not only that, it can also help you spot trouble before it becomes imperative.

For example, if you observe that one of the belts is a little loose one day, and looser still the next day, and then tight the third day, you should stop and check the axis mechanism for loose or broken parts. That is, a gradual decrease in tension may be normal, but a sudden shift from loose to tight or tight to loose means something is wrong.

Visual inspection isn't the only observation technique you can employ. You can observe your printer by listening for odd sounds or being aware of odd smells or any strange movement of the printer. Sometimes a strange sound is fine, but it can also be a precursor to failure or something that will affect your print quality. For example, if you hear a clunk, or a knock, or a similar collision sound, it could mean a portion of one of your axes mechanisms has become loose or out of alignment. Checking for this when you observe the behavior may permit you to fix the anomaly before it becomes an issue.

If your printer starts to move strangely, like returning one or more of the axes to home position or seeming to add extra movement, it isn't always the case that it is the printer at fault. It could be that the print file contains unusual commands. It can also be caused by intermittent errors in your electronics. The bottom line is: if your printer does something strange, pay close attention to what it is doing, stop your print, and diagnose the problem.

BECOME A 3D PRINTER WHISPERER

The more you use your printer, the more familiar you will become with the often strange and sometimes alarming (but normal) noises it makes, how the axes move, or even how it smells when printing.[3] That is, a properly configured printer will make certain noises when the axes are moved; when moving quickly or slowly; and when fans are turned on, off, faster, or slower. In fact, the more you print, the more likely you will become so tuned to the normal sounds and smells that something unusual can manifest as a barely perceptible cue—a sixth sense if you will.

---

[3]Aside from the heated filament odors but those are important too. ABS has a very distinctive odor when overheated. So do electronics when there is too much dust and they overheat.

When I was younger and had more "free" money, I raced motorcycles. I knew my motorcycle. I knew how it smelled when hot, how the engine sounded in the rain or dry, noises it made under acceleration, braking, cornering, and so forth. So in tuned was I to the normal behavior that I could tell when something mechanical wasn't right. Sometimes it was a simple adjustment, and other times it was something more serious. In fact, this technique kept me from a serious crash during practice for the championship race at Road Atlanta, GA.

While at top speed on the (then) long back straight, I grabbed a handful of front brake at my breaking point, but something didn't feel right. There was a small vibration and a slightly different pitch to the sound of the brake pads on the disc. I knew something was wrong but I didn't know what. I was traveling well over 140 mph. I had to make a choice. I could keep applying the front brake and check the bike out later, or I could trust my instincts.

I let off the brake and took the turn really wide, using the pit lane to scrub off speed. It was a good thing too because about the time I got the bike into the straight, the front wheel locked up. The brake caliper bracket had broken, throwing the caliper into the spokes and ruining the front wheel, forks, and what was left of the brakes. Had it not been for that minor, almost imperceptible cue, I would have faced a really bad crash.

I learned this technique from my father who, having been a sailor, taught me to learn the nuances of sailing. He told me to learn the normal sounds, vibrations, and even to feel the movement of the water under the hull and the sound of the wind. He learned this during his tour in the Navy. Indeed, I've met naval officers who could tell you whether their ship was in fresh water, salt water, deep water, or shallow. They couldn't explain—it was just a "feeling" that ran from the keel through the deck and was felt through their feet.

You may develop a similar insight with your printer. Not everyone will achieve this but some will. You may even think this is a bunch of malarkey or a Jedi mind trick, but it really is one of familiarity. The more familiar you are with the sights and sounds of something mechanical, the more likely you are to know when things need attention. So while you are enjoying your printer, pay attention to how it sounds, moves, and smells. That data may come in handy.

Basic Maintenance Tasks

Once again, basic maintenance tasks are those that you should do every time you use your printer and things you should do before each printing session (each day that you use your printer). There are two types of basic maintenance tasks. First, you should inspect your printer for potential problems (loose or broken parts, etc.), and second, there are a few minor adjustments you should perform each time you use your printer or as needed. I say "as needed" because some of these tasks apply to new or newly built (or upgraded) printers and may not be required each and every time you print. I describe each of these types in more detail in the following sections.

Inspection Tasks

The first type of basic maintenance task involves observing the printer—its mechanisms, wiring, frame, filament, and so forth. More specifically, you need to check your printer for anything that looks out of place, and then take action to correct the problem before you start a print. For example, if you observe that one of the belts is loose, you can adjust it so that print quality is not affected. Inspection tasks include the following.

- *Frame*: Checking for loose bolts and alignment
- *Axes*: Checking for loose or misaligned mechanisms
- *Filament*: Measuring the filament to ensure your slicer options are set correctly

- *Extruder*: Checking for broken, worn, or loose parts
- *Belts*: Checking tension
- *Electronics*: Checking for loose connections or broken wires
- *Print surface*: Checking the print surface for damage or wear

For new printers, I recommend performing these tasks each time you print. If you have a new printer or one that you built yourself, it is important to perform these inspections before each print. Doing so will help you make minor adjustments to get the printer broken in. Even if your vendor built your printer, inspecting it before each print will give you a sense of the reliability of your printer.

As you become more familiar with your printer, you may be able to perform these tasks less frequently. However, even if you have printed many objects and your printer is reliable such that adjustments or repairs are infrequent (more than every 50 hours of use), inspecting the printer can help detect when adjustments or repairs may be needed. Thus, for reliable printers, I recommend performing these tasks the first time you use your printer for a given day. For example, if you are going to print a series of objects, inspect the printer before printing the first object.

■ **Tip**   If you keep a journal of your observations, it can help you determine which of these tasks you need to do more frequently than others. For example, if you have never had to tighten your frame bolts, you can delay this task until you perform a preventive maintenance task like lubricating the axes.

Table 9-1 will help you determine when you should perform each of the inspection tasks in the following sections. Notice that I have columns that apply to new printers, including printers that are built from a kit (new); printers that are prebuilt or have not been used much (low usage); and printers that have shown to be reliable without issues over many hours of printing (reliable).

Table 9-1. *Frequency of Inspection Tasks*

Task	Description	New	Low Usage	Reliable
Frame	Check for loose bolts and alignment	Every print	Every 3 or 4 prints	Only when the printer is moved
Axes	Check for loose or misaligned mechanisms	Every print	Once per month	Only when the printer is moved
Filament	Measure filament diameter	Every print	Every 3 or 4 prints	Depends on vendor quality
Extruder	Check for loose bolts, broken parts, a clogged drive pulley (hobbed bolt), and worn gears[4]	Every print	Every print	Every print
Belts	Check for loose belts	Every print	Every first print of the day	Monthly
Wiring	Check for loose connections or broken wirers	Every print	Every first print of the day	Every first print of the day
Print surface	Check the surface for wear or tears	Every print	Every print	Every print

---

[4]This depends on the quality and the type of extruder used; all-metal, direct-driven extruders may not need any adjustment.

Frame

Recall from the discussion about building a 3D printer that the frame is the foundation upon which all other mechanisms are attached. If the frame (some use the term *chassis*) is loose or misaligned, these anomalies will translate to the other mechanisms. For example, if the frame becomes misaligned, it can cause the axes mechanisms to bind, which can translate to poor print quality or, at worse, axis travel failures and ruined prints.

Given that there are so many different 3D printer designs and frame configurations, a complete step-by-step instruction for checking the bolts for tightness and even alignment would be difficult to assemble. However, you don't really need a detailed checklist. You just need to know how your printer is constructed.

That is, you need to locate the parts of the frame that are bolted together. Some of the professional-grade printers have frames that are welded together, and therefore have no parts that could come loose. But the vast majority of printers are constructed from several pieces. RepRap printers, on the other hand, are built from many parts that are bolted together.

Whether you built your printer or purchased one already assembled, you should familiarize yourself with how the frame is assembled. Some manufacturers provide tips on keeping the frame tight and aligned. Some even include illustrations on what parts of the frame should be checked. Even so, take some time to examine your frame and locate all of the fasteners. Make an inventory of the size of wrenches or hex bits you need to tighten the fasteners, and enter that data in your journal.

Tighten Bolts

Check each bolt to make sure that it is tight. Some suggest using your fingers to try to loosen a nut or bolt. The idea is that if you can loosen it with your fingers, it isn't tight enough. I think this is a fine strategy, but it only works for those bolts and nuts that you can get to and can grasp.

I prefer to use tools to check tightness. I simply use the appropriate tool, and rather than try to loosen (which is all too easy), I give each nut and bolt a slight turn to ensure that it is tight. The idea here is that if you can move the bolt or nut with very little effort, it is too loose. When I encounter a bolt or nut like this, I give the tool a one-eighth but no more than a quarter turn to ensure that it is tight. Be sure to not overtighten.

OVERTIGHTENED BOLTS IN PLASTIC FRAME PARTS

If you accidentally overtighten a bolt that secures a plastic part, you will be rewarded with the sound of compressing or breaking plastic. Don't do that. Bolts that secure plastic parts require very little torque. In fact, you need only tighten them to the point where the frame component is rigid and cannot come loose from normal operation of the printer.

However, overtightening bolts, even marginally, can result in a bolt that comes loose frequently. There are several things that contribute to the problem. Most often it is a case where the plastic is compressed just enough to break the internal supports of that part (especially if they are printed with a low fill percentage). When this happens, the part can appear to be solid but has enough flex that can allow the fastener to come loose.

If you find a bolt or nut that has to be tightened frequently, and the part is not overly stressed or is in an area where there should be no flex, you should consider replacing the plastic part and carefully tighten the bolts. If the problem continues to appear, you should consider using a brace or additional frame components to reduce the flex.

Repeat the process until all of the bolts and nuts are checked. It is not unusual for a new printer to have several bolts or nuts that need tightening. But you should not have to retighten them more than once or twice.

If you find a bolt or nut that needs to be tightened frequently, or find bolts or nuts that have fallen out, you either have a stress point that requires a change of fastener or you've overtightened the bolt one too many times. If it is not an overtightening problem, you may need to consider changing or augmenting the fastener.

For instance, you could use Loctite on the threads to help keep bolts in high-stress areas tight, or add a lock washer to keep a nut tight, or change the nut to a self-locking nut (a nut with a nylon ring that grips the threads—sometimes called *nylock* or *nyloc*[5]), which is far less prone to loosening. If the bolt or nut comes loose after that, you should consider reinforcing the area with a brace—or better, isolate the forces that are causing the part to come loose.

Figure 9-1 shows a modification I made to one of my Prusa Mendel i2 printers to keep the frame tight. Interestingly, this printer took longer to get all of the nuts tight. I suspect it is because the plastic parts were printed with slightly larger holes for the threaded rods. That is, the threaded rods have some play—enough that the normal vibrations of regular use can loosen the nuts. I solved the problem with lock nuts. If you choose to use lock nuts, be sure to not overtighten the nuts. It can take a lot of torque to compress the lock nuts completely. So much that it is possible to crush the plastic parts.[6]

Figure 9-1. Checking frame bolts: Prusa Mendel i2

Check Alignment

Aside from tightening the bolts, you should check the alignment of your frame. Normally, the frame should not lose alignment and you would not normally have to do this task. However, if your printer was moved, accidentally bumped, or several parts of the frame have come loose, there is a chance the frame could have become misaligned or twisted.

---

[5]Nyloc is a registered trademark of Forest Fasteners (http://en.wikipedia.org/wiki/Nyloc_nut).
[6]Can you guess how I know this to be true? Yep. Wrench, wrench, crack!

To check alignment, use a square to check that all right angles are still right angles and a straight edge to ensure that parts that form a plane are not twisted. You should also use a ruler to ensure that all parts are at their correct locations. This is especially true for older Prusa variants that use threaded rods for frame components.

You should also make sure that all axes move smoothly without binding or collisions with the frame. RepRap printers are susceptible to minor changes or flexing of the frame. For example, if you move your Prusa Mendel i2 and set it on a surface that is not level (one corner is higher or lower than the others), the weight of the printer can cause the frame to flex and introduce binding in one or more of the axes—most notably the Y axis; this is thought to be the source of bearing holder and clamp failures.

Check for Broken Parts

Finally, examine all of the plastic parts to ensure that they are not cracked or show any signs of stress. The effects of stress can manifest in a number of ways. Most often, the part shows small cracks between the layers, but in the extreme case, you could see discolored sections—or worse, breaks in the plastic. Replace all parts that show any sign of damage.

Once you have performed this inspection to the point where there are no loose bolts and the frame components have not become unaligned, and no parts are broken or loose, you can consider changing the frequency of the inspection. That is, if you haven't tightened a bolt in three or four prints, try making the inspection once a week. If nothing comes loose or misaligned after several weeks, you can consider making the inspection only when the printer is physically moved.

Axes

The axes of your printer are often subjected to small, rapid movement, which can put a lot of stress on the components. New and recently modified printers should be checked frequently to ensure that the axes remain properly aligned. Not only should you check each axis for loose parts, you should also check them for cracked or broken parts as well.

Like the frame, check each bolt to make sure that it is tight, and that pulleys and other moving parts are not loose. Inspect each of the plastic parts carefully to ensure that they are not damaged in any way. That is, if there has been any flexing of the frame, there is also the possibility of plastic parts failure in the axes mechanisms.

Be sure to check the plastic components to make sure that they are not cracked or show any wear. For example, Prusa Mendel i2 X-ends are fragile and can break if the axis is flexed. This can happen if your Z axis crashes into your build plate. In this case, the motors of the Z axis continue to drive the X-ends down once the nozzle strikes the build plate. If the extruder is not in the center of the build plate, one side of the X-end can lower farther than the other flexing the plastic to point of breakage.

You should also check the endstops for damage or loose mounts. An endstop that has moved or can move will make homing your printer difficult and could allow hard parts to collide. Some endstop holders made from PLA may be more brittle than those made with ABS. Endstop holder breakage most often occurs as a result of a malfunction in axis movement that causes the axis to crash into the endstop.

If your printer has been moved or there has been some other event, such as modification of the axes components, you should check the axes for alignment. You can check this quickly for axes that use multiple bearings running on parallel rods (in other words, most printers). The axis should move freely without binding. If there is any friction anywhere along the movement, check the alignment of the axis rods and adjust them until the axis moves freely.

■ **Tip** Whenever you change an axis, be that for loose parts or realignment, always level your print bed to compensate for the changes.

You should check your axis semifrequently (and always after moving the printer from one place to another). Once per each day that you print should be sufficient. On the other hand, if you find you have to adjust the frame, or even realign the axis, you should perform this inspection more frequently.

Filament

The filament is one of the areas that are often overlooked as a source for inspection or even adjustment. More specifically, the diameter of the filament can vary—often changing several times during the spool. Unless your filament vendor has very high standards, you could see variations that can cause some issues with printing.

Recall that we measure the diameter of filament with a caliper. If the measurement is more than a few hundredths of a millimeter larger or smaller than what you specified in your slicer, you may need to change your filament diameter setting, which normally requires reslicing. If you are printing an object you have already sliced, you should consider slicing your object again. We need to do this to ensure that the correct amount of filament is extruded when laying down runs. Too much filament (the actual diameter is larger than your slicer settings) and you risk bulges, stringing, and excess filament in smaller and narrower protrusions. Too little filament (the actual diameter is smaller than your slicer settings) and you risk poor layer adhesion and weak parts.

I recommend changing your slicer settings if you encountered a change in the diameter greater than 0.05 millimeters. Any more than that and you risk the problems stated previously. For example, if you measured your filament at the start of a spool at 1.77mm and find that it varies between 1.74mm and 1.80mm, a setting of 1.75 in your slicer filament settings should be fine.

While you should always check the diameter of the filament before slicing an object for printing, most people forget that the diameter of the filament is a variable in the sliced file. Thus, it is important to make sure that you check the filament diameter regularly and compare it to what is in the sliced file.

If you are using a slicer that produces a .gcode file and it saves the filament diameter (check your slicer to see if this is an option), you can open the file to see the filament size (as follows). If you are using a slicer that produces a binary file (e.g., MakerWare), you may need to remember what the filament size is or make sure that you use high-quality filament.

```
; filament_diameter = 1.75
```

If you are working with spools of filament from a reliable vendor, you may only need to check it once every few prints, or even once each time you start a new spool. However, until you are comfortable with the variance of the filament from your vendor (it may require sampling a number of spools), you should check the diameter every time you print.

Extruder

The extruder is the workhorse of the printer. There are several parts to the extruder, all of which need to be checked for wear or damage. The parts of the extruder include the stepper motor, extruder body, idler bearing or pulley (if equipped), drive and driven gears (if equipped), filament drive gear or hobbed bolt, and wiring for the stepper motor and hot end (if mounted together).

The stepper motor in the extruder is almost always turning, and therefore gets more use than any other stepper motor. In addition, the extruder body endures a lot more heat than the axes movements (unless it is a Bowden setup).

The filament drive gear is one of the top areas that can cause you some trouble. This is because it can become clogged with pieces of filament and start to slip. Furthermore, if the extruder uses a set of gears, the gears will wear over time and should be checked for excessive wear, broken or missing teeth, or loose gears.

There really isn't any way to visibly observe problems with a stepper motor to tell if it needs replacement or has excessive wear (other than complete shutdown in one or both directions). I have seen stepper motors wear out; but the only symptoms were a loss of holding torque where the stepper could not hold its position, or a lack of torque when stepping, such that it missed steps. When this happens, the stepper motor is easier to turn by hand. However, unless the filament is unloaded, you cannot turn the stepper motor. Fortunately, you don't normally have to worry about this until your stepper motor has been used for hundreds of hours of printing.

Rather, the most common wear to the stepper motor is the wiring. If not properly restrained, it is possible for the stepper motor wires to break after many hours of printing. Thus, I recommend that you often check the wiring running to the stepper motor.

The extruder body should be checked for breaks and wear. Some printer owners have reported that the extruder body can wear over time. This is normally associated with multipart extruder bodies. For example, the Greg's Wade extruder uses a hinged door for the idler gear. The pivot point on the door can wear over time. The tension on the bolts that press the idler against the hobbed bolt can put stress on the pivot point, eventually making the hole larger. I have seen this myself a couple of times. The telltale sign is a loose idler door. You can see this visibly whenever you change filament, but you can also see the door flex as the extruder moves. If you see any play in the idler door, you should consider replacing it. Figure 9-2 shows an idler door for a Greg's Wade hinged extruder that has failed.

Figure 9-2. Failed idler door: Greg's Wade hinged extruder

Notice that in the foreground we see that the hole for the bolt is rounded out. This made setting the tension of the idler bearing imprecise. Also, notice in the background that there is a crack in the part. This was due to the wear of the hole for the pivot, which weakened that area of the part.

Even if the extruder body does not have multiple parts, it is a good idea to check it. Look for changes to the way it mounts to the axis, including the carrier to which it is bolted. I have seen a case where the extruder body came loose, which caused some really strange and erratic layer shifts. Thus, always check the extruder body and its mount for loose bolts.

If your extruder uses a set of gears to drive the filament pulley, and if they are 3D-printed parts, you should check the gears for wear and damage. That is, if the gears wear long enough, it is possible that the teeth can become worn down to the point where there is play in the gears. In rare cases, the teeth could break off of the smaller of the two gears. The telltale sign of worn gears is a light dusting of plastic debris in the valleys of the teeth. Figure 9-3 shows a set of gears that have some wear. In this case, the gears have about 125 hours of use.[7]

Figure 9-3. *Inspecting extruder gears: Prusa Mendel i2*

■ **Tip**   You can use a small amount of lithium, silicone, or PTFE grease on the gears to reduce wear, but this can make it harder to detect worn gears.

Notice how the teeth appear a lighter color than the extruder body. The gears in this photo are black. The teeth have a light-gray dusting on them. This is largely normal and should not be a source of alarm. I like to use a soft brush and a vacuum to remove the dust so that I can inspect the teeth more closely. If you see dust spilling over out of the valleys of the gears or packing into the valleys, you need to clean it out, and you should consider checking the gears for excessive play.

Worn teeth can cause excessive play to the point where they no longer mesh properly. To check the gears for play, hold one of the gears stationary and try to turn the other back and forth. You should have no play in the gears. Even a small amount is enough to warrant replacing the gears. The play may not affect your prints, but it is something that will only get worse over time.

Be sure to check the lateral play of the gears as well; more specifically, that the gears are mounted securely. As we saw in an earlier chapter, the larger gear that mounts to a hobbed bolt for a Greg's Wade extruder is susceptible to the nut trap rounding out, causing the gear to wobble and slip back and forth as the gears are rotated in either direction.

---

[7]The gears were printed with PLA, which has shown to be more resistant to wear than ABS.

If your extruder uses an idler bearing (sometimes called the *idler pulley*), you should also check it for play. If the idler bearing uses a modern sealed bearing, you aren't likely to see it fail, but if the mounting point is a 3D-printed part or is mounted to the same, you should check the bolts for tightness and any play. Play in the idler bearing can cause filament extrusion problems if the play is enough to change the tension on the filament. I have seen a case where the play was no more than about 0.04mm, but that was enough to ease tension and cause an extrusion failure. I originally increased the tension to compensate (which does work temporarily), but that only made the problem worse, and eventually resulted in a cracked idler door.

■ **Tip** Any play or loose bolts on the extruder should be corrected immediately.

The filament drive gear, or hobbed bolt, is the one spot on all 3D printers that will eventually require service. If your extruder is constructed so that you can see the filament drive gear or hobbed bolt, check it for filament debris in the teeth. If you see any buildup, you should remove the debris from the teeth or grooves. I discuss this in more detail in the adjustments section.

As I mentioned, the wiring to the extruder is a source of failure caused by being flexed as the extruder moves on the axis. This is known as *wire fatigue*. If you use a strain relief to combat the problem, check the strain relief mounting to make sure that it has not come loose. An improperly mounted strain relief can exasperate the problem by creating yet another stress point. For example, if your strain relief is in the form of a plastic wire wrap and the wrap comes loose on the extruder side where the wires are not restrained, the stiffness of the plastic wire wrap will make the wires flex even more than if there were no wrap at all.

In summary, check the extruder fixed parts for wear, gears for play, filament drive pulley for buildup, and the wiring for any breaks.

Since the extruder gets so much work, I recommend checking it before every print. At the very minimum, you should do a quick look at the extruder body, the stepper motor, the drive and driven gear (if equipped), and the filament drive pulley to ensure that nothing is wrong. Remember, if something goes wrong in the extruder, your print will likely be ruined.

Belts

The belts on your 3D printer can loosen over time. This is normally very little and only after many hours of printing. What is more likely to cause loosening belts is slippage of the securing blocks. This is especially true for printer designs that use clamps on each end of the belt.

Newer RepRap designs and many of the consumer- and professional-grade printers have adapted a more secure mount that prevents slipping. For example, many of the X- and Y-carriage designs for the Prusa i3 have teeth spaced evenly to match the spacing of teeth for the belt, which creates a mounting point that does not slip.

Loose belts are those that have more than about 20mm or more of play (up and down movement perpendicular to the belt travel). Any more than this and the belt can slip on the drive gear. Not only that, but the extra length of the belt can cause minor layer shifts on that axis. For example, a very loose Y-axis belt can manifest as layer shifts on the Y-axis plane (front to back). The amount of play or slack in the belt will depend on how long the belt is, as well as its type. Check your vendor's documentation for the correct threshold for your printer.

To adjust loose belts that are secured at each end (the belt does not form a continuous loop) and that do not include a belt tensioner, you should loosen the clamps that hold the belt, pull the belt tight, and secure the clamp. If your printer has a belt tensioner, you can simply tighten the tensioner to remove the play.

USE AN AUTOMATIC BELT TENSIONER

If your printer does not have a belt tensioner built into it, you should consider adding one. There are a number of belt tensioner designs available on Thingiverse for most common printer designs. I discuss one in particular in Chapter 11 that you can add to a printer to keep a constant tension on the belt. It has a wide range of movement in the spring-loaded arm so that you won't have to make any changes to the belt over many hours of printing.

For closed-loop belts, you should still check the tension. If the belt gets a little loose, you can tighten the belt by loosening the mount of either the idler or driven side of the belt. For example, the MakerBot Replicator 1 and 2 have slotted mounting holes on the driven side (e.g., at the stepper motor mount) that permit you to loosen the four stepper motor mounting bolts and pull out the stepper motor, thereby increasing tension on the belt. You then retighten the bolts to complete the process.

Checking the belts for tension is a very quick test: just press up and down on the belt. I recommend checking belt tension before each print for new printers and for printers that use clamps to secure the belts. If you don't notice any looseness in the belts, you can delay the check to once every day of printing, and if no looseness is detected then, delay the check to once a month.

Wiring

The wiring on your 3D printer is another often overlooked source of problems. Printers built by vendors typically use electronics with connectors that are securely fastened and rarely come loose. However, kit-based printers are more susceptible because most wire connections are press-fit and not secured with tabs, screw terminals, or other forms of keeping the wire in place.

For printers that are assembled from kits, you should make it a priority to check all of the wiring for loose connections. A visible inspection is enough to see a connector that is not seated properly. Check slip and press-fit connections to make sure that they have not become unplugged; screw terminals to ensure that wires are still tight; and look for worn insulation or bare or broken wires at any area where the wiring crosses a metal object. Wiring can loosen due to the normal vibrations of a printer, or it can loosen due to accidental stress on the wiring when performing maintenance.

I once replaced the Z-axis mechanism on one of my Prusa Mendel i2 printers in an effort to test an experimental threaded rod mount. I didn't realize that I had inadvertently pulled on some of the wiring, knocking loose one of the endstops and one of the stepper motors. Unfortunately, it was the Y stepper motor and the Y-axis endstop together. I really scratched my head when I homed the axes, only to discover the Y axis would only move in one direction and wouldn't stop! Since then, I always check the wiring after any maintenance task or upgrade.

■ **Tip**　When moving the axes, especially homing the first time after a major upgrade or electronics change, always keep your hand near the power switch just in case the axis does not stop. It is best to kill the power than risk breaking something. Recall from Chapter 3 that you should also consider testing the endstops by triggering them manually. If the axis movement does not stop, turn off the printer and check your wiring.

But it isn't just the wiring connections that should be checked. I have already mentioned the need to inspect the wiring on the extruder for flexing and signs of breakage, but that is just one of the stress points. Another is the heated print bed. If your printer has a heated print bed that is attached to one of the axes that moves, the wiring on the print bed should be checked for stress in the same manner as the extruder.

■ **Note**   While you would rarely be concerned about soldered connections, if you soldered your own connections and have not had a lot of practice soldering, you may want to check these for the first few prints to make sure the connections are strong.

At least once each day that you start a series of prints, I recommend checking all wiring connections to make sure that they are securely fastened. Otherwise, check the wiring on newly built printers once every print until you are certain that no connections are loose.

Print Surface

The print surface is another wear site. For cases where you are using blue painter's tape or Kapton tape without ABS juice, you only need to replace the print surface when either there are adhesion problems (sudden lifting after many prints without lifting) or when you have torn or gouged the print surface treatment by removing parts. Figure 9-4 shows a print surface that is in need of replacement.

Figure 9-4.   Worn print surface (blue painter's tape)

Notice here that there are small tears and some discoloring in the print surface. Normally, discoloring won't affect adhesion, but any tears will affect adhesion. If your print surface starts looking like this, I recommend changing it. On the other hand, you could just move the start of the print to another portion of the print bed. In Figure 9-4, the surface on either side of the wear is still good.

Recall from a previous chapter that if you use narrower strips of tape, you can replace only those strips that are affected. In Figure 9-4, I needed to replace only the centermost strips.

PATCHING PRINT SURFACES

Some printer owners have suggested patching print surfaces as a means to make supplies last longer. I've tried this, and it can be done, but there is some risk involved when removing the old treatment. For example, if you applied the treatment in strips that run the length of the print surface, you would have to cut out the parts that have to be replaced. Using a hobby knife or other sharp instrument may risk scaring the surface—that is, you could scratch the glass. Doing this with blue painter's tape is a bit easier because your may be able to tear the tape in the middle of the damaged area and pull it away from the print surface before cutting. Regardless, I think it takes a bit of practice to get the new pieces cut just right and then plugged in where they need to go. I'd rather just replace the entire strip—it's easier and far less complicated.

Even if you do not need to replace the print surface, it is a good idea to wipe it with a lint-free cloth to remove any oils from touching it with your hands, as well as any dust that may have accumulated. For Kapton tape, a cloth with a small spot of acetone will remove any filament residue, as well as oils and dust.

Checking the print surface is another easy thing you can do; and, in fact, you should do this before every print. Only a brief glance at the print surface is required to tell if it needs replacing.

Adjustment Tasks

The next type of basic maintenance task includes those things that require minor adjustments on a semiregular basis. I recommend checking to see if you need to do these tasks as your first step when using your printer on any given day. Adjustment tasks don't have to be done before every print (although they can), and printers that have proven to be reliable can have these tasks done on an as-needed basis.

For example, one of my MakerBot printers rarely needs to have the print bed leveled (trammed). As a result, I make this adjustment only when I change print surfaces or build plates (I have three types: the original plastic, a lightweight glass, and a lightweight aluminum build plate).

More importantly, adjustment tasks are those that are most frequently needed to keep your printer running well. Thus, these are tasks you should perform more often, and include the following. I will discuss each in more detail shortly.

- *Level the print bed*: Keep the print bed adjusted properly to ensure high adhesion

- *Set the Z-height*: Adjust the height of the first layer with respect to the print surface

- *Clean the filament drive pulley (gear)*: Remove debris from drive gear

- *Clean the nozzle*: Remove melted filament and contaminants from exterior of nozzle

In the following sections, I provide example procedures for performing these tasks. I have tried to keep them generic enough to be applicable to most printers. That being said, you may find that slightly different steps are needed for your particular printer. For example, your printer may have a different set of screens for its assisted print bed leveling feature or even no such feature. You should still be able to adapt the example to your printer by mimicking the steps by manually jogging the axes.

Table 9-2 will help you determine when you should perform each of the inspection tasks in the following sections. Notice that I provide columns that apply to new printers, including printers that are built from a kit (new); printers that are prebuilt or have not be used much (low usage); and printers that have shown to be reliable without issues over many hours of printing (reliable).

Table 9-2. *Frequency of Adjustment Tasks*

Task	Description	New	Low Usage	Reliable
Level the print bed	Adjust the print bed so that it is parallel (trammed) with the X and Y axes.	Daily	Weekly	When you change the print surface or print bed
Set the Z-height	Adjust the nozzle height over the print bed at the Z-axis home position. Sets first layer height.	Daily	Daily	When you change the print surface or print bed
Clean the filament drive pulley	Remove debris from the gear to make sure that the filament feeds properly and does not slip.	Daily	When you change filament	As needed
Clean the nozzle	Remove extra plastic from the nozzle to prevent droppings on printed parts.	Daily	Weekly	As needed

Level the Print Bed

Recall from Chapter 5 that we need to level (tram) the print bed to ensure that the X axis is always parallel to the print bed (Y-axis) or that the nozzle is the same height above the print bed at all locations of the printable surface area of the print bed.

Some printers incorporate a Z-height adjuster that allows you to control the height of the first layer, or more precisely, how much the first layer is pressed or squished (which can help first-layer adhesion). For these printers, leveling the print bed is a separate procedure. In these cases, you must level your build plate before setting the Z-height. Otherwise, the Z-height could be the correct setting for only one area of the build surface. Printers that do not have a Z-height adjuster incorporate the Z-height setting as part of the print bed leveling procedure.

I presented a procedure for leveling the print bed for a RepRap printer in Chapter 5, but I'd now like to show you a different procedure that is common to printers that incorporate an assisted print bed–leveling feature. The feature is designed to position the axis automatically and guide you along the way as to how to set the nozzle height over the print bed. Demonstrating the procedure will help you adapt it to your own printer, should it vary from the examples in this and previous chapters.

In this example I will use a MakerBot Replicator 1 Dual. This printer has a four-point build plate mount that includes adjusters that tighten or loosen each of the four bolts that suspend the heated print bed on springs. This four-point system is analogous to the construction of most RepRap printer designs.

■ **Note**   Adjusters on the four corners can work against each other by applying too much or too little tension on one corner, which can affect the others. Newer MakerBot and other printers have adapted a three-point mount that makes leveling the print bed easier. Adopting a three-point system allows you to control left/right tilt and front/back tilt without binding or putting stress on the build plate.[8] The assisted print bed–leveling feature is the same on the newer MakerBot Replicator 2, but instead of four adjusters, you use only the three—two in the front and one in the rear.

---

[8]Thus we have the proverbial three-legged stool that never needs shims to keep it from rocking.

To get started leveling the build plate of a MakerBot Replicator 1 (or similar), you first power on the printer and get a sheet of paper ready. I like to use a piece of paper about 3" × 4"—something you can hold onto easily. When you are ready, choose the Utilities menu and then select Level Build Plate.

■ **Tip** You can also use a Post-it note. The sticky portion makes holding the paper a bit easier.

The printer will have you wait until it jogs the axes into position, and then displays the following screens to explain the procedure. You can simply click the M button to skip to the next screen (once you've read it!). Example 9-1 shows the screen text for this step in the procedure.

Example 9-1. Startup Screens for Leveling the Print Bed

```
+----------------------+
| Find the 4 knobs on  |
| the bottom of the    |
| platform and tighten |
| four or five turns   |
+----------------------+

+----------------------+
| I'm going to move    |
| the extruder to      |
| various positions    |
| for adjustment.      |
+----------------------+

+----------------------+
| In each position,    |
| we will need to      |
| adjust 2 knobs at    |
| the same time.       |
+----------------------+

+----------------------+
| Nozzles are at the   |
| right height when    |
| you can just slide a |
| sheet of paper       |
+----------------------+

+----------------------+
| between the nozzle   |
| and the plate.       |
| Grab a sheet of      |
| paper to assist us.  |
+----------------------+
```

Once you press the M button at this point, the printer will display the screen as shown in Example 9-2. Pressing the M button here will move the extruder to the front center position of the build plate. Figure 9-5 shows the location and an example of how you use the sheet of paper to slide under the nozzles. The adjustment knobs are not shown but are located to the left and right of the print bed. Adjust the knobs together until the paper slides snuggly under both nozzles.

Example 9-2. Move to First Point

```
+-----------------------+
| Adjust the front two  |
| knobs until paper     |
| just slides between   |
| nozzle and plate      |
+-----------------------+
```

Figure 9-5. *Leveling the print bed: MakerBot Replicator 1 Dual*

■ **Note** It is important that the paper have the same tension with each nozzle. This will ensure that the print surface is the same height for each nozzle.

Once you have the front two knobs set, press the M button again. You will see the screen message shown in Example 9-3, and the printer will move to the rearmost center (left-to-right) position over the build. Use the two rear adjusters to set the height.

Example 9-3. Move to Second Point

```
+----------------------+
| Adjust the back two  |
| knobs until paper    |
| just slides between  |
| nozzle and plate     |
+----------------------+
```

Once you have the rear two knobs set, press the M button again. You will see the screen message shown in Example 9-4, and the printer will move to the rightmost center position (front-to-back) over the build. Use the two rightmost adjusters to set the height.

Example 9-4. Move to Third Point

```
+----------------------+
| Adjust the right two |
| knobs until paper    |
| just slides between  |
| nozzle and plate     |
+----------------------+
```

It is important to note here that the build plate should not need more than a very minor adjustment of the two rightmost knobs. If you need more than that, you may have a warped print bed or the nozzles may not be at the same height. If this is the case, you must remove the extruder from the printer and adjust the nozzle height. See the MakerBot support page for procedures on how to do this.[9]

Once you have the two rightmost knobs set, press the M button again. You will see the screen message shown in Example 9-5, and the printer will move to the leftmost center position (front-to-back) over the build. Use the two leftmost adjusters to set the height.

Example 9-5. Move to Fourth Point

```
+----------------------+
| Adjust the left two  |
| knobs until paper    |
| just slides between  |
| nozzle and plate     |
+----------------------+
```

Similarly, it is important to note here that the build plate should not need more than a very minor adjustment of the two leftmost knobs. If you need more than that, you may have a warped print bed or the nozzles may not be at the same height. If this is the case, you must remove the extruder from the printer and adjust the nozzle height.

Once you have the two leftmost knobs set, press the M button again. You will see the screen message shown in Example 9-6, and the printer will move to the center of the build plate.

---

[9]You should never have to do this.

Example 9-6. Move to Fifth Point

```
+-----------------------+
| Check that paper      |
| just slides between   |
| nozzle and plate      |
+-----------------------+
```

If the paper slides easily under the nozzles at this point, you are done and your printer is ready to print! If not, you should carefully consider whether the problem is due to a built plate that is not flat. Unless you have a defective plate, it should be flat enough that the nozzles will not press into the build plate. If they do, you may have to compensate by turning each of the four adjusters one-eighth of a turn. Do this and check the nozzle height again; repeat as needed. I would also recommend running the build plate routine again to make sure that you know the effects of this minor adjustment. That is, if the other four points are considerably higher (the paper slides easily with play) or lower (the nozzles hit the build plate), you may have to replace the build plate.

I recommend leveling the print bed for new or unproven printers once each day that you use the printer. Once you have established that the printer is not affected by environment factors—that is, it doesn't need much adjustment from one week to the next, you can adopt a policy of leveling the print bed that is less frequent than once a week. For printers that have been proven reliable and rarely need the print bed leveled, I recommend doing the procedure each time you change the print surface treatment or change the print build plates.

Set the Z-Height

As I mentioned in the previous section, some printers incorporate a Z-height adjuster. I have added this feature to all of my RepRap printers and one of my consumer-grade printers. Once again, a Z-height adjuster allows me to set the Z-height based on conditions such as needing higher first-layer adhesion, using thicker print surface material (like adding ABS juice), and so forth. The basic procedure is as follows. Figure 9-6 shows an example of using the Z-height adjuster on a Prusa Mendel i2.

Figure 9-6. Setting the Z-height: Prusa i2 with separate Z-height adjuster

1. Make sure that your print bed is level and that you home all axes.

2. Use either your printer's LCD menu or printer controller to raise the Z axis by 5mm.

3. Use the same method to position your X and Y axes in the center of the location where you plan to print your object (for instance, in the center of the build platform).

4. Place the sheet of paper under the nozzle and use the printer controller software to home the Z axis.

5. Check the paper for tension and adjust the Z-height adjuster accordingly, and then rehome the Z axis.

6. Repeat step 5 until the height is set.

Notice that the printer also has adjusters to set the print bed height. These are used to level the print bed, which is done prior to this procedure. You may think that the Z-height adjuster is superfluous, given that you can accomplish the same thing with the four adjusters on the print bed. However, the four adjusters would have to be moved exactly the same, else you risk altering the print bed height in one or more corners. The Z-height adjuster is a better alternative because it moves the Z endstop up and down, thereby giving you only one point to adjust—versus four.

■ **Note**   I will cover how to add a Z-height adjuster to your RepRap printer in Chapter 11.

I recommend setting the Z-height once each day that you use the printer, or as needed as dictated by the first layer adhesion. If you are having first-layer adhesion problems not attributable to the print surface, you can set the Z-height a bit lower to help. For printers that have been proven reliable and rarely need the Z-height set,[10] I recommend doing the procedure each time you change the print surface treatment or change print build plates.

Clean the Filament Drive Pulley

Cleaning the filament drive pulley is the first line of offense in correcting the problem of extrusion failure, because most extrusion failures are related to either slipping filament caused by a dirty drive pulley or a blockage. Any time you have an extrusion failure, you should clean the filament drive pulley.

The process for cleaning the filament drive pulley will vary from one printer (extruder) design to another. We saw how to do this for a Greg's Wade extruder in Chapter 7. What follows is a similar procedure for a direct drive extruder. In this case, I am using a MakerBot Replicator 2 with an upgraded extruder mechanism. In the following, I list the procedure and then I present figures that represent each major step.

1. Unload the filament.

2. Disconnect the stepper motor.

3. Remove the extruder fan and heat sink.

4. Remove the stepper motor. Inspect and clean the drive gear.

5. Remove debris from the X-carriage and hot end.

6. Reassemble the extruder and load filament.

---

[10]Only one of my RepRap printers exhibits this characteristic, so I think it is the exception.

■ **Note** This procedure also applies to the MakerBot Replicator 1, Replicator 1 Dual, and Replicator 2X. In the case of dual extruders, the parts are mirrored, but otherwise are removed and installed in the same manner.

The first step is to unload the filament. You can do this by powering on your printer and selecting the Utilities menu, and then the Change Filament menu and the Unload option. Remove the filament guide tube by pulling it straight up, and then pull up the filament very slightly as the filament is ejected. Figure 9-7 shows what this looks like.

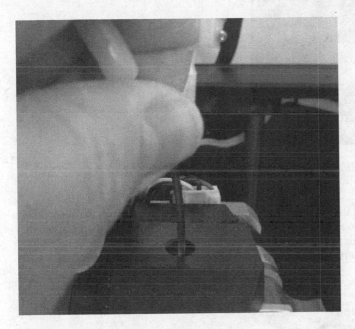

Figure 9-7. *Unloading filament: MakerBot Replicator 2*

■ **Tip** If you are using PLA, check the flexibility of the filament near the end that you removed. You may find that the filament is a bit more flexible than normal. I like to move up the filament (toward the spool) until I find a more brittle place, and then I snap off the filament there, removing the previously heated portion. I've found that filament loads a bit easier if it has not been heated and cooled before.

■ **Note** If your printer does not have an LCD panel, you can use your printer controller software to reverse the extruder once the hot end has reached temperature.

The next step requires you to power off your printer because you will be disconnecting the stepper motor. Failure to turn off your printer first can damage your stepper driver. Just pull up gently on the connector located at the rear of the stepper motor. Figure 9-8 shows the location.

Figure 9-8. *Disconnect stepper motor: MakerBot Replicator 2*

Next, we remove the stepper motor by unbolting the fan guard, fan, spacers, and heat sink. Be sure to cover your print bed with a towel so that falling parts (or tools) do not damage the print surface. Figure 9-9 shows the location of the two bolts. Be careful to not jostle the stepper motor as you remove the last bolt because it can fall onto your print bed. If you remove the bolts slowly, this will not happen. If you want to feel a bit safer, use a piece of blue painter's tape to hold the stepper motor in place.

Figure 9-9. *Removing the extruder fan: MakerBot Replicator 2*

At this point, the small plastic spacers are likely to fall down into your printer. If this happens, be sure to locate them and place them outside of the printer next to the other parts so that you won't lose them. Also, the extruder fan does not need to be disconnected and is fine to dangle from its wiring, provided you don't pull on it in any way.

Next, we remove the stepper motor and examine the filament drive pulley. Remove any loose debris with a vacuum. If there are any bits of plastic stuck in the drive pulley, use a toothpick or sharp hobby knife to remove them and vacuum again. Figure 9-10 shows a filament drive gear in need of cleaning.

Figure 9-10. *Cleaning the extruder drive pulley: MakerBot Replicator 2*

The piece of filament shown in the photo is of a color that I printed before the current filament—that is, it was left over from a previous print run. I was in a bit of a hurry and did not take the time to clean the filament drive gear. In some ways, I was lucky since this extra bit of filament didn't pose any problems and indeed it is quite small. However, if there were several stray bits in there, it could have caused filament to drop down onto my part—or worse, the drive gear to clog and eventually skip. The lesson here is to always check your filament drive gear when you change filament.

■ **Note** The idler shown in Figure 9-10 is an aluminum upgrade, which I will discuss in Chapter 11. It is one of the best upgrades I've found. So much so that I've installed it on my MakerBot Replicator 1 Dual and Replicator 2/2X.

The next step is to examine the X-carriage mount and the top of the hot end for debris. Not surprisingly, I found some stray bits of filament in mine. Figure 9-11 shows an example. Use a vacuum to remove any loose debris. If you see filament stuck to the hot end bar (the light-colored bar that runs parallel to the X axis), use tweezers or a hobby knife to remove it.

Figure 9-11. *Cleaning extruder drive pulley: MakerBot Replicator 2*

Once all of the debris is removed and the gear is clean, reassemble the extruder in the opposite order. It can be a bit of a challenge to keep the spacers in their place. I leave the stepper motor off to give me room to thread the bolts through the fan guard, fan, spacers, and heat sink. Start with the leftmost side. Once you have these parts on the bolt, insert the bolt through the corresponding hole, and then do the same for the right side. Finally, put the stepper motor on and tighten the bolts.

I recommend checking the filament drive pulley once each day that you use the printer. If you do not notice any buildup, you can check it every time you change filament, and clean it when needed. In fact, I always clean the filament drive pulley every time I encounter an extrusion problem.

Clean the Nozzle

The hot end nozzle is one area that many people neglect. Although there isn't anything that needs to be adjusted, it is possible for the nozzle to become dirty over many prints—that is, bits of filament can stick to the outside of the nozzle. This can happen whenever there is stringing from the end of a print, oozing from the nozzle due to higher temperatures, or collisions with objects on the print bed. Figure 9-12 shows a J-head hot end with a brass nozzle. While this specimen is reasonably free of debris, there are some small pieces on the underside.

Figure 9-12. J-head nozzle: Prusa Mendel i2

■ **Caution**   We will be working with a hot end that has been brought up to temperature. When moving around inside the printer, be careful to avoid touching the hot end or nozzle. It will burn you. Also, make sure that the printer is off before using any tools near the nozzle.

Over time, these bits of filament can harden and turn dark—encrusting the nozzle. While some users may say that this isn't a big deal (and I suppose I must admit that it could be OK), I don't like my tools or equipment to get so dirty. And it turns out that if you switch filament often, especially from PLA to ABS and back, some of the extra bits of filament can melt off and fall onto your prints.

I've seen this happen on occasion, and with one particularly gnarly nozzle, it would leave dark spots occasionally on the prints. This is most noticeable when printing with light-colored filament. I observed a very good print from this same printer that was printed in white. There were a total of only four or five tiny black spots that despite their small size, made the part look bad.

You can avoid this ultimate problem by simply cleaning the outside of your nozzle whenever it gets dirty (filament buildup). Best of all, it does not require you to remove the nozzle. Although it may be easy with some printers, with others it is a very involved process. The process to clean the nozzle in place is as follows. As you will see, it is very straightforward and not difficult. I describe the more involved steps in more detail.

1.   Use your printer's LCD menu or printer controller software to position the X and Y axes in the center, and raise the Z axis about 50 to 80mm to give you room to work.

2.   Heat the hot end to the temperature for the filament used.

3.   Turn off the printer and unplug it.

4.   While the hot end is still hot, use tweezers (ESD-safe) to remove the larger pieces of filament.

5.   If your nozzle is oozing, wait for it to cool until it no longer oozes.

6. Use a soft wire brush to remove loose filament while the nozzle is still warm.

7. Vacuum away the loose debris.

8. Soak a small portion of a paper towel with acetone and then wipe the nozzle.

I use ESD-safe tweezers to remove hot filament. This will remove the majority of the loose filament from the nozzle. Figure 9-13 illustrates this process.

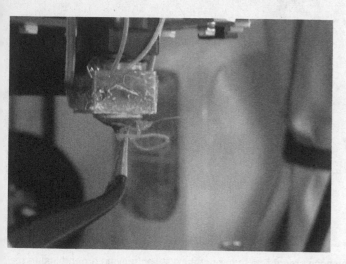

Figure 9-13. *Remove loose filament from the nozzle with tweezers*

While the hot end is still warm, remove any remaining filament residue with a soft wire brush. Figure 9-14 shows this step in progress.

Figure 9-14. *Cleaning the outside of the nozzle with a brush*

Be sure to use a metal brush with bristles of the same or softer metal than the nozzle. A wooden or metal handle[11] is a must. In the photos, for example, I used a brash brush to clean a brass nozzle. You can also use a metal scouring pad, but be sure to use the kind without soap! I do not recommend the use of steel wool because it can deposit several small bits of steel into your printer.

You can scrub the burned-on parts harder, but be sure to not put too much pressure on your hot end. Don't worry about any filament sticking to the brush. You can remove it easily once it is completely cooled.

BURNED FILAMENT: HOW DOES THAT HAPPEN?

If your nozzle has a lot of buildup of melted filament, you may be using temperatures that are too high, and so you should consider lowering the temperature. The buildup can also occur when switching from filament that requires lower heat ranges to those that require higher heat ranges. Thus, always clean your nozzle before switching filament types.

The nozzle also should not be heated to temperature without extruding for extended periods. This is because filament in the nozzle will ooze out and be replaced with an air pocket. This can cause plastic to oxidize inside the nozzle, which can blacken and, in some cases, even clog the nozzle.

To complete the cleaning process, use a towel soaked with a small spot of acetone to clean the nozzle. Fold the towel a couple of times to help absorb the acetone, as well as help protect your fingers if the hot end is still warm. By now, the nozzle should be cool enough to touch. If it is not, wait until it cools some more, and then use the acetone cloth. I use a paper towel to help reduce the temptation to scrub the nozzle. Putting too much force on the nozzle could damage the hot end, its mount, any accessory lighting—or worse, the wiring for the heater core and thermistor. Figure 9-15 shows the use of the towel to clean the nozzle. Notice how close the wiring is to the cloth. Be careful not to damage the wiring.

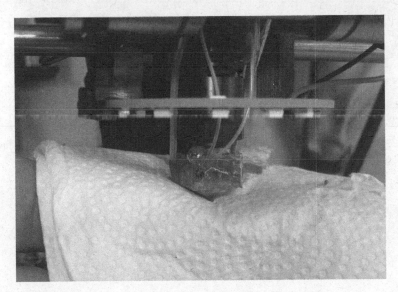

Figure 9-15. *Cleaning the outside of the nozzle with acetone*

---

[11]A plastic handle can melt if you make contact with the nozzle or hot end. This can undo all of your hard work. The best brushes are those with wooden handles.

Once you are done, be sure to vacuum any bits of debris—filament, unidentifiable black flakes (burnt filament), bristles, and so forth, before using the printer.

I recommend cleaning the outside of the nozzle once each day that you use the printer, or as needed. If you are using the proper temperature for your filament and you haven't had any extrusion failures or build failures, you may not need to do this procedure very often. Regardless, buildup is very easy to spot, and except for waiting for the heating and cooling cycles, it is very easy to correct.

Summary

Keeping your printer running well requires some patience and discipline to perform some simple routine tasks. While some tasks are things that make sense and are quite clearly needed, like setting the Z-height or keeping the print bed level (trammed), other tasks—like tightening the frame—may seem mundane, or tasks like keeping the print bed clean and free from debris may not seem like a lot of benefit.

However, failure to do all of these tasks can have a cumulative effect on your printer and you will eventually see some degradation of print quality. That is, if it doesn't break first! You save yourself a lot of time by keeping up with the needs of the printer through inspection and adjustment.

In this chapter, we saw the more common inspection tasks that you can use to help you determine when things need adjustment or repair. We also saw tasks that you need to perform before each print, or once before the first print of the day, in order to keep the printer adjusted properly so that you can continue to enjoy quality prints.

Now that you've seen the common things you need to do to inspect and adjust your printer, the next chapter jumps into the deeper end of 3D printer maintenance. The next chapter will discuss maintenance tasks that you must perform regularly (sometimes called *preventive maintenance*) and describes solutions for some of the more common failures (sometimes called *corrective maintenance*), such as clearing a clogged nozzle and replacing failed parts.

CHAPTER 10

3D Printer Maintenance: Preventive and Corrective Tasks

Maintaining your 3D printer involves a number of simple things you need to do frequently, like checking the condition of the printer for adjustment and breakage. I refer to these tasks as "basic maintenance tasks." Maintenance also involves more complex tasks that need to be done less often to keep the printer running well ("preventive tasks") and tasks that need to be done when something breaks ("corrective tasks").

These may sound like the same thing, but the there is a difference. For example, preventive tasks are things like changing the oil in your engine before the oil degenerates and the moving parts encounter excessive wear. A corrective task is changing a tire when you get a flat.

I presented the basic maintenance tasks in the last chapter. In this chapter, I will present preventive maintenance tasks that you will need to perform periodically and corrective maintenance tasks designed to help you fix things when they wear or break. The following sections describe and list some common tasks for each category.

Preventive Tasks

The goal of preventive maintenance is to execute small tasks frequently to reduce the risk and downtime of equipment failure.[1] More specifically, we take steps to keep our equipment in a condition where it is operating at the highest degree of efficiency possible. This includes making sure that the equipment remains free of debris and dust, that the parts that require lubrication are lubricated properly, and that worn parts are replaced before they fail. Normally these tasks are not time-consuming, but should be performed on a regular basis.

For example, your car requires periodic maintenance. Take a look at your owner's manual and review the maintenance sections.[2] You should find a chart or list that contains many things that need to be attended to at periodic milestones based on mileage driven or time, including replacing the oil and filters, replacing tires and belts when they wear, and even lubricating the chassis.

Fortunately, there aren't many preventive tasks required for maintaining your printer. The following sections describe the preventive tasks you should perform on your printer on a regular basis. As you will see, the frequency will vary from one printer to another, but is based on hours of use and, in some cases, influenced by the environment. I begin with the simplest preventive task: keeping the printer clean.

---

[1]See http://en.wikipedia.org/wiki/Preventive_maintenance.
[2]You have read it, haven't you?

Cleaning the Printer

Keeping your printer clean may not sound like a preventive task. However, depending on the design of your printer, it could be a most vital task in preventing damage. That is, if your printer is a RepRap or similar design without an enclosure, dust and other debris can accumulate on the electronics, making them retain heat. Too much heat—and the electronics will fail.

Dust and dirt can also accumulate on your oiled parts, fouling the lubrication to the point of increasing friction and wear on the bearings and rods. That doesn't mean printers with partial or full enclosures are immune to these effects. It just means the accumulation will be slower.

A bigger concern for printers with enclosures is the accumulation of small bits of plastic falling into the build area (the area around the build platform). This can include brim material, run-off filament from a print, oozing filament from the hot end, and so forth. While it would take an awful lot of plastic bits accumulating in your build area to cause major problems, you should still take the time to clean your build area periodically.

More importantly, you mustn't allow plastic to accumulate on your build platform. Even a small amount of plastic debris on your print surface can cause problems such as uneven first layers and nozzle blockages, leading to extrusion failure.

So how do you clean a 3D printer? You can't put it in a dishwasher or hose it down in the garage.[3] In fact, you should never use any cleansers whatsoever. The only possible exception would be cleaning the outside of your enclosure. Even then, you should use a mild cleanser designed for the material of your enclosure, and do so sparingly. Check your owner's manual for recommended cleaning procedures and cleansers.

DO PRINTERS REALLY GET DIRTY?

You may be wondering why anyone would need to clean a printer. After all, they print with plastic and they don't spew oil or other liquids or generate any particulates (well, mostly). So what is there to clean?

Strictly speaking, all of this is true. However, the accumulation of dust is a concern, as well as the accumulation of bits of plastic from part removal and print bed cleanup. Dust in particular can become a problem for exposed electronics and mechanical movements. Thus, cleaning is mostly about managing dust and debris from normal use.

The specific procedure will vary from one printer design to another, but there are several areas or subtasks you should do to thoroughly clean your printer. These tasks include the following:

- Dust and clean the frame.
- Remove dust from the electronics.
- Remove plastic debris from the build area.
- Clean threaded and smooth rods.

The frequency of when you need to clean the printer and, indeed, what areas you need to clean will depend on how dusty your environment is and how much you use your printer where debris is generated. I recommend checking the printer every 25 hours of use for things that need cleaning. At the very least, I would clean the printer every 50 or 100 hours of printing, depending on how dusty your environment is.

---

[3]Don't do either of these—ever!

Frame

The frame of the printer is one area that some enthusiasts neglect. Especially so when the frame components have been properly tightened and all parts have been seated (they no longer come loose). Part of this has to do with how the frame is constructed.

If the frame is an integral structure like that of the RepRap Prusa variants—where the various moving parts are external to the frame components, the frame isn't something you think about when cleaning the printer and generally isn't cleaned. If the frame is a structure like that of the MakerBot or Ultimaker—where the moving parts are inside a perimeter shell, it is more likely you will notice when it needs to be cleaned.

Another factor is the material that comprises the frame components and how it is finished. Matte painted surfaces and unfinished wood surfaces tend to be less noticeable when they become dusty. Glass, polished metals, acrylic, and gloss painted surfaces will make dust more apparent. Fingerprints may be another concern for glossy finishes, and oils from your skin can smudge some surfaces. Use a soft, dry cloth to wipe away any fingerprints or smudges.

Regardless, you should remove any accumulation of dust on your printer. If your printer has an external frame or enclosure, you can use a simple dry duster to wipe away any accumulation. I find a household-dusting wand or dusting glove works best for most surfaces. If your printer has an internal frame, use a vacuum to remove dust, or use canned air or an air compressor to blow off the dust.

■ **Caution**   If you use a duster, stay away from the electronics! Some dusters can generate electrostatic discharge (ESD), which may damage electronics. It is best to use canned air to clean electronics.

If your vacuum has a dusting brush, you can use it, but be careful using it around any exposed electronics or ports. You should also avoid removing the oil or grease from any of the axis movements while cleaning. Remember, the goal is to remove accumulation of dust, not to sanitize it for food consumption.[4]

If your printer has clear acrylic panels or similar windows, you can remove fingerprints and smudges with a few drops of water applied to a soft cotton or microfiber cloth. You may use acrylic-safe liquid cleaners, but you should apply the spray to the cloth first. Never spray anything directly onto your printer. There are too many areas that can be contaminated.

■ **Tip**   You should never use any liquid cleaners on your printer frame unless expressly recommended by your vendor.

Electronics

The electronics on your printer must also be free from dust and debris. If you allow dust and debris to accumulate on your electronics, you could risk them overheating because the dust can act as insulation. Too much heat and the electronics can fail. Admittedly, it would take a lot of dust to become a danger to some components, but that is no excuse to ignore the danger altogether.

However, cleaning electronics is not as easy as cleaning the frame. Electronics are very sensitive and most dusting devices use static to attract dust. Thus, you should never use anything other than compressed air to blow off the dust.

---

[4]Unless you're printing with chocolate. Yeah, you can do that with the right extruder and hot end (see https://chocedge.com).

I like to use a can of compressed air known as *canned air*. It emits a concentrated blast of air that is very effective at removing dust and small debris. However, you should be aware that some canned air suppliers use chemicals in their products. Those that do are not generally harmful to electronics, but always check the label for applicability before using it to clean electronics.

You should also remove any debris that falls into your electronics. Use a pair of ESD-safe tweezers to remove the larger pieces that cannot be removed by using canned or compressed air.

An electronics enclosure can help with dust build-up. If you choose to use an enclosure for your electronics, be sure to use one with sufficient ventilation or a fan to circulate air over the electronics.

COOL GADGET

If an air compressor is not practical (you cannot fit it into your work area or it's too noisy), canned air may be your only choice for cleaning away dust and debris without touching the device. If you use canned air to clean your printer and other electronics, and you clean often (or have many devices to clean), you could find yourself using up a can of compressed air quickly. Given the expense of canned air, you could be spending a significant amount of money keeping a supply of canned air on hand.

There is another option. Canless Air Systems[5] makes a device called the *O2 Hurricane*. It is about the size of a medium-sized canned air, cordless, and generates a burst of air using a miniature turbine. The battery life is about 15 minutes, but it recharges quickly. It is a bit louder than canned air, though. However, it is safer for the environment because you won't have to dispose of the canned air empties.

---

[5]See `canlessair.com`.

Unlike canned air, you can use the O2 Hurricane in any position and it won't accidentally eject moisture in the form of the propellant and chemicals found in some canned air products. Also, the device isn't quite as powerful as canned air, but it is more than suitable for periodic dusting. For devices with heavy dust accumulation, canned air may be a better choice. Since I clean my devices before dust becomes a problem, the slightly weaker power is not an issue.

The cost of the O2 Hurricane is a bit steep at about $80–$100, but if you use a lot of canned air, it may pay for itself in a short amount of time.

Build Area

One area that can become littered with debris over time (as well as dust) is the build area. As you use your printer, small pieces of filament will be discarded from excess extrusion (before and after a print), which can fall into the build area. If you print with a raft, brim, skirt, or even ABS juice, it is possible for small fragments to break off and also fall into the build area.

While none of these pose an immediate threat to your printer, you should take some time to periodically clean out the build area. I like to vacuum after each day I use the printer. If you use your printer only occasionally, you may not need to vacuum as often. I would recommend cleaning the build area at least once every time you change or clean the print surface. That is, do it weekly.

The best way to do this is to use a small vacuum to remove the debris. I use a long, flat attachment that can reach under the build platform. If your build platform can move in the Z axis (up and down), raise it so that you can vacuum underneath it.

■ **Caution**   Take care when vacuuming your build area. Some vacuums can cause ESD, which can damage electronics. For this reason, some people prefer to use canned air or a compressor to blow out the debris.

You should also take some time to vacuum the area around your printer and the floor underneath your desk or workbench. As I mentioned earlier, the small particles can pose a threat to small animals.

Threaded and Smooth Rods

Most printers use smooth rods as guides for linear or smooth bearings in the axis mechanism. These rods are typically lightly oiled. Some axes also use threaded rods to move the carriage or axis components. In some cases, you may find printers in which the threaded rods are coated with a layer of grease.

Smooth and threaded rods are among the first things in your printer to require cleaning. This is because they have a fine layer of lubrication, which traps dust and small debris. Figure 10-1 shows what this accumulation looks like. Notice that this accumulation is at the minimum range of the axis movement.

Figure 10-1. *Dust accumulation on a smooth rod*

Smooth rods need to be kept free of dust and debris. But doing so requires you to clean them often. If your printer is designed such that the rods are exposed, you should check and clean them at least weekly. If your printer is designed such that the rods are not exposed (they are inside an enclosure), you may not need to clean the rods as often. In that case, you should check and clean them whenever you clean or replace the print surface.

Keeping the smooth rods clean prevents too much accumulation that could damage the seals on some bearings. In fact, those bearing seals are designed to keep dust out.

To clean smooth rods, use a lint-free cloth to wipe away the accumulated dust and debris at each end of the rod. Figure 10-2 shows an example of how the debris can build up at the end of the axis. Notice the area inside the circle. Notice also the use of a cloth to wipe away the accumulated dirt.

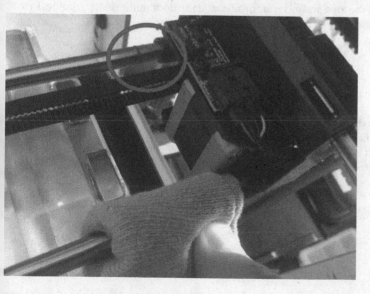

Figure 10-2. *Accumulated debris at axis ends*

Horizontal smooth rods are shown in these photos, however, the vertical smooth rods should also be cleaned but may not get as dirty since dust tends to settle on horizontal surfaces. Be sure to check under the axis for debris. If your printer design permits you to get to this area with the axis raised, you should clean it.

To clean the rest of the smooth rod, fold the cloth so that a clean area can be wrapped around the rod. Slide it up and down the axis to remove any additional debris. Figures 10-2 and 10-3 demonstrate this action.

Figure 10-3. Cleaning smooth rods with a cloth

You should slide the cloth away from the carriage riding on the axis. Clean one side of the axis, move the axis into the cleaned area, and then clean the other side.

Cleaning the threaded rods is a bit more problematic—especially so if the threaded rod is lubricated with grease. In this case, I recommend cleaning the threaded rod only when needed. That is, when the grease becomes dark or shows a lot of accumulation of dust and dirt. In that case, you may be able to use tweezers to remove the majority of the dust (the grease tends to make it clump). If your threaded rods are exposed, this could occur more frequently.

However, if your threaded rods are lubricated with oil and made from steel (including the nut), like what is commonly found on RepRap printers, the threaded rods can become dirty after only a few hours of printing. In most cases, the rods may turn dark as the oil becomes contaminated. While some may feel this doesn't warrant cleaning so long as the rods remain lubricated, I still like to keep them clean.

To clean the threaded rod, use a lint-free cloth coated with a small amount of the same oil or grease you use to lubricate the threaded rod. You might want to use a disposable glove to avoid getting grease on your hands. Check your vendor documentation for the specific lubrication needed. Figure 10-4 shows the application of a small amount of lubrication to a lint-free cloth. You don't need much—a small, 20cm circle is plenty.

Figure 10-4. *Cloth with lubrication for cleaning smooth rods*

■ **Note**   You can also remove your threaded rod to clean it. In this case, you can use a drill to lightly grip the threaded rod and turn the rod slowly to clean the valleys. However, you should be careful to avoid damaging the threads. You also will need to realign your Z axis and level your print bed. You can use more oil this way, because you don't have to worry about getting it on the plastic parts. Just make sure you wipe it clean before reinstalling.

When you are ready, move the axis to either the maximum or minimum position. There are two ways to clean threaded rods: 1) power-off the printer and wrap the cloth around the threaded rod, and then slowly move the axis by hand (this will rotate the threaded rod, allowing the cloth to remove any excess dirt, debris, and lubrication); or 2) power-on the printer and wrap the cloth around the threaded rod, and then use either printer controller software or the utility menu of your printer to move the axis away from the cloth. Figure 10-5 shows the proper positioning of the cloth to clean a threaded rod. Notice that I placed the cloth under the axis. As the axis moves, so too will the cloth.

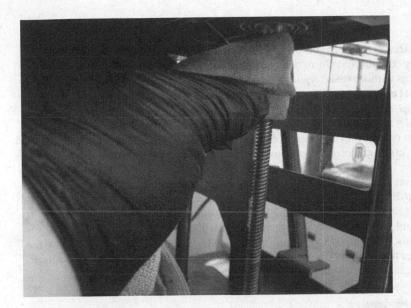

Figure 10-5. Cleaning threaded rods

If you chose the second option—cleaning the threaded rod while moving the axis with the printer powered on—you should take care to avoid obstructing the axis movement. While they may seem tiny, the stepper motors are powerful enough to injure you if you get your hand caught in the mechanism. Thus, you should move the axis away from your hands. The benefit of this option is that it is faster, but it requires extra caution and should not be attempted unless you are comfortable and understand how to move the axis in the correct direction.

■ **Caution**　　Always move the axis away from your hands and toward the endstop.

Once you have cleaned the threaded rods, be sure to lubricate them as described in the next section.

WHAT ABOUT TRACKS AND V-CHANNELS?

If your printer uses an alternative to smooth rods, such as V-channels or tracks, you need to keep them completely free of debris. Unlike some bearings that have seals that can push dust away, channels and tracks generally do not have anything to push away debris.

Dust may not be a problem, but small pieces of filament can be. That is, if a piece of plastic falls into the channel or track, it can cause the carriage to bounce over the obstacle, thereby shifting the axis momentarily. If the piece is large enough, it can cause the axis to stop—or worse, derail.

Thus, you should keep your V-channel and tracks clean, checking them before each print and cleaning them whenever you find any debris.

Lubricating Moving Parts

All 3D printers have metal and other parts that need lubrication. Some are designed to use grease; others light oil, and others still are constructed so that they contain some form of lubrication. For example, some lead screws and threaded rods require grease, some bearings without seals require light oil, and sealed bearings have lubrication inside the seals. There are also bearings that are impregnated with oil in the manufacturing process.[6] What matters most here are the smooth rods and bearings as well as the threaded rods and nuts.

Threaded rods and lead screws typically require either synthetic grease (e.g., PTFE) or lithium or similar grease. As I mentioned in the previous section, you typically do not need to change this grease often. In fact, some vendors suggest doing so after 50 or more hours of printing. I recommend checking the grease every 25 hours or so and replacing the grease every 100 hours.

To change the grease, we first clean away the old grease, as described previously, and then apply new grease using a disposable glove. Use your finger to dip a small portion of grease (about 10mm in diameter) and apply the grease directly to the threads, pressing the grease into the threads over about a 30mm to 40mm section. You do not have to grease the entire section—that would be way too much. A small amount will go a long way.

I like to position the axis to its maximum position, and then apply the grease behind the carriage. I then move the axis through its full movement several times to distribute the grease. Clean away any excess at the minimum position. Figure 10-6 shows an example of applying grease to the lead screw in a MakerBot Replicator 2.

Figure 10-6. *Applying grease to lead screw*

Smooth rods may also need lubrication, depending on what type of bearings you have. If you have bearings that require lubrication, you should apply the lubrication directly to the bearing. Follow your vendor's documentation for doing this. Newer printers use self-lubricating bearings. Regardless, I recommend cleaning the smooth rods as described previously. Figure 10-7 shows an example of a thrust bearing that is not sealed. This bearing will require grease and should be monitored for proper lubrication every 25 hours.

---

[6]See http://en.wikipedia.org/wiki/Oilite.

Figure 10-7. *Unsealed bearing*

WHAT IS A THRUST BEARING?

When working with 3D printers, most bearings are designed to support loads perpendicular to the shaft on which they are mounted. Thrust bearings are designed to support loads parallel to the shaft. Thus, thrust bearings are used at the end of the rod or through a mounting plate.

On the other hand, if the bearings are self-lubricating, you only need to keep the smooth rods lightly oiled. That is, you want the smooth rod to be damp with oil, but not so much that the oil runs or is visible. Most printers have bearings of this type. Thus, I present a method for lubricating the smooth rods.

Take a lint-free cloth and apply a dozen or so drops of the oil recommended by your vendor. I use light machine oil. Figure 10-8 shows the proper amount of oil. Unlike the cleaning process, we need enough oil on the cloth so that it will transfer to the smooth rod.

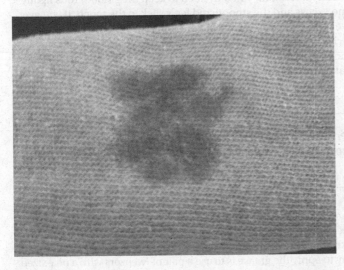

Figure 10-8. *Applying oil to lint-free cloth for lubricating smooth rods*

Once you have the oil on the cloth, wrap it around the smooth rod and move it back and forth. This is the same process as cleaning the smooth rod, but this time we have more oil on the cloth—enough that it will transfer to the smooth rod and distribute evenly. Figure 10-9 demonstrates the technique.

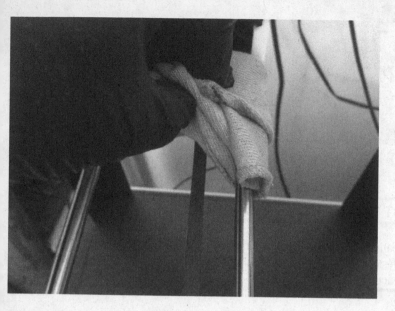

Figure 10-9. *Lubricating smooth rods*

Do this on each side of the carriage. If your axis uses multiple rods, lubricate all of them, checking the cloth to make sure you are not picking up dirt. If you see dirt on the cloth, fold it and continue wiping until the cloth comes away clean. Next, move the axes through its full range of movement a few times. Remove the cloth and examine each end and wipe away any excess oil.

Remember, if you are using bearings that do not need lubrication, you only need to keep the smooth rods lightly oiled. You know you have the right amount if there is no excess and the smooth rod feels slick to the touch. If you ever encounter oil on the build plate or elsewhere, you have used too much oil on your smooth rods.

The frequency for lubricating the smooth rods varies based on when you clean them. That is, you should lubricate the smooth rods after each time you clean them. This is because the cleaning process will remove much of the lubrication. For printers that have smooth rods that do not need cleaning, I recommend cleaning and lubricating them every 50 hours of printing.

■ **Tip**   If your printer uses tracks or grooved channels, the wheels or rollers that ride in these tracks or grooves may need lubrication. If they use sealed bearings, you may not need to lubricate them at all. It is best to check your documentation to make sure.

There is one other possible area where you may need lubrication. Printers using belts or chains to move axes use one or more idler pulleys in the mechanism. These idler pulleys may need lubrication. For example, the MakerBot Replicator 1, 2, and 2X have an idler pulley for the X axis that must be lubricated periodically. MakerBot suggests using the same grease for the lead screw (PTFE). The best way to apply the grease is to use a pair of tweezers with a pea-sized blob of grease. Use tweezers to transfer the grease onto the idler shaft, and then move the idler pulley back and forth to distribute the grease. Figure 10-10 shows the location of the idler pulley.

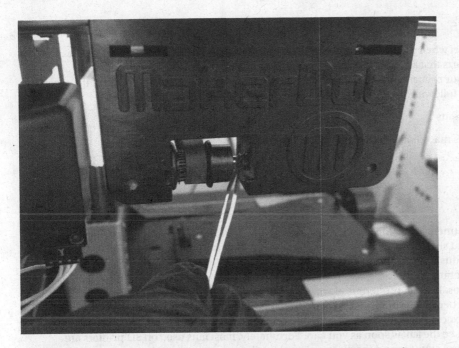

Figure 10-10. *Applying grease to idler pulley (MakerBot Replicator 1, 2, 2X)*

If your idler pulley requires lubrication (check your documentation), I recommend cleaning the idler pulley and reapplying the grease at the same interval you clean and lubricate the lead screw or threaded rods. That is, check it every 25 hours and clean and reapply grease every 100 hours.

WHAT ABOUT MY PRINTER?

The descriptions and procedures presented in this chapter are intentionally vendor neutral.[7] Whereas you should be able to use this information to service your printer, you may want to check your manual for maintenance tasks. Some vendors provide online technical support for maintenance tasks. The best vendors present how-to articles and videos to help you service your printer. Even if your vendor does not provide how-to articles and videos, you should be able to find details on the type of lubrication used on the moving parts. In the rare event you do not find this information on the vendor's web site (or in your manual), contact the vendor to ask.

---

[7]Well, mostly.

Replacing Worn Parts

You should replace any worn part when you discover the problem. As I discussed in the last chapter, periodic inspections can help you find parts that are worn. Whenever you discover a worn part, you should replace it as soon as you can. Continuing to use your printer with worn parts can risk problems with print quality. Some of the most common wear parts include the following:

- Print surface treatments

- Gears and gearboxes made from plastic (printed or otherwise)

- Fans

- Belts

- Bearings

Of course, print surface treatments wear most frequently, and we have already discussed the specifics of inspecting and replacing the print surface. Likewise, we have discussed the signs to watch for wear on gears. Recall that wear normally manifests as dust in the gear valleys and rounding of the teeth. I discuss printing your own replacement gears in the next section.

Fans are one of my pet peeves. I've had numerous electronics projects and a good number of manufactured gear—some very expensive—fail because a small, insignificant fan stopped working. Fans will most likely broadcast potential trouble in the form of excessive noises like high-pitched squeals, rattles, or slow start up. When you encounter these symptoms, replace the fan as soon as you can. Fortunately, most fans used on 3D printers are typically used in only two areas: the extruder and the electronics. Thus, they are easy to get to and normally easy to replace.

Belts are also wear items that may need replacing, but they wear at a much slower rate than gears. Recall that when belts wear, they can stretch—eventually fouling the mating of the teeth and the drive gear. In rare cases, belts can strip teeth or break. However, these are very unlikely events. In fact, unless you use your printer for hundreds to thousands of hours, you may never encounter a problem with worn belts. However, I have seen this happen at least once.

Bearings wear down as well, but like belts, they are unlikely to need replacing. However, when bearings wear, they can start making noises (from lack of lubrication), have excessive play, or even bind or break apart. These events are even less likely than worn belts, but again, if you use your printer a lot or if you fail to keep the bearings lubricated (or they fail from a manufacturing defect), they can fail. Check the bearings at least every 100 hours to ensure that they are in good order.

Now that we have seen some of the maintenance tasks you should perform regularly, and before I get into describing the common corrective tasks you may have to perform, I want to discuss the subject of spare parts that you should have on hand for things that wear or may break.

Got Spares?

Having a store of spare parts is key to keeping your printer running over the long-term. Spares are one of the things a lot of RepRap manuals and blogs discuss, but they often focus on only those plastic parts that you need to maintain RepRap printers. Sadly, some vendors do not mention spare parts at all. That is unfortunate because there are a small number of spares you may want to have on hand if you plan to use your printer for many hundreds of hours. Fortunately, some vendors do offer spare parts for sale. Two of the best examples of ample spare parts availability are Ultimaker and Wanhao.

Ultimaker (https://www.ultimaker.com/t/spare-parts) offers a long list of spare parts you can buy, including fans, belts, gears, and extruder parts—everything you need to keep your printer in top shape.

Wanhao sells printers similar to MakerBot printers. Wanhao (http://wanhaousa.com/pages/parts) offers a complete list of replacement parts that even include many of the molded parts, like X-ends and more.

Don't assume that just because your vendor doesn't offer spares that you will never need to repair your printer. Even if you print only a few hours a week, you will eventually need a spare part. A lot depends on how well the components in your printer were made, how often you perform the required preventive maintenance, and whether events occur that can damage a component.[8]

In my experience, I've had some printers fail as early as within 10 to 20 hours. In one case, a new part failed within an hour. And one of my printers with several hundred hours has yet to fail. However, I must clarify that I replaced a number of worn parts before they failed. The point is that sooner or later you are going to have to replace something that has worn out.

There are two kinds of spares that you should keep on hand. First, there are those components that you can print yourself. This applies mainly to RepRap printers since they are composed of parts printed by other 3D printers. Second, there are electronics and hardware components you should have on hand.

I suggest certain spares in the following sections. The lists are based on my experiences with RepRap, MakerBot, and other commercial-grade printers. The lists for your specific printer may vary from what is presented here. However, you should be able to use the lists to construct your own spares inventory.

But take some care to think through what you need. Taken to the extreme, you could end up with enough parts to build a second printer. For example, the last time I decided to build a RepRap printer, I found that I had everything I needed except the build platform. Of course, once a part has failed I tend to keep a second one on hand just in case it fails again.

■ **Tip** I suggest setting a budget for buying spares. Sometimes a spare part may be too expensive to keep on hand. For example, the electronics board for a MakerBot Replicator is very expensive and (fortunately) rarely fails. On the other hand, if you rely on your printer for your business, you may want to have one on hand so that you don't encounter significant downtime.

Printing Spares

As I mentioned, printed spares are mainly for RepRap printers. However, some commercial- and professional-grade printers use parts that can be printed. For example, you can print new Mk7 Stepstruder (thingiverse.com/thing:53125) extruder bases and idler arms for the MakerBot Replicator 1, 2, and 2X printers.

Printing spares for your printer can be a lot of fun. I recommend printing a set of spare parts as one of your first noncalibration tasks. Not only will you learn a lot about how best to use your printer, you will gain a set of spares to keep the printer running. In fact, you can get carried away to the point where you've printed an entire set of plastic parts—enough to build a new printer. This was one of the main goals of a RepRap printer.

But you don't have to go that far. You need to only print those parts that wear or are prone to breakage. I list these parts in the next section.

---

[8]Basically, your mileage may vary.

Recommended List of Spares

In this section, I present a set of spares you should consider having on hand. If you have the budget to buy a complete set of spares, you should do so. However, if you are budget conscience, you may want to consider finding a source for the spares and saving that information so that when you do need the spares, you can get them quickly. On the other hand, if you are using your printer for a business or cannot afford the downtime to wait for a spare, you should consider investing in a set of spares as soon as your budget permits.

Printed Parts

The following lists the printable spare parts that you should keep on hand. Some of these are applicable to most printers, whereas others are more specific to RepRap printers. Take some time to examine your printer and locate any similar part to determine if you can print the part or you must buy it from your vendor.

- *Extruder gears*: These can be a challenge to print because they must be printed with no lifting or distortion. Thus, printing gears is an excellent way to perfect your technique for eliminating lift.

- *Extruder idler mount*: If you are using a RepRap printer with a Greg's Wade hinged extruder, the idler mount (also called a *door*) can fail over time due to stress. Other extruders may not have this problem, but like the gears, printing a complete extruder body is a good way to practice and fine-tune your printer. However, since some extruder idler mounts are easily broken, you may want to print several spares in case your backup breaks when printing a replacement.

- *Endstop holders*: Endstop holders can take some abuse. Most are rather flimsy, which doesn't help. If your printer uses the same holder for all axes, just print one; otherwise, print a set.

- *X-ends*: The X-ends on RepRap Prusa i2 printers have been known to break from a surprisingly small amount of flex (like from a hot-end crash into the print bed). If you have a Prusa i2, I recommend printing a set of X-ends to have on hand.

- *Bar clamps*: These are among the most fragile parts on RepRap printers. Breakage can occur from the normal shaking of the printer—especially if the rods they support are overtightened. I recommend starting with these and printing a set of four to have on hand. Most print quickly.

- *Belt clamps*: Some older designs use belt clamps that can slip. The natural treatment is to tighten them down, but this act has a tendency to damage the clamps. If you have had to tighten your belt clamps more than once, I recommend printing an extra set or looking for an improved version and replacing the existing clamps with those.

- *Other:* I would also print a spare of any part that breaks. That is, if a part breaks, print two so that you have one as a spare.

Replacement Parts

The following lists spares that you should consider buying if you want to keep your printer running over the long-term. Once again, these may not apply to all printers, but you should buy those that do apply to your printer.

- *Fans*: As mentioned, fans can wear out surprisingly early. Unless your printer is built with exceptionally high-quality fans, you will eventually need a new one.

- *Belts*: Belts are long-wear items. I recommend getting a set once you have had to adjust the belts a couple of times after initial calibration. That is, if you printed for 100 or more hours without having to adjust the belts, and then suddenly have to adjust them, you should have a spare and replace the belt once it begins to need regular adjustment (or it breaks).

- *Nozzle*: The hot-end nozzle is an item that many people have as a spare so that they can change it when it gets clogged. As I have mentioned previously and will demonstrate in the next section, you can clean even the most stubborn clogs. Regardless, having at least one spare[9] will help you keep your printer running should you encounter a clog that cannot be cleared with the cold pull method.

- *Stepper motor*: This is another long-wear item. If you want a complete spare parts supply, I recommend having one on hand. You should not need a complete set unless your printer uses different sizes for each axis (not likely, but I have seen it at least once).

- *Stepper driver*: The stepper driver boards are susceptible to ESD and have been known to fail on occasion. I've had three fail over several hundred hours. If you have a RepRap printer or a printer that has separate stepper drivers, I recommend having at least one spare.

- *Endstop*: Endstops are simple switches and generally have a very long life. However, if the endstop is subjected to axis crashes (where the axis runs into the endstop violently), you could damage the endstop. Given its role, I recommend having one spare.

- *Electronics board*: Commercial- and professional-grade printers generally have proprietary electronics boards that are usually very expensive. If your printer uses one of the more popular general options (RAMPS, Rambo, etc.), and you must rely on your printer, you should have a spare to avoid a lengthy downtime.

- *Build plate*: You should consider having a second build plate to allow you to swap out the build plate when the print surface needs cleaning or if you want to switch from one print surface to another.

If you cannot buy the part from your vendor directly, you will want to ensure that you are getting the correct part for your printer. If you have any concern, be sure to compare the new spare part to the matching existing part. In those cases where the new spare is somewhat different (e.g., not the same supplier), I install the new part and test it, and then put the original part back in when I confirm the replacement is compatible.

Another factor is the cost of the spare part. Some spare parts can be expensive. For example, the electronics board for a MakerBot printer is very expensive, but the electronics board for a RepRap printer is less expensive. You will need to balance the cost of the spare with the availability and time to get the part to decide if you should buy one to have on hand.

Now that I have discussed the spare parts needed for long-term use, I discuss some common and not-so-common repair tasks in the next section.

---

[9]Advanced enthusiasts may also want to have several nozzles of different sizes. This will allow you to experiment with extrusion rates, layer height, and more.

WHAT ABOUT THE FIRMWARE?

There is one other preventive task you may want to consider—upgrading the firmware. Sometimes printer manufacturers will release a new version of the firmware that has fixes or enhancements for the printing process or quality. However, most vendors do not release new versions very often. Firmware changes were common a few years ago, but not so much now.

It is generally a good idea to keep your firmware current, but I would not do it unless I encounter a need for the changes. Check your vendor's support web site for any changes to the firmware, and read the change notes carefully before deciding to upgrade.

If you own a RepRap printer, the firmware is really up to you since it is very much a DIY affair. The same philosophy applies: don't upgrade unless you find changes that you need. If you find that the latest variant of your firmware supports some nifty feature that you want, then upgrade; otherwise, wait. For example, if you want to add Z-probing (auto bed leveling), you will likely need to upgrade the firmware.

Corrective Tasks

This section describes a number of corrective maintenance tasks (repairs) that you may need to do to keep your printer in good working order. I have tried to keep this discussion general, but some of the examples are for specific printers or components. However, you should be able to draw parallels and knowledge from the examples should you need to fix a similar problem.

■ **Caution** When repairing your printer, be sure to turn it off and disconnect it from your computer (if applicable). Unless you are diagnosing a problem, you should not need power to disassemble your printer in the course of a typical repair.

Also, I recommend removing any access panels, enclosure panels, hoods, fans, and so forth, so that you can access the area for the repair. It is also a good idea to remove the build plate if it can be detached—especially if it is made of glass or other materials that are easily scratched or broken. It is all too easy to accidentally drop a sharp tool or part onto the print surface. Even if you aren't concerned about the print surface treatment, the build plate itself may be fragile.

■ **Tip** Whenever you work on your printer, always remove the build plate to avoid damaging the print surface with dropped tools or parts.

As I mentioned in a previous chapter, it is also a good idea to gather the tools you need and place them nearby. If your printer is positioned where access to the repair area requires you to lean over the printer or reach behind it, move the printer to a place where you can access the area more easily. I use a small vintage typewriter stand with a piece of plywood on top as a work stand. Not only does this allow me to move the printer around, it also means I can push the stand out of the way if I don't finish the repair in one sitting.

WHAT'S A TYPEWRITER STAND?

In decades past, typewriters were the laptop of the day. There were special desks designed such that the typewriter was placed in a special drawer that concealed the typewriter in the desk. I've seen some that pop up from under the knee area and others that pull out like a drawer.

There were also special side desks with folding arms that fit under some of the older, large office furniture. The legs are mounted on casters that rotate in all directions; at least two will be locking. The stands were typically made from metal and provided a very sturdy platform for the heavy typewriter. The following shows a typical vintage typewriter stand.

This makes the typewriter stand an excellent choice for supporting a 3D printer. You can find typewriter stands in thrift stores and antique stores, as well as online auction sites. If you look long enough, you should be able to find one in pretty good condition. If you aren't concerned about the antiquity element, you can buy one with heavy patina, and then strip and paint it. The stand in the photo has been refurbished and looks like new.

Corrective tasks—hence, repairs—can take many forms: removing obstructions from the axis movement, cleaning out a hot end, replacing a worn or broken part, or replacing consumables like print surfaces and filters. I discuss some common corrective tasks (repairs) in the following sections.

Clearing a Clogged Nozzle

One of the most frustrating experiences I've encountered is a series of extrusion failures over a short period of time. For example, not being able to complete a print without having an extrusion failure. I discussed the causes of this problem in an earlier chapter. Recall that most of these problems are caused by obstructions in some form: the filament cannot exit the nozzle, the filament tension is too high, or a foreign object has found its way into the hot end. In the last case, the object is larger than the opening in the nozzle, and hence clogs it from within. It is this scenario that I cover in this section.

If you encounter this problem and the cold pull method does not work, you may have to remove the nozzle and clean it out. There are several techniques for doing this. What I present here is the most reliable procedure, but it requires some care to execute safely.

You will need a pair of heat-resistant gloves, the proper tools to remove the nozzle, metal tongs or pliers to hold the nozzle, canned air, a butane torch, a metal trivet or heat-safe place to place the heated nozzle between the procedure steps, and two drill bits—one that is the exact size of your nozzle opening and another that is the same size as the filament chamber (1.75mm or 3mm). The procedure is as follows. I explain each step in more detail afterward.

1. Remove the nozzle.

2. Place the torch on a workbench in an area where there are no combustible liquids or any flammable material.

3. Pick up the nozzle with a pair of metal tongs or pliers.

4. Turn on the torch and turn it up to about a medium setting.

5. Place the nozzle in the flame. Do not heat the nozzle more than a few seconds. You do not want to use so high a flame as to burn the plastic.

6. After 10 to 20 seconds, remove the nozzle from the heat and use the larger drill bit to pull out melted plastic. Let the drill bit and nozzle cool.

7. Reheat the nozzle and repeat step 6 until you cannot get any more plastic.

8. Let the nozzle cool, and then use the small drill bit to clear the nozzle opening.

9. Reheat the nozzle and use canned air to blow out any remaining filament.

10. If you printed with ABS, soak the nozzle in acetone to remove any traces of filament.

■ **Caution**   Never, ever use a powered drill to drive the drill bit. We are only using the bit to grab the plastic, not change the internal structure of the nozzle. You only want to grip plastic and not remove any metal. You should practice this on a nozzle that you have considered a lost cause before trying it on your only nozzle.

You may need to disconnect the heater element, temperature sensor, wiring, and so forth, to remove the nozzle. Some hot ends do not have a removable nozzle (e.g., a Prusa nozzle) and will require removal of the hot end. Others still may require you to disassemble the hot end to get to the core since the nozzle and core are all one piece. Consult your documentation for your hot end for the precise procedure for removing the nozzle.

When you place the nozzle in the flame, move it back and forth to heat the entire nozzle. I like to grip the nozzle by the bottom and let the flame flow over the body. The filament will melt quickly. Some filament may ooze from the opening. This is normal. Figure 10-11 shows how to position the nozzle.

Figure 10-11. *Place the nozzle in the flame*

■ **Caution** You must wear protective gloves while using the torch. Proper eye protection is also prudent, as is having a fire extinguisher nearby in case something goes awry.[10]

Next, use a drill bit that is the same size as the chamber and press it into the melted filament, and then pull it out. Don't use a drill or electric driver for this step. This mimics the cold pull procedure, but in this case we're using the cold drill bit to help grip the plastic and remove it. Figure 10-12 shows the proper size and position of the drill bit. You will want to use the drill bit with one hand while holding the heated nozzle with the tongs or pliers.

---

[10]Such as the "whooshing" sounds of ignition.

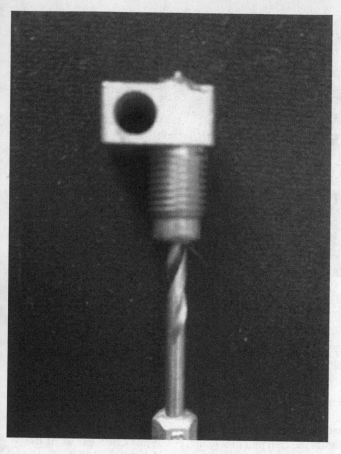

Figure 10-12. *Proper size and location of drill bit for removing plastic*

■ **Caution**   Be very careful when handling the heated nozzle. The nozzle as well as the tool you use to hold it in the flame will get very hot. Also, never use any form of driver or drill in this step. Use your hands to manipulate the drill bit.

Remember, you will be holding the heated nozzle with one hand and your other hand will manipulate the drill bit. Once you have removed some plastic, place the nozzle on a safe surface (e.g., a metal trivet) and allow the drill bit to cool, and then remove the plastic from the drill bit. Reheat the nozzle and try removing more plastic. Do this a few times until no more plastic can be removed.

■ **Caution**   The goal is to remove plastic, not reshape the interior of the nozzle. Thus, you should apply only enough pressure to grasp the filament. If you see metal shavings, you've gone too far.

Once you can no longer get any plastic from inside the chamber, use the small drill bit to gently drill out any plastic from the opening. This step requires a bit of patience and the proper drill size. Be sure to get the properly sized microdrill that matches your nozzle. Figure 10-13 shows the properly sized drill bit and orientation for cleaning the opening.

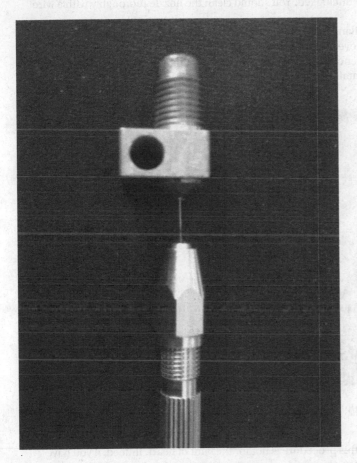

Figure 10-13. *Proper size and location of drill bit for cleaning opening*

Don't apply a lot of pressure here. The drill bit is very small and can break easily. You want to drill out the plastic, not reshape the opening (although you can do that if the opening has been damaged from a crash into the build plate). If this step makes you a bit nervous, that's OK. In that case, try using a drill bit that is slightly smaller than the opening to remove the plastic, and then switch to the correct size once the opening is clear.

At this point, the foreign object should be removed. You should also be able to hold the nozzle up to the light and see a pinpoint of light coming through the opening. If you do not, repeat both drill bit steps until you do see light through the opening.

Return the nozzle to the heat again. Let it heat up for about 20 to 30 seconds, and then position the nozzle so that the opening is facing you and the chamber is facing the workbench (cement or metal floor, metal trash can, etc.) or some area that is safe for melted plastic. Use canned air to blow through the opening. Direct the air through the opening (reverse of the extrusion direction). This will remove the larger of the remaining bits of plastic, such as shavings from the drill bit.

■ **Caution**   Always direct the air away from your body. Hot plastic can burn your skin.

At this point, your nozzle should be completely unclogged. You should clean the nozzle thoroughly with a wire brush before reinstalling it.

If you print with ABS and indeed ABS was the filament used last, you should consider soaking the nozzle in acetone for about an hour. This will completely remove any stray bits of plastic that the previous steps missed. Figure 10-14 demonstrates this step. Notice there is enough acetone to completely submerge the nozzle. Also, the acetone is placed in a glass jar. Any acetone-safe container will work.

Figure 10-14.   Soaking the nozzle in acetone (ABS only)

Now that wasn't so bad, was it? As you can see, this procedure is not for the faint of heart. Indeed, if you have any concerns about performing the procedure, you can always take the easier route and simply replace the nozzle. Replacement nozzles are generally cheaper than an entire hot end (if it is a separate part, like the J-head hot ends), but they are not cheap by any measure.

I recommend buying a replacement nozzle first and then trying this procedure on the original. If you dig too deeply with the drill bit or experience some similar mishap, you will gain practice without so much risk.

■ **Tip**   Until you perfect the procedure, don't try this procedure on your only nozzle!

Replacing Broken or Worn Plastic Parts

If you own a printer that is assembled using printed parts, chances are you will encounter a situation where one of those parts will break or wear out. With RepRap printers, bar clamps, belt clamps, and endstop holders are very common sources of breakage.

Sometimes a broken part can be repaired. That is, if it is made from ABS, you may be able to cement the parts back together. But this isn't always possible if the breakage occurred from an overtightened or undertightened part. In this case, it is possible the movement of the printer itself has weakened the part. Repairing the part may not be the best solution. In these cases, I recommend replacing the part with a new one. If the part was damaged by stress, or if it is not repairable, your only option is to replace the part.

■ **Tip** You can repair ABS parts with acetone-based glue, such as ABS pipe cement. You can also repair PLA parts with a dichloromethane-based solvent glue, such as Weld-On #4.

When parts become worn to the point that they can no longer be tightened, or they wobble or do not function correctly, you have to replace them. For example, the pivot point on the idler mount (the door) for a Greg's Wade hinged extruder can become rounded out over time. When this happens, you may not be able to apply the correct tension to the filament. In this case, you may not be able to print until you replace the idler mount.

If you do not have a replacement part and your printer is still functional or you can secure the broken part temporarily by cementing it back together or using a zip tie or even duct tape,[11] you may be able to hold things together long enough to print a new part.

Replacing the part can sometimes be a little tricky. Depending on where the part is located and how your frame is designed, replacing the part may be as straightforward as unbolting the old one and bolting the new one in its place. If the part is a subcomponent of another part, it may require a lengthier disassembly. For example, if you need to replace a part on a Prusa i2, you may need to partially disassemble the frame to get to the part.

REPLACING PARTS FOR THREADED ROD FRAMES

Printers that use threaded rods use printed parts to connect the parts together. For example, a Prusa i2 uses threaded rods that attach to plastic pieces at the ends of the rods (as well as several that attach to the center). Unfortunately, if one of the plastic pieces break, it can be time-consuming to replace it. This is especially true for pieces that mount toward the center, such as belt clamps, Z-axis clamps, idler pulleys, and Y motor mounts.

In order to replace these or other frame components, you must loosen the nuts on both sides of the threaded rod so that you can move the rod enough to get to the part. For example, to replace a bar clamp for the Y-axis smooth rods, you must first loosen all of the nuts on the rod, and then unthread the rod (left or right—whichever is closest). The figure below shows the location of the belt clamps. The arrows pointing down locate all of the nuts you must loosen or remove and the arrows pointing up locate the two bar clamps.

---

[11]Say it isn't so! Duct tape on a 3D printer. Oh, the horror.

As you can see, there are a lot of things to remove, including ten nuts. However, you don't have to remove all of them. You can loosen them all, and then rotate the threaded rod away from the bar clamp. For example, if replacing the left bar clamp, thread the rod to the right. It is a bit tedious because you have to turn the rod a few turns and then readjust the position of the nuts (blue painter's tape can help here), but it is the only way to replace parts that mount on a threaded rod.

When replacing worn or broken parts, I like to save the part so that if the problem reoccurs, I can compare the failed parts to determine if the problem is the same. This not only helps you diagnose the cause of the failure, it also helps to form a pattern for wear items. That is, if you are wearing out extruder gears, you may be able to detect a pattern to the wear, such as a bent mounting bolt, an overtightened gear, or misalignment between the gears.

When disassembling your printer to remove the part, place the various bolts and nuts away from your tools so that you don't accidentally knock one off onto the floor or drop it into the bowels of your printer. If you are working with a lot of bolts of varying sizes and lengths, make a grid on a piece of paper and label each grid with the location for the bolts. I find this step a necessity when working on smaller electronics such as phones, tablets, and laptops. It is a good habit to form and it will keep you from inserting a bolt that is too long.

BOLT LENGTH DOES MATTER

A professional European car mechanic once taught me to always label bolts with their location. This is extremely important for many high-end sports cars and motorcycles, and especially older European cars. He demonstrated his point by showing me and a few friends what happened when someone reassembled a motor and mixed up some bolts. In this case, there was one bolt 5mm longer than the rest. If you inserted that bolt into one of three places and tightened it down, the bolt would bottom out against a very thin internal casing well which could break off and fall into the oil pan. Needless to say, this would also start a slow and annoying leak, but the major issue is the piece of metal floating around among the gears and pistons. Not good.

However, don't simply replace the part and declare victory. Be sure to examine the printer before you replace the part, and think about what caused the breakage or wear. Knowing what caused the damage can help you avoid the problem in the future. For example, the idler mount for a Greg's Wade hinged extruder can wear more quickly if you use a lot of tension on your filament. Reducing the tension to a minimal setting that still allows for successful and consistent extrusion can help make the idler mount last longer.

I also like to record the repair in my engineering journal in a manner similar to the diagnostic steps from Chapter 7. Be sure to take notes, such as which part it is, what it is made from (ABS or PLA), any pertinent events prior to the failure (such as an axis crash), and the date and time of the repair. It may also help to take photos of the part—both in place and removed. I make a note of the path and name each photo in my notebook so that I can refer to them later. I also tag each part with a piece of blue painter's tape with a note that refers to my notebook entry. Lastly, I write my findings at the end of the entry so that I can affect the same repair should the problem recur.

Repairing Broken ABS Parts

One of the advantages of printing with ABS is that the parts are very easy to repair. In fact, you can join two ABS pieces together using only acetone. If you take two ABS parts and soak each piece in a small amount of acetone (in a depth of about 1mm to 2mm) for 15 seconds, and then press them together, within a few minutes the bond will be strong enough to keep the parts together. Depending on the size of the joint, the part will cure in a few hours. I like to leave the part to cure overnight.

When ABS parts break, they typically break at one or more layers. This can be caused by sheering force, too much stress, overtightening, or simply careless handling. Figure 10-15 shows a part for a Prusa i3. This is a Z-axis motor mount that was accidentally subjected to sheering force. Actually, I was disassembling the X axis and slipped. Oops. Notice how the break is along a single layer but is still attached on one side.

Figure 10-15. *Broken ABS part*

Since the part is still partially attached, the application of soaking in acetone won't work. It is possible to brush the acetone onto the joint, but it is not easy to keep it from running and discoloring the exterior. However, if you dissolve a bit of ABS in the acetone to thicken it, you can brush it on without it running. Plus, brushing acetone doesn't seem to form as strong a joint as the soaking method. Since this part is a motor mount, it needs to be as strong as an original part.

Fortunately, there is an alternative. You can use ABS cement designed for cementing ABS pipe. The most popular ABS plumbing cement has pigment, such as a purple color. This helps the plumber see where the cement is applied so that it is instantly visible whether or not the cement has been applied to the entire surface of the pipe. However, you can get clear ABS plumbing cement. Figure 10-16 shows one example of the cement. It is available from most home improvement and hardware stores that stock plumbing supplies.

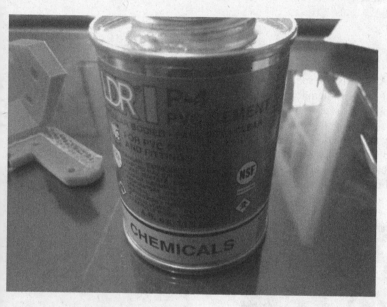

Figure 10-16. *Clear ABS plumbing cement*

There are several advantages to using ABS plumbing cement. First, the cement is thick and easy to apply with a small flat tool like a hobby knife or wooden stirring stick. The consistency means it won't run all over the place like pure acetone. Second, the cement dries very quickly—much quicker than waiting for acetone to evaporate. And finally, the cement forms a very strong bond. Because of these advantages, I use clear ABS plumbing cement for all ABS repairs or multipart assembly. Figure 10-17 shows the repaired motor mount reinstalled.

Figure 10-17. *Repaired ABS part*

Notice that you can see the joint. I was in a bit of a rush when I repaired the part, so I did not apply any finishing techniques to hide the seam. Whether you choose the acetone method or the ABS plumbing cement, you can cover the seam by sanding with fine sandpaper and brushing acetone over the surface. This will make the seam much less noticeable. You may want to consider doing this if the part you are repairing is an aesthetic element.

Replacing Extruder Gears

Extruders that use printed gears are a wear item that should be monitored periodically and replaced when needed. The type of plastic used in printing the gear will have an effect on the longevity of the gears. Gears printed with PLA tend to last longer than those printed with ABS.

Printed gears tend to wear slowly, producing a dust that settles in the valleys of the teeth. The dust isn't a problem (but is good to clean it off once in a while), however the dust is an indication of wear. If you are seeing a lot of dust, you may want to examine the teeth for excessive wear.

One way to do this is to compare the gears to a new set. If you notice rounding or that pieces of the teeth have broken off, you will want to replace the gears. As mentioned in an earlier chapter, if there is any play in the mating of the teeth, you should replace the gears as soon as you can. Figure 10-18 shows a closeup of a gear-driven extruder.

Figure 10-18. *Gears for the Greg's Wade hinged extruder (Prusa i3)*

■ **Tip** If your printer came with gears printed with ABS, I recommend printing replacements with PLA. In my experience, the PLA gears wear much more slowly and are not as susceptible to damage. They also benefit from light lubrication to reduce friction.

Notice the bolts for the stepper motor (one is hidden by the larger gear). These are set in an oblong mount that allows you to adjust the distance of the motor from the larger gear shaft. This is how you would adjust the mating of the gears in this particular extruder body. Other extruders may have similar adjustability—especially if they are variants of the Greg's Wade extruder.

■ **Note** If you decide to use a different set of gears than what your printer came with, check the number of teeth in each gear. If they differ, the gear ratio will be different, which will affect how the extruder works. You can use a different gear ratio, but you will have to change the firmware to match. See Chapter 5 for information about setting the gear ratio in the firmware.

To replace the gears on a typical printed gear-driven extruder, I recommend first unloading the filament. This will allow you to move the gears freely, with the exception of the resistance of the stepper motor. Follow the procedure listed in your documentation to unload the filament. This will involve heating the hot end and then reversing the extruder motor until the filament can pull clear.

Once the filament is unloaded, you can loosen the bolts for the gears. The easiest way to remove the gears is to remove the stepper motor. Typically, the small gear is attached to the stepper motor. Once removed, you can loosen the setscrew (called a *grub screw*) and remove the small gear. You can then remove the nut holding the large gear to take off this gear. Reverse the procedure to install the new gears.

If your extruder has an adjustment feature for the stepper motor mount, be sure to adjust the stepper motor so that the gears mate well. That is, the peaks and valleys close without gaps and there is no play in the gears. To check this, try to turn the gears in opposite directions—first one way and then the other. If there is any play, try moving the stepper motor closer to the large gear.

Replacing Belts

Recall that the belts used in your printer are designed to have teeth or grooves that allow the drive gear to move the belt consistently. If the belt is worn or there are teeth missing, the belt can slip and cause problems with axis shift. If you have monitored your printer over time and notice that the belts become worn (or worse, break), you should replace the belts. The procedure for replacing the belt varies based on the type of belt used.

Some printers use a length of belt with the ends secured to either the carriage, whereas others use continuous or closed belts (they have no break). Most RepRap and similar printers use a length of open belt secured at each end (for example, the X-axis belt for a Prusa i3). MakerBot and other manufactured printers use continuous belts. Some printers use closed belts without clamps. Check your printer manual or the vendor's web site for the specifics on replacing your belts.

■ **Note**   Belts are typically a long-wear item. Depending on how much you use your printer, you may never have to replace the belts. You may have to adjust the tension periodically, but replacing belts is normally for those who use their printers for hundreds of hours per month. I include the procedures in this chapter for completeness.[12]

Replacing Open Belts

Open belts are easier to fix. In this case, you need only to loosen any automatic or manual tensioner, disconnect the belt at both ends, and then pull it out. To install the new belt, thread it over the drive gear and idler, and then attach the ends. You should pull the belt as tight as possible before securing the second end. If you find there is too much slack in the belt—your tension adjustment is at its maximum position—you should set your tension mechanism to its minimum setting then remove one end and pull it tighter before securing it.

Replacing Closed Belts

Closed belts can be a bit more difficult to replace. This is because the belt must be removed from the axis mechanism by partially (or completely) disassembling the axis.

---

[12]And because I've had to do it once myself, and the documentation for the process are hard to find.

If the axis mechanism can be disassembled without removing it from the printer, things aren't so difficult; but if you must remove the axis mechanism, be prepared for a potentially lengthy repair. I recommend taking your time and making notes (assuming your documentation doesn't cover this procedure) so that you can reassemble the mechanism properly.

I will use the closed belts in the MakerBot printers as an example of one of the more complex closed belt replacement tasks. Other printers will require similar steps to replace the belt. Due to the very specific nature of the mechanism, refer to your printer documentation, online support articles, or community member advice for the specifics of replacing the belts in your printer.

X-Axis Belt

Figure 10-19 shows the closed belt for the X axis in a MakerBot Replicator 2/2X. The photo is taken from above. Interestingly, the belt is the same configuration on the MakerBot Replicator 1 Single and Dual.

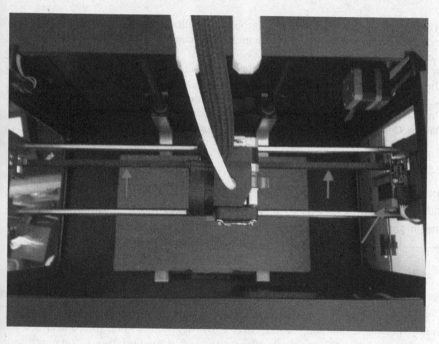

Figure 10-19. X-axis belt (MakerBot Replicator 2)

The arrows in Figure 10-19 point to the belt. Notice that it runs parallel with the X axis. To the right is the X-axis stepper motor, and on the left is the idler pulley. The stepper motor is mounted in slotted holes designed to allow some adjustment for belt tension. There isn't a lot of adjustment; maybe 4mm total, but it is enough to compensate for normal wear.

You can adjust the tension of the belt by loosening the four bolts and pulling the motor to the right (as viewed from the front), and then retightening the bolts. This can take a bit of practice. The best way I've found to do this is to face the right side of the printer and use your left hand to pull the motor toward you and your right to tighten one of the bolts. Once you have one tight, you can release the motor and tighten the others.

Y-Axis Belt

Some printers use multiple belts on one or more axes. For example, the MakerBot Replicator 1, 2, and 2X use three belts for the Y axis; one on each side of the printer and a smaller one in the right rear. The Ultimaker machines use a similar configuration for the X and Y axes.

On the MakerBot Replicator 1, the small belt is connected to the stepper motor, which turns an intermediate shaft at the rear of the printer that has a drive pulley on each side to move the other belts in the same direction. There is a second intermediate shaft in the front of the printer. Figure 10-20 shows the left side belt for the Y axis on a MakerBot Replicator 1 Dual.

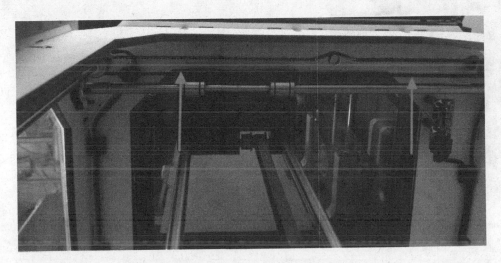

Figure 10-20. Y-axis belt, left side (MakerBot Replicator Dual)

The arrows in Figure 10-20 indicate the belt. Notice the intermediate shaft to the left in the photo. This is the front intermediate shaft. Not shown is a second idler shaft at the rear.

Figure 10-21 shows the right side belt for the Y axis on a MakerBot Replicator 1 Dual.

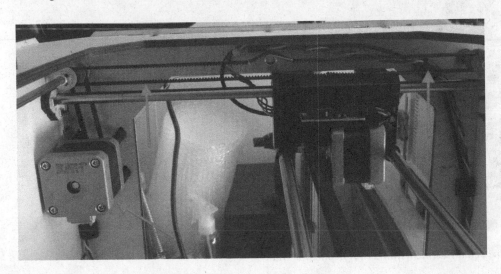

Figure 10-21. Y-axis belt, right side (MakerBot Replicator Dual)

Notice in Figure 10-21 that there are arrows, indicating the belt. If you look at the top center of the photo, you will see a metal loop. This is a belt tensioner, which many MakerBot Replicator and earlier printers used. Newer models do not use the tensioner. There is also an arrow in the left of the photo that shows the stepper motor that drives the Y axis. You can see the drive belt in more detail in Figure 10-22.

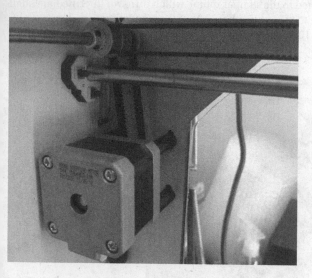

Figure 10-22. Y-axis drive belt (MakerBot Replicator Dual)

Notice that the stepper motor is mounted to the side of the printer. These four bolts are in slots, which allows you to tension the small drive belt. It also allows you to remove the stepper motor, freeing one side of the closed belt. Figure 10-23 shows the outside of the printer and the four bolts for the stepper motor.

Figure 10-23. Y-axis drive belt adjustment (MakerBot Replicator Dual)

The stepper motor mount was changed in the MakerBot Replicator 2/2X. Instead of mounting to the frame directly, the MakerBot Replicator 2/2X Y-axis stepper motor is mounted to a bracket, which is then mounted to the rear of the frame. Figure 10-24 shows the Y-axis stepper motor for a MakerBot Replicator 2/2X.

Figure 10-24. *Y-axis drive belt adjustment (MakerBot Replicator 2/2X)*

You can still adjust the tension, but instead of loosening four bolts, you loosen only two bolts in the rear of the printer.

If you're thinking this example is complex, you're right. It is one of the most complex belt-driven mechanisms you are likely to encounter. I've seen some printers with four belts, but the concept is the same—there are intermediate shafts that allow the stepper motor to be located in a remote place, or like the MakerBot, oriented below the axis.

To replace the Y-axis belts in the MakerBot Replicator 1 printers, you first loosen or remove the Y-axis stepper motor, and then pull the belts out of each side of the X-axis carriages. Simply pull the belt toward you. There are two clamps on each side. Next, remove the intermediate shafts by first loosening the grub screws for all of the pulleys on each shaft, and then removing the shaft covers and sliding the shafts out of the printer. Be sure to catch the pulleys, because they will fall out as you remove the shaft. The belts can then be removed. No, it is not a simple procedure and, yes, it involves a fair amount of work. Figure 10-25 shows the location of the front intermediate shaft. There is a corresponding shaft in the rear. When you remove the shafts, you will push them through these holes.

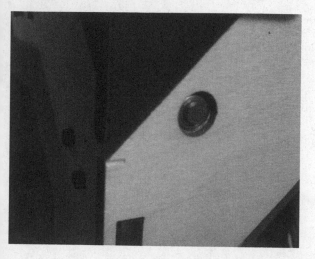

Figure 10-25. *Y-axis intermediate shaft (MakerBot Replicator 1)*

The process is slightly different for the MakerBot Replicator 2/2X. These printers use a single intermediate shaft located at the front of the printer. There are still idler pulleys in the rear, but they ride on a separate shaft that clips into place. Figure 10-26 shows the right-side idler pulley for the Y axis. There is a corresponding pulley on the left side.

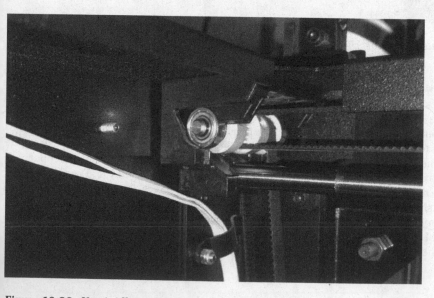

Figure 10-26. *Y-axis idler pulley (MakerBot Replicator 2/2X)*

To remove the idler pulley, you can use a nonmarring tool inserted in the small cavity behind the pulley to carefully pry it out. It should pop out with moderate force.

Similarly, the intermediate shaft in the front can be removed the same way. Figure 10-27 shows the intermediate shaft.

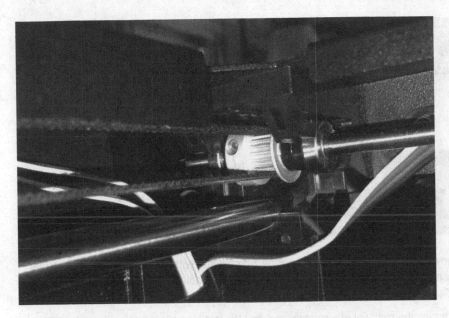

Figure 10-27. *Y-axis intermediate shaft (MakerBot Replicator 2/2X)*

Once the idlers and intermediate shaft are removed, you can replace the belts and reassemble in the reverse order.

Belt Tensioners

The last step in the process of replacing a belt is tensioning it properly. If your printer uses an automatic or adjustable belt tensioner, be sure to loosen the adjuster completely before setting the tension. For example, the Prusa i3 has a Y-axis belt tensioner that includes a bolt to pull the belt tight.

When you replace this belt, you should loosen the bolt completely, install the new belt with as much tension as your can, and then use the adjuster to set the proper tension. Recall the proper tension should be such that you cannot pull the belt away from the drive pulley, or about one-half inch of up/down movement in the center.

MAKERBOT REPLICATOR 2/2X CABLE FIX

The X-axis stepper motor and endstop wires on the MakerBot Replicator 2 and 2X are restrained in such a way that there is a flex point that can damage the wiring. Some people report this happening in as little as 100 hours, but most seem to indicate it will fail around 250 hours.

Fortunately, there is a really easy fix for this. In fact, there are several. The MakerBot web site (`http://makerbot.wikia.com/wiki/Replicator_2_Modifications`) describes the process of removing the retaining pin and using zip ties to secure the wiring so that the flex point is removed.

Another solution that I prefer is one by Home Zillions, which replaces the retaining pin with an aluminum plate. The following photo shows the plate installed in a MakerBot Replicator 2.

Once installed, the cable can move quite freely. The photo shows the X-axis motor with the new shield installed (courtesy of Home Zillions). These are sold primarily on eBay and aren't always available. Search eBay for "X-axis Step Motor Guard for MakerBot".

The installation is very easy, requiring the removal of a single screw and the retaining clip, and then inserting the plate and securing it with the supplied longer screw. If you have a MakerBot Replicator 2 or 2X, you should make this repair a top priority.

Bearings, Bushings, and Rods

Bearings and bushings are normally metal[13] and can withstand many hours of use. There are many forms of bearings and bushings. Most printers use several types. Bearings are typically designed for use on a shaft and have internal parts designed to rotate freely. Bushings are typically a solid part designed to slide over a rod or similar uniform rail. Figure 10-28 shows a number of bearings and bushings that you can find in your printer. There are also many types of plastic bearings and bushings with similar designs and applications.

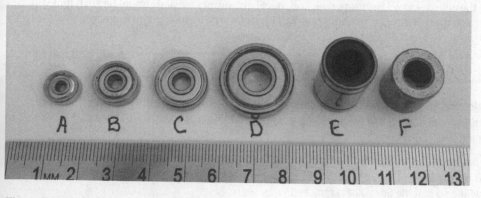

Figure 10-28. *Bearings and bushings*

---

[13] Some have had success in printing bearings, sometimes called a *bushing*, from PLA (thingiverse.com/thing:16813).

Each of these bearings has a standard size that equates to its number, including bore (inner diameter), outer diameter, and length (perpendicular to the shaft or bore). For round bearings, the width is the outer diameter; and for linear bearings and bushings, it is the length. Table 10-1 describes each of the bearings shown. Note that Item F is an oil-infused brass bushing.

Table 10-1. *Some Common Bearings Found in 3D Printers*

Item	Type	Bore	Outer Diameter	Length	Sealed?
A	623ZZ	3mm	10mm	4mm	Yes
B	624ZZ	4mm	13mm	5mm	Yes
C	625ZZ	5mm	16mm	5mm	Yes
D	608ZZ	7mm	22mm	17mm	Yes
E	LM8UU	8mm	15mm	24mm	Yes
F	Common Bushing	8mm	17mm	15mm	No

■ **Note**   Some manufacturers specify "width" as the outer diameter and "thickness" for length.

Replacing Bearings and Bushings

The bearings in your printer are typically of high quality and more than capable of handling the tasks. For example, the common round sealed bearing used in RepRap printers (e.g., 608zz) is also used in skateboards. Clearly, skateboards support a much heavier load than a 3D printer. Unless you encounter a defective bearing or the bearing is subjected to lack of lubrication, you should not need to replace bearings very often. However, if your printer starts making squeaks, grinding, or other metal-on-metal noises, you may have a bad bearing.

Replacing the bearings or bushings can take some time. You will have to take the printer axis apart to get to the bearing, which can include removing the outer panels or enclosure first. Depending on the frame configuration, you may need to remove the axis movement from the printer before you can disassemble it. But sometimes the task can be easier and may involve removing only a few parts.

Replacing Smooth Rods

The smooth rods in your printer should also be made from high-quality metals. Some inexpensive kits have been known to use smooth rods made using softer metals (like aluminum or mild steel) and thus are not suitable for long-term use. These smooth rods may eventually cause problems and degrade from use. However, it is more likely that the surface is not precise enough (it has a consistent diameter throughout its length). The best smooth rods are those made from high-quality materials such as stainless steel. So unless you have a less expensive set of smooth rods, you are not likely to encounter any need to replace them.

If you notice grooves, scratches, or other damage to the surface of the smooth rod, you will need to test it to see if the damage causes binding or variations in the diameter. One way to tell is to move the appropriate-sized bearing or bushing along its length, and if it binds or feels really loose (some play is OK, but you should not be able to wiggle it), you should consider replacing the smooth rod. If you encounter this problem, I recommend replacing all of the rods and their bearings and bushings with higher-quality items. If the bearings and smooth rods are worn significantly, you could be experiencing degraded print quality.

Replacing the smooth rods is the same process as replacing bearings on the affected axis. That is, you may need to partially disassemble the frame and remove the axis in order to replace the smooth rods. For example, if you want to replace the smooth rods for the Z axis in a Prusa i2 or i3, the mounts for the rods are easy to remove; but the X axis is part of the mechanism, so you must either remove it from the printer or suspend it somehow in order to replace the Z-axis rods. The best way to do this is to replace one side at a time.

■ **Note**   If you have to replace bearings or rods for any axis, be advised that you will need to realign the axis, which may include careful calibration and even tramming the print bed.

Replacing Filters

There are at least three reasons a 3D printer would have filters: 1) for fume extraction into the enclosure, 2) for incoming air to cool the electronics, and 3) (more correctly, a cleaner or wipe) to remove dust and debris from filament as it enters the extruder. I describe each of these in more detail. Be sure to check your documentation for the specific procedure to replace the filter.

Fume extraction filters are typically made with charcoal in the filter fabric, or the fibers are coated with a charcoal-based paste. These filters generally have a long lifetime[14] and you would not normally need to replace them. However, if you notice fumes becoming stronger or odors that you did not notice previously, you may want to try replacing the charcoal filter to see if things improve.

Filters for electronics are normally foam or woven fibers that are designed to block dust. They are placed on the intake side of the fan. You should replace the filter whenever there is a significant amount of dust on the filter. To clean the filter, remove it and use a vacuum to remove the dust. Some filters can also be washed. Check with your vendor to see if yours can be washed.

While not specifically a filter in the pure definition of *filter*, there is a device designed to wrap around the filament to remove dust and debris from filament. These cleaners (sometimes incorrectly called filters) can be made from a variety of materials. After filament has passed through the foam, it can be damaged by friction. However, it is more likely that if the filament is dusty, the foam can become dirty, and since there is relatively little surface area, it may require replacement often. Figure 10-29 shows an example of a filament cleaner that needs replacing. The foam in the cleaner was used for over 30 hours.

---

[14]One of my fume extractors, the one I use most often, came with a spare filter—but I've never had to replace it.

Figure 10-29. *Worn filament cleaner foam*

This filament cleaner is made from a kitchen sponge and placed inside a printed cylinder casing (`thingiverse.com/thing:16483`). The sponge is cut half way through longitudinally, and then wrapped around the filament and inserted into the casing. I like this version because it fits just about any printer.

Notice in Figure 10-29 that there is a bit of debris inside the foam. This is mostly trapped dust and small particles. Had I not used the cleaner, all of this would have been sent through my hot end. Any one of the small particles in the foam could have easily caused an extrusion failure. This is clear evidence that filament cleaners really do work.[15] If you don't have one, I suggest that you make it a top priority to add one as soon as you can print it.

If your printer has a filament cleaner, I recommend checking it at least every 10 hours of printing, and replacing it at least every time you change the filament, or 25 hours, whichever comes first.

Summary

Maintaining your 3D printer is thankfully a rather simple task. It doesn't require the changing of any fluids, gaskets, or other messy internal parts, like that of a diesel engine.[16] So long as you watch your printer for signs of wear in the areas mentioned in this and the previous chapter, you should be able to keep your printer running well for as long as you own it.

This chapter covered preventive and corrective tasks associated with 3D printers. Preventive tasks are those in which you do something to keep the part from wearing and eventually failing. Preventive tasks include keeping the printer clean, and the metal parts lubricated and adjusted correctly. Corrective tasks are repairs you need to do to fix the printer when it fails. Corrective tasks include replacing broken or worn parts.

I recommend reading this chapter and the previous chapter before you start using your printer for a long period of time. If you have used your printer for more than 25 hours, take some time to read through these chapters and implement the recommendations for observing, adjusting, and repairing.

The next chapter covers one of my favorite things to do with my 3D printers: upgrading them to improve usability and quality. I will present a number of useful upgrades, as well as some that I feel are must-have items. I group the upgrades by order of necessity, as well as by the type of printer.

---

[15]I've read some commentary that suggests filament cleaners are useless and don't do anything. As is evident here, they are definitely not useless.

[16]A mechanic friend refers to a certain brand of diesel engines as having been "designed by Satan himself," because the maintenance requirements are so frequent, difficult, and expensive.

CHAPTER 11

■ ■ ■

3D Printer Enhancements

There are many things you can do to enhance your printer. You can improve the print quality of your printer, improve usability and maintainability, or simply add new features. For example, you may want to improve vertical layer alignment (for smoother surfaces), add an LCD panel for computerless printing, or automated bed leveling (tramming) and Z-axis probing tasks.

Before you do any of these tasks, you should complete a comprehensive set of calibration tasks like those described in Chapter 4. I cannot stress that enough. You really should complete the calibration process before making any changes to your printer. This is because while some upgrades are designed to improve quality (or known to do so), most are not solutions to calibration problems and can make a small problem a larger one.

■ **Tip**   Be sure to complete calibration before embarking on upgrades that are designed to improve print quality. Failure to do so may end in frustration.

Now that the requisite admonishments are stated, upgrading a 3D printer can be a great deal of fun. Indeed, it is one of my favorite things to do with 3D printers. I am always looking for a better mount, carriage, or mechanism to improve my printers.

Some of the best platforms for upgrading are the many RepRap variants. Most kits come as bare, essential printers. There are typically no features other than those needed to print. That is, you are not likely to have even simple upgrade features such as fans, lights, or Z-height adjusters. While some kit vendors offer these features as upgrades, most do not include them in the kit.

Enhancements fall into three categories: features that add some minor function (farkles), enhancements to existing features that improve quality (enhancements), and upgrades that add completely new features that improve quality as well as usability, maintainability, and in some cases reliability (upgrades).

In this chapter, I discuss each of these categories, as well as some features generic to all printers, and give examples of upgrades for specific printers. If you own one of these printers or are planning to own one, this chapter will be your road map to taking your printer to new heights.

In some cases, the enhancement can be something that prolongs the usefulness of your printer. For example, I purchased a used MakerBot Replicator 1 Dual, and together with the upgrades, have a printer to rival the newer (and current) MakerBot Replicator 2X. Best of all, the total cost of the printer and the upgrades is less than 50% of the price of the new model. How cool is that? I am certain you can achieve similar goals with careful planning and a good bit of frugality.

Types of Enhancements

I like to break enhancements down into categories based on their function and goals, which indirectly relates to their importance or value for the enthusiasts (what you get out of having the enhancement).

The category of least value for print quality, usability, or maintainability includes enhancements for aesthetics and minor functions. I call this category "farkles," because they do add some value, but are mostly for show. The next category includes more useful additions because they are targeted or indirectly equate to improving quality. I call these "quality upgrades." Lastly, anything else that adds a new feature that has some significant improvement for usability, maintainability, or reliability I call simply "feature upgrades."

The following sections discuss each category in more detail and provide examples. Keep your own printer in mind. It may help you decide what you want to do next with your fully calibrated 3D printer!

Farkles

Recall that a farkle is a borrowed term from motorcycling that is a mash-up of "function" and "sparkle."[1] We call something a farkle if it has a specific function but is either not essential to the mission of the device on which it is installed, or it adds more glitz and glamor than function. For example, consider a motorcycle festooned with three GPS devices, a compass, multiple cup holders, and more LED lights than a semitractor truck from those trucker movies from the 1980s. Excess is one of the side effects of farkling. However, some farkles are helpful in some way even if they are not essential.

Beautification

One of the most common farkles is an enhancement to the printer frame and enclosure. Some enthusiasts, especially those who have printers with wooden frames, will stain or paint the frame to add some décor to their printer. This often adds only aesthetics and sometimes no functionally to the printer other than your own taste for adventure and personalization. However, it should be note that sealing a wooden frame can protect it from moisture.

In fact, I painted one of the frames (the threaded rods) of one of my Prusa Mendel i2 printers. I painted it black and used black plastic frame components. It looked pretty good, but I must admit it added no functionality whatsoever—unless you consider the effect on the naïve who see the all-black printer and think it is the newest model.

■ **Caution** If you decide to paint, stain, or otherwise apply decorative coatings to your wooden printer frame, take care to use a finish that will not warp, crack, or otherwise swell (or shrink) the wood. Any distortion in the wood can cause alignment problems that may not be corrected with recalibration. I once stained a small wooden box made from the same thin plywood that some printers use. Once it dried, the lid never closed properly again. Why? The wood warped a tiny bit and caused the lid to deform. You definitely do not want your wooden printer frame to warp.

Similarly, some printer vendors allow you to choose the color of your printer either as a factory option or by providing a set of snap- or bolt-on color panels. This also extends to upgrades. As you will see in a later section, you can replace the panels on the MakerBot Replicator 2/2X with colored panels changing the basic black to green, yellow, blue, red, and so forth.

---

[1] As much as I detest portmanteau words like "framily," I must admit defeat given I use the term "farkle."

LED Lighting

I added an LED light ring to some of my RepRap printers. I did so because they were being used in some low-light areas of my office and workshop. The LED light allowed me to better see the print and more easily see how well the first layer was adhering to the print surface. So while the LED light ring does provide a useful function, it is mostly for show because there is no need to leave it on while printing. The printer doesn't need to see where it's going! Figure 11-1 shows the LED light ring.

Figure 11-1. *LED light ring on a Prusa i2*

It may not be clear in Figure 11-1, but that small ring of LEDs puts out some mighty bright light. Figure 11-2 shows the LED ring on in nearly dark conditions.

Figure 11-2. *LED light ring on a Prusa i2. Illuminatus!*

GOT FARKLES?

So do you farkle your printer or not? That's entirely up to you. If you feel like your printer resembles a plain, sensible machine then you probably won't care about adorning your printer with aesthetics and farkles. However, if you desire something more than a lump of humorless components, you just might be in the farkling state of mind. I say, farkle at will!

   This is all well and good and indeed a lot of fun, but most people will want to work on improving the quality of their printer and print experience.

Quality Enhancements

Improvements designed to bolster quality is the category that gets the most attention and offers a seemingly endless array of possibilities. You may immediately associate this (and rightly so) as how well objects are printed. However, there is more to it. I also include in this category the quality of the printer and the quality of the print experience. In other words, not just how well the printer can print, but how effectively it operates and how well you enjoy using it, or even its ease use.

   Quality enhancements range from added bracing to help wobbly frames, devices designed to reduce or remove backlash, improved electronics, heating, and so forth. One trip through the Thingiverse search engine for your printer will tell you just how many quality-improvement things are available.

   Given its popularity, it should be no surprise that the RepRap variants have countless hits—so many that you have to search for a specific part of the printer to find them all. For example, it is futile to search for "Prusa i2" on Thingiverse. Rather, you should search for what you want to improve. For example, searching with "Prusa i2 filament guide" will list several options to explore for keeping the filament from flopping around and potentially snagging as the extruder pulls it.

Filament Management System

Filament management is one of the largest collections of interesting solutions for printers on Thingiverse. So what is filament management? Recall that one of the potential problems for using your 3D printer is keeping the filament flowing easily so that the extruder isn't working too hard to pull the filament from the spool, which can cause under extrusion or uneven extrusion if the tension waxes and wanes as the spool turns.[2] In extreme cases, it can cause the extruder to lift slightly introducing inconsistent layer heights.

   What is needed is a system where the spool can turn easily with a small amount of friction (just enough to prevent the spool from unraveling), and one or more guides to keep the filament from snagging on other parts of the printer. Figure 11-3 shows a filament management system that I adopted for all of my Prusa Mendel i2 and similar printers.

---

[2]Future 3D printer soap opera or literary gaffe?

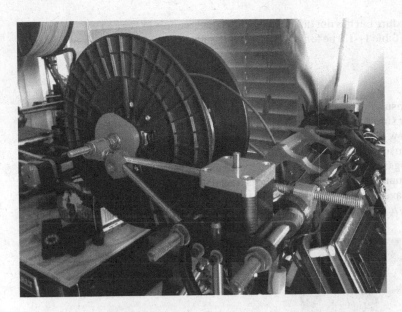

Figure 11-3. *Prusa i2 filament management system*

Notice the spool is mounted above the extruder and at the rear of the printer. The mount is comprised of five threaded rods, some extra Y-axis bar clamps, and a few extra bits to hold it all together. I also use a filament guide that keeps the filament aligned in the center as it is pulled from the spool. The spool is mounted using two cones that ride on 608zz bearings. Best of all, I made this filament management system from things I found on Thingiverse.

If you're thinking, "Hey, I can make one of those for my printer!" you've got the right idea and it is the right attitude to have to get the most out of your printer. I really enjoy downloading things and printing them—especially if it allows me to improve my printer. You can do the same. Just do a search for "<my printer> filament guide" and "<my printer> spool holder" where <my printer> is the brand or design of your printer (e.g., Prusa i3) and you'll get plenty of ideas. Chances are you will be able to put one together like I did without having to modify any of the parts!

The parts that I used for this upgrade are all existing designs I found on Thingiverse. There are several similar solutions on Thingiverse and, in fact, one of the parts I used is from a similar design. Table 11-1 lists all of the components should you wish to make your own.

Table 11-1. *Prusa i2 Filament Management System*

Component	Quantity	Source
Threaded rod about 300mm in length (5/16″, 8mm)	5	Hardware and home improvement stores or spares
Nuts to fit threaded rod (5/16″ or 8mm)	12–16	Hardware and home improvement stores or spares
Bolts for adjustable bar clamps (M3×25)	4	Hardware and home improvement stores or spares
Nuts for adjustable bar clamps (M3)	4	Hardware and home improvement stores or spares
608zz bearings	4	Any 3D printer supplier or online auction site
Spool holder cones	2	thingiverse.com/thing:21850
Twist-on Y-axis bar clamps	4	thingiverse.com/thing:35678
Any-angle bar clamp for brace	4 sets	thingiverse.com/thing:30328
Bar mount for spool holder	2	thingiverse.com/thing:67271
Wide filament guide	1	thingiverse.com/thing:62386

For brevity, I omit the installation procedure but it is not difficult. Just follow the example in Figure 11-3 and read the instructions for each printed object listed in Table 11-1. The longest part of the installation is printing the spool cones.

Insulated Heated Print Bed

Another common quality improvement is insulating the heated print bed. This could be a fix or a cure for some printers that have weaker power supplies or similar power issues where the heated print bed does not remain at a constant temperature. That is, it varies a few degrees as the bed cools (or is cooled by the environment). This fluctuation can cause some quality issues. Insulating the heated print bed can also help printers that take a long time to heat up. In this case, the heaters are losing the battle with the environment to instill enough heat in the bed.

Heated print bed insulation comes in many forms. Some enthusiasts have used materials such as corrugated paper (cardboard), fiberglass, and foam. I have found one of the best materials is from the automotive industry, called *exhaust header wrap* (or simply *exhaust fabric*). Figure 11-4 shows an example of this fabric.

Figure 11-4. Insulation fabric (exhaust header wrap)

Exhaust header insulation is used to wrap headers (the part of the engine where spent gasses are expelled through a collection chamber called the *header* or *manifold*). This material has foil on one side and heat resistant insulation on the other. Threads are interwoven at right angles to give the material extra strength. See thermotec.com/products/14001-aluminized-heat-barrier.html for an example of this form of insulation.

Notice that I cut the corner off. I did this for all four corners. This allows me to place the fabric under the heated print bed without interfering with the print bed adjusters. You may have to trim the corners in a similar manner to make it fit around the bed adjusters/mounts. Figure 11-5 shows the fabric cut to size for a Prusa i3.

Figure 11-5. *Insulation fabric for heated print bed (Prusa i3)*

If your print surface is removable, you can use it to cut the fabric to size by placing the print surface on the fabric and cutting around it. To install the insulation, remove your heated print bed and place the fabric foil-side down on the Y-axis plate. Then put the heated print bed element on top of the fabric and your print surface on top of the heated print bed. Figure 11-6 shows the same fabric mounted on a Prusa Mendel i2.

Figure 11-6. *Insulated heated print bed (Prusa Mendel i2)*

There are many more such improvements that can help print quality or raise the general quality of your printer and thus your experience. Once you achieve the desired quality, you may want to start considering adding new features to your printer in the form of upgrades.

Feature Upgrades

The last category of improvements includes those that provide a new feature or capability for your printer. Unlike farkles, which add a feature that is not essential (but still usable), features are things that add value to your printer either in quality or through expanding its capability.

For example, adding a camera to the printer would enable you to watch the print from a remote location, or perhaps record the print process as a movie, or even make it available online in real time. Clearly, this is a new capability that can add value in the form of entertainment as well as practicality by allowing you to leave your printer in another room and watch it from, say, the living room.

As we saw in a previous chapter, the list of features for 3D printers is long, and most printers don't have them all. However, you can add some of these features to your printer to improve it. For example, if your printer did not come with an LCD panel, adding one will enable you to use the printer without a computer. Similarly, if your printer does not have a fine adjuster for the Z-height, you can add one to help make the setup process easier. I describe each of these features in more detail in the following sections.

LCD Panels

The first printers I built and used did not have any form of display. Sure, there were a few LEDs on the electronics and I added a small buzzer for custom signals to one, but that was about it. That is, unless I wanted to add my own feedback mechanisms. I found several ideas using seven-segment displays (think old alarm clock) to show axes positions and voltages, but these would have been a lot of work.

But feedback isn't really that helpful, given you must have a computer connected to print it, and most printer controller software has the ability to display the current axes positions, temperatures, and more. Even when I added an SD card reader, I still had to use a printer controller application to initiate a print from a file on the SD card.

A display panel will provide much more than simply displaying information about the printer's status. In fact, most add-on display panels are liquid crystal displays, which we simply call LCD panels. These panels are enabled by the firmware to display feedback, as well as provide a host of printer-side controls from homing axes to setting the hot-end temperature, turning on a fan, and even printing from files on an SD card. Figure 11-7 shows an example of an LCD panel for a Prusa Mendel i2.

Figure 11-7. LCD panel (Prusa Mendel i2)

The panel shown in Figure 11-7 is a typical text display capable of displaying 4 lines of 20 characters (called a 4×20 display). Notice that there are some special symbols that may appear as graphics, but they are simply special characters programmed in the firmware. The vast majority of LCD panels are text panels.

There are also graphic LCD panels that allow more freedom for implementing more interesting displays.[3] There are fewer choices for graphic LCD panels, and most are more expensive. Check your firmware or your vendor before adding a graphic LCD panel. Figure 11-8 shows a graphic LCD panel on a Prusa i3.

Figure 11-8. *Graphic LCD panel (Prusa i3)*

As you can see, the display can support up to three extruders, a heated print bed, and a fan. Also displayed are the axes positions and the state of the SD card (% full).

If your printer does not have an LCD panel, check with your vendor to see if they offer an add-on kit. For example, Printrbot has an LCD add-on kit for its line of printers (http://printrbot.com/shop/printrbot-lcd-panel-in-stand/). The kit comes with the panel, a cable, and a stand. Figure 11-9 shows the Printrbot LCD panel.

Figure 11-9. *Printrbot LCD panel kit (courtesy of Printrbot.com)*

If you have a RepRap printer, you may be able to use one of several LCD panels—either text or graphic. Look for one that is designed to work with your electronics. For example, if you have a RAMPS setup, choose one that has an adapter made for the RAMPS shield. In order to activate the LCD panel, you will have to modify the firmware by enabling the corresponding `#define` in the `Configuration.h` file. Listing 11-1 shows an excerpt of the Marlin firmware, listing the types of panels supported. Just uncomment the one that matches your panel, compile, and upload the firmware.

---

[3]The eye of the beholder applies here. I've found some don't like the graphic displays. I like them because they're easier to read.

Listing 11-1. LCD Panel Support in Marlin

```
...
//LCD and SD support
//#define ULTRA_LCD
//#define DOGLCD
//#define SDSUPPORT
//#define SDSLOW
//#define ENCODER_PULSES_PER_STEP 1
//#define ENCODER_STEPS_PER_MENU_ITEM 5
//#define ULTIMAKERCONTROLLER
//#define ULTIPANEL
//#define LCD_FEEDBACK_FREQUENCY_HZ 1000
//#define LCD_FEEDBACK_FREQUENCY_DURATION_MS 100

// The MaKr3d Makr-Panel with graphic controller and SD support
// http://reprap.org/wiki/MaKr3d_MaKrPanel
//#define MAKRPANEL

// The RepRapDiscount Smart Controller (white PCB)
// http://reprap.org/wiki/RepRapDiscount_Smart_Controller
//#define REPRAP_DISCOUNT_SMART_CONTROLLER

// The GADGETS3D G3D LCD/SD Controller (blue PCB)
// http://reprap.org/wiki/RAMPS_1.3/1.4_GADGETS3D_Shield_with_Panel
//#define G3D_PANEL

// The RepRapDiscount FULL GRAPHIC Smart Controller (quadratic white PCB)
// http://reprap.org/wiki/RepRapDiscount_Full_Graphic_Smart_Controller
//
// ==> REMEMBER TO INSTALL U8glib to your ARDUINO library folder:
http://code.google.com/p/u8glib/wiki/u8glib
//#define REPRAP_DISCOUNT_FULL_GRAPHIC_SMART_CONTROLLER
...
```

■ **Tip** If you made any changes to your firmware settings and saved them to memory with the M500 command, use the M503 command via your printer controller software, and write down all of the parameters. You may need to reset these once the firmware is updated.

More recent printers are being shipped with LCD panels as a standard feature. For example, all except one of the newest MakerBot printers have LCD panels. The newest MakerBot Replicator Desktop has a graphic LCD panel.

Z-Height Adjuster

If your printer came with fixed endstops like most RepRap printers, and you did not add any adjusters to the print bed, then you have likely encountered some frustration in printing. Unless your printer is calibrated well and is not affected by changes in your environment, there is little chance you've been spared the frustration.

What I am referring to is the problem of setting the Z-height or the initial layer height of the nozzle above the print surface. Recall that this distance is critical for good adhesion to the print surface and indeed forms the foundation for good quality prints. Figure 11-10 shows one example that I've found works very well (see thingiverse.com/thing:16380).

Figure 11-10. Z-height adjuster (Prusa Mendel i2)

The endstop is indicated with a square box. Notice that it is mounted on an arm that has a knob and is under tension. The knob turns a bolt that is threaded through a nylock nut. This gives the ability to adjust the endstop up or down in very small increments.

Those who have faced this problem typically have to move fixed endstops by loosening one or more clamps, sliding the endstop one way or the other, and then testing the height of the nozzle. But there is a better way. You can install a Z-height adjuster that mounts the Z-axis endstop on a fine adjuster mechanism.

Does this sound like bed leveling? That's because this process is one of the steps, but in the case of bed leveling, we are tramming the print bed with the X and Y axes. The Z-height is part of the equation, but what if your print bed is already leveled (trammed)? How do you set the Z-height—do you adjust each of the bed adjusters? That's too much work. Wouldn't it be better to adjust only the Z-axis endstop?

Perhaps a better question might be why you might need to set the Z-height. It's quite simple and yet rather unintuitive. Depending on the material you are printing with and the condition and type of print surface, you may need a lower Z-height to help with adhesion. I would recommend using the highest setting possible that still permits good adhesion, but sometimes you just need to squish that filament to make it stick (and avoid lifting).

Another and perhaps obscure use for the Z-height adjuster is for printers that have an uneven print surface. If the print surface is too uneven, you will never get a good print; but if it is slightly concave or convex (which is not uncommon for hardware store–quality glass), leveling the bed at the corners leaves the area in the center too low or too high for good prints. Having the Z-height adjuster allows me to position the nozzle in the center of where I want to print and set the Z-height for that area. Of course, the real fix is to throw the bad glass away and get a flat piece. However, if you don't have that option because the surface isn't glass or is very expensive, the Z-height adjuster can help.

If you search Thingiverse, you will find many examples of Z-height adjusters. Just search for "z-height <printer_name>" and you should find plenty of alternatives. Indeed, you should find a number of different mechanisms. Look for the one that is mounted in a position that is favorable to your printer design. For example, there are a lot of examples of Z-height adjusters for RepRap printers, but some are specific to certain variants and some may conflict with other upgrades you might have installed. However, given that the parts are generally small and don't take long to print, you can download and print several, and then choose the one you like best.

■ **Tip**   Look for an adjuster that has a captured fine adjuster (bolt and nut) that is either under tension or uses a nylock nut so that it cannot come loose under normal printing. One of the first designs I used kept loosening after three or four prints, which defeated the advantages by adding more maintenance.

Upgrading Your Printer: Getting Started

I hope that you are excited about the many possibilities and ideas for upgrading your printer. I know I've really enjoyed working on my printers and making them (in some cases far) better. However, you should probably hold off downloading and printing a bunch of parts, or ordering any expensive machined parts, until you figure out what you want to achieve and how to get there. In other words, you need a plan.[4]

Failure to do this could lead to less-than-expected results, wasted time and money, and a great deal more frustration than you ever wanted. For example, resist the temptation to buy the latest and greatest hot end on the market until someone has reviewed it or at least used it for some time. If you fall into this temptation, you could end up with a very nice looking knickknack shaped like a hot end. Yep, I've got one. I suppose several of us do.

Do Your Research: Finding Upgrades

In the previous sections, I mentioned searching Thingiverse for ideas and objects that you can use to effect upgrades and enhancements to your printer. Depending on how long your printer design has been used, you should be able to find solutions that other enthusiasts have created. I recommend starting with those before attempting to develop your own. It will save you a lot of time (and frustration) and could give you ideas for improvements to the design that you can create and also publish for others to use.

The best way to search for upgrades and enhancements is to use search terms that include the name of your printer design (e.g., Prusa i3, Printrbot Simple, MakerBot Replicator, etc.). I would start here as the first search. Chances are you will get a lot of results. If you are not sure what sort of upgrade you're looking for, this may be the best way to find what is available.

On the other hand, if you know what upgrade you are looking for, add it to the search term with the name of your printer design. It is better to use short search terms than long descriptions. That is, to widen your search results, omit as many words as you can. For example, if you are looking for adjustable feet for your Prusa i3, search "Prusa i3 feet".

If you do not find what you are looking for, you can try different search terms. For example, use "Prusa i3 adjuster" if you don't find any hits from using "Prusa i3 feet". I find myself doing several searches and examining the results of each. Sometimes things are named oddly and may not appear in some searches.

Once you find the thing you want to use, check the object page and read all of the information. Pay particular attention to the instructions and any installation tips or requirements for hardware. I typically avoid using things that have little or no information—especially if they are complex, multipart things. For example, I once found a nifty dual extruder for a Prusa i3, but it was made from at least a dozen parts, there were no instructions, and no parts list. Don't make your experience worse by trying to figure out someone else's half-baked idea.

In a previous section I described a filament management system that I mashed together from several spare parts and a small handful of objects that I downloaded from Thingiverse. Before you use any object you find online, be sure to check the license associated with the object to make sure that you are permitted to use it. Fortunately, most things on Thingiverse have few restrictions.

---

[4]Sadly, some of my upgrades have been spontaneous endeavors. With few exceptions, most of these were disappointing. At the very least, set your expectations based on a little research.

CHECK THE LICENSE

Before you use the object, make sure that the use to which you want the object is permitted by the license. Under most licenses, you are typically free to download and print the object, and you can even make minor changes to it, but you are not allowed to claim the derivative as your own. See http://creativecommons.org/licenses/by-sa/3.0/ for an example of a popular license for objects on Thingiverse.

More importantly, never download an object with the intent to monetarily profit on the design. The object creator generally owns the design, and in most cases, the design is free for you to use, but has severe restrictions on what you can do with the result. That is, most designs prohibit selling the printed objects. It is best to check the fine print before downloading an object.

Set Your Goals and Expectations

Once you find an upgrade (or several) that you want to perform on your printer, you need to set your goals and expectations. You should have a clear idea for what you want to upgrade and why. Unless the upgrade is a farkle, you should understand how the upgrade should affect your printer. With this knowledge, you should also be able to set your expectations accordingly.

This applies most appropriately to upgrades found online. Prepackaged upgrade kits from vendors are typically well-sorted out and should work as expected, but things created by the community may or may not be so reliable (but many are). What you do not want to do is find some gee-whiz upgrade, download and print it, and then install it—only to discover it doesn't work or makes your printer worse, or even makes it unusable.

Thus, you should research the upgrade carefully. Pay particular attention to other people who have commented on the upgrade. One indication of the quality or applicability of the upgrade is the number of times it has been downloaded and printed.

Once you have this information, compile it so that you understand what the upgrade will do for you. If the upgrade is designed to improve quality, try to determine how much it will improve quality. I recommend tempering your expectations and avoid the trap of thinking an upgrade will solve all of your problems. Simply put, very few upgrades will fall into this category.

Check Your Calibration

Once you perform an upgrade, always check your printer for proper calibration. Most times this is simply making sure things are still aligned like they are supposed to be. For example, if you have to partially disassemble the frame to install some upgrade, make sure the frame is square and true during reassembly.

Similarly, print at least one test print of an easy object and another of a more difficult object before declaring victory. During the upgrade, sometimes minor and not clearly visible changes can be incurred that affect print quality. These may not have anything to do with the upgrade itself even, but may inadvertently change something enough to cause a problem.

For example, when I installed a Z-height adjuster on my first Prusa i3, I inadvertently repositioned the endstop holder for the Z axis. The first time I homed the printer, the Z axis didn't stop because the plunger I used for the endstop missed the endstop arm by less than a millimeter—but enough to cause the print head to run into the print bed. No, I was not happy. Fortunately, the mistake was minor and I powered the printer off quickly enough to avoid damage to my print surface and axes components.

■ **Tip**   If you change any axis mechanism, endstop, or frame component, keep your hand on the power button the first time you home the printer. At the first sign of trouble—noises, axis not stopping, and so forth, power it off and check your adjustments. You can also trigger the endstops manually to make sure they are in working order.

One Upgrade at a Time

You should resist the temptation to perform multiple upgrades at the same time. This is one way you can make your life much more difficult than it already is. More specifically, if you attempt to upgrade multiple parts of your printer and something goes wrong—or worse, needs recalibration—how do you know which upgrade introduced the problem or even what calibrations need revisiting?

Thus, you should always stick to one upgrade at a time, perfect the installation and calibration, and use the printer for several prints of various difficulty and length before moving on to the next upgrade.

Generic Upgrades: Your First Upgrade

So you've decided to upgrade your printer. That's great! Now, where do you start? I recommend starting small with some simple upgrades that will give you a degree of fun and satisfaction without risking your printer's quality. As such, I will describe some upgrades that apply to almost all printer designs. The following list includes the goals of some generic upgrades that are good choices for a first upgrade. I discuss each in more detail next.

- *Lighting*: Making it easier to see your prints

- *Fans*: Cooling for PLA printing, cooling electronics

- *Adjustable feet:* Stability for uneven (or tilted) work surfaces

Lighting

I described an LED light ring that I added to my Prusa Mendel i2 printers. This ring illuminated the area below and around the nozzle, which makes it easier to see the print and helps determine if there are problems with adhesion.

If you want to use my LED light ring solution, all you need is a 12V 60mm LED light ring (the same used in automotive lights) and a mount for the ring. There are several options available on Thingiverse. My solution is a special standoff for the X-carriage (`thingiverse.com/thing:219419`). You can download the `.scad` file and change it to match your own X-carriage.

You could do something similar and simpler by mounting LEDs to the frame and wiring them to the power supply or via a switch. I recommend searching Thingiverse for LED mounts and switch mounts for your printer. Like most upgrades, you will find a lot of examples.

There are other forms of lighting you may want to consider. For instance, MakerBot printers use LED area lighting to illuminate the build area. Although the LEDs are not bright enough to illuminate the build area (unless it is really dark), it does provide function beyond the mood lighting—a visual cue in the form of changing the LED color to red when the extruder is heating. You could do something similar, but it would require modifying the firmware. Thus, this may be a job for more experienced enthusiasts.

The best part of adding lighting to your printer is it won't affect your printer's capability. You can add the lighting, try it out, change it, and repeat as many times as you want with little risk.

Adjustable Feet

If your workstation or the desk surface where you place your printer is uneven, you may want to consider adding a set of adjustable feet. You've seen these before on furniture and appliances. They are composed of a threaded rod and nut that rides on a wide disc that makes contact with the surface (floor). If you turn the adjuster, you can raise or lower it, and therefore balance the device. You can also use the adjusters to make the device level (not the same as bed leveling and not required for such). Figure 11-11 shows a set of adjustable feet that I made for my MakerBot Replicator 2. You can find these on Thingiverse (thingiverse.com/thing:232984).

Figure 11-11. *Adjustable feet (MakerBot Replicator 2/2X)*

These are great additions because they print quickly, can be modified to fit almost any bolt and nut you have in your spares list (I used some leftover feet from an Ikea purchase), and they don't impede your printer's capabilities. Simply print out four of the mounts, remove the stock feet, thread in your adjusters, and install them. You can finally remove that folded piece of paper from under the one corner to keep the bot from rocking.

Fans

Recall that fans are used to cool components (electronics, stepper motors, etc.) and to cool filament as it exits the extruder, and even to cool the part during printing to keep the temperature even and avoid lifting and cracking. Most printers, especially printer kits, do not come with fans to cool the electronics. However, most that are advertised to print with PLA come with print cooling fans. If your printer has neither of these, you can add them.

Fortunately, there are many options available on Thingiverse for fan mounts, including mounts for electronics and extruders. Figure 11-12 shows a fan mounted on a Prusa Mendel i2. This is composed of a 40mm fan purchased online, a mount for the X-carriage I modified, and a cone to direct the air (thingiverse.com/thing:26650).

Figure 11-12. *Print cooling fan mount (Prusa Mendel i2)*

Installation of the print cooling fan will depend on the mount and cone you use. Notice that in Figure 11-12 the cone fits just under my LED light ring. Had I used a different cone, it would not have fit. Be sure to test fit your parts as you assemble. Fortunately, the mounts and cones print rather quickly, so you can print another if you need to. To connect the fan, you should wire it into your electronics setup. You could wire it directly to the appropriate PSU lead (12v), but you would have to turn it on and off manually (via a switch). However, there is a better way.

Most electronics boards have a connector for a print cooling fan. In fact, the RAMPS shield has terminals that allow you to wire the fan. This is really important because unlike a fan that runs at full speed, the firmware can set the fan speed automatically based on the codes in the print file. More specifically, you can turn on automatic cooling in your slicer that will control how fast the fan spins, depending on the progress of the print. This allows the slicer to use the fan to optimize the print automatically.

So if you are printing with PLA and don't have a fan, do yourself a great favor and download a mount for your printer, and a cone to direct the air. Buy a fan, and then mount it and wire it into your RAMPS board. You won't regret this upgrade and it demonstrates how some upgrades add features that go beyond minor improvements in quality. In this case, the fan can make your potentially miserable PLA printing experience much better.

Which One Should I Choose?

The first two generic upgrades are functional in the sense that they improve the printer but are really farkles. If your printer was sitting on an uneven surface, the adjustable feet may be less of a farkle, but essentially they add a feature that doesn't immediately improve printing. The last generic upgrade, on the other hand, isn't a farkle because it adds to the printer's reliability in the very least, and functionality in the case of a fan for printing with PLA.

If you are looking for an easy project to start with, go with the adjustable feet. Even if your printer is an older Prusa Mendel i2, you will find several solutions and the task will be rewarding. If you want a bit more of a challenge and don't mind working with the wiring of your printer, go with the lighting option. If you would rather upgrade the functionality of your printer—especially if you are trying to print PLA without a fan, print yourself a fan mount and wire up the fan.

Whichever upgrade you decide to start with (or maybe all of them), make sure you follow the preceding advice for planning, implementing, and testing the upgrade. If you are ready to move on to adding other upgrades and features, the next sections will provide you some ideas for upgrades for a series of popular 3D printer models. I haven't listed all possible models or vendors here, but seeing these should give you ideas on how to apply similar upgrades to your printer.

Printer-Specific Upgrades

This section includes examples of common 3D printers that have been heavily modified. Most of the hardware for the upgrades is available worldwide, and some include parts that you can print yourself. I recommend reading through each of these sections because some of the upgrades are repeated. Seeing them applied to different printers will give you an idea of how to upgrade your own printer should you not own one of these. The following printers are included in this section. I offer a short description of the end result of the upgrades.

- *Printrbot Simple*: Improvements to X and Y axes, Z-probing, and LCD panel make this entry-level printer a mid-range printer
- *Prusa Mendel i2*: Numerous upgrades from farkles to feature upgrades take the i2 to its max
- *Prusa i3*: Several key improvements, including Z-probing, improve on the latest Prusa design
- *MakerBot Replicator 1 Dual*: Making an old design new again
- *MakerBot Replicator 2/2X*: Ultimate upgrade path for MakerBot enthusiasts

Printrbot Simple

The Printrbot Simple is an excellent first printer. Whether you buy the kit or a preassembled printer, the Printrbot Simple is all you need to get into the 3D printing world. Given its price point, you won't find advanced features, such as an LCD panel or a heated print bed; these would add significantly to the price. Printrbot has also simplified many of the components in an effort to further minimize cost. So much so that some of the parts from older Simples can be a bit finicky to set up and keep working well. For example, one of the limitations and a source of criticism for older models is the string-drive for the X and Y axes.

■ **Note**   This section refers to the older wooden-frame models.

However, you can improve these features and even add some of the features found on more expensive printers. The following is a list of the upgrades that I have made to my own Printrbot Simple. I include the source for each upgrade. See if you can spot the upgrades in Figure 11-13. I encourage you to explore the links for each of these to see if the upgrade is something you want to perform on your printer. I discuss those upgrades I feel are a must-have for this printer design in more detail in the following sections.

- *LCD panel*: `http://printrbot.com/shop/printrbot-lcd-panel-in-stand/`
- *Onboard LCD mount*:[5] `thingiverse.com/thing:193955`
- *Metal Extruder and print bed*: `http://printrbot.com/shop/printrbot-alu-extruder/`
- *X-axis belt drive*: `thingiverse.com/thing:194686`
- *Y-axis belt drive*: `thingiverse.com/thing:194586`
- *Z-probe (auto leveling)*: `http://printrbot.com/shop/auto-leveling-probe-2/`
- *Z-probe mount*: `thingiverse.com/thing:323442`
- *Tower kit with spool holder*: `http://printrbot.com/shop/printrbot-simple-xl-upgrade-kit/`
- *Power supply upgrade*: `thingiverse.com/thing:383877`

---

[5]The photos for this thing show a very nice enhancement to the wood frame.

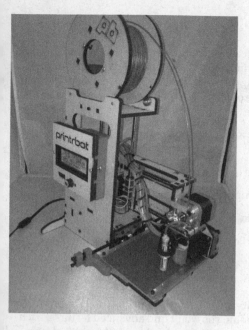

Figure 11-13. *Upgraded Printrbot Simple*

If you implement all of these upgrades, you will turn your entry-level printer into a mid-level printer. It still may not compete with the more sophisticated (and expensive) models, but it will hold its own feature-wise. Thus, if you find you want a bit more from your Printrbot Simple, check out these upgrades. Figure 11-13 shows my heavily upgraded Printrbot Simple.

Belt Drive Upgrades

Aside from the LCD panel, the string and sanding wheel drive for the X and Y axes are the next parts you should upgrade. The main reason for the upgrade is the string can sometimes be finicky to keep tensioned. If you tighten it too much, it can stretch. Too loose, and you have axis movement issues that can affect quality. Perhaps most of all, I found I needed to tighten the string about every three or four prints (even with small prints).

How you upgrade the X and Y axis will depend on what model Printrbot Simple you have. Printrbot has made numerous changes to the Simple over a relatively short period. Currently, the wooden frame Simples are becoming legacy (think last year's model). If you have a Simple made before about February 2014, you can download and print axes upgrade parts from Thingiverse (see thingiverse.com/thing:194686 for the X axis and thingiverse.com/thing:194586 for the Y axis). These are the upgrades shown in Figure 11-13. If you have a newer Printrbot Simple, you can use a special upgrade kit from Printrbot (http://printrbot.com/shop/makers-upgrade-kit/).

Whichever belt drive upgrade you choose, you should consider doing this upgrade only after you have calibrated the printer and have established a stable print quality. I discuss installation specifics in the following sections.

Older Simple Printers

The upgrades available on Thingiverse can be applied to a number of older Simple designs. While the installation is a little tedious, requiring partial disassembly, most enthusiasts should be able to perform the upgrade. If you are new to building 3D printers, you may want to study the documents on Thingiverse before installing, so that you know what you are getting into. I will describe the process here, but the finer details are found in the supplied documents.

The only parts you need to buy for these upgrades are a pair of GT2 16-tooth drive pulleys (they have teeth like a gear) and a length of GT2 belt. I recommend finding a GT2 belt and pulley kit from a RepRap supplier. The cost should be reasonable and you will get everything you need. You will also need (four) 608zz bearings. Again, you can find these at popular RepRap suppliers. The only other things you might need include a few zip ties and a few M3 bolts. Check Thingiverse for specifics on what bolts you need.

You can print most of the parts in these upgrades. For the X axis, you will print five parts; and for the Y axis, you will print 6 parts. Printing the parts for the upgrade will take a couple of hours if you use your Printrbot Simple, but it will be well worth the effort.

Once all of the parts are printed, it's time to install them. Installation for the Y axis is pretty straightforward. You simply remove the existing string and sanding wheel, cut the zip ties holding the Y axis, remove the bolts for the Y-axis motor, and install the new pulley drive. Check the supplied drawings for the proper orientation. Next, you install the pulley and then reassemble the Y axis. Finally, install the bearings, thread the belt, and secure it on each end as directed. The connection on the rear will double as a tensioner. The only issue you may have is the need to trim the opening for the pulley, but I did not have to do that for my Simple (manufactured in January 2014).

Installation of the X axis is a bit more problematic because you have to disassemble about 50% of the printer frame to get the new parts in place. That is, the X-axis motor mount must be replaced. This will require removing all of the panels on the base of the printer. If you are careful and don't tilt the printer too much, you should not lose any nuts from the nut traps. If some fall out, be patient and use blue painter's tape to keep them in place while you thread the bolts.

The last step requires recalibrating the X and Y axes steps per millimeter. Fortunately, you can effect this change without reflashing the firmware. First, use the M503 command to read the existing configuration. Look for the M92 entry in the list and note the values. You need only change the ones for the X and Y axes. Next, issue the M92 command with the new parameters, and then use M500 to write the changes to memory. You can then use the M501 command to see the changes. Listing 11-2 shows a transcript of the commands. I omit some of the output for brevity.

Listing 11-2. Setting the Steps per Millimeter

```
< 8:34:42 PM: echo:Steps per unit:
< 8:34:42 PM: echo:  M92 X84.40 Y84.40 Z2020.00 E96.00
...
< 8:36:47 PM: echo:Settings Stored
< 8:36:49 PM: echo:Stored settings retrieved
< 8:36:49 PM: echo:Steps per unit:
< 8:36:49 PM: echo:  M92 X80.00 Y80.00 Z2020.00 E96.00
...
```

Notice that the original values for the X and Y axes are 84.40 and 84.40. If you use the 16-tooth GT2 pulleys, you need to change this to 80.00 for each, as I have done in Listing 11-2. Recall that we can calculate this using the Prusa online calculator (http://calculator.josefprusa.cz/). Use the calculator to calculate the correct value if you use a different pulley.

Overall, this upgrade is a nontrivial installation. However, you should be able to complete the installation for each axis in about an hour or two if you take your time.

Newer Simple Printers

If you have a newer Printrbot Simple, you can buy Printrbot's belt-driven upgrade. The Maker's Upgrade Kit comes with almost a completely new frame. This is a special design that accommodates the changes to the X and Y axis. Aside from the pulleys, bearings, and belts, the kit also includes a larger stepper motor for the Y axis.

Since most of the frame components are new, installation requires a nearly complete teardown of the frame. Thus, the installation could take an afternoon or more to complete. There is so much work that I would recommend that those who haven't built their Simple printer to carefully consider the installation instructions before attempting the upgrade.

■ **Tip**   There is no installation instruction for the upgrade kit; rather, you can use the instructions for the Makers' Edition Simple (http://help.printrbot.com/Guide/Simple+1405+Assembly/123).

Like the previous upgrade option, you must reset the steps per millimeter for the axes. You can use the same commands as shown in Listing 11-2.

LCD Panel and Onboard Mount

It's hard to deny the convenience of having the ability to use your 3D printer without a computer. The lack of an LCD panel is one thing that might keep enthusiasts new to 3D printers from buying the Printrbot Simple. Fortunately, that is very easy to remedy.

Printrbot offers an LCD upgrade for a reasonable price (http://printrbot.com/shop/printrbot-lcd-panel-in-stand/). The kit comes unassembled, but assembly is not difficult and shouldn't take more than a few minutes. It includes an LCD panel and remote stand (but no SD card reader like those for RepRap printers).

Once the stand is assembled, all you need to do is power-off your printer and plug in the included ribbon cable. When you next power-on the printer, you will be rewarded with a nifty display that you can use to access various menus to manipulate the printer. Another nifty feature is the stand, which can be moved around because it is tethered to the printer via the ribbon cable and not mounted to the frame.

However, if you do not like that (I didn't), and you have the tower upgrade, you can print a different stand that clips to the handle portion of the tower upgrade. The new stand requires printing three parts that reuse the existing hardware from the LCD kit (see thingiverse.com/thing:193955 for details on how to print and assemble the stand). You can see the stand in action in Figure 11-13.

Z-Probe and Mount (Auto Bed Leveling)

One of the hottest upgrades for 3D printers is called *auto bed leveling*.[6] Printrbot offers an upgrade to add this feature to its printers. It is a special probe that uses an induction sensor mounted to the Z axis. The sensor requires you have the metal print bed upgrade. Thus, in order to implement this upgrade, you must first upgrade the print bed.

■ **Tip**   You will need the metal bed upgrade to use the Z-probe.

Installation of the Z-probe requires mounting the Z-probe to the extruder mount using one of several options. Look on Thingiverse for a mount specific to your Simple printer. Mine is an early 2014 model and the mount (thingiverse.com/thing:323442) works well. It mounts the Z-probe to the left of the extruder. Installation was very easy and required only removing the bolts for the extruder to install the mount. Figure 11-13 shows the Z-probe installed on my Printrbot Simple.

Be sure to download and follow the instructions on the product web site. Read all instructions before starting. Printrbot has created a fantastic video that shows the calibration steps (http://youtu.be/1gVmNuwMH68). I recommend watching this video in addition to reading the following procedure.

---

[6]As mentioned in previous chapters, this should be called *auto bed tramming* since there is no leveling—as in making things perpendicular to gravitational force. Also, the process creates a software compensation rather than physically changing the print bed adjustment.

To wire the probe, route the wires to replace the existing Z-axis endstop. To calibrate the Z-probe, power-on the printer and lower the Z axis until the tip of the nozzle just touches the print surface. Then adjust the Z-probe until it is triggered. You can tell it is triggered when the LED on top of the probe illuminates.

The next step requires loading the latest firmware from Printrbot. But first, check the location of your Y-axis endstop. If it is mounted on the front of the chassis, the latest firmware can be downloaded and installed on your Simple without modification. Check the Z-probe product web site for links to the latest firmware. If you are using a Mac, you can download an automatic firmware updater application from printrbottalk.com/wiki/index.php?title=User:PxT.

If your Simple has the Y-axis endstop at the rear of the chassis, things get a little more problematic. You must download the latest Printrbot fork of the Marlin firmware, modify the configuration source file, and compile it. You will need the Arduino IDE and a special library to allow you to compile the firmware for the Printrboard.

If you have a Mac, you can use the prebundled Arduino IDE at printrbottalk.com/wiki/index.php?title=User:PxT. The instructions for modifying the Arduino IDE for other platforms can be found at http://reprap.org/wiki/Printrboard (see the bootloader section).

Additional instructions for downloading, compiling, and loading the firmware can be found at http://printrbot.com/wp-content/uploads/2012/04/Printrbot-Firmware.pdf. I recommend downloading and reading this document in addition to the overview here.

If your Y axis endstop is mounted at the rear of the chassis, the firmware must be changed. This is because the latest firmware is set up to home the Y axis at the maximum position (the endstop is at the maximum position on the Y axis). Older Simples home to the minimum position for the Y axis.

Before you install the new firmware, issue the M503 command via a printer controller application and copy and paste the information shown. You want to capture the values for the M92 command. You will need to set these values and save them to memory after the firmware is loaded.[7]

For some, this may sound like a lot of work and maybe a bit more than they want to go through for this particular upgrade. However, the modifications are not onerous. You need to change only one line in the Configuration.h file. Look for the following line and change it as shown here. You can find the Marlin firmware at https://github.com/PxT/Marlin/tree/leading edge. Click the Download Zip button to download the firmware source code.

```
#define Y_HOME_DIR -1
```

■ **Tip**   Chapter 4 contains a tutorial on Marlin and the Arduino IDE.

Once the code has been changed and compiled, you can then upload the firmware to the printer. Follow the instructions in the preceding links for your specific platform. Essentially, you will need to place a jumper on the Printrboard, power the printer on, and then copy the .hex file (shown at the end of the compilation results) to the bootloader application and follow the instructions. You can then power-off the printer, remove the jumper, and power it back on.

Finally, you can issue the M92, M500, and M501 commands to set the parameters for your printer. This is the same process for the X- and Y-axis upgrade. See Listing 11-2. Note that you can set these values in the firmware if you choose, but it is easier to set them via a printer controller application.

You also need to set the offset for the Z-probe with the M212 command. In this case, you will need to know how far away the probe is from the nozzle. If mounted on the left of the extruder, use a value of 0 for the X axis and measure how far away the probe is in the Y direction. If the probe is behind the nozzle and toward the rear of the platform, use a positive value. If it is in front of the nozzle and toward front of the platform, use a negative value. For the Z axis, it will take some trial and error. Start with a value of –0.9 and adjust as needed.

---

[7]You can modify the parameters in the firmware before compiling as well. See Chapter 4 for a description of configuring Marlin for your printer.

For example, the probe shown in Figure 11-13 is mounted to the left of the extruder and 10mm away from the nozzle in the Y direction. I used the following command to set the values, saved them to memory, and read them to verify the settings.

```
M212 X0 Y10 Z-0.9
M500
M501
```

To use the new feature, you must change your slicer to home the X and Y axes, and then issue the new bed-leveling command. Open your slicer and locate the custom preprint G-code settings and change them as follows. These commands home the X and Y axes, and then take three Z-probe readings and calculate the bed offset based on those points. This compensates for an unleveled (untrammed) bed.

```
G28 X0 Y0
G29
```

Now comes the really fun part. Use your printer controller application to print a small object using the new G-code commands. Keep your hand on the power supply and be ready to pull the cord. Watch the printer carefully. If the nozzle looks like it is going to dig into the print bed, pull the plug and set the Z axis value for the M212 command to a lower value. If the nozzle strikes the print bed, set it to –2.0 and try the print again.

Once you establish a setting where the nozzle is not striking the print bed, repeat the M212 command, adding 0.2 to the value until you get a good first layer adhesion. Repeat these steps until you get a good print. Don't forget to write the values to memory each time with the M500 command. If you get close, you can use a value of 0.1 to fine-tune the position.

If this sounds like a bit of trial and error—you're right, it is. When you reach the point where the Z-probe Z-axis offset is dialed in and your first layer is adhered well, you're all set! Don't forget to reslice your objects to take advantage of the new preprint g-codes.

Power Supply

The power supply included with the Printrbot Simple is a bit fragile. I am not certain how high the failure rate is for the power supply, but it is clear a fair number of them have failed. If you are one of the unfortunate to experience a dead Printrbot Simple power supply, and you have had your printer longer than the warranty coverage, you're facing a pretty expensive replacement if you buy it from Printrbot.

There is an alternative—make your own! When mine failed, I contacted Printrbot technical support for their recommendation for a replacement power supply. Printrbot said a 12v/20a power supply would be more than adequate (and perhaps the max) for the Printrbot Simple.

I created a set of covers for a typical 12v/20a LED power supply and uploaded them to Thingiverse (`thingiverse.com/thing:383877`). These power supplies are very plentiful and can be found on most online electronics stores, auctions sites, and even Amazon.com. Figure 11-14 shows the completed power supply.

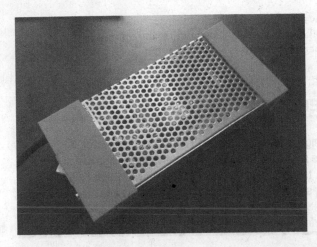

Figure 11-14. *Replacement power supply for the Printrbot Simple*

Other Considerations

I did not list a heated print bed for this printer, but it is possible to add a heated print bed. In fact, if you have the metal bed upgrade (or the all-metal Printrbot Simple; see the upcoming sidebar), there are holes for mounting a heated print bed. The reason I did not list a heated print bed as a must-have upgrade is because it really isn't needed, given the small build volume and onboard fan. I think most people will use PLA exclusively, and even without a heated print bed, the Printrbot delivers very good quality with little lifting.

If you want to add a heated print bed to your Printrbot Simple, you will also need the upgraded power supply because the stock power supply is not adequate for powering a heater. If you upgrade the power supply like I described, you will have enough power to run the heated print bed.

However, there is a trick. You will need to wire a relay in between the Printrboard and the heated print bed. This will allow the Printrboard to trigger power to the heater without drawing power from the board. Some people have success wiring the heated print bed through the Printrboard, but I recommend the use of a relay or perhaps a MOSFET just to be safe. You may also need to change the firmware to limit the switching rate. If you are interested in this upgrade, be sure to Google for solutions and examples.

Another consideration is a good spool holder. It is not essential to get the tower kit I listed earlier, but you should have some form of spool holder to keep the filament feeding smoothly. Check out Thingiverse for a host of spool holders.

THERE'S A NEW SIMPLE IN TOWN

Printrbot may be a smaller company than some other printer vendors, but being a smaller company gives them a huge advantage: they can move new products to market faster. A case in point is the Printrbot Simple. Printrbot is now selling an all-metal version of the Simple complete with a belt-driven X and Y axis. Naturally, the new model is a bit more expensive. If you are in the market for a Printrbot Simple, be sure to check the Printrbot web site for the latest offerings.

Prusa Mendel i2

The Prusa Mendel i2 printer is a great choice for those who want to dive into the RepRap world of open source 3D printers—especially so for anyone seeking to build their own printer. Since this RepRap variant is a few years old, parts are plentiful and kits can be purchased from many vendors.

The platform is also an excellent choice for those who want to make a hobby out of experimenting with upgrades and new technologies for 3D printers. That is, anyone who likes to tinker with augmenting and improving things. I suppose you can toss me into this category because a number of my printers are manifestations of my desire to tinker and improve on existing designs.

ISN'T THE PRUSA MENDEL I2 TOO OLD?

You may be tempted to think that the Prusa Mendel i2 design is too old to be worth considering. However, if you look at the upgrades listed here, you will see there are a lot of opportunities to improve the design and add features. The upgrades won't make the design superior to the newer kits, but given the relatively lower cost of this older design (you can find kits on online auction sites, sometimes at bargain prices) and the large number of things available on Thingiverse for the design, if you are looking for a printer design that you can improve and tinker with, and you are not concerned with absolutely perfect print quality, the Prusa Mendel i2 is a good choice.

One of the downsides to choosing the Prusa Mendel i2 kit is that most kits are bare bones in the sense that they include only those features that you must have to print. Like the Printrbot Simple, there are rarely features like LCD panels, Z-height adjusters, or even adjustable endstops. Some kits don't even come with power supplies or glass for the print bed. However, most do include a heated print bed. What this means is if you buy a kit for this platform, you will probably want to upgrade it soon after you build it.

Fortunately, since the Prusa Mendel i2 has been around a few years, there are hundreds of modifications available with a vast array of designs. Perhaps best of all, most of the latest upgrades are available for this platform. If you search online or on Thingiverse, you will find upgrades ranging from variations on a theme (e.g., Z-axis improvements), new features (e.g., auto bed leveling), and even a number of common upgrades (e.g., LCD panels).

In fact, almost all of the upgrades I've made to my Prusa Mendel i2 printers have been sourced from Thingiverse and online retailers who sell RepRap components. The following lists numerous upgrades and improvements I have made to one of my Prusa Mendel i2 printers. I will discuss those upgrades I feel are a must-have for any Prusa Mendel i2 owner in the following sections. Figure 11-15 shows what my printer looks like today with all of these upgrades installed. See if you can find the upgrades in the photo.

- *Adjustable feet*: thingiverse.com/thing:249932.

- *Print bed adjusters*: thingiverse.com/thing:16428.

- *Borosilicate glass print surface*: Various online retailers.

- *Insulated print bed*: Various online retailers.

- *Z-axis fix*: Replace 608zz bearing with a thrust bearing of the same outer dimensions.

- *Switch mount for accessories*: thingiverse.com/thing:381392.

- *RAMPS fan*: thingiverse.com/thing:30331.

- *Power terminal*: Various online retailers. Clamps are common endstop mounts.

- *LCD panel*: Various online retailers. Mount is from thingiverse.com/thing:84535.

- *RAMPS mount*: thingiverse.com/thing:17912.

- *Power inlet mount and switch*: thingiverse.com/thing:26105.

- *Upgraded Y-axis belt clamps*: thingiverse.com/thing:91370.

- *Onboard power supply mount*: thingiverse.com/thing:57520.

- *Z-height adjuster*: `thingiverse.com/thing:16380`.

- *Print cooling fan*: `thingiverse.com/thing:26650`.

- *LED light ring*: Auto parts stores, `thingiverse.com/thing:219419`.

- *Spool holder and filament guide*: (See the preceding details).

- *Y-axis belt tensioner*: `thingiverse.com/thing:74209`.

- *Filament cleaner*: `thingiverse.com/thing:16483`.

Figure 11-15. Heavily modified Prusa Mendel i2

If you're thinking that is a lot of upgrades, you're right, and they're all on the printer. It isn't my most upgraded printer, but it is close. There are also numerous small tweaks of less significance.

The following sections list those upgrades I feel are essential and must-have to make the Prusa Mendel i2 a very good, stable 3D printing platform. While I consider each one to be a must-have item, I list them in the order of ease of installation. You can use this as a roadmap for your own upgrades. I have discussed some of these previously, but I include them here for anyone looking to improve their Prusa Mendel i2.

LCD Panel

I have discussed the LCD panel and its many virtues and conveniences. Recall that an LCD panel makes it possible to use your printer without the need for a computer. Most also give you the ability to print from an SD card. Figure 11-16 shows an LCD panel mounted on the top-right portion of the frame in front of the right-side Z-axis motor. I find this location very well-suited for right-handed use. Mount it on the left if you prefer left-handed use.[8]

---

[8]I am right-handed and my wife is left-handed. As a result, I often sit on the right. Many of the lamps in our house are awkward for me to use due to their orientation. There is a profound difference in where objects are placed and how they are oriented depending on your dexterity preference.

Figure 11-16. *LCD panel (Prusa Mendel i2)*

Borosilicate Glass Print Surface

One of the easiest upgrades you will ever do is replacing your print surface with higher-quality glass. I have found that Borosilicate glass makes an excellent print surface that transfers heat well, and more importantly, is very flat.

Some enthusiasts have used mirrored glass for their print bed with great success. Again, the key is how flat the surface is. If you want to use mirrored glass, check it carefully for distortions. Only one side of the mirrored glass needs to be perfectly flat—the side without the reflective coating (the top side). Don't be lured into thinking all mirrored glass is flat. Furthermore, I am not so certain the reflective coating can withstand numerous heating and cooling cycles.

Like most other enthusiasts, I used hardware store-grade plate glass for my build surface. But this glass is seldom flat enough for use with 3D printers. There is always some unevenness. That is, the glass has some small amount of wave or bend in it. I found one case where the center was nearly 0.05mm lower than the four corners. Turned over it was nearly 0.08mm higher, so thickness was a problem too.

Distortions like this in the glass can cause bed leveling problems, make Z-height adjustment a nightmare, and cause lifting and poor-quality parts. The only way to discover defects is to use a dial gauge mounted on your X axis to take measurements at the four corners, center, and other points. A good print surface should have no more than about 0.01mm to 0.02mm variance from one spot to the next.

If you are using lower-grade glass for your print bed, you should consider getting a Borosilicate glass plate. You can find these at some 3D printer online vendors and also on popular online auction sites. Be sure to find one sized for your print bed, because it cannot be easily cut to fit. Installation is simple and easy—just remove the old glass and put the new one in place. Just let that puppy cool first if you've been printing lately!

Spool Holder and Filament Guide

I presented a filament management system in great detail in the "Filament Management System" section. I think every printer should have a similar system installed either onboard, like I have built, or as a remote spool holder. Recall that the objective is to reduce the friction on the filament so that it does not cause the extruder to pull the filament unevenly. That is, if the spool catches every now and again, it can affect the quality of the print. In this case, when the spool catches, too little filament could be extruded, causing irregular flow from the nozzle.

If you use the system I described earlier, installation is easy. However, if you do not want to mount the spool holder using the easy-on bar clamps, you may encounter some issues with partially disassembling the frame to get the clamps in place. I strongly recommend using the easy-on clamps.

Print Cooling Fan

Recall that the cooling fan is designed to force air over the print to help PLA parts cool evenly to avoid layer adhesion defects. I discussed a print cooling fan in the "Fans" section. Indeed, you can see the print cooling fan for this printer in Figure 11-12.

■ **Note**   Some hot ends require a fan directed at the top of the hot end. This normally does not direct any air to the print (at least not directly). To distinguish the fans, we call fans directed at the hot end an *extruder fan*. It should be configured to run constantly and not controlled by the firmware like the print cooling fan.

If you plan to print with PLA, you should install print cooling fan. Finding one can be a bit of a challenge. Few of the early Prusa Mendel i2 X-carriages were designed with a fan in mind. Thus, you may need to find a fan mount (like I used) that mounts to the existing belt clamp bolts.

Installing the fan is normally not difficult, with the only challenge being routing the wires along the same path as the hot end, extruder stepper motor, and thermistor. If you have zip-tied everything nice and tight, it may mean taking all of that apart to route the wires. Be sure to mount the wires so that nothing touches moving parts. Recall that the print cooling fan mounts to the electronics board.

Z-height Adjuster

This is another item I've discussed as a generic upgrade. For the Prusa Mendel i2 in particular, it is an absolute must-have. You will find it much easier to get your first layer adhesion dialed in—especially so if your print bed base is wood (many are).

Installation of the adjuster depends on which adjuster you choose. If you go with the one I used, you will need to loosen the left-side smooth rod on the Z axis so that you can slide the adjuster mount onto the rod. Be sure to not move the threaded rods, because you will have to realign the Z axis if you do. You can see the adjuster in Figure 11-10.

Y-Axis Belt Tensioner

The Y-axis belt on Prusa Mendel i2 printers seems more susceptible to slippage than other designs. Or maybe it is just my luck to have several exhibit this behavior. A lot of this has to do with the belt clamps used to hold the ends of the belt. I recommend upgrading to a belt clamp designed to firmly grasp the belt. In other words, one with ridges that match the teeth in the belt. Figure 11-17 shows the belt tensioner installed.

Figure 11-17. *Y-axis belt tensioner (Prusa Mendel i2)*

Notice the switches mounted to the left of the adjuster. These are switches for the LED light ring and the RAMPS fan. This switch mount has been removed from Thingiverse (I don't know why), but there are several others that are similar. If you want one, I suggest making it one of your first designed-from-scratch objects. It isn't difficult to design and it is not trivial. It's good practice for designing more complex objects. Or you can use the one listed earlier (thingiverse.com/thing:381392).

When looking for a belt tensioner, I wanted to find one that did not require dismantling the frame. The one I found is designed to mount around the existing Y-axis idler bearing, making it easy to install. The only issue that you may encounter concerns the belt clamps. I found that I had to loosen the belt to get the tensioner fully seated on the threaded rods. To do that, I had to disassemble the build platform, which is not trivial. It isn't difficult, but it will take some time and it will require you to level your print bed once you reassemble everything. Since you are likely to encounter the same, I suggest replacing those belt clamps while you're at it.

Print Bed Adjusters

Even if you do not have or plan to add a Z-height adjuster, there is one modification you must make to enable leveling the print bed. Most kits include some form of bolts to mount the heated print bed to a plate or subframe for the Y axis. Some, like the kits I used, do not include any form of adjustment. Thus, if you need to level the print bed, you have to use some form of shim or washer to raise the print bed to compensate for print beds that are not level (trammed). Not only is this a lot of work to remove the bolts and insert washers, but it is also imprecise given that the thickness of the washer may be too thick or too thin, leaving the print bed lower or higher on one side. What is needed is a more precise way to raise or lower any corner of the print bed.

There are dozens of examples of adding adjusters in place of the solid mount bolts. Most people tend to use a spring placed over the bolt with the heated print bed next, and then a lock nut on top; or perhaps reversed, where the bolt head is on top and the lock nut is below the print bed. Either way, to adjust the print bed you must use two tools when adjusting each bolt. A variant of this setup fixes the bolt through the Y-axis base and the lock nut on top. This means using fewer tools.

However, wouldn't it be better still to have a solution that doesn't require tools? I decided to make a variant of the spring mount, but not use springs. I threaded the bolts through the Y-axis base and placed a nut on top of the base to hold the bolts fast. I then used a thumb wheel to hold another nut placed below the print bed with a thumb nut on top. Figure 11-18 shows my setup. I use this on all of my RepRap printers.

Figure 11-18. Print bed adjusters (Prusa Mendel i2)

You can use whatever hardware your want (metric or SAE). In this solution, I used a #6 bolt and (two) #6 nuts. The thumb nut on top is a brass #6 nut. All of these are available in most hardware stores. Since the Y-axis base is aluminum, I simply drilled the exiting M3 hole out (I used a #6 tap for my most recent builds). The thumbwheels are available on Thingiverse and there are many varieties. Search Thingiverse for the size that matches your hardware.

■ **Note**   Another benefit from using the spring method is that it permits a bit of cushion for cases where the print head makes contact with the print bed. This may be helpful if you are new to using 3D printers, where accidental Z-axis crashes are more likely.

Installation of print bed adjusters may require removing the print bed and possibly even the Y-axis base plate. Since the goal is to make leveling the print bed easier, the extra work will pay off once you reassemble the Y axis. If you use a toolless solution like mine, you will be able to level your print bed very quickly, and more importantly, you will be able to get the nozzle the same height on all four corners.

Z-Axis Fix

I spoke about Z-axis wobble in an earlier chapter. Recall that most Z-axis wobbles manifest as noticeable ridges in the vertical walls. Figure 11-19 shows two cylinders (they are cylinders like a napkin ring). One was printed on a printer suffering from Z-wobble, and the other on a printer with a Z-axis fix.

Figure 11-19. *Results of Z-axis fix*

Notice the object on top. This is before the Z-axis fix. That is, the Z-axis threaded rods are fixed-mount on both ends. Notice the ridges in the surface. This is the vertical surface of the object. These ridges form a harmonic that will resonate up the vertical surfaces, making them more like Ruffles than high-quality prints.

Now look at the ring on the bottom. This is after the Z-axis fix. Notice how the ridges are almost completely gone. If you look closely, you will see a very small harmonic (I cannot even measure it, but I can see it with a magnifying glass). With the fix in place, the print quality is where it should be and even a bit better than most examples I've seen.

When I first discovered this problem, I tried a number of temporary fixes, including using a flexible coupler on the motors, which helped considerably but did not solve the problem. I also tried to find perfectly straight threaded rods. After visiting a number of hardware stores, I've determined none are perfectly straight. To get precision threaded rods, you have to contact specialty hardware vendors, which means they will be much more expensive.

In the end, none of my attempts really fixed the problem and were merely treating the symptoms. It wasn't until I read Richard Cameron's article, "Taxonomy of Z axis artifacts in extrusion-based 3d printing," in *RepRap Magazine*[9] (http://reprapmagazine.com/issues/1/index.html) that I understood the real problem. It turns out the Z-axis upgrade included in my original kit introduced the problem by fixing both ends of the threaded rods. Thus, any flex, bend, or other irregularity is transmitted to the X axis and manifests as these harmonic distortions in the vertical sides of the object.

So how did I fix the problem? I freed one side of the axis! That is, I made it possible for the threaded rod to shift slightly on the bottom mount. This allows the threaded rod to move around without translating the shifts to the X axis. Figure 11-20 shows the original Z-axis lower mount that came with my kit and a replacement I made to accommodate a thrust bearing.

---

[9]February 2013, Issue 1.

Figure 11-20. Z-axis lower mounts

The part on the left is the original lower Z-axis mount that uses a 608 bearing. The bore for this bearing is 8mm. Typically, two nuts or a single lock nut is used to rest on top of the bearing. Most Prusa Mendel i2 build documents suggest tightening the nuts so that the weight of the axis rests on the bearings. Some printer build documents also suggest using a flex coupling at the motor mount. This helps, but the fixed mount is on the bottom, and since this is closer to where most of the Z-axis travel will be confined (the lower levels), any deformity can translate to the X axis. Yes, there is still flex at the top, but not enough to compensate for threaded rods that are not perfectly straight and properly threaded. Furthermore, the load on the 608 bearing is perpendicular to its specification. Thus, the bearing is the wrong design for this solution.

The mount on the right corrects these errors by using a thrust bearing with a 10mm bore. Not shown is the top bearing washer. This is placed on top of the bearing race. On top of that is an 8mm thrust washer. Two nuts are used to place about half of the load of the X axis on the thrust bearing. This allows the threaded rod to shift around on the thrust bearing. Lastly, I use a flexible coupling at the motor mount to complete the solution. Figure 11-21 shows the solution.

Figure 11-21. Z-axis fix installed

Once again, the goal of my solution was to make it possible for the threaded rod to move around at the bottom, and thus not translate the deformities of the threaded rod to the X axis. The rings shown in Figure 11-19 are from the printer depicted in Figure 11-21. As you can see, the solution improved the Z wobble greatly.

Sadly, installation of this upgrade will take several hours because you must unthread the lower threaded rods to get to the Z-axis lower mount. You will have to remove the crossbar located in the center bottom of the printer as well.

What could make this upgrade even more difficult is if you have additional parts or components mounted to the frame pieces that must be removed. Look at Figure 11-15 again. I had to remove a number of things to get to the Z-axis lower mount. However, I feel the upgrade was absolutely essential and has made this printer far better.

Prusa i3

The Prusa i3 printer is the latest iteration of the Prusa variants of RepRap design. The Prusa i3 improves on previous designs in many ways. Perhaps most important are little or no Z wobble, fewer plastic parts, more frame rigidity,[10] and it is easier to build. Since this RepRap variant is fairly recent, most RepRap vendors will have parts and kits available.

Like the Prusa Mendel i2 kit, most Prusa i3 kits come with the bare minimum for building a 3D printer. Thus, you are likely to find features such as print bed and Z-height adjustment incorporated in the kit. Unlike the Prusa Mendel i2, you may not find as many upgrades. This is due in part to the newness of the Prusa i3.

However, what you will find are several variants of the main plastic parts. The original repository is located at `https://github.com/josefprusa/Prusa3`, but there are several variants available. I prefer to use the source or original design for the plastic parts incorporating variants when needed. More specifically, how do you know the variants improve on the original if you never use the original to know what needs improving. This goes for the upgrades too. You should resist downloading and installing upgrades just because they are labeled "latest," "newest," or "improved." As we saw with the Z-axis lower mount on the Prusa Mendel i2, the latest isn't always best.

That doesn't mean there aren't any options for upgrades. In fact, there are many, and many more being made available every week. I have made a number of improvements, some of my own design, to my Prusa i3 printers. Figure 11-22 shows one printer that I have upgraded recently.

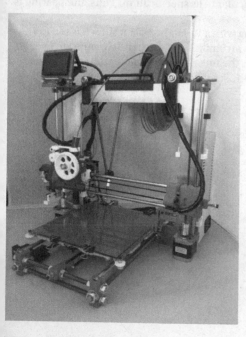

Figure 11-22. Prusa i3 printer

---

[10]With the possible exception of the Z-axis flex on the Y axis for the single-sheet version from a heavy spool mounted on top of the frame. If you plan to mount a spool on top, use some form of brace.

Some of the upgrades are not upgrades in the sense they replace existing parts. Rather, most of the upgrades are improvements in the form of new features. The following lists the upgrades and improvements I've made to the Prusa i3 shown in Figure 11-22. I list links to the parts where available. You may notice some of these are the same as those used on the Prusa Mendel i2.

- *Print bed adjusters*: thingiverse.com/thing:16428.

- *Z-height adjuster*: (See details from earlier list).

- *Borosilicate glass print surface*: Various online retailers.

- *Insulated print bed*: Various online retailers.

- *RAMPS fan*: thingiverse.com/thing:30331.

- *Graphic LCD panel*: Various online retailers. Mount is from thingiverse.com/thing:287633.

- *Power supply mount and cover*: thingiverse.com/thing:396650.

- *Z-probe sled*: thingiverse.com/thing:396692.

- *Relay mount*: thingiverse.com/thing:396653.

- *Endstop holders*: thingiverse.com/thing:82519 and thingiverse.com/thing:82631.

- *Spool holder and filament guide*: (See details from earlier list).

- *USB relocate*: thingiverse.com/thing:237016.

- *Filament cleaner*: thingiverse.com/thing:16483.

- *Filament guide*: thingiverse.com/thing:287608.

- *Y-axis cable strain relief*: thingiverse.com/thing:200704.

- *Z-axis flexible coupler*: Various online retailers. Look for a 5mm to 5mm coupler.[11]

Since this is the latest design for the Prusa design RepRap printer, I present an overview of some of the upgrades in the following paragraphs. I will also describe the must-have upgrades in the following sections in order of difficulty to install.

The LCD panel shown in Figure 11-22 is a graphic LCD from RepRapDiscount. This LCD is a bit larger than the character-based one and therefore a bit easier to read. It also has the ability to display low-resolution images such as symbols for fans, the heated print bed, and extruders. I mounted the LCD panel on the top-left corner of the frame, which makes the panel easier to get to—especially if the printer is on a shelf below desktop-level. Figure 11-23 shows the LCD panel mounting system (the photo was taken from behind the printer). You can find the mounts at thingiverse.com/thing:287633.

---

[11]Most Prusa Mendel i2 use 8mm to 5mm flex couplers. Make sure the flex coupler is designed is for the Prusa i3 that uses a 5mm threaded rod.

Figure 11-23. Graphic LCD panel mount (Prusa i3)

I like to keep my wiring and electronics neat and tidy. One of the things that initially bugged me about building 3D printers was the external power supply arrangement. My early kits used an ATX power supply that rattled around on my worktop in its all-metal case. It was always in the way. Ever since then I try to find some way to attach the power supply to the printer. Some designs don't allow this—there just isn't enough space on the frame to mount it (Printrbot Simple). This is almost true with the Prusa i3, but I observed several solutions that mounted the power supply on the right-side frame. Figure 11-24 shows the solution I made (thingiverse.com/thing:396650).

Figure 11-24. Power supply mount and cover (Prusa i3)

The same is true for the printer electronics. I don't like designs that have the electronics mounted remotely. Fortunately, the Prusa i3 design has included a mounting point for the electronics (at least conceptually if not actually—some frames do not have the mount points drilled). All you do is mount your Arduino or other electronics to the frame, and you're done. If you want to add a fan to your RAMPS like I did, you can take care of bundling the excess wiring at the same time. Figure 11-25 shows the electronics complete with fan (`thingiverse.com/thing:30331`).

Figure 11-25. *RAMPS fan (Prusa i3)*

Now that we've seen a few of the interesting upgrades, let's look at my recommendation for must-have upgrades.

■ **Note** Some of the upgrades that I feel are a must-have item were discussed in the Prusa Mendel i2 section. These include print bed adjusters, the Borosilicate glass print surface, and an LCD panel. For brevity, I will not discuss them here. If you are interested in these, see the references in the list for the part on Thingiverse.

Y-Axis Cable Strain Relief

The X- and Y-axis wiring on 3D printers undergoes a lot of flex during printing. I have discussed how this can cause breaks in the wiring and failure of the components. Most heated print beds have heater plates that mount the wires in the front. More specifically, the lettering on the heater plate is oriented with the wiring at the bottom. Thus, some people route the wiring for the heated print bed from the front of the Y axis, down under the axis movement, and back to the RAMPS. But this places the cable in a precarious position and makes it susceptible to binding by the Y axis. It also creates a lot more bend than is necessary since the wiring must make a nearly 180-degree bend.

You can fix this partially by turning the print bed so that the wiring is in the rear. This allows you to route the wiring to the rear of the printer and to clear the obstructions. However, turning it upside down or left or right makes the orientation of the text awkward. If you're like me, you want everything mounted so that it not only functions well but also looks right. But it also doesn't remove the stress point. The wiring will flex less, but is still a concern.

I found a very nicely designed strain relief on Thingiverse (thingiverse.com/thing:200704) that allows you to route your wiring under the print bed between the Y-axis plate and the heated plate. Since I insulate my heated print bed, the wiring is not subjected to the heat of the heater plate. If you do not use insulation, you can route the wires under the Y-axis base plate and zip-tie it in place.

The part mounts to the Y-axis base plate with a single zip tie. It also has a cutout for a zip tie for the wiring. Figure 11-26 shows the strain relief installed. Notice how the plastic wire loom is secured to the strain relief mount.

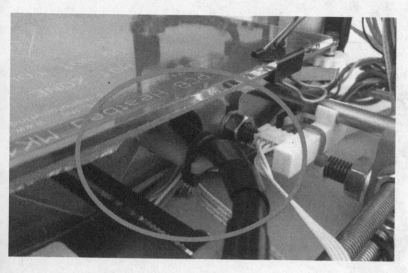

Figure 11-26. Y-axis strain relief (Prusa i3)

Installation is easy, and except for disconnecting the wiring, it does not require disassembly. I recommend mounting the other side of the loom to the rear frame. There is plenty of room for the cable in that area and it keeps it from floating around the back of your printer. If you don't have a setup like this, you should consider making the change before you start any long print jobs.

Flex Coupler

A flex coupler is a nice addition to the Prusa i3. Most kits use a short piece of tubing and zip ties to link the Z-axis motors to the threaded rods. This works, but it doesn't allow as much freedom for flexing as I'd like. Fortunately, there are many examples of aluminum couplers milled with a concentric cut to for a spring-like flex point. Figure 11-27 shows the flex couplers that I used.

Figure 11-27. *Flex coupler on Z axis (Prusa i3)*

You can find these couplers on many RepRap online vendor sites. Installation does require removing the old couplers, lifting the X axis off the motors. If you are careful, you may not need to level your print bed after the installation, but I highly recommend you do so just in case.

USB Cable Relocate

Having the electronics mounted on the back of the frame makes it less likely they will come into contact with your hands or tools as you use your printer. However, the mounting orientation makes plugging in the USB cable difficult. If you move your printer or connect and disconnect it often, you will find this arrangement irritating (at least I did).

Thus, I designed a part to move the USB connector to the front of the printer. I used a USB panel mount cable with a male B-type connector on one end and a female B-type panel mount connector on the other. For me, a 12-inch cable was just about right but I'd recommend an 18-inch cable to give you some extra length. Figure 11-28 shows the part installed.

Figure 11-28. *USB cable relocate (Prusa i3)*

Installation is not difficult, but may require removing your print bed if you cannot move the Y axis far enough back to mount the clamp. I designed the clamp to be slipped over the top Y-axis threaded rod. If you have difficulty pressing the clamp over the threaded rod, you may need to loosen the rod enough to move the rod back to allow you to slide the threaded rod through the clamp. If you have to disassemble the Y axis or the print bed, be sure to level the print bed before you print.

Spool Holder and Filament Guide

A good filament management system is essential for smooth, even extrusion. The negative effects of a spool that has too much friction or even snags can be severe. Recall these can lead to uneven extrusion and poor print quality. In the most severe case, too much tension can cause extrusion failures.

The components of the filament management system are a good spool holder, one or more filament guides to keep the filament away from the moving parts, and a filament cleaner. The spool holder I devised for the Prusa i3 uses threaded rods that clamp to the aluminum single-sheet frame (`thingiverse.com/thing:396669`). Figure 11-29 shows the spool holder frame made from threaded rods, my own frame clamps, and the any angle threaded rod clamp (`thingiverse.com/thing:30328`).

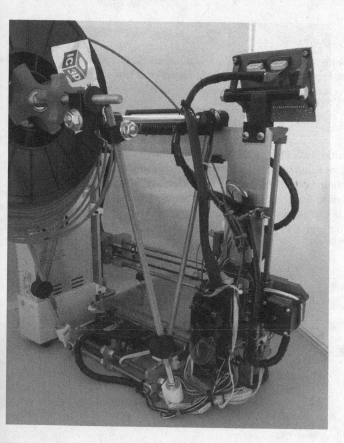

Figure 11-29. Filament management system (Prusa i3)

The spool rides on the same cones from the Prusa Mendel i2 example shown in Figure 11-29 (thingiverse.com/thing:21850), but modified to remove more material. I also designed a wide filament guide that keeps the filament in the middle of the print area (thingiverse.com/thing:287608). It has a slight angle to allow the filament to pull freely and is designed to clamp to the top of the frame. I use the same filament cleaner on all of my printers (see thingiverse.com/thing:16483).

Installation of this upgrade is not difficult and requires assembly of the threaded rod supports. However, the threaded rods required are not a standard length (e.g., 12 inch). You can use standard 12-inch length threaded rods for the top rod, but the rod for the spool holder cones will need to be about 15 inches long. Similarly, depending on how long you make the top threaded rod, the vertical rods may require cutting to a custom length. Cutting the rods to length makes this upgrade a bit harder to do than some. If you don't have any way to cut the threaded rods, use wooden dowels to mockup the build, and then take those measurements to your hardware store and ask them to cut the rods for you (or get a friend with a hacksaw to lend you a hand).

Z-Probe for Auto Bed Leveling

Another must-have upgrade is one that is very popular and indeed still evolving among 3D printer enthusiasts: auto bed leveling (or more correctly auto Z-probing). I demonstrated a similar system for the Printrbot Simple earlier.

There are a number of examples of Z-probe upgrades for the Prusa i3. Most use a servo with the endstop mounted on a short arm to rotate the endstop down when probing, and away or stowed when printing. I never liked this design for two reasons. First, most mount solutions for the servo get in the way of fans and lights, and makes the X-carriage a bit too bulky. Second, you must use a very good quality servo and have almost no noise on your electronics board (RAMPS).[12] That is, most servos I tested either chattered annoyingly or crept into the down position slightly during a long print. For these reasons, I felt there had to be a better way. Figure 11-30 shows my solution.

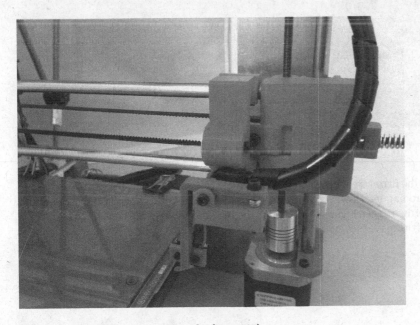

Figure 11-30. Sled mounted Z-probe (Prusa i3)

---

[12]I tried a number of Arduino and RAMPS boards, as well as noise suppression circuitry. The noise suppression helped, but not enough for my expectations.

Notice that there is a new part riding on the X-axis smooth rods. It is a sled with an electromagnet and an arm that has an adjuster for micro changes to the Z-height. What I wanted was a solution that allowed the endstop to be docked when not in use. This sled concept achieves that. When probing the Z axis, the firmware first homes the X axis and then runs the carriage out to the maximum position. Once there, the electromagnet is engaged and attaches magnetically to a metal tab on the X-carriage. The sled is then towed to each position for the probe (all four corners and the center). When probing is complete, the X axis is moved to the maximum position and the electromagnet is disengaged. This docks the endstop out of the way. Figure 11-31 shows a close-up of the sled. The round device mounted in the center is the electromagnet.

Figure 11-31. *Z-probe sled*

The electromagnet is controlled by the firmware via the same pins as the servos. In this case, the pin is set to low or high to engage or disengage the electromagnet. However, since the electromagnet requires 12 volts, not 3 to 5 volts, I use a 12-volt relay with the servo pin as the trigger. Figure 11-32 shows the relay mounted to the back of the frame. You can find the mount on Thingiverse (thingiverse.com/thing:396653).

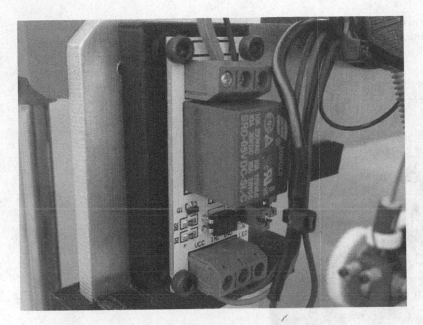

Figure 11-32. *12-volt relay for electromagnet*

Wiring the system requires running wires from the servo pins to the relay, 12-volt power to the relay, and the electromagnet to the relay. The relay should be a board designed to be triggered with a logic signal; that is, about 3 to 5 volts at a maximum amperage of 40mA. You also must run the wires for the endstop to the RAMPS board. As you can see in Figure 11-30, I routed the wires on the right side of the frame to avoid snagging on any parts. Figure 11-33 shows the wiring diagram for the system.

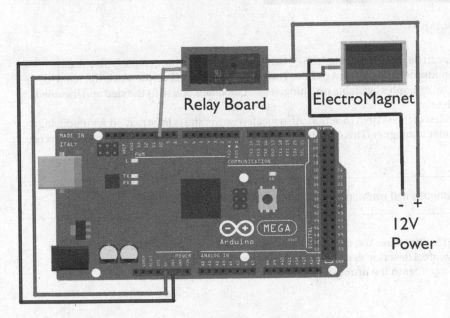

Figure 11-33. *Wiring the electromagnet and relay*

The diagram shows wiring directly to the Arduino for clarity. When you route the wires to the RAMPS board, you will use the servo pins located on the bottom of the RAMPS next to the reset button. Figure 11-34 shows the location of the servo pins.

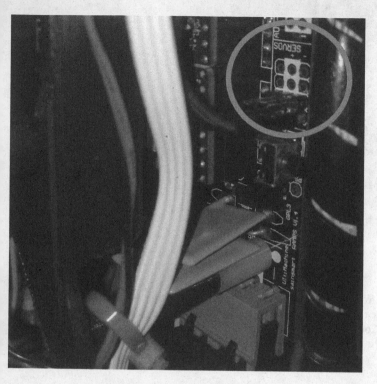

Figure 11-34. *Servo connectors (RAMPS)*

All of the parts for this system can be found on Thingiverse (thingiverse.com/thing:396692). The sled is designed with supports, so you can just download it and print it. The only part not listed on the site is the LM8UU printable bearings. There are several examples available on Thingiverse. I modified one to fit the sled and included the .stl for the bearing on Thingiverse.

You can also find a link to a video of the system in action. Also located on the site is information for modifying your firmware to use the sled and electromagnet. This code is continuing to evolve, so you should check Thingiverse for the latest updates.

■ **Tip** This upgrade is still experimental and evolving. Check Thingiverse for the latest updates.

There are two ways to modify the firmware. You can either modify your own copy of the Marling firmware or use my branch of the Marling firmware. I describe each below. I recommend reading both versions so that you understand how all of the parts fit together in the firmware.

Modifying Your Own Copy

Modifying your own copy of the firmware means you don't have to reconfigure the settings from scratch. You can simply add the code needed to control the sled. The changes to the firmware require adding two new defines to the Configuration.h file and several changes to the Marlin_main.cpp file. The following show the changes to the Configuration.h file.

```
#define Z_PROBE_SLED
#define SLED_DOCKING_OFFSET 5
```

Here we simply define the use of the sled and specify the additional distance the X axis must travel past its maximum to dock the sled. This will vary from one printer to another, so you should run your X axis out to the maximum without the sled installed to check how much space is needed. You need only move the sled so that the endstop does not make contact with print bed when the Z axis is at the minimum position.

You can find the modifications to this file on the Thingiverse site in the form of a difference file (.diff), or simply a patch. To apply the difference file (patch), use the patch command in the Marlin folder. Make sure you are using the latest firmware from https://github.com/ErikZalm/Marlin.

Using the Modified Marlin Firmware

Using my branch of the Marlin firmware may be best for those that are building a new printer or those that have manually configured Marling in the past. It also may be easier to use this branch and copy your settings over if you are not familiar with how to patch source code.

For these cases, I have created a branch of the Marlin firmware that you can use instead of patching your own copy of the firmware. You can get my version of the firmware from https://github.com/oliasmage/Marlin.

Installing and Wiring the Sled

Installation of this upgrade is nontrivial, not only because it requires modifying the firmware, but also because it requires partial disassembly of the Z and X axes. At the minimum, you must remove the smooth and threaded rod from the right side of the frame, and then remove the right-side X-end. To do this, you must remove the X-axis belt. You can then slide the sled onto the smooth rods for the X axis, and then reassemble everything.

Wiring is also an issue, given you have to wire in a relay. However, if you follow the wiring diagram shown in Figure 11-33, you should not have a problem. If you use a different relay or one with pins defined differently, you may have to study the diagram closely and make necessary changes to accommodate your hardware choice.

Once you have the hardware installed, and everything wired and the firmware updated, you will be able to enjoy effortless Z-probing (auto bed leveling). Not only that, but since the Z-probe sled includes an adjuster, you can change the Z-height slightly without need to change the firmware settings or issue any G-code commands. Cool, eh?

MakerBot Replicator 1 Dual

The MakerBot Replicator 1 Dual is a fantastic machine. While it is a bit older than the latest MakerBot Replicator 2X (the only other dual extruder currently available from MakerBot), it is still a viable solution for those seeking to experiment with dual extrusion and printing with ABS. That is, the MakerBot Replicator 1 Dual is optimized for ABS. There are no fans for printing with PLA.

While the list of upgrades I've made to my Replicator 1 Dual is much shorter than the previous printers presented, these upgrades are key upgrades for anyone wanting a high-quality ABS printer on a budget. More specifically, if you want the capabilities of the Replicator 2X (e.g., an enclosure and upgraded extruder) but the cost is too high, you can save a lot of money by buying a slightly used Replicator 1 Dual and installing these upgrades. In fact, my Replicator 1 Dual has a higher print quality than an out-of-the-box Replicator 2X. Figure 11-35 shows a modified Replicator 1 Dual.

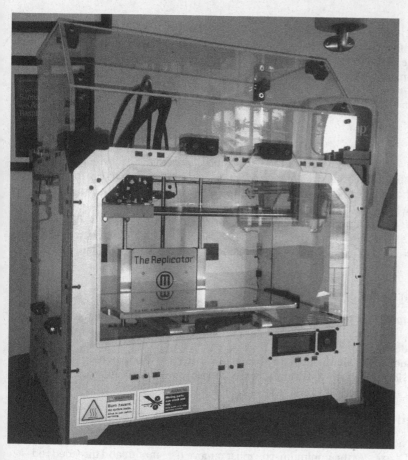

Figure 11-35. *Modified MakerBot Replicator 1 Dual*

The upgrades for the printer shown include the following. Since most of these items are upgrades you can purchase, I also list links to the product web site. I discuss each of the must-have upgrades in the following sections in order of installation complexity.

- *Upgraded heated print bed*: bctechnologicalsolutions.com/HBP/index.html

- *MakerBot Replicator extruder upgrade / filament drive*: Search eBay for the vendor named cred8t

- *AluCarriage Dual*: http://shop.raffle.ch/shop/alucarriage-dual/

- *Aluminum arm upgrade*: bctechnologicalsolutions.com/arm-upgrade/index.html

- *Enclosure*: Hood (thingiverse.com/thing:26063), Windows (thingiverse.com/thing:30311)

- *Adjustable feet*: thingiverse.com/thing:249914

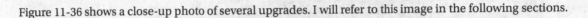

VENDOR SPOTLIGHT: BC TECHNOLOGICAL SOLUTIONS

BC Technological Solutions, also known as Bottleworks, has two key upgrades for the MakerBot Replicator 1, 2, and 2X printers. They offer replacement heated print beds for the Replicator 1 and 2X, as well as the addition of a heated print bed for the Replicator 2. They also have the best and most advanced bed arm replacement. The arms are milled from solid aluminum and completely remove any vibration or sagging found with the stock arms. These two upgrades alone are those that every MakerBot Replicator 1, 2, and 2X owner should have.

Figure 11-36 shows a close-up photo of several upgrades. I will refer to this image in the following sections.

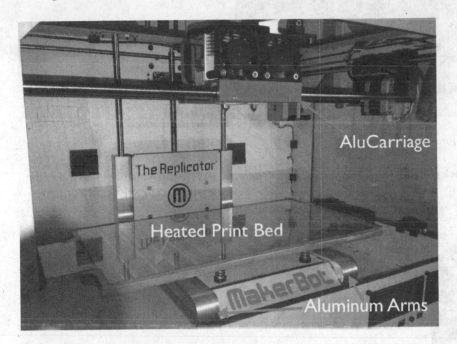

Figure 11-36. Upgraded Replicator 2 parts

MakerBot Replicator Extruder Upgrade / Filament Drive

The extruders in the Replicator 1 are the older Delrin plunger types. These are notorious for being finicky and difficult to keep working well. There are printable solutions available that work much better, but the best way to solve the problem is to upgrade to an all-aluminum plunger design. Figure 11-37 shows the upgrades installed.

Figure 11-37. *Extruder upgrade for Replicator 1 Dual*

The upgrade consists of a back plate, a spring, a lever with a small bearing, and two bolts. Figure 11-38 shows the upgrade installed on the stepper motor. This is the version for the Replicator 2, but the ones for the Replicator 1 are very similar.

Figure 11-38. *Aluminum extruder details*

Installation is pretty easy. You start by unloading the filament from both extruders, disconnect the stepper motors (don't get them reversed!), and remove the bolts holding the fan and stepper motor. Be sure to cover your print bed with a towel in case you drop a bolt or tool.

Take the stepper motors out of the printer and install the new plate and arm as shown in Figure 11-38. The most difficult part is holding the extruder level closed far enough to depress the spring and allow the leftmost bolt to seat. Once done, reassemble and reload your filament. No other adjustments are needed.

If you are struggling with the original Delrin plungers or have upgraded to the printed version (which resembles the aluminum version), you may want to invest in this all-aluminum option. I can say with some authority that most of my extrusion failures with ABS have been solved with this upgrade.

Upgraded Heated Print Bed

The stock heated print bed is sufficient for almost anything you want to print. However, there is one thing I consider a possible design flaw: the build plate is not removable. This makes removing and replacing Kapton tape a difficult and frustrating experience. Fortunately, there is a solution! BC Technologies offers a replacement heated print bed that not only features a removable build plate (print surface), but also comes to temperature a little faster. You can see the new print bed in Figure 11-35.

The heated print bed is a bit longer than the stock unit, and firmware changes would be needed to take advantage of the additional surface area. However, I've found no reason to seek out this modification. Additionally, the vendor recommends keeping the temperature of the surface below 100°C. I set mine to 90°C and it works fine in that range. That is, a bit cooler than the default for the stock unit, so if you decide to get this upgrade, be sure to reset the default in MakerWare.

The removable build plate is really handy. You can buy a second one and treat each with Kapton tape out of the printer using the wet method described earlier in the book. This, I believe, is worth the cost if you use your Replicator 1 Dual often enough to require changing the Kapton tape frequently.[13]

As a bonus, the heated print bed converts your four-post bed level adjusters to the newer three post of the Replicator 2/2X. This requires drilling a small hole in the wooden crosspiece between the arms, but BC Technologies includes a handy template (3D printed, of course).

Installation isn't that difficult, but will require turning the printer on its side to get to the electronics. You will need to remove the electronics cover and disconnect and remove the cable for the stock heated print bed. Disassembly of the stock heated print bed requires removing the adjustable print bed screws and disconnecting the cable. Detailed instructions are included, and with some patience, you can complete the upgrade in under an hour. Naturally, you will need to level your print bed once you're done.

Leveling the print bed with the new three-point system may seem a little awkward at first since the menus and operation of the printer does not change. However, if you follow the menus and ignore the bits about turning the rear left and right adjusters, and only change the one adjuster in the rear, you will adapt quickly.

AluCarriage Dual

The stock X-carriage for the MakerBot printers is made from injection-molded plastic. It holds up well for printing with ABS (and PLA), but if you want to print with filament that requires higher temperatures, such as nylon, the carriage may deform after extended periods of higher temperature extrusion. If you want to print with higher temperature filament, you will need to replace the stock carriage with one made from a material that can withstand higher temperatures. Carl Raffle offers a host of aluminum upgrades for MakerBot printers, including a replacement X-carriage (see the upcoming vendor spotlight sidebar).

Carl calls his upgrade the AluCarriage. It is a single CNC milled piece of aluminum that is a direct replacement for the stock unit. Like all of Carl's products, the AluCarriage is of the highest quality, with an extreme attention to detail. I have several of these. Besides being a perfect fit and solution for higher temperature extrusion, it is a work of art. Carl offers the AluCarriage in a variety of colors. I chose the red option and I must say it looks really good installed.

Better still, the AluCarriage is available for both single and dual extruder models. That is, you can buy one for your MakerBot Replicator 1 Single, Replicator 1 Dual, Replicator 2, or Replicator 2X. Figure 11-39 shows the dual carriage that fits the Replicator 1 Dual and Replicator 2X.

---

[13]I've encountered some who have never changed the Kapton tape.

Figure 11-39. *AluCarriage (courtesy of Carl Raffle)*

Notice the bolt in the background. It has a special clamping aid at the top (3D printed, of course) to aid in securing the stepper motor and hot-end wiring.

The upgrade comes with all the needed parts (e.g., bolts). You will need some small amount of Loctite or similar thread-based adhesive for the small setscrews that hold the bearings in place. Otherwise, the normal tools that come with your printer will suffice for the install. A complete set of instructions are available on the product web site (http://shop.raffle.ch/AluCarriage_InstallationGuide_v2.pdf).

Installation requires removing the stepper motors and hot ends, as well as disconnecting the wiring from the existing top plate. To remove the hot ends, you need only remove the heater block that mounts to the stock carriage using two bolts—one on each side. Again, photos are included in the documentation to help you with each step.

Once the extruders have been disassembled, you then loosen the X-axis belt by loosening the bolts on the X-axis stepper motor and moving it toward the center of the printer. Next, you disconnect the X-axis belt clamp and then pry the stock unit off the bearings. The new carriage is then placed on the bearings and the setscrews are installed to secure the bearings.

Resist the temptation to tighten the setscrews beyond the point where the bearing is seated. This takes surprisingly little torque. Use Loctite to hold the setscrews in place. The best way to test the tension on the bearings is to move the carriage back and forth. It should move freely with very little friction. If it binds, the set screws are either too tight or the bearing is not seated properly (see the underside of the AluCarriage—there is an inset for each bearing).

Once the carriage is mounted on the bearings, you use the provided clamp with a bolt to secure the X-axis belt. Finally, reassemble the extruder and use the new mounting point for the wiring. You will need to level your print bed because the AluCarriage is slightly shorter than the stock carriage.

■ **Tip**   For the Replicator 1 Dual, you may need to omit one of the long bolts for securing the top plate (the part where the PTFE tubes attach). This is because the AluCarriage has only one position for the new retention bolt.

It is possible that you may need to move the Z-axis endstop if the distance needed to raise the print bed is more than the adjusters can handle. That is, you loosen the adjusters to the point where they turn freely and there is no tension from the springs. You need a certain amount of tension to keep the adjusters from coming loose. If this is the case, you can loosen the bolts for the Z-axis endstop (located in the center of the back plate about 4 inches down from the top) and move the endstop up. Move it up[14] only one millimeter, and then tighten all bed adjusters and check the Z-height by homing all axes. If the print bed is still too low, move the endstop another millimeter and check it again. Keep doing this until the nozzle is within 2mm to 3mm of the print bed with the adjusters fully tightened. Once you reach this stage, level the print bed.

Aluminum Arm Upgrade: Replicator 1

There has been quite a lot said about the stock Z-axis arms in the MakerBot Replicator 1, 2, and 2X. Like the X-carriage, they are injection-molded. However, since the arms are designed with a 90-degree (or thereabouts) bend, the combination of the material, length, prolonged use (especially with a heated print bed) and rapid movements of the printer can induce a slight sag—and worse, vibration harmonics that can affect print quality.

Fortunately, there is a solution for the problem. BC Technologies Solutions offers aluminum bed arms that are CNC milled from aluminum. They are a direct replacement for the stock arms and come with all the hardware needed. You can see the aluminum arms in Figure 11-30. A more detailed photo of the arms is shown in Figure 11-40.

Figure 11-40. *Aluminum bed arms for Replicator 1 (courtesy of BC Technologies Solutions)*

Extensive, easy-to-follow installation instructions are included with the upgrade. BC Technologies also installs the new bearings, so you don't have to do that either—but you may need to add the bearing retainers. You also don't need any additional tools. The tools that came with your printer will suffice.

The tricky part of the installation requires turning the printer on its side to remove the cover for the electronics. This isn't difficult, but will require you to secure all loose attachments and accessories (spools, spool holders, glass plates, etc.). You will also need to remove the heated print bed.

The remaining disassembly steps include removing the brass nut for the Z axis, smooth rod covers, and the smooth rods themselves. The process isn't trivial, but you should be able to accomplish it with little consternation. I recommend setting aside about two hours to complete the installation. Once assembled, you will need to level your print bed.

---

[14]Moving the endstop up moves the print bed toward the nozzle when homed. Moving the endstop down moves the print bed away from the nozzle when homed.

The aluminum arm upgrade is a major upgrade, and the price reflects the high-quality machinery that goes into each part. I think the price is reasonable given this and the simple fact that it completely solves the problems with the stock arms. In fact, I think this should be the number-one upgrade for all MakerBot Replicator 1, 2, and 2X printers.

ALTERNATIVE ARM UPGRADES

If the cost and difficulty of replacing the Z-axis arms are too much, there are two other solutions that you may want to consider. Home Zillions offers an aluminum brace that attaches to the stock arms. You can find these on most online auction sites. Performance 3D (p3-d.com) offers a similar solution that is better than the Home Zillions option. It also mounts over the top of the existing arms. The following photo shows the stiffeners mounted on a Replicator 2, but they fit the Replicator 1 as well.

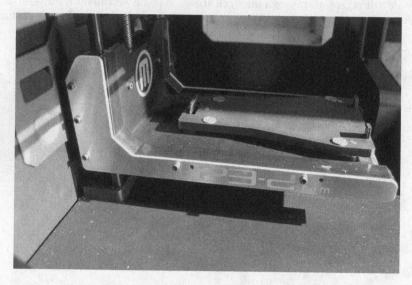

You can purchase the Performance 3D Arm Stiffeners at p3-d.com/aluminum-arm-stiffeners.html.

Enclosure

The final bit that you need to make the Replicator 1 Dual equivalent to the Replicator 2X is an enclosure. The Replicator 2X comes with a hood and windows for the left, right, and front sides. Adding an enclosure to the Replicator 1 Dual not only gives it the same feature available standard on the Replicator 2X, it also helps prevent lifting and similar problems from drafts or unstable ambient temperature around the build area. You can see this upgrade in Figure 11-34.

I list this upgrade last because it requires that you mark, cut, and drill acrylic. If you do not have experience with cutting and forming this material, the build of these upgrades could be a challenge. If you do not feel comfortable cutting acrylic, I recommend asking a friend to help you, or to look online for a set already cut. I have seen several vendors selling complete kits of acrylic. Some are similar to those shown here, but all accomplish the same goals. Unfortunately, I don't see these very often, so you should check online auctions and similar sites regularly.

The hood assembly isn't difficult once the parts are cut and drilled. Printing the supporting parts for the hood can take a few hours (about six to ten, depending on your print speed) but assembling the hood and fitting it is straightforward.

The windows pose a similar challenge for cutting them out. I chose to use the front window from the hood kit and the side windows from the hinged version. In this case, I had to cut two windows from thinner acrylic sheets. The hinges and latches are easy and quick to print, and assembly is easy. I recommend using a small dab of super glue to hold the hinges and latch to the acrylic.

Once the enclosure is complete, you should notice an immediate improvement in several areas. First and foremost, temperature control should be more even, the odor from printing with ABS will be somewhat reduced, and you may see some increase in print quality for larger parts or parts with thin protrusions. For all of these reasons, a full enclosure is a must for a Replicator 1 Dual.

MakerBot Replicator 2 (and 2X)

The release of the MakerBot Replicator 2 (and 2X) printers was a milestone event for professional-grade 3D printers. These models have significant upgrades over the Replicator 1, including a more rigid steel frame, an upgraded print bed system, and a host of smaller changes that, together, make the Replicator 2 a must-have upgrade for owners of the Replicator 1 and anyone who wants a better class of printer. The Replicator 2 is the fourth generation of MakerBot printers.

I have a MakerBot Replicator 2 that I have modified extensively. Figure 11-41 shows my own Replicator 2. No, it isn't a Replicator 2X! It's a Replicator 2 with a full enclosure.

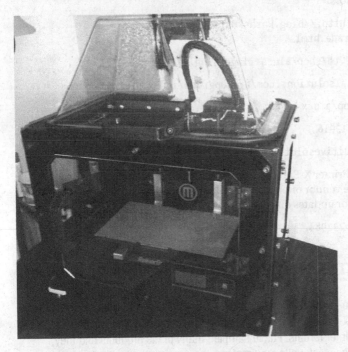

Figure 11-41. Heavily modified MakerBot Replicator 2

Even though MakerBot has since released the fifth-generation printer, which marks yet another step up in sophistication and capability, the Replicator 2 is still a very viable platform for 3D printing. If you are looking for a bit of a price break, you can find many used MakerBot Replicator 2 printers, some with very little hours, on online auction sites. In fact, the price break is so good that you can add a number of upgrades to the Replicator 2 to achieve even better print quality than the newest models—at a discount. Let's see how we can save some money and improve the Replicator 2 at the same time.

On the other hand, if you really want the newest features, such as live video of your build and network printing capability, you may want to invest in the fifth-generation model. Frankly, I've found that these features are still a bit of a novelty (well, maybe not the network connectivity). But if you want these features, you should consider the latest offering from MakerBot.

However, let's say you're like me and those newest gee-whiz features are not tipping the scales of your buying power. The following describes a number of key upgrades you will want to consider if you want to improve your MakerBot Replicator 2 instead of buying the latest model.

■ **Note**   With the exception of the extruder and enclosure upgrades, all of these will fit the Replicator 2 and 2X.

The upgrades for the printer shown are extensive for this model. Indeed, I've taken this printer quite far down the upgrade path. I've upgraded just about everything except the heater block. But there is an upgrade for that too (`http://shop.raffle.ch/shop/hot_end/`). Since there are so many upgrades, I will highlight a few of the more interesting ones, and then discuss each of the must-have upgrades in the following sections in order of installation complexity. Figure 11-41 shows a close-up view of most of the upgrades. I will refer to this figure in the following sections.

- *Upgraded print bed*: Various online vendors.

- *MakerBot Replicator 2 extruder upgrade*: `http://blog.karaskustoms.com/2013/06/makerbot-replicator-2-extruder-upgrade.html`.

- *AluCarriage Single*: `http://shop.raffle.ch/shop/alucarriage-single/`.

- *Aluminum arm upgrade*: `bctechnologicalsolutions.com/arm-upgrade/index.html`.

- *Alu-X-ends*: `http://shop.raffle.ch/shop/alu-x-ends/`.

- *Spool holder*: `thingiverse.com/thing:119016`.

- *Enclosure*: (hood and panels) `http://additivesolutionsllc.com/?cat=3`.

- *X-axis bearing idler*: Search eBay for "3d Printer X-End Idler Kit" and the seller "almws6". You may have to check frequently because the vendor often has limited quantities for sale. Contact the vendor via eBay's messaging system for updates on availability.

- *Adjustable feet*: `thingiverse.com/thing:232984`.

VENDOR SPOTLIGHT: CARL RAFFLE

Carl Raffle (`http://shop.raffle.ch/`) sells custom-made CNC milled upgrades for the MakerBot line of printers (Replicator 1, 2 and 2X). Carl offers new carriages, X-axis ends, heater blocks, and much more. You will find references to his products on many of the online printer forums. I have sampled many of his products and they are truly high quality. Not only are they superior to the stock units they replace, they are aesthetically pleasing. That is, they appear as jewels in your MakerBot crown. Thus, if you are looking for high-quality upgrades for your MakerBot printer, go to Carl's web site and order them. He offers shipping to most of the known world at reasonable prices and surprisingly fast transit times (depending on your location). You will not be disappointed.

One of the most interesting upgrades available for the MakerBot Replicator 2/2X are replacement X-ends. Carl Raffle offers a set of CNC milled aluminum X-ends in a variety of colors (`http://shop.raffle.ch/shop/alu-x-ends/`). Figure 11-42 shows a close-up view of the X-ends installed.

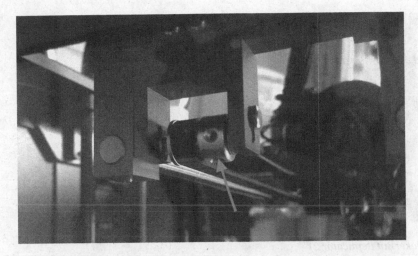

Figure 11-42. Alu-X-ends (MakerBot Replicator 2)

These pieces look great and work better than the stock units. However, the added benefit isn't as dramatic as an extruder or bed arms upgrade. These units will reduce ringing of the X-ends. That is, a minor harmonic effect from the X-ends flexing slightly when the X-carriage changes directions. Granted, the improvement is slight, but if you are seeking perfection with your MakerBot Replicator 2/2X, you should consider this upgrade.

Also shown in the figure is a replacement X-end idler pulley with a small bearing installed. This upgrade will eliminate the need to lubricate the X-end idler pulley. If you use your printer enough to require performing preventative maintenance often, you may want to consider this upgrade. You can find these on popular online auction sites.

Now that we have seen a couple of the more interesting and exotic upgrades, the following describe those that I feel are essential and must-have for owners of the MakerBot Replicator 2 and 2X.

Upgraded Print Bed

The MakerBot Replicator 2 came standard with an acrylic build plate. While the build plate is rather thick and looks cool with the LED lighting, many owners have reported issues with the acrylic plate. Some have reported their build plates are not completely flat. Others have reported that the acrylic plate can sag over time.

The most extreme cases of nonflat build plates are those with concave or convex areas. Needless to say, this condition would make leveling the print bed problematic. That is, you may be able to get the plate close to level, but the convex and concave areas will likely have a compressed first layer (convex) and lifting (concave) problems. Reports of build plate warping are less frequent, but when it does occur, similar issues with leveling the print bed, first-layer compression, and lifting may occur.

Fortunately, there is a very easy fix for this problem. Replacement print beds are available for the MakerBot Replicator 2. Most are glass. There are several variants out there ranging from normal, inexpensive glass that is close to flat (but not likely) but very heavy (much more than the stock plate), to those that use higher-quality glass that is very flat.

However, there is also a plate made from aluminum that I prefer over glass. The eBay vendor cre8it offers a replacement print bed made from aircraft-grade aluminum that is machined to be extremely flat.[15] The aluminum plate is a direct replacement for the acrylic plate. So installation is trivial—just remove the old plate and insert the new one! Figure 11-43 shows the build plate.

---

[15]There is some variance, but the measurement is insignificant. I measured a mere 0.0025mm difference on mine.

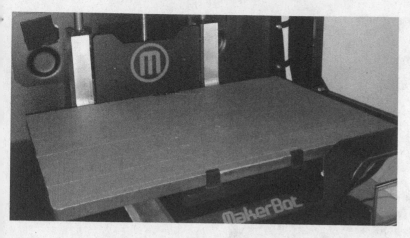

Figure 11-43. Aluminum build plate (MakerBot Replicator 2)

The plates are available in two forms: a solid plate that you can use both sides for printing and a lightened version that has had excess material milled away on one side. The lighter version is considerably lighter, so if you have a weak Z-axis stepper motor or you notice some creep (down) on your Z axis, you may want the lighter version. Some owners have reported that this problem is much worse with the heavier glass replacement. The plates come finished in black with a coating that works well with blue painter's tape.

ALTERNATIVE BUILD PLATES

One example of a glass print bed that is very flat and a good alternative to the aluminum plate is made by Performance 3-d (p3-d.com). This plate is made from thinner, higher-quality glass that uses an adapter to clip onto the stock build plate mount. I tested this plate and found it equivalent in weight, durability, and usability to the aluminum plate. The following figure shows the build plate (courtesy of p3-d.com).

Notice that the glass sits on an adapter. There are two notches to help you align the glass with the adapter. If you are looking for a replacement print bed, and you either prefer glass or want a slightly less expensive option, check out Performance 3-d's web site.

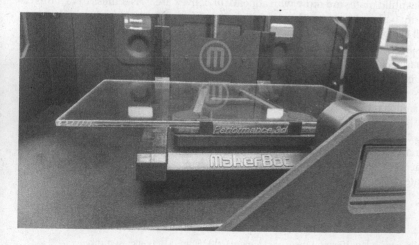

It should be noted that you will find other excellent products for the MakerBot Replicator printers on the MakerBot web site. I have used their low-friction nozzles with great success, and their arm stiffeners are the beefiest and stiffest of the bolt-on solutions.

Whether you like the aluminum plate or a high-quality glass plate, if your stock build plate is not flat, you owe yourself to replace it with one of these alternatives. It won't solve all of your print problems, but it will make your printer much more consistent and easier to set up.

Enclosure

Aside from the dual extruders and the heated build plate (and upgraded power supply), the biggest difference between the MakerBot Replicator 2 and 2X is the enclosure for the Replicator 2X. The Replicator 2 does not come with an enclosure. However, it can benefit greatly from having one.

In fact, my experiments with an enclosure for the Replicator 2 have shown improved lifting control, better adhesion overall, and less sagging for wider bridging. Not to mention I can now use a house fan or place my printer near an HVAC vent without worry of the cooling effects of the air currents. So how do you add an enclosure to the Replicator 2?

You could call MakerBot and order the stock panels and hood from a Replicator 2X. The nice people at MakerBot will happily sell you such parts, but they will be expensive and you may have to request a service ticket to get them. I've ordered frame and panel parts from MakerBot myself. They are very helpful. If you decide to go this route, I recommend stating your intentions upfront. Don't expect to be able to click a link on the web site to order the parts. These are not considered wear or maintenance parts, so you will have to special order them.

However, there is an excellent alternative. You can purchase a set of replacement panels complete with clear windows and a door, as well as a hinged, removable hood from Additive Solutions (http://additivesolutionsllc.com). These are often sold on eBay. Just search for "MakerBot Replicator 2 Panels" or "MakerBot Replicator 2 Hood". The enclosure is so good that I'd say it is better than the stock Replicator 2X enclosure because the door on the front opens to the right (easier to use), and the hood lifts effortlessly and can be removed without tools or removing anything else—it just clips to the frame. The hood is well made and has plenty of room for the filament tube and wire loop. You can see the enclosure and hood in Figure 11-41.

The panels are acrylic and come in a variety of colors. I choose the black panels, but I think the blue and yellow look pretty sharp too (eye of the beholder, of course). The hood is a single piece of Vivak formed to fit on top of the printer. Figure 11-44 shows a better view of the panels.

Figure 11-44. Acrylic panels for the MakerBot Replicator 2 (courtesy of Additive Solutions)

Installation of the panels requires removing the original left, right, and front panels. You then assemble the panels using the instructions included with your order. All of the panels come with protective film, so the longest step in the process is removing the film.

The side panels have four bolts to secure the windows. It is best to thread the bolts so that the heads (hex) are on the inside. This avoids any possibility of snagging in the X-carriage wiring if you used one of the zip-tie solutions to fix the stress point.[16] The front panel requires assembling the door with a handle, and mounting a magnet on the panel and door. The magnet is held in place with instant glue. My advice is to use that stuff sparingly.

The hood takes a bit longer because you have to print the hinge and handle mount. This can take several hours, so if you planned on buying the hood and popping it on when it arrives, you may want to start printing the parts for the hood while you are waiting for delivery. I printed the parts myself using medium resolution, but I think a lower resolution—such as a 0.3mm layer height and faster (115mm) print speeds—would work better. There is no need to make a museum-quality piece because the hinge parts are very large and you really can't see them (they mount to the back of the printer).

Once the parts are printed, you have one more step that requires a bit more skill. You have to drill the holes for the handle mount and hinge. I recommend assembling the hinge and clipping it in place, and then placing the hood over the printer and pressing the hinge to the hood. Use a permanent marker to mark the location of the holes for the hinge. Then remove the hood and drill the holes. Use a drill bit slightly larger than 3mm to give you a bit of room to fine-tune the position. Next, you can use some blue painter's tape to tape the handle mount to the hood and mark the holes accordingly. Drill those out with a bit large enough for the bolts included in the kit.

Installation will take some time and extra effort if you opt for the hood. The results will be readily apparent once you start printing larger objects. You should notice an improvement almost right away. Despite the extra effort, I feel this upgrade is an absolute must for any MakerBot Replicator 2 owner.

---

[16]Can you guess how I know this?

AluCarriage Single

The X-carriage upgrade is the same for the Replicator 2 as it is for the Replicator 1, except that you will order a single extruder carriage instead of the dual. See the preceding "AluCarriage Dual" section for a detailed description of this upgrade. Figure 11-45 shows the AluCarriage Single.

Figure 11-45. AluCarriage Single (courtesy of Carl Raffle)

■ **Note**   If you are upgrading your Replicator 2X, you will be installing the same dual carriage for a Replicator 1 Dual.

Recall that this upgrade permits you to print with higher temperature filament without worry about the carriage deforming from the higher prolonged heat. Installation requires taking the extruder apart and removing the stepper motor, fans, heat sink, and heater bar. You will need to loosen the X-axis stepper motor so that you can unclamp the X-axis belt.

Extruder Upgrade

The extruder upgrade is the same for the Replicator 2 as it is for the Replicator 1, except you only need one set. Of course, if you are upgrading the Replicator 2X, you can use the same set as the Replicator 1 Dual. See the earlier "MakerBot Replicator Extruder Upgrade / Filament Drive" section for a detailed description of this upgrade.

Recall that this upgrade provides improved filament extrusion with fewer failures and more reliable parts. Installation requires unloading the filament and then removing the stepper motor, fan, and heat sink. Once you remove the old extruder parts (e.g., the Delrin plunger mechanism), you can install the new parts and reassemble it. The total upgrade time should be about an hour.

Aluminum Arm Upgrade: Replicator 2/2X

Like the extruder upgrade, the aluminum arm upgrade is the same as that for the Replicator 1. However, the arms are slightly different, so make sure that you order the correct parts. See the "Aluminum Arm Upgrade: Replicator 1" section for a detailed description of this upgrade.

Recall that the arms will help reduce vibration and will not sag like the stock arms. Installation on the Replicator 2/2X takes a bit longer because unlike the Replicator 1, the smooth rods on the Replicator 2/2X are captured in a subassembly that must be removed as a unit. This will take you a bit longer than a similar upgrade for the Replicator 1. However, the instructions included with the upgrade are excellent and walk you through every step. Give yourself about three to four hours to complete the upgrade. Don't forget to level your print bed when you're done reassembling.

Summary

Owning a 3D printer can be a lot of fun. Whether you print gifts, solutions for your home or auto, or just enjoy tinkering with designs, a good 3D printer won't let you down. However, if you want to take the printer a bit further or you want to save some money by adding features to your current printer, upgrading can also be a lot of fun.

This chapter covered the types of upgrades available, as well as suggestions for optimizing your upgrade experience. I also presented descriptions of several upgrades for several popular printer models. Even if your printer wasn't listed, reading through the descriptions will help you see what is possible for your own printer.

The next chapter begins the final part of this book. The next two chapters are designed to provide you with the information you need to take your 3D printing experience beyond the stage of printing the test objects and canned objects you've downloaded from the Internet.[17]

Thus, the next chapter begins the journey with a look at how to create simple objects, combine several existing objects, and even how to finish your object by applying several techniques for sanding, painting, and improving your prints.

---

[17]Even though I design many of my own objects, I never stop looking for things to print. If someone else has designed something I need (and it is licensed appropriately), I use it!

PART 4

■ ■ ■

Mastering Your Craft

Now that you have become the master of your 3D printer, it is time to take your skills to the people. That is, to contribute your knowledge to the community. This section presents techniques on creating your own objects with OpenSCAD, creating new objects from existing objects, finishing your objects to improve their aesthetic appeal, and even how to contribute your new designs for others to use. Finally, examples of solutions to real-world problems are presented to give you fuel for sparking your own creativity.

CHAPTER 12

■ ■ ■

Working with Objects

Seeing your 3D printer generate objects is really cool. When you create solutions and things you can use every day, the experience is even greater. However, there is more to 3D printing than just downloading and printing things. Indeed, most things on Thingiverse can be downloaded and printed with no changes. However, sometimes you need the same thing, only with a hole in a different place or maybe a bit longer or wider.

Also, most things you print can be used with little or no work, but some things will require trimming, reaming out holes, and so forth. If you are creating things for decoration or personal wear, you may want the surface to be perfectly smooth or at least without the telltale layering effect. You may even want to change the color of your thing. That is, you may not have the right color filament, or the color of the filament just isn't the right shade.

I address all of these topics in this chapter. I begin with a short tutorial on how to create your own objects (it's really easy), I next discuss how to make modifications to existing objects (sometimes called a *mashup*) and joining multipart objects, and then I discuss various techniques for completing your object by applying finishing touches.

Creating Objects

If you haven't used Thingiverse by now, you really should give it a try. You will find many thousands of things that you can download and print. If you have used Thingiverse or a similar web site, chances are you have already printed a number of objects that others have created. However, sometimes the right thing just isn't out there on Thingiverse. Perhaps you can find something similar, but it just isn't quite right—maybe it's too long or the bore holes are the wrong size or in the wrong place.

Wouldn't it be great if you could create your own object or modify objects uploaded by others? The short answer is you can! But it will depend on what CAD software was used to create the object and the format of the object file. If you have experience with the CAD that was used to create the object, that's great and you can do whatever you want to make the object your own.

However, if you have little or no experience with the specific CAD software, what can you do? Fortunately, you are not alone and there is a solution. Indeed, a lot of enthusiasts don't have extensive knowledge in CAD software and yet they have created a lot of objects on Thingiverse. How did they do it? They used a much simpler, easier-to-use object creation software called OpenSCAD (openscad.org).

Recall from an earlier chapter that OpenSCAD uses a programming-like environment to generate a script that can be compiled to render the object. But don't let the programming element discourage you. You don't have to have an advanced degree in computational sciences to learn how to use OpenSCAD.[1] In fact, all you need to create objects in OpenSCAD is the ability to envision an object as a step-wise build. That is, you will be using commands (shape primitives and controls) to generate an object from several other parts.

---

[1]You won't have to count in hexadecimals, work with memory, or any such advanced topic. You need only a step-wise mindset to solving problems. Read on.

Let's dive into a short tutorial on OpenSCAD. The following won't give you magical powers, but it will get you everything you need to start making your own objects in OpenSCAD. I present the most basic things that you need to know to get started with OpenSCAD. I encourage you to download OpenSCAD (`openscad.org/downloads.html`) and experiment with the code presented in the tutorial.

OpenSCAD Tutorial

OpenSCAD is an amazing tool for those of us who want to create our own objects, but don't have the time to master a complex CAD application. OpenSCAD uses a relatively small number of commands (called *statements*) that you can use to build an object in a programmatic way. The files you create therefore are code files (plain text) that are very small compared to most CAD application binary object files. Indeed, I have seen some files from popular CAD applications that were quite large. Perhaps the best quality of OpenSCAD is that it is open source and supported by a growing community of enthusiasts.

You may be surprised by the number of objects that are available on Thingiverse as OpenSCAD files. I did a quick query and found over 3,000 things that mention `.scad`[2]—and that's just searching on the title! So there are plenty of examples out there. We typically save OpenSCAD (or simply SCAD) files with the extension `.scad`.

Before jumping in, let's consider one of the key concepts you must master to get the most out of OpenSCAD: coordinates.

Coordinates

One of the biggest challenges to coding your own objects is keeping a sense of the orientation of the object in the coordinate system. We are working in three-dimensions. The OpenSCAD-rendered object screen has a diagram or key to show you the orientation of the axes. Figure 12-1 shows the key.

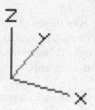

Figure 12-1. Coordinate key in OpenSCAD

When you render (compile) your object (code), you will see the result on the right side of the OpenSCAD dialog. The default orientation has the X axis left-to-right, the Y axis front-to-back, and the Z axis up-and-down. You can zoom and rotate the object to see all sides. The key for the axes moves with the object, so you can always keep the perspective.

However, sometimes it can be confusing as to which parameter you want to change or set in some of the code statements. Fortunately, most statements that use coordinates as parameters list them by X, Y, and Z. As long as you keep that in mind, you can provide the right parameters. If you make a mistake, it will be rather obvious when you compile the code. For example, if you wanted an object 20mm wide (on the X axis), 10mm long (on the Y axis), and 40mm high but reversed the X and Y parameters, you would see the object is 10mm wide and 20mm long instead.

---

[2]Including a d20. Got crit?

■ Note   All measurements in OpenSCAD are unitless, but when you export the STL, the 3D software will interpret the units as millimeters.

Since the result is a compilation of the code, all you need to do is fix the parameters and recompile. I encourage you to experiment with the cube() statement to see how the axes are oriented. Recall the cube() statement is one of several primitive solid statements that take the coordinates as a list specified by square brackets. The following shows the correct code for the example.

```
cube([20,10,40]);
```

I have already shown you a very simple code file for creating a simple shape. The following shows another small example that creates a small object made from two parts. Figure 12-2 shows the OpenSCAD environment with the code pane on the left, an object view on the right, and a feedback area in the lower right.

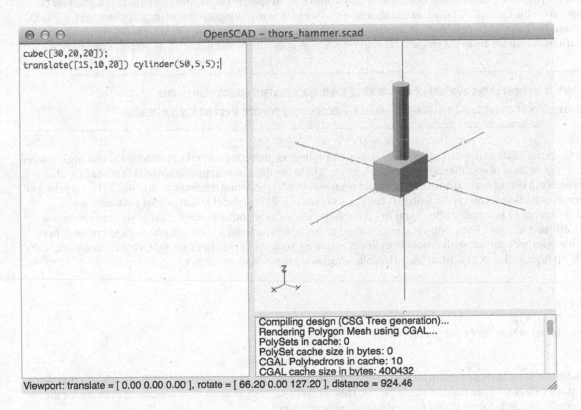

Figure 12-2. *Object in OpenSCAD*

The object is a hammer in its most basic design—a large block for the head and a tall cylinder for the shaft. Notice the code. Here I used a cube object to create the head and a cylinder for the shaft (or handle). The one command that may seem strange is the translate() statement. It is one of several transformation statements that allow you to change the origin or starting point for the object. The default starting point is the center (0,0,0) position. If I had not used the translate() statement, the shaft would have been placed in the wrong location.

The use of translate() also shows how you can combine graphic operations with shape statements. That is, the translation is executed for the next statement (or shape). Notice that the cylinder() statement, which is another primitive solid statement, that takes three parameters. In order, they are height, radius of the base, and radius of the top. If you're thinking, hey, that means I can create a cone, you're right, you can.

One feature that is not commonly used is the ability to specify the parameters by name. For example, I could have used the following to code the cylinder for the shaft.

```
translate([15,10,20]) cylinder(r1=5,h=50,r2=5);
```

Notice that here I specified the parameters out of order. So long as you reference them by name, you can put the parameters in any order. If you do not reference them by name, you must put them in the order that is listed in the documentation.

Notice also that each statement is made up of one or more statements and must end (terminate) with a semicolon. There are statements that don't use a semicolon for a terminator, but those are things like code blocks and modules (as we will see later).

So how do you know which statements are available and how to specify the parameters? There is a good set of documentation on the OpenSCAD site that you should spend some time exploring (openscad.org/documentation.html). What I present here in this tutorial will get you going, but there is much more to OpenSCAD. That is, there are many more statements available from 2D shapes, 3D shapes, Boolean operations, and many other graphics operations.

■ **Tip** There is a cheat sheet available that lists all of the major standard coding statements (openscad.org/documentation.html#cheat-sheet). I recommend printing this and keep it nearby.

Aside from the basic geometric shapes like cubes and cylinders, there are several key statements you must master to achieve a higher level of sophistication for your objects. These are the Boolean operations difference() and union(), which are two of several constructive solid geometry (CSG) modeling statements. You would be surprised at the number of objects you can create with just cube(), cylinder(), difference(), and union() statements.

The difference() statement allows you to take a shape and subtract other shapes. That is, you can create one object and subtract another. For example, if you wanted to create an electronics standoff, you need to create a short tube, which is a larger cylinder with a smaller cylinder removed from the center. Let's say you want to create standoffs that are 10mm high and accept a 3mm bolt. The following code creates such an object.

```
m3_diameter = 3.75;
difference() {
  cylinder(10,4,4);
  cylinder(10,m3_diameter/2,m3_diameter/2);
}
```

OK, there are several things going on here. The first statement is an example of how to define variables that you can use to store values that are used in many places. Here I used a variable to store the diameter of the bore for the standoff. I made it slightly larger than I needed to give me some room.

The next statement is the difference() statement. Notice that we use a set of curly braces to define the body (or block) of the statement. The difference() works by generating the object listed first, and then subtracting the objects listed after that. That is, you can subtract multiple objects from another object. Think about a larger object with several holes for bolts or rods. You can use the difference() to draw the object, and then remove the holes (cylinders) in one pass (within the curly braces).

Recall that the cylinder() statement takes three parameters in the order of height, radius of the bottom, and radius of the top. In the second statement in the difference statement, I specify the same height but need to convert the diameter of the hole to radius, which is a simple division. Thus, you can specify mathematical formulas in place of the parameters. Cool, eh?

■ **Note** You can specify only two parameters for cylinder() if you specify the parameters r=N and d=N. In this case, r will be the radius value for both r1 and r2.

Now, to create the object, we compile the code. Click the Design ➤ Compile menu. After a very brief pause (more complex objects with many statements could take a while to compile, but it is usually very fast). Figure 12-3 shows the preceding code compiled. Once you have compiled this object, notice something in the drawing. The cylinders are very coarse. In fact, the center hole resembles a hexagon rather than a cylinder.

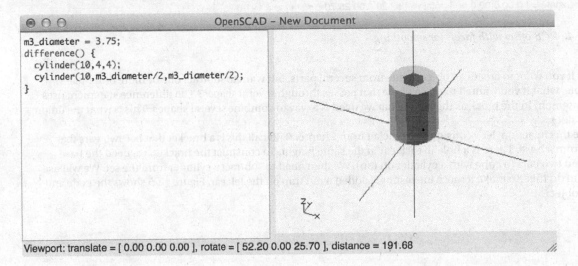

OpenSCAD – New Document

```
m3_diameter = 3.75;
difference() {
  cylinder(10,4,4);
  cylinder(10,m3_diameter/2,m3_diameter/2);
}
```

Viewport: translate = [0.00 0.00 0.00], rotate = [52.20 0.00 25.70], distance = 191.68

Figure 12-3. PCB offset

You can fix this with a special variable, $fn=n, which allows you to specify the number of facets (or fragments) used in rendering. You can add this to shapes to help smooth the shape. For example, if I add the variable as a parameter to the cylinder statements, the object generated is much smoother. I find a value of 32 or 64 makes for very smooth shapes.

You can also control the angle of the facet with $fa and the size of the face with $fs, which will let OpenSCAD decide the facets to use based on the size of the shape. See http://en.wikibooks.org/wiki/OpenSCAD_User_Manual/Other_Language_Features for more information about these special variables.

However, it should be noted that the more facets you specify, the longer the object will take to compile. This may not matter for small objects, but it may for larger objects. Figure 12-4 shows the updated code and compiled object. Notice that the hole is now a cylinder as expected.

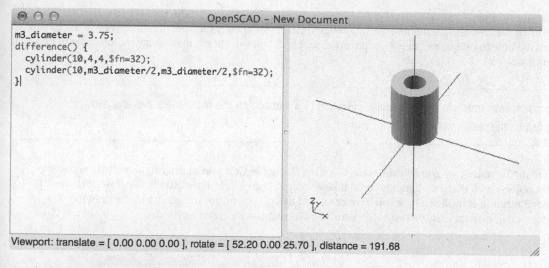

```
m3_diameter = 3.75;
difference() {
  cylinder(10,4,4,$fn=32);
  cylinder(10,m3_diameter/2,m3_diameter/2,$fn=32);
}|
```

Viewport: translate = [0.00 0.00 0.00], rotate = [52.20 0.00 25.70], distance = 191.68

Figure 12-4. *PCB offset with facets for smoothing*

What if you want to create an object made from several parts, but want to subtract one or more other parts? For example, what if you wanted to place a hole that passes through several shapes? The difference statement uses the first statement in the block as the base. What we need is a way to combine several shapes. This is what the union statement does.

To see this in action, let's consider the bracket from Chapter 9. Recall this is a bracket that has two ears that protrude from a base. There is a hole in each ear at the same height. To construct the bracket, we need the base (a cube) and two ears (a cube with a cylinder on top). We then need to subtract a cylinder from the set. We will use the union to do this. To make it more interesting, I added a nut trap on the left ear. Figure 12-5 shows the code and compiled object.

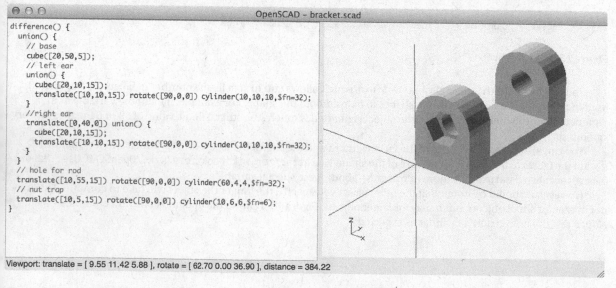

```
difference() {
  union() {
    // base
    cube([20,50,5]);
    // left ear
    union() {
      cube([20,10,15]);
      translate([10,10,15]) rotate([90,0,0]) cylinder(10,10,10,$fn=32);
    }
    //right ear
    translate([0,40,0]) union() {
      cube([20,10,15]);
      translate([10,10,15]) rotate([90,0,0]) cylinder(10,10,10,$fn=32);
    }
  }
  // hole for rod
  translate([10,55,15]) rotate([90,0,0]) cylinder(60,4,4,$fn=32);
  // nut trap
  translate([10,5,15]) rotate([90,0,0]) cylinder(10,6,6,$fn=6);
}
```

Viewport: translate = [9.55 11.42 5.88], rotate = [62.70 0.00 36.90], distance = 384.22

Figure 12-5. *Complex object: bracket*

■ **Note** The hole and nut trap are not to scale. They are exaggerated (larger) to show detail.

The most interesting part of this example to me is the use of only two shapes to create this part: the cube and cylinder. Even if you never master any other shapes, these two can be used to create almost any part.

However, this example is more complex than the previous examples. But part of that was elective on my part. Notice the use of the union() statement. I added these to each ear to demonstrate how you can nest statements. That is, put a statement inside the operational segment of another.

Take a look at the code again. Notice the statements that start with two slashes (//). These are comment statements. You should use these to denote certain important sections of code. You can also make a block of comments (multiple lines) placed inside /* and */. As you can see in the example, I use comments to identify the parts of the object. This makes it a lot easier to find the part should you ever want to modify it. For example, if you wanted the hole for the rod to be larger, it would be easy to locate if it were identified.

■ **Tip** Always add comments to your code so that others will know what each part is. Sometimes this isn't so obvious. Even a short comment is better than none.

I used another new statement in the example. This is one of those key items you should learn to use. Often it is the case that you need to reorient a part. For example, you want to have a cylinder that goes along the Y axis rather than the Z axis. The rotate() statement is another transformation statement that allows you to rotate any statement (shape) in any direction. You specify a list of the coordinates (X,Y,Z). In this example, I wanted the mounting rod to travel along the Y axis. Thus, I rotated the cylinder 90 degrees on the X axis with rotate([90,0,0]). Think of it as "rotate around" rather than on the axis. Thus, rotating around the X axis means the cylinder will be horizontal and parallel with the Y axis. The rotate() statement works the same way as the translate() statement—it affects the next statement in the file and only the next statement.

The difference statement is a CSG modeling statement used to remove the cylinder that makes up the hole for the rod as well as the nut trap. If you look at the translate statement for the hole, you will see that I made the origin 5mm longer and the cylinder itself 10mm longer so that the cylinder removed passes through both ears. Sometimes if you use the difference statement and align the origin of the part that is being subtracted (removed), OpenSCAD may show an incomplete hole. Moving the origin a bit further out and making the cylinder longer avoids this.

Notice how I created the nut trap. I used the cylinder() statement but specified the $fn variable with a value of 6. This creates a perfect hexagon for holding a nut. Since this part is also subtracted from the union of the base and ears, it appears as removed in the compiled image. Recall the difference statement removes parts listed after the first statement, and in this case I use a union for the base and ears that effectively forms a single statement.

Finally, notice also the indentation for the statements. You should always use indentation to help readability. I like to use two spaces, but you can use tabs if you prefer. Just don't forget to use indentation. This a pet peeve for many programmers, and rather annoying when encountered in the community. To me, not using indentation makes the code less appealing and a bit amateurish. We don't want that.

In the next section, I present another example, but this time it is something you can actually use or give away as a gift. If you haven't tried to print any of the previous examples, try this one. I will show you have to generate the .stl file so you can print it yourself. You will also see how to envision the object and how to construct it from several parts.

Example: Creating a Thread Spool

Now it is time to put what we have learned into practice. Let's create an object that can be used in the home. If you know anyone who sews, you can create this object and give it as a gift. We will be creating a thread spool. Much like the spool for filament, a thread spool allows you to coil thread for use in a sewing machine. Sometimes you need an extra spool to load some thread or move thread to another machine. Let's begin with a description of the part.

There are several characteristics of thread spools. First, they have a hole in the center for mounting on a rod on the sewing machine. Second, they have beveled edges, and third, there is a small slit on each side to hold the end of the thread.

So with this in mind, we need to build the spool with six cylinders. One on the top and bottom for the outer diameter of the spool, one on the inside of each that forms the bevel, and a center cylinder to form the body. Finally, we need a cylinder for the bore through the center. We also need a cube to make the slit. Listing 12-1 shows the code needed to make this object.

Listing 12-1. Code for Defining a Thread Spool

```
difference() {
  union() {
    // bottom
    cylinder(2,15,15,$fn=64);
    translate([0,0,2]) cylinder(2,15,12,$fn=64);
    // center
    translate([0,0,4]) cylinder(32,12,12,$fn=64);
    // top
    translate([0,0,36]) cylinder(2,12,15,$fn=64);
    translate([0,0,38]) cylinder(2,15,15,$fn=64);
  }
  // hole
  cylinder(40,3,3,$fn=64);
  // cut
  translate([12,0,0]) cube([3,0.25,40]);
}
```

Once again, I used only the basic cube, cylinder, translate, difference, and union statements to create the object. I also used the facet special variable so that the shape appears smooth. Recall you must compile the code before you can generate the `.stl` file by using the File ➤ Export ➤ Export as the STL menu option.

I assembled the code the same way I envisioned the finished object sliced into parts. I started at the bottom with a cylinder set to the maximum outer diameter (30mm), and then I placed a cylinder on top of that (via translate) with one side the same diameter and the topside smaller to make the depth of the spool (3mm). You can see this in the Listing 12-1 code on the first statement with a translate directive. This forms a short cone. I then added the center portion as a simple cylinder on top, followed by another cone and disc to complete the object. Lastly, I removed the center hole and a sliver from the outer beveled edge for the slit.

Do you notice something about this code? Let me phrase it this way: how tall is this thread spool? Can you tell? You'd have to add up the height of each part to find out.[3] Wouldn't it be a lot easier to read and discern the measurements if we used variables to hold the values? Furthermore, wouldn't it be easier to make another spool using the same code by changing a few variables? This is referred to as making the object *parametric* or providing parameters for making a range of objects with different sizes for key values. The best objects on Thingiverse provide parametric OpenSCAD code files.

---

[3] It's 2+2+36+2+2 = 40mm.

Make It Parametric: Enable Adaptation

If you want to make your object usable for a lot of people, or you want to be able to resize the object quickly without having to hunt around in the code and change all of the parameters individually (usually very tedious and often frustrating for code like that shown in Listing 12-1), you will want to use variables for any repeated value or values that can change to make different objects from the same code.

Let's take a look at the same code changed to use variables for all of the key values. Listing 12-2 shows the modified code. Here I have placed all of the commonly used variables at the top and assigned them values. Now it is easy to see how large this spool will be when compiled.

Listing 12-2. Parametric Code Using Variables

```
diameter=30;
height=40;
depth=3;
hole_radius=6;
radius = diameter/2;
center_height = height-8;
difference() {
  union() {
    // bottom
    cylinder(2,radius,radius,$fn=64);
    translate([0,0,2]) cylinder(2,radius,radius-depth,$fn=64);
    // center
    translate([0,0,4]) cylinder(center_height,radius-depth,radius-depth,$fn=64);
    // top
    translate([0,0,height-4]) cylinder(2,radius-depth,radius,$fn=64);
    translate([0,0,height-2]) cylinder(2,radius,radius,$fn=64);
  }
  // hole
  cylinder(height,hole_radius/2,hole_radius/2,$fn=64);
  // cut
  translate([(diameter/2)-depth,0,0]) cube([depth,0.25,height]);
}
```

This is much better, but there is another statement you can use to make it even easier to change. You can make the code a module (similar to making your own statement or shape). In this case, we use the module directive, give it a name, and then provide parameters. You "call" the module by specifying its name and providing values for the parameters—much like you do for other statements. Listing 12-3 shows the improved code.

Listing 12-3. Improved Parametric Code

```
module thread_spool(diameter=30,height=40,depth=3,hole_radius=3) {
  radius = diameter/2;
  center_height = height-8;
  difference() {
    union() {
      // bottom
      cylinder(2,radius,radius,$fn=64);
      translate([0,0,2]) cylinder(2,radius,radius-depth,$fn=64);
```

```
      // center
      translate([0,0,4]) cylinder(height-8,radius-depth,radius-depth,$fn=64);
      // top
      translate([0,0,height-4]) cylinder(2,radius-depth,radius,$fn=64);
      translate([0,0,height-2]) cylinder(2,radius,radius,$fn=64);
   }
   // hole
   cylinder(height,hole_radius,hole_radius,$fn=64);
   // cut
   translate([(diameter/2)-depth,0,0]) cube([depth,0.25,height]);
 }
}

thread_spool(30,40,3);
```

Notice here that I did not provide all of the values as parameters to the module. Rather, I specified only those that would likely be changed. Those variables listed inside the module statement are not visible outside of the module. Thus, if you create a second module, you cannot access these variables inside it. This is called *scope*. Suffice it to say, you just need to remember to make those variables you want to use anywhere at the top of the code.

Notice also that I called the module by specifying its name. In this way, you can create .scad files that provide modules for reuse. Indeed, most files that you download (sometimes called *libraries*) are made up of modules that you can reuse. To use the module, the file must reside in the same directory and you use the use statement to import the file (or specify the path if it is in a different directory), as shown.

```
use <thread_spool.scad>;
thread_spool(30,40,4);
```

The use statement requires a file name of the code file to open. You can then call the statements in that code file directly as shown. For example, the code file for the module is named thread_spool.scad. This is a very powerful mechanism that you can use to reuse others work.

Document Your Work

The example shown in the previous section is a good example of creating a parametric object. However, it lacks sufficient documentation. While it may be obvious from the name of the parameters what each is and how it is used, this isn't always going to be the case. Indeed, sometimes people use single letter names for their variables, or perhaps they use another language (Creole, Klingon, etc.).

To make the code fully usable and understandable by others, we place comments at the start of the file to describe the intended purpose of the object, as well as what each parameter does. You should also consider adding your contact information to help others contact you if they have questions. This not only helps to document who created the code and why, but it also gives others a chance to read about the code in plain language rather than trying to decipher the code itself. Listing 12-4 shows the fully documented and improved parametric code.

Listing 12-4. Completed Code for the Thread Spool

```
/*
  Module: thread_spool

  Description: This module creates a spool used for winding thread. The
  spool is constructed so that there are beveled sides that slope inward
  toward a center cylinder. The parameters include the following.
```

```
    diameter - the outer diameter of the spool.
    height - the outer height of the spool including the bevel edges.
    depth - depth of the bevel. Inner cylinder diameter = diameter - depthx2
    hole_radius - radius of center hole

    Date Created: 2014-07-27

    Created by: Charles Bell
*/
module thread_spool(diameter=30,height=40,depth=3,hole_radius=3) {
    radius = diameter/2;
    center_height = height-8;
    difference() {
      union() {
        // bottom
        cylinder(2,radius,radius,$fn=64);
        translate([0,0,2]) cylinder(2,radius,radius-depth,$fn=64);
        // center
        translate([0,0,4]) cylinder(height-8,radius-depth,radius-depth,$fn=64);
        // top
        translate([0,0,height-4]) cylinder(2,radius-depth,radius,$fn=64);
        translate([0,0,height-2]) cylinder(2,radius,radius,$fn=64);
      }
      // hole
      cylinder(height,hole_radius,hole_radius,$fn=64);
      // cut
      translate([(diameter/2)-depth,0,0]) cube([depth,0.25,height]);
    }
}

thread_spool(30,40,4);
```

Doesn't that make the code much nicer? You should always document your code in this manner. It never hurts and always makes the code look more professional.

ADDITIONAL TUTORIALS

If you want to learn more about OpenSCAD, go over to openscad.org/documentation.html or http://en.wikibooks.org/wiki/OpenSCAD_User_Manual and check out the numerous tutorial articles and videos. You will find many examples that can help you discover the specialized statements and techniques for creating more complex objects.

Modifying Objects

You may not always find the object you need on Thingiverse. In fact, you may find some that are close, but just aren't oriented correctly, or maybe some of the holes aren't in the right place, or it is missing a tab or some other portion of the part. Whatever the reason, most times you can augment the part. This is especially true if the author created the object in OpenSCAD (and uploaded the code). However, you can also modify objects from the .stl file. While a bit more limited in function, it is still a powerful way to modify objects to your needs. I will demonstrate both of these techniques in the following sections.

Modifying OpenSCAD Files

In the previous section, we saw how you can reuse OpenSCAD modules with the use statement. If you are fortunate enough to find a code file that has been constructed with modules, you can use those modules in your own code. That is, sometimes you find a code file that has multiple modules (which is not only permitted, but also encouraged). You can use these modules the same way—using the use statement and calling the module by name.

However, sometimes the code isn't exactly what you want or need, and therefore you have to modify it. If it has sufficient documentation, this can be very easy. Modifying the object is as simple as making the change to the code and recompiling. But since every object will be different, showing a specific example may not be helpful. Rather, I list several tips and suggestions for you to follow when modifying the code others have generated.

- *Check prerequisites*. Some use libraries or other source files. You may need to find these and download them if they are not bundled with the code you downloaded.

- *Mark your update*. If you modify a code file, use comments to preserve the original statements. I like to copy the statement before I modify it and then comment one of the lines. That is, placing the comment symbol (//) at the start of the line effectively disables that line of code. This allows me to return the code to its original state.

- *Resist the temptation to copy*. Making wholesale copies of modules should be avoided. It is best to make changes and comment them than making copies. If you make too many copies of a module, each with small changes, you can mistake one for another.

- *Contribute your modifications*. Whereas most objects are licensed in such a way as to allow you to modify at will, some require you to donate your changes to the owner. Even if there is no license that requires it, if you create an interesting derivation or improvement, you should share it so others can benefit.

The next section discusses a unique form of modification with OpenSCAD: using existing .stl files to create new objects.

Object Mashup

Let's say you want to make a part for your MakerBot Replicator 2 and let's say the part you want is a set of adjustable feet. There are several things on Thingiverse that are replacements for the stock feet, but (let's assume) there are none that are height adjustable.[4]

What we want is to use one of the existing stock feet replacements, but to add an adjuster so that we can make our MakerBot Replicator 2 sit on an unlevel/uneven surface. I created an object to do this. I started with the existing object (thingiverse.com/thing:219127), downloaded and imported it in OpenSCAD, and added my new part. You must also download the base object and place the file in the same directory as your code (Machine_feet_for_the_Replicator_2_and_2X.stl). Otherwise, the object will not be imported when you compile. Figure 12-6 shows the completed object compiled in OpenSCAD.

---

[4]The part in this example is thingiverse.com/thing:232984.

Figure 12-6. *Adjustable feet (MakerBot Replicator 2)*

Notice that I have the original foot augmented with a cube area and a small space near the bottom for a nut. The large cylinder to the left is a pad that I can use to attach to a bolt and thread through the nut in the new part. Sounds like magic, eh? Let's look at the code. Listing 12-5 shows the OpenSCAD code to create these objects.

Listing 12-5. MakerBot Replicator 2 Adjustable Feet

```
// This script creates an adjustable foot for the MakerBot Replicator 2 and 2X.
// It uses an m8 bolt and nut to form the foot and a mashup of another thing.
//
// Instructions:
//
// We're going to do a mashup of the new base and a replacement foot made
// by Creative Tools: http://www.thingiverse.com/thing:219127
//
// 1) Download and place the .stl file in the same directory as this file.
// 2) Compile, save, and print (4) sets
// 3) For each base, remove the interior cylinder with a hobby knife.
//     This prevents the need to use support material.
// 4) For each foot, press the bolt into the foot and either cement
//     in place or (better) heat the bolt and press it into the plastic and
//     fold over the small collar to hold it in place (easy when bolt is hot).
// 5) Assemble each adjuster by threading the foot into the base.
```

```
//  6) Carefully remove the feet from your Replicator 2 and press the new
//     feet into place and level the unit.
//
// Enjoy!

import("Machine_feet_for_the_Replicator_2_and_2X.stl");

module foot(shaft=8.6, nut_dia=15.2, nut_h=7.1) {
  difference() {
    union() {
      cylinder(6,25,25);
      cylinder(10,13,13);
      cylinder(12,(nut_dia/2)+1,(nut_dia/2)+1);
    }
    translate([0,0,3]) cylinder(nut_h+3,nut_dia/2,nut_dia/2,$fn=6);
  }
}

module adjustable_base(shaft=8.6, nut_dia=15.2, nut_h=7.1, nut_flat=13.2) {
  difference() {
    // base
    cube([20,20,20]);
    // shaft
    translate([10,10,-1]) cylinder(25,shaft/2,shaft/2);
    // nut trap
    translate([10,10,2]) cylinder(nut_h,nut_dia/2,nut_dia/2,$fn=6);
    translate([0,3.3,2]) cube([nut_flat,nut_flat,nut_h]);
    // bevel for mashup
    translate([20,-2.75,0]) rotate([0,0,45]) cube([4,4,25]);
  }
  // support (cut away)
  difference() {
    translate([10,10,2]) cylinder(nut_h,(shaft/2)+.25,(shaft/2)+.25);
    translate([10,10,-1]) cylinder(25,shaft/2,shaft/2);
  }
}

translate([2.5,22.5,0]) rotate([0,0,-90]) adjustable_base();
translate([0,-30,0]) foot();
```

The key to reusing an existing .stl file is the import statement. I imported the .stl file, and then built and oriented the part I wanted to add so that the parts overlap. When you compile and export the new .stl file, the parts will be one piece.

Notice also that I have a fully documented code file that explains the prerequisite (the original foot replacement), and instructions for using the new part. Take some time to read through this code and notice how I created two complex objects with only a small number of statements. Once again, you can create almost anything in OpenSCAD with very little in-depth knowledge and a very short learning curve.

Now that we have seen how to create objects, let's look at the other end of the process and discuss some ways we can make printed objects better.

Post-Print Finishing

Most things that you print will be usable with very little cleanup. More specifically, if it was designed for 3D printing, it should have been designed to eliminate or reduce the need for support, bridging, and other challenges. Most things on Thingiverse have this characteristic, but some do not. If it is not obvious in the description, ask the creator what settings you should use to print it.

If you printed with supports, a brim, or a raft, you may have some cleaning up to do, but most times it is simply cutting away the unwanted bits. However, you may not be satisfied with how the thing looks. That is, you may want a completely smooth surface for the vertical sides (rather than the layered look). You also may want a thing that is a slightly different color or even a thing made from several other things.

This section discusses techniques you can use to achieve a better-finished thing. I begin with some key preparation steps, and then discuss how to paint your thing and assemble an object from parts. I conclude the section with a look at a special technique for making the surface of ABS parts glossy and uniform.

Preparation Is Key

Ask anyone who has worked with paint, stains, and other finishes their secrets for a perfect finish and they will tell you that preparation is the number-one contributor to their success. They will also say it requires plenty of care, patience, and experience.

The process for finishing printed parts is very similar for that of wood and other materials. We begin with basic cleanup of the part—removing excess material, sanding, and applying any pretreatments and finishes to the surface. The following describes each of these in more detail as it applies to printed objects.

Cleanup

The first step is to clean up your print. You should remove any rafting, brims, and support material. I like to remove the material by hand first so that I don't accidentally gouge the object with a knife or some other tool. Once the large bits are removed, I then use a hobby knife to carefully cut away the remaining bits. Be careful not to cut away too much.

■ **Tip** Trimming ABS is easier than trimming PLA. So if you need to print a complex object with lots of support, ABS might be a better choice for cleanup.

If you printed supports in a cavity such as a nut trap or bearing space, you may need to do a bit more cleanup. Sometimes the supports are difficult to remove from smaller or tighter spaces. I like to use a pair of thin needle-nose pliers to remove the supports. Not only can I reach into the space easier, the pliers make it easier to twist the support material to break it away from the part. This is also where having a hobby-knife kit with many shapes of blades comes in handy. You can use differently shaped blades to get into the hard-to-reach areas.

Be sure to remove any extraneous blobs, strings, and other artifacts that may have accumulated on your part. You should also check any holes for the proper size. I often find I need to ream out holes. They aren't necessarily too small (that would be a calibration problem), but I find running a properly size drill through the hole will remove any excess filament, and thus make it easier to assemble. If nothing else, it makes the holes uniform; so if you have any small amount of warp, reaming will compensate and make the part useable.

■ **Tip** If you have more than a few tenths of material to remove, try running the drill in reverse to avoid the bit biting into the plastic. This will also help if you need to ream out a hole that does not go all the way through the part. Also, be sure to secure the part before drilling. It is not advisable to hold it with your hand while using an electric drill to ream out the part.[5] Any slippage, and your part can become an erzats propeller.

Some authors create supports into their models. I have found this to be a very helpful practice. Rather than allow the slicer to generate supports, which is usually a series of thin walls, I add additional thin walls of planes and cylinders in strategic locations. Not only does this make the part easier and faster to print without sagging or failed overhang, it also makes the part easier to clean up.

By way of example, let's look at the bracket example again. Let's say I really want to print the bracket vertically so that the sheering force is minimized (the layers running perpendicular to the load). The problem is that the ear at the top will be hanging in space, and thus will need to be printed with supports. I can do that, but there will be a lot of supports to remove. Also, recall there is a nut trap on this part. If I print it so that the nut trap is on the bottom, there will be bridging needed, and if I turn on support, the support will be printed inside the nut trap, making it harder to print and clean up.

Rather than do that, if I orient the part so that the nut trap is on the top, and add two thin cylinders between the ears, the part will print with less support (and therefore a bit faster) and will be easier to clean up. Figure 12-7 shows the new part with the cylinders added. I leave how to add the support cylinders to you as an exercise. Hint: Make one the same size as the bore, and another one the same size as the curved part of the ear.

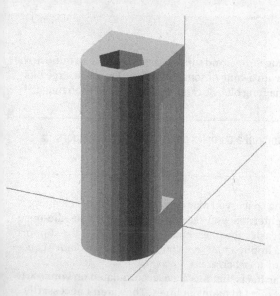

Figure 12-7. Bracket remix with support

OK, so I'll give you another hint. You need to use the difference statement to create a thin-walled cylinder of about 0.25mm. Figure 12-8 shows a cross section of what the new built-in supports would look like.

---

[5]Guilty as charged. Do as I say, not as I do.

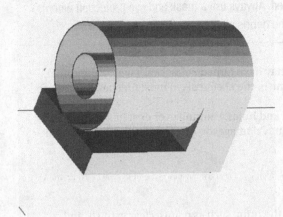

Figure 12-8. *Detail of built-in supports (cutaway)*

Notice the thin cylinders. The gap between the cylinders is only a few millimeters and should be no problem for most printers to bridge. You can always add a center cylinder if you experience sagging. Regardless, removing two thin-walled sections like this is much easier and faster than the typical supports generated. Try it and see!

■ **Tip** One of the best resources for how to finish printed parts are hobby stores. They typically carry a range of how-to books on modeling. Look for books on plastic modeling and finishing. All of the techniques listed there apply to printed parts. Cool!

Sanding

Once you have removed all of the extra bits, it's time to do some sanding. If you skip this step and try to apply a surface treatment, you are likely to see the layered effect, the imprint from the print surface, and the top surface showing through. That is, it will look exactly like it did when you printed it—only with paint on it. That's not good.

The effect we're after here is to prepare the surface for painting. That is, to remove any irregularities. How well you do this—or how smooth you make the surface—depends on how you want to finish the print. If you want a glossy finish, you would need to make the surface as smooth as possible. If you are looking for a nonglossy finish, some irregularities may be fine. Plus, some surface treatments—such as certain paints—can cover sanding marks and small imperfections more easily than others.

There are many techniques for sanding, and most depend on the material you are sanding. For most well-calibrated printers, you won't need to use very coarse sandpaper to remove a lot of plastic. You can typically start with 120-grit (coarse) sandpaper to remove the larger imperfections. A quick pass of several seconds of sanding on each side should do.

I like to use canned air to blow away the debris (dust) and check the surface. You can also use a damp cloth, but you should let the part dry before continuing to sand or applying a surface treatment. I would repeat the sanding on any side that still shows irregularities. But don't sand away too much material!

Once the major irregularities are removed, you can switch to 320-grit sandpaper to give the surface a smoother finish. This will remove any of the small gouges or swirls from the coarse sandpaper. Once again, use canned air or a cloth to wipe away the dust.

■ **Caution** Dust from sanding can be harmful or an irritant if inhaled. Always use a mask and eye protection when sanding. To avoid contact in the future, you should also vacuum up the debris as soon as you finish.

At this point, your part may look a little dull and the plastic may have turned color. Don't worry about that. If you want to use a surface treatment such as a clear paint or varnish, the chemicals in most finishes will restore the color.

Also, be sure to remove any buildup of dust from small areas and holes. Painting over dust in small areas can result in having to clean it out again before assembly, which may damage the finish you're working so hard to perfect.

Surface Treatments

Simply stated, surface treatments are any coating that you apply to the print, such as paints, clear varnish, and so forth. But it can also include any chemical treatment you want to apply. There are many to choose from. Here I list a few of the more popular surface treatments, followed by some helpful tips.

- *Paint*: Use acrylic paints for ABS or PLA. They work great.

- *Clearcoat*: Use any acrylic varnish only. You can get matte, semigloss, and gloss versions.

- *Chemicals*: For ABS, you can warm the part and brush on a thin layer of acetone to restore the color of the plastic after sanding. Keep the temperature below about 50 °C. You can allow it to dry and then apply another coat to increase the sheen from semigloss to gloss. You can also heat acetone to form a vapor to finish a printed part with little or no sanding (see the upcoming "Acetone Vapor Bath" section).

■ **Tip** Applying acetone on cool parts can cause the ABS to turn cloudy. Applying too much heat can cause the surface to become too soft and potentially bubble as the acetone boils. It is best to experiment with discarded prints before trying this on your final product.

Painting

Some web sites and articles I've read seem to tell more of a horror story than present a helpful reference when it comes to painting parts. Some have stated that you simply cannot paint printed parts because the paint will melt the plastic, cause bubbles on the surface, or otherwise cause catastrophic failures of the surface. That might be true if you try to use certain paints with chemicals that dissolve or disrupt the properties of ABS or PLA. However, it is not true with acrylic paint in particular.

You can use acrylic paint to paint your ABS or PLA parts, including different tints and even the clear coats to give it sheen. So if you don't like the color of your filament, or it just doesn't match your décor, you can paint it! I've done both myself and there have been no ill effects. Indeed, so long as I took my time and applied several thin layers, the paint turned out pretty well.

■ **Tip** If you plan to paint your part, don't worry about the color of the filament. In fact, you can use whatever color you have the most of and save your favorite colors for other prints that you won't be painting.

You can use brush-on paint, like those for modeling, or paint in spray cans. Just check the spray paint for the sort of propellant used. It is still possible to find some that are corrosive to ABS or PLA, but these are normally the industrial paints and those from vendors that are not so keen on the environment. Avoid those.

You may be able to use some water-based paints, but I've not found them to be as good as the acrylic-based paints. Clean up of brushes with acrylic paint require a solvent (e.g., paint thinner), so be aware that you may need to let your brushes dry in a well-ventilated area after you clean them and before you store them.

If you plan to use spray paint, be sure to wear a mask, gloves, and some work clothes in case you miss or bump up against wet paint. Trust me, it doesn't come off too easily.

Before you get started painting, there is some additional preparation needed. I like to make sure that I have an area free of contaminants, without any air currents, and some place I don't mind getting messy. Spray paint in particular is messy. You will want to use a drop cloth, an old bedsheet, or a large piece of cardboard to place your part on so that you don't get paint on anything from the overspray.

You should also place your part on an elevated platform, riser, or wire rack to avoid the case where the paint sticks to the underlayment. That is, paint sticks really well to cardboard, and if you have any runoff at all, it may tear when you try to pull the part off. Likewise, paint will stick to cloth and make the part one with the cloth. A riser or wire rack will avoid that. I sometimes use thin strips of wood (left over from other projects) to place my parts on, but a wire rack works just as well.

To get the best out of your paint, apply several thin layers, allowing each layer to dry for at least an hour. Follow the instructions on the can to prep the surface, if needed. Specifically, if the manufacturer suggests a primer coat, apply it first and allow the part to dry completely before continuing.

When I use spray paint, I find that the best technique is one where I trigger the spray away from the part, and then move the spray across the part and release once I've cleared the part. Only do this twice on each face of the part. Resist the temptation to completely cover the part in one spray session. That will lead to runs, which are horrible to try to repair.[6] Similarly, don't try to get the paint into every nook and cranny. That's what multiple layers are for. Once the part is dry, you can reposition it to make another pass that will cover that piece you missed. Repeat this process as many times as you need to completely cover the part in paint.

■ **Tip** Use several thin layers of paint. Don't glob it on thinking one coat will do—even if the can reads, "Covers in one coat."

If you want a glossier finish, you can lightly sand the paint with 500-grit or higher sandpaper. Do this on a completely dry part—and don't bear down. A light buff is all you need. Be sure to wipe off the dust, and then apply another thin layer on top. Repeat as needed until you get the sheen you desire.

■ **Tip** If you are painting parts that will need to be joined together with glue, mask the areas that make contact with blue painter's tape so that the glue will adhere.

Overall, if you take your time, you will find painting your prints a rewarding experience. But it does take some time, patience, and a bit of practice if you've never painted small parts.

---

[6]Can you guess how I know this?

ABS Acetone Vapor Bath

The best technique I've found for treating ABS parts to get a good, glossy finish that removes all signs of printing (layers, etc.), is an acetone vapor bath. Essentially, we heat acetone until it changes to vapor, and then allow the ABS part to sit in the vapor. The vapor then dissolves the outer layers of the part, making it all flow together, which is very similar in effect to powder coating. Once it glosses, the powder flows together, forming a shell.

There is a caveat. Well, several as you shall see. Recall that acetone is flammable and its vapor can be an irritant for some people. You should take extreme care when performing this technique. There is no risk of explosion, but there is risk of fire if an ignition source is nearby. I would highly recommend you treat this procedure with care, making sure that there are no ignition sources in the area.[7]

■ **Caution**   Acetone is flammable and potentially toxic if inhaled! Use your vapor bath in a well-ventilated area, preferably outside. Never place the heating unit near an open flame, sparks, or similar ignition sources. Although acetone vapor is heavier than air, you can still accidentally inhale it, which may be harmful. Always wear a mask designed to filter harmful vapors when working with acetone vapor. And always have a fire extinguisher nearby.

The good news is that this technique does not require any specialized, expensive hardware. All you need is a used, small deep-fryer; some Kapton tape; and acetone. I used a Presto multicooker, as shown in Figure 12-9. Be sure to get one that has a basket and a clear lid like the one shown. You can find these units on popular online discount stores, online auction sites, and even occasionally in thrift and used goods stores. A used unit is fine so long as the internal coating is intact, it has the basket and lid, and it works. Thus, you need not spend a lot of money on it. Mine was less than $20 and it was still in its original box. Wire baskets are OK, but the Kapton tape doesn't adhere quite as well.

Figure 12-9. *A Presto multicooker used as an acetone vapor vessel*

---

[7]Open flames, gas heaters, energetic cats on pile carpeting, and so forth.

What Does It Do?

You may be wondering just what this process does. I've stated that it makes the surface smooth, but how smooth? Let's take a look at before and after photos. Figure 12-10 is the object before treatment.

Figure 12-10. *Before treatment*

As you can see, this print is rough and the layers are clearly visible. Figure 12-11 is the object after treatment.

Figure 12-11. *After treatment*

As you can see, the after image has a nice glossy finish. Best of all, I did not have to even sand it! However, sanding will make the surface better (glossier). Furthermore, you don't need to go so far as to use the really fine sandpaper. Just a light sanding of medium grade sandpaper is all you need.

Preparation

There is some preparation needed. You must cover the bottom and about 30cm of the sides of the basket with Kapton tape. This keeps the part from sticking to the basket, but more importantly, it keeps acetone from splashing onto the part while it is heated. Figure 12-12 shows a properly prepared basket.

Figure 12-12. *Lining the basket with Kapton tape*

■ **Caution**   Never, ever reuse the deep fryer for food preparation once you have used it for acetone. Keep it locked away in your workshop and label it appropriately to warn others.

For best results, use some short standoffs mounted to the bottom of the basket to lift the basket away from the acetone. You can see this in the figure. Notice the bolts in the small pockets in the bottom of the basket. I used threaded brass connectors, but you can use any similar item made of metal. Just make sure that the feet and basket still fit so that the lid can be securely set on the fryer (it closes well).

Next, you need to find a place where there are no ignition sources and is well ventilated. If you attempt this indoors, you may encounter an untenable state when the acetone vapors are released. It is best to do this in an area that is either very large and has open areas (like a porch or an open garage) or, better, outside. You will need to plug the fryer in—so if you use an extension cord, be sure to use one of an appropriate size for the distance (in other words, the heavier, the better). Lastly, make sure you have a fire extinguisher ready and at least one other person in the area that is aware of what you are doing.[8]

---

[8]Have I frightened you? Don't be. Just be cautious.

Vapor Bath Process

The process is rather simple. We simply pour some acetone into the fryer, add our part, and turn on the heat. We don't need a lot of heat and it won't be for a long period—about a minute is all that is needed. You can repeat this process several times if the part doesn't gloss like you want. The process is as follows.

1. Prepare the object by doing light sanding on it to remove the larger imperfections.

2. Set up the fryer in a well-ventilated area, removing the basket.

3. Pour 2 to 3 ounces of acetone into the fryer.

4. Place the part in the basket that has been coated with Kapton tape. If your lid has a handle in the center, the bolt point can be a source for the acetone vapor to condensate and drip. Thus, you should place the object and basket away from the center, as shown in Figure 12-13.

Figure 12-13. Placing the object in the basket

5. Place the basket in the fryer and cover it with the lid.

6. Plug in the fryer and turn the temperature to around 300°F or 325°F.

7. Wait 60 to 90 seconds or until the boiling sounds stop. Turn off the fryer and unplug it. Never let it heat for more than 90 seconds.

■ **Caution**   Be sure to watch the process carefully. If anything goes wrong, turn off the fryer!

---

8. Wait 1 hour to remove the lid and allow the vapor to dissipate.

9. Wait 1 more hour for the part to harden a bit and inspect the part.

10. Repeat steps 2–8 until the part is completely glossed.

When satisfied with the finish, allow the part to dry overnight before removing it from the basket or handling in any way. Until the acetone evaporates, it will be soft and can be molded or blemished with fingerprints.

■ **Note**   Depending on the size of the object, it may take more than 1 hour for it to cure completely. Do not handle the part until it has set overnight and hardened (all of the acetone has evaporated).

When you add acetone, you don't need to add very much. You need only a couple of ounces. There is no magical formula. Just cover about one-third of the bottom of the fryer.

When heating, don't turn up the temperature more than about 325°F. This may be tempting because we start the fryer cold (at room temperature). Thus, it may take about 30 seconds to reach temperature, which is fine because it only takes about 30 to 60 seconds for the acetone to turn to vapor.

You should see the clear lid fog a bit when the temperature is reached. This is normal and nothing to be alarmed about; it isn't smoke, it's acetone vapor. On the other hand, if you see acetone condensing on the top, you have used too much acetone. This could be a problem if the acetone accumulates enough to drip on the part. This is why you should watch the process carefully, so that you can abort if something like that happens. To do so, cut the power and lift the lid straight up. Allow the vapors to dissipate and wipe the lid clean, and then restart the process.

Cleanup

The vapor bath is very corrosive to the adhesive on the Kapton tape, which can cause it to lose adhesion to the basket. I find I have to replace the Kapton tape about every three to four uses. Also, if you leave the part in the vapor too long, it has a tendency to stick to the Kapton tape and tear when you remove it.

There is no other cleanup necessary, other than taking the precaution to allow the fryer and basket to cool completely before storing. If you have any acetone remaining in the fryer, you can either pour it back into its container (only when the fryer is cool) or simply allow it to evaporate. Having some left over after 2 hours means you have used too much acetone. Try using about half an ounce less next time.

Be sure to store your fryer in a place where others cannot accidentally encounter it and attempt to use it for preparing food. In other words, don't store it in your home! Keep it in a garage, shed, workshop, or if you have none of those, ask a neighbor or friend who does if you can store it there.

Assembling Multipart Things

If you print an object that has multiple parts, such as a sculpture, model kit, or object that has been divided into parts to fit your build volume, you have to take a bit more care when finishing the parts. This includes making sure the parts fit together, as well as how to apply the surface treatment. This section provides some tips to help make your finishing of multipart things easier.

SPLITTING INTO PARTS TO FIT BUILD VOLUME

If you encounter a thing you want to print, but it is larger than your build volume (it won't fit within the confines of your axes movement), you can split the thing into parts. There are several techniques for doing this and it is beyond the scope of this book to list them all. One quick way to do it is to import the object into OpenSCAD and use the difference mechanism to slice the part by masking it with a large cube, and then reorienting the segment so that it lays flat. Repeat this as many times as needed, and you have a multipart set of objects that you can print and then reassemble.

You should not apply any surface treatment (e.g., paint) to the areas that are joined. If you are gluing the parts together, the glue may not stick to the surface treatment. You should also make sure the parts fit together very well prior to applying the surface treatment. I like to test fit all parts during the sanding process so that I can remove any extra plastic as needed. This way, if I slip or make a mistake, I won't ruin the surface treatment (I won't scratch the nice paint job).

Also, it may be that you can assemble the parts prior to applying the surface treatment. If you have parts that are joined but you do not want the joint to show through the surface treatment, you can fill in the joint prior to painting.

If you are printing with ABS, you can dissolve some ABS in acetone, making a paste-like substance that you can apply with a hobby knife (kind of like a trowel and spackling). Once the ABS evaporates and you sand it, the part will appear as a solid piece.

If you are using PLA, you can do the same with epoxy made for plastic. It isn't nearly as nice, and the epoxy is hard to sand and to get the same texture as the rest of the part. Thus, it may show more once the part is painted. However, you need to take care here because some epoxy can melt or weaken PLA. It is best to experiment with scrap PLA parts until you find an epoxy that works well.

Perhaps the best advice is to sand and trim the parts so that they fit together as tight as possible. The tighter the seam, the less likely you may need to cover it up.

Finally, I'd like to impart a technique for assembling metal bits and plastic parts; more specifically, how to save some time getting those nut traps, slots, and other areas cleaned up and prepped for assembly. If you make a part with a nut trap, try to make the shape the correct size. It is often OK to make it slightly smaller and use the technique here, but making it too large can be a problem—the nut may not sit properly and turn or strip the plastic.

The best way to fit nuts and bolts (the hex heads) into plastic parts prior to assembly is to heat the nut or bolt with a butane torch, and then insert the heated metal into the part. This is really great if the opening is just a tad too small, as it will make a very tight setting for the nut or bolt. I use this technique a lot and it saves me a great deal of time trimming those tiny M3 nut traps to fit.

Summary

Once you have printed several parts and have mastered your printer's configuration and calibration, you may start to wonder if there is more that you can do with 3D printers. Indeed there is! There is a whole world of finishing options to consider—from sanding and smoothing, to applying surface treatments such as painting, to making multipart prints fit together to appear as a single piece.

This chapter has presented all of these topics in a series of tips and techniques for you to get started finishing your prints and taking them to the next level—to become something more than a few dozen layers of plastic.

The next chapter completes the journey of 3D printing by challenging you to expand your 3D printing hobby beyond your own workshop. I will discuss sharing objects with the world, as well as presenting ideas for how you can put your 3D printing hobby to practical use by solving real-world problems.

CHAPTER 13

■ ■ ■

Taking It to the Next Level

Mastering your 3D printing hobby can be a very rewarding achievement, and once you do, it is time to take things to the next level. The 3D printing community has evolved around several principles. Most notably it is one of sharing your work with others. That is, you should desire to share what you have learned and what you make with others.

Indeed, the RepRap movement in particular was founded and fueled by members of the community who shared a desire to make the 3D printing world as open as possible. Thus, I hope you feel an obligation and a desire to share your designs with others.

Furthermore, you will likely reach a plateau where you begin to look for ways to put your 3D printer to work to solve real-world problems. That is, you will desire to print more than the occasional whistle, stretchy bracelet, and figurine (although all of those are really cool things to print).

This chapter completes our journey through the 3D printing world by presenting suggestions and guidelines for contributing your own 3D models, as well as presenting ideas for solving real-world problems. I also discuss a rather interesting application from the RepRap world: spawning a new printer.

Contributing 3D Models

As more and more free thinkers drive hobbies like 3D printing, the more prevalent the concept of sharing becomes. This is no accident. Many of the founders of the 3D printing movement are open source advocates. This applies not only to hardware and software, but it also applies to other intellectual products, such as 3D printing models ("things" in the Thingiverse vernacular).

Many feel designs for objects (models) should be free for anyone to use and modify with reciprocal expectations. For example, if you modify someone else's design, you should share not only the improved design but also credit the originator. In some cases, this is as simple as listing the original author, but other times it may mean giving the original author your modifications. So long as you follow the guidelines of the license, all is fair and well in sharing.

■ **Note** I use the terms *model*, *object*, and *things* to mean the same: a set of files for 3D printing. There may be some specifics that delineate, but that is not a concern for this discussion.

However, depending on how the model was created, there may be some limitation to what can be shared. For example, it may not be possible to share a model made by a proprietary CAD application. While you may be the creator of the object, you do not own the file format and the application that created it. You most likely can share the file with others, but modification of the file format may be restricted to the CAD application.

Sharing your models also means placing them someplace where others can find them. You may want to make them freely available to anyone or you may want to sell your objects. Fortunately, there are web sites that can handle either quite well.

It is a really good feeling to see one of your things being liked, used, and made by others. Thingiverse[1] has a feature that allows you to show the world something you've made that others have designed and shared by adding a photo of your print. While little used, this feature has a huge feedback aspect because it shows the original author that her thing was put to use by someone else. If you download and make someone's thing—and you like the outcome—post a picture of the printed thing by visiting Thingiverse and clicking "I Made One".

The next section focuses on how to go about sharing your objects—either for free or fee.

How We Share

You may be wondering why anyone would want to give away something they have worked on for hours. While it is true that the expectation is you should share your cool things with others, it isn't a hard and fast rule. In fact, there are some who have made their things available for a fee. But the vast majority of enthusiasts share their things for free. I discuss each of these options in this section.

Selling Your Things

It is possible to sell your things for profit. There is nothing wrong with that and there are people doing it now. There are even web sites you can use to sell your own designs.

For example, MakerBot Industries now has an online thing store called the Digital Store (https://digitalstore.makerbot.com), where you can purchase things (models) for downloading and printing. Prices are relatively low and the models are of the highest quality. Currently, there are many things available (mostly toys) and many more being added every week.

If you are thinking you'd like to do the same, there are web sites you can use. The RedPah web site (redpah.com) is a site for people to upload designs (much like Thingiverse) and set a fee for people to purchase the right to use the design for printing. Like the Digital Store, most things are inexpensive and there are even some things that are free. The idea is that you can check out someone's free things before deciding to buy their other things. This allows you to evaluate the quality and appropriateness of the design, which will tell you if it is worth purchasing other things from the same designer. All you need to do to post your thing on RedPah is to set up an account and agree to the usage license agreement. If you want to sell items, you may also be required to set up a payment vehicle. RedPah will get a percentage of your sale (that is how they make their money).

■ **Tip**   Selling your things will require you to pay someone to host them for you. You can build your own web site, but you won't have the market exposure that the professionals can provide.

There is also a site called Shapeways (shapeways.com) that allows you to upload your designs for sale. However, unlike RedPah, Shapeways provides a 3D printing service. Yes, that's right. They have a huge assortment of industrial 3D printers that can print anything from plastic to advanced metal-based powder fusion. In fact, you can upload your thing for sale and people can have it made from steel, nickel, and even some precious metals. How cool is that?

Best of all, you can browse the site's catalog of things and print many exciting objects—from rings to larger objects of art, function, and form. I've found some designs that I'd like to have printed myself. However, the price is considerably higher than a site where you download the thing and print it yourself. As you can imagine, the fee for hosting your object is also higher than sites like RedPah. However, if you design some object that you've prototyped in plastic but want it made from platinum, Shapeways is the place for you.

---

[1]The originators were thinking the "Universe of Things" when they named this site and its very core is about sharing things.

Giving to Others

As I mentioned, making your things free for others to use is the more popular method of sharing 3D things. I have used Thingiverse (`thingiverse.com`) as an example of a repository for free things. However, there are others. The following lists a few alternatives to Thingiverse. Most are repositories, but some provide some rather unique features. I give a brief overview of each. If you are looking for something other than Thingiverse, you may want to check out some of these.

- *Bld3r* (`bld3r.com`): A community-driven site for 3D printing tinkerers. Provides a forum for members to vote for the best designs and rate each design based on quality. Largely member-driven.

- *Yeggi* (`yeggi.com`): A search engine for finding 3D models. If there is a model to match your description, Yeggi will find it for you.

- *Repables* (`repables.com`): A 3D print file repository.

- *YouMagine* (`youmagine.com`): An online 3D printing community featuring a repository, a blog, and forums for discussion. Community-driven and provided by Ultimaker.

- *Cuboyo* (`cuboyo.com`): A 3D print file repository.

There are many more alternatives and more being added. Only time will tell which ones will endure or become as popular as Thingiverse (or as well advocated and advertised). Those that were not created and directly funded by the community are likely to have been started by a 3D printing company. Two popular examples are Treasure Island (`http://treasure.is/#/products`) and 123D's Gallery (`123dapp.com/Gallery/content/all`). Most sites sponsored by companies tend to cater to their own brands. So if you use these sites, be aware that they may have a specific slant or viewpoint.[2]

However, no matter which site you choose (and the choice is yours), there are some things you must understand about sharing objects. I discuss the etiquette or code of conduct in the following section.

Sharing Etiquette

Believe it or not there is a set of rules—some written, some not—that you are expected to follow should you decide to embrace the community of 3D printing or any similar community. The following lists some guidelines (rules) you would do well to heed when sharing your ideas, things, and commentary with the community.

Keep Your Designs Original

Nobody likes a copycat. You didn't like it when you were five and you won't appreciate it when you see something you designed and shared for free being presented as the "design of the month" credited to someone else.

Thus, you must do your homework to make sure your design is unique. You don't have to purposefully alter your design so that it doesn't resemble someone else's thing, but you should do due diligence and at least search for similar objects.

In the rare case that it so happens that your design is nearly identical to another design, so long as your work is your own, there shouldn't be a problem. In fact, this happened to me once. My response and that of the other designer were something like, "Cool thing. Like-minds, eh?" Once again, there is nothing wrong with that, provided you both acknowledge the resemblance and there are no licensing issues.

---

[2]Which is partly why some people don't like sites like Thingiverse and Autodesk 123D.

If the other thing like yours is truly the same design but was licensed differently, you may have to negotiate with the other designer. This can happen when things are licensed for ownership (e.g., commercial property), but it is rare given that most 3D printing repositories are sites where people share their designs for free.

Let's look at another example. What is the likelihood that a dozen different cases for a Raspberry Pi will be similar in size, have the same openings for ports, and perhaps even assemble the same way (snap together)? Very likely, yes? Does this mean that there is one original and eleven copies? No, certainly not. This is not what I am talking about.

What I mean by *unique* is that of those twelve cases, you should be able to identify some differences among them. Be that how they print (e.g., orientation on the build platform), whether they are made from several parts, whether they have designs on the top or ventilation, and so forth. Even if all twelve designers started at the same time, there will be some minor differences. More importantly, each is its own work. That is, no one used the design of another to pass off as his own.

However, using another's work to create a new version with an alteration creates a new thing. This is permissible and encouraged. Consider a thirteenth sample of the Raspberry Pi case. Let's say you like one of the twelve, but you wanted to add feet to it so that it could be raised off the work surface. Rather than start your design from scratch, you decide to download and use the one you like.

When it comes time to share your design, you must annotate your thing, giving credit to the original designer. That is, you state unequivocally that your thing is a derivation of the original (a "remix" in Thingiverse vernacular). You should list a link to the original design, along with your modifications. That is, this assumes the license permits it (most things on Thingiverse do with the share-and-share-alike license).

Check the License

I mentioned licensing of things in a previous chapter under the aspect of downloading and printing things. Recall that most repositories will require you to specify a license for your thing. This permits the repository to host your thing and communicate to everyone what your intentions are regarding ownership, permissions to use, and so forth.

As I stated previously, you need to check the license before using any design. If you plan to modify it, you need to pay close attention to the license. The vast majority of licenses will allow you to use the design and most will allow you to modify it.

However, some licenses differ where it concerns the ownership of the modifications. Some open source licenses, like GPL, permit modifications but require you to surrender those modifications to the original owner (the person or organization that created and licensed it) if you plan to distribute those changes. That is, you can modify it at will for personal use, but once you distribute those changes, you have to give them to the owner of the license.

I have only run into this a couple of times, but in those cases, the designer was prototyping designs for a commercial product. The license and indeed the text of the thing made it clear she was looking for help with the design, but that the design would not be made public. Watch out for this and tread lightly. Any work you do could be for the benefit of the owner and not yours to keep or profit from.

■ **Tip**   When in doubt about a license, contact the originator and ask him or her directly.

Since most things are licensed for sharing and free modification, you normally don't have to worry too much. However, I recommend you check the license before using anyone else's object in your own design.

Keep It Appropriate

The most vivid imaginations among us have come up with ways to use 3D printing to print things that some may consider inappropriate or even obscene. No matter what your own views are, you should strive to tolerate the views of others.[3] That doesn't mean you must compromise your own views, just be aware yours may offend, and strive to minimize the offense.

More specifically, don't upload inappropriate things to sites that are viewable by everyone. It's fine to upload some design for a thing that promotes a theme, ideal, and so forth (provided there are no copyright violations), just don't upload things that are clearly offensive or intended to cause harm.

For example, if you consider the fact that 3D printing is being used in schools to teach children the technology and techniques of 3D design and printing, you shouldn't upload things that parents may deem as inappropriate. The most obvious, of course, are offensive language, adult themes, and slanderous images.

You should check the usage and user agreement for the site that hosts your chosen repository as part of the post/no-post decision. Make sure you read the section about what is and what is not appropriate, and adhere to that. On Thingiverse, for example, it is not permitted to upload designs for firearms.

There is another angle to consider. You should avoid uploading designs that are or could potentially be illegal or unlawful. This may be difficult to discern considering the 3D printing community includes the entire globe. However, most sites will have language to suggest what is and what is not permitted. And some have language in the agreement that gives them (the site) the right to remove things they deem inappropriate.

For example, I once saw a design for something that had a very adult theme. It wasn't something one could get in serious trouble for downloading, or even using, but it was just a bit too adult for most young children (in my opinion). I decided to test the site to see what would happen. I did nothing but wait. I checked the site the following day and found the thing had been removed. There was no trace of it and its link was broken (content missing).

So before you upload a design, make sure you understand and agree to the terms of the user agreement as to what is and what is not appropriate. Most times, a misunderstanding is not something that will get you into trouble, but if you do it more than once, chances are that someone at the site will want to speak with you or restrict your access. Which brings me back to the opening of this section: be sure to respect the views of others and especially the intended audience of the site. If you disagree, find another site.

Annotate Your Work

One of the ways I can tell if a thing is good or of high quality is how it is annotated. That is, how well the designer described the thing on its site. If I encounter a thing that looks appealing, only to discover the designer didn't bother to describe the thing with more than seven words (or less), didn't provide any instructions, or worse—didn't present any photos of the actual resulting print, I won't use the thing.

Thus, you should strive to provide as full a description as possible. You don't have to write a novel, novella, or a dissertation on the thing, but you should provide enough information to describe the intended use, what problem it solves, as well as a set of instructions for how to print or modify it (if you made it parametric).

The only exception is a case where you are still working on a thing or you plan to make changes before finalizing it. In this case, you should mark (annotate) the thing with some verbiage about it being a work in progress, being experimental, and so forth. If your repository has a feature to mark the thing as such, use that. This way, others will know your thing isn't quite ready. One reason for doing this may be to get feedback from others. I've done this myself with mixed results. Mostly, people like the thing but don't comment, or if they do, however encouraging, don't suggest any changes.

---

[3]Be careful here. The ultimate path of tolerance is anarchy and chaos, so clearly there must be limits. Where those limits are, I have no clue.

I would also suggest you provide some level of contact information so that others who have questions can contact you. Most sites make it easy for viewers to contact you through the site, but you may want to provide other forms of contact (e.g., e-mail). You may not want to provide your home address and phone number (don't do that), but an e-mail address is a nice way to make yourself open to the community. For example, I have seen things where people have posted their IRC handles, e-mail addresses, and even in one case a business phone number. While I may not go quite that far, I like to provide an e-mail address so that I can communicate with people who like my designs. Sometimes they needed some help using it, other times they have made practical—and in at least one case, profound—suggestions for improving the design. Plus it's nice to connect one-on-one with someone to discuss 3D printing!

Be a Good Citizen

Suppose you run across a design for a thing that not only isn't high quality but is also (in your opinion) engineered incorrectly. Should you immediately comment on the thing and crush the designer's ego with a flippant remark about how dumb the thing is? No, certainly not!

What I would do (most likely) is ignore the thing altogether. I mean, why make things worse by pointing out the defects? I have found the community at large (there are some exceptions) will likely do the same and ignore the thing and not comment. Recall that one of the keys to determining whether a thing is well designed (good) is the number of people who use it. Typically, there is a counter on the site that allows you to check for this. If no one has liked it, or even downloaded it, you can be sure it won't make it to the top of any search lists or as "thing of the month."

On the other hand, if you feel compelled to comment, be sure to either contact the designer privately or be as constructive as you possibly can. The goal should be to help the designer improve his designs, not challenge his intellect (or pride).

When I do comment on things I find strange and perhaps flawed (and it is rare), I generally phrase my comments in the form of a question. A question normally doesn't put someone on the defensive, and if worded properly, it should also not offend.

For example, I may ask, "How have you found the thing may break when using it in a moving vehicle?" This is a nice way of asking if the designer has tested his thing under conditions that you expect it to fail. This is good, constructive criticism in a most intellectual form. I am certain that if you think about what you are about to say, you can find other and perhaps more elegant ways of helping people improve their designs.

Example: Uploading a Thing to Thingiverse

Let's look at an example of how to make things available for others on Thingiverse. In this case, I want to share a mount for a dial gauge for a Prusa i3. It allows you to use a dial gauge to level your print bed. It is designed to clip to the X-axis rods and hold the dial gauge firmly. Figure 13-1 shows my finished design. The following sections guide you through the process of uploading the design.

Figure 13-1. Prusa i3 dial gauge

Prepare the Design

I decided to use OpenSCAD to create the model (object). I also decided, based on my experience with dial gauges, to allow users to change the size of the hole for the dial gauge because not all dial gauges have the same diameter shaft. Furthermore, the dial gauge needs to be mounted firmly so that the tension of the depth rod doesn't dislodge it from the mount. Thus, I decided to make the object as a module and provide a parameter for the tool diameter.

■ **Note**   This thing can be found on the Thingiverse site (thingiverse.com/thing:232979).

I also wanted to provide comments in the file to include why the object was created and how to use it. As it turns out, I also decided to provide additional information about how to use the dial gauge for leveling the print bed. Listing 13-1 shows an abbreviated set of the comments I added to the top of the file.

Listing 13-1. Comments for Prusa i3 Dial Gauge

```
// Dial Gauge Mount for Prusa i3
//
// This thing is designed to allow you to use a typical dial guage
// for tramming (leveling) the print bed.
//
// Notes
//
// The only parameter you should have to change is the diameter of
// the tool itself. The hole for the tool should be snug so that
// the tool does not get dislodged when raising or lowering the
// Z-axis. If it is too snug, you can use a rolled up piece of
```

```
// sand paper to make the hole a bit larger. You can also change
// the parameter to the method and recompile the object if the
// tolerance is too large.
//
// Instructions for Use
//
// To use the thing, move the extruder to the center of the X-axis
// (not by hand!), insert your gauge into the mount, and clip the
// mount onto the X-axis to the left of your extruder. Press the
// top on first then swing the bottom until it lightly clicks onto
// the lower bar.
//
// Move the Z-axis (not by hand!) so that the dial tip makes contact
// with the print bed. Move it closer a few millemeters to ensure
// the dial gauge will have a good range of motion.
//
// To tram your print bed, move the gauge to the left-most edge of
// the print bed and move your Y-axis to the home position (not by
// hand!). This should be the [0,0,0] corner (home) of your print
// bed. Note the value (I like to turn the dial so the gauge reads
// 0. Make sure your bed adjuster is not too far out of the middle
// range.
//
// Next, move the Y-axis (not by hand!) to the MAX point and adjust
// the bed until the dial reads '0' or as close to it as your
// patience will permit. ;) Now you see why I move the dial to '0'!
//
// Next, move the gauge to the other side of the X-axis carefully
// so as to not change the position of the tool in the mount or the
// position of the dial. Measure and adjust the MAX/MAX point for X/Y.
//
// Finally, move the Y-axis to 0 (not by hand!) and measure and
// adjust the last corner.
//
...
// Created by: Charles Bell
//
// Enjoy!
```

As you can see, the comments are quite long. However, you will notice that I listed the purpose, usage notes, and even instructions on how to use the thing. You don't have to be quite as verbose as this, but you should be sure to include all of the information someone needs to use your thing. The more complete you make the comments, the more likely someone will like it and make one.

The next step is to generate the .stl file. Recall that we do this by compiling the code in OpenSCAD. This step is required before exporting it to graphic file format. We then export the file as an .stl by clicking the File ➤ Export ➤ Export as STL. . . menu item. Figure 13-2 shows the rendered object.

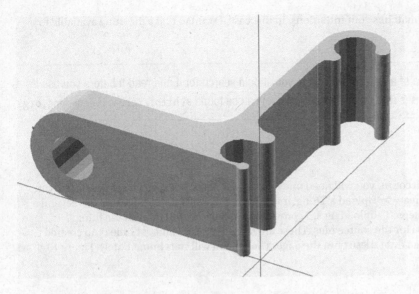

Figure 13-2. *Compiled object*

At this point, you should have a set of files to upload. In this example, I have the OpenSCAD file
(dial_gauge_mount.scad) and the .stl file (dial_gauge_mount.stl).

Choose a License

Once the object has been prepared, you need to consider which license you want to use. I chose the Creative
Commons—Attribution—Share Alike license. Figure 13-3 shows the license options Thingiverse allows you
to choose.

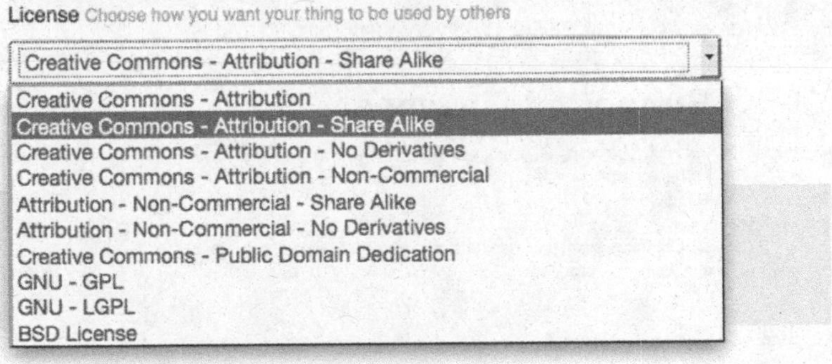

License Choose how you want your thing to be used by others

Creative Commons - Attribution - Share Alike
Creative Commons - Attribution
Creative Commons - Attribution - Share Alike
Creative Commons - Attribution - No Derivatives
Creative Commons - Attribution - Non-Commercial
Attribution - Non-Commercial - Share Alike
Attribution - Non-Commercial - No Derivatives
Creative Commons - Public Domain Dedication
GNU - GPL
GNU - LGPL
BSD License

Figure 13-3. *License options*

Be sure to choose the one that best matches your intentions. In this case, I want to make the thing available to anyone to use and remix.

■ **Tip**   If you are not sure about the use of a particular license, you should search for it and read it before you use it. For example, the Creative Commons licenses (the most common choice) can be found at `http://creativecommons.org`.

Create the Site

If you don't already have a Thingiverse account, you will need one to upload objects. Once you have registered, you can log in to Thingiverse and click the Create ➤ Upload a Thing! menu item. This will open a page that has several areas for you to fill out. There are three steps: 1) upload files, 2) provide the details, and 3) publish the thing.

The first screen you see prompts you for the source files. These are the OpenSCAD and `.stl` files you created when you completed your design. You can drag these onto the page. The upload will start immediately. Figure 13-4 shows a snapshot of the screen.

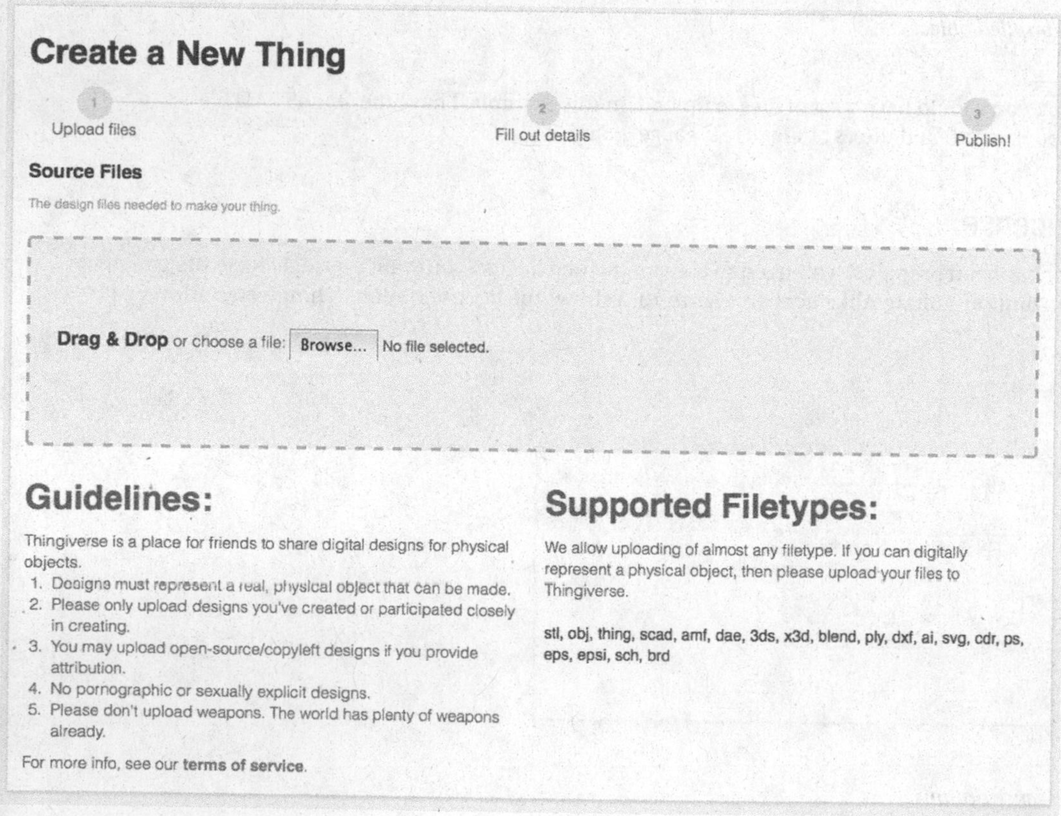

Create a New Thing

1 Upload files   2 Fill out details   3 Publish!

Source Files

The design files needed to make your thing.

Drag & Drop or choose a file: Browse... No file selected.

Guidelines:

Thingiverse is a place for friends to share digital designs for physical objects.

1. Designs must represent a real, physical object that can be made.
2. Please only upload designs you've created or participated closely in creating.
3. You may upload open-source/copyleft designs if you provide attribution.
4. No pornographic or sexually explicit designs.
5. Please don't upload weapons. The world has plenty of weapons already.

For more info, see our **terms of service**.

Supported Filetypes:

We allow uploading of almost any filetype. If you can digitally represent a physical object, then please upload your files to Thingiverse.

stl, obj, thing, scad, amf, dae, 3ds, x3d, blend, ply, dxf, ai, svg, cdr, ps, eps, epsi, sch, brd

Figure 13-4. Upload source files

Note the discussion at the bottom left of the form that provides guidelines for uploading things. You should read this list and adhere to its restrictions. Indeed, by creating the thing, you are agreeing to the terms of service—see the link at the bottom of the list. Listed to the right are the supported file types.

Once the files are uploaded, you will see the form expand to allow you to upload a photo of your thing (highly recommended), as well as sections to add a name and description, choose a category and license, and optionally provide instructions. I highly recommend you add the instructions. There is also a check box to tick for marking the thing as a work in progress. Lastly, you should add any tags you deem appropriate. For this thing, I chose dial_gauge, mount, and Prusa_i3. You can use whatever you want and is appropriate.

At the bottom of the form is a place for you to identify any design that you used to create your thing. That could be a thing you downloaded and included, or perhaps it is a design that you re-created and augmented. Whatever the case, always list the sources for your design here. If you created it yourself without any inspirational examples, you can leave it blank, but that is only for those ideas that are truly unique.

For example, if you created a new X-end for a RepRap printer, even if you dreamed up the design yourself, the fact of the matter is that the original X-end already exists. In fact, there are many variants. You should choose the one that best matches your idea and list it here. You should also note this in the description. It is fine to say, "Inspired by" in the description to indicate it isn't a direct variant (remix), but it is good taste to give credit to your inspiration.

You should also choose a name that correctly identifies your thing. Resist the temptation to glorify it with something like, "Chuck's amazing, wonderful, absolutely beautiful thing." That isn't very descriptive and some may take offense at the egotistical spin (however well intended as humor). Rather, you should use a name that is short and completely describes your thing by using keywords. I chose "Prusa i3 Dial Gauge". It is short and precise.

To give you an idea of what I would consider the bare minimum for a description and instruction, the following is what I included when I created the site for this thing.

Description
This is a dial gauge to fit the Prusa i3 X-axis. See the .scad file for more details on customizing it to fit your dial gauge.

UPDATE: Added lower version for printers with taller hot ends.

Instructions

Print the gauge holder and insert the dial gauge. When you want to use it, simply attach it to the X-axis smooth rods. Snap it onto the top rod and then swivel it down to snap onto the lower rod.

See the .scad file for a complete description of how to use the dial gauge to tram the print bed.

■ **Note**   The tool size is 9.75mm. If you need it larger, use the .scad file and enlarge the mounting hole per the instructions.

As you can see, it is very terse but it serves to communicate everything one needs to know. Notice that I refer to the OpenSCAD file for anyone who would like to learn how to use the dial gauge. I reasoned that those searching for a dial gauge would likely know how to use it, and thus I spared them from having to ponder all that text.

Once you have all of the information entered and the options selected, you can click Save Draft to save it so that you can edit it later (for example, you want add more pictures), or click Publish to publish the thing. Figure 13-5 shows an excerpt of the thing site.

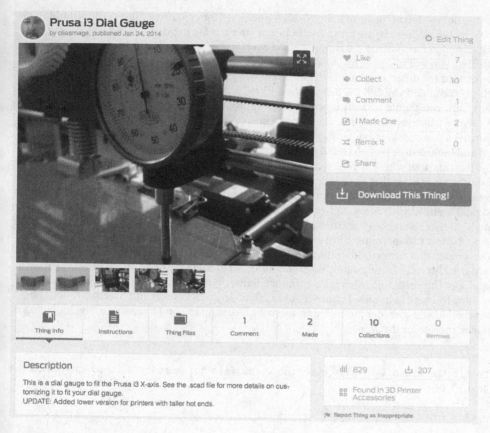

Figure 13-5. *Site for dial gauge*

Notice that visitors to this site can view your description, instructions, and files, and even leave you comments. What this page doesn't show is the number of visits and downloads. At this time, there were 96 views and 30 downloads. Not the most successful thing on Thingiverse, but clearly a couple dozen people liked it enough to download it!

Monitor Feedback

Once your thing is published, you have one more task to do to be a responsible community member. You should check back periodically for any comments, and respond where appropriate. When you are logged in, you will see a tab labeled Dashboard at the top. If anyone has liked your thing, left a comment, made an example, a remix, and so forth, you will see a red box with a number that indicates the number of events for your things.

Be sure to check back every couple of days or at least weekly to see if there are comments, and respond to them. As for me, I check Thingiverse daily, so if you comment on one of my things, I am likely to respond within 24 hours. There is no unspoken rule about that; just make sure that you do respond—especially if someone has asked you a question.

Ideas for Using Your 3D Printer

Unlike other 3D printing books, I have saved the discussion of "What can you do with your 3D printer?" to last. I don't like reading 3D printing books that place it at the front. It makes me feel like I'm reading the ending before the rest of the story. In this section, I give you some ideas of the many things you can make with your 3D printer. More specifically, I would like to encourage you to consider using your 3D printer to solve real-world problems. I hope to convey this by showing you some of the ways I have done so in my home. I begin by presenting one of the original uses for RepRap printers—creating another printer.[4]

Spawning a New Printer

One of the most satisfying tasks that I've used my 3D printers for was to print the parts to make another printer. Originally one of the tenets of RepRap printers, printing a new printer (sometimes called *spawning*) can be a lot of fun. This is especially true once the set of parts are ready, and made sweeter when the build is complete. Even if you don't want to make a hobbyist career of building 3D printers, you should give it a go with at least one build. You will learn a lot.

In this section, I present a different design for a 3D printer. It's called a Smartrap and is sponsored by Smartfriendz (smartfriendz.com). Figure 13-6 shows a completed Smartrap printer.

Figure 13-6. *Smartrap printer (courtesy of* smartfriendz.com*)*

I chose this design as an example because the plastic components are small and can be printed with PLA in about 8 to 12 hours, depending on the feed rate of your printer. It is also easier to assemble than some of the popular Prusa designs, requiring only a couple of screwdrivers and an Allen wrench.

---

[4]Every home needs another 3D printer, right?

What Is a Smartrap?

The Smartrap is a RepRap variant that is designed around a minimalistic view. There are no large frame components, complex axis mechanisms, or even an enclosure. In fact, rather than an external frame, the plastic parts bolt to a wooden plank to provide a solid foundation. The frame therefore is formed from the plastic parts that mount the various components together, namely the stepper motors—three of which are mounted on the bottom. It resembles a Printrbot Simple in form factor.

What I like most about the Smartrap is its mad scientist look—with the bare electronics mounted under a glass build plate and wires running here and there. Overall, it's a really cool-looking printer.

But the best part is that it is fully supported by a vendor, Smartfriendz. Not only that, but the files for printing the plastic parts are both available online and open source. As a result, you will find that there is a growing community of people creating features and upgrades. Indeed, many are on Thingiverse.

Smartfriendz has a storefront where you can purchase fully assembled printers, complete kits, and partial kits. Thus, Smartfriendz is a hobbyist-grade provider. However, their web site is complete with documentation, a forum for getting help, build files and videos, an FAQ, and more. So in many ways, Smartfriendz is closer to a consumer-grade provider. They are an excellent example of what RepRap vendors should strive to become.

Printing the Plastic Parts

The plastic parts for the Smartrap can be found on Thingiverse (thingiverse.com/thing:177256). You will find four files on this site. There is a bill of materials file and three .stl files that make up the set of plastic parts.

The three .stl files are subsets of the plastic parts laid out to fit on a typical RepRap printer build platform. More specifically, they can fit on the Smartrap platform. All you need to do is take the .stl files, slice them, and print them. Figure 13-7 shows the set of plastic parts needed.

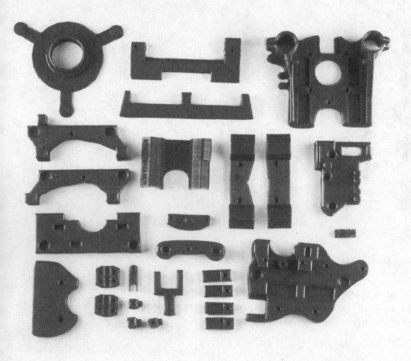

Figure 13-7. Plastic parts for a Smartrap (courtesy of smartfriendz.com)

Notice that there are 27 parts that you need to print. None of them are very large, so printing them in three groups should not be a problem for most printers. For example, each group fits easily on a MakerBot Replicator 2 platform and takes about 2 to 3 hours to print.

However, if you want to print each part separately, you can. All you need to do is load the .stl file in a slicer, split (ungroup) it, and save the individual parts. You can do this easily with Slic3r. I leave this as an exercise for anyone who wants to break up the sets.

I would recommend printing the parts with a lower resolution of about 0.3mm layer height and 20% infill. This will enable you to print each .stl file in a few hours. In fact, you can print all of the parts over a weekend, easily, and still have time to watch the big game.[5]

If you plan to print the plastic parts over some time, say during your ever-shrinking free time, I would recommend waiting to acquire the hardware and electronics until your set of plastic parts is complete.

Don't forget that you may need to clean up some of the parts by removing any supports and reaming out the holes for proper fitting.

Acquiring the Hardware and Electronics

As I mentioned, you can purchase the entire hardware and electronics kits from Smartfriendz. But you don't have to. If you have leftover parts (spares even) from building other RepRap printers, you can use those for your Smartrap. In fact, the Smartrap uses many of the same parts as the Prusa variants.

For example, you will need four NEMA 17 stepper motors (you need five for a Prusa i3), some smooth and threaded rods, linear bearings, belts, and various metric bolts. See the bill of materials for a complete list. As for the electronics, most people use a RAMPS setup with one of several popular hot ends.

So if you want to acquire the components yourself, you need to get the bill of materials and make a list of the vendors near you that have the components in stock. Of course, you could just order what you need from smartfriendz.com.

Building

Rather than present a complete build guide for the Smartrap, I encourage you to visit the Smartfriendz site and download the build guide (http://reprap.org/wiki/Smartrap_Build_Manual), which is maintained by the RepRap community. You will find that it is very well written and easy to follow. You should also refer to Chapter 3 for additional tips on building 3D printers.

Overall, the build should go well and fairly quickly. None of the assembly is overly difficult, and with needing so few tools, you should not encounter any problems. If you do, be sure to visit the Smartfriendz web site for help.

Now that you've seen a brief overview of an example printer, you can create one yourself by generating a set of plastic parts, you should be ready to go forth and spawn your own 3D printer.

Practical Household Solutions

Have you ever found something broken in your home? Maybe a hook, handle, or pull has become loose, stripped, or cracked. Wouldn't it be nice to replace it with a part you made yourself? With enough creativity and a bit of work with a CAD application and your 3D printer, you should be able to make almost anything.

Perhaps you have had ideas for things you could make out of plastic, but you didn't have the tools or information needed to make it happen. Now that you have a deeper understanding of your printer and its capabilities, as well as some new skills at making your own objects, you can make these things a reality.

---

[5]That is, if you don't have any print failures and someone doesn't kick the power strip out of the wall.

WHAT DOES 3D PRINTING COST?

You may be wondering how much it costs to print something vs. buying a manufactured one in the store. The answer depends on a number of factors. If you exclude your own time and effort, and focus on only the cost of the plastic, you may be surprised to learn printing your own parts won't necessarily save you a lot of money.

For example, consider a typical small household hardware item that costs $4.[6] Now consider that you print the same part and it weighs a mere 3 ounces (which is a lot of plastic). Further, consider that the cost of a spool of filament is $45 (an average cost) and it weighs approximately 2 pounds (32 ounces). Simple division gives you 45/32 = $1.40 per ounce. Now, at 3 ounces, we have a printed part that costs about $4.20. It's close, right? Well, not really. If you factor in the additional time to make the part vs. the time it would have taken to get it from a store, the printed part isn't such a good bargain.

However, if you consider the wow factor and joy you get from seeing a creation realized, that printed part becomes priceless—especially so if you are creating a part that just isn't available (see the upcoming gate hinge). Imagine when someone asks about it. You can say, "I made that."

Rather than take you down a path of listing all manner of suggestions without substantial information, I will present three solutions from the many things I've made for my own home. By reading through these, I hope to inspire your own creativity rather than present something for you to go forth and print (although you are welcome to do so).

I will begin with some tips on how to go about building parts that work. This is because it isn't always as simple as measuring something, printing a part to match, and installing it. Many times, the part needs fine-tuning to get it correct. Indeed, I've found that I need to print samples of key portions of the part in order to get things to work correctly. That is, I find printing a hinged portion of the part helps solve problems like one side being a bit too large, or a hole that is too small. How do I do this? I use my 3D printer for printing prototypes of the part.[7] The following are recommendations for prototyping your solutions.

Prototyping Tips

When you make things intended to be installed or used in some manner other than a knickknack or curiosity, especially those things that bolt or mount to other things, you would do well to measure, re-measure, and then measure again.[8] Imagine designing and printing a complex shape, only to discover the spacing of the holes or size is slightly off—either due to measuring mistakes or a mistake when coding the OpenSCAD file. I can say with some certainty that printing an object for three hours, only to discover a minor error in the CAD process, is very disappointing and even frustrating. Wouldn't it be better if you could print only a part of the object to test the fit?

This is a form of prototyping—making test pieces (prints) to check fit so that you can adjust the object and avoid printing the completed product. Not only does this mean the pieces are faster to print, it also means that when you do print the entire object, it will be fit correctly and be ready to use.

I've done this before with things I've printed by aborting the print after a few layers. However, this only works for testing fit for features on the bottom. What do you do if you want to test a portion of an object on a different plane?

Enter the ever-versatile OpenSCAD. Even if all you have is an .stl file, you can use OpenSCAD to mask out part of the object and print the remaining parts. You can even use this technique to mask the object in stages, creating several parts.

---

[6]While that may sound like a random number, I've come to realize when buying small hardware items at a home improvement store, if I add up the number of items in my cart and multiply by 4, I get a number that is pretty close to the total cost of all of the items. Weird.
[7]This is one of the primary uses of 3D printers in industry!
[8]In carpentry terms: measure twice, cut once.

The vehicle at work here is the `difference()` statement. Recall that it allows us to subtract (erase) portions of an object that are overlapped by one or more other shapes. Let's see an example.

Let's suppose we want to test the fit of a piece that has some holes and a channel for mounting on a piece of wood. Rather than print the entire object, we can use the `difference()` statement to erase or mask the parts we don't want to print. Figure 13-8 shows the code for this (comments omitted for brevity). We will see this object later in the chapter.

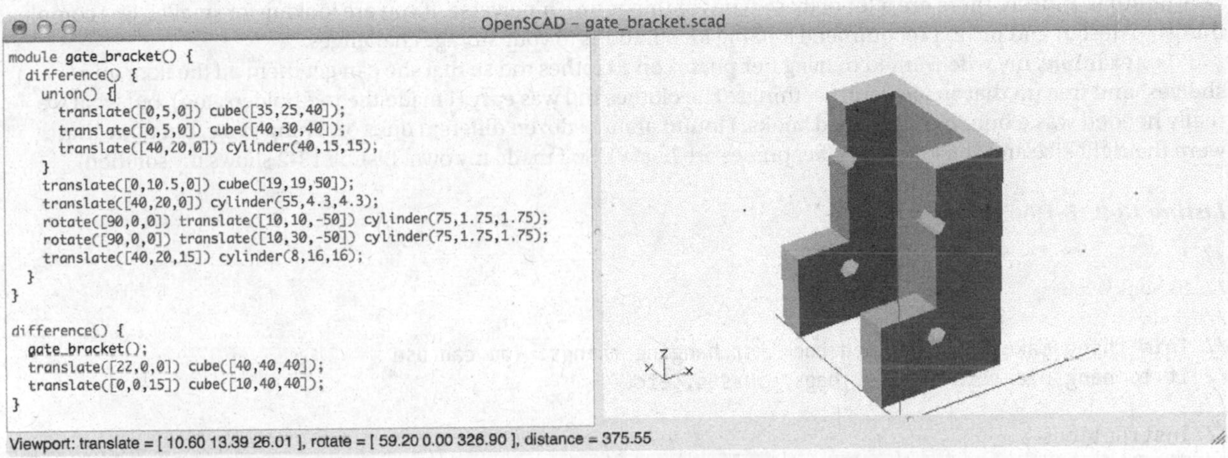

```
OpenSCAD – gate_bracket.scad

module gate_bracket() {
  difference() {
    union() {
      translate([0,5,0]) cube([35,25,40]);
      translate([0,5,0]) cube([40,30,40]);
      translate([40,20,0]) cylinder(40,15,15);
    }
    translate([0,10.5,0]) cube([19,19,50]);
    translate([40,20,0]) cylinder(55,4.3,4.3);
    rotate([90,0,0]) translate([10,10,-50]) cylinder(75,1.75,1.75);
    rotate([90,0,0]) translate([10,30,-50]) cylinder(75,1.75,1.75);
    translate([40,20,15]) cylinder(8,16,16);
  }
}

difference() {
  gate_bracket();
  translate([22,0,0]) cube([40,40,40]);
  translate([0,0,15]) cube([10,40,40]);
}
```

Viewport: translate = [10.60 13.39 26.01], rotate = [59.20 0.00 326.90], distance = 375.55

***Figure 13-8.** Masking for prototyping*

Notice that I used two cubes to cut away most of the object. What is left is a much smaller test piece that I can print quickly to test the location of the holes, as well as the depth and width of the groove to ensure that it fits. If adjustments are needed, I can make the adjustments to the code, compile, export, and reprint the prototype.

■ **Note**   You may be able to use `intersect()` to achieve the same goal. Check the OpenSCAD documentation for how to use this method.

Another helpful technique for prototyping is changing the slicing parameters to generate lower fill and thinner walls. This saves you a bit of plastic, because the strength of the prototyped part is normally not an issue—it will never be installed! Thus, there is no need to print with higher quality, additional shells (thicker vertical and horizontal walls), or even a high fill factor. I recommend using 0.3mm layer height, no more than two shells, 10% infill, and the fastest print speed allowed. Again, the look of the part isn't important. We're mainly testing fit and alignment.

As you may surmise, the color of the filament is also not important, so you can use whatever filament you have the most of and save your chosen filament for the final product.

■ **Note**   Some printers may exhibit dramatically poorer print quality at higher speeds and higher layer heights. Be sure to consider this because these effects can cause part warping and the distortion of smaller areas that affect fit. In this case, some trimming and cleanup may be needed if the anomalies are not too severe.

I have found this technique to be extremely handy when creating unique parts, replacement parts, or new parts that need to fit or be assembled with other parts. As I mentioned, you can also use the technique of breaking a part into several pieces.

Closet Accessories

Making closet accessories, and to some extent, accessories for the bathroom, such as shelves, hooks, and hangers, is very popular. Indeed, there are a lot of these types of things on Thingiverse. If you are looking for smaller, less complex things to design and print, I recommend looking for solutions to your storage challenges.

For example, my wife wanted to hang her purses on a clothes rod so that she can get them off the floor and shelves[9] and free up that space for other things. The clothes rod was easy (I made the rod holders, too), but what we really needed was a bunch of S-shaped hooks. I found about a dozen different ones on Thingiverse, but none that were the right size and thickness (leather purses are heavy). So I made my own. Listing 13-2 shows my solution.

Listing 13-2. S-Hook Code

```
//
// S-hook
//
// This thing makes an S-shaped hook for hanging things. You can use
// it to hang planters, belts, bags, purses, etc.
//
// Instructions
// Simply compile, export, and print! If you want to make the hooks
// a different size, use the following parameters to alter the size.
//
// - The diameter parameter sets the outer diameter of the loops.
// - The thickness is the height and width of the cross section of
//   the loops.
//
// Created by: Charles Bell
//
// Enjoy!
//
module s_hook(diameter=40,thickness=5) {
  radius=diameter/2;
  difference() {
    cylinder(thickness,radius,radius,$fn=64);
    cylinder(thickness,radius-thickness,radius-thickness,$fn=64);
    translate([0,-radius,0]) cube([radius,radius,thickness]);
  }
  translate([0,thickness-diameter,0]) difference() {
    cylinder(thickness,radius,radius,$fn=64);
    cylinder(thickness,radius-thickness,radius-thickness,$fn=64);
    translate([-radius,0,0]) cube([radius,radius,thickness]);
  }
}

s_hook();
```

---

[9]No, she doesn't have that many, but you'd be surprised by how much space only a few can consume.

Prototyping this object was easy. I simply halted the print after a couple of layers. This allowed me to check the fit of the S-hook to see if it fit over the clothes rod. Figure 13-9 shows the finished product installed.

Figure 13-9. Closet S-hooks

Notice the hook in the center. This was a metal hook from a hardware store that came in a pack of two for about $2.00. I printed almost a dozen S-hooks for about $0.20 each. If you are wondering about the elasticity of plastic, don't. These hooks were printed with ABS in early 2013 and have held the purses without sagging.

If you are looking for something to design and print, look in your closet and bathroom for ways you can improve organization by making hooks, small containers, and similar devices.

Mechanical Hardware

Another area where your 3D printer can solve real-world problems is by making mechanical hardware. This could be something that you want or need to attach something to a wall, floor, or ceiling, or perhaps a new knob, clip, or similar miscellaneous bit.

For example, sometimes you may find you can print a replacement part for something that breaks. I once made a replacement handle for a shower door. The original was over 30 years old and not available for purchase. Rather than try to find something at the hardware store that I could trim, drill, or otherwise modify to fit, I just created one and printed it! Best of all, I chose to print it in translucent clear PLA, which most closely matched the faded opaque original.

While fixing things is a lot of fun, creating new solutions is even more fun.[10] However, it can also be a lot of work if you need to create a part to fit into or be mounted on something. Let's look at an example.

---

[10]In a geeky, mad-scientist way.

473

■ **Note** This is the same part shown in the example in the prototyping section.

Suppose you have children or small pets, and your home has a steep stairwell that you don't want them to explore. What do you use? A baby gate of course. What if the area where you want to install the baby gate has two locations that you want to block, but only one at a time. The mounting hardware for the gate works well for securing the gate, but has no ability to pivot. Rather than install two sets of hardware, you decide what you need is a hinge. More specifically, one side of the gate is mounted so that it can be swung from one locking position to another. Figure 13-8 shows the code to create the hinge (you need two of them). Figure 13-10 shows the hinge installed.

Figure 13-10. Gate hinge

Notice that there is an eyehook in the center of the hinge, which the hinge pivots on. I used a simple pin to secure the hinge to the eyehook, and screws to mount the hinge to the gate. Of course, this required removing the original hardware that was mounted at the same location. Therefore, the hinge was made large enough to cover the holes from the original hardware and to fit onto the wooden gate without modifying the gate itself (other than removing the hardware).

To design the part, I prototyped the slot and hole location for the mounting point on the gate, and printed a prototype of the left side to ensure that it fit the eyehook and could swing like I expected. Once I had those prototypes sorted out, I printed the complete hinge and tested it. It worked! Figure 13-11 shows the gate in operation in each of its positions.

Figure 13-11. *Completed swinging gate*

Objects in this category tend to be more complex, but once you've created a few less-complex solutions, you will be ready to take on projects like this one.

Furniture

You can also print solutions for building and accessorizing furniture. My wife received as a gift a replica of a Chesapeake skiff made by one of her uncles. He had been a waterman for some time and built his own boats. The replica is true to his original designs (only much smaller) and it turned out great—so much so that we decided to use the boat as a coffee table by mounting a piece of glass over the boat.

However, being boat-shaped, it was not so easy to get glass to fit. Fortunately, we found a glass shop that agreed to cut the odd shape if I made a template of the surface. Rather than mount a piece of glass that floated on top of the boat, we decided to make a piece to fit within the gunwales. But this presented another problem. There were no cross members to mount the glass. We need a solution that mounted to the gunwales in such a way that it looked like it fit and was also as unobtrusive as possible. Figure 13-12 shows the final design of the solution.

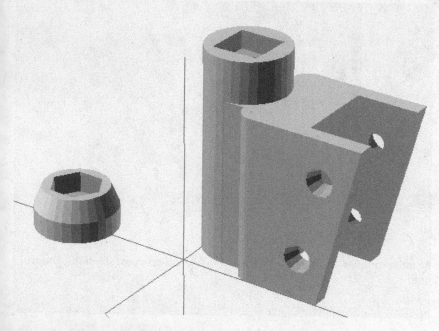

Figure 13-12. *Riser design for glass shelf*

I used four of these mounts with a bolt and nut to complete the riser. It is a fairly minimal solution, but more importantly, it looks like it has always been part of the boat. Figure 13-13 shows the completed solution. The risers are noted with circles. Hard to see, aren't they? Success!

Figure 13-13. Chesapeake skiff coffee table with glass top

As you can see, the mount is designed to use a bolt and nut to form the adjustable riser. The mount was designed to attach to one of the ribs with counter-sink wood screws. The ribs are slanted to form the sides of the boat, so I had to make an angled slot. I made the ears of the slot longer so that it would fit the differing angles of the fore and aft ribs.[11]

Overall, the project was fun and it shows off how 3D printing can be used to solve problems where there are no commercial solutions. I am certain I could have eventually cobbled together some strange bits from the hardware store, but at least I didn't have to wander for hours up and down the aisle deflecting "May I help you?" a dozen times. Plus, it looks great and was entirely homemade—except for the glass.

---

[11]"Front and back" to landlubbers.

MAKERBOT DESKTOP SOFTWARE

There is one other tool that you can put in your 3D printing arsenal to take your 3D printing to the next level. Recently, MakerBot released a new software application called the MakerBot Desktop. This application is a one-stop application for browsing Thingiverse, purchasing things on the Digital Store, and organizing your own library of things. It combines the ability to find and organize things with the ability to prepare things for printing, print them, and control the printer.

If you have downloaded or created as many things as I have, the organization feature is a very valuable addition. The organizational feature alone makes it worth checking out this app. You can manage your own things that you've uploaded to Thingiverse, search for things on Thingiverse, browse things you have downloaded, and buy things from the Digital Store.

Furthermore, if you have the MakerBot Digitizer, you can connect to it to scan your image, upload it, and even print it. The following is a snapshot of the software.

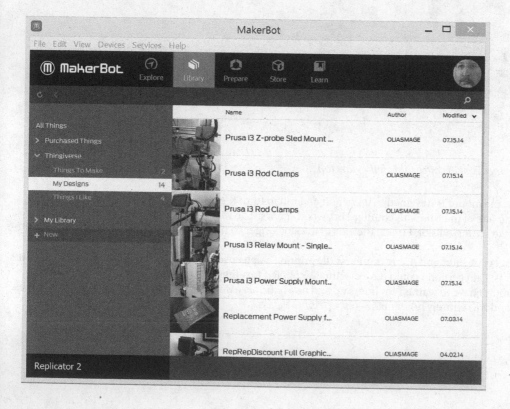

The software is currently available in beta and for the Mac, Windows, and Linux platforms. Furthermore, only the most recent MakerBot printers are supported, going back to the MakerBot Replicator 2 and 2X. Older printers are not supported.

The MakerBot Desktop software is an excellent example of how 3D printing companies are bundling features that were previously separate applications into a 3D printing environment; an IDE for 3D printing. I cannot wait to watch this software (and others like it) evolve. I can envision having a single application that covers the entire 3D printing tool chain. We're almost there!

There is one more bit of coolness at MakerBot. Check out their MakerBot Printshop for iPad. This is a 3D printing suite for your iPad that allows you to browse and print things. It also provides the ability to customize certain objects. It's still very new, but it looks very promising.

If you have a recent MakerBot printer, you should consider downloading and installing the MakerBot Desktop, and if you have an iPad, try out the new MakerBot Printshop.

Summary

Owning a 3D printer is a lot of fun. You can increase that enjoyment by extending your printing endeavors from printing knickknacks, small boxes, and miscellaneous curiosities to printing solutions that solve real-world problems. With your newfound knowledge and experience, you can also become a contributing member of the 3D printing community.

This chapter presented discussions in these areas. You saw how to become a productive member of the community by learning how to participate and share your designs. The chapter also presented some ideas and suggestions for things you can print around the house by way of demonstration of actual solutions. This means you weren't shown an image of a 3D printed bunny, only to be told, "Now go print your own steam engine." This book has given you all of the tools you need to design and print your own objects. All you need is imagination and creativity!

Now that you've discovered these things, you have all of the knowledge you need to get the most out of your 3D printer. So ends our journey through the 3D printing world. May all of your 3D printing endeavors be successful.

■■■

Common Problems and Solutions

This appendix contains a quick reference guide for many of the common problems you may encounter when using 3D printers. Tables A-1, A-2, A-3, and A-4 provide descriptions of problems, sources of the problems, and solutions. I have divided the categories of problems into sections for easier reference.

The best way to use these tables is to look for the problem description that best matches the problem you are experiencing, identify which of the possible sources apply, and then execute the remedy lists. Note that there can be more than one remedy per problem and source. Further, some problems may be remedied by changes to hardware or software. It is best to test each solution one at a time. Some remedies may be worded such that you can repeat the action. For example, lowering the hot-end temperature by 5 degrees can be applied repeatedly until the problem is solved.

■ **Tip** Well, there is a limit to this. Clearly, reducing the temperature a dozen times by 5 degrees would likely be excessive. The same is true with raising the temperature. In either case, you will reach a threshold where the process is no longer applicable. Use these techniques as a guide rather than a literal instruction.

Adhesion Problems

This category of problems includes those that relate to how the object adheres to the build plate, as well as other layer adhesion problems.

Table A-1. *Adhesion Problems and Solutions*

Problem	Cause	Solution
Objects lift on one side or at corners on one side. The object is adhered well on other sides.	Bed not level	If the bed is not level, the side that is lower can induce lift. Check and re-level the print bed.
		Use a raft.
	Draft or air currents	Use walls (blue tape, printed) to control slight air currents.
		Move printer away from vents, open windows and other sources of air currents.
		Place printer in an enclosure or investigate the possibility of adding a hood and doors.
Object is not sticking to print surface or comes loose during printing.	Z-height too high	Check and set Z-height lower.
	Heated bed too cold	Raise temperature of heated print bed by 5 degrees.
	Print surface dirty or worn	Clean print surface. Inspect for damage and replace if worn or you have used it for more than 10 prints in the same area.
		Use a raft.
		Use a brim.
	First layer print speed too high	Slow the first layer speed. Slower first-layer print speeds can help first-layer adhesion. You should not lower the first layer speed to less than 75% of the normal print speed.
	Hot end too cold	Raise the temperature of the hot end by 5 degrees.
Object lifts on several sides or in several places around the perimeter.	Heated bed too cold	Raise the temperature of heated print bed by 5 degrees.
	Strong air currents or drafts	Turn off all fans and HVAC vents, and close windows and doors.
		Use an enclosure or add a hood and doors to block air currents.
	Ambient temperature too cold	Increase ambient temperature. Best to keep it stable during printing.
	Object has very thin protrusions	Add helper disks to increase surface area that contacts the print surface. Some slicers have an option for this feature. You can always add them using the .stl mashup procedure described in an earlier chapter.
Object cracks at higher layers.	Strong air currents or drafts	Turn off all fans and HVAC vents, and close windows and doors.
		Use an enclosure or add a hood and doors to block air currents.
	Ambient temperature too cold	Increase ambient temperature. Best to keep it stable during printing.

Extrusion Problems

This category of problems includes those related to the extruder, hot end, and filament.

Table A-2. Extrusion Failures

Problem	Cause	Solution
Filament jams in extruder or extruder drive pulley/bolt strips filament	Hot end too cold	Raise hot end temperature by 5 degrees.
	Contaminated filament	Check filament for damage or stress (filament will show lighter color) and remove damaged section.
		Check for dusty or dirty filament and clean filament with a lint-free cloth.
		Use a filament filter to remove dust and small debris.
		If failures continue, discard filament (or return to vendor for partial refund).
	Nozzle obstruction	Remove nozzle and clean it using the cold pull method. Remove any obstructions on the build platform.
	Wrong nozzle size	Check your slicer settings. If your slicer settings have a value that is too low, the extruder can jam by pressing more filament through the hot end than it can handle.
	Too much tension on spool	Make sure spool can feed with as little friction as possible. Use a spool holder with rollers or bearings for smooth movement.
	Wrong tension on extruder door or clamp	Check and adjust tension. Too much tension can cause the filament to compress. Too little tension can permit the filament to slip.
Filament curls when exiting hot end	Damaged nozzle	Check the nozzle to ensure there is no debris, burr, or other damage to the opening. Replace the nozzle if damaged.
Burning smell from extruder	Hot end too hot	Lower hot end temperature by 5 degrees.
Filament oozes excessively from hot end	Hot end too hot	Lower hot end temperature by 5 degrees. Note: Some oozing is normal, but it should not run out like the extruder is running.

(continued)

Table A-2. (*continued*)

Problem	Cause	Solution
Filament extrudes unevenly	Hot end too cold	Raise hot end temperature by 5 degrees.
	Extruder stepper motor overheating	Check stepper driver current and adjust to match stepper motor.
	Extruder stepper motor current too high	
	Extruder stepper motor current set too low	
	Loose, stripped, or worn gears	Tighten loose gears and set screws. Replace worn or broken extruder gears.
	Nozzle obstruction	Check, clean, or replace nozzle.
Popping or spitting noises when printing	Contaminated filament	Filament may have too much moisture. Use a drying agent to dry the filament for at least 24 hours.
Steam from hot end	Contaminated filament	Filament may have too much moisture. Use a drying agent to dry the filament for at least 24 hours.

Print Quality Problems

This category includes problems you can encounter that cause print quality to suffer.

Table A-3. *Print-Quality Issues*

Problem	Cause	Solution
Object layers break apart or appear thin and weak	Wrong nozzle size	Check your slicer settings and choose the correct nozzle size.
	Wrong filament size	Measure your filament and ensure the correct size is specified in your slicer.
Slight variances in layer alignment	Loose or worn belts on axis	Adjust belt tension.
	Loose frame components	Tighten loose bolts. Use lock washers or Loctite (blue) to keep bolts and nuts from coming loose from vibration.
		Reduce print speed to reduce vibration.
Object appears squished and smaller (Z axis) than desired	Heated bed too hot	Lower heated print bed by 5 degrees.
Object has thick runs of filament	Too much filament extruded	Check diameter of filament and change slicer settings to match.
Blobs and clumps	Too much filament extruded	Check diameter of filament and change slicer settings to match.
Holes slightly too small	Too much filament extruded	Check diameter of filament and change slicer settings to match.
Circular areas oblong	Loose or worn belts on axis	Adjust belt tension.
Object layers shift in one direction	Loose or worn belts on axis	Adjust belt tension.
	Stepper motor failure	Check stepper driver voltage. If correct, replace stepper motor.
	Stripped belt drive gear	Replace belt drive gear.
	Acceleration too high	Lower acceleration parameters in firmware.
	Obstruction in axis movement	Remove obstruction.
	Plastic part failure	Check all axis parts for damage and replace as needed.
	Damaged bearings	Check all bearings for proper lubrication and replace loose or worn bearings.

Mechanical or Electrical Problems

This category includes a host of mechanical and electrical failures that can cause any number of print failures. Some are severe. Always use caution when working with electronic components and especially mains power.

Table A-4. *Mechanical and Electrical Failures*

Problem	Cause	Solution
Printing pauses or halts while printing	Loss of communication with computer	If printing from computer, check USB connection.
	Corrupt SD card/file	Check SD card for corrupted files. Replace SD card or replace corrupt file.
	Overheating electronics	Mount fans to cool electronics.
		Check stepper driver for correct voltages.
Hot end or heated print bed stops heating	Heating element failed	Replace heating element.
	Electronics board failure	Replace electronics board.
	Power supply failure	Check power and replace if no power to electronics. For example, it is possible for the 12v power to fail, making motors and heaters inoperable.
	Broken wire	Check all wiring for stress fractures and loose connectors. Replace as needed.
	Blown fuse	Check and replace fuse.
Stepper motor stops working	Stepper driver failure	Replace stepper driver.
	Power supply failure	Check power and replace if no power to electronics. For example, it is possible for the 12v power to fail making motors and heaters inoperable.
	Broken wire	Check all wiring for stress fractures and loose connectors. Replace as needed.
	Blown fuse	Check and replace fuse.
Stepper motor overheats	Wrong voltage on stepper driver	Measure voltage and set it to match stepper motor.
Extruder gears turn but filament pauses before it extrudes	Worn or damaged gears	Check gears for damage and replace.
	Rounded-out nut trap	Check large gear for rounded-out nut trap and replace gear.
	Loose hobbed bolt	Tighten hobbed bolt.
Extruder stepper motor turns but no filament extrudes	Loose gears	Tighten or replace gears.
	Extruder jammed	Check Table A-1 and repair extruder jam.

(continued)

Table A-4. (*continued*)

Problem	Cause	Solution
Squeaks, creaks, scratching, or clunking sounds when axes move	Insufficient lubrication	Perform regular maintenance to clean and lubricate axis movement.
	Loose axis mechanism	Check, replace, and tighten axis mechanism.
Axis does not stop at endstop	Broken switch	Replace endstop.
	Broken or disconnected wire	Check and replace as needed.
Burning smell from electronics	Short or electronics failure	Turn computer off immediately. Check electronics for damage. Remove 12v power and connect USB cable to check low-voltage operation. Replace all damaged components.
Sparks, clicking, or smoke from electronics	Short or electronics failure	Turn computer off immediately. Check electronics for damage. Remove 12v power and connect USB cable to check low-voltage operation. Replace all damaged components.
No lights or LCD display	Power supply failure	Replace power supply.
Unexplained noises when axes move—not related to axis mechanism	Loose frame components	Check all frame components and tighten as needed.
Axis runs into max stop	Improper homing	Make sure you home all axis before printing.
Metal screech from Z-axis rods	Insufficient lubrication	Ensure threaded rods are lubricated with the proper lubrication. (e.g., PTFE grease). Check your manual for the correct type to use.
Printer vibrates excessively so that it moves across table	Loose frame components	Check all frame components and tighten as needed.
	Acceleration too high	Check acceleration settings in firmware. Reduce by 10%.
	Print speed too high	Lower infill print speed.

Index

■ R

■ S

■ T

Get the eBook for only $10!

> Now you can take the weightless companion with you anywhere, anytime. Your purchase of this book entitles you to 3 electronic versions for only $10.

This Apress title will provè so indispensible that you'll want to carry it with you everywhere, which is why we are offering the eBook in 3 formats for only $10 if you have already purchased the print book.

Convenient and fully searchable, the PDF version enables you to easily find and copy code—or perform examples by quickly toggling between instructions and applications. The MOBI format is ideal for your Kindle, while the ePUB can be utilized on a variety of mobile devices.

Go to www.apress.com/promo/tendollars to purchase your companion eBook.

All Apress eBooks are subject to copyright. All rights are reserved by the Publisher, whether the whole or part of the material is concerned, specifically the rights of translation, reprinting, reuse of illustrations, recitation, broadcasting, reproduction on microfilms or in any other physical way, and transmission or information storage and retrieval, electronic adaptation, computer software, or by similar or dissimilar methodology now known or hereafter developed. Exempted from this legal reservation are brief excerpts in connection with reviews or scholarly analysis or material supplied specifically for the purpose of being entered and executed on a computer system, for exclusive use by the purchaser of the work. Duplication of this publication or parts thereof is permitted only under the provisions of the Copyright Law of the Publisher's location, in its current version, and permission for use must always be obtained from Springer. Permissions for use may be obtained through RightsLink at the Copyright Clearance Center. Violations are liable to prosecution under the respective Copyright Law.